D0764474

ACT® Prep Plus 2019

PUBLISHING

New York

ACT® is a registered trademark of ACT, Inc.

© 2018 by Kaplan, Inc.

Published by Kaplan Publishing, a division of Kaplan, Inc.
750 Third Avenue, 7th Floor
New York, NY 10017

All rights reserved. The text of this publication, or any part thereof, may not be reproduced in any manner whatsoever without written permission from the publisher.

Printed in the United States of America

10 9 8 7 6 5 4 3 2

ISBN-13: 978-1-5062-3510-3

Kaplan Publishing books are available at special quantity discounts to use for sales promotions, employee premiums, or educational purposes. For more information or to order books, please call the Simon & Schuster special sales department at 866-506-1949.

Table of Contents

Additional resources available at www.kaptest.com/actbookresources

UNIT FIVE: INTEGRATING ESSENTIAL SKILLS

UNIT SIX: HIGHER MATH

UNIT SEVEN: READING INTRODUCTION

UNIT EIGHT: ACT READING

UNIT NINE: SCIENCE INTRODUCTION

UNIT TEN: SCIENCE

INTRODUCTION TO THE ACT

The first step to achieving ACT success is to learn about the structure of the test and why it's so important for your future. The ACT, like any standardized test, is predictable. The more comfortable you are with the test structure, the more confidently you will approach each question type, thus maximizing your score.

ACT STRUCTURE

The ACT is 2 hours and 55 minutes long, or 3 hours and 35 minutes long if you choose to complete the optional Writing test. It consists of a total of 215 scored multiple-choice questions and one optional essay.

Test	Allotted Time (min.)	Question Count
English	45	75
Math	60	60
Reading	35	40
Science	35	40
Writing (optional)	40	1
Total	175 *or* 215 (w/Writing)	215 *or* 216 (w/Writing)

ACT SCORING

The ACT is scored differently from most tests that you take at school. Your ACT score on a test section is not reported as the total number of questions you answered correctly, nor does it directly represent the percentage of questions you answered correctly. Instead, the test makers add up all of your correct answers in a section to get what's called your *raw score*. They then use a conversion chart, or scale, that matches up a particular raw score with what's called a *scaled score*. The scaled score is the number that gets reported as your score for that ACT subject test. For each version of the ACT administered, the test makers use a unique conversion chart that equates a particular raw score with a particular scaled score.

ACT scaled scores range from 1 to 36. Nearly half of all test takers score within a much narrower range: 17–23. Tests and scores on different dates vary slightly, but the information below is based on a recent administration of the test and can be considered typical.

ACT Approximate Percentile Rank	Scaled (or Composite) Score	Percentage of Questions Correct
99%	33	90%
90%	28	75%
74%	24	63%
56%	21	53%
30%	17	43%

Notice that to earn a score of 21 (the national average), you need to answer only about 53% of the questions correctly. On most tests, getting just a bit more than half the questions right would not be a passing grade, let alone an average score. Not so on the ACT. A score of 21 puts you in the middle range of test takers.

> ✔ **Expert Tip**
>
> **Just a few questions right or wrong on the ACT can make a big difference. Answering only five extra questions correctly on each subject test can move you from the bottom of the applicant pool into the middle or from the middle up to the top.**

The score table includes two very strong scores: 28 and 33. Either score would impress almost any college admissions officer. A 28 would put you in the top 10% of the students who take the exam, and a 33 would put you in the top 1%. Even a 33 requires getting only about 90% of the questions right! So the best-scoring students will probably get at least a dozen questions wrong but will still get the scores they need to get into a highly competitive college.

If you earn a score of 24, you'll be in about the 74th percentile. That means that you did as well as or better than 74% of the test takers—in other words, you're in the top quarter of people who took the ACT. That's a strong score, but notice that to earn this score, you need to get only about 63% of the questions correct. On most tests, a score of 63% is probably a D or lower. But on the ACT, it's about a B+.

HOW MANY ACT SCORES WILL YOU GET?

The ACT scaled score we've talked about so far is technically called the Composite score—when people say "I got ___ on the ACT," this is what they're talking about. While the Composite score is really important, you'll see more scores and reporting categories when you get your ACT results: the Composite score, subject scores, reporting categories, and domain scores. Though the subject scores can play a role in decisions or course placement at some schools, the reporting categories and domain scores usually aren't as important as the Composite.

Here's the full battery of ACT scores (1–36) you'll receive:

Subject	Reporting Categories / Domain Scores	Concepts Tested
English score (1–36)	Reporting categories: 1. Production of Writing 2. Knowledge of Language 3. Conventions of Standard English	1. Topic development; organization, unity, and cohesion 2. Precision; concision; style and tone 3. Punctuation; usage; sentence structure and formation

Mathematics score (1–36)	Reporting categories:
	 1. Preparing for Higher Mathematics
	  1A. Number & Quantity
	  1B. Algebra
	  1C. Functions
	  1D. Geometry
	  1E. Statistics & Probability
	 2. Integrating Essential Skills
	 3. Modeling
		1. Use algebra as a general way of expressing and solving equations
		  1A. Real and complex number systems
		  1B. Solving, graphing, and modeling expressions
		  1C. Function definition, notation, representation, and application
		  1D. Knowledge of shapes and solids; understanding composition of and solving for missing values of figures
		  1E. Center and spread of distributions; applying and analyzing data collection methods; understanding and modeling bivariate data relationships; probabilities
		 2. Rates and percentages; average and median; expressing numbers in different ways
		 3. Producing, interpreting, understanding, evaluating, and improving models

Subject	Reporting Categories / Domain Scores	Concepts Tested
Reading score (1–36)	Reporting categories: 1. Key Ideas and Details 2. Craft and Structure 3. Integration of Knowledge and Ideas	1. Central ideas and themes; summarizing information and ideas; understanding relationships and drawing logical inferences and conclusions; understanding sequential, comparative, and cause-effect relationships 2. Word and phrase meanings; understanding authors' word choices, purposes, and perspectives; analyzing text structure and characters' points of view 3. Understanding authors' claims; differentiating between facts and opinions; using evidence to make connections between different texts
Science score (1–36)	Reporting categories: 1. Interpretation of Data 2. Scientific Investigation 3. Evaluation of Models, Inferences, and Experimental Results	1. Manipulating and analyzing scientific data presented in tables, graphs, and diagrams 2. Understanding experimental tools, procedures, and design; comparing, extending, and modifying experiments 3. Judging the validity of scientific information; formulating conclusions and predictions based on information presented
(Optional) Writing score (2–12)	Domain scores: 1. Ideas and Analysis 2. Development and Support 3. Organization 4. Language Use and Conventions	1. Generating productive ideas and engaging critically with multiple perspectives on a given issue 2. Discussing ideas, offering rationale, and supporting an argument 3. Organizing ideas with clarity and purpose 4. Using written language to clearly convey arguments

HOW DO COLLEGES USE YOUR ACT SCORE?

The most important score is typically the Composite score (which is an unweighted average of the four major subject scores). This is the score used by most colleges and universities in the admissions and scholarship process. The subject scores and subscores may be used for advanced placement or occasionally for scholarships, but they are primarily used by college advisers to help students select majors and first-year courses.

Although many schools deny that they use benchmark scores as cutoffs, students have had mixed experiences, and it's well worth understanding the impact of all of your scores. Highly competitive universities generally decline to accept students with any Composite scores below 22 or 23. For less competitive schools, the benchmark score may be lower than that; for some very selective schools, the cutoff may be higher.

To be clear, no school uses the ACT as an absolute or stand-alone bar to admission; for most applicants, though, a low ACT score can be decisive. As a rule, only students whose backgrounds are extremely unusual or who have overcome enormous disadvantages are accepted if their ACT scores are below the school's benchmark.

HOW DO SCHOOLS USE THE OPTIONAL WRITING TEST?

The ACT Writing test may be used for either admissions or course placement purposes, and sometimes both. Students who take the Writing test will receive a subject-level writing score reported on a range of 2-12, based on an analytic scoring rubric. An image of your essay will be available to your high school and the colleges to which you have ACT report your scores from that test date.

WHERE AND WHEN TO TAKE THE ACT

The ACT is offered every year on multiple Saturday test dates. Typically, exams are offered in September, October, December, February, April, and June. (The February date is not available in the state of New York.) You can take the ACT multiple times. Some states offer special administrations of the ACT on different dates. Sunday tests are available by request for students requiring religious or other exemptions. The ACT is administered at high schools around the country that serve as testing centers. Your high school may or may not be a testing center. Check www.act.org for a list of testing centers near you. Note that you must register for the ACT approximately one month in advance to avoid paying a late fee.

CAN YOU RETAKE THE TEST?

You can take the ACT as many times as you like before you need to finish and submit your college applications. If you take it more than once, you can select whichever test score you prefer to be sent to colleges when you apply. However, you can only take advantage of this option if, at the time you register for the test, you do not designate certain colleges to receive your scores automatically. Thus, if you are even possibly interested in taking the test more than once, it is crucial that you not designate any colleges when you register for the test. You can (for a small additional fee) have ACT scores sent to colleges at any time after the scores are reported.

Therefore, if you can afford the small extra fee to send your scores again, give yourself the freedom to retake the test. (An exception would be if you're taking the test at the last minute and need your scores to reach your target schools as soon as possible.) What this means, of course, is that even if you don't get the score you're looking for the first time, you can give yourself another chance without the schools of your choice seeing every score. The ACT is one of the few areas of your academic life in which you get a second chance. Still, keep in mind that your goal is to get your desired score as soon as possible by using your Kaplan Strategies and Methods. Once you get the score you're looking for, you can breathe a little easier about your college applications!

> **✔ Expert Tutor Tip**
>
> The ACT is offered many times per year, so plan your prep and testing around the date that will give you the most time to prepare. Consider activities, class tests, and personal plans when setting your prep and test schedule so you can give your ACT preparation the attention it deserves.

COMMON TESTING MYTHS

In this section, we'll dispel some of the most common ACT myths. As always, you can find the most up-to-date information about the ACT at the official website (https://www.act.org).

Myth: Answer choice C/H is most likely to be the correct answer.

Fact: This rumor has roots in human psychology. Apparently, when people such as high school teachers, for example, design an exam, they have a slight bias toward answer choice C/H when assigning correct answers. While humans do write ACT questions, a computer randomizes the distribution of correct choices; statistically, therefore, each answer choice is equally likely to be the correct answer.

Myth: **The ACT is just like another test in school.**

Fact: While the ACT covers some of the same content as your high school English, math, literature, and science classes, it also presents concepts in ways that are fundamentally different. While you might be able to solve a math problem in a number of different ways on an algebra test, the ACT places a heavy emphasis on working through questions as quickly and efficiently as possible.

Myth: **You can't prepare for the ACT.**

Fact: While the ACT is designed to test students fairly regardless of preparation, you can gain a huge advantage by familiarizing yourself with the structure and content of the exam. By working through the questions and practice tests available to you, you'll ensure that nothing on the ACT catches you by surprise and that you do everything you can to maximize your score. Your Kaplan resources help you structure this practice in the most efficient way possible and provide you with helpful strategies and tips as well.

KEYS TO ACT SUCCESS

There are four basic keys to achieving ACT success. Following any of these by itself will improve your score. Following all four together will get you to where you want to be.

1. LEARN THE TEST

The ACT is very predictable. The test makers are excellent at crafting the types of challenges that show what they're trying to see in your score. As a result, the same kinds of questions, testing the same skills and concepts, appear every time the ACT is given. This is to your considerable advantage.

Because the test specifications rarely change, you can learn in advance what to expect on every section. Just a little familiarity can make an enormous difference. Here are a few ways learning the test will boost your score:

- **You'll know the directions.** Why waste valuable time reading directions when you can have them down pat beforehand? You need every second during the test to answer questions and get points.

- **You'll know the difficulty range of questions.** Every question on the ACT is worth the same number of points, and the questions aren't in any order of difficulty. Knowing this, you can plan your approach to recognize the points you can earn quickly and move past the questions that will take too long until you can get back to them. Doing the questions in the order the ACT gives them to you isn't a strategy. Finding every last point you can get *is*.

- **You'll get extra points by guessing.** Unlike some other standardized tests, the ACT has no wrong-answer penalty. Knowing how to apply that fact can boost your score significantly. You miss 100 percent of shots you don't take. So if you can't answer a question, guess.

- **You'll know how to write a high-scoring essay.** If you are taking the optional Writing test, learning how it is evaluated will help you get a top score.

2. LEARN THE KAPLAN METHODS AND STRATEGIES

The ACT isn't like the exams you take in school. Most school exams test your memory for what you've just been taught. Instead, the ACT tests your problem-solving skills and how you use them, mostly on unfamiliar content. So instead of worrying about what you do or don't know, focus on learning the Kaplan problem-solving Methods and Strategies to earn you points!

Students miss a lot of ACT questions for no good reason. They see a tough-looking question, say to themselves, "Uh oh, I don't remember how to do that," and start to gnaw on their No. 2 pencils.

However, most ACT questions can be answered without perfect knowledge of the material being tested. Often, all you need to do to succeed on the ACT is to think strategically and creatively. We call this kind of strategic, creative frame of mind the ACT Mindset.

How do you put yourself into the ACT Mindset? You continually ask yourself questions such as "What am I being asked? What does this mean? How can I put this into a form I can understand and use? How can I do this faster?" Once you develop some savvy test-taking skills, you'll find yourself capable of working out problems that, at first reading, might have seemed unsolvable. In fact, we'll show you how you can sometimes get right answers when you don't even understand the questions.

There are many, many specific strategies you can use to boost your score. Here are just a few things you'll learn:

Strategy A: Triaging the Test

You do not need to complete questions on the ACT in order. Every student has different strengths and should attack the test with those strengths in mind. Your main objective on the ACT should be to score as many points as you can. While approaching questions out of order may seem counterintuitive, it is a surefire way to achieve your best score.

Just remember, you can skip around within each section, but you cannot work on a section other than the one you've been instructed to work on.

To triage the test effectively, do the following:

- First, work through all the easy questions that you can do quickly. Skip questions that are hard or time-consuming.

- Second, work through the questions that are doable but time-consuming.

- Third, work through the hard questions.

- If you run out of time, choose your Letter of the Day for remaining questions.

A Letter of the Day is an answer choice letter (A/F, B/G, C/H, or D/J) that you choose before Test Day to select for questions you guess on.

> ✔ **Expert Tip**
>
> For the English and Reading tests, start with the passage you find most manageable and work toward the one you find most challenging—you do not need to go in the order of the passages.

Strategy B: Elimination

Even though there is no wrong-answer penalty on the ACT, elimination is still a crucial strategy. If you can determine that one or more answer choices are definitely incorrect, you pare down the number of choices to select from and increase your chances of getting the right answer.

To eliminate answer choices, do the following:

- Read each answer choice.

- Cross out the answer choices that are incorrect.

Strategy C: Guessing

Each multiple-choice question on the ACT has either four or five answer choices and no wrong-answer penalty. That means if you have no idea how to approach a question, you have a 20–25% chance of randomly choosing the correct answer. Even though there's a 75–80% percent chance of selecting the incorrect answer, you won't lose any points for doing so. The worst that can happen on the ACT is that you'll earn zero points on a question, which means you should *always* at least take a guess, even when you have no idea what to do.

When guessing on a question, do the following:

- Always try to strategically eliminate answer choices before guessing.

- If you run out of time, or have no idea what a question is asking, choose your Letter of the Day.

3. LEARN THE MATERIAL TESTED

The ACT is designed to test skills and concepts learned in high school and needed for college. But familiarity with the test, coupled with effective test-taking strategies, will take you only so far. For your best score, you need to sharpen the skills and content knowledge that the ACT tests.

The good news is that most of the content on the ACT is covered by sophomore year at most high schools, with the majority taught even earlier than that. So you've probably already learned most of what the ACT expects you to know, but you may need to spend some time remembering or finding better ways to approach the information. That's partly what this book is for—to remind you of the knowledge you already have and to build and refine the specific skills you've developed so far. Here are just a few of the things we'll review:

- How to read graphs and tables efficiently for the Science test

- The rules for grammar and punctuation (yes, there are consistent and absolute rules, and we'll tell you what they are)

- Math rules for triangles, probabilities, algebraic expressions, and more

- The difference between generalizations and details and between inferences and summaries, as well as how to make a Passage Map that saves you more time than it takes to make it

- What goes into an excellent persuasive essay, what to leave out, and what to choose to write about if you're running out of time.

4. PRACTICE, PRACTICE, PRACTICE

Practice creates confidence. On Test Day, you need to have the Kaplan Methods and Strategies and the tested concepts ready to go—and you need to be relaxed enough to let them all work. So reading and understanding the contents of this book are key, but there's one more step: you need to make the Kaplan Methods part of your everyday routine. The best way to do that is to practice as much as possible.

Test Day will bring its own challenges—you have to be up early to take a long test, in a room full of people you may or may not know, with everyone in a state of anticipation and nervousness—and the anxiety is contagious! You'll be the one who doesn't let nerves take over and make you forget what you know about doing well. Your best ally is the confidence practice gives you.

Note: If you don't have time to practice with all of the sections of this book, you can (and should!) practice in the areas you feel weakest.

So here are your four keys to ACT success:

1. Learn the test.
2. Learn the strategies.
3. Learn the material tested.
4. Practice, practice, practice.

Follow these steps, and you'll find yourself just where you want to be: in full command of your ACT test-taking experience, ready to get your highest score. Count on it.

HOW TO USE THIS BOOK

WELCOME TO KAPLAN!

Congratulations on taking this important step in your college admissions process! By studying with Kaplan, the official partner of Online Prep Live instruction for the ACT®, you'll maximize your score on the ACT, a major factor in your overall application.

Our experience shows that the greatest ACT score increases result from active engagement in the preparation process. Kaplan will give you direction, focus your preparation, and teach you the specific skills and effective test-taking strategies you need to know for the ACT. We will help you achieve your top performance on Test Day, but your effort is crucial. The more you invest in preparing for the ACT, the greater your chances of achieving your target score and getting into your top-choice college.

Are you registered for the ACT? Kaplan cannot register you for the official ACT. If you have not already registered for the upcoming ACT, talk to your high school guidance counselor or visit the official website at www.act.org to register online and for information on registration deadlines, test sites, accommodations for students with disabilities, and fees.

PRACTICE TESTS

Kaplan's practice tests are just like the actual ACT. By taking practice exams, you will prepare yourself for the actual Test Day experience. One of your practice tests is included in this book and the other four can be accessed online; see the Digital Resources section to learn how to access these. We recommend you complete these online practice tests as you make your way through the content of this book. You can score your tests by hand using the score conversion tables in this book, or log into your online resources for easy online scoring. When scored online, Kaplan provides you with a detailed score report. Use this summary to help you focus and review the content areas that comprise your greatest areas of improvement.

Kaplan also provides detailed answers and explanations for an official practice test. We encourage you to visit the ACT website, download and take the exam, and return to your online resources to see how you performed. Doing so will help you familiarize yourself with the official test directions.

EXTRA PRACTICE

You need to reinforce what you learn in each chapter by practicing the Kaplan methods and strategies. Each chapter contains a section called "On Your Own" that features additional practice problems reinforcing the concepts explained in that chapter. These questions are great practice for the real ACT. Answers and Explanations are provided in the back of the book.

SMARTPOINTS

Each chapter contains a breakdown of SmartPoints. By studying the information released by the ACT, Kaplan has been able to determine how often certain topics are likely to show up on the test, and therefore how many points these topics are worth on Test Day. If you master a given topic, you can expect to earn the corresponding number of SmartPoints on Test Day. The breakdown of SmartPoints for English, Math, Reading, and Science are summarized in the following tables. You can also see how these topics align to chapters in this book.

English			
SmartPoints Category	**# of Points**	**Sub-Categories**	**ACT Chapter(s)**
Sentence Structure and Formation	8		Ch. 2
Punctuation	5		Ch. 3
Usage	6		Ch. 4
Organization, Unity, and Cohesion	5	Passage Organization, Transitions	Ch. 5
Topic Development	6	Writer's Purpose, Supporting Material	Ch. 6
Knowledge of Language	6	Ambiguity, Concision, Precision, Style and Tone	Ch. 7
TOTAL	**36**		

Math			
SmartPoints Category	**# of Points**	**Sub-Categories**	**ACT Chapter(s)**
Essential Skills	14	Rates, Percents, Proportions, and Unit Conversion; Numbers and Operations; Expressions and Equations; Geometry; Statistics and Probability	Ch. 9
Higher Math	22	Number and Quantity; Algebra; Functions; Geometry; Statistics and Probability	Ch. 10, Ch. 11, Ch. 12, Ch. 13, Ch. 14
TOTAL	**36**		

Reading			
SmartPoints Category	**# of Points**	**Sub-Categories**	**ACT Chapter(s)**
Key Ideas and Details	21	Global, Inference, Detail	Ch. 16, Ch. 17
Craft and Structure	11	Vocab-in-Context, Function, Writer's View	Ch. 17, Ch. 18
Integration of Knowledge and Ideas	4	Synthesis	Ch. 19
TOTAL	**36**		

Science		
SmartPoints Category	# of Points	ACT Chapter(s)
Interpretation of Data	17	Ch. 21
Scientific Investigation	9	Ch. 22
Evaluation of Models, Inferences, and Experimental Results	10	Ch. 23
TOTAL	36	

DIGITAL RESOURCES

To access the online resources that accompany this book, follow the steps below.

1. Go to kaptest.com/booksonline.
2. Have this book available as you complete the onscreen instructions.

ACT Videos and Quizzes

In addition to practice tests, your ACT online resources include a variety of videos and quizzes. The following icons indicate what is available for you online.

Video: A short instructional video from Kaplan ACT experts

Quiz: A series of test-like questions to practice for Test Day

Join a Live Online Event

Kaplan's ACT Live Online sessions are interactive, instructor-led prep lessons that you can participate in from anywhere you have Internet access.

ACT Live Online sessions are held in our state-of-the-art visual classroom: Actual lessons in real time, just like a physical classroom experience. Interact with your teacher using chat, whiteboards, and polling. Just like courses at Kaplan centers, ACT Live Online sessions are led by top Kaplan instructors.

To register for an ACT Live Online event, visit https://www.kaptest.com/ACT/enroll. From here you can view all of our ACT course offerings—from prep courses, to tutoring, to free events.

ACT Live Online events are scheduled to take place throughout the year. Please check the registration page with dates and times.

ENGLISH INTRODUCTION

BY THE END OF THIS UNIT, YOU WILL BE ABLE TO:

1. Identify the format and timing of the ACT English test

2. Apply tips and strategies to the ACT English test

CHAPTER 1

ACT English

CHAPTER OBJECTIVES

By the end of this chapter, you will be able to:

1. Identify the six ACT English question types

2. Use SmartPoints to determine the highest-yield question types

INSIDE THE ACT ENGLISH TEST

The English test is 45 minutes long and includes 75 questions. The test includes five essays, or passages, each of which includes 15 questions. This means you only have 9 minutes to spend on each passage, or 30–40 seconds on each question. Because time is limited, the Kaplan Method for ACT English will be invaluable in helping you answer the questions strategically within the time allowed.

THE FORMAT

ACT English Passages

English passages will be about a variety of subjects and may be written in numerous styles: persuasive, explanatory, narrative, etc. Recognizing the style of an English passage helps you focus on the questions as they relate to the passage's general purpose. Knowing the overarching aim of the passage will help you answer questions more efficiently and accurately.

> **✔ Expert Tip**
>
> Correct answers must be consistent with a passage's overall style.

TEST DAY DIRECTIONS AND FORMAT

The directions on the English test illustrate why there's an advantage to knowing them beforehand—they're long and complicated, and if you learn them now, then on Test Day, you'll already be racking up points while everyone else is reading the directions. Although the exact wording might vary, here's what the English directions could look like:

Directions: Each passage has certain words and phrases that are underlined and numbered. The questions in the right column will provide alternatives for the underlined segments. Most questions require you to choose the answer that makes the sentence grammatically correct, concise, and relevant. If the word or phrase in the passage is already the correct, concise, and relevant choice, select Choice A, NO CHANGE. Some questions will ask a question about the underlined segment. When a question is presented, choose the best answer.

Some questions will ask about part or all of the passage. These questions do not refer to a specific underlined segment. Instead, these questions will accompany a number in a box.

For each question, choose your answer and fill in the corresponding bubble on your answer sheet. Read the passage once before you answer the questions. You will often need to read several sentences beyond the underlined portion to be able to choose the correct answer. Be sure to read enough to answer each question.

If you would like to read through the exact wording you will see on Test Day, visit the test maker's website and download the Preparing for the ACT guide.

QUESTION TYPES

Most ACT English questions consist of underlined words, phrases, or sentences that are embedded within the passage itself. These questions follow the order of the passage and ask you to choose which answer choice best replaces the underlined portion (or to select "NO CHANGE"). Some questions within the passage will contain a question stem, which will correspond to either an underlined segment or a numbered box in the passage text. Other questions refer to the passage as a whole. These questions appear at the end of the passage after a box with the instructions "Questions # and # ask about the preceding passage as a whole."

OUTSIDE KNOWLEDGE

The ACT English test thoroughly covers rules from a variety of common English topics, mostly from courses students typically complete by the end of the 11th grade. The needed English "facts" are addressed in the strategic discussion throughout the English chapters in this book.

THE INSIDE SCOOP

The ACT is designed to test your understanding of the conventions of written English—punctuation, grammar, sentence structure—and of general rhetorical skills. (Rhetorical skills are more strategic concepts like organizing the text and making sure it's consistently styled and concise.)

The questions *do not* get harder as you proceed through the test.

TIMING

Plan to spend 9 minutes on each passage. That way, when time is called, you should have looked at all 75 English questions and made sure you have gridded in at least a guess for every question.

Have an organized approach. Because of the passage-based format, we recommend that you *do not* skip around in the English subject test. Move straight from beginning to end, answering all of the questions as you go. Unlike some sections, in English you'll usually have at least a sense of what the right answer should be rather quickly. But remember, even the correct answer will start to sound wrong if you think about it too much!

WHEN YOU'RE RUNNING OUT OF TIME

If you have no time left to even read the last few questions, choose the shortest answer for each one. Remember that DELETE, when it appears, counts as the shortest answer. For questions not based on clarity, pick a "letter of the day" and just use that. No choice is more likely than any other, so pick one letter and use it for all questions you can't work on.

SCORING

You will receive an English subject score—from 1 to 36—for the entire English subject test. This score will be averaged into your ACT Composite Score, equally weighted with your scores on the other three major subject tests. You will also receive three other scores based on specific knowledge and concepts. These are called reporting categories and consist of:

- Conventions of Standard English
- Production of Writing
- Knowledge of Language

QUICK TIPS

Mind-Set

- **When in doubt, take it out.** Make sure that everything is written as concisely as possible. If you think something doesn't belong in a sentence, it probably doesn't, so choose an answer that leaves it out. Between two grammatically correct and relevant choices, the shorter one will always be right. Not just better—*right*.

- **Make sure it makes sense.** When switching phrases in and out, it's easy to find grammar but lose logic. Consider sentence formation, making sure that sentences are complete and not fragments and that ideas relate logically. For an answer to be correct in ACT English, it must create a sentence that is logically *and* grammatically correct.

- **Trust your eyes and ears.** Mistakes in grammar often look or sound wrong—trust that instinct. Don't choose the answer that "sounds fancy." Choose the one that sounds *right*.

SPECIAL STRATEGIES: IF YOU GET STUCK ...

A few questions will require you to rearrange the words in a sentence, the sentences in a paragraph, or even the paragraphs in a passage. Others may ask questions about the meaning of all or part of the passage or about its structure. Your approach to these questions should be:

1. **Determine your task.** What are you being asked to do?

2. **Consider the passage as a whole.** Read the sentences around the numbered question to get the big picture—you need to know the points made there. Most passages will have a well-defined theme, laid out in a logical way, so choose the answer that expresses the arrangement of elements that best continues the "flow" of the passage.

3. **Predict your answer.** As you'll see again in the Reading section, making a prediction will give you an idea of what the answer is before you look at the choices.

SMARTPOINTS BREAKDOWN

By studying the information released by the ACT, Kaplan has been able to determine how often certain topics are likely to show up on the test and, therefore, how many points these topics are worth on Test Day. If you master a given topic, you can expect to earn the corresponding number of SmartPoints on Test Day.

Here is a brief overview of what exactly to expect and how much of it you should be expecting.

CONVENTIONS OF STANDARD ENGLISH—19 POINTS

Conventions of Standard English questions make up 51–56% of the English test. The questions in this category require an understanding of English grammar, usage, and mechanics. You will need to be able to identify errors, revise, and edit text.

Sentence Structure and Formation—8 Points

The test will require you to identify improper sentence structure and formation in a text. You'll need to make revisions to improve the text. Some concepts you will be tested on include, but are not limited to:

- Run-on sentences and fragments
- Misplaced modifiers
- Inappropriate grammatical shifts in the construction of verb and pronoun phrases

Punctuation—5 Points

The test will present common problems with standard English punctuation and require you to make revisions to improve the writing. Some concepts you will be tested on include, but are not limited to:

- Inappropriate use of punctuation within sentences
- Unnecessary punctuation
- Inappropriate use of possessive nouns and pronouns

Usage—6 Points

The test will present common problems with standard English usage and require you to make revisions to improve the writing. Some concepts you will be tested on include, but are not limited to:

- Errors in agreement between subject and verb, between pronoun and antecedent, and between modifiers and the word modified
- Errors in verb tense, pronoun case, and comparative and superlative modifiers
- Frequently misused words and idioms

PRODUCTION OF WRITING—11 POINTS

Production of Writing questions make up 29–32% of the English test. The questions in this category require an understanding of the purpose and focus of a piece of writing. You will need to be able to identify errors as well as to revise and edit text.

Organization, Unity, and Cohesion—5 Points

The test will require you to use various strategies to ensure that a text is logically organized, flows smoothly, and has an effective introduction and conclusion. Some concepts you will be tested on include, but are not limited to:

- Logical order of a text's information and ideas within each paragraph

- Logical order of a text's information and ideas within the passage as a whole

- Transition words, phrases, or sentences used to introduce, conclude, or connect information and ideas

Topic Development—6 Points

The test will require you to demonstrate an understanding of, and control over, the rhetorical aspects of texts. You'll need to identify the purposes and parts of texts, determine whether a text or part of text has met its intended goal, and evaluate the relevance of materials in terms of a text's focus. Some concepts you will be tested on include, but are not limited to:

- The effect of adding, revising, or deleting information within a passage

- Appropriate phrasing in relation to a passage's purpose, unity, or focus

- The purpose of an English passage, including whether the text accomplishes this purpose

KNOWLEDGE OF LANGUAGE—6 POINTS

Knowledge of Language questions make up 13–19% of the English test. The questions in this category require you to demonstrate effective language use through ensuring precision and concision in word choice and through maintaining a consistent tone. You will need to be able to identify errors as well as to revise and edit text. Some concepts you will be tested on include, but are not limited to:

- Elements in a passage that are wordy, redundant, or not relevant to a passage's topic and purpose

- Exactness or content appropriateness of word choice

- Consistency of style and tone with a passage's purpose

UNIT TWO

CONVENTIONS OF STANDARD ENGLISH

BY THE END OF THIS UNIT, YOU WILL BE ABLE TO:

1. Apply the Kaplan Method for English
2. Identify and correct errors in sentence structure and formation
3. Identify and correct punctuation errors
4. Identify and correct usage errors

CHAPTER 2

The Kaplan Method for ACT English & Sentence Structure and Formation

CHAPTER OBJECTIVES

By the end of this chapter, you will be able to:

1. Apply the Kaplan Method for ACT English

2. Recognize and correct run-ons and fragments

3. Recognize and correct misplaced and incorrect modifiers

4. Recognize and correct inappropriate grammatical shifts in the construction of verb and pronoun phrases

SMARTPOINTS

Point Value	SmartPoints Category
Point Builder	The Kaplan Method for ACT English
8 Points	Sentence Structure

THE KAPLAN METHOD FOR ACT ENGLISH

The Kaplan Method for ACT English is the method you will use to boost your score on the English test. By understanding what the question is looking for, how it relates to the passage, and the questions you should ask yourself on Test Day, you will maximize the number of points you earn. Use the Kaplan Method for ACT English for every ACT English test passage and question you encounter, whether practicing, completing your homework, working on a Practice Test, or taking the actual exam on Test Day.

The Kaplan Method for ACT English has three steps:

> **Step 1: Read the passage and identify the issue**
>
> **Step 2: Eliminate answer choices that do not address the issue**
>
> **Step 3: Plug in the remaining answer choices and select the most correct, concise, and relevant one**

Let's take a closer look at each step.

Step 1: Read the passage and identify the issue

Rather than reading the whole passage and then answering all of the questions, you can answer questions as you read because they are mostly embedded in the text itself.

When you see a number, stop reading and look at the question. If you can answer it with what you've read so far, do so. If you need more information, keep reading until you have enough context to answer the question.

Step 2: Eliminate answer choices that do not address the issue

Eliminating answer choices that do not address the issue increases your odds of getting the correct answer by removing obviously incorrect answer choices.

Step 3: Plug in the remaining answer choices and select the most correct, concise, and relevant one

Correct, concise, and **relevant** means that the answer choice you select:

- Makes sense when read with the correction

- Is as short as possible while retaining the information in the text

- Relates well to the passage overall

Correct answers do NOT:

- Change the intended meaning of the original sentence, paragraph, or passage
- Introduce new grammatical errors

> ✔ **Expert Tip**
>
> Occasionally, more than one answer choice will be grammatically correct. When this is the case, ask yourself which answer choice most concisely conveys the relevant information.

When you encounter an English question, use the Kaplan Method, asking yourself a series of strategic thinking questions. By asking these strategic thinking questions, you will be able to select the correct answer choice more easily and efficiently. Pausing to ask yourself questions before answering each question may seem like it takes a lot of time, but it actually saves you time by preventing you from weighing the four answer choices against each other; it's better to ask questions that lead you directly to the correct answer than to debate which of four answers seems the least incorrect.

> ✔ **Expert Tip**
>
> If you have to guess, eliminate answer choices that are clearly wrong and then choose the shortest one—the ACT rewards students who know how to be concise.

FRAGMENTS AND RUN-ONS

Run-ons and fragments create grammatically incorrect sentences. The ACT requires that you know the specific rules governing sentence construction.

Fragments

A complete sentence must have a subject and a predicate verb in an independent clause that expresses a complete thought. If any one of these elements is missing, the sentence is a fragment. You can recognize a fragment because the sentence does not make sense as written.

Missing Element	Example
Subject	*Running down the street.*
Predicate verb	*Seth running down the street.*
Complete thought	*While Seth was running down the street.*

Run-ons

If a sentence has more than one independent clause, the clauses must be properly joined. Otherwise, the sentence is a run-on. There are several ways to correct a run-on such as *I recently learned how to cook a few basic dinners, I plan to try more difficult recipes soon.*

To Correct a Run-on	Example
Use a period to separate into two sentences	*I recently learned how to cook a few basic dinners. I plan to try more difficult recipes soon.*
Use a semicolon	*I recently learned how to cook a few basic dinners; I plan to try more difficult recipes soon.*
Make one clause dependent	*Because I recently learned how to cook a few basic dinners, I plan to try more difficult recipes soon.*
Add a FANBOYS conjunction: For, And, Nor, But, Or, Yet, So	*I recently learned how to cook a few basic dinners, and I plan to try more difficult recipes soon.*
Use a dash	*I recently learned how to cook a few basic dinners—I plan to try more difficult recipes soon.*

Work through the Kaplan Method for English step-by-step to answer the questions that accompany the following English passage excerpt. The table below the excerpt contains two columns. The column on the right features the strategic thinking a test expert employs when approaching passages and related questions.

The Bebop Movement

For a jazz musician in New York City <u>in the early 1940s. The most interesting place</u> to spend the
₁
hours between midnight and dawn was probably a Harlem nightclub called Minton's. After finishing their jobs at other clubs, young musicians like Charlie Parker, Dizzy Gillespie, Kenny Clarke, and Thelonious Monk would gather at Minton's and have "jam" sessions, or informal performances featuring lengthy group and solo <u>improvisations, the all-night sessions</u> resulted in the birth of modern jazz as these African
₂
American artists together forged a new sound, known as bebop.

Questions	Strategic Thinking
1. **A.** NO CHANGE **B.** in the early 1940s; the most interesting place **C.** in the early 1940s, the most interesting place **D.** in the early 1940s, it was when the most interesting place	**Step 1: Read the passage and identify the issue** The underlined portion is a fragment. **Step 2: Eliminate answer choices that do not address the issue** Eliminate A because fragments are grammatically incorrect. Replacing the period with a semicolon does not fix the fragment, so B is incorrect. **Step 3: Plug in the remaining answer choices and select the most correct, concise, and relevant one** Choice (C) fixes the fragment by joining the dependent clause "For a jazz musician in New York City in the early 1940s" and the independent clause "the most interesting place to spend the hours between midnight and dawn was probably a Harlem nightclub called Minton's" with a comma. Choice D corrects the fragment but is unnecessarily wordy. Choice (C) is correct.

Questions	Strategic Thinking
2. **F.** NO CHANGE **G.** improvisations and the all-night sessions **H.** improvisations, the all-night sessions, **J.** improvisations. The all-night sessions	**Step 1: Read the passage and identify the issue** The underlined portion includes a run-on. **Step 2: Eliminate answer choices that do not address the issue** Eliminate F because run-ons are grammatically incorrect. Eliminate G because replacing the comma with a FANBOYS word (in this case the word *and*) does not fix the run-on. Adding a comma after *sessions* does not fix the run-on, so H is also incorrect. **Step 3: Plug in the remaining answer choices and select the most correct, concise, and relevant one** Choice (J) correctly separates two independent clauses with a period and a capital letter.

PARALLELISM

Parallelism questions on the ACT test your ability to revise sentences to create parallel structure. Items in a series, list, or compound must be parallel in form. Series, lists, and compounds may contain nouns, adjectives, adverbs, or verb forms.

Check for parallelism if the sentence contains:

Feature	Example	Parallel Form
A list	*Chloe **formulated** a question, **conducted** background research, and **constructed** a hypothesis before starting the experiment.*	3 verb phrases
A compound	***Hunting** and **fishing** were essential to the survival of midwestern Native American tribes such as the Omaha.*	2 gerund verb forms
A correlative	*Kaylee remembered **to hydrate** and **to stretch** before the lacrosse game started.*	2 infinitive verb forms
A comparison	*Garrett enjoys a short **sprint** as much as a long-distance **run**.*	2 nouns
Related nouns	***Students** who review their practice **tests** are more likely to earn high **scores** on Test Day.*	3 related plural nouns

Work through the Kaplan Method for English step-by-step to answer the question that accompanies the passage below. The table below the passage contains two columns. The left column contains test-like questions. The column on the right features the strategic thinking a test expert employs when approaching the passage and questions presented.

Unlike "swing," the enormously popular jazz played in the 1930s, bebop was not dance music. Often, it had been blindingly fast, incorporated tricky, irregular rhythms, and featured discordant sounds that jazz audiences had never heard before. Earlier jazz, like practically all of Western music up to that time, used an eight-note scale. Bebop, in contrast, was based on a 12-note scale, thereby opening up vast new harmonic opportunities for musicians.

Questions	Strategic Thinking
3. A. NO CHANGE B. Often, it was going to be blindingly fast, incorporated tricky, irregular rhythms, and featuring discordant sounds that jazz audiences had never heard before. C. Often, it was blindingly fast, incorporated tricky, irregular rhythms, and featured discordant sounds that jazz audiences had never heard before. D. Often, it was blindingly fast, incorporated tricky, irregular rhythms, and featuring discordant sounds that jazz audiences had never heard before.	**Step 1: Read the passage and identify the issue** The sentence includes items in a list that are not in parallel form. **Step 2: Eliminate answer choices that do not address the issue** Choice A is incorrect because it includes a parallelism error. Eliminate B and D, which do not offer three parallel verb phrases. **Step 3: Plug in the remaining answer choices and select the most correct, concise, and relevant one** Choice (C) correctly uses three past-tense verb phrases.

Questions	Strategic Thinking
4. **F.** NO CHANGE **G.** Earlier jazz, like practically all of Western musicians up to that time, used an eight-note scale. **H.** Earlier jazz instruments, like practically all of Western musicians up to that time, used an eight-note scale. **J.** Earlier jazz music, like practically all of Western musicians up to that time, used an eight-note scale.	**Step 1: Read the passage and identify the issue** The word *like* indicates that the author is making a comparison. Check to make sure the comparison is logical. **Step 2: Eliminate answer choices that do not address the issue** Eliminate G and J because they make illogical comparisons between music and musicians. Choice H compares instruments to musicians, which is equally illogical. **Step 3: Plug in the remaining answer choices and select the most correct, concise, and relevant one** Choice (F) is correct because the sentence logically compares *jazz* with *Western music*.

MODIFIERS

A modifier is a word or a group of words that describes, clarifies, or provides additional information about another part of the sentence. Modifier questions on the ACT require you to identify the part of a sentence being modified and use the appropriate modifier in the proper place. In many cases, an introductory phrase or clause will modify the first noun that follows. Use context clues in the passage to identify the correct placement of a modifier; a misplaced modifier can cause confusion.

Modifier/ Modifying Phrase	Incorrect	Correct
nearly	*Andre **nearly** watched the play for four hours.*	*Andre watched the play for **nearly** four hours.*
in individual containers	*The art teacher handed out paints to students **in individual containers**.*	*The art teacher handed out paints **in individual containers** to students.*
A scholar athlete	***A scholar athlete**, maintaining high grades in addition to playing soccer were expected of Maya.*	***A scholar athlete**, Maya was expected to maintain high grades in addition to playing soccer.*

Work through the Kaplan Method for English step-by-step to answer the questions that accompany the following English passage excerpt. The table below the excerpt contains two columns. The column on the right features the strategic thinking a test expert employs when approaching passages and related questions.

The musicians who pioneered bebop shared two common elements: a vision of the new music's possibilities and astonishing improvisational skill—the ability to play or compose a musical line on the spur of the moment. As the essence of jazz, <u>paramount is improvisation within the context of a group setting.</u> Parker, perhaps the greatest instrumental genius jazz has known, was a <u>brilliantly improviser.</u>
5
He often played twice as fast as the rest of the band, but his solos were always in rhythm and exquisitely shaped, revealing a harmonic imagination that enthralled his listeners.

Questions	Strategic Thinking
5. A. NO CHANGE B. improvisation within the context of a group setting is paramount C. improvisation within the context is paramount of a group setting D. within the context of a group setting is paramount improvisation	**Step 1: Read the passage and identify the issue** The modifying phrase "As the essence of jazz" must be followed by the noun or pronoun it is modifying. **Step 2: Eliminate answer choices that do not address the issue** Eliminate A and D because they do not feature the word *improvisation* directly after the modifying phrase. **Step 3: Plug in the remaining answer choices and select the most correct, concise, and relevant one** Eliminate C because the phrase *is paramount* is incorrectly placed in the middle of the sentence. Choice (B) is correct because it places the noun *improvisation* directly after the modifying phrase and places *is paramount* at the end of the sentence.

Questions	Strategic Thinking
6. **F.** NO CHANGE 　　**G.** brilliantly, improviser 　　**H.** brilliant, improviser 　　**J.** brilliant improviser	**Step 1: Read the passage and identify the issue** The underlined portion includes an adverb (*brilliant*) and a noun (*improviser*), both of which must be used properly. **Step 2: Eliminate answer choices that do not address the issue** Eliminate F and G because it is grammatically incorrect to use an adverb to modify a noun. **Step 3: Plug in the remaining answer choices and select the most correct, concise, and relevant one** Eliminate H because it adds an unnecessary comma. Choice (J) correctly uses an adjective to modify a noun and does not introduce a new error.

SHIFTS IN VERB TENSE AND PRONOUN CASE

On the ACT English test, you will be asked to identify and replace unnecessary shifts in verb tense and pronoun case. Because these shifts may occur within a single sentence or among multiple sentences, you will need to read around the underlined portion to identify the error. The underlined segment must logically match the other parts of the sentence as well as the passage as a whole.

Shifts in Verb Tense

Verb tense places the action or state of being described by the verb into a place in time: present, past, or future. Each tense has three forms: simple, progressive, and perfect.

Form	Past	Present	Future
Simple: Actions that simply occur at some point in time	*Connor **planted** vegetables in the community garden.*	*Connor **plants** vegetables in the community garden.*	*Connor **will plant** vegetables in the community garden.*
Progressive: Actions that are ongoing at some point in time	*Connor **was planting** vegetables in the community garden this morning before noon.*	*Connor **is planting** vegetables in the community garden this morning before noon.*	*Connor **will be planting** vegetables in the community garden this morning before noon.*

Form	Past	Present	Future
Perfect: Actions that are completed at some point in time	*Connor **had planted** vegetables in the community garden every year until he gave his job to Jasmine.*	*Connor **has planted** vegetables in the community garden since it started five years ago.*	*Connor **will have planted** vegetables in the community garden by the time the growing season starts.*

Shifts in Pronoun Case

Pronouns replace nouns in sentences. A pronoun must agree with the noun it is replacing in person and number. The ACT will test your ability to recognize and correct inappropriate shifts in pronoun usage.

Person	Refers to	Singular Pronouns	Plural Pronouns
First person	the person speaking	*I, me, my*	*we, us, our*
Second person	the person spoken to	*you, your*	*you, your*
Third person	the person or thing spoken about	*he, she, it, him, her, his, hers, its*	*they, them, theirs*
Indefinite	a nonspecific person or group	*anybody, anyone, each, either, everyone, someone, one*	*both, few, many, several*

Work through the Kaplan Method for English step-by-step to answer the questions that accompany the following English passage excerpt. The table below the excerpt contains two columns. The column on the right features the strategic thinking a test expert employs when approaching passages and related questions.

Like many revolutions, unfortunately, <u>the bebop movement encounters</u> heavy resistance. Opposition
7
came from older jazz musicians initially, but also, later and more lastingly, from a general public alienated
by the music's complexity and sophistication. Furthermore, due to the government ban on recording that
was in effect during the early years of World War II <u>(you often forget that records were made of vinyl, a</u>
8
<u>petroleum product that was essential to the war effort)</u>, the creative ferment that first produced bebop
8
remains largely undocumented today.

Questions	Strategic Thinking
7. **A.** NO CHANGE **B.** the bebop movement encountering **C.** the bebop movement is encountering **D.** the bebop movement encountered	**Step 1: Read the passage and identify the issue** The underlined portion includes a present-tense verb, but the surrounding text is written in past tense. **Step 2: Eliminate answer choices that do not address the issue** As written, the sentence uses the wrong verb tense, so eliminate A. Choice B creates a fragment. Choice C is a complete sentence, but it uses the incorrect tense. **Step 3: Plug in the remaining answer choices and select the most correct, concise, and relevant one** Choice (D) correctly uses the past tense.
8. **F.** NO CHANGE **G.** (they often forget that records were made of vinyl, a petroleum product that was essential to the war effort) **H.** (I often forget that records were made of vinyl, a petroleum product that was essential to the war effort) **J.** (records were made of vinyl, a petroleum product that was essential to the war effort)	**Step 1: Read the passage and identify the issue** The underlined portion includes the pronoun *you*, which needs to match the surrounding text in person and number. **Step 2: Eliminate answer choices that do not address the issue** Eliminate F because the writer does not address the audience as *you* anywhere else in the essay. Choice G is incorrect because it is unclear whom *they* refers to and ambiguous pronouns are grammatically incorrect. Eliminate H because the word *I* is too personal to reflect the author's informative tone. **Step 3: Plug in the remaining answer choices and select the most correct, concise, and relevant one** Choice (J) is correct; it reflects the author's tone and is the most concise option.

Chapter 2: The Kaplan Method for ACT English & Sentence Structure and Formation

You have seen the ways in which the ACT tests you on Sentence Structure and Formation in English passages and how an ACT expert approaches these types of questions. Use the Kaplan Method for English to answer the questions that accompany the following English passage excerpts. Remember to look at the strategic thinking questions that have been provided for you—some of the answers have been filled in, but you will have to complete the answers to others. Use your answers to the strategic thinking questions to select the correct answer, just as you will on Test Day.

Women's Suffrage

The Nineteenth Amendment, which granted all American women the right to vote, was passed by Congress on June 4, 1919, nearly fifty years after the birth of the women's suffrage movement. In 1848, the Seneca Falls Convention provided a platform for a wide array of criticisms and demands that were initially considered too radical and demanding to be feasible. As a way of gaining broader support and increasing their constituency, suffragists <u>were finding it</u> necessary to streamline and slightly alter their
9
positions.

Question	Strategic Thinking
9. **A.** NO CHANGE **B.** were to find it **C.** finding it **D.** found it	**Step 1: Read the passage and identify the issue** The underlined verb phrase is in progressive past tense, but the surrounding text is written in past tense. **Step 2: Eliminate answer choices that do not address the issue** Eliminate A because it is incorrect as written. Eliminate C because it creates a run-on sentence. **Step 3: Plug in the remaining answer choices and select the most correct, concise, and relevant one**

Instead of arguing for equality based on principle, suffragists insisted that the ways in which women and men differ were <u>precisely why women in government must be allowed to participate</u>. In an attempt to
10
appease opponents, suffragists bolstered their argument for a woman's right to vote with an overt emphasis on traditional views about women's roles; <u>suffragists insisted that the female vote would help to purify politics, enacting reforms, outweighing less desirable votes</u>. Even though anti-suffragists insisted that
11
11
women's shared interests would encourage them to vote together and terribly alter the world of politics, the positive outcome of a female voting bloc, suffragists insisted, would be a government that reflected a woman's position as protector of the home, family, and society.

Questions	Strategic Thinking
10. **F.** NO CHANGE **G.** precisely why women must in government be allowed to participate **H.** precisely why women must be allowed to participate in government **J.** precisely in government why women must be allowed to participate	**Step 1: Read the passage and identify the issue** The modifying phrase "in government" is not correctly placed within the underlined portion. **Step 2: Eliminate answer choices that do not address the issue** Eliminate F because it is incorrect as written. Eliminate G because it would require two commas—"must, in goverment,"—to be grammatically correct. **Step 3: Plug in the remaining answer choices and select the most correct, concise, and relevant one** _____ _____

Questions	Strategic Thinking
11. **A.** NO CHANGE **B.** suffragists insisted that the female vote would help to purify politics, enacting reforms, and outweighing less desirable votes **C.** suffragists insisted that the female vote would help to purify politics, enact reforms, and outweigh less desirable votes **D.** suffragists insisted that the female vote would help to purify politics, to enact reforms, and outweighing less desirable votes	**Step 1: Read the passage and identify the issue** Items in a list must be in parallel form. **Step 2: Eliminate answer choices that do not address the issue** _____ _____ **Step 3: Plug in the remaining answer choices and select the most correct, concise, and relevant one** _____ _____

Despite anti-suffragist objections, the suffrage movement finally achieved its ultimate goal, but only after offering its participants a political education and a sense of taking an active role in the nation's history, which in turn helped to convince the rest of the country of the worth of the woman's vote. Much to the anti-suffragists' surprise, it was soon apparent that women, in fact, did not vote together as a bloc; <u>voting as individuals and in smaller proportions than men.</u>
12

Questions	Strategic Thinking

12. F. NO CHANGE
   G. women voted as individuals and in smaller proportions than men
   H. women voting as individuals and in smaller proportions than men
   J. voting both as individuals and in smaller proportions than men
	Step 1: Read the passage and identify the issue
	
	The underlined segment follows a semicolon, which is used to separate two independent clauses.
	
	Step 2: Eliminate answer choices that do not address the issue
	
	_____
	_____
	
	Step 3: Plug in the remaining answer choices and select the most correct, concise, and relevant one
	
	_____
	_____

Chapter 2: The Kaplan Method for ACT English & Sentence Structure and Formation   **29**

> Early 20th-century women did not necessarily vote as a united caucus, they felt a new sense of
>
> 13
>
> empowerment. They were, by law, participants in a democracy that could no longer exclude them.
>
> 13
>
> Women, indeed, were a gathering force that proved impossible for you to ignore.
>
> 14

Question	Strategic Thinking
13. A. NO CHANGE **B.** Early 20th-century women did not necessarily vote as a united caucus but they felt a new sense of empowerment. **C.** Early 20th-century women did not necessarily vote as a united caucus they felt a new sense of empowerment. **D.** While early 20th-century women did not necessarily vote as a united caucus, they felt a new sense of empowerment.	**Step 1: Read the passage and identify the issue** The underlined sentence is a run-on. **Step 2: Eliminate answer choices that do not address the issue** _____ _____ **Step 3: Plug in the remaining answer choices and select the most correct, concise, and relevant one** _____ _____
14. F. NO CHANGE **G.** proved impossible to ignore **H.** proved impossible for them to ignore **J.** proved impossible for us to ignore	**Step 1: Read the passage and identify the issue** _____ _____ **Step 2: Eliminate answer choices that do not address the issue** _____ _____ **Step 3: Plug in the remaining answer choices and select the most correct, concise, and relevant one** _____ _____

Answers and Explanations are provided at the end of the book.

Now try a test-like ACT English passage and question set on your own. Give yourself 6 minutes to read the passage and answer the questions.

Espresso 89

For years, friends in my neighborhood complained

<u>in the area</u> about the lack of a good coffee shop.
15

15. Which of the following is the best placement for the underlined phrase?

   A. Where it is now

   B. After the word "friends"

   C. After the word "neighborhood"

   D. After the word "shop" (ending the sentence with a period)

The discussions at times became <u>passionate, and it</u>
16
seemed that my neighbors believed that a coffee shop

would cure just about any problem our suburban

neighborhood faced. Not a coffee drinker,

16. Which of the following replacements for the underlined segment of the sentence would NOT be acceptable?

   F. passionate it

   G. passionate; it

   H. passionate. It

   J. passionate—it

<u>my friends who thought that a place to buy coffee would</u>
17
<u>make such a difference were hard for me to understand.</u>
17
Then, a coffee shop called Espresso 89 finally opened in

the neighborhood. Six months after it opened, I

understand what all of the fuss was about.

17. A. NO CHANGE

   B. my friends thinking a place to buy coffee would make such a difference was hard for me to understand.

   C. having a hard time understanding why my friends thought a place to buy coffee would make such a difference.

   D. I had a hard time understanding why my friends thought a place to buy coffee would make such a difference.

It's not as though I've suddenly converted to a daily

diet of lattes and cappuccinos. (However, <u>one can get</u> in
18
the habit of buying chai, a delicious spiced tea.) Instead,

18. F. NO CHANGE

   G. I have gotten

   H. you can get

   J. we have gotten

I have discovered that a coffee shop can be about more than coffee. Ingrid and Gus, the owners of <u>Espresso 89</u> <u>running</u> their shop as something of a community center for the area.

      They began by inviting a local artist to display her paintings on the walls of the shop and holding a "gallery" opening for the occasion. They encouraged other local artists to sign up for future opportunities to share their work with the coffee-drinking public.

      <u>Two or three nights a week, Espresso 89 hosts music or literary events that provide entertainment and the opportunity for local artists to share their craft.</u> Another public performance is the weekly children's story hour, when one corner of the shop is filled with parents and their toddlers listening to storybook after storybook read by a retired elementary school teacher.

      The owners of the shop have also made Espresso 89 available to different groups for <u>a small meeting</u>.

19.
  A. NO CHANGE
  B. Espresso 89. Run
  C. Espresso 89, run
  D. Espresso 89, running

20.
  F. NO CHANGE
  G. To create evenings that provide entertainment and the opportunity to host music or literary events, local artists share their craft with Espresso 89 two or three nights a week.
  H. To provide entertainment and the opportunity to share their craft, two or three nights a week local artists at Espresso 89 host created evenings.
  J. Sharing their craft, evenings hosted by Espresso 89 provide entertainment and an opportunity for local artists two or three nights a week.

21.
  A. NO CHANGE
  B. a small meetings
  C. small meetings
  D. a meeting

Readers gather for book clubs, crafters have been
                                    22
connecting to work on group projects, and even an
                                    22
American Sign Language organization meets there on
                                    22
a regular basis. Every so often, local politicians hold
      22
events at the shop, sharing information with or

explaining government services to constituents.

22. **F.** NO CHANGE

G. Readers have been gathering for book clubs, crafters connect to work on group projects, and even an American Sign Language organization meets there on a regular basis.

H. Readers gather for book clubs, crafters connect to work on group projects, and even an American Sign Language organization has been meeting there on a regular basis.

J. Readers gather for book clubs, crafters connect to work on group projects, and even an American Sign Language organization meets there on a regular basis.

Answers and Explanations are provided at the end of the book.

ON YOUR OWN

The following questions provide an opportunity to practice the concepts and strategic thinking covered in this chapter. While many of the questions pertain to Sentence Structure and Formation, some touch on other concepts tested on the English test to ensure that your practice is test-like, with a variety of question types per passage.

Liberal Arts Education

[1]

Although the concept of liberal arts has existed since the time of ancient Greece, the parameters <u>over the centuries have remained relatively unchanged</u>
<u>of liberal arts study.</u> [A] In essence, liberal arts are
      1
defined as "any study given to reflection and free inquiry."

<u>This not always being the case, however.</u>
                    2

[2]

In medieval times, the seven liberal arts were divided into two parts: the Trivium ("the three roads") and the Quadrivium ("the four roads"). [B] The Trivium consisted of grammar, rhetoric, and <u>logic, the Quadriv-</u>
                                              3
<u>ium consisted of arithmetic, geometry, astronomy, and</u>
                    3
<u>harmonics.</u> However, the description of a liberal arts
    3
college is somewhat more limiting.

1. **A.** NO CHANGE
    B. over the centuries of liberal arts study have remained relatively unchanged.
    C. of liberal arts study have remained relatively unchanged over the centuries.
    D. of liberal arts study remaining relatively unchanged over the centuries.

2. **F.** NO CHANGE
    G. This has not always been the case, however.
    H. Although this has not always been the case.
    J. Although this not always been the case.

3. **A.** NO CHANGE
    B. logic; while the Quadrivium consisted of arithmetic, geometry, astronomy, and harmonics.
    C. logic, so the Quadrivium consisted of arithmetic, geometry, astronomy, and harmonics.
    D. logic; the Quadrivium consisted of arithmetic, geometry, astronomy, and harmonics.

A liberal arts college generally awarded a Bachelor of
                                                    4
Arts degree after four years of study, primarily enrolls
                                                      4
full-time students between the ages of 18 and 24, typi-
                                                   4
cally had between 800 and 1,800 students, and does not
                                        4
provide professional or vocational preparation.
                        4

4. **F.** NO CHANGE

    G. A liberal arts college generally awarded a Bachelor of Arts degree after four years of study, primarily enrolled full-time students between the ages of 18 and 24, typically had between 800 and 1,800 students, and does not provide professional or vocational preparation.

    H. A liberal arts college generally awarded a Bachelor of Arts degree after four years of study, primarily enrolled full-time students between the ages of 18 and 24, typically had between 800 and 1,800 students, and would not have provided professional or vocational preparation.

    J. A liberal arts college generally awards a Bachelor of Arts degree after four years of study, primarily enrolls full-time students between the ages of 18 and 24, typically has between 800 and 1,800 students, and does not provide professional or vocational preparation.

[3]

The liberal arts have been the primary focus of
                  5
undergraduate education in the United States since it

was a British colony. [C] The number of liberal arts

colleges in the United States steady increased through-
                                 6
out the 20th century as private universities, state

universities, and community colleges all sought to

give their undergraduates a broad education. [D]
7

5. **A.** NO CHANGE

    B. The liberal arts has been

    C. The liberal arts having been

    D. The liberal arts being

6. **F.** NO CHANGE

    G. steadily increased

    H. increased in a steady fashion

    J. increased in a steadily fashion

7. **A.** NO CHANGE

    B. give its

    C. giving their

    D. gave its

[4]

The content of liberal arts study still focuses on the
arts, humanities, and <u>sciences, and the basic notion of</u>
                                              8
<u>forming well-rounded students</u> in these areas is still the
          8

concept behind liberal arts education today. <u>There is</u>
                                                          9
<u>some concern, however, that the philosophy is out of</u>
                          9
<u>step with the times in which today's students are</u>
                      9
<u>living behind liberal arts education.</u> Responding to this
          9

concern, <u>courses in computer science and information</u>
                                  10
<u>technology have been added to the curriculum of many</u>
                          10
<u>colleges and universities.</u> Does this mean the end of
          10

8. **F.** NO CHANGE

   G. sciences; and the basic notion of forming well-rounded students

   H. sciences. And the basic notion of forming well-rounded students

   J. sciences: and the basic notion of forming well-rounded students

9. **A.** NO CHANGE

   B. There is some concern, however, that behind liberal arts education the philosophy is out of step with the times in which today's students are living.

   C. There is some concern, however, that the philosophy behind liberal arts education is out of step with the times in which today's students are living.

   D. There is some concern, however, that the philosophy is out of step with the times behind liberal arts education in which today's students are living.

10. **F.** NO CHANGE

   G. computer science and information technology courses have been added to the curriculum of many colleges and universities.

   H. computer science and information technology are the subject of courses that have been added to the curriculum of many colleges and universities.

   J. many colleges and universities have added courses in computer science and information technology to the curriculum.

liberal arts education as it has been practiced since the

days of Martianus Capella? <u>I don't believe so.</u>
                                        11

11. **A.** NO CHANGE

　　B. Many educators don't think so.

　　C. You wouldn't believe so.

　　D. We don't believe so.

<u>Most liberal arts colleges award Master's and doctoral</u>
                            12
<u>degrees as well.</u> The study of liberal arts may have to
　12
evolve with the times, but its basic premise—that

12. **F.** NO CHANGE

　　G. Master's and doctoral degrees are awarded by most liberal arts colleges as well.

　　H. Most degrees awarded by liberal arts colleges are Master's and doctoral ones.

　　J. DELETE the underlined portion.

well-rounded students are well-educated students—<u>remain</u>
                                                        13
<u>as valid today</u> as it was in medieval times.
　13

13. **A.** NO CHANGE

　　B. remaining as valid today

　　C. remains as valid today

　　D. remained as valid today

Questions 14 and 15 ask about the passage as a whole.

---

14. The writer is considering adding the following sentence to the essay:

The late 1800s saw an expansion of liberal arts colleges as the right to education began to include minorities and women.

If the writer were to add this sentence, it would most logically be placed at Point:

　　F. A in Paragraph 1.

　　G. B in Paragraph 2.

　　H. C in Paragraph 3.

　　J. D in Paragraph 3.

15. Suppose the writer's primary purpose had been to write an essay summarizing the history of higher education in the United States. Would this essay accomplish this purpose?

　　A. Yes, because it discusses the natural evolution of liberal arts, which is taught only at the collegiate level.

　　B. Yes, because it explains how most liberal arts colleges award Master's and doctoral degrees as well.

　　C. No, because it does not mention higher education anywhere.

　　D. No, because liberal arts is just one type of higher education offered in the United States.

Answers and Explanations are provided at the end of the book.

CHAPTER 3

Punctuation

CHAPTER OBJECTIVES

By the end of this chapter, you will be able to:

1. Recognize and correct inappropriate uses of punctuation within sentences

2. Recognize and omit unnecessary punctuation

3. Identify and correct inappropriate uses of possessive nouns and pronouns

SMARTPOINTS

Point Value	SmartPoints Category
5 Points	Punctuation

WITHIN-SENTENCE PUNCTUATION

The ACT English test requires you to identify and correct inappropriate commas, semicolons, colons, and dashes when they are used to indicate breaks in thought within a sentence.

You can recognize Punctuation questions because the underlined portion of the text will include a punctuation mark. The answer choices will move that punctuation mark around, replace it with another punctuation mark, or remove it altogether. When you identify a Punctuation question, check to make sure the punctuation is used correctly in context.

Commas

Use commas to...	Example
Separate independent clauses connected by a FANBOYS conjunction (For, And, Nor, But, Or, Yet, So)	*Jess finished her homework earlier than expected, so she started a project that was due the following week.*
Separate an introductory or modifying phrase from the rest of the sentence	*Knowing that soccer practice would be especially strenuous, Tia spent extra time stretching beforehand.*
Set off three or more items in a series or list	*Jeremiah packed a sleeping bag, a raincoat, and a lantern for his upcoming camping trip.*
Separate nonessential information from the rest of the sentence	*Professor Mann, who is the head of the English department, is known for the extensive assignments in his courses.*
Separate an independent and dependent clause	*Tyson arrived at school a few minutes early, which gave him time to organize his locker before class.*

> ✔ **Expert Tip**
>
> When you see an underlined comma, ask yourself, "Could the comma be replaced by a period or a semicolon?" If yes, the comma is grammatically incorrect and needs to be changed.

Semicolons

Use semicolons to...	Example
Join two independent clauses that are not connected by a FANBOYS conjunction	*Gaby knew that her term paper would take at least four more hours to write; she got started in study hall and then finished it at home.*
Separate items in a series or list if those items already include commas	*The team needed to bring uniforms, helmets, and gloves; oranges, almonds, and water; and hockey sticks, pucks, and skates.*

✔ **Expert Tip**

When you see an underlined semicolon, ask yourself, "Could the semicolon be replaced by a comma?" If yes, the semicolon is grammatically incorrect and needs to be changed. If the semicolon is separating two independent clauses and can be replaced with a period, it is grammatically correct.

Colons

Use colons to...	Example
Introduce and/or emphasize a short phrase, quotation, explanation, example, or list	*Sanjay had two important projects to complete: a science experiment and an expository essay.*

Dashes

Use dashes to...	Example
Indicate a hesitation or a break in thought	*Going to a history museum is a good way to begin researching prehistoric creatures—on second thought, heading to the library would likely be much more efficient.*
Set off explanatory elements within a sentence	*Rockwell's Space Transportation Systems Division handled all facets—design, development, and testing—of the reusable orbiter.*

✔ **Expert Tip**

When you see an underlined colon or dash, ask yourself, "Has the author included a new idea by introducing or explaining something, or by breaking his or her thought process?" If yes, the punctuation is often grammatically correct.

UNNECESSARY PUNCTUATION

The ACT will ask you to recognize instances of unnecessary punctuation, particularly commas.

Do NOT use a comma to...	Incorrect	Correct
Separate a subject from its predicate	*The diligent student council, meets every week.*	*The diligent student council meets every week.*
Separate a verb from its object or its subject, or a preposition from its object	*The diligent student council meets, every week.*	*The diligent student council meets every week.*
Set off elements that are essential to a sentence's meaning	*The, diligent student, council meets every week.*	*The diligent student council meets every week.*
Separate adjectives that work together to modify a noun	*The diligent, student council meets every week.*	*The diligent student council meets every week.*

✔ **Expert Tip**

✔ **Expert Tip**

To determine whether information is nonessential, read the sentence without the information. If the sentence still makes sense and has the same intended meaning without the omitted words, then those words need to be set off with punctuation.

Work through the Kaplan Method for English step-by-step to answer the questions that accompany the following English passage excerpt. The table below the excerpt contains two columns. The column on the right features the strategic thinking a test expert employs when approaching passages and related questions.

Medusa

For more than two thousand <u>years; Medusa</u> has been a prominent image in the world of art and the
          1
world of myth. As far back as 200 BCE, images of <u>Medusa—the defeated Gorgon, abounded</u>. The shield of
                             2
Alexander the Great, for example, was graced with an image of the mythical Medusa with her locks of live
<u>serpents, and</u> a gaze that could turn men into stone.
   3

Question	Strategic Thinking

1. **A.** NO CHANGE
   B. years, Medusa
   C. years Medusa
   D. years. Medusa
	Step 1: Read the passage and identify the issue
	
	The underlined segment includes a semicolon, but the first part of the sentence is not an independent clause. The first part of the sentence is an introductory phrase and must be punctuated accordingly.
	
	Step 2: Eliminate answer choices that do not address the issue
	
	Eliminate A because the semicolon neither joins two independent clauses nor separates items containing commas in a series or list. Eliminate C because it removes punctuation altogether, creating a run-on sentence. Eliminate D because it creates a fragment.
	
	Step 3: Plug in the remaining answer choices and select the most correct, concise, and relevant one
	
	Choice (B) is correct because it separates an introductory phrase from the rest of the sentence with a comma.

Question	Strategic Thinking
2. **F.** NO CHANGE **G.** Medusa the defeated Gorgon, abounded **H.** Medusa the defeated Gorgon abounded **J.** Medusa—the defeated Gorgon—abounded	**Step 1: Read the passage and identify the issue** The underlined segment sets off the nonessential phrase "the defeated Gorgon" with one comma and one dash. **Step 2: Eliminate answer choices that do not address the issue** Eliminate G and H because they do not provide punctuation on both sides of the nonessential phrase. **Step 3: Plug in the remaining answer choices and select the most correct, concise, and relevant one** Eliminate F because either two commas or two dashes are used to set off a nonessential phrase; using one of each is not correct. Choice (J) is correct.
3. **A.** NO CHANGE **B.** serpents; and **C.** serpents and **D.** serpents: and	**Step 1: Read the passage and identify the issue** The underlined segment includes a comma, so check to make sure it is used properly. **Step 2: Eliminate answer choices that do not address the issue** Eliminate A and B; "a gaze that could turn men into stone" is not an independent clause, so neither a comma and FANBOYS conjunction nor a semicolon is appropriate. **Step 3: Plug in the remaining answer choices and select the most correct, concise, and relevant one** Eliminate D because a colon is used to introduce a short phrase, quotation, explanation, example, or list. Choice (C) is correct; no punctuation is needed.

POSSESSIVE NOUNS, PRONOUNS, AND APOSTROPHES

Possessive nouns and pronouns refer to something that belongs to someone or something. Each follows different rules, and the ACT will test both. These ACT questions will also require you to identify both the singular and plural forms.

Possessive Nouns and Pronouns

To spot errors in possessive noun or pronoun construction, look for...	Example
Two nouns in a row	The **professor's lectures** were both informative and entertaining.
Pronouns with apostrophes	It is in **one's** best interest to plan ahead.
Words that sound alike	The three friends decided to ride **their** bicycles to the park over **there** where **they're** going to enjoy a picnic lunch.

Apostrophes

Use an apostrophe to...	Example
Indicate the possessive form of a single noun	My oldest **sister's** soccer game is on Saturday.
Indicate the possessive form of a plural noun	My two older **sisters'** soccer games are on Saturday.
Indicate a contraction (e.g., *don't, can't*)	**They've** won every soccer match this season.

> ✔ **Expert Tip**
>
> To check whether *it's* is appropriate, replace it in the sentence with *it is* or *it has*. If the sentence no longer makes sense, *it's* is incorrect.
>
> *The tree frog blends perfectly into its surroundings. When it holds still, it's nearly invisible.*

Work through the Kaplan Method for English step-by-step to answer the questions that accompany the following English passage excerpt. The table below the excerpt contains two columns. The column on the right features the strategic thinking a test expert employs when approaching passages and related questions.

Medusa was surely one of the most threatening <u>figure's</u> of ancient Greek mythology. One of the
                                              4
three Gorgon sisters, she had been known for her beauty. However, she aroused the anger of the goddess
Athena, who turned <u>Medusas</u> once lovely hair to snakes. With the power to turn anyone who looked upon
                        5
her into stone, Medusa was feared and thought impossible to defeat.

Nevertheless, Medusa finally did meet her end at the hands of Perseus. Perseus was helped by Athena and Hermes, another major Greek god. Perseus was given a powerful sword, a helmet that made him invisible, winged sandals that enabled him to fly, and a highly polished shield. Using these gifts, Perseus was able to invisibly sneak up on the sleeping Gorgon, use the shield as a mirror to protect himself from **6** Medusa's direct gaze, and cut off the monster's head. **6**

Question	Strategic Thinking
4. F. NO CHANGE **G.** figures' **H.** figure **J.** figures	**Step 1: Read the passage and identify the issue** The underlined apostrophe indicates that this is a Punctuation question. The sentence does not require a possessive noun, so the punctuation must be changed. **Step 2: Eliminate answer choices that do not address the issue** Eliminate F because it incorrectly uses a singular possessive noun. Eliminate G because the sentence does not require a plural possessive noun. **Step 3: Plug in the remaining answer choices and select the most correct, concise, and relevant one** Choices H and (J) eliminate the apostrophe, but H incorrectly uses a singular noun. Choice (J) is correct.

Question	Strategic Thinking
5. **A.** NO CHANGE **B.** Medusa's **C.** Medusas' **D.** Medusa	**Step 1: Read the passage and identify the issue** The underlined segment needs to show singular possession because the "once lovely hair" belonged to Medusa. **Step 2: Eliminate answer choices that do not address the issue** Eliminate A and D because they are not possessive nouns. **Step 3: Plug in the remaining answer choices and select the most correct, concise, and relevant one** Choices C and (B) both use apostrophes to show possession, but C incorrectly makes the word a plural possessive noun. Choice (B) is correct because *Medusa's* is a singular possessive noun.

English

Question	Strategic Thinking
6. **F.** NO CHANGE **G.** Using these gifts, Perseus was able to invisibly sneak up on the sleeping Gorgon, use the shield as a mirror to protect himself from Medusa's direct gaze, and cut off the monsters head. **H.** Using these gifts, Perseus was able to invisibly sneak up on the sleeping Gorgon, use the shield as a mirror to protect himself from Medusas direct gaze, and cut off the monsters head. **J.** Using these gifts, Perseus is able to invisibly sneak up on the sleeping Gorgon, uses the shield as a mirror to protect himself from Medusa's direct gaze, and cuts off the monster's head.	**Step 1: Read the passage and identify the issue** The underlined sentence includes two apostrophes. To answer this Punctuation question correctly, you must verify the use of both. The *direct gaze* is Medusa's and the *head* is the monster's, so two singular possessive nouns are necessary. **Step 2: Eliminate answer choices that do not address the issue** Eliminate G and H because they do not include the necessary singular possessive nouns *Medusa's* and *monster's*. **Step 3: Plug in the remaining answer choices and select the most correct, concise, and relevant one** Eliminate J because even though it punctuates the possessive nouns correctly, it changes the verbs to present tense, which is grammatically incorrect given the context of the rest of the passage. The sentence is correct as written, so (F) is the answer.

You have seen the ways in which the ACT tests you on Punctuation in English passages and how an ACT expert approaches these types of questions. Use the Kaplan Method for ACT English to answer the questions that accompany the following English passage excerpt. Remember to look at the strategic thinking questions that have been laid out for you—some of the answers have been filled in, but you will have to complete the answers to others. Use your answers to the strategic thinking questions to select the correct answer, just as you will on Test Day.

Mary's Attic

I thought the tour of my <u>friend's</u> new house was finished as we came to a stop outside her bedroom on
7
the third floor. But Mary had something else in mind. "Do you want to go up to the attic?" she asked me, her eyes sparkling with mischief. "My dad says no one has gone there for forty years!"

I wasn't thrilled about the idea of exploring the dark, musty space overhead. <u>In the past: I hesitated</u>
8
<u>whenever</u> Mary suggested risky or dangerous activities, but this time I just nodded, trying to appear non-
8
chalant. Mary yanked on the cord dangling from the wooden <u>door—as if by magic, a staircase</u> unfolded,
9
the bottom step landing directly in front of my feet. I looked up into the looming darkness, imagining cobwebs crawling with eight-legged monsters, and shuddered.

I took a deep breath, <u>hoping, Mary wouldn't notice and</u> gripped the ladder. As I placed my foot on the
10
bottom rung, I wondered how my best friend had failed to remember I had a terrible fear of spiders. "The sooner you get this over with, the better," I whispered to myself.

Question	Strategic Thinking
7. **A.** NO CHANGE **B.** friends **C.** friends' **D.** friends,	**Step 1: Read the passage and identify the issue** The underlined apostrophe indicates that this is a Punctuation question. The sentence requires a singular possessive noun, because the house belongs to the narrator's friend. **Step 2: Eliminate answer choices that do not address the issue** Eliminate B and D because they are not possessive nouns. **Step 3: Plug in the remaining answer choices and select the most correct, concise, and relevant one** _____ _____

Question	Strategic Thinking

8. **F.** NO CHANGE
   G. In the past
      I hesitated, whenever
   H. In the past,
      I hesitated whenever
   J. In the past;
      I hesitated whenever
	Step 1: Read the passage and identify the issue
	
	The underlined segment incorrectly uses a colon. Colons are only tested on the ACT in only one way: to introduce a brief explanation, definition, or list.
	
	Step 2: Eliminate answer choices that do not address the issue
	
	Eliminate F because it misuses a colon. Eliminate J because the semicolon neither joins two independent clauses nor separates items containing commas in a series or list.
	
	Step 3: Plug in the remaining answer choices and select the most correct, concise, and relevant one
	
	_____
	
	_____

9. **A.** NO CHANGE
   B. door: as if by magic,
      a staircase
   C. door as if, by magic
      a staircase
   D. door; as if by magic,
      a staircase
	Step 1: Read the passage and identify the issue
	
	The underlined portion includes the only dash in this sentence, which does not indicate a hesitation or a break in thought.
	
	Step 2: Eliminate answer choices that do not address the issue
	
	_____
	
	_____
	
	Step 3: Plug in the remaining answer choices and select the most correct, concise, and relevant one
	
	_____
	
	_____

Question	Strategic Thinking
10. F. NO CHANGE **G.** hoping Mary wouldn't notice; and **H.** hoping Mary wouldn't notice: and **J.** hoping Mary wouldn't notice, and	**Step 1: Read the passage and identify the issue** _____ _____ **Step 2: Eliminate answer choices that do not address the issue** _____ _____ **Step 3: Plug in the remaining answer choices and select the most correct, concise, and relevant one** _____ _____

Answers and Explanations are provided at the end of the book.

Now try a test-like ACT English passage and question set on your own. Give yourself 6 minutes to read the passage and answer the questions.

Gregory Hines, a Beloved Icon

During the last five decades of the

20th <u>century; Gregory</u> Hines enriched musical theater
11

11. A. NO CHANGE

    B. century, Gregory

    C. century Gregory

    D. century—Gregory

with his performances as <u>a dancer, singer, and star</u>
12
of the Broadway stage. A multitalented

12. F. NO CHANGE

    G. a dancer, singer, and star,

    H. a dancer singer and star

    J. a dancer; singer, and star

<u>artist—he</u> was also employed as
13

13. A. NO CHANGE

    B. artist; he

    C. artist, he

    D. artist he

<u>an: actor a director, and a producer</u> in television and
14
film.

14. F. NO CHANGE

    G. an actor, a director, and a producer

    H. an actor a director, and a producer

    J. an actor a director and a producer

Hines began performing as a dancer when he was

five, touring professionally in nightclubs across the

country with his older <u>brother Maurice, as the duo</u> The
15
Hines Kids. Both brothers studied dance with famous

tap dancer Henry LeTang and performed regularly at

the Apollo Theater in New York City. In addition to

learning from LeTang, Hines improved his art by watch-

ing fellow performers such as the Nicholas Brothers and

Sandman Sims.

15. A. NO CHANGE

    B. brother: Maurice, as the duo

    C. brother, Maurice, as the duo

    D. brother, Maurice as the duo:

<u>At eight, he</u> made his Broadway debut and
16
remained a star of the stage in a variety of musicals,

including *Eubie!*, *Sophisticated Ladies*, and *Comin'*

Uptown. He received a Tony award for Best Actor for his

work in <u>*Jellys* Last Jam</u> in 1993, as well as three
17

Tony <u>nominations, from</u> 1979 to 1981.
18

16. **F.** NO CHANGE

    G. At eight—he

    H. At eight he

    J. At eight; he

17. **A.** NO CHANGE

    B. *Jellies*

    C. *Jelly*

    D. *Jelly's*

18. **F.** NO CHANGE

    G. nominations; from

    H. nominations from

    J. nominations: from

Answers and Explanations are provided at the end
of the book.

English

ON YOUR OWN

The following questions provide an opportunity to practice the concepts and strategic thinking covered in this chapter. While many of the questions pertain to Punctuation, some touch on other concepts tested on the English test to ensure that your practice is test-like, with a variety of question types per passage.

The History of Marbles

<u>Taws, alleys and flints</u> are the names of particular
1
kinds of marbles. The names of marbles may originate

1. **A.** NO CHANGE
    B. Taws, alleys, and flints
    C. Taws alleys, and flints
    D. Taws alleys; and flints

from <u>their appearance, as in "cloudies"; their use, as in</u>
2
<u>"shooters"; or their original material.</u>
2

2. **F.** NO CHANGE
    G. their appearance, as in "cloudies," their use, as in "shooters," or their original material.
    H. their appearance as in "cloudies"; their use, as in "shooters," or their original material.
    J. their appearance: as in "cloudies," their use, as in "shooters"; or their original material.

<u>"Alleys," for example were</u> once made of alabaster.
3
Marbles may be made from many different materials.

3. **A.** NO CHANGE
    B. "Alleys" for example, were
    C. "Alleys," for example: were
    D. "Alleys," for example, were

<u>In the eighteenth century: marbles</u> were actually made
4
from marble chips.

4. **F.** NO CHANGE
    G. In the eighteenth century, marbles
    H. In the eighteenth century—marbles
    J. In the eighteenth century; marbles

Nowadays, <u>its' more common for marbles</u> to consist of
                              5
glass, baked clay, steel, onyx, plastic, or agate. Perhaps,

the key word regarding marbles is "variety."

    Marbles can be manipulated in a variety of ways.

"Knuckling" is a <u>technique in which the</u> knuckles of the
                              6
hand are balanced against the ground while a marble

placed against the forefinger is shot outward by the

thumb.

Marbles can also be <u>thrown, rolled; dropped, and even</u>
                                  7
<u>kicked.</u>
  7

    There are also many varieties of marble games. The

most common American version involves winning

<u>opponents marble's</u> by knocking them out of a designated
       8

area with <u>ones'</u> own marbles. Another popular game is
             9

<u>taw also known as ringtaw or ringer,</u> the object of which
               10
is to shoot marbles arranged like a cross out of a large

ring. Players in a pot game such as moshie try to knock

one another's marbles into a hole. In nineholes, or

bridgeboard, players shoot <u>his or her marbles</u> through
                                      11
numbered arches on the board.

5. A. NO CHANGE
    B. its' more common for marble
    C. it's more common for marble
    D. it's more common for marbles

6. F. NO CHANGE
    G. technique, in which, the
    H. technique in, which the
    J. technique in which; the

7. A. NO CHANGE
    B. thrown, rolled, dropped—and even
        kicked.
    C. thrown rolled, dropped and even kicked.
    D. thrown, rolled, dropped, and even kicked.

8. F. NO CHANGE
    G. opponents marbles
    H. opponent marbles'
    J. opponents' marbles

9. A. NO CHANGE
    B. one's
    C. ones
    D. one

10. F. NO CHANGE
    G. taw; also known as ringtaw or ringer,
    H. taw, also known as ringtaw or ringer,
    J. taw also known as: ringtaw or ringer

11. A. NO CHANGE
    B. your marbles
    C. their marbles
    D. our marbles

The popularity of marbles spans c<u>enturies</u> and
                                    12
crosses cultural boundaries. The first marble games

took place in antiquity. <u>It was played with</u> nuts, fruit
                                    13
pits, or pebbles. Even the great Augustus Caesar,

<u>in addition with</u> his Roman playmates, was known to
        14
have played marble games as a child. During Passover,

Jewish children have customarily used filberts as

marbles. Several traditional Chinese games are also

played with marbles.

So, although most people consider the game of

marbles to be just for children, it actually has a <u>complex</u>
                                                        15
<u>history.</u> If anyone accuses you of having marbles in your
    15
head, you might ask what kind.

12. **F.** NO CHANGE
    G. span centuries
    H. spanning centuries
    J. spans hundreds of years

13. **A.** NO CHANGE
    B. They were played with
    C. They were playing with
    D. It plays with

14. **F.** NO CHANGE
    G. additionally with
    H. along with
    J. having the addition of

15. **A.** NO CHANGE
    B. it actual has a complex history.
    C. the history that they have is actually complex.
    D. it has a history that is actually complex.

Answers and Explanations are provided at the end
of the book.

CHAPTER 4

Usage

CHAPTER OBJECTIVES

By the end of this chapter, you will be able to:

1. Recognize and correct errors in agreement between subject and verb, between pronoun and antecedent, and between modifiers and the word modified

2. Revise text as necessary to correct verbs, pronoun case, and comparative and superlative modifiers

3. Recognize and correct idiom errors and frequently misused words

SMARTPOINTS

Point Value	SmartPoints Category
6 Points	Usage

AGREEMENT

Subject-Verb Agreement

A verb must agree with its subject in person and number:

>Singular: *The apple tastes delicious.*

>Plural: *Apples taste delicious.*

The noun closest to the verb is not always the subject: *The chair with the cabriole legs is an antique.* The singular verb in this sentence, *is*, is closest to the plural noun *legs*. However, the verb's actual subject is the singular noun *chair*, so the sentence is correct as written.

Only the conjunction *and* forms a compound subject requiring a plural verb form:

>*Saliyah and Taylor are in the running club.*

>*Either Saliyah or Taylor is in the running club.*

>*Neither Saliyah nor Taylor is in the running club.*

Pronoun-Antecedent Agreement

A pronoun is a word that takes the place of a noun. Pronouns must agree with their antecedents not only in person and number but also in gender.

Gender	Example
Feminine	*Because Yvonne had a question,* **she** *raised her hand.*
Masculine	*Since* **he** *had lots of homework, Rico started working right away.*
Neutral	*The rain started slowly, but then* **it** *became a downpour.*
Unspecified	*If a traveler is lost,* **he** *or* **she** *should ask for directions.*

Modifier Agreement

A modifier is a word or group of words that describes, clarifies, or provides more information about another part of the sentence.

Adjectives are single-word modifiers that describe nouns and pronouns: *Ian conducted an* **efficient** *lab experiment.*

Adverbs are single-word modifiers that describe verbs, adjectives, or other adverbs: *Ian* **efficiently** *conducted a lab experiment.*

Work through the Kaplan Method for English step-by-step to answer the questions that accompany the following English passage excerpt. The table below the excerpt contains two columns. The column on the right features the strategic thinking a test expert employs when approaching passages and related questions.

Music in the Park

Some people think of classical music as too boring, too academic, or simply too long to enjoy. They feel that music without lyrics <u>are</u> lacking in emotion or is just too difficult to focus on. For many years,

1
I was among those who thought that classical music wasn't for <u>him or her.</u> But when a friend took me to

2
see the New York Philharmonic in Central Park—a free performance <u>usual</u> scheduled twice each

3
summer—my whole perception of orchestras and classical music changed.

Question	Strategic Thinking

1. **A.** NO CHANGE
   B. are often
   C. is
   D. is,
	Step 1: Read the passage and identify the issue
	
	The verb *are* does not agree with the subject *music*.
	
	Step 2: Eliminate answer choices that do not address the issue
	
	Eliminate A and B because the plural verb *are* does not match the singular subject *music*.
	
	Step 3: Plug in the remaining answer choices and select the most correct, concise, and relevant one
	
	Choices (C) and D both include a singular verb, but D introduces an unnecessary comma. Choice (C) is correct.

2. **F.** NO CHANGE
   G. them.
   H. he or she.
   J. him.
	Step 1: Read the passage and identify the issue
	
	The singular pronoun phrase *him or her* does not match the plural antecedent *those*.
	
	Step 2: Eliminate answer choices that do not address the issue
	
	Eliminate F, H, and J because they contain singular pronouns that do not match the plural antecedent.
	
	Step 3: Plug in the remaining answer choices and select the most correct, concise, and relevant one
	
	Choice (G), containing a plural pronoun, is correct.

Question	Strategic Thinking

3.   **A.** NO CHANGE
    B. usual,
    C. usually, nearly without exception,
    D. usually
	Step 1: Read the passage and identify the issue
	
	The adjective *usual* is modifying the verb *scheduled*.
	
	Step 2: Eliminate answer choices that do not address the issue
	
	Eliminate A and B because adjectives cannot modify verbs.
	
	Step 3: Plug in the remaining answer choices and select the most correct, concise, and relevant one
	
	Both C and (D) correctly modify the verb *scheduled* with the adverb *usually*, but (D) offers a clearer and more concise option.

VERBS, PRONOUN CASE, COMPARATIVE/SUPERLATIVE

Verbs

Verb tense indicates when an action or state of being took place: past, present, or future. Each tense has three forms: simple, progressive, and perfect. Don't worry about the names of verb tenses, just their correct usage.

	Past	Present	Future
Simple: Actions that occur at some point in time	She **studied** two extra hours before her math test.	She **studies** diligently.	She **will study** tomorrow for her French test.
Progressive: Actions that are ongoing at some point in time	She **was studying** yesterday for a French test today.	She **is studying** today for her math test tomorrow.	She **will be studying** tomorrow for her physics test next week.
Perfect: Actions that are completed at some point in time	She **had studied** two extra hours before she took her math test yesterday.	She **has studied** diligently every day this semester.	She **will have studied** each chapter before her physics test next week.

Pronoun Cases

There are three pronoun cases, each of which is used based on the context of the sentence.

Case	Pronouns	Example
Subjective: The pronoun is used as the subject	I, you, she, he, it, we, you, they, who	*Rivka is the student **who** will lead the presentation.*
Objective: The pronoun is used as the object of a verb or a preposition	me, you, her, him, it, us, you, them, whom	*With **whom** will Rivka present the scientific findings?*
Possessive: The pronoun expresses ownership	my, mine, your, yours, his, her, hers, its, our, ours, their, theirs, whose	*Rivka will likely choose a partner **whose** work is excellent.*

> ✔ **Expert Tip**
>
> When there are two pronouns or a noun and a pronoun in a compound structure, drop the other noun or pronoun to confirm which case to use. For example: *Leo and me walked into town.* Would you say, "Me walked into town"? No, you would say, "I walked into town." Therefore, the correct case is subjective, and the original sentence should read: *Leo and I walked into town.*

Comparative/Superlative

When comparing like things, use adjectives that match the number of items being compared. When comparing two items or people, use the comparative form of the adjective. When comparing three or more items or people, use the superlative form.

Comparative (two items)	Superlative (three or more items)
better, more, newer, older, shorter, taller, worse, younger	best, most, newest, oldest, shortest, tallest, worst, youngest

Work through the Kaplan Method for English step-by-step to answer the three questions that accompany the following English passage excerpt. The table below the excerpt contains two columns. The column on the right features the strategic thinking a test expert employs when approaching passages and related questions.

> I knew that there would be a large audience for the performance, but I didn't think the atmosphere would be festive. In contrast to my expectations, I wasn't the <u>youngest</u> of the audience members. The
> 4
> audience wasn't made up of retirees and studious types; there were people on dates, families with small children, and groups of friends <u>whom</u> were enjoying a summer picnic. Thousands of people had spread
> 5
> out blankets to relax and experience the music. As the sky turned pink and purple with the setting sun, the musicians <u>are tuning</u> their instruments in preparation for the show.
> 6

Question	Strategic Thinking

4. F. NO CHANGE
  G. youngest,
  H. younger
  J. younger,
	Step 1: Read the passage and identify the issue
	
	The adjective *youngest* is in the superlative form, which is used when comparing three or more items or people.
	
	Step 2: Eliminate answer choices that do not address the issue
	
	Eliminate H and J because *younger* is in the comparative form, which is only used to compare two items or people, not a group of people such as an audience.
	
	Step 3: Plug in the remaining answer choices and select the most correct, concise, and relevant one
	
	Both (F) and G correctly use the superlative adjective *youngest*, but G adds an unnecessary comma. Choice (F) is the correct answer

5. A. NO CHANGE
  B. who, in actuality,
  C. who
  D. of whom
	Step 1: Read the passage and identify the issue
	
	The antecedent for *whom* is *groups of friends*, which is part of the sentence's subject. The pronoun *whom* is incorrect because it is objective.
	
	Step 2: Eliminate answer choices that do not address the issue
	
	Eliminate A and D, which contain objective pronouns.
	
	Step 3: Plug in the remaining answer choices and select the most correct, concise, and relevant one
	
	Both B and C include the proper subjective pronoun *who*, but (C) offers a clearer, more concise option.

English

Question	Strategic Thinking

6. **F.** NO CHANGE
   G. tune
   H. were tuned
   J. tuned
	Step 1: Read the passage and identify the issue
	
	The verb phrase *are tuning* is present tense, but the actions in this passage took place in the past.
	
	Step 2: Eliminate answer choices that do not address the issue
	
	Eliminate F and G because they contain present-tense verbs.
	
	Step 3: Plug in the remaining answer choices and select the most correct, concise, and relevant one
	
	Both H and (J) include past tense verbs. However, *were tuned* does not make sense when plugged into the sentence; it makes it seem as if the musicians, not the instruments, were the ones being tuned. *Tuned* is the most correct, concise verb for this sentence. The correct answer is (J).

IDIOMS AND MISUSED WORDS

Idioms

An idiom is a combination of words that must be used together to convey either a figurative or literal meaning. Idioms are tested in three ways on the ACT:

1. Proper Preposition Usage in Context: The preposition must reflect the writer's intended meaning.

   *She waits **on** customers.*

   *She waits **for** the bus.*

   *She waits **with** her friends.*

2. Idiomatic Expressions: Some words or phrases must be used together to be correct.

> Simone will **either** bike **or** run to the park.

> **Neither** the principal **nor** the teachers will tolerate tardiness.

> This fall, Shari is playing **not only** soccer **but also** field hockey.

3. Implicit Double Negatives: Some words imply a negative and therefore cannot be paired with an explicit negative.

> Janie **can hardly** wait for vacation.

Frequently Tested Prepositions	Idiomatic Expressions	Words That Can't Pair with Negative Words
at by for from of on to with	as . . . as between . . . and both . . . and either . . . or neither . . . nor just as . . . so too not only . . . but also prefer . . . to	barely hardly scarcely

Misused Words

English contains many pairs of words that sound alike but are spelled differently and have different meanings.

Accept: to take or receive something that is offered	My niece **accepts** her pile of birthday gifts with great enthusiasm.
Except: with the exclusion of	All of the presents are toys **except** for a box containing a popular book series.

Affect: to act on, to have influence on something	The dreary, rainy weather negatively **affected** Rahul's mood.
Effect: something that is produced by a cause; a consequence	A recent study explored the **effects** of weather on mental well-being.

Lay: to put or place something	I **laid** the report on my boss's desk before leaving for the day.
Lie: to rest or recline	After a long day of work, I just want to **lie** down on the couch.

Raise: to build or lift up something; to support the growth of someone	Many books are dedicated to the topic of **raising** children.
Rise: to get up	Ted likes to **rise** early in the morning to exercise before his children wake up.

English

Its: a possessive pronoun for singular, gender-neutral noun or pronoun	*A sunflower is not just a pretty plant;* ***its*** *oil and seeds are quite useful.*
It's: a contraction for "it is"	***It's*** *common for some sunflower varieties to grow as tall as 12 feet.*

Whose: a possessive pronoun	***Whose*** *uniform shirt is this?*
Who's: a contraction meaning "who is"	***Who's*** *responsible for ordering new uniforms?*

Their: a possessive pronoun for a plural noun or pronoun	*The college students plan to travel internationally after* ***their*** *graduation.*
They're: a contract for "they are"	***They're*** *going to visit several countries in East Asia.*
There: at a certain point or place	*The students are excited to experience the foods and cultures* ***there.***
There's: a contraction for "there is"	***There's*** *a tour of an ancient palace that they're looking forward to seeing.*

Other words do not sound alike, but they have similar meanings that are often confused.

Among: in a group of, or surrounded by, multiple things or people	*Navya was* ***among*** *many doctoral candidates who visited the university.*
Between: distinguishing one thing from one other thing	*Navya had to decide* ***between*** *her top two doctoral program choices.*

Amount: sum or quantity of multiple things that cannot be counted	*The* ***amount*** *of pollution in the ocean is affecting dolphin populations.*
Number: sum or quantity of a finite collection that can be counted	*Scientists report that the* ***number*** *of dolphins has decreased significantly.*

Less: a smaller extent or amount of things that cannot be counted	*The common supermarket sign "10 items or* ***less***" *is actually incorrect.*
Fewer: of a smaller number, referring to things that can be counted	*Since the items can be counted, the sign should read "10 items or* ***fewer.***"

Much: great in quantity, referring to things that cannot be counted	*My sister has* ***much*** *more patience than I have.*
Many: great in quantity, referring to things that can be counted	***Many*** *of her friends admire her ability to stay calm in difficult situations.*

Good: satisfactory in quality, quantity, or degree; adjective	*Dakota considered both the* ***good*** *and bad effects of standardized testing before composing her essay.*
Well: To perform an action in a satisfactory manner; adverb	*Dakota wrote her essay so* ***well*** *that her professor used it as an example of excellent persuasive writing.*

Work through the Kaplan Method for English step-by-step to answer the three questions that accompany the following English passage excerpt. The table below the excerpt contains two columns. The column on the right features the strategic thinking a test expert employs when approaching passages and related questions.

By the end of the first piece, Mendelssohn's *Symphony No. 4 in A Major*, I was hooked. The sounds of the orchestra's many instruments captured the attention of everyone in the park, including me. The second piece was Tchaikovsky's *1812 Overture*, and the <u>members in the audience</u> hushed their already whispered
7
conversations to hear the work's interplay <u>between</u> the brass, strings, woodwinds, and percussion. <u>It's</u>
8   9
emotional ending, punctuated with booming cannons and church bells, made me realize that classical music didn't have to be boring at all.

Question	Strategic Thinking

7. **A.** NO CHANGE
   B. members of the audience
   C. members for the audience
   D. member in the audiences
	Step 1: Read the passage and identify the issue
	
	The underlined phrase includes the preposition *in*, which indicates this is an idiom question.
	
	Step 2: Eliminate answer choices that do not address the issue
	
	The preposition *in* is not correct within the context of the underlined phrase. Eliminate A and D.
	
	Step 3: Plug in the remaining answer choices and select the most correct, concise, and relevant one
	
	"Members of the audience" conveys the proper meaning of the idiomatic phrase. Choice (B) is correct.

Question	Strategic Thinking

8. **F.** NO CHANGE
    G. among,
    H. between all of
    J. among
	Step 1: Read the passage and identify the issue
	
	The preposition *between* refers to only two people or items.
	
	Step 2: Eliminate answer choices that do not address the issue
	
	There are more than two items in the list "brass, strings, woodwinds, and percussion." Eliminate F and H.
	
	Step 3: Plug in the remaining answer choices and select the most correct, concise, and relevant one
	
	Choices G and (J) include the correct preposition *among*, which is used for three or more items, but G introduces an unnecessary comma. Therefore, (J) is the correct answer.

9. **A.** NO CHANGE
    B. Its'
    C. Their
    D. Its
	Step 1: Read the passage and identify the issue
	
	The sentence calls for a possessive pronoun for the word *work*, mentioned in the previous sentence.
	
	Step 2: Eliminate answer choices that do not address the issue
	
	Eliminate A and B because *it's* and *its'* are not possessive pronouns. (*Its'* is never correct.)
	
	Step 3: Plug in the remaining answer choices and select the most correct, concise, and relevant one
	
	Their is a possessive pronoun, but it is plural. *Its* is a singular possessive pronoun. Choice (D) is correct.

You have seen the ways in which the ACT tests you on Usage in English passages and the way an ACT expert approaches these types of questions. Use the Kaplan Method for ACT English to answer the questions that accompany the following English passage excerpts. Remember to look at the strategic thinking questions that have been laid out for you—some of the answers have been filled in, but you will have to complete some of the answers. Use your responses to the strategic thinking questions to select the correct answer, just as you will on Test Day.

Questions 10–17 are based on the following passage.

Galloping Gertie

For four months in the fall of 1940, citizens of the Puget Sound area of Washington <u>was using</u> one
10
of the <u>most illustrious, and most dangerous,</u> suspension bridges ever built. The Tacoma Narrows Bridge,
11
or "Galloping Gertie," enjoyed a <u>relative short life</u> compared to similar structures in the United States. In
12
its short career, "Gertie" taught important lessons on what to do—and what not to do—when building a

suspension bridge.

Question	Strategic Thinking
10. F. NO CHANGE G. used H. are using J. is using	**Step 1: Read the passage and identify the issue** The subject of the sentence, *citizens*, is plural, but the verb phrase *was using* is singular. **Step 2: Eliminate answer choices that do not address the issue** Eliminate F and J, since they contain singular verb phrases. **Step 3: Plug in the remaining answer choices and select the most correct, concise, and relevant one**

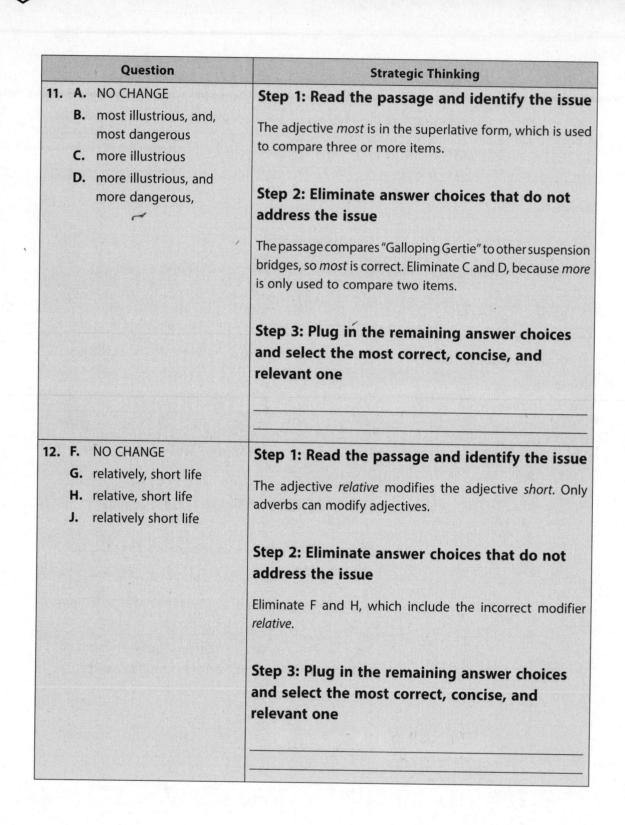

Question	Strategic Thinking
11. **A.** NO CHANGE **B.** most illustrious, and, most dangerous **C.** more illustrious **D.** more illustrious, and more dangerous,	**Step 1: Read the passage and identify the issue** The adjective *most* is in the superlative form, which is used to compare three or more items. **Step 2: Eliminate answer choices that do not address the issue** The passage compares "Galloping Gertie" to other suspension bridges, so *most* is correct. Eliminate C and D, because *more* is only used to compare two items. **Step 3: Plug in the remaining answer choices and select the most correct, concise, and relevant one** _____ _____
12. **F.** NO CHANGE **G.** relatively, short life **H.** relative, short life **J.** relatively short life	**Step 1: Read the passage and identify the issue** The adjective *relative* modifies the adjective *short*. Only adverbs can modify adjectives. **Step 2: Eliminate answer choices that do not address the issue** Eliminate F and H, which include the incorrect modifier *relative*. **Step 3: Plug in the remaining answer choices and select the most correct, concise, and relevant one** _____ _____

State officials in Washington saw <u>a need in a bridge</u> across Puget Sound to connect the city of Tacoma,

13

on the mainland, with the Olympic Peninsula on the other side of the Sound. The closest point was the

Tacoma Narrows, a windy 2,800-foot gap that, at the time, appeared to be the ideal place for a suspension

bridge. Construction began in November of 1938, and the bridge was officially opened on July 1, 1940.

Spanning the length of the Narrows, the Tacoma Narrows Bridge was the third-largest span in the world at

the time and <u>is hailed</u> by the public as a triumph of engineering.

14

Questions	Strategic Thinking

13. **A.** NO CHANGE
   B. a need with a bridge
   C. a need for a bridge
   D. a need, and a bridge
	Step 1: Read the passage and identify the issue
	
	The underlined phrase includes the preposition *in*, which indicates this is an idiom question.
	
	Step 2: Eliminate answer choices that do not address the issue
	
	_____
	_____
	
	Step 3: Plug in the remaining answer choices and select the most correct, concise, and relevant one
	
	_____
	_____

Questions	Strategic Thinking
14. F. NO CHANGE **G.** was hailed **H.** was hailed, at the time, **J.** is being hailed	**Step 1: Read the passage and identify the issue** This sentence requires past tense verbs. The verb phrase *is hailed* is present tense. **Step 2: Eliminate answer choices that do not address the issue** **Step 3: Plug in the remaining answer choices and select the most correct, concise, and relevant one**

Even during construction, though, the bridge acquired its ominous nickname. Although they knew about form and structure, the bridge's engineers failed to take into account aerodynamics, particularly the gusts of the Narrows and <u>their effect</u> on the roadway. Because the roadbed was made of solid, stiffening plate

15
girders, <u>they could not</u> absorb the winds of the Sound. Instead, the road acted like a giant sail, collecting the

16
force of the gusts. The narrowness of the bridge—it was only two lanes wide—made it extremely flexible. Therefore, on any windy day, the roadway buckled and contorted, or "galloped"—<u>hence, its' nickname.</u> The

17
undulation became so severe that the bridge was eventually closed to traffic.

Question	Strategic Thinking
15. A. NO CHANGE **B.** its effect **C.** their affect **D.** its affect	**Step 1: Read the passage and identify the issue** The underlined segment contains the commonly misused word *effect*. **Step 2: Eliminate answer choices that do not address the issue** **Step 3: Plug in the remaining answer choices and select the most correct, concise, and relevant one**
16. F. NO CHANGE **G.** they cannot **H.** it cannot **J.** it could not	**Step 1: Read the passage and identify the issue** **Step 2: Eliminate answer choices that do not address the issue** **Step 3: Plug in the remaining answer choices and select the most correct, concise, and relevant one**

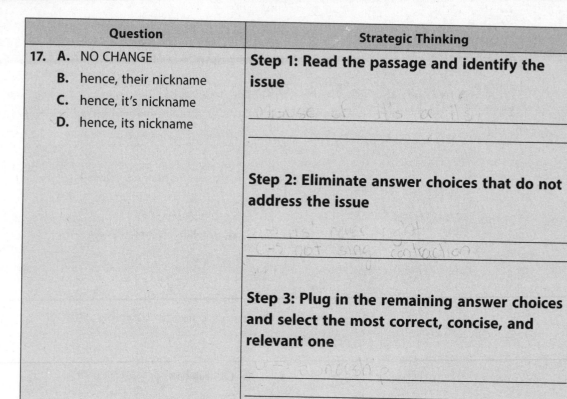

Question	Strategic Thinking
17. **A.** NO CHANGE 　　**B.** hence, their nickname 　　**C.** hence, it's nickname 　　**D.** hence, its nickname	**Step 1: Read the passage and identify the issue** _Use of it's a its._ **Step 2: Eliminate answer choices that do not address the issue** _it's never right_ _C - not sing contraction_ **Step 3: Plug in the remaining answer choices and select the most correct, concise, and relevant one** _V = ownership_

Answers and Explanations are provided at the end of the book.

Now try a test-like ACT English passage and question set on your own. Give yourself 5 minutes to read the passage and answer the questions.

> Questions 18–26 are based on the following passage.

Basketry

Basketry may be the world's oldest handicraft.

The earlier examples of basketry are 10,000 years old.
             18

18. **F.** NO CHANGE
    G. earlier examples in basketry
    H. earliest examples of basketry
    J. earliest examples for basketry

These ancient fragments, which have been preserved good
                                         19
in the dry environment of Danger Cave, Utah, show that

19. **A.** NO CHANGE
    B. has been preserved well
    C. has been preserved good
    D. have been preserved well

early Native Americans know the art of weaving
                        20
semi-rigid materials into useful objects. The remains

of baskets are also found on every continent.

20. **F.** NO CHANGE
    G. knew
    H. knew:
    J. know that

Materials, rather than technique or decoration,

is oftentimes most useful in identifying a basket's origin.
            21
Willow, just pliant enough to be either woven or plaited,

is the favored basket-making material of northern

Europe. In other areas, basket makers use relatively rigid

materials, such as bamboo and rattan. Africa has yielded

many basket-making materials, including palm leaves,
            22
tree roots, and grasses.

21. **A.** NO CHANGE
    B. is oftentimes most used
    C. are oftentimes most useful
    D. was oftentimes most useful

22. **F.** NO CHANGE
    G. many basket-making materials:
    H. much basket-making materials;
    J. much basket-making materials,

Watching a craftsperson weave a basket can be a marvelous experience. The craftsperson, who works <u>quick and gracefully,</u> passes the weft over and under the
23
foundation element, or warp. Although each culture has

23. A. NO CHANGE
   B. quickly and gracefully,
   C. quick and graceful,
   D. quickly and graceful,

<u>its own</u> unique basket-making patterns, the most
24
common and most beautiful patterns worldwide are twillings and twinings.

24. F. NO CHANGE
   G. it's own
   H. their own
   J. they're own

Unfortunately, the traditional art of basket making has been eroded by the pressures of commercialism. Many modern craftspeople must choose <u>among</u>
25
traditional artistry and financial security.

25. A. NO CHANGE
   B. along with
   C. in between
   D. between

Sadly, factory-made baskets today <u>are a far cry for</u>
26
the delicate, geometric designs of the solitary artisan. Indeed, the handmade basket has become an "artwork." Now, collectors who prize the work of the traditional basket maker may fly thousands of miles in order to purchase genuine designs. Under such financial pressure, how long will basketmakers be able to preserve their standards?

26. F. NO CHANGE
   G. are a far cry from
   H. are a far cry: for
   J. are a far cry of

Answers and Explanations are provided at the end of the book.

ON YOUR OWN

The following questions provide an opportunity to practice the concepts and strategic thinking covered in this chapter. While many of the questions pertain to Usage, some touch on other concepts tested on the English test to ensure that your practice is test-like, with a variety of question types per passage.

Frankenstein

[1]

The character of Frankenstein did not originate in Hollywood. Rather, the legendary mad scientist <u>whom sought to reanimate</u> lifeless bodies was the creation of Mary Wollstonecraft Shelley,
₁

1. A. NO CHANGE
   B. whom seeks to reanimate
   C. who sought in reanimating
   D. who sought to reanimate

<u>who's</u> married to famed poet Percy Bysshe Shelley. Her
₂
Frankenstein, or the Modern Prometheus, published in

2. F. NO CHANGE
   G. who had
   H. who was
   J. whose

1818, is considered <u>one of the greater</u> horror tales of all
₃
time.

3. A. NO CHANGE
   B. one of her greater
   C. one of the greatest
   D. the greatest

[2]

Mary Shelley created her nightmarish subject in response to a bet. [A] <u>Her, her husband, Lord Byron, and</u>
₄
<u>Byron's physician</u> had a contest to see who could write
₄
the best ghost story.

4. F. NO CHANGE
   G. She, her husband, Lord Byron, and Byron's physician
   H. She herself, her husband, Lord Byron, and his physician
   J. Her, her husband Lord Byron, and Lord Byron's physician

Although <u>it was begun whimsical,</u> her tale became
                        5
a serious examination of the fate of an individual who

decides to overstep moral and social bounds. [B]

[3]

Shelley's novel tells the story of a scientist,

Dr. Victor Frankenstein, who discovers the secret

of bringing corpses <u>back from life</u> and
                        6

creates a monster with material from graveyards,
<u>creates a monster</u>
       7
dissecting rooms, and slaughterhouses.

<u>Similar to</u> the monster's gruesome appearance, he is
       8
basically good. [C] After being rejected by

Dr. Frankenstein and all other people

<u>with whom he comes into contact,</u> the monster becomes
                        9
violent. One by one, the monster murders the people

Dr. Frankenstein cares for the most: <u>his younger</u>
                                            10
<u>brother, and his best friend, and he even killed his wife.</u>
                        10

5. **A.** NO CHANGE

    B. it began whimsical,

    C. it was begun whimsically, but

    D. it was begun whimsically,

6. **F.** NO CHANGE

    G. back through life

    H. back to life

    J. back into life

7. **A.** NO CHANGE

    B. creating a monster,

    C. created a monster,

    D. created a monster

8. **F.** NO CHANGE

    G. Although

    H. Despite

    J. Because of

9. **A.** NO CHANGE

    B. with whom he contacts,

    C. who he comes into contact with,

    D. whom he comes into contact with

10. **F.** NO CHANGE

    G. his younger brother, and his best friend, and his wife.

    H. his younger brother, best friend, and his wife.

    J. his younger brother, his best friend, and his wife.

[D] The tale ends as Dr. Frankenstein chases the monster to the North Pole, <u>where each of them eventually die.</u>
11

[4]

[1] The critical acclaim and continued popularity of the story is also evidenced by the numerous films that have been based on it. [2] Although it is a horror story, Mary Shelley's *Frankenstein* is respected by many as a literary classic. [3] Some versions, like *Young Frankenstein*, <u>provide a humorous retelling of the story.</u>
12

[4] Other versions, like the most recent *Mary Shelley's Frankenstein*, attempt to be faithful to the original. 13

11. **A.** NO CHANGE
    B. where both of them eventually dies.
    C. where each of them eventually have died.
    D. where each of them eventually dies.

12. **F.** NO CHANGE
    G. provide a humorous, retelling of the story.
    H. provides a humorous retelling of the story.
    J. humorously provide a comedic retelling of the story.

13. The correct order of the sentences in Paragraph 4 is:
    A. NO CHANGE
    B. 3, 4, 1, 2
    C. 2, 1, 3, 4
    D. 2, 3, 4, 1

14. The writer wants to add the following sentence to the essay:

    > The monster, who is nameless, only becomes evil when his creator refuses to accept and care for him.

    The sentence would most logically be placed at Point:
    F. A in Paragraph 2.
    G. B in Paragraph 2.
    H. C in Paragraph 3.
    J. D in Paragraph 3.

Question 15 asks about the passage as a whole.

15. Suppose the writer's primary purpose had been to write an essay analyzing the film adaptations of Mary Shelley's *Frankenstein*. Would this essay accomplish this purpose?

A. Yes, because it compares and contrasts various film versions of the story.

B. Yes, because it critiques how closely film versions follow the original story.

C. No, because it only focuses on one type of film adaptation of the story.

D. No, because the film adaptations are one point in an overall discussion of the story.

Answers and Explanations are provided at the end of the book.

PRODUCTION OF WRITING & KNOWLEDGE OF LANGUAGE

BY THE END OF THIS UNIT, YOU WILL BE ABLE TO:

1. Evaluate the organization, effectiveness, and clarity of an ACT English passage

2. Identify proper and effective language use

CHAPTER 5

Organization, Unity, and Cohesion

CHAPTER OBJECTIVES

By the end of this chapter, you will be able to:

1. Organize a text's information and ideas into the most logical order

2. Evaluate whether transition words, phrases, or sentences are used effectively to introduce, conclude, or connect information and ideas as well as make revisions to improve text as needed

SMARTPOINTS

Point Value	SmartPoints Category
5 Points	Organization, Unity, and Cohesion

ORGANIZATION, UNITY, AND COHESION

Organization, Unity, and Cohesion questions require you to assess the logic and coherence of an English passage. These questions differ in scope; you might be asked to organize the writing at the level of a sentence, a paragraph, or even an entire passage.

Transitions

If a transition word is underlined, you must determine the writer's intended meaning and find the transition that best conveys this meaning. Writers use transitions to show relationships such as contrast, cause and effect, continuation, emphasis, and chronology. Knowing which types of words convey each type of transition will help you choose the correct word on Test Day.

Contrast Transitions	Cause-and-Effect Transitions	Sequential Transitions	Emphasis Transitions
although, but, despite, even though, however, in contrast, nonetheless, on the other hand, rather than, though, unlike, while, yet	as a result, because, consequently, since, so, therefore, thus	after, also, before, first (second, etc.), furthermore, in addition	certainly, in fact, indeed, that is

Passage Organization

Organizing Ideas

Some Organization questions ask you to either reorder the sentences in a paragraph or reorder the paragraphs in a passage to ensure that information and ideas are logically conveyed. When reordering, begin by determining which sentence or paragraph most logically introduces the paragraph or passage, respectively.

Adding Information

Some Organization questions ask you to insert new ideas into a passage. When inserting new information into a passage, begin by determining which paragraph of the passage most logically accompanies the new idea. If more than one answer choice includes the paragraph you have in mind, plug in each new idea to see how it fits within the context. Choose the answer that best reflects the writer's tone and purpose.

Opening, Transitional, and Closing Sentences

Some Organization questions task you with improving the beginning or ending of a paragraph or passage. The transition words, phrases, or sentences must be used effectively not only to connect information and ideas but also to maintain logical structure. To answer these questions effectively, determine the writer's intended purpose, eliminate answer choices that do not reflect this purpose, and choose the most correct and relevant option.

> ✔ **Note**
>
> While conciseness is important, it should not be a primary goal when answering Organization questions. Instead, focus on picking answer choices that make the most sense logically, given your understanding of the writer's tone and purpose.

Work through the Kaplan Method for English step-by-step to answer the questions that accompany the following English passage excerpt. The table below the excerpt contains two columns. The column on the right features the strategic thinking a test expert employs when approaching passages and related questions.

Symbiotic Relationships

The following paragraphs may or may not be in the most logical order. Each paragraph is numbered in brackets, and question 4 will ask you to choose where Paragraph 3 should most logically be placed.

[1]

Usually regarded as pests, the termites of south Florida provide an excellent illustration of nature at work. In the natural world, when two or more different organisms coexist to each other's benefit, they are involved in a symbiotic relationship. [A] The dominant member of the symbiotic pair or group is known as the "host," while the smaller, less dominant member is a "parasite."

[2]

[A] A classic symbiotic relationship of this kind takes place in the digestive tract of Florida wood-eating termites. [B] The protozoa provide the termite with a service necessary to its survival: they digest the cellulose in the wood that the termite consumes. [C] We think of a termite as being able to digest wood, but, <u>consequently</u>, it cannot. [D] The termite plays host to parasitic protozoa, single-celled organisms that live in the termite's gut. [2]

[3]

If this all sounds very strange, consider the fact that humans have their own symbiotic relationship with bacteria in their digestive tracts. Humans rely on bacterial activity in the large intestine to provide several vitamins, including vitamin K, vitamin B$_{12}$, thiamin, and riboflavin. [B] Vitamin K is particularly important because it plays a role in blood clotting, and humans do not normally get enough vitamin K in their diet.

[4]

That is far from the whole story, however. The only movement that protozoa are capable of on their own is spinning; they cannot move around inside the termite's intestine to reach the cellulose. This problem is solved by the presence of another parasite, the third member of the partnership. [C] Each protozoan harbors a colony of thousands of bacteria that are attached to its surface. Only two to three micrometers long each, the bacteria are grouped in parallel rows end-to-end over the 150-micrometer length of each protozoan's outer membrane. Whip-like tentacles on the surfaces of the bacteria (known as flagella) overlap to form continuous strands that wave back and forth and propel each host protozoan forward. [D] These bacteria may do more than just drive the protozoan around. Some bacteria can be found inside the protozoan and are thought to help with the digestion of tiny wood particles. 3

Question	Strategic Thinking

1.   **A.** NO CHANGE
     B. however
     C. in fact
     D. therefore
	Step 1: Read the passage and identify the issue
	
	The underlined word is a cause-and-effect transition, which doesn't make sense in context.
	
	Step 2: Eliminate answer choices that do not address the issue
	
	Eliminate A and D because this sentence does not call for a cause-and-effect transition. Eliminate B because *however* along with *but* would be redundant.
	
	Step 3: Plug in the remaining answer choices and select the most correct, concise, and relevant one
	
	Choice (C) contains the correct emphasis transition and fits within the context of the sentence.

Question	Strategic Thinking
2. The correct order for the sentences in paragraph 2 is: **F.** NO CHANGE **G.** A, C, D, B **H.** D, A, C, B **J.** D, C, B, A	**Step 1: Read the passage and identify the issue** When the ACT asks you to reorder the sentences in a paragraph, first determine which sentence logically introduces the main topic for that paragraph. **Step 2: Eliminate answer choices that do not address the issue** The current first sentence, [A], properly introduces the topic of the paragraph: the symbiotic relationship that aids in termites' digestion. Eliminate H and J, which do not start with proper introductory sentences. **Step 3: Plug in the remaining answer choices and select the most correct, concise, and relevant one** Choice F includes the correct introductory sentence, but the next sentence discusses "the protozoa" as if this information had already been explained. The correct answer is (G), which contains the most logical order.
3. The writer would like to add the following sentence: This allows the protozoan to move around and to continue consuming cellulose within the termite. The sentence would be most logically placed at point: **A.** A in Paragraph 1. **B.** B in Paragraph 3. **C.** C in Paragraph 4. **D.** D in Paragraph 4.	**Step 1: Read the passage and identify the issue** The writer would like to add a sentence that elaborates on the mechanism that aids the protozoan's movement. Begin by determining which paragraph most logically accompanies this sentence's idea. **Step 2: Eliminate answer choices that do not address the issue** Paragraph 4 discusses protozoa in depth. Eliminate A and B because paragraphs 1 and 3 do not primarily address the topic of protozoa. **Step 3: Plug in the remaining answer choices and select the most correct, concise, and relevant one** Choice C's placement does not make sense in context. Choice (D) correctly places the additional sentence directly after a sentence that introduces the mechanism protozoa use to move around.

Question	Strategic Thinking
4. For the sake of logic and coherence, Paragraph 3 should be: F. where it is now. G. before Paragraph 1. H. after Paragraph 1. J. after Paragraph 4.	**Step 1: Read the passage and identify the issue** When asked to check for proper passage organization, check the main idea of each paragraph as well as the transitions from one paragraph to another. **Step 2: Eliminate answer choices that do not address the issue** Paragraph 3 discusses humans' symbiotic relationship with bacteria. There is no transition to this either from Paragraph 2 or in the introduction to Paragraph 3, so you can eliminate F. Eliminate G and H because both Paragraphs 1 and 2 discuss symbiotic relationships in termites, not humans. Additionally, Paragraph 3's opening statement, "If this all sounds very strange," makes for an apt concluding paragraph. **Step 3: Plug in the remaining answer choices and select the most correct, concise, and relevant one** Paragraph 3 should be placed after Paragraph 4 to make the passage flow logically. The correct answer is (J).

You have seen the ways in which the ACT tests you on Organization, Unity, and Cohesion in English passages and how an ACT expert approaches these types of questions. Use the Kaplan Method for English to answer the questions that accompany the following English passage excerpts. Remember to look at the strategic thinking questions that have been provided for you—some of the answers have been filled in, but you will have to complete the answers to others. Use your answers to the strategic thinking questions to select the correct answer, just as you will on Test Day.

Eva Salazar: Master Weaver

The Kumeyaay Indians are a Native American community that has thrived in San Diego, California, for 12,000 years. They have retained a rich cultural and social life <u>in the event that</u> a forced split
5
approximately 140 years ago, when some Kumeyaay were driven across the border into Mexico. Now resettled in the small farming community of San José de la Zorra, the families have not forsaken their traditional way of life.

Question	Strategic Thinking
5. **A.** NO CHANGE **B.** because of **C.** despite **D.** however	**Step 1: Read the passage and identify the issue** The underlined transition indicates cause and effect, but the sentence needs a contrast transition. **Step 2: Eliminate answer choices that do not address the issue** Eliminate A and B, since they do not contain contrast transitions. **Step 3: Plug in the remaining answer choices and select the most correct, concise, and relevant one** <u>C - contrast transition</u> _____

[1] It is in this remote valley that Eva Salazar learned the ancient art of basket weaving from her tribal elders. [2] Among the Kumeyaay, as is common in many Native American groups, women have the crucial responsibility of making baskets, which are important artifacts of everyday life. [3] Kumeyaay baskets are tightly woven with expressive designs. They are made mostly for utilitarian uses: cooking, storing food products, and gathering ingredients. [4] As traditional objects of art, they are also valued for their aesthetic beauty. 6

Following in her ancestor's footsteps, Eva Salazar uses native materials to weave her intricate baskets, primarily the strong, sharp reed known as juncus, as well as yucca, sumac, and other native plants. She colors the reeds with black walnut, elderberry, and other natural dyes. Eva specializes in coiled baskets, and her shapes and decorations echo traditional forms.

Questions	Strategic Thinking
6. For the sake of logic in this paragraph, Sentence 1 should be placed: F. where it is now. G. after Sentence 2. H. after Sentence 3. J. after Sentence 4.	**Step 1: Read the passage and identify the issue** Determine whether the current placement introduces this paragraph and connects it to the previous paragraph. **Step 2: Eliminate answer choices that do not address the issue** The previous paragraph discusses the location of the Kumeyaay Indians. Sentence 1 connects this location to Eva Salazar's art. **Step 3: Plug in the remaining answer choices and select the most correct, concise, and relevant one** _____ _____

Questions	Strategic Thinking
7. If the author were to delete the underlined portion, the sentence would primarily lose: **A.** nothing. **B.** a key detail that explains Eva Salazar's relationship to the Kumeyaay. **C.** an explanation as to why Eva Salazar used the Kumeyaay method in her work. **D.** the reason why the Kumeyaay value Eva Salazar's work.	**Step 1: Read the passage and identify the issue** Determine the importance of the underlined phrase. **Step 2: Eliminate answer choices that do not address the issue** _____ _____ **Step 3: Plug in the remaining answer choices and select the most correct, concise, and relevant one** _____ _____

Though she is best known for her baskets, Eva Salazar also makes dolls, willow bark skirts, nets, and
8
shell necklaces. Her most ambitious work is a basket measuring almost three feet in diameter. The basket

took her two years to weave and represents a masterpiece of Native American art.

Surprisingly, Eva is heralded as a master weaver. Now an American citizen living in San Diego, she
9
remains focused on traditional tribal arts and teaches basket weaving at local reservations and colleges.

Her baskets continue to represent the height of Kumeyaay basket weaving artistry.
10

English

Questions	Strategic Thinking
8. **F.** NO CHANGE **G.** Because **H.** Nonetheless **J.** On the other hand	**Step 1: Read the passage and identify the issue** Check to make sure the underlined transition accurately conveys the author's intent. **Step 2: Eliminate answer choices that do not address the issue** _____ _____ **Step 3: Plug in the remaining answer choices and select the most correct, concise, and relevant one** _____ _____
9. **A.** NO CHANGE **B.** Today, **C.** On the contrary, **D.** For example,	**Step 1: Read the passage and identify the issue** _____ _____ **Step 2: Eliminate answer choices that do not address the issue** _____ _____ **Step 3: Plug in the remaining answer choices and select the most correct, concise, and relevant one** _____ _____

Questions	Strategic Thinking
10. Which choice most effectively concludes the passage? **F.** NO CHANGE **G.** She is famous for not letting the Kumeyaay traditions be lost. **H.** Her work has inspired countless artists to follow in her footsteps. **J.** She will be remembered for her unique adaptations of the Kumeyaay traditions.	**Step 1: Read the passage and identify the issue** _____ _____ **Step 2: Eliminate answer choices that do not address the issue** _____ _____ **Step 3: Plug in the remaining answer choices and select the most correct, concise, and relevant one** _____ _____

Answers and Explanations are provided at the end of the book.

Now try a test-like ACT English passage and question set on your own. Give yourself 5 minutes to read the passage and answer the questions.

The Victorian Way of Life

The following paragraphs may or may not be in the most logical order. Each paragraph is numbered in brackets, and question 16 will ask you to choose where Paragraph 3 should most logically be placed.

---

[1]

The Victorian Era stretched from the coronation of Queen Victoria in 1837 to her death in 1901. Over her 63-year reign, her influence on Britain was enormous. Politics and international affairs aside, manners, morals, and even dress conformed to Victoria's straightlaced concepts of what was and was not acceptable. Despite
11
the upper classes, propriety and reputation had to be spotlessly maintained.

11. A. NO CHANGE
     B. Especially for
     C. Regardless of
     D. Occasionally among

[2]

Unmarried men and women were strictly supervised to keep improprieties, such as a slight touch of a hand, from occurring. Proper introductions were mandatory; a woman would not presume to converse with a gentleman to whom she had not been formally introduced. Courtship was formal and lengthy, and it was conducted only when approved by parents or guardians, who were probably nervous about their teenagers
12
getting into trouble.
12

12. F. NO CHANGE
     G. who took their responsibility super seriously.
     H. who were often very loyal to both their country and their queen.
     J. who had the final word on marriage as well.

English

[3]

Early in the era, men wore tight-fitting calf-length frock coats with linen shirts underneath. As the decades progressed, three-piece suits became popular, tie fashions changed, and the blazer became acceptable for informal activities. Hats, from top hats for upper-class men to bowlers for the working man, were an essential piece of clothing.

[4]

Fashion styles were similarly prescribed. In the 1840s, women's dresses were relatively simple, albeit with a number of stiff petticoats. Thirty years later, restricting corsets were worn to pull in the waist to the smallest width possible <u>while</u> still leaving the wearer room to breathe. Hats and gloves were expected for all occasions.
¹³

13. **A.** NO CHANGE
    B. rather than
    C. therefore
    D. thus

[5]

Most upper-class women were educated only to the point of literacy, with household management and domestic arts such as needlework heavily emphasized. <u>Because of this,</u> some women were quite well schooled,
¹⁴
depending on their fathers' opinion about the propriety of educated females. Queen Victoria, in fact, fell somewhere in the middle of that spectrum; she was well versed in English, French, and German but did not learn any political theory or philosophy.

14. **F.** NO CHANGE
    G. Therefore,
    H. Indeed,
    J. On the other hand,

[6]

It is a mark of the length, importance, and impact of Queen Victoria's reign that this period of British history is known as the Victorian Era. She left her indelible mark not only on society and culture <u>as well as</u> on British influence throughout the world.
15

15. **A.** NO CHANGE
    B. therefore
    C. but also
    D. and also

Question 16 asks about the passage as a whole.

16. For the sake of the logic and coherence of this essay, Paragraph 3 should be placed:

    F. where it is now.
    G. after Paragraph 1.
    H. after Paragraph 4.
    J. after Paragraph 5.

Answers and Explanations are provided at the end of the book.

ON YOUR OWN

The following questions provide an opportunity to practice the concepts and strategic thinking covered in this chapter. While many of the questions pertain to Organization, Unity, and Cohesion, some touch on other concepts tested on the English test to ensure that your practice is test-like, with a variety of question types per passage.

Early 19th-Century Women in New England

> The following paragraphs may or may not be in the most logical order. Each paragraph is numbered in brackets, and question 15 will ask you to choose where Paragraph 5 should most logically be placed.

[1]

In the early 19th century, the market economy expanded, and the home became a haven <u>from the developed commercialism.</u> During this time, middle-class wives and mothers in New England assumed the role of protectors and leaders of home life.

With men working in <u>factories;</u> women were responsible for housekeeping, providing religious education, and raising children.

[2]

<u>Rather than</u> a broader degree of autonomy and a new sense of authority within their homes, women were given opportunities for wage work; this included producing goods, such as palm-leaf hats and straw-braided items, for wider consumption. Wage work provided women with the ability to live at home <u>while</u> earning money to supplement the family's income.

1. **A.** NO CHANGE
   B. from developed commercialism.
   C. from the developing commercialism.
   D. from commercialism.

2. **F.** NO CHANGE
   G. factories,
   H. factories—
   J. factories

3. **A.** NO CHANGE
   B. Therefore,
   C. In addition to
   D. Despite

4. **F.** NO CHANGE
   G. even though
   H. in spite of
   J. thus

[3]

[1] Shoemaking was another source of income for women, <u>being that</u> their work was socially and physi-
5
cally isolated from the shoe binding that took place in cobblers' shops.

5. **A.** NO CHANGE
    B. but
    C. because
    D. in the event that

[2] <u>Also,</u> when increased demand for shoes required the
6
use of sewing machines to speed up the pace of produc-
tion, women organized a small-scale movement that trained young women to use sewing machines in their homes.

6. **F.** NO CHANGE
    G. Indeed,
    H. Thus,
    J. However,

[3] <u>Despite</u> this bold move, women who worked at home
7
as shoe binders remained isolated and vulnerable to competition from the more lucrative and efficient factories. [4] Women were also denied craft status and admis-
sion into unions, which limited their influence. 8

7. **A.** NO CHANGE
    B. More importantly,
    C. Even more than
    D. Due to

8. For the sake of logic, Sentence 4 should be placed:
    F. where it is now.
    G. before Sentence 1.
    H. before Sentence 2.
    J. before Sentence 3.

[4]

Women <u>working</u> in factories were also prohibited
9
from joining unions, allowing factories such as the Lowell Mills to exploit their labor.

9. **A.** NO CHANGE
    B. that worked
    C. who worked
    D. whom worked

<u>As a result,</u> female factory workers were offered a type of
10
work outside of the home

10. **F.** NO CHANGE
    G. Rather,
    H. However,
    J. Hence,

and away from their families, <u>which provided</u> them with
11
a new level of independence.

11. **A.** NO CHANGE
    B. that provided
    C. provided
    D. while providing

[5]

For many women, the <u>changes in womens roles</u>
12
during the first half of the 19th century were a part of

a positive and liberating transformation. For others,

though, either their roles remained quite traditional

<u>nor</u> their new endeavors, such as working in factories,
13
were not as freeing as they had hoped.

12. **F.** NO CHANGE
    G. changing womens'
    H. changes in
    J. changes in women's

13. **A.** NO CHANGE
    B. nor,
    C. or
    D. or,

Women <u>knows</u> they still had a long way to go, but many
14
were prepared, and some were even eager, for the jour-

ney ahead.

14. **F.** NO CHANGE
    G. knew
    H. knowing
    J. know

Question 15 asks about the passage as a whole.

15. For the sake of the logic and coherence of this
essay, Paragraph 5 should be placed:

    A. where it is now.

    B. before Paragraph 1.

    C. before Paragraph 2.

    D. before Paragraph 4.

Answers and Explanations are provided at the end
of the book.

CHAPTER 6

Topic Development

CHAPTER OBJECTIVES

By the end of this chapter, you will be able to:

1. Identify whether material is appropriate in relation to a passage's purpose, unity, or focus

2. Determine the effect of adding, revising, or deleting information in a passage

3. Determine whether an English passage accomplishes a certain purpose

SMARTPOINTS

Point Value	SmartPoints Category
6 Points	Topic Development

TOPIC DEVELOPMENT

Topic Development questions test your ability to determine why a passage is written and whether particular information helps accomplish that purpose. There are two subcategories within Topic Development: Supporting Material and Writer's Purpose.

Supporting Material questions may ask you to:

- Evaluate whether material maintains the focus and unity of the passage
- Identify the purposes of parts of the passage
- Determine the effect of adding, revising, or deleting information

Writer's Purpose questions may ask you to:

- Determine whether a sentence or a paragraph has met the writer's intended goal
- Determine whether an entire passage has met the writer's intended goal

SUPPORTING MATERIAL

Focus and Unity

When determining the focus, or the author's subject matter and particular emphasis within that subject matter, of a passage, ask yourself what the passage is discussing. Often, the first paragraph and the topic sentences of the remaining paragraphs reveal the main focus of the passage.

In order to be unified, a passage must maintain a consistent focus on its subject matter. Information that is not relevant to the focus of the passage should be deleted. Keep in mind that each paragraph has its own main idea and all the information in the paragraph should relate to this main idea. Even information that relates to the overall subject of the passage should be deleted if it does not match the focus of the paragraph in which it appears.

Purpose

Once you've determined a passage's focus, identifying the purpose of the passage or a portion of the passage will be much easier. To determine the purpose of a passage, ask yourself what the author is trying to achieve by writing the passage. The writer selects particular wording and examples to support the focus of the passage while maintaining a consistent tone and purpose.

Effect of Adding, Revising, or Deleting Information

When asked about adding or revising a selection, consider what new information the selection provides and whether that information: (a) matches the writer's focus and (b) helps express the purpose of the sentence or paragraph. When asked about deleting a selection, consider what the passage might be missing if the proposed revision were made. To answer these questions, read the passage both ways—with and without the proposed change—to see which sounds more cohesive. Be sure to read the sentences before and after the proposed revision to best assess the change in context.

> ✔ **Expert Tip**
>
> When the question has a question stem, you are not being tested on concision, or expressing an idea in the fewest words possible, even when asked about deleting information. The test shows no preference for deleting information on Writing Strategy questions, so don't automatically think that deleting is the best option! When you see a question stem, focus on relevance rather than concision.

Work through the Kaplan Method for English step-by-step to answer the questions that accompany the following English passage excerpt. The table below the excerpt contains two columns. The column on the right features the strategic thinking a test expert employs when approaching passages and related questions.

Internet Advertising

Twenty years ago, large companies hoped to reach their target markets through advertisements in national magazines and network television. Smaller companies utilized local newspapers, phone books, and radio stations to reach their customers. Of course, companies <u>large and small</u> still buy advertisements
1
in mass media outlets that reach large numbers of consumers. However, companies now have the opportunity to reach their intended audience in a different way. [2]

Now, businesses can use Internet advertising, including company websites, banner advertisements, and ads generated by search engines, to reach more specifically targeted audiences. Small, local business-es have benefited greatly from the marketing opportunities presented by the Internet. [3]

Question	Strategic Thinking
1. The primary purpose of the underlined portion is to provide: ✓ **A.** a connection between the advertising methods of small and large companies. **B.** information about how companies can differ in size. **C.** a description of what makes a company large or small. **D.** an opinion about the importance of maintaining a variety of business sizes.	**Step 1: Read the passage and identify the issue** The question asks about the primary purpose of a portion of the passage, so it is testing Topic Development/Supporting Material. Consider why the author has used the particular words "large and small." In the previous sentences, the author discussed how large companies advertise differently from small companies. **Step 2: Eliminate answer choices that do not address the issue** Eliminate B because the information that companies can differ in size is not new to the paragraph. Eliminate C because the phrase does not describe what makes a company large or small. Eliminate D because the writer is not providing an opinion about the size of businesses. **Step 3: Plug in the remaining answer choices and select the most correct, concise, and relevant one** Choice (A) reflects the purpose of the phrase because it describes the way "large and small" connects the ideas in the first two sentences of the paragraph. This choice is correct.

Question	Strategic Thinking
2. In the preceding sentence, the writer is considering replacing "their intended audience" with "people." Should the writer make this revision? F. Yes, because it is more inclusive. G. Yes, because it clarifies to whom the companies want to advertise. H. No, because it loses the emphasis on whom a company can reach with its advertising. J. No, because it inaccurately portrays the purpose of advertising.	**Step 1: Read the passage and identify the issue** When a question asks whether the writer should make a revision, it's testing Topic Development/Supporting Material. Consider whether the proposed revision adds or detracts from the main focus of the paragraph. **Step 2: Eliminate answer choices that do not address the issue** The paragraph emphasizes the different advertising venues utilized by large and small companies. Because the original phrase emphasizes the different groups that could be reached by these various methods, it is a better choice than the proposed revision. Eliminate F and G. **Step 3: Plug in the remaining answer choices and select the most correct, concise, and relevant one** Eliminate J, which uses faulty reasoning. Choice (H) is correct.

Question	Strategic Thinking
3. The writer is considering adding the following sentence: Small specialty shops once were relatively limited to serving local populations of customers, but today those same shops can have customers from around the world. Should the writer make this addition here? **A.** Yes, because it explains why small businesses benefit from Internet advertising. **B.** Yes, because it clarifies the kind of advertising being discussed. **C.** No, because it does not explain why small shops should use Internet advertising. **D.** No, because it is unnecessarily specific.	**Step 1: Read the passage and identify the issue** When the question asks whether to add a sentence, the issue is Topic Development/Supporting Material. Consider what the sentence might contribute to the paragraph as a whole. **Step 2: Eliminate answer choices that do not address the issue** The paragraph describes the benefits of Internet advertising, focusing on the benefits to small businesses. The additional sentence illustrates this benefit, so it should be added to the paragraph. Eliminate C and D. **Step 3: Plug in the remaining answer choices and select the most correct, concise, and relevant one** Choice B advocates adding the sentence, but for an incorrect reason. The correct answer is (A).

WRITER'S PURPOSE

Some Topic Development questions ask explicitly about the purpose of a part of the passage or of the passage as a whole. When asked which choice best accomplishes the purpose of a part of the passage, consider the scope and function of that part. For example, a good conclusion is designed to summarize the passage, and a good paragraph transition clearly connects the ideas between the paragraphs.

Some questions ask whether the essay as a whole accomplishes a certain purpose. These questions appear at the end of the passage. In order to answer these questions, consider the overall purpose and scope of the passage. Is the passage meant to persuade the reader, or is it more neutral and explanatory? What is the main topic of the passage? Be careful not to select answer choices that are either too narrow or too broad. For example, a passage discussing the history of European fairy tales could not accurately be described as an essay on the history of literature; that description is too broad. On the other hand, describing it as an essay on one particular fairy tale would be too narrow. Incorrect answer choices that are too narrow often describe the focus of one paragraph while not capturing the scope of the entire passage.

Work through the Kaplan Method for English step-by-step to answer the questions that accompany the following English passage excerpt. The table below the excerpt contains two columns. The column on the right features the strategic thinking a test expert employs when approaching passages and related questions.

No longer are national chains the only companies that enjoy a wide range of customers. With a website and a few well-placed Internet advertisements, a small company can make itself known to potential customers who, regardless of where they live, are excited about the company's products. Internet advertising has opened up a world of possibility for companies.

Question	Strategic Thinking
4. Suppose the writer's goal had been to write an essay about how the Internet has changed the world. Would this essay accomplish that goal? F. Yes, because it describes how businesses use the Internet. G. Yes, because it emphasizes the broad impact the Internet has had. H. No, because it suggests that companies would have changed without the Internet. J. No, because it focuses on advertising rather than the overall impact of the Internet.	**Step 1: Read the passage and identify the issue** The issue is Topic Development / Writer's Purpose. When asked whether the passage accomplishes a certain purpose, watch out for purposes that are too narrow or too broad. **Step 2: Eliminate answer choices that do not address the issue** The focus of the passage is how Internet advertising has affected businesses, so the stated purpose is too broad. Eliminate F and G. **Step 3: Plug in the remaining answer choices and select the most correct, concise, and relevant one** The passage does not make the suggestion described in H. Choice (J) is correct.

You have seen the ways in which the ACT tests you on Topic Development in English passages and how an ACT expert approaches these types of questions. Use the Kaplan Method for English to answer the questions that accompany the following English passage excerpts. Remember to look at the strategic thinking questions that have been provided for you—some of the answers have been filled in, but you will have to complete the answers to others. Use your answers to the strategic thinking questions to select the correct answer, just as you will on Test Day.

Humphrey Bogart

Although the screen appeal of Humphrey DeForest Bogart has seemingly grown exponentially in the years following his death in 1957, the early stages of his career were not marked by success. In fact, when one considers Bogart's early academic pursuits and formative years, it is perhaps surprising that he made it onto the stage at all.

Born in New York City in 1899 as the son of a prominent surgeon, young Humphrey was quickly put on the academic track to medical school. After finishing his early schooling, he was sent to the prestigious Phillips Academy in Andover, Massachusetts. Bogart, however, was not inclined toward academics, and he was often described during his adolescent years as a frequent instigator of trouble. 5 In the spring of 1918, Bogart chose to enter the navy. It was in the service that he received an injury to his mouth that partially paralyzed his upper lip, creating a distinctive snarl that would come to be the signature of his stardom. 6

Question	Strategic Thinking
5. At this point, the writer is considering adding the following true statement: Indeed, soon after he had arrived at Andover, he ran into disciplinary problems and was eventually expelled. Should the writer make this addition here? **A.** Yes, because it explains Bogart's rise to stardom. **B.** Yes, because it adds details that support the previous sentence. **C.** No, because it deviates from the passage's focus on fame. **D.** No, because it distracts from the emphasis on Bogart's academic accomplishments.	**Step 1: Read the passage and identify the issue** When asked to consider adding a statement, determine the focus of the paragraph in which it would appear. **Step 2: Eliminate answer choices that do not address the issue** This paragraph discusses Bogart's troubles with pursuing an academic track. The proposed statement adds additional information about these troubles, so it relates to the paragraph. Eliminate C and D. **Step 3: Plug in the remaining answer choices and select the most correct, concise, and relevant one** _____
6. In the preceding sentence, the writer is considering replacing *stardom* with *eventual stardom*. Should the writer make this revision? **F.** Yes, because it emphasizes Bogart's slow rise to fame. **G.** Yes, because it adds a new detail to the passage. **H.** No, because it places too much emphasis on Bogart's past. **J.** No, because it fails to describe how Bogart became famous.	**Step 1: Read the passage and identify the issue** When considering whether to revise a phrase, determine what, if anything, the revision would add. **Step 2: Eliminate answer choices that do not address the issue** The proposed revision places greater emphasis on how far Bogart was from fame, which supports the main idea expressed in Paragraph 1. Thus, the writer should make the revision. Eliminate H and J. **Step 3: Plug in the remaining answer choices and select the most correct, concise, and relevant one** _____

[7] He contacted a family friend in the business who hired him to work in a theater office in New York. Bogart eventually became a stage manager and finally worked himself into some minor roles on the stage. <u>His inexperience showed, however, and</u> he struggled to find any substantive parts. In the early
                                                                8
1930s, Bogart set out for Hollywood, and although he quickly signed a contract with Fox Pictures, he appeared, marginally, in only three films.

Question	Strategic Thinking
7. Which of the following true statements would provide the best transition from the preceding paragraph to this paragraph? **A.** Bogart eventually became a well-known actor. **B.** Bogart did not see his navy service as a lifelong career, and he served for only two years. **C.** When Bogart was released from the navy in 1920, he turned his attention toward the theater. **D.** Bogart's time in the theater was next.	**Step 1: Read the passage and identify the issue** The issue is Topic Development/Supporting Material. Read the surrounding sentences to determine what content the passage is transitioning between. A transition should connect the previous paragraph with the content of the current paragraph. **Step 2: Eliminate answer choices that do not address the issue** _____ _____ **Step 3: Plug in the remaining answer choices and select the most correct, concise, and relevant one** _____ _____

Question	Strategic Thinking
8. If the writer were to delete the underlined portion (adjusting capitalization as necessary), the sentence would primarily lose: **F.** details about Bogart's success. **G.** a warning against changing careers. **H.** an example illustrating Bogart's lack of expertise. **J.** a reason for Bogart's slow start in the theater.	**Step 1: Read the passage and identify the issue** When asked what would be lost if a phrase were deleted, consider what the phrase adds to the surrounding text. **Step 2: Eliminate answer choices that do not address the issue** _____ _____ _____ **Step 3: Plug in the remaining answer choices and select the most correct, concise, and relevant one** _____ _____

Frustrated with his stagnant career, he returned to the Broadway stage and finally caught his break as Duke Mantee in the play *The Petrified Forest*. [9] Bogart's performance as the quintessential tough guy soon catapulted his career. Bogart consistently created rich and complex screen images punctuated by his hangdog expressions, perennial five o'clock shadow, and world-weary attitude. From his early gangster roles to his consummate portrayal of the reluctant hero, Bogart's performances came to personify male elegance on the screen, and it is unlikely that his illustrious career will ever be forgotten.

Question	Strategic Thinking
9. The writer is considering adding the following sentence: *The Petrified Forest* was set in a U.S. desert. Should the writer make this addition here? **A.** Yes, because it adds a detail that supports the main point of the paragraph. **B.** Yes, because it provides an example of the setting for Bogart's acting. **C.** No, because it detracts from the focus on Bogart's career. **D.** No, because it distracts from the emphasis on films.	**Step 1: Read the passage and identify the issue** _the information helps the focus of the paragraph_ **Step 2: Eliminate answer choices that do not address the issue** _not the___ act or not_ **Step 3: Plug in the remaining answer choices and select the most correct, concise, and relevant one**
10. Suppose the writer's primary purpose had been to describe the life of someone who struggled before finding success. Would this essay accomplish that purpose? **F.** Yes, because it describes Bogart's perseverance in response to people who doubted his talent. **G.** Yes, because it depicts several setbacks Bogart experienced before he found a lasting career. **H.** No, because it focuses mainly on the reasons for Bogart's success. **J.** No, because it does not describe Bogart's troubles in detail.	**Step 1: Read the passage and identify the issue** _the essay accomplish the goal_ **Step 2: Eliminate answer choices that do not address the issue** _the essay DID ___ accomplish a goal_ **Step 3: Plug in the remaining answer choices and select the most correct, concise, and relevant one**

Answers and Explanations are provided at the end of the book.

Now try a test-like ACT English passage and question set on your own. Give yourself 6 minutes to read the passage and answer the questions.

Community-Supported Agriculture

This spring, my family joined our local community-supported agriculture, or CSA, association. We wanted to eat more organic, locally grown foods, and this seemed like a natural place to start. [11] The CSA works like this: Before the growing season begins on the farm, people have the opportunity to buy a "share" of the year's crop. Then the farm delivers a box of vegetables and fruit each week. The box is filled with the farmer's harvest.

[12] The farmer is guaranteed payment for the year, no matter what variables the growing season presents, and share members are guaranteed regular access to a

11. The writer is considering adding the following sentence:

> We thought about joining in the winter, but we waited until spring.

Should the writer make this addition here?

A. Yes, because it adds interesting context for the main idea.

B. Yes, because it gives an example of the decisions the family made.

C. No, because it does not provide a reason for the delay.

D. No, because it distracts from the focus on the CSA.

12. In the preceding sentence, the writer is considering replacing "the farmer's harvest" with "whatever was harvested that week on the farm." Should the writer make this revision?

F. Yes, because it adds a detail that is relevant to the point being made in the paragraph.

G. Yes, because it emphasizes the benefits of the CSA.

H. No, because it is less concise than the original wording.

J. No, because it is more ambiguous than the original wording.

variety of local, organic fruits and vegetables. ⬚13

Right away, we discovered that fresh, in-season food is delicious. I had never liked broccoli before, but one bunch <u>that came in our second June box</u> changed my
14
mind. My younger brother is usually reluctant to try new foods, but so far he has tried and liked both kale and

turnips from the CSA. <u>Of the four people in my family,</u>
15
<u>my mother is definitely the most accomplished cook.</u>
15

13. The writer is considering deleting the phrase "no matter what variables the growing season presents" from the preceding sentence. If the writer were to delete this phrase, the paragraph would primarily lose:

   A. information that explains why the narrator's family joined the CSA.

   B. an additional explanation of why farmers sell to CSAs.

   C. a contrast between farmers who sell to CSAs and those who do not.

   D. nothing, because the essay focuses on the members' experience in the CSA, not the farmer's.

14. If the writer were to delete the underlined portion, the sentence would primarily lose a detail that:

   F. explains when the family participated in the CSA.

   G. exemplifies the kind of produce the family received.

   H. connects the broccoli bunch to the topic of the passage.

   J. clarifies the main idea of the paragraph.

15. Given that all the choices are true, which one provides a conclusion to this paragraph that is most consistent with the other information in the paragraph?

   A. NO CHANGE

   B. Before we joined the CSA, the most unusual vegetable my brother was willing to eat was a carrot.

   C. The cardboard boxes are recycled each week, and the CSA even provides composting services on-site.

   D. We pick up our vegetables from the farmer's delivery every Thursday afternoon.

We have, however, run into a minor problem with the CSA vegetable boxes. That problem is zucchini, and lots of it. Each week in July, we received at least six zucchini in our box. First we just grilled the zucchini. [16] By the third week, when we received ten zucchini, it was time to get creative. We found and tried out recipes for zucchini soup, zucchini casserole, zucchini bread,

zucchini pizza, and zucchini brownies. [17] Though everything has been rather tasty, except for the brownies, we'll all be a bit relieved when zucchini season is over. By then, though, tomato season will have begun, and we'll have to figure out how to prepare countless tomatoes each week. I hope we don't have to resort to tomato brownies!

16. At this point, the writer is considering adding the following true statement:

Then we made pasta with sautéed zucchini.

Should the writer make this addition here?

F. Yes, because it helps to establish the range of the family's cooking skills.

G. Yes, because it helps to emphasize the main idea of this paragraph.

H. No, because it is unnecessarily repetitive.

J. No, because it does not specify what type of pasta the family made.

17. In the preceding sentence, the writer is considering replacing *zucchini brownies* with *even zucchini brownies*. Should the writer make this revision?

A. Yes, because it emphasizes how creative the family needed to get.

B. Yes, because it shows that the family baked zucchini brownies.

C. No, because it places too much emphasis on baking.

D. No, because it distracts from the focus on zucchini.

Question 18 asks about the passage as a whole.

18. If the writer's goal were to write a brief essay about the purpose and organization of community-supported agriculture, would this essay successfully accomplish that goal?

   F. Yes, because it explains how community-supported agriculture works.

   G. Yes, because it fully describes both the benefits and drawbacks of community-supported agriculture.

   H. No, because it focuses instead on one family's experience with community-supported agriculture.

   J. No, because it fails to provide an overview of how membership in a community-supported agriculture association works.

Answers and Explanations are provided at the end of the book.

ON YOUR OWN

The following questions provide an opportunity to practice the concepts and strategic thinking covered in this chapter. While many of the questions pertain to Topic Development, some touch on other concepts tested on the English test to ensure that your practice is test-like, with a variety of question types per passage.

The Library System

In the past ten years, library systems have undergone increasing computerization, a trend that <u>have</u> led to speculation about the future
1
of libraries. Some people believe that not only the card catalog, but also the library stacks themselves, will eventually be rendered obsolete. It is quite likely, they say, that in the next decade or so, electronic data will replace books as we know them. ☐2

This thought presents an interesting picture of the future. Instead of spending a cozy evening with a good

book, we may be <u>looking at</u> a laptop computer. With
3
all the intriguing possibilities the future holds, we are

1. **A.** NO CHANGE
   B. has
   C. having
   D. had

2. In the previous sentence, the writer is considering replacing the phrase "in the next decade or so" with *soon*. Should the writer make this revision?

   F. Yes, because it is easier to understand.
   G. Yes, because it clarifies when the change might take place.
   H. No, because it is too concise.
   J. No, because it removes a relevant detail.

3. Which choice best emphasizes the coziness of reading while maintaining the essay's positive tone?

   A. NO CHANGE
   B. next to
   C. stuck with
   D. curling up with

inclined to ignore the past. <u>We should not ignore the</u>
                                          4
<u>past, because it helps make us who we are.</u>
                                          4

Libraries may have originated as early as the

third millennium BCE in Babylonia. There, clay

tablets were used for record-keeping purposes and

stored in a temple. <u>In the seventh century BCE,</u> the
                                5
King of Assyria organized an enormous collection of

<u>records approximately</u> 20,000 tablets and fragments
              6
have been recovered. The first libraries to store books

were fourth-century BCE Greek temples established in

4. Given that all the choices are true, which one provides the best transition to the rest of the essay?

F. NO CHANGE

G. Libraries have a past as well as a future, both of which are important to keep in mind when thinking about them.

H. The future of libraries is something perhaps none of us can fully predict, and we shouldn't try.

J. While predicting the future state of the library system may be interesting, the library has a rich history as well.

5. If the writer were to delete the underlined portion (adjusting capitalization as necessary), the paragraph would primarily lose:

A. a sense of the chronology of library developments.

B. an emphasis on the seventh century BCE over other centuries.

C. a detail connecting the King of Assyria to the people of Babylonia.

D. an example that strengthens the central claim of the paragraph.

6. F. NO CHANGE

G. records; approximately

H. records, approximately

J. records and approximately

conjunction with the various schools of philosophy. [7]

7. At this point, the writer is considering adding the following true statement:

> In the second century CE, libraries were founded in monasteries.

Should the writer make this addition here?

A. Yes, because it adds a relevant detail.

B. Yes, because it supports the main idea of religious contributions to libraries.

C. No, because it does not say where the monasteries were.

D. No, because it distracts from the emphasis on books.

Not until the thirteenth <u>century were</u> university libraries
  8
created.

8. F.   NO CHANGE

G. century, were

H. century; were

J. century—were

[9] The emergence of a middle class, a growth in literacy, and the invention of the printing press all played a role. However, wars and revolutions served to hinder the development of the library system in England.

9. Given that all the choices are true, which one provides the best transition into the rest of the paragraph?

A. The institution of the library continued to change over time.

B. Many societal changes occurred in the Renaissance.

C. During the Renaissance, a series of societal changes began to transform the library system into the form we have today.

D. The Renaissance was a rebirth of classical ideas and artistic styles.

10 For example, Henry VIII ordered the destruction of countless manuscripts and disbanded some monastic

10. If the writer were to delete the preceding sentence, the paragraph would primarily lose:

    F. details that support the preceding sentence.

    G. a link between Henry VIII's actions and libraries.

    H. an introduction of the details in the following sentence.

    J. an emphasis on library developments after the thirteenth century.

libraries. 11

11. At this point, the writer is considering adding the following true statement:

    Henry VIII was married six times.

    Should the writer make this addition here?

    A. Yes, because it supports the claim in the previous sentence.

    B. Yes, because it provides an interesting anecdote that adds to the main point.

    C. No, because it is in conflict with the main claim of the passage.

    D. No, because it does not relate to the purpose of the passage.

In the days of King Henry—many English citizens
12
were pondering the fate of the nascent library system.

Today's societal changes are likewise causing some of us

to consider and think about the same thing,
13

12. **F.** NO CHANGE

    G. Henry, many

    H. Henry: many

    J. Henry; many

13. **A.** NO CHANGE

    B. consider

    C. consider while thinking about

    D. consider and be thinking about

although in ways that medieval readers could never
14
have imagined. Have we progressed from clay tablets

to paperbacks only to trade our paperbacks in for

microchips?

14. **F.** NO CHANGE

   G. despite

   H. also

   J. consequently

Question 15 asks about the passage as a whole.

15. Suppose the writer's primary purpose had
    been to develop a prediction about the future
    of libraries. Would this essay accomplish that
    purpose?

   A. Yes, because it gives evidence in favor of
   thinking that libraries will change.

   B. Yes, because it treats the past as
   unimportant.

   C. No, because it focuses on the history of
   libraries.

   D. No, because it emphasizes the struggles
   of libraries throughout history.

Answers and Explanations are provided at the end
of the book.

CHAPTER 7

Knowledge of Language

CHAPTER OBJECTIVES

By the end of this chapter, you will be able to:

1. Identify and correct elements in a passage that are wordy, redundant, or not relevant to a passage's topic and purpose

2. Revise text as needed to improve the exactness or content appropriateness of word choice

3. Improve the consistency of style and tone with a passage's purpose as necessary

SMARTPOINTS

Point Value	SmartPoints Category
6 Points	Knowledge of Language

KNOWLEDGE OF LANGUAGE

Good writing must be concise, precise, and consistent in tone. The ACT rewards your ability to identify and correct these Knowledge of Language issues.

Concision

A concise sentence includes no unnecessary words: avoid phrasing that is wordy or redundant. Each word must contribute to the meaning of the sentence; otherwise, it should be eliminated.

Wordy/Redundant Sentence	Concise Sentence
The superb musical score **added enhancement to the experience of** the play's development.	The superb musical score **enhanced** the play's development.
I **did not anticipate** the **surprising, unexpected** plot twist.	I **did not anticipate** the plot twist.
The students **increased some of their knowledge of** Tuscan architecture.	The students **learned about** Tuscan architecture.

Work through the Kaplan Method for English step-by-step to answer the questions that accompany the passage below. The table below the passage contains two columns. The column on the right features the strategic thinking a test expert employs when approaching passages and related questions.

International Model United Nations

For many years, the Hague has been the stage of The European International Model United Nations (TEIMUN), <u>which is a model of the United Nations.</u> TEIMUN started in 1987, when a group of
1
American students who were on an exchange program in the Netherlands organized the first conference as a part of their focus on international relations. The organizers hoped to educate participants about the workings of an international organization in order to combat <u>a growing sense of isolationism</u> among
2
European youth.

Question	Strategic Thinking
1. **A.** NO CHANGE **B.** being a model of the United Nations. **C.** which is a model UN. **D.** DELETE the underlined portion and change comma after "(TEIMUN)" to a period.	**Step 1: Read the passage and identify the issue** The underlined portion repeats information that is already expressed in the name of TEIMUN, so this is a Knowledge of Language / Concision issue. **Step 2: Eliminate answer choices that do not address the issue** Eliminate A, B, and C, which all repeat information that is expressed in the name of TEIMUN. **Step 3: Plug in the remaining answer choices and select the most correct, concise, and relevant one** The correct answer is (D).
2. Which of the following alternatives to the underlined portion would NOT be acceptable? **F.** a growing sense of separation **G.** a growing sense of both isolationism and separation **H.** the growing isolationism **J.** the increasing isolationism	**Step 1: Read the passage and identify the issue** When the underlined portion contains no grammatical or punctuation errors, the question could be testing Knowledge of Language. Check whether the proposed alternatives are precise, concise, and consistent in tone. **Step 2: Eliminate answer choices that do not address the issue** The question stem asks for the unacceptable alternative. Eliminate choices F, H, and J, which do not introduce errors and would therefore be acceptable alternatives. **Step 3: Plug in the remaining answer choices and select the most correct, concise, and relevant one** Choice (G) is wordy and redundant and therefore unacceptable. The correct answer is (G).

English

Precision

Words should convey their meaning precisely, so be on the lookout for language that is vague or ambiguous. The ACT rewards your ability to distinguish between clear and unclear language.

Words within passages should be not only necessary but also relevant to the main point of the paragraph in which they occur. Make sure that no sentence includes phrases that detract from the main point. If "DELETE the underlined portion" is an answer choice, ask yourself whether the underlined portion enhances the meaning and clarity of the passage.

Ambiguous Pronouns

A pronoun is ambiguous if its antecedent (the noun to which it refers) is either missing or unclear. The ACT tests your ability to identify and correct either of those issues. When you see an underlined pronoun, make sure you can identify the noun to which it refers and check whether the pronoun clearly refers to that noun.

Ambiguous Pronoun Use	Clear Pronoun Use
*Anthony walked with Cody to the ice cream shop, and **he** bought a banana split.*	*Anthony walked with Cody to the ice cream shop, and **Cody** bought a banana split.*

Word Choice

Some questions test your knowledge of the correct word to use in context. The ACT does not primarily test difficult vocabulary; rather, the ACT tests your ability to identify whether the author has used the correct word(s) to convey the intended meaning. The ACT may explicitly ask you to identify which choice conveys a certain meaning. The test may also ask you to identify how well a sentence fits with the main point of the paragraph. Make sure the underlined portion or answer choice clearly conveys the intended meaning and fits with the rest of the content.

Work through the Kaplan Method for English step-by-step to answer the questions that accompany the passage below. The table below the passage contains two columns. The left column contains test-like questions. The column on the right features the strategic thinking a test expert employs when approaching the passage and questions presented.

There were many hurdles to overcome, for students' attitudes in Europe toward simulations of the United Nations were not favorable. Hence, drumming up interest was a struggle. The Americans also wanted to ensure there were methods for helping students from less developed countries to participate. Through the American students' perseverance, hard work, and dedication, TEIMUN prospered and attracted <u>them.</u> Over the years, TEIMUN has gained acceptance <u>somewhat</u>. The TEIMUN conference has
                    3   4
become one of the biggest and most important model United Nations on the European continent, with participants from over 65 countries registering for the conference.

Question	Strategic Thinking

3. **A.** NO CHANGE
   B. those.
   C. the Americans.
   D. more participants.
	Step 1: Read the passage and identify the issue
	
	The underlined portion is a pronoun, and it is unclear to whom this pronoun refers.
	
	Step 2: Eliminate answer choices that do not address the issue
	
	Choices A and B are both ambiguous pronouns; eliminate them.
	
	Step 3: Plug in the remaining answer choices and select the most correct, concise, and relevant one
	
	Choice C has a specific noun, but it changes the meaning of the sentence. It is the Americans who were trying to attract other participants. The correct answer is (D).

4. Which choice best emphasizes the smooth increase in the acceptance of TEIMUN over time?
   F. NO CHANGE
   G. steadily
   H. dramatically
   J. entirely
	Step 1: Read the passage and identify the issue
	
	The question asks which word best conveys a certain meaning, so the issue is word choice.
	
	Step 2: Eliminate answer choices that do not address the issue
	
	Choice F conveys a small increase rather than a smooth increase. Choice H emphasizes the quickness of the increase rather than the smoothness. Choice J emphasizes the extent of the increase rather than the smoothness.
	
	Step 3: Plug in the remaining answer choices and select the most correct, concise, and relevant one
	
	Choice (G) emphasizes the smoothness of the increase and is therefore correct.

Style and Tone

An author's style and tone are conveyed by word choice, rhetorical devices, and sentence structure. An author may write informally, as though speaking with friends; academically, as though speaking to experts; or persuasively, as though trying to convince the reader. The ACT requires you to revise a text to ensure that its style and tone are consistent. Some Style and Tone questions have question stems, whereas others do not. Even if the question lacks a question stem, check to ensure that the wording matches the style and tone of the passage as a whole.

Style

An important element of style is the voice of the passage: whom the passage is directed toward and whether the author refers to himself or herself. One indicator of style is the type of pronouns the author uses.

Style	Pronoun Use in Passage
Somewhat informal	First-person pronouns such as *I* and *my*
More informal	Second-person pronouns such as *you* and *your*
Formal	Third-person pronouns such as *one* and *one's*

Different voices are appropriate for different subject matter and purposes. Within a passage, style—including how it is expressed with pronouns—must be consistent.

Tone

Tone includes the features of the text that reflect the author's point of view. The tone of the text should match the author's purpose. For example, the phrase "this mind-blowing new treatment" might fit well in a passage whose purpose is to recommend a course of action, but it would not fit the tone of a passage whose purpose is to give an objective description of the treatment. Some Tone questions include a question stem that asks which choice best maintains the essay's tone. Whether or not there is a question stem, make sure that the underlined portion matches the overall purpose and the author's point of view.

> Participation in a TEIMUN can be a very exciting, yet challenging, experience. The goal of the conference is to enhance participants' negotiation and oratory skills and to broaden the participants' views about and knowledge of the world. Students are confronted with the need to set aside their personal opinions and take up the official policy of the countries they have chosen to represent. Furthermore, <u>you are faced with the very difficult dilemma of choosing your countries' positions</u> or participating in international cooperation.
>
> 5

> Students still direct and organize each yearly conference. They seek new ways to attract enthusiastic participants, and they strongly believe that TEIMUN is <u>a powerful outlet</u> for fostering an interest in diplomacy among Europe's youth. Countless alumni have gone on to pursue careers in international policy after first encountering the art of diplomacy during their years in TEIMUN.
>
> 6

Question	Strategic Thinking
5. A. NO CHANGE B. they are faced with the dilemma of choosing their countries' positions C. you need to choose your countries' positions D. the countries' positions must be chosen	**Step 1: Read the passage and identify the issue** The pronouns *you* and *your* do not appear elsewhere in the passage. Therefore, the style is inconsistent. **Step 2: Eliminate answer choices that do not address the issue** Eliminate A and C because both include the pronoun *you*. **Step 3: Plug in the remaining answer choices and select the most correct, concise, and relevant one** Choice D introduces a new error of passive voice and creates a sentence fragment. Choice (B) is correct.
6. Which choice maintains the essay's positive tone and most strongly supports the idea presented in the concluding sentence? F. NO CHANGE G. a place H. a good place J. all right	**Step 1: Read the passage and identify the issue** The question stem mentions the essay's positive tone, so check that the underlined segment conveys a consistent tone. **Step 2: Eliminate answer choices that do not address the issue** Eliminate G and J, which are too neutral to maintain the essay's positive tone. **Step 3: Plug in the remaining answer choices and select the most correct, concise, and relevant one** Choice H does not support the idea that countless alumni have pursued careers in diplomacy as strongly as (F) does, so (F) is correct.

English

You have seen the ways in which the ACT tests you on Knowledge of Language in English passages and how an ACT expert approaches these types of questions. Use the Kaplan Method for ACT English to answer the questions that accompany the following English passage excerpts. Remember to look at the strategic thinking questions that have been laid out for you—some of the answers have been filled in, but you will have to complete the answers to others. Use the strategic thinking questions to select the correct answer, just as you will on Test Day.

Native American Sweat Lodges

The 21st century has seen a marked increase in the popularity of natural medicines and therapies. The most widely used of these is believed to be the Native American sweat lodge. Nearly every culture has adopted this practice in some form, including the Finnish sauna and the Turkish steam room. The basic purpose of <u>them</u> is to raise the body's core temperature to between 102 and 106 degrees Fahrenheit. At
7
this temperature, bacterial and viral infections <u>within the body</u> cannot easily survive. The heat can also
8
ease muscle tension and soreness, and the resulting perspiration flushes the system of toxins.

Question	Strategic Thinking
7. **A.** NO CHANGE **B.** those **C.** this popularity **D.** these therapies	**Step 1: Read the passage and identify the issue** The underlined portion is a pronoun, and it is unclear to what *them* refers. **Step 2: Eliminate answer choices that do not address the issue** Eliminate A and B, since they both contain ambiguous pronouns. **Step 3: Plug in the remaining answer choices and select the most correct, concise, and relevant one** _____ _____

Question	Strategic Thinking
8. Which of the following alternatives would NOT be acceptable? **F.** NO CHANGE **G.** within your very own body **H.** within one's body **J.** within a body	**Step 1: Read the passage and identify the issue** The answer choices contain pronouns that express different tones. **Step 2: Eliminate answer choices that do not address the issue** Choices F, H, and J all fit the tone of the passage. The question stem says to select the choice that is not acceptable, so eliminate F, H, and J. **Step 3: Plug in the remaining answer choices and select the most correct, concise, and relevant one** G → "your" is slightly informal and therefore doesn't match

A traditional Native American sweat lodge is built of willow; its bark is considered medicinal and, indeed, contains the same analgesic as aspirin. Though they were <u>totally</u> covered with animal skins, the

9

lodges today are more likely to be made with canvas or blankets. In many traditions, the entrance of the sweat lodge faces east, with a <u>clear and unobstructed</u> view of the sacred fire pit where the stones are

10

heated before being brought inside the lodge. Facing east allows observers to acknowledge the power of the sun, which is considered the source of life, power, and wisdom. Between the fire and the entrance to the sweat lodge is an altar barrier, which prevents participants from accidentally falling into the fire pit when they emerge from the lodge.

Questions	Strategic Thinking

9. Which choice best conveys the contrast between traditional sweat lodges and those of today?
  A. NO CHANGE
  ✓**B.** originally
  C. finally
  D. essentially
	Step 1: Read the passage and identify the issue
	
	The question stem asks which choice best conveys a certain meaning, so precision is the issue.
	
	Step 2: Eliminate answer choices that do not address the issue
	
	C → it's a past tense sentence
	A → doesn't flow in sentence
	
	Step 3: Plug in the remaining answer choices and select the most correct, concise, and relevant one
	
	B → contrast in diff time periods show

10. **F.** NO CHANGE
  G. crystal and clear
  H. clearly unobstructed
  ✓**J.** clear
	Step 1: Read the passage and identify the issue
	
	The words *clear* and *unobstructed* are redundant.
	
	Step 2: Eliminate answer choices that do not address the issue
	
	F + G + H → redundant
	
	Step 3: Plug in the remaining answer choices and select the most correct, concise, and relevant one
	
	J → simple + concise

Prior to entering the lodge, people are often smudged with the smoke of burning sage, sweetgrass, or cedar to signify <u>the person's cleanliness.</u> Once participants are inside the lodge, the Stone People
                                            11
spirits are called upon, and the sweat leader sounds the Water Drum. <u>Often,</u> a sweat typically includes
                                                                              12
four sessions, each lasting 30 to 45 minutes. The rounds reflect four distinct themes: the spirit world, cleanliness and honesty, individual prayer, and growth and healing.

The original sweat lodge ceremonies, which often included songs, prayers, and chants, were believed to purify not only the body but also the mind. "Healing comes on a spiritual level," wrote Dr. Lewis Mehl-Madrona in his book *Coyote Medicine*. "Ceremony and ritual provide the means of making ourselves available."

Question	Strategic Thinking
11. Which choice best matches the author's emphasis on the symbolic aspects of the experience? **A.** NO CHANGE **B.** being clean. **C.** ritual cleanliness. **D.** one's newfound cleanliness.	**Step 1: Read the passage and identify the issue** *style maintenence issue* **Step 2: Eliminate answer choices that do not address the issue** *A + B + D → no symbolic representation* **Step 3: Plug in the remaining answer choices and select the most correct, concise, and relevant one** *C → "ritual" implies a symbolic feel*

Question	Strategic Thinking
12. F. NO CHANGE **G.** More often, **H.** Occasionally, ✓**J.** DELETE the underlined portion and capitalize the word *A*.	**Step 1: Read the passage and identify the issue** wordiness problem **Step 2: Eliminate answer choices that do not address the issue** F + G + H → keep being redundant with the word "typically **Step 3: Plug in the remaining answer choices and select the most correct, concise, and relevant one** J → "often" conflicts with the already used word "typically

Answers and Explanations are provided at the end of the book.

Now try a test-like ACT English passage and question set on your own. Give yourself 5 minutes to read the passage and answer the questions.

Early Writing Careers

Many well-known writers began their professional careers while they were still attending high school or college. Stephen King, for example, not only wrote for his high school newspaper but also began submitting short stories to science fiction magazines when he was <u>the young age of just thirteen years old.</u> Mary
13
Shelley completed her novel *Frankenstein* before the age of twenty, and Helen Keller published her first autobiography, *The Story of My Life*, while still in college. If you are serious about a career as a writer or journalist, you can submit your work to a number of publications that accept unsolicited manuscripts. It is best, however, to submit a query letter first.

A query letter is a one-page document in which you introduce yourself to the editors of the publication and ask if they <u>would like to read it.</u> Begin by telling the
14

editor a little bit about <u>oneself.</u> Don't pretend to be a
15
seasoned professional; you won't fool anyone, and your age may actually

13. **A.** NO CHANGE
   B. the young age of thirteen years old.
   C. a younger age of thirteen.
   D. just thirteen years old.

14. **F.** NO CHANGE
   G. would like to read something you have written.
   H. have read it.
   J. would like to read them.

15. **A.** NO CHANGE
   B. who one is.
   C. yourself.
   D. myself.

work to your advantage. Include a paragraph or two
16
outlining the story you've written or the article you'd

like to write. If you've taken any creative writing courses,

be sure to include that information. If you've won any

prizes for your writing or had any of your writings

published, tell the editor about that, too. Don't forget to

thank the editor for taking the time to read it.
17

You probably won't sell your first story or article,

but don't get discouraged. Stephen King didn't sell his
18
first submission either. In fact, he is quoted as saying

that as a teenager, "The nail in my wall would no longer

support the weight of the rejection slips impaled upon

it. I replaced the nail with a spike and kept on writing."

Stephen King didn't persevere, and neither should you.
19

16. Which choice best maintains the essay's casual tone while emphasizing the benefits of being young?

F. NO CHANGE

G. be of utmost importance.

H. convey great personal benefit.

J. be fine.

17. A. NO CHANGE

B. your letter.

C. what you wrote.

D. itself.

18. F. NO CHANGE

G. discouraged or disheartened.

H. a discouraging attitude.

J. feelings of discouragement.

19. Which choice best conveys King's persistence in continuing to write?

A. NO CHANGE

B. stop plodding on and on

C. keep going

D. give up

Question 20 asks about the passage as a whole.

20. This essay is written in the second person (*you, your*). If this essay were revised so that the second-person pronouns were replaced with the pronouns *one* and *one's*, the essay would primarily:

F. gain a friendlier, more approachable tone.

G. gain a sense of applying to every reader.

H. lose its accessible, encouraging appeal to the reader.

J. lose its light, humorous tone.

Answers and Explanations are provided at the end of the book.

ON YOUR OWN

The following questions provide an opportunity to practice the concepts and strategic thinking covered in this chapter. While many of the questions pertain to Knowledge of Language, some touch on other concepts tested on the English test to ensure that your practice is test-like, with a variety of question types per passage.

Thomas Paine

Compared to most of America's other Founding Fathers, Thomas Paine is not nearly as well-known. <u>However,</u> there are many Americans who have either
₁
never even heard

1. **A.** NO CHANGE
   B. In fact,
   C. Rather,
   D. Because of this,

of him or cannot recall his <u>significance in</u> history.
₂

2. **F.** NO CHANGE
   G. being in
   H. famousness in
   J. absence from

Paine was born in 1737 as the son of a <u>corseter: a tailor</u>
₃
<u>specializing in corsets and other undergarments</u> and
₃
grew up in rural Thetford, England.

3. **A.** NO CHANGE
   B. corseter, a tailor specializing in corsets and other undergarments;
   C. corseter—a tailor specializing in corsets and other undergarments—
   D. corseter a tailor specializing in corsets, and other undergarments,

As a young man, Paine worked as a corseter, sailor, and minister but only found his <u>one true calling</u> when
₄
he moved to the British colonies in America.

4. **F.** NO CHANGE
   G. truest of callings
   H. very truest calling
   J. true calling

Paine first gained recognition as the editor of

Pennsylvania Magazine, as political turmoil engulfed the
5
colonies,

he became more <u>vocal.</u> In 1776, Paine anonymously
6
published a book called *Common Sense* that argued

forcefully for American independence from Britain.

<u>Its</u> popularity spread like
7

<u>peanut butter;</u> soon there were 200,000 copies in
8
circulation.

Thomas Paine's influence continued far beyond

sparking the Revolutionary War. Once the war began,

Paine published a series of pamphlets called *The*

American Crisis, which, in the midst of a bloody war,

helped keep <u>their morale</u> up. In addition to his
9
achievements as a writer,

5. A. NO CHANGE
    B. *Pennsylvania Magazine—as*
    C. *Pennsylvania Magazine;* and as
    D. *Pennsylvania Magazine,* and as

6. Which choice best conveys Paine's increased fame?
    F. NO CHANGE
    G. prominent.
    H. understandable.
    J. divisive.

7. A. NO CHANGE
    B. Their
    C. The book's
    D. Britain's

8. Which choice best conveys the rapid increase in popularity and is consistent with the writer's tone?
    F. NO CHANGE
    G. wildfire.
    H. eagle's wings.
    J. pages in a book.

9. A. NO CHANGE
    B. the morale of the troops
    C. his morale
    D. someone's morale

Thomas Paine is also <u>credited</u> with conceiving the name
10
"The United States of America." Because Thomas Paine was

<u>a writer,</u> Thomas Jefferson and John Adams drew
11
heavily on his work when drafting the Declaration of

Independence. Later in life, Paine wrote other,

highly controversial works. [12] In 1797, Paine did his

part to inspire what would become Social Security. He

suggested a system of social insurance for the young and

the elderly in his last great work, *Agrarian Justice*.

Given Thomas Paine's contributions to America,

he deserves recognition as one of our <u>more important</u>
13
Founding Fathers.

10. **F.** NO CHANGE
    G. tasked
    H. helped
    J. noted

11. Which choice maintains the essay's positive tone regarding Paine and best describes why Jefferson and Adams used his work?
    A. an extremely talented writer,
    B. the best writer in the colonies,
    C. an adequate author,
    D. an author of controversial content,

12. The writer is considering adding the following sentence:

    He was even exiled from England and imprisoned in France for his writings.

    Should the writer make this addition here?

    F. Yes, because the passage focuses on Paine's international relations.

    G. Yes, because it adds an interesting detail that contributes to the purpose of the paragraph.

    H. No, because it detracts from the emphasis on controversy.

    J. No, because it does not describe Paine's writings.

13. **A.** NO CHANGE
    B. very most important
    C. mostly important
    D. most important

Whether you think of him as a patriot who named

a whole entire nation or a controversial activist who
            14
lobbied for socialist ideas, he should at the very least be

remembered as a seminal figure in the development of a

new, autonomous nation.

14. **F.** NO CHANGE

   G. a whole nation itself

   H. an entire nation

   J. the entire, whole nation

Question 15 asks about the passage as a whole.

15. Suppose the writer's primary purpose had
    been to advocate placing a greater emphasis
    on Thomas Paine's contributions to American
    history. Would this essay accomplish that
    purpose?

   A. Yes, because it praises Paine's influence.

   B. Yes, because it is a thorough treatise on
   American history.

   C. No, because it does not establish that
   Paine's contributions were beneficial.

   D. No, because it focuses too much on the
   American Revolution.

Answers and Explanations are provided at the end
of the book.

MATH INTRODUCTION

BY THE END OF THIS UNIT, YOU WILL BE ABLE TO:

1. Identify the format and timing for the ACT Math test

2. Identify the three primary ACT Math question types

3. Apply tips and strategies to the ACT Math test

CHAPTER 8

ACT Math

CHAPTER OBJECTIVES

By the end of this chapter, you will be able to:

1. Identify the categories into which ACT Math questions fall

2. Use SmartPoints to determine the highest-yield Math categories

INSIDE THE ACT MATH TEST

The Math test is 60 minutes long and includes 60 questions. That works out to 1 minute per question, but you'll wind up using more time on some questions and less on others.

The Format

All of the Math questions have the same basic multiple-choice format, with a stand-alone question and five possible answers (unlike questions on the other subject tests, which have only four choices each). Occasionally, you may encounter a set of two or three questions that share a table, graph, or other relevant information.

The questions cover a wide range of math topics, from pre-algebra to coordinate geometry and even a little bit of trigonometry. More emphasis is placed on earlier-level math skills (such as order of operations, working with variables, solving basic equations, and geometry) and less on higher-level math (such as sequences, logarithms, and matrices).

Test Day Directions and Format

Although the exact wording might vary, here's what the Math directions could look like:

Directions: Choose the correct solution to each question and fill in the corresponding bubble on your answer sheet.

Do not continue to spend time on questions if you get stuck. Solve as many questions as you can before returning to any if time permits.

You may use a calculator on this test for any question you choose. However, some questions may be better solved without a calculator.

Note: Unless otherwise stated, you can assume:

1. Figures are NOT necessarily to scale.

2. Geometric figures are two-dimensional.

3. The word *line* indicates a straight line.

4. The word *average* indicates arithmetic mean.

If you would like to read through the exact wording you will see on Test Day, visit the test maker's website and download the Preparing for the ACT guide. Either way, when it comes to directions on the ACT, the golden rule is this: Don't read anything on Test Day you already know! Familiarize yourself with everything now to save time later.

The Math directions don't really tell you much anyway. Of the four special notes at the end of the Math directions, #2, #3, and #4 almost go without saying. Note #1 is pretty important, though—while this rule "bends" a little bit when you have to guess, it's important to know that your eyes *don't* tell you what you need to know about figures; you really do have to do the math. What a figure *looks like* won't reliably get you the right answer.

Question Types

The types of questions you'll see on the ACT can be divided into three main types—those that include a diagram (or for which you need to draw one), story problems, and concept questions.

Diagram Questions

About one-third of the Math questions either give you a diagram or describe a situation that should be diagrammed. For these questions, the diagrams are crucial—you don't get any points for solving questions in your head, so draw *everything* out.

Example

1. The figure below contains five congruent triangles. The longest side of each triangle is 4 meters long. What is the area of the whole figure in square meters?

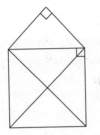

   A. 12.5

   B. 15

   C. 20

   D. 30

   E. Cannot be determined from the given information

Getting to the Answer: The key to this question is to let the diagram tell you what you need to know: Each triangle represents one-quarter of the area of the square, and the sides of the *square* are 4 meters (you can figure this out because the top side of the square is the hypotenuse of the triangle that makes the "roof"). Because the area of a square can be found by squaring its side length, the area of the square is 16 square meters. Thus, each triangle has an area that is one-fourth as much, or 4 square meters. Because the whole figure consists of *five* triangles, each with area 4, the total area is $5 \times 4 = 20$ square meters. The answer is (C).

✔ Expert Tip

In ACT Math questions, the choice "cannot be determined" is rare. When it does appear, it's rarely the right answer, and is almost always incorrect in a question that comes with a diagram or for which you can draw one.

Math

Story Problems

About another third of the Math questions are story problems, which are also referred to as modeling questions. Here's an example:

Example

2. Evan drove halfway home at 20 miles per hour, then sped up and drove the rest of the way at 30 miles per hour. What was his average speed for the entire trip?

    F. 20 miles per hour

    G. 22 miles per hour

    H. 24 miles per hour

    J. 25 miles per hour

    K. 28 miles per hour

Getting to the Answer: A good way to comprehend—and resolve—a story problem like this is to think of a real situation like the one in the story. Imagining an actual trip with miles and speeds may make the question more approachable. For example, what if Evan had 60 miles to drive? (You should pick a distance that's easily divisible by both rates.) He would go 30 miles at 30 mph, then 30 miles at 20 mph. How long would it take? Consider each leg of the trip: 30 miles at 30 mph is 1 hour, and 30 miles at 20 mph is 1.5 hours. That's a total of 60 miles in 2.5 hours; 60 divided by 2.5 gives an average speed of 24 mph. The correct answer is (H).

> ✔ **Expert Tip**
>
> Don't let variables or abstract stories confuse you. When you see them, stay calm and make them simpler by putting real numbers in for the variables. You'll learn more about this Picking Numbers strategy a bit later.

Concept Questions

Finally, about one-third of ACT Math questions directly ask you to demonstrate your knowledge of specific math concepts.

Example

3. If angles *A* and *B* are supplementary, and the measure of angle *A* is 57°, what is the measure, in degrees, of angle *B* ?

    A. 33

    B. 43

    C. 47

    D. 123

    E. 147

Getting to the Answer: This question requires that you know the concept of supplementary angles: Two angles are *supplementary* when they form a straight line—in other words, when they add up to 180°. Thus, question 3 boils down to this: What number, added to 57, makes 180? The answer is (D), 123.

These three types of Math questions, of course, will be discussed more fully in the Math chapters that follow.

Outside Knowledge

The ACT Math test thoroughly covers rules from a variety of common Math topics, mostly from courses students typically complete by the end of the 11th grade. The needed math "facts" are addressed in the strategic discussion throughout the math chapters in this book.

The Inside Scoop

The ACT Math test is designed to measure problem solving and logical reasoning, along with basic computational skills. Covered topics include:

- Rates, percents, proportions, and unit conversion
- Number properties
- Number operations
- Algebra
- Functions
- Graphing
- Geometry and trigonometry
- Statistics and probability

Although Math questions aren't ordered in terms of difficulty, questions drawn from elementary or middle school curricula tend to come earlier in the test, while those from high school curricula tend to come later. But this doesn't mean that the easy questions come first and the hardest ones come later. We've found that high school subjects tend to be fresher in most students' minds than things they were taught years ago, so you may actually find the later questions easier.

TIMING

You have an average of 1 minute to spend per question. Ideally, you'll be able to spend significantly less time on easy questions so you can buy more time for the hard questions.

Spend about 45 minutes on your first pass through the Math subject test. Do the easier questions, guess on the questions you suspect aren't going to come to you no matter what, and mark the tough ones that you'll want to come back to. Spend the last 15 minutes picking up those questions you skipped on the first pass.

We recommend you grid your answers at the end of every page or two. Don't wait until the end of the test or you may run out of time. And make sure that you have an answer (even if it's a blind guess) gridded for every question by the time the test is over.

Don't worry if you have to guess on a lot of the Math questions. You can miss a lot of questions on the Math test and still get a great score. Remember that the average ACT test taker gets fewer than half of the Math questions right!

When You're Running Out of Time

If at some point you realize you have more questions left than you have time for, be willing to skip around, looking for questions you understand right away. Pick your points and concentrate on the questions you have the best chance of correctly answering. Just be sure to grid an answer—even if it's just a wild guess—for every question.

SCORING

You will receive a Math subject score—from 1 to 36—for the entire Math subject test. This score will be averaged into your ACT Composite Score, equally weighted with your scores on the other three major subject tests. You will also receive eight other scores based on specific knowledge and concepts. These are called reporting categories and consist of:

- Integrating Essential Skills

- Preparing for Higher Mathematics, which also includes separate scores for Number and Quantity, Algebra, Functions, Geometry, and Statistics and Probability

- Modeling

QUICK TIPS

Mind-Set

- **The end justifies the means.** Your goal is to get as many points as possible, not to demonstrate how great you are at any particular math area, or show all your work, or get all the "hard" questions—just to get points, plain and simple. That means getting as many correct answers as quickly as possible. If the best way to get this done is to do straightforward questions in a straightforward way, that's fine. But many questions can be solved faster by using Kaplan strategies, such as Backsolving and Picking Numbers, which will make you both faster and more accurate.

- **Take time to save time.** It sounds paradoxical, but to go your fastest on the Math test, you sometimes have to slow down. Don't just dive in headlong, wildly crunching numbers or manipulating equations without first giving the question some thought. Remember your priority is the whole section, not just one particular question.

- **When in doubt, shake it up.** ACT Math questions are not always what they seem at first glance. Sometimes all you need is a new perspective to break through the disguise. Take a step back and look at the question another way.

Special Strategies: If You Get Stuck ...

If after a few moments of thought you find you still can't come up with a reasonable way of doing a question, try one of these techniques:

- **Restate.** When you get stuck, try looking at the question from a different angle. Try rearranging the numbers, changing decimals to fractions, changing fractions to decimals, multiplying out numbers, factoring problems, redrawing a diagram, or doing anything that might help you to look at the information you've been given a bit differently.

- **Remove the disguise.** Find out what the question is really asking—it might not be obvious at first glance.

- **Find the objective** and circle it. This is especially helpful when you're confused.

- **Try eyeballing.** Even though the directions warn you that diagrams are "not necessarily" drawn to scale, eyeballing is a surprisingly effective guessing strategy. You won't be able to get specifics without doing the math, sometimes, but you will be able to rule some answers out or get a better idea of what you're looking for.

SMARTPOINTS BREAKDOWN

By studying the information released by the ACT, Kaplan has been able to determine how often certain topics are likely to show up on the test and, therefore, how many points these topics are worth on Test Day. If you master a given topic, you can expect to earn the corresponding number of SmartPoints on Test Day.

Here is a brief overview of what exactly to expect and how much of it you should be expecting.

Essential Skills—14 Points

Approximately 40–43% of the Math test will be Essential Skills questions. These questions test your knowledge and skill level associated with concepts you likely learned in middle school. Topics include but are not limited to:

- Numbers and operations

- Rates, percents, proportions, and unit conversion

- Expressions and equations

- Basic geometry

- Basic statistics and probability

Many of the concepts that you'll see in Essential Skills questions will also be present in Higher Math questions—the questions in the latter group will just be more advanced and will require more steps to arrive at a final solution. For example, an Essential Skills question may involve finding the mean of a list of numbers. A related Higher Math question may involve calculating a mean from a bar graph or a frequency table—the underlying concept is the same, but getting to the final answer requires significantly more work and finesse.

Higher Math—22 Points

Approximately 57–60% of the test will consist of Higher Math questions. These questions capture the mathematics that you most likely learned more recently, or are learning right now, in high school. This category is divided into the five subcategories described next.

Number and Quantity—3 Points

Number and Quantity questions make up about 7–10% of the Math test. These questions test your knowledge of the real and complex number systems. You will need to understand, reason about, and use numerical quantities in various forms, including integer and rational exponents, and matrices and vectors. Number and Quantity questions require that you understand the behavior of numbers, particularly evens and odds and positives and negatives. These questions are ripe for Picking Numbers, which will be discussed in the next chapter. You'll also need to use properties of divisibility, such as factors, multiples, and prime numbers. Tested operations include all parts of the PEMDAS order of operations (parentheses, exponents, multiplication, division, addition, and subtraction). Rarer questions test basic knowledge of radical and imaginary numbers.

Algebra—5 Points

Algebra questions make up about 12–15% of the Math test and extensively test your ability to solve for an unknown quantity given a wide range of information of varying complexity. The simplest questions are pulled from elementary algebra and require you to solve for a single variable. They build up to more advanced algebra, asking you to solve systems of equations, equations involving absolute value, inequalities, and quadratic equations. These questions also test your ability to write the equation of a line given certain types of information. The slope-intercept form of a line is the most important equation to remember here, and slope in general is paramount. You may even see radical and rational expressions and equations sprinkled in among the more typical polynomial equations.

Functions—5 Points

Functions questions make up about 12–15% of the Math test. You'll need to know how to interpret function notation and recognize the different ways in which functions can be represented. You will also be tested on function operations, which include adding, subtracting, multiplying, dividing, and finding compositions. Questions in this category will also involve using functions to solve problems about real-world scenarios and describing important features of graphs of functions. The types of functions you may see include but are not limited to linear, polynomial, radical, rational, exponential, logarithmic, trigonometric, and piecewise functions. Finally, the Functions category includes questions involving arithmetic and geometric sequences.

Geometry—5 Points

Geometry includes coordinate geometry, plane geometry, and solid geometry. Geometry questions make up about 12–15% of the Math test. These questions test your ability to graph equations and inequalities in the coordinate plane and to solve problems related to lines, angles, and figures. Triangles—specifically right triangles—and circles are the two most commonly tested shapes, but you can expect to see questions on a variety of polygons, as well as complex 2-D and simple 3-D shapes. The test will ask you to break down complex figures into recognizable shapes and use problem-solving skills to transfer information throughout a figure. Fortunately, as on the rest of the ACT Math test, the number of rules to remember is limited. The test will ask questions that require knowledge of the Midpoint and Distance formulas, and occasionally you will need to work with the graphs of simple shapes such as triangles and circles in the coordinate plane.

Statistics and Probability—4 Points

Statistics and Probability questions make up about 8–12% of the Math test. These questions test your ability to interpret and/or use data presented in a variety of forms. Common questions include finding or using averages and describing or analyzing the center or spread of a set of data. You'll also see questions involving counting techniques, such as combinations and permutations, as well as questions about Venn diagrams. Finally, you'll have to calculate simple and conditional probabilities that are based on a description of a scenario, data presented in a two-way table or other type of chart or graph, or a probability distribution function.

A Note About Modeling

Together, Essential Skills and Higher Math questions make up 100% of the Math test. However, there is a third category, Modeling, to be aware of, although it doesn't have a SmartPoints value associated with it. The test maker has indicated that more than 25% of the test will involve modeling, but don't let this fact intimidate you. *Modeling* just means using mathematical equations, graphs, diagrams, scatterplots, etc. to represent real-world scenarios. Word problems certainly fit within this category, but you'll also see some concept questions that fit within the Modeling category. Every modeling question will also be counted in the reporting categories described earlier.

INTEGRATING ESSENTIAL SKILLS

BY THE END OF THIS UNIT, YOU WILL BE ABLE TO:

1. Apply the Kaplan Method for ACT Math
2. Use properties of real numbers to answer questions and perform basic operations
3. Use proportional relationships to answer questions
4. Solve basic linear equations and inequalities
5. Answer basic coordinate geometry questions
6. Answer basic plane geometry questions involving lines and angles
7. Answer basic statistics and probability questions

CHAPTER 9

Essential Skills

CHAPTER OBJECTIVES

By the end of this chapter, you will be able to:

1. Use strategies such as Picking Numbers and Backsolving as part of the Kaplan Method for ACT Math

2. Perform basic operations using rational numbers

3. Apply properties of factors and multiples, including prime factorization, to answer questions

4. Use rates, ratios, proportions, and percents to answer real-world scenario questions

5. Solve arithmetic problems that involve converting units of measure

6. Evaluate and simplify algebraic expressions

7. Apply properties of lines and angles to answer geometry questions

8. Calculate simple probabilities

9. Analyze simple data sets using descriptive statistics (mean, median, and mode)

SMARTPOINTS

Point Value	SmartPoints Category
Point Builder	The Kaplan Method for ACT Math
Point Builder	Picking Numbers
Point Builder	Backsolving
14 Points	Essential Skills

THE KAPLAN METHOD FOR ACT MATH

Step 1: What is the question?

First, focus on the *question stem* (the part before the answer choices) and make sure you understand the question. ACT Math questions can have complicated phrasing, and if you don't know *precisely* what you're looking for, you aren't likely to find it. So first, locate the end goal—the objective—and circle it. Do you need to solve for *x*? Find an odd number? Maybe it's a story problem and you need to find how many adults were admitted to an exhibit or the number of girls in a classroom. If it is a word problem and you get lost, break the question into pieces and make sure you come away with a clear understanding of what you're looking for. What is the end objective of your work? Again, *circle the question*, or objective as stated in the question stem, when you've found it.

Step 2: What information am I given?

Look through the question stem again and *underline the pieces of information provided*. Ask yourself whether you have everything you'll need to solve the problem or if there are intermediary steps you'll have to take. By underlining everything, you'll have a place to start, even if you're lost, as the ACT rarely provides information you don't need to solve the problem. Then, examine the format of the answer choices. This can help you determine your strategy. For example, you may think you need to solve for *x* in an equation, but then you see that all of the answers are given *in terms of x*, so you don't actually need to find *x*. Instead, you just need to come up with a different expression. As another example, if you are given information in fractions and see answers in decimals, you'll know you need to convert from one to the other at some point.

Step 3: What can I do with the information?

Now that you've gathered the information, it's time to answer the question. Decide on a plan of attack:

- **Straightforward math.** Do you know how to answer the question using your math skills? Go for it!

- **Picking Numbers.** Are there variables in the answer choices? If so, is there a way to pick some easy-to-use numbers you can plug in for the variable to help you get to the right answer? (This strategy is discussed in depth in the Point Builders section.)

- **Backsolving.** Are there numbers in the answer choices? What is the question asking for? Is there a way to use the answer choices to get to the right answer? (This strategy is also discussed in the Point Builders section.)

- **Guess strategically.** If you're really not sure, you can guess—you don't lose points for incorrect answers on the ACT. Try to eliminate as many incorrect choices as you can before guessing. Also, mark the question in your booklet so you can return to it at the end of the Math test and try again. If you still can't answer the question, bubble in your Letter of the Day.

Math

A Letter of the Day is an answer choice letter that you choose before Test Day to select for all questions you guess on. You'll need to select one letter from A, B, C, D, E and one from F, G, H, J, K.

Step 4: Am I finished?

In Step 1, you circled the objective. Check what you circled now. Is that what you found? Have you fully answered the question? Some questions may require several steps, and you may miss the last step if you don't check before you select. The ACT will frequently offer tempting answer choices for students who don't recheck the question. For example, you may need to find the area of a circle and you've only determined the radius—and the radius might be an answer choice! Because you will have identified and marked the question in Step 1, double-checking that you're finished should take only a few seconds, and it can make a real difference on Test Day. If you're stuck, circle the problem in your test book and come back later—always get through the easy questions first.

POINT BUILDERS

As promised, there are many ways to view questions. Here are the top two ways to think outside the box about how to answer some math questions on the ACT.

Picking Numbers

This strategy relates to questions that contain variables. You can Pick Numbers to make abstract problems—ones that insist on dealing with variables rather than numbers—more concrete. **Use this strategy when there are variables in the answer choices.** You may not even need to solve for the variables, but rather just determine how they would behave if they were real numbers. Thus, don't assume—pick a real number and see for yourself. Follow these guidelines:

Step 1: Pick a simple number to stand in for the variables, making sure it follows the criteria stated in the question stem. Does the number have to be even or odd? Positive or negative? Be careful when using 0 and 1, as they behave differently than most other numbers, but always pick easy-to-use numbers.

Step 2: Solve the *question* using the number(s) you picked.

Step 3: Test each of the *answer choices* using the number(s) you picked, eliminating those that give you a result that is different from the one you're looking for.

Step 4: If more than one choice remains, pick a different set of numbers and repeat steps 1–3.

Picking Numbers is the perfect strategy to apply to story problems that ask for an expression that represents a given scenario. This is called *modeling*. Let's use this strategy to answer the modeling question that follows.

> Money collected by c charities is to be divided equally among those charities. A trust fund has been set up to collect and distribute the money. According to donation records, p people gave d dollars each. Which expression represents the amount of money each charity will receive?
>
> **A.** $\dfrac{c}{pd}$
>
> **B.** $\dfrac{pd}{c}$
>
> **C.** $pd + c$
>
> **D.** $\dfrac{dc}{p}$
>
> **E.** $(p - c)d$

Getting to the Answer: If the mere thought of this question gives you a headache, Picking Numbers can provide you with a safe way to quickly get to the answer. The key is to choose numbers that make the math easy for you. Because the money will be divided evenly among the charities, pick numbers that relate easily to each other to make the math go smoothly. Try 2 for *p*, 4 for *c*, and 8 for *d*. Now the question asks: If 2 people each donated $8 to a trust fund that will distribute the money equally among 4 charities, how much money, in dollars, did each charity receive? So, this becomes $16 divided by 4. The answer to this question would be $4. Now replace *p* with 2, *d* with 8, and *c* with 4 in each of the answer choices and see which one comes out to 4.

Choice A: $\dfrac{c}{pd} = \dfrac{4}{2 \times 8} = \dfrac{4}{16} = \dfrac{1}{4}$ Eliminate.

Choice B: $\dfrac{pd}{c} = \dfrac{2 \times 8}{4} = \dfrac{16}{4} = 4$ Keep.

Choice C: $pd + c = 2 \times 8 + 4 = 16 + 4 = 20$ Eliminate.

Choice D: $\dfrac{dc}{p} = \dfrac{8 \times 4}{2} = \dfrac{32}{2} = 16$ Eliminate.

Choice E: $(p - c)d = (2 - 4) \times 8 = (-2) \times 8 = -16$ Eliminate.

Only (B) works, so it must be correct.

Math

Questions that involve properties of numbers (even/odd, prime/composite, rational/ irrational, etc.) are another example where Picking Numbers can make your life easier. Let's give the next question a try.

If a is an odd integer and b is an even integer, which of the following must be odd?

F. $2a + b$

G. $a + 2b$

H. ab

J. a^2b

K. ab^2

Getting to the Answer: Rather than trying to think this one through abstractly, it may be easier to Pick Numbers for a and b. There are rules that predict the evenness or oddness of sums, differences, and products, but there's no need to memorize those rules.

The question states that a is odd and b is even, so let $a = 3$ (remember, 1 can be used, but is not typically helpful) and $b = 2$. Plug those values into the answer choices, and you'll find that only one choice will be odd:

Choice F: $2a + b = 2(3) + 2 = 8$ Eliminate.

Choice G: $a + 2b = 3 + 2(2) = 7$ Keep.

Choice H: $ab = (3)(2) = 6$ Eliminate.

Choice J: $a^2b = (3)^2(2) = 18$ Eliminate.

Choice K: $ab^2 = (3)(2)^2 = 12$ Eliminate.

Choice (G) is the only odd result when $a = 3$ and $b = 2$, so it *must* be the one that's odd no matter *what* odd number a and even number b actually stand for. Even if you're not positive (G) will always be right, you know for a fact that all the others are definitely wrong, which is just as good!

> ✔ **Note**
>
> Had more than one of the answer choices returned an odd value, you would simply try another pair of numbers, such as $a = 5$ and $b = 8$. Very rarely would you need to pick more than two sets of numbers before you find the correct answer.

BACKSOLVING

On the ACT, you know for certain that one of the answer choices is correct (as opposed to a fill-in-the-blank test). Therefore, with some ACT Math problems, it may actually be easier to try out each answer choice until you find the one that works, rather than attempt to solve the problem and then look among the choices for the answer. This approach is called Backsolving. Let's try it out.

> Suppose 200 tickets were sold for a particular concert. Some tickets cost $10 each, and the others cost $5 each. If total ticket sales were $1,750, how many of the more expensive tickets were sold?
>
> **A.**   20
>
> **B.**   75
>
> **C.**   100
>
> **D.**   150
>
> **E.**   175

There are ways to solve this problem by setting up an equation or two, but if you're not comfortable with the algebraic approach to this one, why not just try out each answer choice? You know one of them will work.

Here's the next part you need to know: **When Backsolving, always start with the middle answer choice**. The numerical answer choices on the ACT are always either in ascending or descending order. If you solve for the one in the middle and it comes out too big, you can eliminate it *and the two larger numbers*, and the same if it's too small. So trying *one* answer choice can eliminate *three* options.

Getting to the Answer: Start with C. If 100 tickets were sold for $10 each, then the other 100 have to have been sold for $5 each: 100 at $10 is $1,000, and 100 at $5 is $500, for a total of $1,500—too small. There *must* have been more than 100 tickets sold at the higher price point ($10).

This is great news! If you know it's not C, and you know C is too small, you can eliminate A and B as well. By solving for one value, you've eliminated three answer choices. Even if you had to stop and guess now, you'd be picking from two answers, not five! So, which answer do you try next? More good news—it doesn't actually matter. If you solve for D and it's wrong, the answer must be E; you don't even have to solve for E to know that. So either remaining answer works equally well. That being the case, you should solve for whichever one looks easier, because it's just about doing the math. In this case, 150 looks a little bit easier to work with than 175, so try D.

If 150 tickets went for $10, then the other 50 went for $5. Do the math: 150 tickets at $10 is $1,500, and 50 tickets at $5 is $250, for a total of $1,750—that's it! The answer is (D), no need to go any further.

✔ Expert Tip

Backsolving your way to the answer may not be a method you'd show your algebra teacher, but your algebra teacher won't be watching on Test Day. Remember, all that matters is correct answers—it doesn't matter how you get them.

Now it's time to dig into the Essential Skills that you'll be expected to demonstrate on Test Day. These questions test your knowledge and skill level associated with concepts you likely learned in middle school, and they make up about 40–43% of the Math test. Many of the concepts that you'll encounter in Essential Skills questions will also be tested in Higher Math questions—those questions will just be more advanced and will require more steps to arrive at a final solution.

NUMBERS AND OPERATIONS

Math questions in this category test your knowledge of the real number system and fundamental math concepts and operations. Being comfortable with how numbers look and work can make your life easier on all sorts of math question types on the ACT.

Number Properties

Here are some essential rules and definitions to know:

- **Integers** include 0 and negative whole numbers. If a question says "x and y are integers," it's not ruling out numbers like 0 and −1.

- **Evens and odds** include 0 and negative whole numbers. Zero and −2 are even numbers; −1 is an odd number.

- **Prime numbers** do not include 1. The technical definition of a prime number is a positive integer with exactly two distinct positive integer factors. Two is prime because it has exactly two positive factors: 1 and 2. It is the smallest, and the only even, prime number. Four is not prime because it has three positive factors (1, 2, and 4)—too many! And 1 is not prime because it has only one positive factor (1)—too few!

- **Remainders** are integers left over when dividing. If a question asks for the remainder when 15 is divided by 2, don't say "15 divided by 2 is 7.5, so the remainder is 0.5." What you should say is: "15 divided by 2 is 7 with a remainder of 1."

- **The $\sqrt{}$ symbol** represents the positive square root only. The equation $x^2 = 9$ has two solutions: 3 and −3. But when you see $\sqrt{9}$, it means positive 3 only.

Let's practice using these rules and the Kaplan Method to work through a tricky Number Properties question. Keep in mind that the Kaplan Method isn't intended to be a rigid procedure, but rather a set of guidelines that will keep you on track, moving quickly and evading traps.

1. If the sum of five consecutive even integers is equal to their product, what is the greatest of the five integers?

   A. 4

   B. 10

   C. 14

   D. 16

   E. 20

Work through the Kaplan Method for ACT Math step-by-step to answer this question. The following table shows Kaplan's strategic thinking on the left, along with suggested math scratchwork on the right.

Strategic Thinking	Math Scratchwork
Step 1: What is the question? Put the question stem into words you can understand. What is the question stem really saying here?	When you add up the five consecutive even integers, you get the same thing as when you multiply them.
Step 2: What information am I given? Are you given any specific numbers to work with?	No, but you are told that you'll be working with consecutive even integers.
You are also given five answer choices. What do these represent?	Five numbers that *could* be the final term of the five-even-number sequence
What does the word *even* tell you?	The difference between each integer in this sequence will be 2.
Step 3: What can I do with the information? Straightforward math? You could set up an equation. That would work, but it's a huge equation and very difficult to solve, so try another approach.	$x + (x-2) + (x-4) + (x-6) + (x-8)$ $= x(x-2)(x-4)(x-6)(x-8)$
Pick Numbers?	There are no variables in the answer choices, so not this time.
Backsolving?	That should work, but it's going to take a bit of patience.
The question asks which is the greatest of the integers, so you have to start with the greatest answer choice: E—if you start with any other, even if it works, you won't know whether it's the *largest*.	Try E: $20 + 18 + 16 + 14 + 12 = 80$ $\quad 20 \times 18 \times 16 \times 14 \times 12$ is way *too big*! Try C: $14 + 12 + 10 + 8 + 6 = 50$ $\quad 14 \times 12 \times 10 \times 8 \times 6$ is still way *too big*! Try (A): $4 + 2 + 0 + (-2) + (-4) = 0$ $\quad$ Anything times $0 = 0$
Step 4: Am I finished? You found the largest of the five consecutive even integers, so you're all done!	Choice (A) is correct.

Math

Factors, Multiples, and Prime Factorization

The Numbers and Operations category also includes questions about divisibility, which involve factors (including greatest common factor), multiples (including least common multiple), and prime numbers (including prime factorization).

Let's review some definitions:

- A **factor** of an integer is any number that divides precisely into that integer (with no remainder).

- A **multiple** of an integer is that integer times any number. In other words, factor × factor = multiple.

- A **prime number** is a positive integer that is divisible without a remainder by only 1 and itself. The number 2 is the smallest prime number and the only even prime number; 1 is not considered prime.

- To find the **prime factorization** of an integer, use a factor tree to keep breaking the integer up into factors until all the factors are prime numbers. To find the prime factorization of 36, for example, you could begin by breaking it into 4 × 9. Then break 4 into 2 × 2 and break 9 into 3 × 3. The prime factorization of 36 is 2 × 2 × 3 × 3.

- The **greatest common factor (GCF)** of two numbers is the highest number that divides precisely into each of them without a remainder. To find the greatest common factor, break down both numbers into their prime factorizations and take all the prime factors they have in common. For example, try 36 and 48: 36 = 2 × 2 × 3 × 3 and 48 = 2 × 2 × 2 × 2 × 3. What they have in common is two 2s and one 3, so the GCF is 2 × 2 × 3 = 12.

- The **least common multiple (LCM)** of two numbers is the smallest multiple both of those numbers divide into. To find the LCM of two or more numbers, check out the multiples of the larger number until you find one that's also a multiple of the smaller. For example, to find the LCM of 12 and 15, begin by taking the multiples of 15: 1 × 15 = 15, which is not divisible by 12; 2 × 15 = 30, not divisible by 12; nor is 45, which is 3 × 15. But the next multiple of 15, 4 × 15 = 60, is divisible by 12, so it's the LCM.

- Two integers are **relative primes** if they share no prime factors. To determine whether two integers are relative primes, break them both down to their prime factorizations. For example, 35 = 5 × 7 and 54 = 2 × 3 × 3 × 3. They have no prime factors in common, so 35 and 54 are relative primes.

> ✔ **Note**
>
> All numbers are both factors and multiples of themselves. Six is a factor of 12, and 24 is a multiple of 12. Twelve is both a factor (12 ÷ 12 = 1) and a multiple (12 × 1 = 12) of itself.

> ✔ **Expert Tip**
>
> You can always get a common multiple of two numbers by multiplying them, but unless the two numbers are relative primes, the product will not be the least common multiple. For example, to find a common multiple for 12 and 15, you could just multiply: 12 × 15 = 180.

These concepts are occasionally tested directly, but more often, a thorough understanding of each will help you navigate through more complex questions from different categories. Let's try a quick one now to test what you've learned:

2. If $2 \leq M \leq 100$, and M is a multiple of 10 and 45, what is M?

   F.   1

   G.   5

   H.   45

   J.   90

   K.   450

Work through the Kaplan Method for ACT Math step-by-step to answer this question. The following table shows Kaplan's strategic thinking on the left, along with suggested math scratchwork on the right.

Strategic Thinking	Math Scratchwork
Step 1: What is the question? Restate the question in your own words to make sure you understand exactly what you're trying to find.	You need to find a common multiple of 10 and 45 that is between 2 and 100.
Step 2: What information am I given? You're given three facts about M.	$2 \leq M \leq 100$ M is a multiple of 10. M is a multiple of 45.
Step 3: What can I do with the information? Start listing multiples of the larger number (45) until you find one that is also a multiple of the smaller number (10). Remember, all multiples of 10 end in 0.	45 × 1 = 45 Not a multiple of 10. 45 × 2 = 90 Stop.
Step 4: Am I finished? Check that your value for M is between 2 and 100. It is, so you're all set.	Choice (J) is correct.

✔ **Expert Tip**

Watch out for trap answers! Choice K is likely to tempt you because 450 is the most obvious common multiple of 10 and 45, but 450 is not between 2 and 100.

Math

Rational Number Operations

Many of the questions you'll encounter on Test Day will surely involve fractions and decimals, so you'll want to review these in advance.

Any number that can be expressed as a fraction or a repeating decimal is a **rational number**. This includes numbers like 3, $\frac{2}{5}$, −0.1666, or $0.\bar{3}$. **Irrational numbers** cannot be expressed precisely as a fraction or decimal. For the purposes of the ACT, the most important irrational numbers are $\sqrt{2}$, $\sqrt{3}$, and π. You'll learn more about irrational numbers in a later chapter. Here's what you need to know for now:

irr #'s

- Generally speaking, when you work with fractions on the ACT, you'll need to put them in **lowest terms**. This means the numerator and the denominator are not divisible by any common integer greater than 1. The fraction $\frac{1}{2}$ is in lowest terms, but the fraction $\frac{3}{6}$ is not, because 3 and 6 are both divisible by 3. The process used to write a fraction in lowest terms is called **reducing**, which simply means dividing out any common multiples from both the numerator and denominator. This process is also commonly called **canceling.**

- To add or subtract fractions, first find a **common denominator** and then add or subtract the numerators. Finding a common denominator often involves multiplying one or more of the fractions by a number so that the denominators will be the same:
$$\frac{2}{15} + \frac{3}{10} = \frac{4}{30} + \frac{9}{30} = \frac{4+9}{30} = \frac{13}{30}.$$

- To **multiply fractions**, multiply straight across—numerator times numerator and denominator times denominator: $\frac{5}{7} \times \frac{3}{4} = \frac{5 \times 3}{7 \times 4} = \frac{15}{28}.$

- To **divide fractions**, invert the fraction in the denominator and multiply:
$$\frac{1}{2} \div \frac{3}{5} = \frac{1}{2} \times \frac{5}{3} = \frac{1 \times 5}{2 \times 3} = \frac{5}{6}.$$ *Keep, change, change*

- To **convert a mixed number**, which is a whole number with a fraction, to an improper fraction, which is a fraction where the numerator is bigger than the denominator, multiply the whole number part by the denominator, then add the numerator. The result is the new numerator (over the same denominator). To convert $7\frac{1}{3}$, first multiply 7 by 3, then add 1 to get the new numerator of 22. Put that over the same denominator, 3, to get $\frac{22}{3}$.

- To **convert an improper fraction** to a mixed number, divide the denominator into the numerator, and the remainder will be the numerator of the fraction part, with the same denominator. For example, to convert $\frac{108}{5}$, first divide 5 into 108, which yields 21 with a remainder of 3. Therefore, $\frac{108}{5} = 21\frac{3}{5}$.

- The **reciprocal** of a fraction is the inverse of that fraction. To find the reciprocal of a fraction, switch the numerator and the denominator. The reciprocal of $\frac{3}{7}$ is $\frac{7}{3}$. The reciprocal of 5 (or $\frac{5}{1}$ because all whole numbers can be written over 1) is $\frac{1}{5}$. The product of two reciprocals is always 1.

- One way to **compare fractions** is to manipulate them so they have a common denominator. For instance, compare $\frac{3}{4}$ and $\frac{5}{7}$:

  $\frac{3}{4} = \frac{21}{28}$ and $\frac{5}{7} = \frac{20}{28}$; $\frac{21}{28}$ is greater than $\frac{20}{28}$, so $\frac{3}{4}$ is greater than $\frac{5}{7}$.

  Another way to compare fractions is to convert them both to decimals: $\frac{3}{4}$ converts to 0.75, and $\frac{5}{7}$ converts to approximately 0.714, and 0.75 is greater than 0.714.

- To **convert a fraction to a decimal**, divide the numerator by the denominator. To convert $\frac{5}{8}$, divide 5 by 8, yielding 0.625. Often, these numbers will start repeating, such as with $\frac{1}{6}$. When 1 is divided by 6, the decimal starts repeating almost right away, 0.16666666..., so it can be written as $0.1\overline{66}$ (the line over the 66 means "repeating"). To find a particular digit in a repeating decimal, note the number of digits in the cluster that repeats. If there are two digits in that cluster, then every second digit is the same. If there are three digits in that cluster, then every third digit is the same. And so on.

- The **absolute value** of a number (integers, fractions, and decimals alike) is its distance from zero on the number line, which is why absolute value is always positive. Treat absolute value signs a lot like parentheses. Do what's inside them first and then take the absolute value of the result. Don't take the absolute value of each piece between the bars before calculating. In order to calculate $|(-12) + 5 - (-4)| - |5 + (-10)|$, first do what's inside the bars to arrive at $|-3| - |-5|$, which is $3 - 5$, or -2.

Let's try another question about numbers:

3. When $\frac{1}{27}$ is expressed as a decimal number, what is the 50th digit after the decimal point?

   A. 0
   B. 1
   C. 2
   D. 3
   E. 7

Work through the Kaplan Method for ACT Math step-by-step to answer this question. The following table shows Kaplan's strategic thinking on the left, along with suggested math scratchwork on the right.

Strategic Thinking	Math Scratchwork
Step 1: What is the question? You need to find the 50th digit after the decimal point when $\frac{1}{27}$ is written as a decimal number.	
Step 2: What information am I given? You're given a fraction and told to express it as a decimal number instead.	To convert the fraction to a decimal, divide the numerator by the denominator.
Step 3: What can I do with the information? How can you convert the fraction to a decimal quickly?	Use your calculator to save some time.
Do you need to write out all 50 digits after the decimal point? Write the number with a bar so you can "see" the pattern. There are three digits in the repeating cluster, so every third digit is the same: 7.	No, just enough to establish a pattern. The decimal equivalent of $\frac{1}{27}$ is 0.037037037… $0.\overline{037}$
To find the 50th digit, look for the multiple of 3 just less than 50—that's 48.	The 48th digit is 7, and with the 49th digit the pattern repeats with 0. So, the 50th digit is 3.
Step 4: Am I finished? You found the 50th digit after the decimal point, so move on to the next question.	Choice (D) is correct.

Order of Operations (PEMDAS) and Rules of Exponents

You'll also want to practice using the order of operations and exponent rules before Test Day. A quick review follows:

PEMDAS = Please Excuse My Dear Aunt Sally.

$L \rightarrow R$ $L \rightarrow R$

P = Parentheses		M = Multiplication		A = Addition
E = Exponents	then	D = Division	then	S = Subtraction

Multiplication and division are ordered from left to right. Similarly, addition and subtraction are ordered from left to right.

> ✔ **Expert Tip**
>
> If an expression has parentheses within parentheses, work from the innermost out.

The most challenging element of those basic operations is exponents. The ACT tests exponents in a variety of ways. By remembering a few simple rules, you can make your life much easier when dealing with exponents. You'll also be well on your way to understanding more advanced concepts, like radicals and logarithms. Here are those rules:

- An **exponent** refers to the number of times a base is multiplied by itself. For example, $4^3 = 4 \times 4 \times 4$. An integer times itself is the **square** of that integer (5×5 is 5^2), and an integer times itself twice is the **cube** of that integer ($4 \times 4 \times 4$ is 4^3).

- To **multiply** two terms with the same base, keep the base and add the exponents.

  Write it out: $2^2 \times 2^3 = (2 \times 2)(2 \times 2 \times 2) = 2 \times 2 \times 2 \times 2 \times 2 = 2^5$
  Use the rule: $2^2 \times 2^3 = 2^{2+3} = 2^5$

- To **divide** two terms with the same base, keep the base and subtract the exponent of the denominator from the exponent of the numerator.

  Write it out: $5^4 \div 5^2 = \dfrac{5 \times 5 \times \cancel{5} \times \cancel{5}}{\cancel{5} \times \cancel{5}} = \dfrac{5 \times 5}{1} = 5^2$

  Use the rule: $5^4 \div 5^2 = 5^{4-2} = 5^2$

- To raise a **power to another power**, multiply the exponents.

  Write it out: $(3^2)^4 = (3 \times 3)^4 = (3 \times 3)(3 \times 3)(3 \times 3)(3 \times 3) = 3^8$

  Use the rule: $(3^2)^4 = 3^{2 \times 4} = 3^8$

- To evaluate a **negative exponent**, take the reciprocal of the base and change the sign of the exponent: $2^{-3} = \left(\dfrac{1}{2}\right)^3 = \dfrac{1}{2^3} = \dfrac{1}{8}$.

- Any nonzero number raised to the zero power is equal to 1. For example, $7^0 = 1$.

Math

How about some practice? Take your time and follow the correct order of operations.

4. What is the value of $30 - 5 \times 4 + (7 - 3)^2 \div 8$?

F. 3.25

G. 12

H. 15

J. 102

K. 105

$30 - 5 \times 4 + (4)^2 \div 8$
$30 - 5 \times 4 + 16 \div 8$
$30 - 20 + 2$
$10 + 2$
12

Work through the Kaplan Method for ACT Math step-by-step to answer this question. The following table shows Kaplan's strategic thinking on the left, along with suggested math scratchwork on the right.

Strategic Thinking	Math Scratchwork
Step 1: What is the question?	
You need to find the value of the given expression.	
Step 2: What information am I given?	
You're given a numerical expression with several operations, grouping symbols, and an exponent.	$30 - 5 \times 4 + (7 - 3)^2 \div 8$
Step 3: What can I do with the information?	
Use PEMDAS. Start with the parentheses.	$30 - 5 \times 4 + 4^2 \div 8$
Evaluate terms with exponents next.	$30 - 5 \times 4 + 16 \div 8$
Then, do all multiplication and division from left to right.	$30 - 20 + 2$
Finally, do all addition and subtraction from left to right.	$10 + 2 = 12$
Step 4: Am I finished?	
Choice (G) is a match, so your job is done.	Choice (G) is correct.

RATIOS, PROPORTIONS, RATES, AND UNIT CONVERSIONS

Many of the story problems you're likely to see on the ACT will involve ratios, proportions, rates, and unit conversions. These are concepts you probably learned in middle school, so be sure to dust them off and refresh your memory before Test Day.

Ratios and Proportions

A **ratio** is a comparison of one quantity to another. In a ratio of two numbers, the numerator is often associated with the word *of*, and the denominator with the word *to*. For example, the ratio of 3 *to* 4 is $\dfrac{of\ 3}{to\ 4} = \dfrac{3}{4}$.

A **part-to-part ratio** can be turned into two **part-to-whole ratios** by putting each number in the original ratio over the sum of the parts. If the ratio of males to females is 1 to 2, then the males-to-people ratio is $\dfrac{1}{1+2} = \dfrac{1}{3}$ and the females-to-people ratio is $\dfrac{2}{1+2} = \dfrac{2}{3}$. This is the same as saying $\dfrac{1}{3}$ of all the people are male and $\dfrac{2}{3}$ are female.

You can also **combine ratios**. If you have two ratios, *a:b* and *b:c*, you can derive *a:c* by finding a common multiple of the *b* terms. Take a look at the following table to see this in action. Suppose the ratio of *a* to *b* is 3:4 and the ratio of *b* to *c* is 3:5. What's the ratio of *a* to *c*?

a	:	*b*	:	*c*
3	:	4		
		3	:	5
9	:	12		
		12	:	20
9		:		20

What's a common multiple of the *b* terms? The number 12 is a good choice because it's the least common multiple of 3 and 4 and so will reduce the need to simplify later. Where do you go from there? Multiply each ratio by the factor (use 3 for *a:b* and 4 for *b:c*) that will get you to *b* = 12. The ratio of *a* to *c* equals 9:20. Notice we didn't merely say *a:c* is 3:5; this would be incorrect on Test Day (and likely a wrong-answer trap!).

A **proportion** is two ratios set equal to each other. Proportions are an efficient way to solve certain problems, but you must exercise caution when setting them up. Watching the units of each piece of the proportion will help you with this. To solve a proportion, cross-multiply:

$$\frac{x}{5} = \frac{3}{4}$$

$$4x = 5(3)$$

$$x = \frac{15}{4} = 3.75$$

Rates and Unit Conversions

A **rate** is any "something per something"—days per week, miles per hour, dollars per gallon, etc. Pay close attention to the units of measurement, because often the rate is given in one measurement in the question and a different measurement in the answer choices. This means you need to convert the rate to the other measurement before you answer the question.

You can use the **factor-label method** to convert rates and their units. The factor-label method is a simple yet powerful way to ensure you're doing your calculations correctly and getting an answer with the requested units. For example, suppose you're asked to find the number of cups in two gallons. First, identify your starting quantity's units (gallons) and then identify the end quantity's units (cups). The next step is to piece together a path of relationships (called unit conversions) that will convert gallons into cups, canceling out units as you go. Keep in mind that you will often have multiple stepping stones between your starting and ending quantities, so don't panic if you can't get directly from gallons to cups.

Follow along as we convert from gallons to quarts to pints to cups using the factor-label method:

$$2 \text{ gal} \times \frac{4 \text{ qt}}{1 \text{ gal}} \times \frac{2 \text{ pt}}{1 \text{ qt}} \times \frac{2 \text{ cups}}{1 \text{ pt}} = (2 \times 4 \times 2 \times 2) \text{ cups}$$

$$= 32 \text{ cups}$$

Average rate is *not* simply the average of two rates. It's the average of the total amounts. The most common rate is speed—distance over time—and the most common question about average rates is average speed—total distance over total time.

$$\text{Average } A \text{ per } B = \frac{\text{Total } A}{\text{Total } B}$$

$$\text{Average speed} = \frac{\text{Total distance}}{\text{Total time}}$$

For example, if the first 120 miles of a journey is at 40 mph and the next 120 miles is at 60 mph, what is the average speed? Don't just average the two speeds. Instead, figure out the total distance and the total time. The total distance is $120 + 120 = 240$ miles. The times are 3 hours for the first leg and 2 hours for the second leg, or 5 hours total. The average speed, then, is $\frac{240}{5} = 48$ miles per hour.

✔ **Expert Tip**

Be sure to get comfortable with the DIRT equation before Test Day: **D**istance **I**s **R**ate times **T**ime. You can use a manipulation of this equation to solve most rate questions.

Time to exercise your brain again. Here's a ratio question for you to try.

5. The ratio of girls to boys in a class is 3:5. If the total number of students is 32, how many more boys are there than girls?

   A. 3
   B. 5
   C. 8
   D. 12
   E. 20

Work through the Kaplan Method for ACT Math step-by-step to answer this question. The following table shows Kaplan's strategic thinking on the left, along with suggested math scratchwork on the right.

Strategic Thinking	Math Scratchwork
Step 1: What is the question?	
You need to find how many more boys there are than girls.	
Step 2: What information am I given?	
You're given the ratio of girls to boys in the class.	girls:boys = 3:5
You're also given the total number of students.	32 students in all
Step 3: What can I do with the information? Because you're given the total number of students, rewrite the part-to-part ratio as a part-to-whole ratio.	If there are 3 parts girls and 5 parts boys, there are 8 parts total. girls:total = 3:8
Set up a proportion that relates the number of girls (g) to the total number of students. Then cross-multiply to solve for g.	$\dfrac{3}{8} = \dfrac{g}{32}$ $8g = 3(32)$ $g = \dfrac{3(32)}{8} = 12$
Step 4: Am I finished?	
No! Choice D is a trap. Review what the question is asking for: how many more boys there are than girls. If there are 32 students in all, and 12 are girls, then 20 are boys. Now answer the question.	There are 20 − 12 = 8 more boys than girls. Choice (C) is correct.

Math

Percents

Percents are one of the most commonly used mathematical relationships and are quite popular on the ACT. *Percent* is just another word for *hundredth*. For example, 27% (27 percent) means:

27 hundredths $\dfrac{27}{100}$ 0.27

27 out of every 100 things
27 parts out of a whole of 100 parts

> ✔ **Note**
>
> In percent questions, whether you need to find the part, the whole, or the percent, use the same three-part percent formula: Part = percent × whole.

When you work with a percent in a formula, be sure to convert the percent into decimal form:

Example: What is 12% of 25 ?
Setup: Part = 0.12 × 25

Example: 15 is 3% of what number?
Setup: 15 = 0.03 × whole

Example: 45 is what percent of 9 ?
Setup: 45 = percent × 9

Here are some other types of questions that may involve percents:

- To **increase a number by a percent**, add the percent to 100%, convert to a decimal, and multiply. For example, to increase 40 by 25%, add 25% to 100%, convert 125% to 1.25, and multiply by 40. The result is 1.25 × 40 = 50. To decrease, just subtract the percent from 100%, convert to a decimal, and multiply.

- To calculate a **percent increase** (or decrease), use the formula:

$$\text{Percent change} = \frac{\text{amount of change}}{\text{original amount}} \times 100\%$$

- When there are **multiple percent increases** and/or decreases, and the question asks for the combined percent increase or decrease, the easiest and most effective strategy is to pick 100 for the original value and see what happens.

Example: A price went up 10% one year, and the new price went up 20% the next year. What was the combined percent increase over the two-year period?

Setup: First year: 100 + (10% of 100) = 110.
                Second year: 110 + (20% of 110) = 132.
                That's a combined 32% increase.

Math

- To find the **original whole before a percent increase or decrease,** set up an equation with a variable in place of the original number. Suppose you have a 15% increase over an unknown original amount, say *x*. You would follow the same steps as always: 100% plus 15% is 115%, which is 1.15 when converted to a decimal. Then multiply by the number, which in this case is *x*, and you get 1.15*x*. Finally, set that equal to the new amount.

  Example: After a 5% increase, the population was 59,346. What was the population *before* the increase?

  Setup: $1.05x = 59{,}346 \rightarrow x = 56{,}520$

Ready to try a percent question?

6. In 1960, scientists estimated a certain animal population in a particular geographical area to be 6,400. In 2000, the population had risen to 7,200. If this animal population experiences the same percent increase over the next 40 years, what will the approximate population be?

   F. 8,000
   G. 8,100
   H. 8,240
   J. 8,400
   K. 8,600

Work through the Kaplan Method for ACT Math step-by-step to answer this question. The following table shows Kaplan's strategic thinking on the left, along with suggested math scratchwork on the right.

Strategic Thinking	Math Scratchwork
Step 1: What is the question? You need to find the approximate population of the animal population 40 years after 2000.	
Step 2: What information am I given? You know the population in 1960 and in 2000. You're told that the *percent increase* over the next 40-year period will be the same.	1960 population = 6,400 2000 population = 7,200

Strategic Thinking	Math Scratchwork
Step 3: What can I do with the information?	
First, use the percent change formula to find the percent increase over the first 40-year period.	$\% \text{ change} = \dfrac{\text{amount of change}}{\text{original amount}} \times 100\%$ $= \dfrac{7{,}200 - 6{,}400}{6{,}400}$ $= \dfrac{800}{6{,}400} = 0.125 = 12.5\%$
Apply the same percent increase to the 2000 population to estimate the population 40 years later.	$7{,}200 \times 1.125 = 8{,}100$
Step 4: Am I finished?	
You found the approximate population 40 years later, so you're all done.	Choice (G) is correct.

BASIC ALGEBRA

You'll get to practice lots of Algebra in a later chapter, but for now, let's review the basics.

Expressions, Equations, and Inequalities

Evaluating an expression typically involves substituting a given value (or values) for the variables into the expression and then simplifying. For example, the value of $3x + 4y$ when $x = 5$ and $y = -2$ is $3(5) + 4(-2) = 15 - 8 = 7$.

To **solve an equation**, isolate the variable. As long as you do the same thing to both sides of the equation, the equation is still balanced. To solve $5x - 12 = -2x + 9$, first get all the x terms on one side by adding $2x$ to both sides: $7x - 12 = 9$. Then add 12 to both sides: $7x = 21$. Finally, divide both sides by 7 to get $x = 3$.

Solving an inequality means finding the set of all values that satisfy the given statement. They work just like equations: Your task is to isolate the variable on one side of the inequality symbol. The only significant difference is that if you multiply or divide by a negative number, you must reverse the direction of the inequality symbol.

> ✔ **Expert Tip**
>
> If the variable ends up on the right-hand side of the symbol when you solve an inequality, be careful when matching it to an answer choice. For instance, $3 > x$ can be rewritten as $x < 3$. Notice that the small end of the symbol stays pointed at x.

The solution to an inequality can be represented on a number line. For example, $x > 4$ could be graphed like this:

Notice the open dot at 4, indicating that 4 is not a solution to the inequality. This is called a **strict** inequality. By contrast, the graph of $x \leq 4$ looks like this:

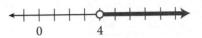

Notice the closed (solid) dot, indicating that 4 should be included in the solution set for the inequality.

>   **Note**
>
> To help remember which way to shade, read the $<$ symbol as "less than," which tells you to shade to the left of the dot. Note the Ls: Less than means shade Left.

Modeling

Writing an expression or equation to **model** a real-world scenario involves translating from English into math. To do this, look for key words and work from left to right, turning phrases into algebraic expressions and sentences into equations. Be careful about order, especially when subtraction is called for.

Example: The charge for a phone call is r cents for the first 3 minutes and s cents for each minute thereafter. What is the cost, in cents, of a call lasting exactly t minutes, assuming $t > 3$?

Setup: The charge begins with r, and then something more is added, depending on the length of the call. The amount added is s times the number of minutes past 3 minutes. If the total number of minutes is t, then the number of minutes past 3 is $t - 3$. So the charge is $r + s(t - 3)$.

The following table shows some of the phrases and mathematical equivalents you're most likely to see on the ACT.

Math

Translating from English into Math	
English	**Math**
equals, is, equivalent to, was, will be, has, costs, adds up to, the same as, as much as	=
times, of, multiplied by, product of, twice, double, by	×
divided by, per, out of, each, ratio	÷
plus, added to, and, sum, combined, total, increased by	+
minus, subtracted from, smaller than, less than, fewer, decreased by, difference between	−
a number, how much, how many, what	x, n, etc.

✔ **Expert Tip**

Questions in which you must simply match an expression or equation to a scenario are great opportunities to use the Picking Numbers strategy.

Let's try an algebra question before moving on to geometry.

7. If $4x + 3 = 9x - 4$, then $x = ?$

    A. $\dfrac{7}{5}$

    B. $\dfrac{5}{7}$

    C. $\dfrac{7}{15}$

    D. $\dfrac{1}{5}$

    E. $-\dfrac{1}{5}$

$$4x + 3 = 9x - 4$$
$$ +4 +4$$
$$4x + 7 = 9x$$
$$-4x -4x$$
$$7 = 5x$$
$$5 -5$$
$$\boxed{7/5 = x}$$

Work through the Kaplan Method for ACT Math step-by-step to answer this question. The following table shows Kaplan's strategic thinking on the left, along with suggested math scratchwork on the right.

Strategic Thinking	Math Scratchwork
Step 1: What is the question? You need to find the value of *x*.	
Step 2: What information am I given? You have an equation with variables on both sides and constants on both sides.	
Step 3: What can I do with the information? Could you Backsolve?	There are numbers in the answer choices, so Backsolving is an option.
Should you Backsolve?	The answer choices are all fractions which will make the computations slow and tedious. Straightforward algebra will be faster.
Isolate the variable by either subtracting 4x from both sides of the equation and then adding 4 to both sides, or by subtracting 9x from both sides of the equation and then subtracting 3 from both sides.	$4x + 3 = 9x - 4$ $3 = 5x - 4$ $7 = 5x$
Then divide both sides by the coefficient of *x*.	$x = \dfrac{7}{5}$
Step 4: Am I finished? You found the value of *x*, so you're done.	Choice (A) is correct.

Math

BASIC GEOMETRY

Geometry is a highly tested area on the ACT. This includes Coordinate Geometry and Plane Geometry. The more sophisticated topics are presented in a later chapter, but over the next couple of pages, we'll review some of the fundamental properties that you need to know.

Graphing on the Coordinate Plane

Basic two-dimensional graphing is performed on a **coordinate plane**. There are two axes, x and y, that meet at a central point called the origin. Each axis has both positive and negative values that extend outward from the origin at evenly spaced intervals. The axes divide the space into four sections called quadrants, which are labeled I, II, III, and IV. Quadrant I is always the upper-right section, and the rest follow counterclockwise.

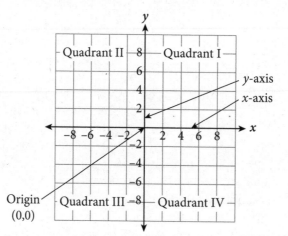

To **plot points** on the coordinate plane, you need their coordinates. The **x-coordinate** is where the point falls along the x-axis, and the **y-coordinate** is where the point falls along the y-axis. The two coordinates together make an ordered pair written as (x,y). When writing ordered pairs, the x-coordinate is always listed first (think alphabetical order). Four points are plotted in the following figure as examples.

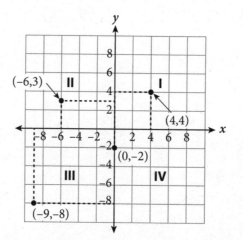

When two points are vertically or horizontally aligned, calculating the **distance** between them is easy. For a horizontal distance, only the *x*-value changes; for a vertical distance, only the *y*-value changes. Take the positive difference of the *x*-coordinates (or *y*-coordinates) to determine the distance. Two examples are presented here.

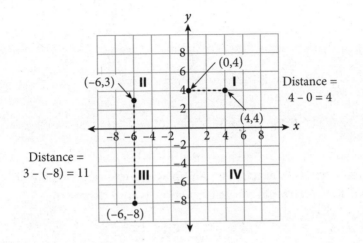

The **midpoint** of a line segment with endpoints (x_1, y_1) and (x_2, y_2) is simply the average of the *x*-coordinates and the average of the *y*-coordinates. You should recognize and be able to use the midpoint formula: $M = \left(\dfrac{x_1 + x_2}{2}, \dfrac{y_1 + y_2}{2} \right)$.

Plane Geometry: Lines and Angles

A **line** is a one-dimensional geometric abstraction—infinitely long with no width. It is not physically possible to *draw* a line, as any physical line would have a finite length and some width, no matter how long and thin we tried to make it. Two points determine a straight line: Given any two points, there is exactly one straight line that passes through them.

A **line segment** is a section of a straight line, of finite length with two endpoints. A line segment is named for its endpoints, as in segment *AB*. The **midpoint** is the point that divides a line segment into two equal parts.

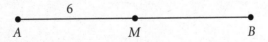

Example: In the figure shown, *A* and *B* are the endpoints of $\overline{AB}$ and *M* is its midpoint $\left(\overline{AM} = \overline{MB} \right)$. What is the length of *AB* ? $\overline{AM}$ is 6, meaning $\overline{MB}$ is also 6, so $\overline{AB} = 6 + 6 = 12$.

Two lines are **parallel** if they lie on the same plane and will never intersect each other regardless of how far they are extended. If line ℓ_1 is parallel to line ℓ_2, you write $\ell_1 \parallel \ell_2$. Parallel lines have the same slope, which is why they never intersect.

Math

An **angle** is formed whenever two lines or line segments intersect at a point. The point of intersection is called the **vertex** of the angle. Angles are measured in degrees (°).

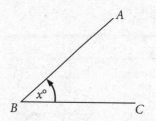

Angle x, $\angle ABC$, and $\angle B$ all denote the same angle in the diagram shown above.

An **acute angle** is an angle whose degree measure is between 0° and 90°. A **right angle** is an angle whose degree measure is exactly 90°. An **obtuse angle** is an angle whose degree measure is between 90° and 180°. A **straight angle** is an angle whose degree measure is exactly 180°.

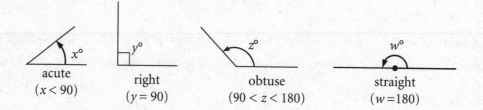

The sum of the measures of the angles on one side of a straight line is 180°.

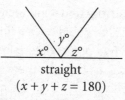

The sum of the measures of the angles around a point is 360°.

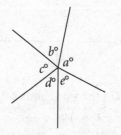

$$a + b + c + d + e = 360$$

Two lines are **perpendicular** if they intersect at a 90° angle. The shortest distance from a point to a line is a perpendicular line segment drawn from the point to the line. If line ℓ_1 is perpendicular to line ℓ_2, you write $\ell_1 \perp \ell_2$. If $\ell_1 \perp \ell_2$ and $\ell_2 \perp \ell_3$, then $\ell_1 \parallel \ell_3$:

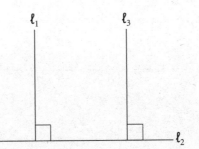

Two angles are **supplementary** if together they make up a straight angle, i.e., if the sum of their measures is 180°. Two angles are **complementary** if together they make up a right angle, i.e., if the sum of their measures is 90°.

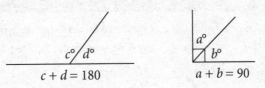

A line or line segment **bisects** an angle if it splits the angle into two equal halves. In the following figure, $\overline{BD}$ bisects $\angle ABC$, meaning $\angle ABD$ has the same measure as $\angle DBC$. The two smaller angles are each half the size of $\angle ABC$.

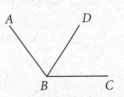

Vertical angles are a pair of opposite angles formed by two intersecting line segments. At the point of intersection, two pairs of vertical angles are formed. In the following figure, angles a and c are vertical angles, as are b and d.

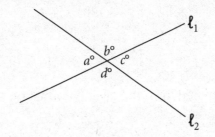

The two angles in a pair of vertical angles have the same degree measure. In the diagram shown above, $a = c$ and $b = d$. In addition, since ℓ_1 and ℓ_2 are straight lines, $a + b = c + d = a + d = b + c = 180$. In other words, each angle is supplementary to each of its two adjacent angles.

If two parallel lines intersect with a third line (called a *transversal*), each of the parallel lines will intersect the third line at the same angle. In the following figure, $a = e$ (corresponding angles along a transversal), $a = c$ (vertical angles), and $e = g$ (vertical angles). Therefore, $a = c = e = g$ and $b = d = f = h$.

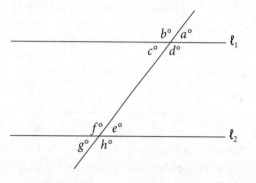

✔ **Expert Tip**

Restating the previous property results in a very useful fact: When two parallel lines intersect with a third line, all acute angles formed are equal, all obtuse angles formed are equal, and any acute angle is supplementary to any obtuse angle.

Now that you know the rules associated with lines and angles, try the next question.

8.   Lines *E*, *F*, and *G* are parallel lines cut by transversal *H* as shown below. What is the value of $a + b + c + d$?

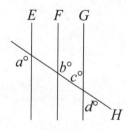

   F.   180

   G.   270

   H.   360

   J.   540

   K.   Cannot be determined from the given information

Work through the Kaplan Method for ACT Math step-by-step to answer this question. The following table shows Kaplan's strategic thinking on the left, along with suggested math scratchwork on the right.

Strategic Thinking	Math Scratchwork
Step 1: What is the question? The question asks for the value of $a + b + c + d$.	
Step 2: What information am I given? You know that line H is a transversal through lines E, F, and G. What do you know about these lines?	The lines are parallel.
Step 3: What can I do with the information? There are no angle measures given, so you'll need to think about properties of parallel lines. What do you know about the angles? What is true about the relationship between the acute angles and the obtuse angles formed when a transversal cuts parallel lines? Now do the math.	The angles labeled $a°$ and $b°$ are obtuse angles; the angles labeled $c°$ and $d°$ are acute angles. Angle a must be supplementary to angle d, and angle b must be supplementary to angle c. $a + d = 180$; $b + c = 180$ $a + b + c + d = 180 + 180 = 360$
Step 4: Am I finished? You found the sum of the four angle measures, so select your answer and move on.	Choice (H) is correct.

✔ **Note**

Notice that you didn't (in fact, you couldn't) find the measure of any one of the angles. Don't be tempted by the "Cannot be determined" option. It's very rarely the correct answer.

Triangle Basics

A **triangle** is a closed figure with three angles and three straight sides.

The sum of the measures of the angles in a triangle is 180°.

Each **interior angle** is supplementary to an adjacent **exterior angle**. The degree measure of an exterior angle is equal to the sum of the measures of the other two angles of the triangle (the two not next to the exterior angle), or 180° minus the measure of its adjacent interior angle.

In the figure shown here, a, b, and c are interior angles, so $a + b + c = 180$. Further, d is supplementary to c, so $d + c = 180$, $d + c = a + b + c$, and $d = a + b$. Thus, the exterior angle d is equal to the sum of the two remote interior angles—a and b.

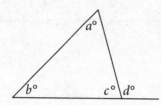

You'll get to practice your triangle expertise in a later chapter, so let's wrap up with some basic statistics and probability.

> ✔ **Note**
>
> Some geometry questions about perimeter, area, and volume may also be considered Essential Skills questions, depending on the complexity of the question. We'll save those for the Geometry chapter where you'll have a chance to really dig in.

STATISTICS AND PROBABILITY

Depending on the situation, questions about data can be very quick or very time-consuming. Just to get your feet wet, let's review a few basic definitions and formulas, and then we'll try out a less complicated Statistics question.

Statistical Measures of Center

While there are entire high school and college courses devoted to the study of statistics, the ACT will (fortunately) only test you on a few basic statistical concepts. Using an example from high school, let's take a look at the sort of concepts the ACT expects you to be familiar with.

Suppose you took five quizzes in an algebra class and earned scores of 85, 92, 85, 80, and 96. Descriptions of three fundamental statistical measures you can find for this data set follow:

- **Mean (also called average):** The sum of the values divided by the number of values. For your algebra class, the mean of your quiz scores is $\dfrac{85 + 92 + 85 + 80 + 96}{5} = \dfrac{438}{5} = 87.6$.

- **Median:** The value that is in the middle of the set *when the values are arranged in order (ascending or descending)*. The test scores in ascending order are 80, 85, 85, 92, and 96, making the median 85. Be careful: The ACT could give you a set of numbers that is not in order. Make sure you properly arrange them before determining the median.

- **Mode:** The value that occurs most frequently. The score that appears more than any other is 85 (twice vs. once), so it is the mode. If more than one value appears the most often, that's okay: A set of data can have multiple modes.

✔ **Note**

To find the median of a data set that contains an even number of terms, arrange the terms in ascending order, then find the average of the two middle terms.

9. If the average of 292, 305, 415, and x is 343, what is the value of x ?

  A. 292

  B. 343

  C. 360

  D. 415

  E. 1,355

Work through the Kaplan Method for ACT Math step-by-step to answer this question. The following table shows Kaplan's strategic thinking on the left, along with suggested math scratchwork on the right.

Strategic Thinking	Math Scratchwork
Step 1: What is the question?	
You need to find the value of x.	
Step 2: What information am I given?	
You are given three numbers, along with the average of those three numbers and one missing value, x.	292, 305, 415, x average = 343
Step 3: What can I do with the information?	
If the variable makes the average seem difficult to calculate, consider the sum instead.	average of 4 numbers = 343 sum of 4 numbers = 4 × 343 = 1,372
Three of the numbers are 292, 305, and 415, so the final number must be the difference between the sum of all four numbers and the sum of these three.	1,372 – (292 + 305 + 415) = 1,372 – 1,012 = 360
Step 4: Am I finished?	
You found the missing number, 360, which is the value of x you're looking for.	Choice (C) is correct.

✔ **Note**

You could also use Backsolving to answer the preceding question if you're not sure how to work it out formally.

Probability

Probability measures the likelihood of an event taking place. It can be expressed as a fraction ("The probability of snow tomorrow is $\frac{1}{2}$"), a decimal ("There is a 0.5 chance of snow tomorrow"), or a percent ("The probability of snow tomorrow is 50%").

To compute a probability, divide the number of desired outcomes by the number of possible outcomes.

$$\text{Probability} = \frac{\text{number of desired outcomes}}{\text{number of possible outcomes}}$$

Example: If you have 12 shirts in a drawer and 9 of them are white, what is the probability of picking a white shirt at random?

Setup: When picking a shirt in this situation, there are 12 possible outcomes, 1 for each shirt. Of these 12, 9 of them are white, so there are 9 desired outcomes. Therefore, the probability of picking a white shirt at random is $\frac{9}{12} = \frac{3}{4}$. The probability can also be expressed as 0.75 or 75%.

A **probability of 0** means that the event has no chance of happening. A **probability of 1** means that the event will always happen.

Thus, probability is just another ratio, specifically a part-to-whole ratio. How many parts desired? How many total parts? Finding the probability that something *won't* happen is simply a matter of taking the other piece of the pie.

If the probability of picking a white shirt is $\frac{3}{4}$, the probability of not picking a white shirt is $\frac{1}{4}$, or 1 minus the probability that it will happen. These two events are called **complementary events**.

To find the probability that **two separate events** will both occur, *multiply* the probabilities.

Let's take a look at an example of a typical ACT probability question. Beware—there's a twist, but that's not unusual.

10. Nancy is picking apples from a display at the grocery store. Of the apples in the display, 24 are red. She randomly picks an apple to purchase. If the probability that she picks a red apple is $\frac{3}{4}$, how many apples are in the display?

    F. 6

    G. 18

    H. 24

    J. 32

    K. 48

Work through the Kaplan Method for ACT Math step-by-step to answer this question. The following table shows Kaplan's strategic thinking on the left, along with suggested math scratchwork on the right.

Strategic Thinking	Math Scratchwork
Step 1: What is the question? You need to find the total number of apples in the display.	
Step 2: What information am I given? You're told the number of red apples and the probability of picking a red apple.	# of red apples = 24; $P(red) = \frac{3}{4}$
Step 3: What can I do with the information? Assign a variable to the total number of apples. Set up a proportion using the definition of probability. Then solve for a.	Let a = number of apples. $P(red) = \dfrac{\text{\# of red apples}}{\text{total \# of apples}} = \dfrac{3}{4}$ $\dfrac{3}{4} = \dfrac{24}{a}$ $3a = 96$ $a = 32$
Step 4: Am I finished? You found the total number of apples in the display, 32, so you're finished.	Choice (J) is correct.

Now you'll have a chance to try a few test-like questions in a scaffolded way. We've provided some guidance, but you'll need to fill in the missing parts of the explanation or the step-by-step math to get to the correct answer. Don't worry—after going through the worked examples at the beginning of this section, these questions should be completely doable.

11. Which of the following orders the numbers 0.6, 0.07, and $\frac{3}{4}$ from least to greatest?

   A. $0.6 < 0.07 < \frac{3}{4}$

   B. $0.07 < 0.6 < \frac{3}{4}$

   C. $0.07 < \frac{3}{4} < 0.6$

   D. $\frac{3}{4} < 0.07 < 0.6$

   E. $\frac{3}{4} < 0.6 < 0.07$

Use the following scaffolding as your map through the question. If you aren't sure where to start, fill in the blanks in the table as you work from top to bottom.

Strategic Thinking	Math Scratchwork
Step 1: What is the question? Order the three numbers from least to greatest.	
Step 2: What information am I given? You're given two decimal numbers and one fraction.	$0.6, 0.07,$ and $\frac{3}{4}$
Step 3: What can I do with the information? It's easiest to compare numbers when they are written in the same form. Decimals convert readily to fractions over 10 and 100. Because $\frac{3}{4}$ doesn't convert easily to tenths, write each number as a fraction with a denominator of 100. Now order the fractions based on the size of the numerators. Finally, put the original numbers back into the inequality and look for a match in the answer choices.	$0.6 = \dfrac{\quad}{10} = \dfrac{\quad}{100}$ $0.07 = \dfrac{\quad}{100}$ $\dfrac{3}{4} = 0.75 = \dfrac{\quad}{100}$ $\dfrac{\quad}{100} < \dfrac{\quad}{100} < \dfrac{\quad}{100}$ $\underline{\quad} < \underline{\quad} < \underline{\quad}$
Step 4: Am I finished? Did you get $0.07 < 0.6 < \frac{3}{4}$? If so, you're correct!	*Choice* $\underline{\quad}$ *is correct.*

12. Raymond is reading a road map. On the map, $\frac{1}{4}$ inch represents 12 miles. Approximately how many miles apart are two cities that are $3\frac{1}{2}$ inches apart on Raymond's map?

    F.   12

    G. 48

    H. 96

    J.   132

    K. 168

Use the following scaffolding as your map through the question. If you aren't sure where to start, fill in the blanks in the table as you work from top to bottom.

Strategic Thinking	Math Scratchwork
Step 1: What is the question? You need to find the distance between two cities that are $3\frac{1}{2}$ inches apart on the map.	
Step 2: What information am I given? You're given the map scale. You're also told how far apart the cities are on the map.	_____ inches = _____ miles map distance between cities = _____ in.
Step 3: What can I do with the information? Questions about map scales almost always involve setting up a proportion. Fractions within fractions can be confusing, so write the fractions as decimals. Set up the proportion as $\frac{\text{map}}{\text{actual}} = \frac{\text{map}}{\text{actual}}$. Call the unknown number of miles between the cities m. Solve by cross-multiplying.	$\frac{1}{4} = $ _____ $3\frac{1}{2} = $ _____ $\dfrac{\_\_\_ \text{ inches}}{\_\_\_ \text{ miles}} = \dfrac{\_\_\_ \text{ inches}}{m \text{ miles}}$ $\_\_\_ \, m = \_\_\_ \times \_\_\_$ $m = \_\_\_$ miles
Step 4: Am I finished? Was your final answer 168 miles? Super!	Choice _____ is correct.

Math

13. At the end of the season, a team's ratio of wins to losses was 3:5. If there were no ties, what percentage of its games did the team win?

A. $33\frac{1}{3}$%

B. $37\frac{1}{2}$%

C. 40%

D. 60%

E. 75%

Use the following scaffolding as your map through the question. If you aren't sure where to start, fill in the blanks in the table as you work from top to bottom.

Strategic Thinking	Math Scratchwork
Step 1: What is the question? You need to find the percentage of its games that the team won.	
Step 2: What information am I given? You're given a ratio. What kind of ratio is it? To find the percentage of *all* the games the team won, what kind of ratio do you need?	The ratio of wins to losses is a _____ to _____ ratio. Need a _____ to _____ ratio.
Step 3: What can I do with the information? Rewrite the ratio in the form that you need. What is the ratio of games won to games played? Write the ratio as a fraction and divide to find the percentage (as a decimal). Multiply by 100%.	_____ : _____ $\dfrac{\Box}{\Box} = $ _____ _____ × 100% = _____ %
Step 4: Am I finished? Hopefully, you got $37\frac{1}{2}$%.	Choice _____ is correct.

14. If $ax + y = 23$, $3x - y = 9$, and $x = 8$, what is the value of a?

    F.   1

    G.   3

    H.   5

    J.   8

    K. 15

Use the following scaffolding as your map through the question. If you aren't sure where to start, fill in the blanks in the table as you work from top to bottom.

Strategic Thinking	Math Scratchwork
Step 1: What is the question? You need to find the value of a.	
Step 2: What information am I given? You're given two equations that involve three different variables and the value of one of those variables.	$ax + y = 23$ $3x - y = 9$ $x =$ _____
Step 3: What can I do with the information? Could you Backsolve? Would it be a good idea? You already have enough information to solve the second equation for y. Plug in 8 for x and do the algebra. Now that you know the value of y (and you already knew the value of x), you can find the value of a. Plug in 8 for x and the value you found for y and solve for a.	Yes you can, but it's likely to be very slow. $3x - y = 9$ $3(\underline{\quad}) - y = 9$ $\underline{\quad} - y = 9$ $y = \underline{\quad}$ $ax + y = 23$ $a(\underline{\quad}) + \underline{\quad} = 23$ $\underline{\quad}\, a = \underline{\quad}$ $a = \underline{\quad}$
Step 4: Am I finished? Did you wind up with $a = 1$? That's exactly right!	Choice _____ is correct.

15. In the figure below, points *A*, *B*, and *C* are on a straight line. What is the measure of angle *DBE* ?

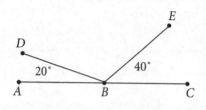

A. 60°

B. 80°

C. 100°

D. 120°

E. 140°

Use the following scaffolding as your map through the question. If you aren't sure where to start, fill in the blanks in the table as you work from top to bottom.

Strategic Thinking	Math Scratchwork
Step 1: What is the question? You need to find the measure of angle *DBE*.	
Step 2: What information am I given? You're given the measures of two angles that together with the missing angle form a straight line. What does this tell you?	∠*ABC* is a _____ angle m∠*ABC* = _____ °
Step 3: What can I do with the information? Write an equation that relates the angle measures and the sum of the angles. Use *x* to represent the missing angle measure. Solve the equation using an inverse operation.	m∠*ABD* + m∠*DBE* + m∠*EBC* = _____ ° _____ ° + _____ ° + _____ ° = _____ ° *x* = _____ °
Step 4: Am I finished? Did you get 120°? If so, great job!	Choice _____ is correct.

16. Nancy and Meghan are playing a game that involves flipping a 2-sided coin designated heads and tails and rolling a 6-sided die numbered 1 through 6. What is the probability of getting heads on the coin and an even number on the die?

F. $\dfrac{1}{2}$

G. $\dfrac{1}{4}$

H. $\dfrac{1}{6}$

J. $\dfrac{1}{8}$

K. $\dfrac{1}{12}$

Use the following scaffolding as your map through the question. If you aren't sure where to start, fill in the blanks in the table as you work from top to bottom.

Strategic Thinking	Math Scratchwork
Step 1: What is the question? You are looking for the probability of getting heads on the coin and an even number on the die.	
Step 2: What information am I given? The game involves flipping a 2-sided coin.	Number of possible outcomes when flipping the coin is _____ .
The game also involves rolling a 6-sided die, numbered 1 through 6.	Number of possible outcomes when rolling the die is _____ .
The desired outcome is getting a heads and rolling an even number.	Number of desired outcomes when flipping the coin is _____ .
The even numbers on the die are 2, 4, and 6.	The number of desired outcomes when rolling the die is _____ .

Strategic Thinking	Math Scratchwork
Step 3: What can I do with the information? Find the probability of each event separately. Remember, the probability is the number of desired outcomes over the number of possible outcomes. The probability that two independent events will both happen is the probability of the first times the probability of the second.	$P(heads) = $ _____ $P(even\ number) = $ _____ _____ × _____ = _____
Step 4: Am I finished? Is your final answer $\frac{1}{4}$? Excellent!	Choice _____ is correct.

Now that you've seen the variety of ways in which the ACT can test you on Essential Skills, try the following questions to check your understanding. Give yourself 3 minutes to answer these 4 questions. Make sure you use the Kaplan Method for ACT Math as often as you can. Remember, you want to emphasize speed and efficiency in addition to simply getting the correct answer.

17. Artie owns two dogs. Each day, one dog eats $1\frac{1}{2}$ scoops of dog food, and the other eats $2\frac{3}{4}$ scoops of the same dog food. If one bag of this dog food contains about 340 scoops, how many days should it last the two dogs?

　A. 80

　B. 85

　C. 92

　D. 100

　E. 120

18. A particular asteroid moves at a speed of 55,000 miles per hour. How many hours will it take the asteroid to travel a distance of 4.62×10^5 miles?

　F. 6.8

　G. 8.4

　H. 11.9

　J. 1.19×10^6

　K. 2.54×10^{10}

19. What is the value of $\dfrac{|5 - 2x| - 13}{-x}$ when $x = 3$?

　A. $-12\frac{2}{3}$

　B. -6

　C. -4

　D. 4

　E. $4\frac{2}{3}$

20. If the measures of the angles of a triangle are in the ratio 2:3:7, what is the measure in degrees of the largest angle?

　F. 15

　G. 30

　H. 45

　J. 84

　K. 105

Answers and Explanations are provided at the end of the book.

ON YOUR OWN

The following questions provide an opportunity to practice the concepts and strategic thinking covered in this chapter.

1. Of the participants at a certain conference, $\frac{1}{3}$ are anthropologists, $\frac{1}{2}$ are biologists, and the remaining 12 participants are chemists. Each participant specializes in only one field. What is the total number of participants at the conference?

   A. 36

   B. 48

   C. 60

   D. 72

   E. 76

2. Which of the following expressions will produce an odd number for any integer a ?

   F. a^2

   G. $a^2 + 1$

   H. $2a^2 + 1$

   J. $3a^2 + 2$

   K. $4a^2 + 4$

3. How many different integer values of n satisfy the inequality $\frac{1}{11} < \frac{3}{n} < \frac{1}{9}$?

   A. 5

   B. 4

   C. 3

   D. 2

   E. 1

4. If 60 is written as a product of its prime factors, what is the sum of all the numbers?

   F. 12

   G. 15

   H. 16

   J. 19

   K. 24

5. The ratio of men to women on the First-Year College Experience Committee at a certain university is 5:3. If there are a total of 24 people on the committee, how many women are there?

   A. 12

   B. 11

   C. 10

   D. 9

   E. 8

6. Ernesto is shopping at a store that is having a clearance sale. Everything in the store is 25% off. If Ernesto buys a shirt originally priced at $22.00 and a 6% sales tax is added, what will be the total price of the shirt?

   F. $29.15

   G. $23.10

   H. $18.66

   J. $17.49

   K. $16.50

7. At 350°F, an oven can cook approximately 3 pounds of turkey per hour. At 450°F, it can cook approximately 4.5 pounds per hour. In 10 minutes, how many more ounces of turkey can the oven cook at 450° than at 350°? (1 pound = 16 ounces)

    A.   4

    B.   6

    C.   8

    D.   10

    E.   12

8. An aquarium contains dolphins, sharks, and whales. There are twice as many dolphins as whales and 8 fewer sharks than dolphins and whales combined. If there are x whales, which of the following represents the number of sharks?

    F. $5x$

    G. $3x - 8$

    H. $10 + x$

    J. $3x^2 - 8x$

    K. $3\sqrt{2x - 8}$

9. If $5x + 3 = -17$, then $x = $?

    A. -25

    B. -7

    C. -4

    D. $\dfrac{1}{3}$

    E.   4

10. Which of the following inequalities is equivalent to $-2 - 4x \le -6x$?

    F. $x \ge -2$

    G. $x \ge 1$

    H. $x \ge 2$

    J. $x \le -1$

    K. $x \le 1$

11. What is the length in units of side BC in the diagram that follows?

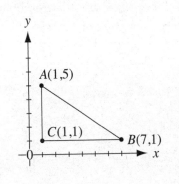

    A. $\sqrt{6}$

    B. $\sqrt{13}$

    C.   6

    D.   8

    E.   12

12. In the figure shown here, line t crosses parallel lines m and n. What is the degree measure of $\angle x$?

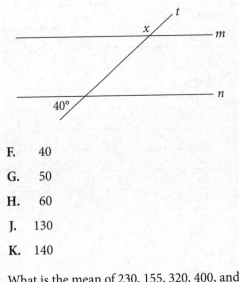

    F.   40

    G.   50

    H.   60

    J.   130

    K.   140

13. What is the mean of 230, 155, 320, 400, and 325?

    A.   205

    B.   286

    C.   288

    D.   300

    E.   430

Math

14. In a game, 20 small squares of paper are numbered 1 through 20. If Egan randomly selects 1 piece of paper, what is the probability that he will select a multiple of 4 ?

F. $\dfrac{1}{20}$

G. $\dfrac{1}{16}$

H. $\dfrac{3}{20}$

J. $\dfrac{1}{5}$

K. $\dfrac{1}{4}$

15. Jordan owns a small car dealership. The numbers of different types of vehicles on his car lot are given in the table that follows. What fraction of the vehicles on Jordan's lot are NOT luxury vehicles?

Vehicle Type	Number on Lot
Subcompact	64
Compact	30
Midsize	61
Full-size	58
Luxury	35
SUV	44
Truck	28
Total	320

A. $\dfrac{17}{160}$

B. $\dfrac{7}{64}$

C. $\dfrac{59}{80}$

D. $\dfrac{57}{64}$

E. $\dfrac{143}{160}$

16. If $\left(\dfrac{1}{2} + \dfrac{1}{6}\right) - \left(\dfrac{1}{12} + \dfrac{1}{3}\right)$ is calculated and the result is reduced to simplest terms, what is the numerator of this fraction?

F. 1

G. 2

H. 3

J. 4

K. 5

17. What value of x solves the following proportion?

$$\dfrac{2}{9} = \dfrac{x}{15}$$

A. $2\dfrac{2}{5}$

B. 3

C. $3\dfrac{1}{3}$

D. $4\dfrac{1}{3}$

E. $5\dfrac{1}{2}$

18. Dr. Hasenpfeffer's physics midterm has 60 questions. He scores the test as follows: For each correct answer, he gives 2 points; for each incorrect answer, he subtracts $\dfrac{2}{3}$ of a point; for unanswered questions, he neither gives nor subtracts points. If Denise scored a 68 and did not answer 2 of the questions, how many questions did she answer correctly?

F. 34

G. 36

H. 38

J. 40

K. 42

19. The temperature, t, in degrees Fahrenheit, in Summerville on an August day satisfies the inequality $|t - 94| \leq 10$. Which of the following temperatures, in degrees Fahrenheit, is NOT in this range?

    A. 82

    B. 90

    C. 96

    D. 98

    E. 104

20. If 125% of a number is 470, what is 50% of the number?

    F. 168

    G. 188

    H. 208

    J. 228

    K. 248

21. A certain television set is discounted 20% on Monday and then discounted another 25% on Tuesday. What is the total percent discount applied to the price of the television on Monday and Tuesday?

    A. 22.5%

    B. 40%

    C. 45%

    D. 50%

    E. 55%

22. If $x = -2$, then $14 - 3(x + 3) = ?$

    F. −1

    G. 11

    H. 14

    J. 17

    K. 29

23. If paintbrushes cost $1.50 each and canvases cost 6 times that much, which of the following represents the cost, in dollars, of p paintbrushes and c canvases?

    A. $7.5pc$

    B. $10.5pc$

    C. $9c + 1.5p$

    D. $7.5(p + c)$

    E. $10.5(p + c)$

24. In the figure below, $\overline{CD}$ is parallel to $\overline{AB}$ and $\overline{PQ}$ intersects $\overline{CD}$ at R and $\overline{AB}$ at T. If the measure of $\angle CRP$ is 110°, what is the measure of $\angle ATQ$?

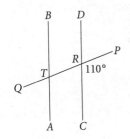

    F. 30°

    G. 50°

    H. 70°

    J. 90°

    K. 110°

25. On the number line that follows, point G is the midpoint of $\overline{FH}$ and $HJ = JK$. If $HK = 18$, what is the length of GJ ?

    A. 13

    B. 18

    C. 22

    D. 24

    E. 26

Math

26. Suppose $\overline{PQ}$ is perpendicular to $\overline{RS}$ and Q is a point on $\overline{RS}$. If L is in the interior of $\angle PQS$, which of the following could be the measure of $\angle LQR$?

  F. 110°

  G. 90°

  H. 70°

  J. 50°

  K. 30°

27. Randy scored 150, 195, and 160 in 3 bowling games. What should she score on her next bowling game if she wants to have an average score of exactly 175 for the 4 games?

  A. 205

  B. 195

  C. 185

  D. 175

  E. 165

28. A jar contains 8 red marbles, 14 blue marbles, 11 yellow marbles, and 6 green marbles. If a marble is selected at random, what is the probability that it will be green?

  F. $\dfrac{2}{39}$

  G. $\dfrac{2}{13}$

  H. $\dfrac{8}{39}$

  J. $\dfrac{3}{13}$

  K. $\dfrac{11}{39}$

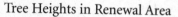

Use the following information to answer questions 29–30.

A scientist measured all of the trees in an area that was once a waste dump and is now being returned to nature. The scientist made the histogram that follows to show the heights of the trees.

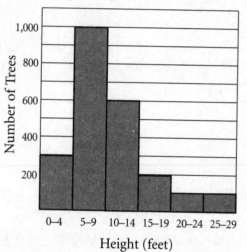

29. According to the data, how many trees did the scientist measure?

  A. 1,000

  B. 2,200

  C. 2,300

  D. 22,000

  E. 23,000

30. Which range of heights contains the median of the data?

  F. 0–4

  G. 5–9

  H. 10–14

  J. 15–19

  K. Cannot be determined from the given information

Answers and Explanations are provided at the end of the book.

HIGHER MATH

BY THE END OF THIS UNIT, YOU WILL BE ABLE TO:

1. Use number properties to simplify, compare, and evaluate expressions

2. Add, subtract, and multiply complex numbers, matrices, and vectors

3. Answer questions involving linear equations, linear inequalities, and systems of linear equations

4. Perform arithmetic operations on polynomials, including factoring quadratic expressions

5. Solve polynomial and absolute value equations

6. Solve simple, compound, absolute value, and quadratic inequalities

7. Evaluate and analyze graphs of functions, including trigonometric functions and transformations

8. Analyze and extend arithmetic, geometric, and recursively defined sequences

9. Answer questions involving coordinate and plane geometry

10. Apply basic trigonometric ratios to answer questions involving right triangles

CHAPTER 10

Number and Quantity

CHAPTER OBJECTIVES

By the end of this chapter, you will be able to:

1. Answer questions involving number properties
2. Apply rules of exponents to simplify expressions and to manipulate numbers written in scientific notation
3. Simplify numerical expressions that contain square roots and cube roots
4. Apply properties of rational exponents
5. Perform arithmetic operations on complex numbers
6. Add, subtract, and multiply matrices
7. Answer questions involving addition, subtraction, and scalar multiplication of vectors

SMARTPOINTS

Point Value	SmartPoints Category
3 Points	Number and Quantity

Approximately 60% of the ACT Math test will consist of Higher Math questions. These questions capture the mathematics that you most likely learned recently, or are learning right now, in high school. Higher Math is divided into five subcategories, covered in this unit. The first subcategory is Number and Quantity.

NUMBER AND QUANTITY

Number and Quantity questions make up about 7–10% of the Math test. These questions test your knowledge of the real and complex number systems. You will need to understand, reason about, and use numerical quantities in various forms, including integer and rational exponents, imaginary numbers, and matrices and vectors. Number and Quantity questions also require that you understand the behavior of numbers, particularly evens and odds and positives and negatives.

Number Properties

In the Essential Skills chapter, we reviewed some of the basic number properties you'll need to know. Let's add to that list now.

Know This About Odds and Evens on the ACT

Even $\times$ Even = Even	Even $\pm$ Even = Even
Even $\times$ Odd = Even	Odd $\pm$ Odd = Even
Odd $\times$ Odd = Odd	Even $\pm$ Odd = Odd
Even $^{\text{Positive Integer}}$ = Even Odd $^{\text{Positive Integer}}$ = Odd	

Know This About Positives and Negatives on the ACT

Positive $\times$ Positive = Positive Negative $\times$ Negative = Positive Positive $\times$ Negative = Negative	Subtracting a negative number is the same as adding a positive number
Negative $^{\text{Even Exponent}}$ = Positive Negative $^{\text{Odd Exponent}}$ = Negative	Positive Fraction $^{\text{Positive Integer}}$ = Smaller Positive Fraction (assuming the fraction is between 0 and 1 and the exponent is greater than 1)

Let's practice using these rules and the Kaplan Method for ACT Math to work through a Number and Quantity question.

1. Which of the following will result in an odd integer for any integer n?

   A. n^2

   B. $3n^2$

   C. $4n^2$

   D. $3n^2 + 1$

   E. $4n^2 + 1$

Work through the Kaplan Method for ACT Math step-by-step to answer this question. The following table shows Kaplan's strategic thinking on the left, along with suggested math scratchwork on the right.

Strategic Thinking	Math Scratchwork
Step 1: What is the question?	
You need to find the expression that will always yield an odd integer.	
Step 2: What information am I given?	
You're told that n is an integer. What does that mean?	n could be positive or negative or zero. n could be even or odd.
Step 3: What can I do with the information?	
Could you use Picking Numbers here?	The answers contain variables, so Picking Numbers is definitely an option.
Take a peek at the answer choices—each one contains an n^2, so start with that. Remember, n can be any integer, so pick easy values to start with.	If $n = 2$, then: $n^2 = 2^2 = 4$, even. Eliminate A. $3n^2 = 3(4) = 12$, even. Eliminate B. $4n^2 = 4(4) = 16$, even. Eliminate C. $3n^2 + 1 = 12 + 1 = 13$, odd. Keep D. $4n^2 + 1 = 16 + 1 = 17$, odd. Keep E.
To decide between D and E, pick another value for n. This time, pick an odd value. (You can worry about negative numbers if this doesn't settle the matter.)	If $n = 3$, then: $3n^2 + 1 = 3(9) + 1 = 28$, even. Eliminate D and choose (E) as your answer.
If you feel you must, you can check (E), but it's not necessary.	If $n = 3$, then $4n^2 + 1 = 4(9) + 1 = 37$, which is indeed odd.

Strategic Thinking	Math Scratchwork
Step 4: Am I finished? You didn't rule out every single option for values of n, but only one answer choice can be correct, and (E) is the only one that consistently produces an odd result.	Choice (E) is correct.

✔ Expert Tip

To answer this question logically, think about when a product is odd and when it is even. Any time you multiply an integer by an even integer, the resulting product is even. Thus, $4n^2$ is an even integer for any integer n. What happens when you add 1 to an even integer? The sum will always be odd, so $4n^2 + 1$ will result in an odd integer given any integer n.

Rules of Exponents

We reviewed the rules of exponents in the Essential Skills chapter. Now let's see what happens to certain types of numbers when they are raised to powers. Compare the locations and values of the variables and numbers on the following number line to the results in the table.

$$\begin{array}{ccccccc} w & -1 & x & 0 & y & 1 & z \end{array}$$

Quantity	Even Exponent Result	Odd Exponent Result	Example
w	positive, absolute value increases	negative, absolute value increases	$(-5)^2 = 25$ $(-5)^3 = -125$
-1	always 1	always -1	n/a
x	positive, absolute value decreases	negative, absolute value decreases	$\left(-\dfrac{1}{2}\right)^2 = \dfrac{1}{4}$ $\left(-\dfrac{1}{2}\right)^3 = -\dfrac{1}{8}$
0	always 0	always 0	n/a
y	positive, absolute value decreases	positive, absolute value decreases	$\left(\dfrac{1}{4}\right)^2 = \dfrac{1}{16}$ $\left(\dfrac{1}{4}\right)^3 = \dfrac{1}{64}$
1	always 1	always 1	n/a
z	positive, absolute value increases	positive, absolute value increases	$3^2 = 9$ $3^3 = 27$

Scientific Notation

Scientific notation is used to express very large or very small numbers. A number written in scientific notation is a number that is greater than or equal to 1, but less than 10, raised to a power of 10. For example, 3.64×10^8 is written in scientific notation, while 36.4×10^7 is not. The two numbers are equivalent, but the second doesn't meet the definition of scientific notation because 36.4 is not between 1 and 10.

To write a number in scientific notation, move the decimal point (to the right or to the left) until the number is between 1 and 10. Count the number of places you moved the decimal point—this tells you the power of 10 that you'll need. If the original number was a tiny decimal number (which means you had to move the decimal to the right), the exponent will be negative; if the original number was a large number (which means you had to move the decimal point to the left), the exponent will be positive.

> *Examples:* $0.000000819 = 8.19 \times 10^{-7}$
>
> $14{,}250{,}000{,}000 = 1.425 \times 10^{10}$

You can **add and subtract** numbers written in scientific notation as long as the power of 10 in each term is the same. Simply add (or subtract) the numbers and keep the same power of 10. Be careful—you may have to adjust the final answer if it is no longer written in scientific notation.

> *Example:* $(4.3 \times 10^5) + (8.2 \times 10^5) = (4.3 + 8.2) \times 10^5 = 12.5 \times 10^5$

Because 12.5 is not between 1 and 10, move the decimal one place to the left and adjust the power of 10 to get 1.25×10^6.

You can **multiply and divide** numbers written in scientific notation using rules of exponents. Simply multiply (or divide) the numbers and add (or subtract) the powers of 10. As before, you may have to adjust the final answer if it is no longer written in scientific notation.

> *Example:* $(12 \times 10^9) \div (3 \times 10^2) = (12 \div 3) \times 10^{9-2} = 4 \times 10^7$

Ready to try a question that involves exponents?

2.   What is the value of $\dfrac{10^5 \times 100^7}{1{,}000^6}$?

   F.   1
   G.   10
   H.   100
   J.   1,000
   K.   10,000

Work through the Kaplan Method for ACT Math step-by-step to answer this question. The following table shows Kaplan's strategic thinking on the left, along with suggested math scratchwork on the right.

Strategic Thinking	Math Scratchwork
Step 1: What is the question? You're asked to find the value of the expression, which means you need to simplify it.	
Step 2: What information am I given? You're given an expression that contains different bases with different exponents.	$\dfrac{10^5 \times 100^7}{1{,}000^6}$
Step 3: What can I do with the information? You can't combine the bases or the exponents of the expression as written. However, you know that $100 = 10^2$ and $1{,}000 = 10^3$, so rewrite the numerator and denominator to reflect these relationships. To raise a power to a power, multiply the exponents. To simplify the numerator, add the exponents. Once finished, subtract the exponent of the number in the denominator.	$\dfrac{10^5 \times 100^7}{1{,}000^6} = \dfrac{10^5 \times \left(10^2\right)^7}{\left(10^3\right)^6}$ $= \dfrac{10^5 \times 10^{14}}{10^{18}}$ $\dfrac{10^{5+14}}{10^{18}} = \dfrac{10^{19}}{10^{18}} = 10^{19-18} = 10$
Step 4: Am I finished? The expression is completely simplified, so you're all set.	*Choice (G) is correct.*

Radicals and Rational Exponents

A **radical** expression is any expression that contains a radical ($\sqrt{\ }$) symbol. This is often referred to as a *square root* symbol, but keep in mind that it can also be used to describe a cube root ($\sqrt[3]{\ }$), a fourth root ($\sqrt[4]{\ }$), or higher. The little number outside the radical is called the **index**.

You already know that addition and subtraction (and multiplication and division) are inverse operations; similarly, raising a number to a power and taking the root of the number are inverse operations. Specifically, when you raise a term to the nth power, taking the nth root will return the original term. Consider for example $3^4 = 3 \times 3 \times 3 \times 3 = 81$. If you take the fourth root of 81 (that is, determine the number that can be multiplied by itself four times to get 81), you will arrive at the original term: $\sqrt[4]{81} = \sqrt[4]{3 \times 3 \times 3 \times 3} = 3$.

Radicals can be intimidating at first, but remembering the basic rules for radicals can make them much easier. The following table contains all the formulas you'll need to know to achieve "radical" success on the ACT.

Rule	Example
When a fraction is under a radical, you can rewrite it using two radicals.	$\sqrt{\dfrac{a}{b}} = \dfrac{\sqrt{a}}{\sqrt{b}}$ $\sqrt{\dfrac{4}{9}} = \dfrac{\sqrt{4}}{\sqrt{9}} = \dfrac{2}{3}$
Two factors under a single radical can be rewritten as separate radicals multiplied together.	$\sqrt{ab} = \sqrt{a} \times \sqrt{b}$ $\sqrt{75} = \sqrt{25} \times \sqrt{3} = 5\sqrt{3}$
A radical can be written using a fractional exponent.	$\sqrt{a} = a^{\frac{1}{2}}, \sqrt[3]{a} = a^{\frac{1}{3}}$ $\sqrt{225} = 225^{\frac{1}{2}} = 15$
When you have a fractional exponent, the numerator is the power to which the base is raised, and the denominator is the root to be taken (power over root).	$a^{\frac{b}{c}} = \sqrt[c]{a^b}$ $8^{\frac{2}{3}} = \sqrt[3]{8^2} = \sqrt[3]{64} = 4$

✔ Note

Note this difference: By definition, the square root of a number is positive. However, when you take the square root to solve for a variable, you get two solutions, one that is positive and one that is negative. For instance, by definition $\sqrt{4} = 2$. However, if you are solving $x^2 = 4$, x will have two solutions: $x = \pm 2$.

To **simplify a square root**, factor out the perfect squares under the radical, square root them, and put the result in front of the part left under the square root symbol (the non-perfect-square factors):

$$\sqrt{12} = \sqrt{4 \times 3} = \sqrt{4} \times \sqrt{3} = 2\sqrt{3}$$

You can **add or subtract radicals** only if the part under the radicals is the same. In other words, treat terms with radicals like terms with variables. Just as $2x + 3x = 5x$ (where you add the coefficients of x):

$$2\sqrt{3} + 3\sqrt{3} = 5\sqrt{3}$$

In other words, you add or subtract the numbers in front of the square root symbol—the numbers under the radical stay the same.

It is not considered **proper notation** to leave a radical in the denominator of a fraction. However, it's sometimes better to keep radicals there throughout intermediate steps to make the math easier (and sometimes the radical is eliminated along the way). Once all manipulations are complete, the denominator can be **rationalized** to remove a remaining radical by multiplying both the numerator and denominator by that same radical.

1. Original Fraction	2. Rationalization	3. Intermediate Math	4. Resulting Fraction
$\dfrac{\sqrt{2}}{\sqrt{5}}$	$\dfrac{\sqrt{2}}{\sqrt{5}} \times \dfrac{\sqrt{5}}{\sqrt{5}}$	$\dfrac{\sqrt{2 \times 5}}{\sqrt{5 \times 5}} = \dfrac{\sqrt{10}}{\sqrt{25}}$	$\dfrac{\sqrt{10}}{5}$

Sometimes, you'll have an expression such as $2 + \sqrt{5}$ in the denominator. To rationalize this, multiply by its conjugate, which is found by negating the second term; in this case, the conjugate is $2 - \sqrt{5}$.

> ✔ **Note**
>
> When you rationalize a denominator, you are not changing the value of the expression; you're only changing the expression's appearance. This is because the numerator and the denominator of the fraction that you multiply by are the same, which means you're simply multiplying by 1.

Ready to take on a test-like question that involves radicals? Take a look at the following:

3. Which of the following is equivalent to $\dfrac{1}{\sqrt{3}} + \dfrac{8}{\sqrt{2}}$?

A. $\dfrac{\sqrt{2} + 8\sqrt{3}}{\sqrt{6}}$

B. $\dfrac{8\sqrt{2} + \sqrt{3}}{\sqrt{6}}$

C. $\dfrac{9}{\sqrt{3} + \sqrt{2}}$

D. $\dfrac{9}{\sqrt{5}}$

E. $\dfrac{9}{\sqrt{6}}$

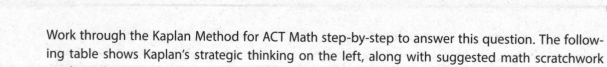

Work through the Kaplan Method for ACT Math step-by-step to answer this question. The following table shows Kaplan's strategic thinking on the left, along with suggested math scratchwork on the right.

Strategic Thinking	Math Scratchwork
Step 1: What is the question? You need to find the expression that is equivalent to the sum of the two given radical terms.	
Step 2: What information am I given? You have two radical terms and answer choices that also contain radicals.	$\dfrac{1}{\sqrt{3}} + \dfrac{8}{\sqrt{2}} = ?$
Step 3: What can I do with the information? Do you need to rationalize the denominators before you add the expressions? You add fractions that contain radicals the same way you add regular fractions—find a common denominator. Then, multiply each fraction by whatever it takes to get that denominator. Once that's done, add the numerators and keep the same denominator.	No, the answer choices also have radicals in the denominators, so there is no need to rationalize anything. common denominator: $\sqrt{3} \cdot \sqrt{2} = \sqrt{6}$ $\dfrac{1}{\sqrt{3}}\left(\dfrac{\sqrt{2}}{\sqrt{2}}\right) + \dfrac{8}{\sqrt{2}}\left(\dfrac{\sqrt{3}}{\sqrt{3}}\right)$ $= \dfrac{\sqrt{2}}{\sqrt{6}} + \dfrac{8\sqrt{3}}{\sqrt{6}}$ $= \dfrac{\sqrt{2} + 8\sqrt{3}}{\sqrt{6}}$
Step 4: Am I finished? There is a perfect match among the answer choices, so you're done!	Choice (A) is correct.

✔ **Note**

You could also use your calculator to find the decimal equivalent of the given expression (which is approximately 3.9831) and each of the answer choices until you find a match, but you must enter the expressions very carefully and this could take a bit of time.

Let's try one more tricky radical question.

4. Which of the following is equivalent to the product $\sqrt{3} \times \sqrt[6]{3}$?

    F. $\sqrt[6]{3}$

    G. $\sqrt[7]{3}$

    H. $\sqrt[6]{6}$

    J. $\sqrt[3]{9}$

    K. It is not possible to multiply the two numbers.

Work through the Kaplan Method for ACT Math step-by-step to answer this question. The following table shows Kaplan's strategic thinking on the left, along with suggested math scratchwork on the right.

Strategic Thinking	Math Scratchwork
Step 1: What is the question? You need to multiply the two radicals.	
Step 2: What information am I given? You're given two radical numbers, but they are not the same kinds of roots.	The first number is a square root; the second number is a sixth root.
Step 3: What can I do with the information? Even though the numbers under the radical symbols are the same (3), you can't multiply radicals that have different indices. Is there another way you can express the radicals? Now multiply the numbers using rules of exponents. You'll need to find a common denominator so you can add the exponents.	Express the radicals using fraction exponents. $\sqrt{3} = 3^{\frac{1}{2}}$ $\sqrt[6]{3} = 3^{\frac{1}{6}}$ $3^{\frac{1}{2}} \times 3^{\frac{1}{6}} = 3^{\frac{1}{2}+\frac{1}{6}}$ $= 3^{\frac{3}{6}+\frac{1}{6}}$ $= 3^{\frac{4}{6}} = 3^{\frac{2}{3}}$
Step 4: Am I finished? The answers are written in radical form, so use the saying "power over root" to convert your answer back to a radical.	$3^{\frac{2 \to power}{3 \to root}} = \sqrt[3]{3^2} = \sqrt[3]{9}$ Choice (J) is correct.

Math

Imaginary Numbers

Until you reached more advanced math classes like Algebra 2 and Trigonometry, you were likely taught that it is impossible to take the square root of a negative number. There is some truth to this, as the result isn't a real number. What you get instead is an **imaginary number**.

To take the square root of a negative number, it is necessary to use *i*, which is defined in math as the square root of -1. Take $\sqrt{-49}$ as an example. To simplify this expression, rewrite $\sqrt{-49}$ as $\sqrt{-1 \times 49}$, take the square root of -1 (which is by definition *i*) and then take the square root of 49, which is 7. The end result is 7*i*.

✔ **Expert Tip**

The simplification $i^2 = \left(\sqrt{-1}\right)^2 \rightarrow i^2 = -1$ also comes in handy when working with imaginary numbers.

✔ **Note**

Be particularly careful when multiplying two radicals that contain negative numbers. The first step is *always* to rewrite each quantity as the square root of the product of -1 and a positive number. Take the square root of -1 and then multiply the resulting expressions. For example, if you're asked to simplify $\sqrt{-16} \times \sqrt{-25}$, you must first rewrite the expression as $i\sqrt{16} \times i\sqrt{25}$, which becomes $4i \times 5i = 20i^2 = -20$. Combining the two radicals into one and canceling the negative signs to give $\sqrt{16 \times 25}$ is incorrect and will likely lead to a trap answer.

When a number is written in the form $a + bi$, where *a* is the real component and *b* is the imaginary component (and *i* is $\sqrt{-1}$), it is referred to as a **complex number**. The realm of complex numbers encompasses all numbers, including those that do not have an imaginary component (such as 5, π, and $\sqrt{2}$), in which case $b = 0$, and those that do not have a real component (such as 3*i*), in which case $a = 0$. When writing complex numbers, the real part is typically written first, followed by the imaginary part.

Operations on Complex Numbers

You can add, subtract, multiply, and divide complex numbers just as you do real numbers.

- To **add (or subtract)** complex numbers, simply add (or subtract) the real parts and then add (or subtract) the imaginary parts.

- To **multiply** complex numbers, treat them as binomials and use FOIL. To simplify the product, use the simplification $i^2 = -1$ and combine like terms.

- To **divide** complex numbers, write them in fraction form and then rationalize the denominator (just as you would for a fraction with a radical in the denominator) by multiplying top and bottom by the conjugate of the complex number in the denominator.

Rationalizing the Denominator of a Complex Number

Because *i* is defined as a radical, it's not considered proper notation to leave an *i* in the denominator of a fraction. To avoid this, you'll occasionally need to **rationalize the denominator** of a complex number (just as you did earlier with radicals). Suppose you're asked to simplify the expression $\frac{21}{3 + 5i}$. The conjugate of $3 + 5i$ is $3 - 5i$, so you would multiply the expression by $\frac{3 - 5i}{3 - 5i}$. This is the same as multiplying by 1, so you're not changing the value of the expression. The result is this:

$$\frac{21}{3 + 5i} \times \frac{3 - 5i}{3 - 5i} = \frac{21(3 - 5i)}{(3 + 5i)(3 - 5i)} = \frac{63 - 105i}{9 - 25i^2}$$

You know $i^2 = -1$, so the expression simplifies to:

$$\frac{63 - 105i}{9 - (25)(-1)} = \frac{63 - 105i}{34}$$

> **✔ Note**
>
> If you don't see your answer among the choices, you may have to separate the complex expression into its real and imaginary components. In the previous example, you can write each of the terms in the numerator over the denominator in separate fractions, yielding $\frac{63}{34} - \frac{105}{34}i$.

Powers of i

When an imaginary number is raised to a power, you can use the pattern shown below to determine what the resulting term will be. Knowing the cycles of *i* will save you time on Test Day.

When you have ...	i^1	i^2	i^3	i^4
... it becomes:	i	$\sqrt{-1} \times \sqrt{-1} = -1$	$i^2 \times i = -i$	$i^2 \times i^2 = -1 \times -1 = 1$

So, the cycles of *i* are i, -1, $-i$, 1, then repeat (try a few more if you're not convinced). When you have *i* raised to an exponent greater than 4, divide the exponent by 4. The remainder will dictate the final answer. Take i^{63} as an example. Divide 63 by 4 to get 15 with a remainder of 3. This means that $i^{63} = (i^4)^{15} \times i^3 = 1^{15} i^3$. Because $i^3 = -i$, i^{63} becomes $-i$.

Math

Ready to try some test-like questions involving imaginary numbers? Check out the next two problems.

5. Which of the following is the correct simplification of the expression $(2 + 7i) - (4 - 3i)$?

   A. $-2 - 10i$

   B. $-2 - 4i$

   C. $-2 + 10i$

   D. $2 - 4i$

   E. $2 + 10i$

Work through the Kaplan Method for ACT Math step-by-step to answer this question. The following table shows Kaplan's strategic thinking on the left, along with suggested math scratchwork on the right.

Strategic Thinking	Math Scratchwork
Step 1: What is the question? You must correctly simplify the expression given.	
Step 2: What information am I given? You are given two complex numbers, each written in the form $a + bi$.	
Step 3: What can I do with the information? Use straightforward math to simplify. Distribute the negative sign and then combine like terms.	$(2 + 7i) - (4 - 3i)$ $= 2 + 7i - 4 + 3i$ $= -2 + 10i$
Step 4: Am I finished? You've correctly simplified the expression, so move on to the next question.	Choice (C) is correct.

6. Given that $i = \sqrt{-1}$, which of the following is equal to $(11 + 4i)(2 - 5i)$?

   F. 2

   G. 42

   H. $2 - 75i$

   J. $22 - 20i$

   K. $42 - 47i$

Work through the Kaplan Method for ACT Math step-by-step to answer this question. The following table shows Kaplan's strategic thinking on the left, along with suggested math scratchwork on the right.

Strategic Thinking	Math Scratchwork
Step 1: What is the question? You need to multiply the two expressions and then simplify the result.	
Step 2: What information am I given? You are given two complex numbers, each written in the form $a + bi$. You are also given some information about i, which may or may not be useful.	$i = \sqrt{-1}$
Step 3: What can I do with the information? The two factors in the product are binomials, so use FOIL to multiply them. You're given that $i = \sqrt{-1}$. That's not very useful as written, but if you square both sides, you'll be able to use the result: $i^2 = -1$.	$(11 + 4i)(2 - 5i)$ $= (11)(2) + (11)(-5i) + (4i)(2) + (4i)(-5i)$ $= 22 - 55i + 8i - 20i^2$ $= 22 - 47i - (20)(-1)$ $= 22 - 47i + 20$ $= 42 - 47i$
Step 4: Am I finished? You can't simplify any further, so look for a match among the choices.	*Choice (K) is correct.*

Matrices

Matrices look intimidating, but they're really not that difficult. You can think of them as tables with no borders around the cells. Although many complex operations can be performed using matrices, you'll only encounter the most basic of these on the ACT—addition, subtraction, and perhaps a multiplication problem here or there.

So first the basics:

- A **matrix** is a rectangular arrangement of numbers, symbols, or expressions, formatted in rows and columns.

- The **size** (also referred to as the dimensions) of a matrix is given by the number of rows and the number of columns, in that order.

$$\begin{bmatrix} a & b \\ c & d \\ e & f \end{bmatrix}$$ is a 3 × 2 matrix because it has 3 rows and 2 columns.

$[\; g \quad h \quad j \quad k \;]$ is a 1 × 4 matrix because it has 1 row and 4 columns.

- You can multiply an entire matrix by a number by multiplying each entry in the matrix by that number. This is called **scalar multiplication** and works exactly the way you would expect.

$$3\begin{bmatrix} 5 & -2 \\ 1 & 7 \end{bmatrix} = \begin{bmatrix} 3(5) & 3(-2) \\ 3(1) & 3(7) \end{bmatrix} = \begin{bmatrix} 15 & -6 \\ 3 & 21 \end{bmatrix}$$

- To **add (or subtract)** matrices, the matrices must be exactly the same size. The operation itself is very straightforward: Add (or subtract) the corresponding entries (the numbers that sit in the same spots). The size of the resulting matrix will be the same as that of the original matrices.

$$\begin{bmatrix} -3 & 6 \\ 2 & -9 \end{bmatrix} + \begin{bmatrix} 5 & -1 \\ 0 & 3 \end{bmatrix} = \begin{bmatrix} -3+5 & 6+(-1) \\ 2+0 & -9+3 \end{bmatrix} = \begin{bmatrix} 2 & 5 \\ 2 & -6 \end{bmatrix}$$

- To **multiply** matrices, the inner dimensions of the sizes of the matrices must match. (This sounds much worse than it is.) For example, you can multiply a 3 × **2** matrix by a **2** × 5 matrix because the 2s in the middle match. The product of the matrices will be a 3 × 5 matrix (the outer numbers in the two matrix sizes). Surprisingly, you cannot multiply a 3 × **2** matrix by a **3** × 2 matrix (even though they are the same size) because the two middle numbers don't match.

- The **process of multiplying matrices** is fairly complex and is best explained by working through an example. The general idea is this: To find the entry in the first row and first column of the product matrix, find the sum of the products of the entries in row 1 of the first matrix times the entries in column 1 of the second matrix; to find the entry in the first row and second column of the product matrix, find the sum of the products of the entries in row 1 of the first matrix times the entries in column 2 of the second matrix; and so on. Let's see this in action:

$$\begin{bmatrix} a & b \\ c & d \\ e & f \end{bmatrix}\begin{bmatrix} u & v & w \\ x & y & z \end{bmatrix} = \begin{bmatrix} au+bx & av+by & aw+bz \\ cu+dx & cv+dy & cw+dz \\ eu+fx & ev+fy & ew+fz \end{bmatrix}$$

$$\underline{3} \times ②\quad ② \times \underline{3} \quad = \qquad\qquad \underline{3} \times \underline{3}$$

✔ Note

The order in which two matrices are multiplied matters. In other words, unlike regular multiplication, matrix multiplication is not commutative: *AB* very rarely equals *BA*. In fact, sometimes one product can be calculated while the other cannot.

Let's try a few questions that involve matrices.

7. If $A = \begin{bmatrix} 4 & 0 & 3 \\ 0 & -2 & 1 \end{bmatrix}$ and $B = \begin{bmatrix} 1 & 5 & -2 \\ 0 & 0 & 4 \end{bmatrix}$, then $2A + B = ?$

A. $\begin{bmatrix} 9 & 5 & 4 \\ 0 & -4 & 6 \end{bmatrix}$

B. $\begin{bmatrix} 9 & 5 & 4 \\ 0 & 0 & 4 \end{bmatrix}$

C. $\begin{bmatrix} 9 & 5 & 4 \\ 0 & -2 & 4 \end{bmatrix}$

D. $\begin{bmatrix} 8 & 0 & 6 \\ 0 & -4 & 2 \end{bmatrix}$

E. $\begin{bmatrix} 5 & 5 & 1 \\ 0 & -2 & 5 \end{bmatrix}$

Work through the Kaplan Method for ACT Math step-by-step to answer this question. The following table shows Kaplan's strategic thinking on the left, along with suggested math scratchwork on the right.

Strategic Thinking	Math Scratchwork
Step 1: What is the question?	
You need to find the matrix that represents the sum of twice the first matrix plus the second matrix.	
Step 2: What information am I given?	
You're given two 2 × 3 matrices and an expression that tells you how to combine them.	$2A + B$ means to double A then add B.
Step 3: What can I do with the information?	
Break the question into two parts: First multiply all the entries in matrix A by 2.	$2A = \begin{bmatrix} 8 & 0 & 6 \\ 0 & -4 & 2 \end{bmatrix}$
Now add B to this new matrix by adding the corresponding entries.	$\begin{bmatrix} 8 & 0 & 6 \\ 0 & -4 & 2 \end{bmatrix} + \begin{bmatrix} 1 & 5 & -2 \\ 0 & 0 & 4 \end{bmatrix}$ $= \begin{bmatrix} 8+1 & 0+5 & 6+(-2) \\ 0+0 & -4+0 & 2+4 \end{bmatrix}$ $= \begin{bmatrix} 9 & 5 & 4 \\ 0 & -4 & 6 \end{bmatrix}$
Step 4: Am I finished?	
This is a perfect match for (A).	Choice (A) is correct.

Now let's give multiplication a try.

8. If $\begin{bmatrix} 1 & 2 & 3 \end{bmatrix} \begin{bmatrix} x \\ 2x \\ 3x \end{bmatrix} = 42$, what is the value of x ?

    F. 2

    G. 3

    H. 4

    J. 6

    K. 7

Work through the Kaplan Method for ACT Math step-by-step to answer this question. The following table shows Kaplan's strategic thinking on the left, along with suggested math scratchwork on the right.

Strategic Thinking	Math Scratchwork
Step 1: What is the question?	
You need to find the value of *x*.	
Step 2: What information am I given?	
You are given a 1 × 3 matrix, a 3 × 1 matrix, and the result of multiplying the two matrices.	
Step 3: What can I do with the information?	
There's not a lot to go on here, so just multiply the two matrices and see what happens.	$\begin{bmatrix} 1 & 2 & 3 \end{bmatrix} \begin{bmatrix} x \\ 2x \\ 3x \end{bmatrix}$ $= 1(x) + 2(2x) + 3(3x)$ $= x + 4x + 9x$ $= 14x$
You're told in the question stem that the product is equal to 42, so this becomes an algebra problem.	$14x = 42$ $x = 42 \div 14 = 3$
Step 4: Am I finished?	
You determined that $x = 3$, so your job is done.	*Choice (G) is correct.*

Vectors

A **vector** is represented visually by a line segment with an arrow on one end. The length of the segment represents the **magnitude** of the vector, and the arrow represents the **direction** of the vector (the arrow does not mean that it continues forever). All vectors must have *both* magnitude and direction.

In two dimensions, vectors have an *x*- and *y*-component (just like ordered pairs) and are written in the form $\mathbf{v} = \langle 2,5 \rangle$. The easiest way to draw a vector is to start from a given location (usually the origin) and use the components of the vector to move horizontally and vertically from that location. For $\mathbf{v} = \langle 2,5 \rangle$, you would move 2 units to the right and 5 units up.

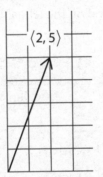

Here's what you'll need to know about vectors for Test Day:

- To **add (or subtract)** two vectors, simply add (or subtract) the *x*-components and add (or subtract) the *y*-components. For example:

$$\langle 2, -1 \rangle + \langle 3,7 \rangle = \langle 2 + 3, \ -1 + 7 \rangle = \langle 5,6 \rangle$$

$$\langle 2, -1 \rangle - \langle 3,7 \rangle = \langle 2 - 3, \ -1 - 7 \rangle = \langle -1,-8 \rangle$$

- To **multiply a vector by a number** (called scalar multiplication), multiply each component of the vector by the number. For example:

$$\frac{2}{3}\langle 6, -15 \rangle = \left\langle \frac{2}{3} \cdot 6, \ \frac{2}{3} \cdot -15 \right\rangle = \langle 4,-10 \rangle$$

> **✔ Expert Tip**
>
> There's nothing to memorize here. These vector operations work exactly as you would expect them to, so don't panic when you see a vector question.

Let's wrap up this chapter with a complicated-looking—but not hard to answer—question about vectors.

Math

9. The component forms of vectors **v** and **w** are given by $\mathbf{v} = \langle 1,4 \rangle$ and $\mathbf{w} = \langle 2,3 \rangle$. If $4\mathbf{v} + (-5\mathbf{w}) + \mathbf{z} = 0$, what is the component form of **z** ?

    A. $\langle -12,35 \rangle$

    B. $\langle -6,1 \rangle$

    C. $\langle -3,-7 \rangle$

    D. $\langle 6,-1 \rangle$

    E. $\langle 12,-35 \rangle$

Work through the Kaplan Method for ACT Math step-by-step to answer this question. The following table shows Kaplan's strategic thinking on the left, along with suggested math scratchwork on the right.

Strategic Thinking	Math Scratchwork
Step 1: What is the question?	
You need to find the component form of **z**.	
Step 2: What information am I given?	
You're given the component forms of two vectors.	$\mathbf{v} = \langle 1,4 \rangle$ $\mathbf{w} = \langle 2,3 \rangle$
You're also given an equation that relates the sum of those two vectors and the vector you're interested in, **z**.	$4\mathbf{v} + (-5\mathbf{w}) + \mathbf{z} = 0$
Step 3: What can I do with the information?	

Break the equation into pieces. First, find 4**v** by multiplying each component of **v** by 4. Then repeat for −5**w**.	$4\mathbf{v} = \langle 4\cdot 1, 4\cdot 4 \rangle$
	  $= \langle 4,16 \rangle$
	
	 $-5\mathbf{w} = \langle -5\cdot 2, -5\cdot 3 \rangle$
	  $= \langle -10,-15 \rangle$

The first part of the equation is 4**v** + (−5**w**), so do that next.	$4\mathbf{v} + (-5\mathbf{w})$ $= \langle 4,16 \rangle + \langle -10,-15 \rangle$ $= \langle 4+(-10), 16+(-15) \rangle$ $= \langle -6,1 \rangle$
Don't stop! This is not the answer. This sum plus **z** equals 0, so the corresponding components of **z** must have opposite signs.	$\langle -6,1 \rangle + \mathbf{z} = 0 \rightarrow \mathbf{z} = \langle 6,-1 \rangle$
Step 4: Am I finished?	
The components of **z** are $\langle 6,-1 \rangle$.	Choice (D) is correct.

Now you'll have a chance to try a few test-like questions in a scaffolded way. We've provided some guidance, but you'll need to fill in the missing parts of the explanation or the step-by-step math to get to the correct answer. Don't worry—after going through the worked examples at the beginning of this section, these questions should be completely doable.

10. Which of the following is equivalent to $\sqrt{24} + \sqrt{150}$?

F. $\sqrt{174}$

G. $7\sqrt{6}$

H. $29\sqrt{6}$

J. $36\sqrt{7}$

K. $36\sqrt{29}$

Use the following scaffolding as your map through the question. If you aren't sure where to start, fill in the blanks in the table as you work from top to bottom.

Strategic Thinking	Math Scratchwork
Step 1: What is the question? You need to add the two given radicals.	
Step 2: What information am I given? You're given two square roots with different numbers under the radical symbol. The answer choices are also radicals.	
Step 3: What can I do with the information? To add square roots, the numbers under the radical symbol must be the same. This means you need to simplify each of the terms before you can add. To do this, look for perfect squares that you can remove from the square roots.	$\sqrt{24} = \sqrt{\underline{} \cdot \underline{}}$ $\sqrt{150} = \sqrt{\underline{} \cdot \underline{}}$ $= \sqrt{\underline{}} \cdot \sqrt{\underline{}}$ $= \sqrt{\underline{}} \cdot \sqrt{\underline{}}$ $= \underline{}\sqrt{\underline{}}$ $= \underline{}\sqrt{\underline{}}$
Now that the numbers under the radicals are the same, add the coefficients and keep the same radical part.	$\underline{}\sqrt{\underline{}} + \underline{}\sqrt{\underline{}} = \underline{}\sqrt{\underline{}}$
Step 4: Am I finished? Did you get $7\sqrt{6}$? If so, nice work!	Choice _____ is correct.

11. Written in scientific notation, $820{,}000{,}000 + 500{,}000{,}000 = ?$

    A. 1.32×10^{-9}

    B. 1.32×10^{-8}

    C. 1.32×10^{8}

    D. 1.32×10^{9}

    E. 132×10^{15}

Use the following scaffolding as your map through the question. If you aren't sure where to start, fill in the blanks in the table as you work from top to bottom.

Strategic Thinking	Math Scratchwork
Step 1: What is the question? You need to add the two numbers and express the sum in scientific notation.	
Step 2: What information am I given? You're given two large numbers written in standard form.	$820{,}000{,}000 + 500{,}000{,}000 = ?$
Step 3: What can I do with the information? Write the numbers vertically so you can add them quickly. To write the sum in scientific notation, place a decimal point after the last 0 in the number. Then move the decimal until the number is between 1 and 10. To determine the power on 10, count the number of places you moved the decimal point. Did you move left or right? And what does that tell you about the sign of the exponent?	$820{,}000{,}000$ $+\ 500{,}000{,}000$ $\boxed{}$ ___ . ___ $\times 10^{?}$ *Moved* ___ *places to the* ___ . *The exponent will be* ___ . ___ . ___ $\times 10^{-}$
Step 4: Am I finished? Your final answer should be 1.32×10^{9}. Is that what you got?	*Choice* ___ *is correct.*

12. Which of the following values of n satisfies the inequality $\frac{4}{5} < n < 1$?

F. $\dfrac{\sqrt{10}}{5}$

G. $\dfrac{\sqrt{14}}{5}$

H. $\dfrac{\sqrt{18}}{5}$

J. $\dfrac{\sqrt{26}}{5}$

K. $\dfrac{\sqrt{30}}{5}$

Use the following scaffolding as your map through the question. If you aren't sure where to start, fill in the blanks in the table as you work from top to bottom.

Strategic Thinking	Math Scratchwork
Step 1: What is the question? You need to find the value of n that is greater than $\frac{4}{5}$ and less than 1.	
Step 2: What information am I given? You're given an inequality that contains "plain" numbers and answer choices that have radicals in them.	
Step 3: What can I do with the information? Each answer choice has a denominator of 5, so rewrite the inequality to match. Each answer choice has a radical in the numerator, so rewrite the inequality again to match. Based on the rewritten inequality, the number under the radical in the numerator must be between what two integers? Which number meets this requirement?	$\dfrac{4}{5} < n < \dfrac{\overline{\quad}}{5}$ $\dfrac{\sqrt{\overline{\quad}}}{5} < n < \dfrac{\sqrt{\overline{\quad}}}{5}$ $\underline{\qquad} <$ numerator $< \underline{\qquad}$ $\underline{\qquad}$
Step 4: Am I finished? Were you able to determine that $\frac{\sqrt{18}}{5}$ is the only number that satisfies the inequality? If so, great job!	Choice $\underline{\qquad}$ is *correct*.

13. For the complex number i such that $i^2 = -1$, which of the following represents $\dfrac{1}{3-i}$ written in the form $a + bi$?

A. $\dfrac{3}{10} + \dfrac{1}{10}i$

B. $\dfrac{1}{3} - \dfrac{1}{i}$

C. $\dfrac{3}{8} + \dfrac{1}{8}i$

D. $3 + i$

E. $3 - i$

Use the following scaffolding as your map through the question. If you aren't sure where to start, fill in the blanks in the table as you work from top to bottom.

Strategic Thinking	Math Scratchwork
Step 1: What is the question? You need to rewrite the given complex number in the form $a + bi$. In other words, you need to separate it into its real part and its imaginary part.	
Step 2: What information am I given? You're given a complex number that is not separated into its real part and its imaginary part. You're also given some information about i^2.	$i^2 = -1$
Step 3: What can I do with the information? Start by rationalizing the denominator (getting the i out). To do this, multiply top and bottom by the conjugate of the denominator. To simplify the denominator, FOIL. You can simplify further by plugging -1 in for each i^2.	$\dfrac{1}{3-i} \times \underline{\hspace{2cm}}$ $= \underline{\hspace{3cm}}$ $= \underline{\hspace{3cm}}$ $= \underline{\hspace{2.5cm}}$ $= \underline{\hspace{2.5cm}}$
Step 4: Am I finished? This isn't one of the answer choices, so split the number into its real part and its imaginary part by writing each of the terms in the numerator over 10.	$= \underline{\hspace{1cm}} + \underline{\hspace{1cm}}i$ Choice $\underline{\hspace{1cm}}$ is correct.

14. Four matrices are shown here.

$$A = \begin{bmatrix} 1 & 2 \\ 3 & 4 \end{bmatrix} \quad B = \begin{bmatrix} 5 & 6 & 7 \\ 8 & 9 & 0 \end{bmatrix} \quad C = \begin{bmatrix} 2 \\ 4 \end{bmatrix} \quad D = \begin{bmatrix} 3 & 5 \end{bmatrix}$$

Which matrix product is not possible?

F. AB

G. AC

H. BC

J. CD

K. DA

Use the following scaffolding as your map through the question. If you aren't sure where to start, fill in the blanks in the table as you work from top to bottom.

Strategic Thinking	Math Scratchwork
Step 1: What is the question? You need to determine which product cannot be calculated.	
Step 2: What information am I given? You're given four matrices, all different sizes.	
Step 3: What can I do with the information? You only have to decide whether each product is possible. To do this, do you have to perform the multiplication? Matrix multiplication is only possible when the sizes of the two matrices match up nicely (the inner dimensions must match). Start by jotting down the size of each matrix. Now, check each product until you find one that is not possible. You can stop when you find one that doesn't work.	___ A B ___ × ___ ___ × ___ C D ___ × ___ ___ × ___ AB = ___ × ___ times ___ × ___ AC = ___ × ___ times ___ × ___ BC = ___ × ___ times ___ × ___ CD = ___ × ___ times ___ × ___ DA = ___ × ___ times ___ × ___
Step 4: Am I finished? Did you find that BC doesn't work? Great job!	Choice _____ is correct.

15. The number of employees at a company by age group can be shown by the following matrix.

18–24	25–34	35–44	45–54
[30	20	60	10]

The Human Resources Department estimates the proportion of current employees who will utilize the company's health plan more than one time in the next year with the following matrix.

18–24	0.3
25–34	0.5
35–44	0.2
45–54	0.4

Given these matrices, what is the Human Resource Department's estimate of the number of current employees between the ages of 18 and 54 who will utilize the company's health plan more than one time in the next year?

A. 27

B. 35

C. 42

D. 49

E. 53

Use the following scaffolding as your map through the question. If you aren't sure where to start, fill in the blanks in the table as you work from top to bottom.

Strategic Thinking	Math Scratchwork
Step 1: What is the question? You need to determine the number of employees, ages 18–54, who are likely to utilize the company's health plan more than one time in the next year.	
Step 2: What information am I given? You're given two matrices—one provides information on the number of employees in each age group, and the other provides information on the proportion of employees in each age group who are expected to utilize the company's health plan more than one time in the next year.	

Strategic Thinking	Math Scratchwork
Step 3: What can I do with the information? Think logically based on how the matrices are set up. How many employees in the 18–24 age range fit the description? How many employees in the 25–34 age range fit the description? You can continue with this logic or simply multiply the two matrices. Use whichever method you're more comfortable with. Don't forget to find the sum.	18–24: _____ × _____ = _____ 25–34: _____ × _____ = _____ 35–44: _____ × _____ = _____ 45–54: _____ × _____ = _____ ___ + ___ + ___ + ___ = ___
Step 4: Am I finished? Did you get a total of 35 employees? That's exactly right!	*Choice* _____ *is correct.*

16. If **u** = $\langle 8,-24 \rangle$ and **v** = $\langle 4,6 \rangle$, then $-\frac{1}{2}($**u** + **v**$) = ?$

  F. $\langle -6,-9 \rangle$

  G. $\langle -6,9 \rangle$

  H. $\langle -6,18 \rangle$

  J. $\langle 0,18 \rangle$

  K. $\langle 6,-9 \rangle$

Use the following scaffolding as your map through the question. If you aren't sure where to start, fill in the blanks in the table as you work from top to bottom.

Strategic Thinking	Math Scratchwork
Step 1: What is the question? You need to find the equivalent vector form of the given expression.	
Step 2: What information am I given? You're given two vectors and an equation that tells you how to combine the vectors and then scale the result.	(**u** + **v**) → _____ the vectors. $-\frac{1}{2}($**u** + **v**$) \rightarrow$ _____ each component of the sum by _____ .
Step 3: What can I do with the information? You could distribute the $-\frac{1}{2}$ to the components of each vector and then add the resulting vectors, but the quicker route is to add the vectors first. Then, multiply each component of the sum by $-\frac{1}{2}$.	**u** + **v** = $\langle$ ___ + ___ , ___ + ___ $\rangle$ = $\langle$ ___ , ___ $\rangle$ $-\frac{1}{2}($**u** + **v**$)$ = $\left\langle -\frac{1}{2} \cdot \underline{\quad} , -\frac{1}{2} \cdot \underline{\quad} \right\rangle$ = $\langle$ ___ , ___ $\rangle$
Step 4: Am I finished? If you got $\langle -6,9 \rangle$, you're exactly right!	Choice _____ is correct.

Math

Now that you've seen the variety of ways in which the ACT can test you on Number and Quantity, try the following questions to check your understanding. Give yourself 4 minutes to answer these 4 questions. Make sure you use the Kaplan Method for ACT Math as often as you can. Remember, you want to emphasize speed and efficiency in addition to simply getting the correct answer.

17. Which of the following numbers is NOT a real number?

   A. $-\sqrt{9}$

   B. 3^{-2}

   C. $\sqrt{-9}$

   D. $\sqrt{3}$

   E. $(-3)^2$

18. The value of $\dfrac{x+m}{n}$ is an integer when $m = 2$ and $n = 3$. Which of the following is a possible value of x?

   F. -1

   G. 0

   H. 4

   J. 6

   K. 12

19. When the complex number i is defined as $i = \sqrt{-1}$, it follows that $i^2 = -1$. Based on this information, which of the following is equivalent to $\dfrac{i^3 + 4i}{\sqrt{-9}}$?

   A. -1

   B. 1

   C. 3

   D. i

   E. $3i$

20. Given the matrix product

   $$\begin{bmatrix} 1 & 2 \\ 3 & 4 \end{bmatrix}\begin{bmatrix} -1 & -2 \\ -3 & -4 \end{bmatrix} = \begin{bmatrix} x & y \\ z & w \end{bmatrix},$$

   what is the value of $x + y$?

   F. -17

   G. -14

   H. -5

   J. 0

   K. 4

Answers and Explanations are provided at the end of the book.

Math

ON YOUR OWN

The following questions provide an opportunity to practice the concepts and strategic thinking covered in this chapter.

1. Which of the following is equivalent to $7^{77} - 7^{76}$?

   A. 7
   B. 7^{77-76}
   C. 7^{77+76}
   D. $7(77-76)$
   E. $7^{76}(6)$

2. If $\frac{x}{2} - \frac{x}{6}$ is an integer, which of the following statements must be true?

   F. x is positive.
   G. x is odd.
   H. x is even.
   J. x is a multiple of 3.
   K. x is a perfect square.

3. What is the value of $(-2)^{-3} + (-3)^{-2}$?

   A. $-\dfrac{17}{72}$
   B. $-\dfrac{1}{72}$
   C. 0
   D. $\dfrac{1}{72}$
   E. $\dfrac{17}{72}$

4. What is the value of $9^{-\frac{3}{2}}$?

   F. -27
   G. $-13\dfrac{1}{2}$
   H. $\dfrac{-1}{27}$
   J. $\dfrac{1}{27}$
   K. $13\dfrac{1}{2}$

5. Given that $x > 0$, which of the following is equivalent to $\sqrt{0.0016x^2}$?

   A. $0.08x$
   B. $0.04x$
   C. $0.004x$
   D. $0.0008x$
   E. $0.0004x$

6. The complex number i is defined such that $i^2 = -1$. What is the value of $(2i - 3)^2$?

   F. -13
   G. 5
   H. $-3 - 4i$
   J. $9 + 4i$
   K. $5 - 12i$

7. If $i = \sqrt{-1}$, then which of the following has the greatest value?

   A. $i^4 + i^2$

   B. $i^8 + i^6$

   C. $i^{12} + i^6$

   D. $i^{16} + i^{12}$

   E. $i^{20} + i^{10}$

8. If $\begin{bmatrix} x & 6 \\ 13 & x \end{bmatrix} + \begin{bmatrix} 2 & 3y \\ 5 & y \end{bmatrix} = \begin{bmatrix} 6 & 12 \\ 18 & z \end{bmatrix}$, what is the value of z?

   F. -6

   G. 6

   H. 8

   J. 22

   K. 24

9. The product $\begin{bmatrix} 1 & 2 & 3 \end{bmatrix} \cdot \begin{bmatrix} -1 \\ -2 \\ -3 \end{bmatrix} = ?$

   A. -14

   B. 0

   C. 14

   D. $\begin{bmatrix} -1 & 0 & 0 \\ 0 & -4 & 0 \\ 0 & 0 & -9 \end{bmatrix}$

   E. $\begin{bmatrix} 0 & 1 & -1 \\ 2 & 0 & -2 \\ 3 & -3 & 0 \end{bmatrix}$

10. If the vector **u** is given by $\mathbf{u} = \langle 25, -30 \rangle$, which of the following represents $-\dfrac{2}{5}\mathbf{u}$?

    F. $\langle -10, -30 \rangle$

    G. $\langle -10, 12 \rangle$

    H. $\langle -10, -12 \rangle$

    J. $\langle 10, -12 \rangle$

    K. $\langle 10, 12 \rangle$

11. What is the greatest integer smaller than $\sqrt{250}$?

    A. 15

    B. 16

    C. 17

    D. 19

    E. 20

12. When $\dfrac{4}{11}$ is written as a decimal, what is the 100th digit after the decimal point?

    F. 3

    G. 4

    H. 5

    J. 6

    K. 7

Math

13. Which of the following is equivalent to

$$\frac{\left(3.0 \times 10^4\right)\left(8.0 \times 10^9\right)}{1.2 \times 10^6}?$$

A. 2.0×10^6

B. 2.0×10^7

C. 2.0×10^8

D. 2.0×10^{30}

E. 2.0×10^{31}

14. Which of the following is equivalent to the product $\left(\sqrt{8} + \sqrt{6}\right)\left(\sqrt{8} - \sqrt{6}\right)$?

F. 1

G. 2

H. $\sqrt{7}$

J. $\sqrt{14}$

K. 7

15. What is the value of $\left(5\sqrt{3}\right)^2$?

A. 15

B. $10\sqrt{3}$

C. $25\sqrt{3}$

D. 30

E. 75

16. If $x > 1$, then which of the following must be true?

F. $\frac{\sqrt{x}}{x} - 1 < 0$

G. $\frac{x}{\sqrt{x}} < 1$

H. $2\sqrt{x} < x$

J. $\sqrt{x} + x > x^2$

K. All of the choices are true.

17. If $x^4 = 90$ (and x is a real number), then x lies between which two consecutive integers?

A. 3 and 4

B. 4 and 5

C. 5 and 6

D. 7 and 8

E. 9 and 10

18. If $i^2 = -1$, which of the following is a square root of $8 - 6i$?

F. $3 + i$

G. $3 - i$

H. $3 - 4i$

J. $4 + 3i$

K. $4 - 3i$

19. The number of employees at a company in each division can be modeled using the following matrix.

Marketing	Public Relations	Development	Recruitment
[300	200	600	100]

The head of recruitment estimates the proportion of current employees who will leave within the next year using the following matrix:

Marketing	
Marketing	0.13
Public Relations	0.15
Development	0.12
Recruitment	0.14

Given these matrices, what is the head of recruitment's estimate of the number of current employees in these departments who will leave within the next year?

A. 140

B. 155

C. 188

D. 210

E. 245

20. If **u** and **v** are vectors such that $\mathbf{u} = \langle 2,0 \rangle$ and $\mathbf{v} = \langle 0,-2 \rangle$, which of the following represents $\mathbf{u} + \mathbf{v}$?

F. $\langle -2,-2 \rangle$

G. $\langle -2,2 \rangle$

H. $\langle 0,0 \rangle$

J. $\langle 2,-2 \rangle$

K. $\langle 2,2 \rangle$

Answers and Explanations are provided at the end of the book.

CHAPTER 11

Algebra

CHAPTER OBJECTIVES

By the end of this chapter, you will be able to:

1. Determine the slope and/or intercepts of a line from its equation

2. Write the equation of a line given certain information about the line

3. Solve systems of two linear equations, including those that are used to represent real-world scenarios

4. Add, subtract, and multiply polynomials

5. Factor quadratic expressions

6. Use the quadratic formula and other techniques to solve quadratic equations

7. Solve absolute value equations

8. Solve an equation in terms of a specified variable

9. Solve compound, absolute value, and simple quadratic inequalities and match the solutions with their graphs on a number line

SMARTPOINTS

Point Value	SmartPoints Category
5 Points	Algebra

ALGEBRA

Algebra questions make up about 12–15% of the Math test and extensively test your ability to solve for an unknown quantity given a wide range of information of varying complexity. You can expect to solve systems of equations, quadratic equations, absolute value equations, and a variety of inequalities.

Algebra questions will also test your ability to write the equation of a line given certain types of information. The slope-intercept form of a line is the most important equation to remember here, and understanding slope in general is crucial to success on Test Day, so let's start with those.

Lines and Their Equations

You can glean a lot of information about a line from its equation. For example, you can determine the line's slope and where it crosses the horizontal and vertical axes on a coordinate plane without having to graph the line. Similarly, you can use information about a line's graph to determine its equation.

The important equations to remember for lines are:

- **Standard form:** $Ax + By = C$. From this equation, you can find intercepts fairly quickly by substituting 0 for the *other* variable. For example, to find the *x*-intercept, substitute 0 for *y*.

- **Slope-intercept form:** $y = mx + b$, where *m* is the slope and *b* is the *y*-intercept of the line.

- **Slope formula:** $m = \dfrac{y_2 - y_1}{x_2 - x_1}$, where (x_1, y_1) and (x_2, y_2) are two ordered pairs through which the line passes.

When dealing with **parallel** and **perpendicular** lines, remember that parallel lines have the same slope and perpendicular lines have opposite reciprocal slopes. For example, if the slope of a given line is 5, the slope of a parallel line is also 5. However, the slope of a line perpendicular to these lines is $-\dfrac{1}{5}$.

> ✔ **Note**
>
> Also, remember that horizontal lines have a slope of zero and vertical lines have a slope that is undefined.

Math

Let's try a question that involves these concepts.

1. What is the *y*-intercept of the line that passes through the points (1,21) and (4,42) ?

   A.   0

   B.   7

   C.   9

   D.   14

   E.   19

Work through the Kaplan Method for ACT Math step-by-step to answer this question. The following table shows Kaplan's strategic thinking on the left, along with suggested math scratchwork on the right.

Strategic Thinking	Math Scratchwork
Step 1: What is the question? The question asks for the *y*-intercept.	
Step 2: What information am I given? You know two points on the line.	(1,21) and (4,42)
Step 3: What can I do with the information? You're looking for the *y*-intercept, so use slope-intercept form. Unfortunately, you can't find *b* without finding *m*, so you need to find the slope. Identify x_1, y_1, x_2, and y_2. Now use the slope formula. Substitute 7 for *m* and plug in the values of either point to find *b*. It's typically easier to use the smaller numbers, as long as they're not negative numbers, so use (1,21).	$y = mx + b$ Looking for *b*. (1,21) and (4,42) ↓ ↓　　↓ ↓ x_1 y_1　x_2 y_2 $m = \dfrac{y_2 - y_1}{x_2 - x_1} = \dfrac{42 - 21}{4 - 1} = \dfrac{21}{3} = 7$ $y = mx + b$ $21 = 7(1) + b$ $21 = 7 + b$ $b = 21 - 7 = 14$
Step 4: Am I finished? You don't need to write out the equation of the line. You found *b*, and that's all you need.	Choice (D) is correct.

Systems of Linear Equations

You can get numerical solutions for more than one unknown if you are given the same number of equations as unknowns. The test maker likes systems of equations questions because they take a little thought to answer. Solving a system of equations almost always involves somehow combining the equations, but you have to figure out what's the best way to do so.

Substitution is the most straightforward method for solving systems, and it can be applied in every situation. Unfortunately, it is often the longer and more time-consuming route, especially when none of the variables has a coefficient of 1. To use substitution, solve the simpler of the two equations for one variable and then substitute the result into the other equation.

Combination involves adding the two equations together to eliminate a variable. In many cases, one or both of the equations must be multiplied by a constant before they are added together. Combination is often the best technique to use to solve a system of equations as it is usually faster than substitution.

> ✔ **Note**
>
> If it's convenient, you can also subtract one equation from the other, but you must be particularly careful to subtract all the terms. It's very easy to get confused when subtracting an entire equation.

Let's review the two methods by looking at an example of each.

Method I: Substitution

Example: Solve for m and n when $m = 4n + 2$ and $3m + 2n = 16$.

1. Because m is already written in terms of n, you can substitute $4n + 2$ for m in the second equation.

$$3\boxed{m} + 2n = 16$$
$$3\boxed{(4n + 2)} + 2n = 16$$
$$12n + 6 + 2n = 16$$

2. Solve for n.

$$14n = 10$$
$$n = \frac{10}{14} = \frac{5}{7}$$

3. Substitute $\frac{5}{7}$ for n in the first equation to solve for m.

$$m = 4\boxed{n} + 2$$
$$m = 4\boxed{\frac{5}{7}} + 2$$
$$= \frac{20}{7} + \frac{14}{7} = \frac{34}{7}$$

Method II: Combination

Example: If $3a + 2b = 12$ and $5a + 4b = 23$, what is the value of a ?

> ✔ **Expert Tip**
>
> Before diving into the process, consider which variable you want to keep and which one you want to eliminate. This could save valuable time on Test Day.

1. Start by lining up the equations, one under the other.

   $$3a + 2b = 12$$
   $$5a + 4b = 23$$

2. You want to keep a, so multiply the top equation by -2, to get $-4b$, which will cancel with the $4b$ in the bottom equation (leaving only the a terms).

   $$-2(3a + 2b = 12) \rightarrow -6a - 4b = -24$$
   $$5a + 4b = 23 \rightarrow 5a + 4b = 23$$

3. Add to eliminate the b terms.

   $$-6a - \cancel{4b} = -24$$
   $$+ \quad 5a + \cancel{4b} = 23$$
   $$\overline{\qquad -a = -1}$$
   $$a = 1$$

> ✔ **Expert Tip**
>
> Don't do more work than you have to on Test Day. You don't always have to find the value of each variable to answer a system of equations question, so pay careful attention to what the question is asking you to find.

Even though most students are more familiar with substitution, problems on the ACT are often designed to be quickly solved using combination. To really boost your score on Test Day, practice combination as much as you can on Practice Tests and in homework problems so that it becomes second nature.

Translating Word Problems into Multiple Equations

While solving systems of equations can be relatively straightforward once you get the hang of it, sometimes you'll encounter a complex word problem and need to translate it into a system of equations and then solve. This sounds scarier than it actually is. The key is to use variables that make sense in the context of the question. Let's give one a try.

2. At a certain toy store, tiny stuffed zebras cost $3 and giant stuffed zebras cost $14. The store doesn't sell any other sizes of stuffed zebras. If the store sold 29 stuffed zebras and made $208 in revenue in one week, how many tiny stuffed zebras were sold?

   F. 8

   G. 11

   H. 14

   J. 18

   K. 21

Work through the Kaplan Method for ACT Math step-by-step to answer this question. The following table shows Kaplan's strategic thinking on the left, along with suggested math scratchwork on the right.

Strategic Thinking	Math Scratchwork
Step 1: What is the question? You need to find the number of tiny stuffed zebras that were sold.	
Step 2: What information am I given? You're given the price of each item. You're also given the total number sold and the amount of money collected.	tiny zebra = $3; giant zebra = $14 total sold = 29 total collected = $208
Step 3: What can I do with the information? Translate all information into math. Because both toys are zebras, z is likely to be a confusing choice for a variable. Instead, use t for tiny and g for giant.	t = # of tiny zebras g = # of giant zebras

Strategic Thinking	Math Scratchwork
Break off each piece of relevant information into a separate phrase. Translate each phrase into a math equation.	"sold 29 stuffed zebras" $t + g = 29$ "made \$208 in revenue" # tiny × cost + # giant × cost = total \$ $3t + 14g = 208$
You now have a system of equations. You want to keep t, so use combination to eliminate g. Multiply the first equation by -14 and add the result to the second equation. Then solve for t.	$-14(t + g = 29) \rightarrow -14t - 14g = -406$ $3t + 14g = 208 \rightarrow \underline{\quad 3t + 14g = 208}$ $\qquad\qquad\qquad\qquad -11t = -198$ $\qquad\qquad\qquad\qquad\quad t = 18$
Step 4: Am I finished?	
Yes! Don't waste time finding the value of g. The question only asks for the number of tiny stuffed zebras, so you're done.	Choice (J) is correct.

> ✔ **Note**
>
> You could also use Backsolving to answer this question. Start with H: If 14 tiny zebras were sold, then $29 - 14 = 15$ giant zebras were sold. This would result in a revenue of $14(\$3) + 15(\$14) = \$252$. This is too much, so choose the next larger number of tiny zebras (because they cost less). If 18 tiny zebras were sold, then $29 - 18 = 11$ giant zebras were sold. This would result in a revenue of $18(\$3) + 11(\$14) = \$208$. Perfect!

Polynomials

By now you're used to seeing equations, exponents, and variables. Another important topic you are sure to see on the ACT is polynomials. A **polynomial** is an expression made up of variables, exponents, and coefficients, where the only operations involved are addition, subtraction, multiplication, division (by constants *only*), and non-negative integer exponents. A polynomial can have one or multiple terms. The following table contains examples of polynomial expressions and non-polynomial expressions.

Polynomial	$23x^2$	$\dfrac{x}{5} - 6$	$y^{11} - 2y^6 + \dfrac{2}{3}xy^3 - 4x^2$	47
Not a Polynomial	$\dfrac{10}{z} + 13$	x^3y^{-6}	$x^{\frac{1}{2}}$	$\dfrac{4}{y - 3}$

> ✔ **Note**
>
> Remember that a constant, such as 47, is considered a polynomial; this is the same as $47x^0$. Also, keep in mind that for an expression to be a polynomial, division by a constant is allowed, but division by a variable is not.

Identifying **like terms** is an important skill that will serve you well on Test Day. To simplify polynomial expressions, you combine like terms just as you did with linear expressions and equations (x-terms with x-terms, constants with constants, etc.). To be like terms, the types of variables present and their exponents must match. For example, $2xy$ and $-4xy$ are like terms; x and y are present in both, and their corresponding exponents are identical. However, $2x^2y$ and $3xy^2$ are not like terms because the exponents on corresponding variables do not match. A few more examples follow:

Like terms	$7x, 3x, 5x$	$3, 15, 900$	$xy^2, 7xy^2, -2xy^2$
Not like terms	$3, x, x^2$	$4x, 4y, 4z$	$xy^2, x^{2y}, 2xy$

You can **evaluate** a polynomial expression (just like any other expression) for given values in its domain. For example, suppose you're given the polynomial expression $x^3 + 5x^2 + 1$. At $x = -1$, the value of the expression is $(-1)^3 + 5(-1)^2 + 1$, which simplifies to $-1 + 5 + 1 = 5$.

A polynomial can be described based on its **degree**. For a single-variable polynomial, the degree is the highest power on the variable. For example, the degree of $3x^4 - 2x^3 + x^2 - 5x + 2$ is 4 because the highest power of x is 4. For a multi-variable polynomial, the degree is the highest sum of the exponents on any one term. For example, the degree of $3x^2y^2 - 5x^2y + x^3$ is 4 because the sum of the exponents in the term $3x^2y^2$ equals 4.

On Test Day, you might be asked about the number or the nature of the **zeros** or **roots** of a polynomial. Simply put, the roots are the x-intercepts of the polynomial's graph, which can be found by setting each factor of the polynomial equal to 0. If the degree of a polynomial is n, then the polynomial can have at most n roots. For example, a 4th-degree polynomial can have 0, 1, 2, 3, or 4 roots.

Adding and subtracting polynomials involve combining like terms. To combine like terms, keep the variable part unchanged while adding or subtracting the coefficients (numbers): $2a + 3a = (2 + 3)a = 5a$. Here's a slightly more complex example:

$$\left(3x^2 + 5x - 7\right) - \left(x^2 + 12\right)$$
$$= \left(3x^2 - x^2\right) + 5x + (-7 - 12)$$
$$= 2x^2 + 5x - 19$$

Multiplying polynomials is just like multiplying ordinary numbers, except you want to pay special attention to distributing and combining like terms. To multiply monomials, multiply the numbers and the variables separately: $2a \times 3a = (2 \times 3)(a \times a) = 6a^2$.

Math

To multiply binomials, use **FOIL**—**F**irst, **O**uter, **I**nner, **L**ast:

Example: Multiply $(y + 3)(y + 4)$.
Steps: First multiply the **F**irst terms: $y \times y = y^2$.
Next the **O**uter terms: $y \times 4 = 4y$.
Then the **I**nner terms: $3 \times y = 3y$.
And finally the **L**ast terms: $3 \times 4 = 12$.
Then combine like terms: $y^2 + 4y + 3y + 12 = y^2 + 7y + 12$.

✔ **Expert Tip**

To square a binomial, first rewrite the problem as multiplication and then use FOIL. For example, write $(3x + 5)^2$ as $(3x + 5)(3x + 5)$.

FOIL works only when you want to multiply two binomials (an expression with two terms). If you want to multiply polynomials with more than two terms, make sure you multiply each term in the first polynomial by each term in the second. Take the expression $(3x^3 + 5x)(2x^2 + x - 17)$ as an example. Distribute the $3x^3$ first, then repeat with $5x$.

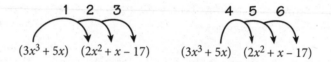

Now, write out each product and combine any like terms.

$$6x^5 + 3x^4 - \mathbf{51}x^3 + \mathbf{10}x^3 + 5x^2 - 85x$$

$$= 6x^5 + 3x^4 - 41x^3 + 5x^2 - 85x$$

✔ **Expert Tip**

When you have lots of terms to keep up with, consider arranging your work vertically, aligning like terms underneath each other.

Time to try out a question about polynomials. Be patient and take your time! It's easy to miss a term or a negative sign.

3. For all a and b, what is the product of $(a - b)^2$ and $(a + b)$?

   A. $a^2 - b^2$

   B. $a^3 - b^3$

   C. $a^3 - 2a^2b + b^3$

   D. $a^3 - ab^2 + a^2b - b^3$

   E. $a^3 - a^2b - ab^2 + b^3$

Work through the Kaplan Method for ACT Math step-by-step to answer this question. The following table shows Kaplan's strategic thinking on the left, along with suggested math scratchwork on the right.

Strategic Thinking	Math Scratchwork
Step 1: What is the question? You need to find the product of $(a-b)^2$ and $(a+b)$.	
Step 2: What information am I given? You're working with the square of a binomial and another binomial.	
Step 3: What can I do with the information? There are variables in the question stem and the answer choices, so you could use Picking Numbers, but that's not going to be pretty. Break the question into two parts. First, write the squared binomial as multiplication and use FOIL. Then, multiply the result by the remaining factor, $a+b$, and simplify once again by combining like terms.	Straightforward algebra will be the quickest route to the answer. $(a-b)^2 = (a-b)(a-b)$ $\quad = a^2 - ab - ab + b^2$ $\quad = a^2 - 2ab + b^2$ $(a^2 - 2ab + b^2)(a+b)$ $= a^2(a+b) - 2ab(a+b) + b^2(a+b)$ $= a^3 + a^2b - 2a^2b - 2ab^2 + ab^2 + b^3$ $= a^3 - a^2b - ab^2 + b^3$
Step 4: Am I finished? Look at the answer choices carefully. This is a perfect match for (E).	Choice (E) is correct.

Factoring Quadratic Expressions

You can think of factoring as undoing multiplication. A factor common to all terms of a polynomial can be **factored out**. For example, all three terms in the polynomial $3x^3 + 12x^2 - 6x$ contain a factor of $3x$. Pulling out the common factor yields $3x(x^2 + 4x - 2)$. Remember that if you factor a term out completely, you are still left with 1. For example, in the expression $6x^2 + 9x + 3$, you can factor a 3 out of everything. You're left with $3(2x^2 + 3x + 1)$. The most common type of polynomial that you'll need to factor on the ACT is a quadratic. There are several techniques that you'll want to review before Test Day.

Math

Classic quadratics: One of the test maker's favorite classic quadratics is the **difference of squares**. These are easy to spot because both terms are perfect squares and they're separated by subtraction. The general rule is $a^2 - b^2 = (a - b)(a + b)$. As an example, $x^2 - 9$ factors to $(x - 3)(x + 3)$. Occasionally, you'll find a difference of squares hiding in another binomial—just keep an eye out for two terms separated by a minus sign. For example, factoring a 7 out of the quadratic expression $28x^2 - 700$ yields $7(4x^2 - 100)$ which factors as $7(2x - 10)(2x + 10)$.

There are two other classic quadratics, each a **square of a binomial**, that occur regularly on the ACT:

$$a^2 + 2ab + b^2 = (a + b)^2$$
$$a^2 - 2ab + b^2 = (a - b)^2$$

For example, $4x^2 + 12x + 9$ factors to $(2x + 3)^2$, and $n^2 - 10n + 25$ factors to $(n - 5)^2$.

Recognizing a classic quadratic can save a lot of time on Test Day—be on the lookout for these patterns. (HINT: Any time you have a quadratic and one of the numbers is a perfect square, you should check for one of these three patterns.)

FOIL in reverse: To factor a quadratic expression written in the form $x^2 + bx + c$, think about what binomials you could FOIL to get that quadratic expression. For example, to factor $x^2 - 5x + 6$, think about what **F**irst terms will produce x^2, what **L**ast terms will produce $+6$, and what **O**uter and **I**nner terms will produce $-5x$. When there is no number in front of the first term, you are looking for two numbers that add up to the middle term and multiply to the third term. So here, you'd want two numbers that add up to -5 and multiply to 6. (Pay attention to signs—negative vs. positive makes a big difference here!) The correct factors are $(x - 2)(x - 3)$.

> ✔ **Expert Tip**
>
> Factoring is easiest when the leading coefficient is 1, so whenever possible, try to simplify the expression so that is the case. In addition, if you see nice-looking numbers (integers or simple fractions) in the answer choices, this is a clue that factoring is possible. If you're ever not sure that you've done your factoring correctly, go ahead and FOIL to check your work. You should get the expression you started with.

Math

Factoring quadratics when $a \neq 1$: Although less commonly seen than other strategies, **grouping** is useful when factoring more challenging quadratics, especially when the leading coefficient (the value of a) is not 1. You'll need two x terms to use this route. The goal of grouping is to identify the greatest common factor (GCF) of the first two terms, repeat for the second two terms, then finally combine the two GCFs into a separate binomial. Check out the following example.

Step	Scratchwork
Expression to factor:	$2x^2 - 7x - 15$
You need to split the x term in two; the sum of the new terms' coefficients must equal b, and their product must equal ac.	$a \times c = 2 \times (-15) = -30, b = -7$ new x term coefficients: 3 and -10 $2x^2 - 10x + 3x - 15$
What's the GCF of the first pair of terms? How about the second pair of terms?	GCF of $2x^2$ and $-10x$ is $2x$ GCF of $3x$ and -15 is 3
Factor out the GCFs for each pair of terms.	$2x^2 - 10x + 3x - 15$ $2x(x - 5) + 3(x - 5)$
Factor out the newly formed binomial and combine the GCFs into another factor.	$\mathbf{2x}(x - 5) + \mathbf{3}(x - 5)$ $(\mathbf{2x + 3})(x - 5)$

Let's try a couple of factoring questions. Everyone could use a little practice in this area before Test Day.

4. Which of the following linear expressions divides evenly into $6x^2 + 7x - 20$?

    F. $3x - 10$

    G. $3x - 5$

    H. $3x - 4$

    J. $3x - 2$

    K. $3x - 1$

Work through the Kaplan Method for ACT Math step-by-step to answer this question. The following table shows Kaplan's strategic thinking on the left, along with suggested math scratchwork on the right.

Strategic Thinking	Math Scratchwork
Step 1: What is the question? You need to determine which binomial divides evenly into the quadratic.	
Step 2: What information am I given? You're given a quadratic expression and answer choices that are binomials.	The answer choices provide a hint—factor the quadratic expression.
Step 3: What can I do with the information? Think about whole numbers: A number divides evenly into another number when the smaller number is a **factor** of the larger number. The leading coefficient of the equation is not 1, so you'll need to use grouping to factor the equation.	$6x^2 + 7x - 20$
Multiply a times c.	$6 \times (-20) = -120$
Look for two factors of -120 whose sum is equal to the coefficient of the middle term, $+7$. Try numbers that end in 0s and 5s first (because 120 ends in a 0).	$10 \times (-12) = -120$ and $10 + (-12) = -2$ ✗ $-10 \times (12) = -120$ and $-10 + (12) = +2$ ✗ $8 \times (-15) = -120$ and $8 + (-15) = -7$ ✗ $-8 \times (15) = -120$ and $-8 + (15) = +7$ ✔
Break the middle term ($7x$) into two terms using the numbers you found, then factor by grouping.	$6x^2 + 7x - 20$ $= 6x^2 - 8x + 15x - 20$ $= 2x(3x - 4) + 5(3x - 4)$ $= (2x + 5)(3x - 4)$
Step 4: Am I finished? $3x - 4$ is a factor, so it must divide evenly into the expression.	Choice (H) is correct.

Although it's certainly possible that you'll be asked a straightforward question about factoring, you could also encounter one that's camouflaged as something else. Take a look at this question, which is really all about factoring.

5.   Which of the following is the simplified form of $\dfrac{x^2 - 4x + 4}{2x^2 + 4x - 16}$?

   A. $\dfrac{1}{2}$

   B. $\dfrac{x}{x + 4}$

   C. $\dfrac{x - 2}{2(x + 4)}$

   D. $\dfrac{x + 2}{2(x - 8)}$

   E. $\dfrac{x^2 - 4x + 1}{x^2 + 2x - 4}$

✔ **Expert Tip**

When you encounter a quadratic expression in the numerator and/or denominator of a rational expression, try to factor the quadratics. Chances are that one or more factor in the numerator will cancel with one or more factor in the denominator. Always factor the easier quadratic first, which may provide a hint as to how to factor the more difficult quadratic.

Work through the Kaplan Method for ACT Math step-by-step to answer this question. The following table shows Kaplan's strategic thinking on the left, along with suggested math scratchwork on the right.

Strategic Thinking	Math Scratchwork
Step 1: What is the question? You need to find the simplified expression that is equivalent to the one given.	
Step 2: What information am I given? You're given a rational expression, but don't panic! Both the numerator and denominator are quadratic expressions, and you know how to factor those.	$\dfrac{x^2 - 4x + 4}{2x^2 + 4x - 16}$

Math

Strategic Thinking	Math Scratchwork
Step 3: What can I do with the information? There are a couple of x^2 terms, so you should be thinking about quadratics and factoring. Examine the numerator first: It's an example of a perfect square trinomial, so it's easy to factor. The denominator is a bit more involved. First factor out a 2 to get 1 for the x^2 coefficient. Then factor the quadratic as usual. If the numerator and denominator have any factors in common, cancel those factors.	$\dfrac{x^2 - 4x + 4}{2x^2 + 4x - 16} = ?$ $\dfrac{(x - 2)(x - 2)}{2x^2 + 4x - 16}$ $\dfrac{(x - 2)(x - 2)}{2(x^2 + 2x - 8)}$ $= \dfrac{(x - 2)\cancel{(x - 2)}}{2(x + 4)\cancel{(x - 2)}}$ $= \dfrac{x - 2}{2(x + 4)}$
Step 4: Am I finished? This looks exactly like one of the answer choices, so there is no more work to be done.	*Choice (C) is correct.*

Solving Quadratic Equations

You can solve a quadratic equation using a number of different methods. To be as efficient as possible, you should always consider which method will get you to the answer the quickest. Here are the three most popular methods.

Factoring: If an equation is factorable, set it equal to 0, factor it into two binomials, set each of the binomials equal to 0, and solve.

Example: $x^2 - 3x + 2 = 0$

To find the solutions, or roots, start by doing what we did just a bit ago—factor the quadratic. You can factor $x^2 - 3x + 2$ into $(x - 2)(x - 1)$, making the quadratic equation $(x - 2)(x - 1) = 0$.

You now have an equation in which the product of two binomial factors equals 0. This can only be the case when at least one of the factors is 0. Therefore, to find the roots, set the two binomials equal to 0 and solve each for x. In other words, either $x - 2 = 0$ or $x - 1 = 0$, so solving for x yields $x = 2$ or $x = 1$. To check the math, plug 1 and 2 back into the original equation and make sure that both variables satisfy it.

Square rooting: If there are perfect squares on each side of the equal sign, take the square root of each side, split the resulting equation into two pieces, and solve each piece.

Example: $(x + 4)^2 = 25$

Taking the square root of both sides gives $x + 4 = \pm 5$. You can split this into two equations: $x + 4 = 5$ and $x + 4 = -5$. Solving both equations yields $x = 1$ or $x = -9$.

> ✔ **Expert Tip**
>
> Square rooting is a super fast way to solve a quadratic equation (if the equation is set up correctly). However, if you didn't think of using this method, you could also FOIL the left side of the equation, set the equation equal to 0 by subtracting 25 from both sides, and then factor. There are always options!

Quadratic formula: The quadratic formula can be used to solve any quadratic equation. However, because the math often gets complicated, use this as a last resort or when you need to find exact (e.g., not rounded, fractions, and/or radicals) solutions. If you see square roots in the answer choices, this is a clue to use the quadratic formula.

The quadratic formula that follows yields solutions to a quadratic equation that is written in standard form, $ax^2 + bx + c = 0$:

$$x = \frac{-b \pm \sqrt{b^2 - 4ac}}{2a}$$

The $\pm$ sign that follows $-b$ indicates that you will have two solutions, so remember to find both.

The expression under the radical ($b^2 - 4ac$) is called the **discriminant**, and its value determines the number of real solutions. If this quantity is positive, the equation has two distinct real solutions; if it is equal to 0, there is only one distinct real solution; and if it's negative, there are no real solutions.

> ✔ **Note**
>
> Being flexible and familiar with your strengths on Test Day is essential. By doing so, you can identify the path to the answer that is the most efficient for you.

Math

It's time to solve a quadratic equation. Ready?

6. If $3x^2 - 12x - 18 = 18$, what are the possible values for x?

    F.   4, 12

    G.   −6, 2

    H. −6, −2

    J.   6, 2

    K.   6, −2

Work through the Kaplan Method for ACT Math step-by-step to answer this question. The following table shows Kaplan's strategic thinking on the left, along with suggested math scratchwork on the right.

Strategic Thinking	Math Scratchwork
Step 1: What is the question? The question asks for the possible values of x.	
Step 2: What information am I given? You know that $3x^2 - 12x - 18 = 18$. You know that the answer choices are nice integers.	Notice that the equation isn't set = 0. This is a clue that you can factor.
Step 3: What can I do with the information? Start by setting the equation equal to 0. This is necessary for both factoring and using the quadratic equation, and square rooting is definitely not an option here. Be careful—the 18s do not cancel! The answer choices are integers, so factoring is the quickest route. You could factor right away, but it will be much easier if you pull a 3 out of each term first. Divide both sides of the equation by 3 (which still leaves 0 on the right side), then set each factor equal to 0 and solve for x.	$3x^2 - 12x - 18 = 18$ $3x^2 - 12x - 36 = 0$ $3(x^2 - 4x - 12) = 0$ Need the factors of −12 that sum to −4. That's −6 and 2. $3(x - 6)(x + 2) = 0$ $(x - 6)(x + 2) = 0$ $x - 6 = 0 \rightarrow x = 6$ $x + 2 = 0 \rightarrow x = -2$
Step 4: Am I finished? You've found the possible values for x, so move on to the next question.	Choice (K) is correct.

> **✔ Note**
>
> If factoring isn't your strong suit, you could also use Backsolving to answer the previous question.

Now solve another quadratic equation using a different approach.

7. Which of the following are the roots of the equation $x^2 + 8x - 3 = 0$?

    A. $-8 \pm \sqrt{19}$

    B. $-4 \pm \sqrt{19}$

    C. $-4 \pm \sqrt{3}$

    D. $4 \pm \sqrt{19}$

    E. $8 \pm \sqrt{19}$

Work through the Kaplan Method for ACT Math step-by-step to answer this question. The following table shows Kaplan's strategic thinking on the left, along with suggested math scratchwork on the right.

Strategic Thinking	Math Scratchwork
Step 1: What is the question? You need to find the roots of the given equation.	
Step 2: What information am I given? You are given a quadratic equation with integer coefficients. The answer choices contain radicals.	*Factor? No, check out the answers.* *Square roots in the answer choices tell you to use the quadratic formula.*
Step 3: What can I do with the information? The answer choices contain radicals, so use the quadratic formula. First, jot down the values for a, b, and c. You should also jot down the formula itself so you're not trying to recall it and plug in values at the same time. Carefully substitute the values into the formula and simplify.	$x = \dfrac{-b \pm \sqrt{b^2 - 4ac}}{2a}$ $a = 1, b = 8, c = -3$ $x = \dfrac{-(8) \pm \sqrt{(8)^2 - 4(1)(-3)}}{2(1)}$ $= \dfrac{-8 \pm \sqrt{64 + 12}}{2}$ $= \dfrac{-8 \pm \sqrt{76}}{2}$

Strategic Thinking	Math Scratchwork
Step 4: Am I finished? This is not one of the answer choices, which tells you that you need to simplify the radical. To simplify the radical, look for a perfect square that divides into 76 and take its square root.	$$x = \frac{-8 \pm \sqrt{4 \times 19}}{2}$$ $$= \frac{-8 \pm 2\sqrt{19}}{2}$$ $$= -4 \pm \sqrt{19}$$ Choice (B) is correct.

Solving Absolute Value Equations

To solve an **absolute value equation**, think about the two different cases—when what is inside the absolute value sign equals a positive number and when it equals a negative number.

For example, to solve the equation $|x - 12| = 3$, think of it as two equations: $x - 12 = 3$ or $x - 12 = -3$. Adding 12 to both sides of each equation gives $x = 15$ or $x = 9$. You may have to perform some preliminary operations before you get to this point, so think of the absolute value symbols as parentheses until you're ready to split the equation into two.

> **✔ Expert Tip**
>
> Just as with quadratic equations, equations with absolute value signs will have two possible solutions. Keep in mind that although the absolute value of a number can never be negative, there can be a negative solution to an absolute value equation.

Ready to give one a try? Remember—one inverse operation at a time.

8. Which value(s) of x satisfy the equation $5|2x - 6| + 3 = 13$?

   F. −2

   G. 2

   H. 4

   J. −2 and 4

   K. 2 and 4

Work through the Kaplan Method for ACT Math step-by-step to answer this question. The following table shows Kaplan's strategic thinking on the left, along with suggested math scratchwork on the right.

Strategic Thinking	Math Scratchwork
Step 1: What is the question? You need to solve the equation for x.	

Strategic Thinking	Math Scratchwork
Step 2: What information am I given? You're given an equation that contains an absolute value.	$5\lvert 2x - 6 \rvert + 3 = 13$
Step 3: What can I do with the information? Do easy operations first. You can worry about getting rid of the absolute value signs once you've isolated that term. You could start by dividing everything by 5, but that would produce messy fractions, so subtract 3 from both sides first. Now that the absolute value has been isolated, split it into two equations and drop the absolute value signs.	$5\lvert 2x - 6 \rvert + 3 = 13$ $5\lvert 2x - 6 \rvert = 10$ $\lvert 2x - 6 \rvert = \dfrac{10}{5}$ $\lvert 2x - 6 \rvert = 2$ $2x - 6 = 2$ or $2x - 6 = -2$ $\quad 2x = 8 \qquad\qquad 2x = 4$ $\quad\ \ x = 4 \qquad\qquad\ \ x = 2$
Step 4: Am I finished? You found the possible values for x, so your job is complete.	Choice (K) is *correct*.

✔ **Note**

You could use Backsolving to answer the previous question, but the equation has a lot of parts, so this strategy may be time-consuming. If you do choose this method, be sure to take into account that J and K each contain two possible answers, so you'll need to check both for at least one of them.

Solving Equations and Formulas in Terms of a Given Variable

When you convert a linear equation from standard form, $Ax + By = C$, to slope-intercept form, $y = mx + b$, you're solving the first equation **in terms of** y. That simply means you're isolating y on one side of the equation.

If you've ever taken a chemistry or physics course, you probably noticed that many real-world situations can't be represented by simple linear equations. There are frequently radicals, exponents, and fractions galore. For example, the root-mean-square velocity for particles in a gas can be described by the following equation:

$$v = \sqrt{\dfrac{3kT}{m}}$$

In this equation, v represents the root-mean-square velocity, k is a constant, T is the temperature in degrees Kelvin, and m is the mass of one molecule of the gas. It's a great equation if you have k, T, and m and are looking for v. However, if you're looking for a different quantity, having that unknown buried under the radical can be unnerving. Fortunately, unearthing it is easier than it appears. Suppose you want to solve the equation for T instead. First, square both sides to eliminate the radical; the result is $v^2 = \dfrac{3kT}{m}$. Next, isolate T by multiplying both sides by m and dividing by $3k$. In terms of T, the equation is $\dfrac{mv^2}{3k} = T$.

✔ **Note**

Note that it doesn't matter which side of the equation the variable of interest ends up on, as long as it's by itself.

---

9. If $a = \dfrac{b + x}{c + x}$, what is the value of x in terms of a, b, and c?

A. $\dfrac{a - bc}{a - 1}$

B. $\dfrac{b - ac}{a - 1}$

C. $\dfrac{a + bc}{a + 1}$

D. $\dfrac{ac + b}{a + 1}$

E. $\dfrac{ac - b}{a}$

Work through the Kaplan Method for ACT Math step-by-step to answer this question. The following table shows Kaplan's strategic thinking on the left, along with suggested math scratchwork on the right.

Strategic Thinking	Math Scratchwork
Step 1: What is the question? You need to solve the equation in terms of x. In other words, you need to get x by itself.	
Step 2: What information am I given? You're given an equation that has four different variables, one of which is x.	$a = \dfrac{b + x}{c + x}$
Step 3: What can I do with the information? You want to get x on one side by itself. The first thing to do is eliminate the denominator by multiplying both sides of the equation by $c + x$. Once there, distribute to simplify the left side.	$a = \dfrac{b + x}{c + x}$ $a(c + x) = \left(\dfrac{b + x}{c + x}\right)(c + x)$ $ac + ax = b + x$
Next, move all terms with x to one side and all terms without x to the other.	$ac + ax = b + x$ $ax - x = b - ac$
Now factor x out of the left side and divide both sides by the other factor to isolate x.	$ax - x = b - ac$ $x(a - 1) = b - ac$ $x = \dfrac{b - ac}{a - 1}$
Step 4: Am I finished? You should find a match among the answer choices, so you're all done.	*Choice (B) is correct.*

Solving Compound Inequalities

You may occasionally see an inequality that consists of three pieces, such as $-4 < x < 1$, with the variable sandwiched in the middle. This is called a **compound inequality**. Solving a compound inequality is much like solving a regular inequality. The only big difference is that whatever you do to one piece, you must do to all three pieces. As always, if you multiply or divide by a negative number, you must reverse the inequality symbols (both of them). Let's take a look at this in action.

Math

10. Which of the following represents the solution set for $-15 \leq 2x - 13 < 3$?

F. $-1 \leq x < 8$

G. $-2 \leq x < 16$

H. $-5 \leq x < -1$

J. $-14 \leq x < 8$

K. $-28 \leq x < 16$

Work through the Kaplan Method for ACT Math step-by-step to answer this question. The following table shows Kaplan's strategic thinking on the left, along with suggested math scratchwork on the right.

Strategic Thinking	Math Scratchwork
Step 1: What is the question? You're asked to find the solution set for the inequality.	
Step 2: What information am I given? You're given a compound inequality.	$-15 \leq 2x - 13 < 3$
Step 3: What can I do with the information? Straightforward algebra is required here. Perform one inverse operation at time. Don't forget—whatever you do to one piece, you must do to all three pieces.	First step: Add 13 to all three pieces $-2 \leq 2x < 16$
Now that you have the variable term by itself in the middle, divide everything by its coefficient, 2.	$\dfrac{-2}{2} \leq \dfrac{2x}{2} < \dfrac{16}{2}$
Simplify the result, and you're all done.	$-1 \leq x < 8$
Step 4: Am I finished? There is an exact match among the answer choices, so your work is done.	Choice (F) is correct.

Solving Absolute Value Inequalities

About the most complicated algebraic solving you'll have to do on the ACT Math test will involve inequalities and absolute value signs. Fortunately, there are two firm rules you can remember to make the process easier.

Rule 1 (Greater): To solve an inequality in the form $|\text{whatever}| > p$, where $p > 0$, just put that "whatever" outside the range $-p$ to p (because its distance from 0 is greater than p):

$$|\text{whatever}| > p \text{ means: whatever} < -p \quad \text{OR} \quad \text{whatever} > p$$

For example, $|3x + 5| > 7$ becomes $3x + 5 < -7$ OR $3x + 5 > 7$. In most cases, the graph of an "or" scenario will be a split number line, part of which is shaded to the left and part shaded to the right.

Rule 2 (Less): To solve an inequality in the form $|\text{whatever}| < p$, where $p > 0$, just put the "whatever" inside the range $-p$ to p (because its distance from 0 is less than p):

$$|\text{whatever}| < p \text{ means: } -p < \text{whatever} < p$$

For example, $|x - 5| < 14$ becomes $-14 < x - 5 < 14$. This one should look familiar—it's a compound inequality, and you already know how to solve it. In most cases, the graph of a compound inequality will be a number line shaded between two numbers.

> ✔ **Note**
>
> Rules 1 and 2 also apply to the symbols $\leq$ and $\geq$.

11. Which of the following represents the solution to the inequality $|2x - 5| > 11$?

A.

B.

C.

D.

E.

Work through the Kaplan Method for ACT Math step-by-step to answer this question. The following table shows Kaplan's strategic thinking on the left, along with suggested math scratchwork on the right.

Strategic Thinking	Math Scratchwork
Step 1: What is the question? You need to find the number line that matches the solution to the given inequality.	
Step 2: What information am I given? You're given an absolute value inequality with a > symbol.	Pay close attention to the symbol. You'll be using Rule 1 here.
Step 3: What can I do with the information? Whenever you encounter an absolute value inequality, you must rewrite it without the absolute value signs. The symbol here is >, so this will become two inequalities separated by an "or."	$\lvert 2x - 5 \rvert > 11$ $2x - 5 < -11$ OR $2x - 5 > 11$

Solve each inequality separately.	$2x - 5 < -11$ OR $2x - 5 > 11$
	    $2x < -6$ $2x > 16$
	    $x < -3$ $x > 8$

Before looking at the answer choices, picture what the solution should look like.	$x < -3$ should be shaded to the left of -3. $x > 8$ should be shaded to the right of 8.
Step 4: Am I finished? Find the number line that matches, and you've done it.	Choice (A) is correct.

Solving Quadratic Inequalities

Solving a quadratic inequality is a bit more complicated than solving a linear inequality. Consider this inequality: $(x + 2)(x - 5) < 0$. If the first factor is negative and the second factor is positive, the product will be negative and therefore less than 0. The same is true of the reverse: If the first factor is positive and the second factor is negative, the product will be negative. However, if both factors have the same sign, so both are either positive or both are negative, then the product will be greater than 0. That's a lot to think about. Fortunately, there's a strategy for solving these that doesn't require so much thinking.

To solve a quadratic inequality, follow these steps:

Step 1: Replace the inequality symbol with an equal sign, factor, and solve.

Step 2: Draw a test line, placing only the two solutions on the line (in order). This divides the number line into intervals (usually three intervals).

Step 3: Pick a number from each interval and test it in the factored form of the inequality. If the result is true, that interval is a solution to the inequality.

> ✔ **Note**
>
> You could also test numbers in the original inequality (unfactored), but this almost always takes longer. You don't need to find the actual value, just whether it is positive (> 0) or negative (< 0).

To see this process in action, work out an example.

12. Which of the following gives the solution set for $x^2 - 8x - 20 < 0$?

    F. $-10 < x < 2$

    G. $-2 < x < 10$

    H. $2 < x < 10$

    J. $x < -10$ or $x > 2$

    K. $x < -2$ or $x > 10$

Work through the Kaplan Method for ACT Math step-by-step to answer this question. The following table shows Kaplan's strategic thinking on the left, along with suggested math scratchwork on the right.

Strategic Thinking	Math Scratchwork
Step 1: What is the question? You need to solve the given inequality.	
Step 2: What information am I given? You're given a quadratic inequality that contains a less than symbol.	*Less than 0 means negative.*
Step 3: What can I do with the information? Replace the inequality symbol with an equal sign, factor, and solve. To factor, look for factors of −20 that sum to −8; the factors are −10 and 2.	$x^2 - 8x - 20 = 0$ $(x + 2)(x - 10) = 0$ $x = -2$ and $x = 10$
Draw a test line, placing only the two solutions, −2 and 10, on the line (in order).	*(test line with −2 and 10)*
Pick a number from each interval and test it in the factored form of the inequality. If the result is true, that interval is a solution to the inequality.	$(-3+2)(-3-10)$ $(0+2)(0-10)$ $(11+2)(11-10)$ $(-)(-)=+$ $(+)(-)=-$ $(+)(+)=+$ Test −3 Test 0 Test 11 −2 10
You want values that are less than 0, so choose the interval or intervals that produce a negative result.	x is between −2 and 10 $-2 < x < 10$
Step 4: Am I finished? You bet! There's a match among the answer choices.	*Choice (G) is correct.*

✔ Expert Tip

Thinking about a quadratic inequality graphically can make finding the solution even easier. Assuming that the coefficient of the squared term is positive and that the equation has two real solutions, the graph of the equation will be a parabola (a U shape) that opens upward. The left and right edges of the parabola will be above the x-axis ($y > 0$), and the dip in the middle that contains the vertex will be below the x-axis ($y < 0$). The change from positive to negative and back again occurs at the x-intercepts of the graph.

Now you'll have a chance to try a few test-like questions in a scaffolded way. We've provided some guidance, but you'll need to fill in the missing parts of the explanation or the step-by-step math to get to the correct answer. Don't worry—after going through the worked examples at the beginning of this section, these questions should be completely doable.

13. Line t has a y-intercept of -3 and is parallel to the line having the equation $3x - 5y = 4$. Which of the following is an equation for line t?

    A. $y = -\dfrac{3}{5}x - 3$

    B. $y = -\dfrac{5}{3}x - 3$

    C. $y = \dfrac{3}{5}x + 3$

    D. $y = \dfrac{5}{3}x + 3$

    E. $y = \dfrac{3}{5}x - 3$

Use the following scaffolding as your map through the question. If you aren't sure where to start, fill in the blanks in the table as you work from top to bottom.

Strategic Thinking	Math Scratchwork
Step 1: What is the question?	
You need to find the equation for line t.	
Step 2: What information am I given?	
You know the y-intercept of line t.	y-intercept = -3
You also know that line t is parallel to another line.	parallel to $3x - 5y = 4$
Step 3: What can I do with the information?	
To write the equation of a line, you need two things: the slope and the y-intercept. You already know the y-intercept, so you can eliminate two of the choices. Which ones?	$y = mx + b$ $b =$ _____ Eliminate _____ and _____.
To choose between the remaining equations, think about slope. What do you know about the slopes of parallel lines?	Parallel lines have _____ slopes.
To find the slope of the given line, rewrite it in slope-intercept form, $y = mx + b$.	$3x - 5y = 4 \rightarrow -5y =$ _____ $x + 4$ $y =$ _____ $x +$ _____
What is the slope of the given line and, consequently, the slope of line t?	$m =$ _____
Step 4: Am I finished?	
Almost done. Which of the remaining equations has the correct slope?	Choice _____ is correct.

14. If $2x + 5y = 49$ and $5x + 3y = 94$, then the product of x and y = ?

  F. 17

  G. 34

  H. 42

  J. 48

  K. 51

Use the following scaffolding as your map through the question. If you aren't sure where to start, fill in the blanks in the table as you work from top to bottom.

Strategic Thinking	Math Scratchwork
Step 1: What is the question? You need to find the product of x and y.	
Step 2: What information am I given? You're given two equations, each with two variables. (Go ahead and line them up vertically.)	____ + ____ = ____ ____ + ____ = ____

Step 3: What can I do with the information?
 	
Solving for either variable will result in messy fractions, so combination will likely be faster than substitution here.
 	
Suppose you want to eliminate x. The coefficients of x are 2 and 5. Unfortunately, you can't multiply 2 by an integer to get 5 or vice versa, so you'll have to multiply both equations by numbers that will produce a common term. Don't forget to make one of them negative.
 	
Carry out combination as usual, being especially careful with the larger numbers.
 	
Plug your y-value back into one of the original equations and solve for x.
	$2x + 5y = 49$
	$5x + 3y = 94$
	
	____ (____ + ____ = ____)
	____ (____ + ____ = ____)
	
	  ____ + ____ = ____
	+ ____ + ____ = ____
	_____
	   ____ = ____
	    $y =$ ____
	
	$x =$ ____

Step 4: Am I finished? No! You need to multiply x and y together. If you got 51, you're exactly right!	____ × ____ = ____ Choice ____ is correct.

15. If A and B are polynomial expressions such that $A = 24xy + 13$ and $B = 8xy + 1$, how much greater is A than B?

    A. $32xy - 14$

    B. $16xy - 14$

    C. $16xy + 12$

    D. $32xy + 12$

    E. $32xy + 14$

Use the following scaffolding as your map through the question. If you aren't sure where to start, fill in the blanks in the table as you work from top to bottom.

Strategic Thinking	Math Scratchwork
Step 1: What is the question? You're asked to determine how much greater A is than B.	
Step 2: What information am I given? You're given two polynomial expressions.	$A =$ _____ and $B =$ _____
Step 3: What can I do with the information? The first step is to interpret the question (figure out which operation to use). To determine how much greater 20 is than 10, what would you do? Now that you know which operation to use, set up an expression that represents that operation. Distribute the negative sign and combine like terms.	Circle one of the following: add / subtract / multiply / divide $A \boxed{} B$ (_____) $\boxed{}$ (_____) ____ + ____ − ____ − ____ = _____
Step 4: Am I finished? Did you get $16xy + 12$? Excellent job!	Choice _____ is correct.

16. A projectile is launched from a cannon on top of a building. The height of the projectile in feet can be modeled using the quadratic equation $h = -16t^2 + 128t + 320$, where h represents the height and t represents the number of seconds after the projectile was launched. After it is launched, how long will it take the projectile to hit the ground?

F. 2 seconds

G. 4 seconds

H. 8 seconds

J. 10 seconds

K. 12 seconds

Use the following scaffolding as your map through the question. If you aren't sure where to start, fill in the blanks in the table as you work from top to bottom.

Strategic Thinking	Math Scratchwork
Step 1: What is the question? You need to find the amount of time it takes for the projectile to hit the ground.	
Step 2: What information am I given? You're given a quadratic equation (buried in a word problem) and information about what each variable represents.	$h = -16t^2 + 128t + 320$ $h =$ _____ , $t =$ _____
Step 3: What can I do with the information? First you need to interpret how the question that is being asked relates to the equation. Which variable are you solving for? At what height will the projectile be when it hits the ground? Plug the height into the equation and solve for t. Start by factoring the -16 out. Then factor the new quadratic into binomial factors. Finally, set each binomial factor equal to 0 and solve for t.	Looking for _____ , so solve for _____. On the ground means $h =$ _____. _____ $= -16t^2 + 128t + 320$ _____ $= -16($ _____ $)$ _____ $= -16($ _____ $)($ _____ $)$ _____ $= 0 \rightarrow t =$ _____ _____ $= 0 \rightarrow t =$ _____
Step 4: Am I finished? Time must be a positive number, so select the positive result as your answer.	Choice _____ is correct.

17. How many distinct real roots does the equation $3x^3 + 30x^2 + 75x = 0$ have?

   A. 0

   B. 1

   C. 2

   D. 3

   E. 5

Use the following scaffolding as your map through the question. If you aren't sure where to start, fill in the blanks in the table as you work from top to bottom.

Strategic Thinking	Math Scratchwork
Step 1: What is the question? You need to find the number of distinct real roots for the given equation.	
Step 2: What information am I given? You are working with a third-degree polynomial.	$3x^3 + 30x^2 + 75x = 0$
Step 3: What can I do with the information? Try to eliminate answers that can't possibly be correct. What is the maximum number of solutions a third-degree polynomial can have? Notice that each term has an x in it and each is divisible by a certain number. What is the GCF that you can factor out here? You should now have a quadratic inside the parentheses. Factor the quadratic into binomial factors. Don't forget to carry the GCF along as well. Then set each factor equal to 0 and solve. Count the number of distinct real roots.	____ Eliminate ____ . GCF = ____ ____ (_____) = 0 ____ (_____)(_____) = 0 _____ = 0 → x = ____ _____ = 0 → x = ____ _____ = 0 → x = ____ There are ____ distinct real roots.
Step 4: Am I finished? Did you get 2 distinct real roots? Excellent!	Choice ____ is correct.

18. How many integers are in the solution set of $|4x + 3| < 8$?

    F.   0

    G.   2

    H.   3

    J.   4

    K.   Infinitely many

Use the following scaffolding as your map through the question. If you aren't sure where to start, fill in the blanks in the table as you work from top to bottom.

Strategic Thinking	Math Scratchwork
Step 1: What is the question? You need to determine *how many integers* are in the solution set of the given inequality.	
Step 2: What information am I given? You are given an absolute value inequality where the symbol is $<$.	$\|4x + 3\| < 8$
Step 3: What can I do with the information? You need to rewrite the statement without the absolute value signs. The inequality symbol is less than, so $4x + 3$ is within 8 units of 0 on a number line (in other words, between -8 and 8). To solve for x, start by subtracting 3 from all three pieces of the new inequality. Next, divide each piece by 4. Simplify the result by converting to decimal numbers to make them easier to work with.	____ $< 4x + 3 <$ ____ ____ $< 4x <$ ____ $\dfrac{\square}{4} < \dfrac{\square}{4} < \dfrac{\square}{4}$ ____ $< x <$ ____
Step 4: Am I finished? You're not quite finished. You need to count the number of integers in the range you found. The integers are -2, -1, 0, and 1. How many is that?	*Choice* ____ *is correct.*

Now that you've seen the variety of ways in which the ACT can test you on Algebra, try the following questions to check your understanding. Give yourself 4 minutes to answer these 4 questions. Make sure you use the Kaplan Method for ACT Math as often as you can. Remember, you want to emphasize speed and efficiency in addition to simply getting the correct answer.

19. If the equation of a line is $4x - 7y = 14$, what is the slope of the line?

A. -7

B. $-\dfrac{4}{7}$

C. $\dfrac{4}{7}$

D. $\dfrac{7}{4}$

E. 7

20. At a school trivia competition, contestants can answer two kinds of questions: easy questions and hard questions. Easy questions are worth 3 points, and hard questions are worth 5 points. Nicole knows that she correctly answered 21 questions and that she had a total of 79 points. How many hard questions did she answer correctly?

F. 7

G. 8

H. 12

J. 13

K. 15

21. What is the sum of the values of x for which $2x^2 = 2x + 12$?

A. -2

B. -1

C. 0

D. 1

E. 2

22. Which of the following is an irrational solution to $|x^2 - 28| - 8 = 0$?

F. $2\sqrt{-5}$

G. $2\sqrt{5}$

H. $\sqrt{6}$

J. $6i$

K. 6

Answers and Explanations are provided at the end of the book.

Math

ON YOUR OWN

The following questions provide an opportunity to practice the concepts and strategic thinking covered in this chapter.

1. The graph below represents which of the following equations?

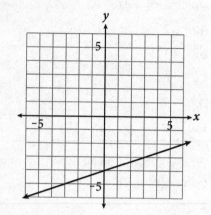

A. $y = -3x + 4$

B. $y = -3x - 4$

C. $y = -\dfrac{1}{3}x + 4$

D. $y = \dfrac{1}{3}x - 4$

E. $y = 3x - 4$

2. In the xy-coordinate plane, lines m and n are perpendicular. If line m contains points $(0,0)$ and $(-3,1)$, and if line n contains points $(-3,1)$ and $(0,z)$, then what is the value of z?

F. -10

G. -8

H. $-\dfrac{1}{3}$

J. 3

K. 10

3. Which of these is an equation of the line that crosses through $(-3,4)$ and $(3,6)$?

A. $x + 3y = -15$

B. $x - 3y = -15$

C. $\dfrac{1}{3}x - y = 5$

D. $3x + y = 5$

E. $-3x + y = 5$

4. Which of the following represents all the values of x that satisfy the inequality $2 \le 3 - \dfrac{x}{4} \le 4$?

F. $x \le -16$

G. $x \ge 4$

H. $x \ge 16$

J. $-4 \le x \le 4$

K. $x \le -4 \text{ or } x \ge 4$

5. The formula for converting a Fahrenheit temperature reading to Celsius is $C = \dfrac{5}{9}(F - 32)$, where C is the reading in degrees Celsius and F is the reading in degrees Fahrenheit. Which of the following is the Fahrenheit equivalent to a reading of 95° Celsius?

A. 35°F

B. 53°F

C. 63°F

D. 203°F

E. 207°F

6. If $x = \frac{1}{3}t + 2$ and $y = 4 - t$, which of the following expresses y in terms of x?

   F. $y = 2 - \frac{1}{3}x$

   G. $y = 4 - x$

   H. $y = 10 - 3x$

   J. $y = -2 - 3x$

   K. $y = 6 - 3x$

7. What are the (x,y) coordinates of the point of intersection of the line representing the equation $5x + 2y = 4$ and the line representing the equation $x - 2y = 8$?

   A. $(2,3)$

   B. $(-2,3)$

   C. $(2,-3)$

   D. $(-3,2)$

   E. $(3,-2)$

8. At a local theater, adult tickets cost $8 and student tickets cost $5. At a recent show, 500 tickets were sold for a total of $3,475. How many adult tickets were sold?

   F. 125

   G. 200

   H. 325

   J. 400

   K. 450

9. What is the resulting coefficient of x when $-x + 6$ is multiplied by $2x - 3$?

   A. -15

   B. -2

   C. 3

   D. 9

   E. 15

10. If $x^2 + 8x = 48$ and $x > 0$, what is the value of $x - 5$?

    F. -9

    G. -1

    H. 4

    J. 7

    K. 9

11. Which of the following are solutions to the quadratic equation $(x + 1)^2 = \frac{1}{25}$?

    A. $x = -6, x = 4$

    B. $x = -\frac{24}{25}$

    C. $x = -\frac{6}{5}, x = -\frac{4}{5}$

    D. $x = -\frac{4}{5}, x = \frac{6}{5}$

    E. $x = \frac{4}{5}, x = \frac{6}{5}$

12. What is the value of $2x + y$ given that $4x^2 + 6xy + 2y^2 = 32$ and $x + y = 4$?

    F. 4

    G. 5

    H. 6

    J. 7

    K. 8

13. What is the solution set for the equation $|2x - 3| = 13$?

    A. $\{-8\}$

    B. $\{-8, 8\}$

    C. $\{-5\}$

    D. $\{-5, 8\}$

    E. $\{5, -8\}$

14. If the number line below shows the range of possible values for some number b, which of the following shows the same possible values for b?

F. $|b - 5| \leq 1$

G. $|b - 5| \leq 2$

H. $|b - 2| \leq 5$

J. $|b - 2| \leq 3$

K. $|b - 1| \leq 5$

15. For what values of x is $x^2 - 5x + 6 < 0$?

A. $2 < x < 3$

B. $-2 < x < 3$

C. $-3 < x < -2$

D. $-2 < x$ or $x > 3$

E. $-3 < x$ or $x > 2$

16. What is the slope of the line given by the equation $-12x - 2y = 14$?

F. -7

G. -6

H. $-\dfrac{1}{6}$

J. $\dfrac{1}{6}$

K. 6

17. What is the y-intercept of the line that passes through the points $(1, -13)$ and $(-10, 31)$?

A. -9

B. -4

C. 0

D. 4

E. 9

18. If $k - 3 = -\dfrac{5}{3}$, then $3 - k = ?$

F. $-\dfrac{5}{3}$

G. $-\dfrac{3}{5}$

H. $\dfrac{3}{5}$

J. $\dfrac{5}{3}$

K. $\dfrac{7}{3}$

19. If $\dfrac{3}{zy} = \dfrac{2y}{x}$, then x is equal to which of the following?

A. $\dfrac{2zy^2}{3}$

B. $\dfrac{3zy^2}{2}$

C. $\dfrac{2z}{3}$

D. $\dfrac{3}{2zy^2}$

E. $6zy^2$

20. If $-3x + 7 \leq 4$ and x is an integer, which of the following statements must be true?

F. $x > 0$

G. $x \geq -1$

H. $x \leq 1$

J. $x \leq 0$

K. $x \leq 3$

21. Brandy has a collection of comic books. If she adds 15 to the number of comic books in her collection and multiplies the sum by 3, the result will be 65 less than 4 times the number of comic books in her collection. How many comic books are in her collection?

   A. 50

   B. 85

   C. 100

   D. 110

   E. 145

22. The toll for driving a segment of a certain freeway is $1.50 plus 25 cents for each mile traveled. Joy paid a $25.00 toll for driving a segment of the freeway. How many miles did she travel?

   F. 75

   G. 94

   H. 96

   J. 100

   K. 106

23.

Price of One Pound	Projected Number of Pounds Sold
$1.20	15,000
$1.40	12,500
$1.60	10,000
$1.80	7,500
$2.00	5,000
$2.20	2,500

Which of the following equations best describes the linear relationship shown in the table, where r represents the number of pounds of rice sold and d represents the price in dollars of one pound of rice?

   A. $r = 1.2d + 12,500$

   B. $r = 12,500d + 15,000$

   C. $r = -12,500d + 17,500$

   D. $r = 12,500d + 30,000$

   E. $r = -12,500d + 30,000$

24. What is the solution for x in the system of equations below?

$$\begin{cases} 3x + 4y = 31 \\ 3x - 4y = -1 \end{cases}$$

   F. 4

   G. 5

   H. 6

   J. 9

   K. 10

Math

25. What are the roots of the polynomial given by the equation $y = 2(x + 5)(x - 1)(x - 4)$?

    A. $-5, 1, 4$

    B. $-4, -1, 5$

    C. $2, -5, 1, 4$

    D. $2, -4, -1, 5$

    E. $0, 2, -5, 1, 4$

26. Which of the following is a factor of $6x^2 - 13x + 6$?

    F. $2x + 3$

    G. $3x - 2$

    H. $3x + 2$

    J. $6x - 2$

    K. $6x + 2$

27. Which of these is equivalent to $(4x - 1)(x + 5)$?

    A. $4x^2 + 8x$

    B. $4x^2 - 10x - 5$

    C. $4x^2 + 15x + 5$

    D. $4x^2 + 19x - 5$

    E. $4x^2 + 19x + 5$

28. If $a = 4$, what is the value of $\dfrac{4a^4 + 64b}{16}$?

    F. $\dfrac{1}{4} + 4b$

    G. $4 + 16b$

    H. $64 + 4b$

    J. $32 + 16b$

    K. $16 + 64ba$

29. For all $x \neq 8$, $\dfrac{x^2 - 11x + 24}{8 - x} = $?

    A. $3 - x$

    B. $8 - x$

    C. $x - 3$

    D. $x - 8$

    E. $x - 11$

30. For all $x > 0$, $\dfrac{1}{1 + \dfrac{1}{x}} = $?

    F. $x + 1$

    G. $\dfrac{x}{x + 1}$

    H. $x + 2$

    J. $\dfrac{x}{x + 2}$

    K. $\dfrac{x}{2}$

31. Which of the following values of x satisfy the equation $|2x - 6| = -4$?

    A. -1

    B. 1

    C. 5

    D. 1 and 5

    E. There are no values of x for which the equation is true.

32. How many integer values of x satisfy the inequality $|2x + 5| > 11$?

    F. None

    G. Two

    H. Three

    J. Four

    K. Infinitely many

280 **Unit Six: Higher Math**

33. For what values of x is $x^2 + 9 < 0$?

    A. $x < -3$

    B. $x > 3$

    C. $-3 < x < 3$

    D. $x < -3$ or $x > 3$

    E. There are no values of x for which the inequality is true.

34. If $x \neq 4$ and $x \neq -4$, then the expression $\dfrac{4x}{x^2 - 16} - \dfrac{3x}{x - 4}$ is equivalent to which of the following?

    F. $\dfrac{x}{x^2 - x - 20}$

    G. $\dfrac{x}{x^2 - 20}$

    H. $\dfrac{-5x}{x^2 - 16}$

    J. $\dfrac{-3x^2 - 8x}{x^2 - 16}$

    K. $\dfrac{-3x^2 + 16}{x^2 - 16}$

35. What is the value of x if $\dfrac{x + 1}{x - 3} - \dfrac{x + 2}{x - 4} = 0$?

    A. -2

    B. -1

    C. 0

    D. 1

    E. 2

Answers and Explanations are provided at the end of the book.

CHAPTER 12

Functions

CHAPTER OBJECTIVES

By the end of this chapter, you will be able to:

1. Use function notation and evaluate functions at integer values, including compositions of functions

2. Find the domain and range of polynomial and rational functions

3. Analyze and draw conclusions based on graphs of functions, including transformations of graphs

4. Apply a definition of an operation for whole numbers (e.g., m ¥ $n = m^2 + n$)

5. Analyze and extend arithmetic, geometric, and recursively defined sequences

6. Apply properties of exponential and logarithmic functions

7. Match graphs of basic trigonometric functions with their equations

8. Use trigonometric concepts and basic identities to solve problems, including problems based on the unit circle

SMARTPOINTS

Point Value	SmartPoints Category
5 Points	Functions

FUNCTIONS

Functions questions make up about 12–15% of the Math test. You'll need to know how to interpret function notation and recognize the different ways in which functions can be represented. You will also be tested on function operations, which include adding, subtracting, multiplying, dividing, and finding compositions. Questions in this category will also include using functions to solve problems about real-world scenarios and describing important features of graphs of functions. The types of functions you may see include but are not limited to linear, polynomial, rational, exponential, logarithmic, trigonometric, and piecewise functions. Finally, the Functions category includes questions involving arithmetic and geometric sequences.

Function Basics

Lots of students are afraid of functions. But there's nothing especially difficult about them. They just look scary. Once you "get" the conventions, however, you'll never be afraid of functions again. Here's a quick and painless review of the basic things you need to know about functions.

A **function** is a process or rule that turns a number (an input) into another number (an output). Squaring is an example of a function. For any number you can think of, there is a unique number that is its square. The conventional way of writing this function is $f(x) = x^2$. Don't be too concerned about "x"—it's just there as a placeholder to show where the input goes and what happens to it.

> ✔ **Note**
>
> There's nothing inherently difficult about functions. There aren't a lot of formulas or theorems to remember. Getting comfortable with functions just means understanding the symbolism and conventions.

Evaluating a Function

The most straightforward Functions questions you'll encounter on the ACT are questions that ask you to simply apply a function to some number or expression. This is called **evaluating a function**. When you apply the function to some particular number, such as -5, you write it this way: $f(-5)$. To find the value of $f(-5)$, you plug $x = -5$ into the rule. Let's use our squaring function from before:

$$f(x) = x^2$$
$$f(-5) = (-5)^2 = 25$$

If you must apply a function to an expression, such as $x + h$, you just need to be careful that you distribute where necessary. Using the same squaring function as before:

$$
\begin{aligned}
f(x+h) &= (x+h)^2 \\
&= (x+h)(x+h) \\
&= x^2 + 2xh + h^2
\end{aligned}
$$

Ready to try a Functions question? Be patient, this one will take a bit of work, but only because the algebra is tricky.

1. If $f(x) = x^2 + \dfrac{x}{2}$, then $f(a + 2) = ?$

   A. $a^2 + \dfrac{a}{2}$

   B. $a^2 + \dfrac{5a}{2} + 2$

   C. $a^2 + \dfrac{5a}{2} + 5$

   D. $a^2 + \dfrac{9a}{2} + 2$

   E. $a^2 + \dfrac{9a}{2} + 5$

Work through the Kaplan Method for ACT Math step-by-step to answer this question. The following table shows Kaplan's strategic thinking on the left, along with suggested math scratchwork on the right.

Strategic Thinking	Math Scratchwork
Step 1: What is the question? You need to find $f(a + 2)$.	
Step 2: What information am I given? You're given the rule for a function and an expression for an input value.	$f(x) = x^2 + \dfrac{x}{2}$ $f(a + 2) = ?$
Step 3: What can I do with the information? To find $f(a + 2)$, plug $a + 2$ into the rule for each x. Substituting an algebraic expression for x is a little more complicated than substituting a number for x, but the idea's the same. To square the binomial, write it as multiplication and use FOIL. To simplify the fraction, split it into two terms. To add the a terms, write $4a$ as $8a$ over 2 so you have a common denominator.	$f(x) = x^2 + \dfrac{x}{2}$ $f(a + 2) = (a + 2)^2 + \dfrac{a + 2}{2}$ $= (a + 2)(a + 2) + \dfrac{a + 2}{2}$ $= a^2 + 2a + 2a + 4 + \dfrac{a}{2} + 1$ $= a^2 + \dfrac{8a}{2} + \dfrac{a}{2} + 4 + 1$ $= a^2 + \dfrac{9a}{2} + 5$
Step 4: Am I finished? You've found $f(a + 2)$, so you're all done.	*Choice (E) is correct.*

Combining Functions

The letter *f* is not the only letter used to designate a function, though it is the most popular. Second in popularity is the letter *g*, which is generally used in a question that includes two different functions.

There are several ways in which the ACT might ask you to juggle multiple functions simultaneously. Fortunately, the rules governing what to do are easy to understand. To start, we'll look at how to combine functions. This technique simply involves **adding, subtracting, multiplying, and/or dividing functions**. Check out the following table for a synopsis of how to combine functions with the four basic operations (and make them look less intimidating).

When you see ...	... convert it to:
$(f + g)(x)$	$f(x) + g(x)$
$(f - g)(x)$	$f(x) - g(x)$
$(fg)(x)$	$f(x) \times g(x)$
$\left(\dfrac{f}{g}\right)(x)$	$\dfrac{f(x)}{g(x)}$

You'll have a chance to answer a question involving combined functions shortly.

A more challenging type of question that you're likely to see is a **composition of functions** or **nested functions** question. Questions involving a composition of functions require that you find an output value for one function and use the result as the input for another function to get the final solution. A composition of functions can be written as $f(g(x))$ or $(f \circ g)(x)$. The first is read as *f of g of x*, and the second, *f composed with g of x*. To answer these questions, start with the innermost parentheses and work your way out.

Suppose $f(x) = 8x$ and $g(x) = x + 3$. To find the value of $f(g(1))$, your steps would be as follows:

1. Determine $g(1)$, the innermost function when $x = 1$.

2. By substituting 1 for x in $g(x)$, you find that $g(1) = 1 + 3 = 4$. This output becomes your new input for *f*.

3. Find $f(4)$, the outer function when $x = 4$. Substituting 4 for x in function *f*, the final answer is $8(4) = 32$.

> ✔ **Note**
>
> Note that $f(g(x))$ does *not* equal $g(f(x))$. Not only is interchanging these incorrect, but this practice might also lead to a trap answer on Test Day.

Math

Take a look at the next example:

2.   If $p(x) = x^2 - 4x + 8$ and $q(x) = x - 3$, what is the value of $\dfrac{q(p(5))}{p(q(5))}$?

    F.   0

    G.   0.4

    H.   1

    J.   2.5

    K.   10

Work through the Kaplan Method for ACT Math step-by-step to answer this question. The following table shows Kaplan's strategic thinking on the left, along with suggested math scratchwork on the right.

Strategic Thinking	Math Scratchwork
Step 1: What is the question? You're asked for the value of $\dfrac{q(p(5))}{p(q(5))}$.	
Step 2: What information am I given? You're given rules for two functions and an initial input value of 5.	$p(x) = x^2 - 4x + 8,\ q(x) = x - 3$
Step 3: What can I do with the information? The numerator and denominator look quite similar, so keep track of your calculations. Start with the numerator: Compute the inner-most set of parentheses first and then work your way outward.	$p(5) = 5^2 - 4(5) + 8$ $\quad\quad = 25 - 20 + 8 = 13$ $q(13) = 13 - 3 = 10$ $q(p(5)) = 10$
Repeat this process with the denominator.	$q(5) = 5 - 3 = 2$ $p(2) = 2^2 - 4(2) + 8$ $\quad\quad = 4 - 8 + 8 = 4$ $p(q(5)) = 4$
Once finished, combine the final values in the original expression.	$\dfrac{q(p(5))}{p(q(5))} = \dfrac{10}{4} = 2.5$
Step 4: Am I finished? Yep! You found the requested value.	Choice (J) is correct.

✔ **Expert Tip**

When it comes to combining functions, pay close attention to order and parentheses.

Modeling with Functions

You learned in the Algebra chapter that equations can be used to model real-world scenarios in convenient ways, and the same is true for functions.

For example, suppose a homeowner wants to determine the cost of installing a certain amount of carpet in her home. Suppose also that the carpet costs $2.99 per square foot, the installer charges an $89 installation fee, and the sales tax on the total cost is 6%. The total cost of the project can be expressed as a function. The following table summarizes what each piece of the function would represent in the scenario.

English	Total cost	Square footage	Material cost	Installation fee	With sales tax
Math	C	f	$2.99f$	89	1.06

Using your algebra skills and function knowledge, you can build the function $C(f) = 1.06(2.99f + 89)$, where $C(f)$ is shorthand for "cost as a function of square footage." Using the function, it would be simple to calculate different costs based on various square footages. For example, suppose the homeowner wants to carpet a rectangular room that measures 12 feet by 16 feet, which means she needs a total of $12 \times 16 = 192$ square feet of carpet. The total cost, then, would be $C(192) = 1.06(2.99 \times 192 + 89)$ which simplifies to $702.86.

> ✔ **Note**
>
> Why does a 6% tax translate to 1.06? Using 0.06 would only provide the sales tax due. Because the function is meant to express the total cost, 1.06 is used to retain the carpet cost and installation fee while introducing the sales tax. Think of it as 100% (the original price) + the 6% sales tax on top. In decimal form, $1 + 0.06 = 1.06$.

Let's give a modeling question a try.

3. A Pep Club is keeping track of how many students show up to home football games wearing their school colors. To encourage participation, there is a prize giveaway at each game. As the prizes get more exciting, participation begins to increase. If x represents the game number and $f(x)$ represents the number of students wearing school colors at game x, which of the following functions best models the information in the table?

Game	1	2	3	4	5	6	7	8
Number of students	5	11	21	35	53	75	101	131

A. $f(x) = x + 4$

B. $f(x) = 2x + 3$

C. $f(x) = 6x - 1$

D. $f(x) = x^2 + 4$

E. $f(x) = 2x^2 + 3$

Work through the Kaplan Method for ACT Math step-by-step to answer this question. The following table shows Kaplan's strategic thinking on the left, along with suggested math scratchwork on the right.

Strategic Thinking	Math Scratchwork
Step 1: What is the question? The question asks which function shows the relationship between the game number and how many students show up wearing school colors.	
Step 2: What information am I given? The question stem tells you what $f(x)$ and x represent and provides a table relating the two variables.	$f(x) = \#$ of students wearing school colors $x =$ game number
Step 3: What can I do with the information? You can eliminate three choices right away based on the pattern in the table. The game numbers are going up by 1 each time, while the number of students is going up by varying amounts (6, then 10, then 14, and so on). What does this tell you?	The function cannot be linear because the rate of change is not constant. Eliminate A, B, and C.
Try plugging a pair of data points from the table into the remaining choices.	Try (1,5): D → $5 = 1^2 + 4$ ✓ Keep for now. E → $5 = 2(1)^2 + 3$ ✓ Keep for now.
You may have to try more than one pair to find the correct function, but you don't have to try all the pairs.	Try (2,11): D → $11 = 2^2 + 4$ X Eliminate. E → $11 = 2(2)^2 + 3$ ✓ Correct!
Step 4: Am I finished? You've found the only function that works for all the pairs of values, so you're done.	Choice (E) is correct.

Two-Variable Functions

Occasionally, you may encounter a function that is defined in terms of two independent variables. These functions behave just as you would expect them to. For example, suppose $g(x,y) = 3x + 2y$. To evaluate $g(-1,5)$, you would substitute -1 for x and 5 for y to get $g(-1,5) = 3(-1) + 2(5) = 7$.

You might even see **operations defined using symbols**. This is really the same as a two-variable function. The previous example might be written like this:

Let $x ⚜ y = 3x + 2y$. Which of the following is the value of $-1 ⚜ 5$?

The solution would be exactly the same as before—the only difference is the way in which the rule has been defined. (So $-1 \circledast 5 = 7$ if you want to double-check.)

Let's try one before moving on.

4.   Let $a \mathbin{\triangle} b = \dfrac{\sqrt{a+b}}{ab}$. Which of the following is the value of $14 \mathbin{\triangle} 35$?

   F. $\dfrac{1}{70}$

   G. $\dfrac{1}{10}$

   H. 7

   J. 49

   K. 490

Work through the Kaplan Method for ACT Math step-by-step to answer this question. The following table shows Kaplan's strategic thinking on the left, along with suggested math scratchwork on the right.

Strategic Thinking	Math Scratchwork
Step 1: What is the question?	
You need to find the value of $14 \mathbin{\triangle} 35$.	
Step 2: What information am I given?	
You are given a rule for combining the two numbers.	$a \mathbin{\triangle} b = \dfrac{\sqrt{a+b}}{ab}$
Step 3: What can I do with the information?	
Don't panic. This is nothing more than a plug-and-chug question. Plug in 14 for each a and 35 for each b.	$14 \mathbin{\triangle} 35 = \dfrac{\sqrt{14+35}}{14(35)}$
All that's left to do is simplify.	$= \dfrac{\sqrt{49}}{490} = \dfrac{7}{490} = \dfrac{1}{70}$
Step 4: Am I finished?	
Short and sweet. You're done!	*Choice (F) is correct.*

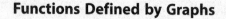
Math

Functions Defined by Graphs

The ability to interpret the graph of a function will serve you well on Test Day. To interpret graphs of functions, you'll need to utilize the same skills you use to interpret "regular" equations on the coordinate plane, so this material shouldn't be completely foreign.

You know from the first part of this chapter that a function is merely a dressed-up equation, so translating from function to "regular" notation or vice versa is a straightforward process. Consider the following brief example.

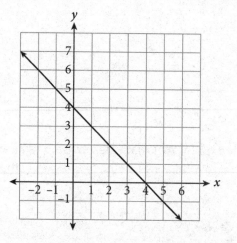

Suppose the graph represents $f(x)$ and you're asked to find the value of $f(3)$. Translating to plain English, this means you need to find the y-value on the graph when $x = 3$. So locate 3 on the horizontal axis and trace up until you hit the graph: The y-value at that point is 1. Thus, $f(3) = 1$. This also gives you a point on the graph, (3,1).

Now suppose you're asked to find the value of x for which $f(x) = 6$. Because $f(x)$ represents the output value, or range, translate this as "When does the y-value equal 6?" To answer the question, find 6 on the y-axis, then trace over to the function (the line). Read the corresponding x-value: It's -2, so when $f(x) = 6$, x must be -2. This corresponds to another point on the graph, $(-2,6)$. You could do this all day, right?

The ACT might also present functions in the form of tables. These may or may not have an equation associated with them, but regardless, you'll need to be adept at extracting the information necessary to answer questions. Most of the time the table will have just two columns, one for the domain (inputs) and another for the range (outputs).

> ✔ **Note**
>
> Remember: A value of $f(x)$ corresponds to a location along the y-axis. A value of x corresponds to a location on the x-axis.

Domain and Range

If you think of a function as a set of ordered pairs $(x, f(x))$, then for each value of x, there is one and only one value of $f(x)$. To make the notation less cumbersome, you can also write the ordered pairs as (x, y).

The set of all allowable x-values (inputs) is called the **domain** of the function. For many functions, such as polynomial functions, the domain is simply all real numbers. For example, the domain of $p(x) = 4x^3 - 3x^2 + 25$ is all real numbers because any number (positive, negative, fraction, decimal, etc.) can be plugged into $p(x)$ and will yield a result. Other functions, though, such as radical and rational functions, have **restricted domains**. For example, the domain of the rational function $r(x) = \dfrac{2}{x - 5}$ is the set of all real numbers such that $x \neq 5$ because 5 would result in division by 0, which is not possible.

> ✔ **Note**
>
> When graphed, the function $r(x) = \dfrac{2}{x - 5}$ has a vertical asymptote at $x = 5$. A vertical **asymptote** is a dashed line that the function will get very close to but never touch. As a general rule, a rational function has vertical asymptotes at all values of x for which the denominator is zero. The only time this is not the case is when factors that are common to the numerator and the denominator cancel each other.

The corresponding set of all y-values (outputs) is called the **range** of the function. It's harder to think algebraically about what the range of a function will be. Instead, think about what the function looks like graphically. For example, the range of the function $f(x) = 3x^2 + 5$ is the set of all real numbers such that $y \geq 5$ because the graph is a parabola that has been shifted up 5 units and opens upward. (Don't worry, we'll review parabolas a bit later.) If a question asks about the maximum or minimum value of a function, it's really asking about the upper or lower bound on the range.

> ✔ **Expert Tip**
>
> To keep domain and range straight, just think about alphabetical order: x comes before y, and *domain* comes before *range*. So the domain of a function is the set of all possible x-values, and the range is the set of all y-values.

Let's take a minute to visualize domain and range. Consider the graph that follows:

First the domain: There are no holes or gaps in the graph and there are arrows on both the left and right side, so the domain (the set of *x*-values) is all real numbers.

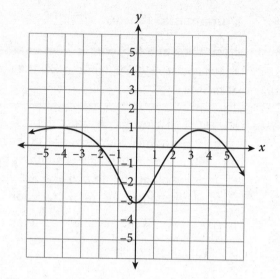

Identifying the range is more challenging—you must look very carefully. In plain English, you need to describe the spread between the lowest possible *y*-value and the highest possible *y*-value. There is a downward dip to −3, but is this the lowest *y*-value? Based on the two arrows at the ends of the graph (which point downward), the graph will eventually decrease to negative infinity, so there is no lowest *y*-value. However, the highest *y*-value on either side of the graph is 1, so the range is the set of all real numbers such that $y \leq 1$.

Piecewise-Defined Functions

On Test Day, you might see **piecewise functions**. A piecewise function is a function that is defined, literally, by multiple pieces. What breaks a function into pieces are different rules that govern different parts of the function's domain. Here's an example:

In the function shown, the behavior of the graph depends on the domain. Each "rule" is written inside the open bracket in "pieces." To the right of the "if" is the domain interval for which each "rule" applies. On the graph, an open dot indicates that a point is not included in the interval; a closed dot indicates one that is. Note that the different inequality signs dictate whether a dot is open or closed on the graph. For a single-point interval, an equal sign is used.

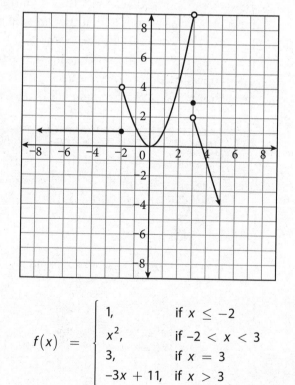

To **evaluate** a piecewise function, first determine to which piece of the domain the input value belongs. Then, substitute the value into the corresponding rule. For example, in this function, $f(2) = (2)^2 = 4$, because the input value 2 is between −2 and 3 (the second piece of the domain). Similarly, $f(5) = -3(5) + 11 = -4$ because the input value 5 is greater than 3 (the last piece of the domain). You can confirm these values by looking at the graph. At $x = 2$, the point on the graph is (2,4), and at $x = 5$, the point on the graph is (5,−4).

$$f(x) = \begin{cases} 1, & \text{if } x \leq -2 \\ x^2, & \text{if } -2 < x < 3 \\ 3, & \text{if } x = 3 \\ -3x + 11, & \text{if } x > 3 \end{cases}$$

Now let's try a test-like example.

5. In the figure shown here, what is the value of $f(0) + g\left(\dfrac{1}{2}\right)$?

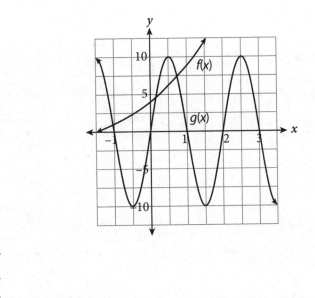

A. −4

B. 4

C. 6

D. 10

E. 14

Work through the Kaplan Method for ACT Math step-by-step to answer this question. The following table shows Kaplan's strategic thinking on the left, along with suggested math scratchwork on the right.

Strategic Thinking	Math Scratchwork
Step 1: What is the question? You're asked to determine the value of $f(0) + g\left(\dfrac{1}{2}\right)$.	
Step 2: What information am I given? You're given a graph that shows the functions $f(x)$ and $g(x)$.	Read the graph to find the function values you're looking for.

Math

Strategic Thinking	Math Scratchwork
Step 3: What can I do with the information? One of the values you need is $f(0)$. Locate $x = 0$ on the graph (it's the y-axis). Run your finger up the y-axis until you intersect the graph of f. At that point, the y-value appears to be about 4. (Always pay careful attention to the axis labels when reading graphs.)	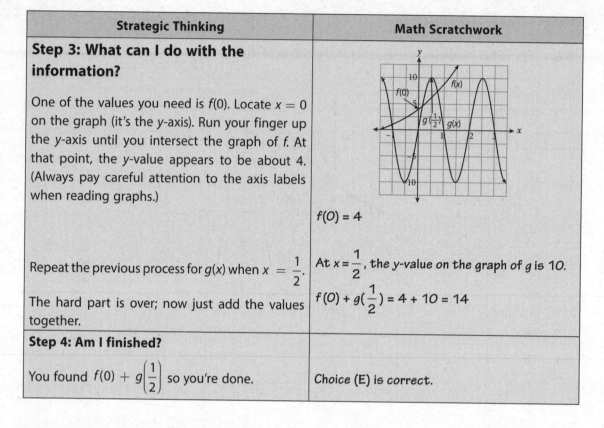 $f(0) = 4$
Repeat the previous process for $g(x)$ when $x = \dfrac{1}{2}$. The hard part is over; now just add the values together.	At $x = \dfrac{1}{2}$, the y-value on the graph of g is 10. $f(0) + g\left(\dfrac{1}{2}\right) = 4 + 10 = 14$
Step 4: Am I finished?	
You found $f(0) + g\left(\dfrac{1}{2}\right)$ so you're done.	*Choice (E) is correct.*

Describing Function Behavior

When describing the graph of a function or an interval (a specific segment) of a function, the trend of the relationship between the x- and y-values while reading the graph from left to right is often important. Three terms you are sure to see in more difficult function questions are **increasing**, **decreasing**, and **constant**. Let's look at what these terms mean and how they apply to ACT questions.

- **Increasing** functions have y-values that *increase* as the corresponding x-values increase (slant upward from left to right).

- **Decreasing** functions have y-values that *decrease* as the corresponding x-values increase (slant downward from left to right).

- **Constant** functions have y-values that *stay the same* as the x-values increase (horizontal segment or line).

The ACT can ask about function trends in a variety of ways. The most basic would be to examine a function's behavior and determine whether (and where) the function is increasing, decreasing, or constant. Tougher questions might ask you to identify the trend and then explain what it means in the context of a real-life situation presented in the question, or to identify the effect a transformation would have on the trend of a function.

Function Families and Transformations

A **family of functions** is a group of functions that have the same basic shape and characteristics. The simplest function in a family is called the **parent function**. Learning the basic shapes of these parent functions can help you to recognize or write equations for more complex functions in the same family.

You should make mental notes about the characteristics of the parent functions. For example, the first six functions in the table that follows all pass through (0,0). This can be a very convenient point to track. For the absolute value and quadratic functions, (0,0) is the vertex. For the square root function, the graph actually begins at (0,0), so the domain is $x \geq 0$ and the range is $y \geq 0$. Knowing little tidbits of information like this can save you time on Test Day.

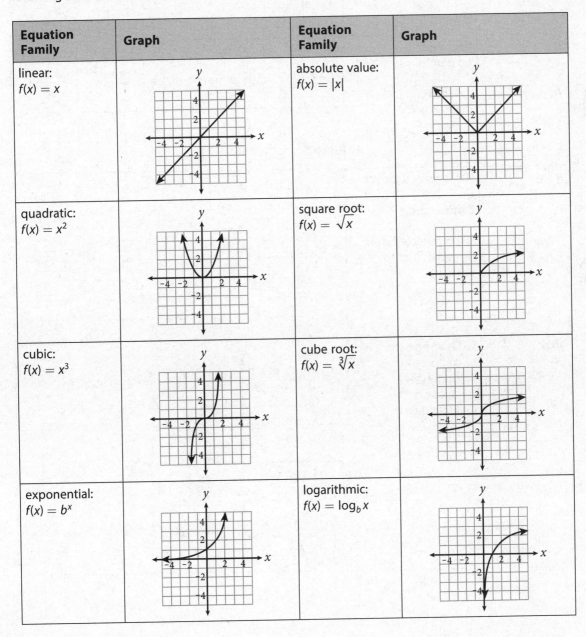

Equation Family	Graph	Equation Family	Graph
linear: $f(x) = x$		absolute value: $f(x) = |x|$	
quadratic: $f(x) = x^2$		square root: $f(x) = \sqrt{x}$	
cubic: $f(x) = x^3$		cube root: $f(x) = \sqrt[3]{x}$	
exponential: $f(x) = b^x$		logarithmic: $f(x) = \log_b x$	

Math

A **transformation** occurs when a change is made to the function's equation or graph. The most commonly tested transformations are translations (moving a graph up/down, left/right) and reflections (flips about an axis or other line). How do you know which is occurring? The following table provides some rules for altering the cubic function $f(x) = x^3$.

Algebraic Change	Corresponding Graphical Change	Graph
$f(x + a)$	$f(x)$ moves left a units	
$f(x - a)$	$f(x)$ moves right a units	
$f(x) + a$	$f(x)$ moves up a units	
$f(x) - a$	$f(x)$ moves down a units	
$f(-x)$	$f(x)$ is reflected over the y-axis (left to right)	
$-f(x)$	$f(x)$ is reflected over the x-axis (top to bottom)	
$af(x)$	$f(x)$ is stretched or compressed vertically (the y-values are multiplied by a)	

✔ **Note**

Pay careful attention to horizontal translations—they are opposite of what they look like: $+a$ shifts to the left, while $-a$ shifts to the right.

✔ **Expert Tip**

Do you notice a pattern in the way the transformations work? Adding or subtracting inside the parentheses of a function results in a horizontal translation; if the alteration is outside the parentheses, the result is a vertical translation. The same is true for reflections: When the negative is inside the parentheses (with the x), the reflection is horizontal; when the negative is outside the parentheses (away from the x), the reflection is vertical.

If you forget what a particular transformation looks like, you can always plug in a few values for x and plot the points to determine the effect on the function's graph.

Check out the next two questions related to function transformations.

6. The graph that follows shows a transformation of the absolute value function, $f(x) = |x|$. Which equation best describes the transformation?

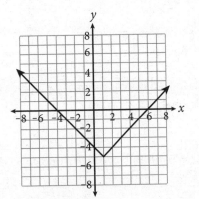

F. $y = f(x + 1) - 5$

G. $y = f(x - 1) - 5$

H. $y = f(x - 1) + 5$

J. $y = -f(x + 1) - 5$

K. $y = -f(x - 1) - 5$

Work through the Kaplan Method for ACT Math step-by-step to answer this question. The following table shows Kaplan's strategic thinking on the left, along with suggested math scratchwork on the right.

Strategic Thinking	Math Scratchwork
Step 1: What is the question? You need to choose the equation that represents the transformation shown in the graph.	
Step 2: What information am I given? You're told that the function is the absolute value function. You're also given a graph to examine.	$f(x) = \lvert x \rvert$
Step 3: What can I do with the information? Start by picturing the parent function.	The absolute value graph is a V with its vertex at (0,0).
The graph shown is still a V, so it has not been reflected vertically (turned upside down). This means you can eliminate two choices.	Eliminate J and K.
The vertex of the V has been shifted to the right 1 unit. How does this change the equation?	$y = f(x - 1)$, so eliminate F.
The vertex of the V has also been shifted down 5 units. How does this change the equation?	$y = f(x - 1) - 5$, so eliminate H.
Step 4: Am I finished? You've found the transformed equation, so you're all done.	Choice (G) is correct.

✔ **Note**

You may wonder why the equations in the answer choices don't include absolute value signs. The answer is this: The presence of f (which is defined in the question stem as the absolute value function) encompasses the absolute value signs. In other words, it's built into the equations by referring to f.

7. Suppose a polynomial function $p(x)$ has roots of -4 and 7. If $q(x)$ is a translation of $p(x)$ such that $q(x) = p(x - 2)$, through which two points must the graph of $q(x)$ pass?

   A. $(-4,0)$ and $(7,0)$

   B. $(-4,2)$ and $(7,2)$

   C. $(-4,-2)$ and $(7,-2)$

   D. $(-2,0)$ and $(9,0)$

   E. $(-6,0)$ and $(5,0)$

Work through the Kaplan Method for ACT Math step-by-step to answer this question. The following table shows Kaplan's strategic thinking on the left, along with suggested math scratchwork on the right.

Strategic Thinking	Math Scratchwork
Step 1: What is the question? Your job is to determine which two points $q(x)$ passes through.	
Step 2: What information am I given? You are given the roots for $p(x)$ and a rule for translating $p(x)$ to get $q(x)$.	roots of $p(x)$ are -4 and 7 $q(x) = p(x - 2)$
Step 3: What can I do with the information? The answer choices are ordered pairs, so translate the roots into points to make them easier to compare. The translation is inside the parentheses, so it is a horizontal shift, and horizontal shifts are the opposite of how they look, so $q(x)$ is $p(x)$ shifted to the right 2 units.	root of -4 = x-intercept at $(-4,0)$ root of 7 = x-intercept at $(7,0)$ To perform a translation to the right 2 units, add 2 to the x-coordinates of the points. $(-4,0) \rightarrow (-4 + 2,0) \rightarrow (-2,0)$ $(7,0) \rightarrow (7 + 2,0) \rightarrow (9,0)$
Step 4: Am I finished? You found the two points through which $q(x)$ must pass. Well done!	Choice (D) is correct.

✔ **Note**

It's not unusual for questions on the ACT to combine concepts. Here, you needed to use your algebra skills to translate *roots* of a polynomial into ordered pairs, and then you used what you know about functions to perform the translation.

Math

Patterns and Sequences

A **sequence** is a list of numbers or expressions in which there is a pattern. Knowing the basic parts of a sequence will make questions of this type seem less daunting.

- Each number in a sequence is called a **term** and is named by, or is a function of, its position in the sequence.

- The first term in a sequence is called a_1, the nth term is called a_n, and the term after that is a_{n+1}. So a general sequence looks like $a_1, a_2, a_3, \ldots a_{n-1}, a_n, a_{n+1}, \ldots$.

- You can also write a sequence using function notation: $f(1), f(2), f(3), \ldots, f(n-1), f(n), f(n+1), \ldots$.

An **arithmetic sequence** is a sequence in which the same number is **added** to get from one term to the next. For example, 1, 4, 7, 10, … is an arithmetic sequence because you add 3 each time, and 12, 7, 2, −3, … is also an arithmetic sequence because you add −5 each time (always think about what is being added, not subtracted). The difference between any two terms is called the **common difference**, and is usually represented by the variable d. There are two formulas that you should review before Test Day:

- Finding the **n^{th} term**: $a_n = a_1 + (n-1)d$, where n is the number of the term, a_1 is the first term, and d is the common difference between terms. For example, the 50th term of the arithmetic sequence 1, 4, 7, 10, … is found like this:

$$n = 50, a_1 = 1, d = 3$$

$$
\begin{aligned}
a_{50} &= 1 + (50 - 1)3 \\
&= 1 + 49(3) \\
&= 1 + 147 \\
&= 148
\end{aligned}
$$

- Finding the **sum of the first n terms**: $S_n = \dfrac{n(a_1 + a_n)}{2}$, where n is the number of the term, a_1 is the first term, and a_n is the nth term (the last term you're adding in the sequence). For example, the 50th term of the arithmetic sequence 1, 4, 7, 10, … is found like this:

$$n = 50, a_1 = 1, a_{50} = 148$$

$$
\begin{aligned}
S_{50} &= \frac{50(1 + 148)}{2} \\
&= \frac{50(149)}{2} \\
&= 25(149) = 3{,}725
\end{aligned}
$$

✔ Expert Tip

In the previous example, we had to use a_{50}, which we'd already calculated, to find S_{50}. This is often the case when finding a sum. There is another formula for finding a sum that allows you to skip this step, but the formula itself is longer and more complicated to remember: $S_n = \frac{n}{2}(2a_1 + (n-1)d)$.

A **geometric sequence** is a sequence in which the same number is **multiplied** to get from one term to the next. For example, 2, 6, 18, 54, ... is a geometric sequence because you multiply by 3 each time, and 48, 24, 12, 6, ... is also a geometric sequence because you multiply by $\frac{1}{2}$ each time (always think about what you're multiplying by, not dividing by). The number that you're multiplying by is called the **common ratio**, and it is usually represented by the variable r. To find the common ratio, divide any term by the term before it. There are two formulas that you should review before Test Day:

- Finding the **n^{th} term**: $a_n = a_1 r^{n-1}$, where n is the number of the term, a_1 is the first term, and r is the common ratio.

- Finding the **sum of the first n terms**: $S_n = \dfrac{a_1(1 - r^n)}{1 - r}$, where n is the number of the term, a_1 is the first term, and r is the common ratio.

✔ Note

A sequence can be neither arithmetic nor geometric. For example, the sequence 1, 8, 27, 64, 125, ... has a pattern (perfect cubes) but it is not arithmetic and it is not geometric.

Ready to give a sequence a try?

8. If the first term in a geometric sequence is 3, the third term is 48, and all terms are positive integers, what is the 11th term?

   F. 228

   G. 528

   H. 110,592

   J. 3,145,728

   K. 12,582,912

Work through the Kaplan Method for ACT Math step-by-step to answer this question. The following table shows Kaplan's strategic thinking on the left, along with suggested math scratchwork on the right.

Strategic Thinking	Math Scratchwork
Step 1: What is the question? You need to find the 11th term in the sequence.	
Step 2: What information am I given? You're told that the sequence is geometric and that the first term is 3 and the third term is 48. You also know that all the terms are positive integers.	$a_1 = 3$ $a_3 = 48$ geometric sequence
Step 3: What can I do with the information? To find the nth term of a geometric sequence, you need to know the first term (here given as 3), and you need to know the ratio r between consecutive terms. You're not given consecutive terms but rather the first term and the third term. The second term would be the first term times r, and the third term would be the second term times r. Now use the formula for finding the nth term, where $n = 11$.	$r = ?$ All the numbers are positive integers, so r must be a positive integer. $a_1 \times r \times r = a_3$ $a_1 r^2 = a_3$ $3r^2 = 48$ $r^2 = 16$ $r = 4$ $a_{11} = a_1 r^{11-1}$ $= (3)(4^{10})$ $= 3{,}145{,}728$
Step 4: Am I finished? You bet! You found the 11th term.	Choice (J) is correct.

Explicit Formulas and Recursive Sequences

A formula that allows you to find any term in a sequence by plugging in the position of the term is called an **explicit formula**. For example, the 10th term in the sequence whose formula is $f(n) = 5n + 2$ is $5(10) + 2 = 52$.

A formula in which each term is found using the previous term or terms is called a **recursive formula**. For example, if $a_1 = 2$ and $a_n = a_{n-1} + 3$, then $a_2 = a_1 + 3 = 2 + 3 = 5$, and $a_3 = a_2 + 3 = 5 + 3 = 8$, and so on. In general, at least the first term of the sequence must be given.

> ✔ **Note**
>
> When you build a sequence using a recursive formula, you cannot find the 10th term without knowing the 9th term, which requires the 8th term, and so on. You must build the sequence from a known term.

9. Which function could be used to generate the sequence that begins −7.5, −7, −6.5, −6, −5.5, … ?

   A. $f(n) = -7 + \dfrac{n+1}{2}$

   B. $f(n) = -7 - \dfrac{n}{2}$

   C. $f(n) = -8 + n$

   D. $f(n) = -8 + \dfrac{n}{2}$

   E. $f(n) = -8 - \dfrac{n}{2}$

Work through the Kaplan Method for ACT Math step-by-step to answer this question. The following table shows Kaplan's strategic thinking on the left, along with suggested math scratchwork on the right.

Strategic Thinking	Math Scratchwork
Step 1: What is the question? You need to find the function that could be used to create the given sequence.	
Step 2: What information am I given? You are given a sequence of numbers and answer choices that have variables in them.	−7.5, −7, −6.5, −6, −5.5, …
Step 3: What can I do with the information? The functions are written using explicit formulas, so choose values of n and test them, eliminating choices as you go. Start with $n = 1$ (the first term) and look for the function that yields −7.5.	A: $-7 + \dfrac{\boxed{1}+1}{2} = -7 + 1 = -6$ Eliminate. B: $-7 - \dfrac{\boxed{1}}{2} = \boxed{-7.5}$ Keep. C: $-8 + 1 = -7$ Eliminate. D: $-8 + \dfrac{\boxed{1}}{2} = \boxed{-7.5}$ Keep. E: $-8 - \dfrac{\boxed{1}}{2} = -8.5$ Eliminate.

Strategic Thinking	Math Scratchwork
Try $n = 2$ in the remaining functions. This time, you're looking for a result of -7. That only leaves (D).	B: $-7 - \dfrac{\boxed{2}}{2} = -7 - 1 = -8$ Eliminate. D: $-8 + \dfrac{\boxed{2}}{2} = -8 + 1 = \boxed{-7}$ Keep.
Step 4: Am I finished? All done! You found the correct function.	Choice (D) is correct.

Logarithmic Functions

A **logarithm** is the power to which a number must be raised in order to get some other number. Logarithms exist so that exponential functions have inverses. You can rewrite an exponential equation of the form $y = b^x$ using the notation $\log_b y = x$. That's the most important thing to remember about logarithms, so let's look at several examples.

Exponential Form	Logarithmic Form
$b^x = y$	$\log_b y = x$
$2^3 = 8$	$\log_2 8 = 3$
$4^2 = 16$	$\log_4 16 = 2$
$5^{-2} = \dfrac{1}{25}$	$\log_5 \dfrac{1}{25} = -2$

✔ **Expert Tip**

It's easy to get the order of the numbers mixed up in logarithmic form, so keep two things in mind: The base in exponential form becomes the base of the logarithm, and the exponent goes to the outer edge of the logarithmic equation (notice the e's in exponent and edge).

$$2^{\overset{\text{exp}}{3}} = 8 \Leftrightarrow \log_{\underset{\text{base}}{2}} 8 = \overset{\text{edge}}{3}$$

To solve a basic logarithmic equation (one that has a single logarithm), rewrite the equation in exponential form and solve for the variable. Here are two examples:

Example 1:   If $\log_x 81 = 2$, then $x = ?$
Rewrite: $x^2 = 81$, so $x = 9$

Example 2:   If $\log_2 (x + 1) = 3$, then $x = ?$
Rewrite: $2^3 = x + 1 \rightarrow 8 = x + 1 \rightarrow x = 7$

You could possibly encounter a slightly more involved question that requires knowledge of the following **logarithmic properties**:

$$\log_b(xy) = \log_b x + \log_b y$$

$$\log_b\left(\frac{x}{y}\right) = \log_b x - \log_b y$$

$$\log_b x^y = y \log_b x$$

$$\log_b b = 1$$

These properties are simply the inverses of exponent rules (assuming terms have the same bases). When you multiply with exponents, you add them; when you add with logarithms, you multiply. When you divide with exponents, you subtract them; when you subtract logarithms, you divide. When you raise an exponent to another exponent, you multiply; when you multiply a number times a logarithm, you raise it as an exponent. Finally, any base raised to the first power is itself, so $\log_b b = 1$.

> **✔ Note**
>
> Logarithms are not hard once you're familiar and experienced with them and know the rules. If you're a long way from fully understanding logs, don't worry about them for this test. Logs will probably account for no more than one question. It's not worth spending a lot of time and effort figuring out logs when they appear so infrequently on the test.

Try giving one logarithm question your best effort.

10. If $\log_3(x + 5) = 2$, then $x = ?$

    F.   3

    G.   4

    H.   7

    J.   9

    K.   14

Work through the Kaplan Method for ACT Math step-by-step to answer this question. The following table shows Kaplan's strategic thinking on the left, along with suggested math scratchwork on the right.

Math

Strategic Thinking	Math Scratchwork
Step 1: What is the question?	
You need to find the value of *x*.	
Step 2: What information am I given?	
You're given a basic logarithmic equation.	$\log_3 (x + 5) = 2$
Step 3: What can I do with the information?	
Rewrite the equation in exponential form: The base is 3, and the exponent is 2. Then solve for *x*.	$3^2 = x + 5$ $9 = x + 5$ $4 = x$
Step 4: Am I finished?	
You found the value of *x*, so on to the next question.	Choice (G) is correct.

Did you notice how easy the algebra was in the previous example? Most logarithm questions hinge on rewriting the equation in exponential form. The rest is usually a piece of cake!

Trigonometric Functions and Their Graphs

The ACT may ask you to recognize the graphs of the sine, cosine, and tangent functions, which are presented in the table below. You may also be asked to apply transformations to these graphs.

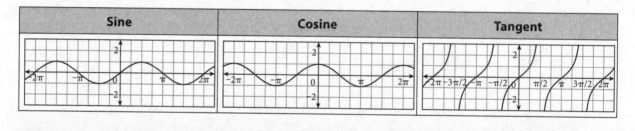

Sine	Cosine	Tangent

✔ **Note**

The tangent function at all positive and negative multiples of $x = \dfrac{\pi}{2}$ is undefined. As a result, the graph of the tangent function has vertical asymptotes at $x = \pm\dfrac{\pi}{2}, \pm\dfrac{3\pi}{2}, \pm\dfrac{5\pi}{2}, \dots$.

The domain of the sine and cosine functions is all real numbers, but notice that their graphs oscillate (bounce back and forth) between $y = -1$ and 1. This means the range of $y = \sin x$ and also $y = \cos x$ is $-1 \le y \le 1$. This is not true for tangent, whose range is all real numbers. In other words, the **maximum** value of a standard sine or cosine function is 1 and the **minimum** value is -1, while the tangent function has no maximum or minimum.

You are also likely to see words such as *amplitude* and *period* in questions about trig functions. The **amplitude** of a wave function (such as sine and cosine) is the vertical distance from the center line (the horizontal at rest line) to the maximum or minimum value. For the standard sine and cosine function, the amplitude is 1. The **period** of the standard sine and cosine function is 2π because their graphs repeat every 2π units. The period of the standard tangent function is π.

How about trying a trig question?

11. What is the amplitude of the function $f(x) = 4\sin(2x + \pi)$?

A. $\dfrac{1}{4}$

B. $\dfrac{1}{2}$

C. 2

D. π

E. 4

Work through the Kaplan Method for ACT Math step-by-step to answer this question. The following table shows Kaplan's strategic thinking on the left, along with suggested math scratchwork on the right.

Strategic Thinking	Math Scratchwork
Step 1: What is the question?	
You need to find the amplitude of the given function.	
Step 2: What information am I given?	
You are given a trigonometric function that includes several transformations.	$f(x) = 4\sin(2x + \pi)$
Step 3: What can I do with the information?	
First, recall what the amplitude of the standard sine function is. What is the distance from the center line to the highest point?	$y = \sin x \rightarrow$ amplitude = 1
Next, think about transformation rules. Which one(s) could affect the amplitude?	$(2x + \pi) \rightarrow$ inside parentheses with the x so changes are horizontal $4 \rightarrow$ multiplies all y-values by 4, so new amplitude = 4(1) = 4
Step 4: Am I finished?	
You found the amplitude of the transformed function, so you're done.	Choice (E) is correct.

Math

Math

> ✔ **Note**
>
> The amplitude of a sine (or cosine) function of the form $f(x) = A \sin(bx \pm c) \pm d$ is $|A|$. Although the $\pm d$ is a vertical change, it only shifts the graph up or down. It does not change the "height" of the waves.

Reciprocal Trig Functions and Trig Identities

There are three reciprocal trig functions, secant (sec), cosecant (csc), and cotangent (cot). Their values are the reciprocals of the sine, cosine, and tangent functions, as shown below:

$$\csc x = \frac{1}{\sin x}$$

$$\sec x = \frac{1}{\cos x}$$

$$\cot x = \frac{1}{\tan x}$$

To find the value of one of these functions, you can simply flip the relationships given by SOHCAHTOA (which are covered in the Geometry chapter):

$$\csc x = \frac{\text{hypotenuse}}{\text{opposite}}$$

$$\sec x = \frac{\text{hypotenuse}}{\text{adjacent}}$$

$$\cot x = \frac{\text{adjacent}}{\text{opposite}}$$

In addition to these definitions, there are just a few more trig relationships that you'll need to know. (There are actually a *lot* more trig relationships, but if a question on the ACT involves one of the less common identities, it will be provided within the question stem.) Here are the three **most common identities**:

Complementary angles have a special relationship relative to sine and cosine.

- $\sin x = \cos\left(\dfrac{\pi}{2} - x\right)$ or $\sin x = \cos(90° - x)$

- $\cos x = \sin\left(\dfrac{\pi}{2} - x\right)$ or $\cos x = \sin(90° - x)$

In plain English, this translates as: The sine of an acute angle is equal to the cosine of the angle's complement, and vice versa. For example, $\cos 30° = \sin 60°$, $\cos 45° = \sin 45°$, and $\cos 60° = \sin 30°$. Understanding how trig functions of complementary angles work can help you learn the unit circle and answer trig questions on Test Day.

Two other particularly useful relationships are that $\tan x = \dfrac{\sin x}{\cos x}$ and the **Pythagorean identity**: $\sin^2 x + \cos^2 x = 1$. (Notice that it resembles the Pythagorean theorem.)

> ✔ **Note**
>
> A note about notation: $\sin^2 x$ is the same as $(\sin x)^2$. It is *not* the same as $\sin x^2$, where only the x is squared.

Math

The Unit Circle

The **unit circle** is a circle with a radius of 1 centered at the origin. Below is such a circle that contains an example triangle.

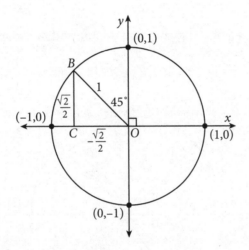

Suppose you were asked to determine sin 135° and cos 135°. Draw a radius at 135° (which is 45° past the *y*-axis in the second quadrant) and then add a vertical line from where the radius intersects the circle down to the *x*-axis. Because this radius, $\overline{OB}$, is within the unit circle, its length is 1. Triangle *OBC* is a 45°-45°-90° triangle, so each of its legs has a length of $\dfrac{\sqrt{2}}{2}$. This means sin 135° is $\dfrac{\frac{\sqrt{2}}{2}}{1} = \dfrac{\sqrt{2}}{2}$. Note that because $\overline{OC}$ lies on the negative part of the *x*-axis, you should use $-\dfrac{\sqrt{2}}{2}$ as the "measure" of the adjacent side. Therefore, $\cos 135° = \dfrac{-\frac{\sqrt{2}}{2}}{1} = -\dfrac{\sqrt{2}}{2}$. Notice that if you were to label point *B* on the unit circle, its (*x,y*) coordinates would correspond to (cos 135°, sin 135°).

Radians

Most geometry questions present angle measures in degrees. In trigonometry, however, you will encounter a different unit: the radian. As you saw earlier in this chapter, when trigonometric functions are graphed, the horizontal axis is almost always measured in radians. Don't let the prospect of learning a new measure scare you, though; just remember that $180° = \pi$ radians. For instance, if you're asked to convert 90° into radians, use this relationship as a conversion factor with the factor-label method: $90° \times \dfrac{\pi \text{ radians}}{180°} = \dfrac{\pi}{2}$ radians (notice that 180° is in the denominator, so the degrees will cancel). This conversion works in the opposite direction as well: To convert radians to degrees, multiply by $\dfrac{180°}{\pi \text{ radians}}$. (Typically, angles given in radians are written without units, so you're more likely to see $\dfrac{\pi}{2}$ than $\dfrac{\pi}{2}$ radians.)

> ✔ **Note**
>
> Most graphing calculators have both degree and radian modes. Make sure you're in the correct mode when using a calculator to answer trig questions!

Here is a handy unit circle diagram with common degree and radian measures.

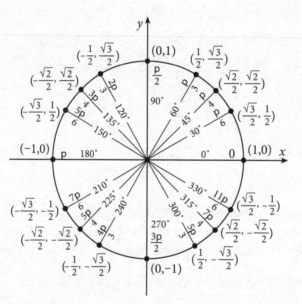

To find the trig values for angles that measure greater than 2π (greater than 360°), you can repeatedly subtract 2π (or 360°) until the angle measure is between 0 and 2π (because 2π is one full circle). These are called **coterminal angles**. Similarly, to find the trig values for angles that measure less than 0π (less than 0°), you can repeatedly add 2π (or 360°) until the angle measures are between 0 and 2π.

> ✔ **Expert Tip**
>
> Knowing the trig values for the most commonly tested "benchmark" angles (multiples of 30° and 45°) will save time on Test Day.

Let's wrap up this chapter with one final trig question.

12. If $x = -\cos(11\pi)$, what is the value of x?

    F. -1

    G. $-\dfrac{\sqrt{3}}{2}$

    H. 0

    J. $\dfrac{\sqrt{3}}{2}$

    K. 1

Work through the Kaplan Method for ACT Math step-by-step to answer this question. The following table shows Kaplan's strategic thinking on the left, along with suggested math scratchwork on the right.

Strategic Thinking	Math Scratchwork
Step 1: What is the question? You need to find the value of x.	
Step 2: What information am I given? You're given a trigonometric expression for x.	$-\cos(11\pi)$
Step 3: What can I do with the information? The angle measure, 11π, is greater than 2π, so subtract 2π as many times as necessary to get the angle measure between 0 and 2π. Now use your unit circle expertise. Don't forget to multiply by -1.	$11\pi - 5(2\pi) = 11\pi - 10\pi = \pi$ $-\cos(11\pi) = -\cos(\pi)$ $\cos(\pi) = -1$, so $-\cos(\pi) = -(-1) = 1$
Step 4: Am I finished? Congratulations, you found the value of x.	*Choice (K) is the correct answer.*

✔ **Note**

You could also use your calculator to answer this question. Just make sure it is set to radian mode.

Now you'll have a chance to try a few test-like questions in a scaffolded way. We've provided some guidance, but you'll need to fill in the missing parts of the explanation or the step-by-step math to get to the correct answer. Don't worry—after going through the worked examples at the beginning of this section, these questions should be completely doable.

13. A company uses the function $P(x) = 150x - x^2$ to determine how much profit the company will make when it sells 150 units of a certain product that sells for x dollars per unit. How much more profit per unit will the company make if it charges $25 for the product than if it charges $20?

   A. $ 3.50

   B. $ 35

   C. $ 52.50

   D. $350

   E. $525

Use the following scaffolding as your map through the question. If you aren't sure where to start, fill in the blanks in the table as you work from top to bottom.

Strategic Thinking	Math Scratchwork
Step 1: What is the question? You need to find how much more profit per unit the company makes at $25 per unit instead of $20 per unit.	
Step 2: What information am I given? You're given a function that represents the profit when the company sells 150 units. You're also given two price points to compare.	$P(x) = 150x - x^2$ first price: $x = \$$ _____ second price: $x = \$$ _____
Step 3: What can I do with the information? Evaluate the profit function at $25. Don't forget to follow the correct order of operations. Evaluate the profit function at $20. Find the difference in the profit amounts.	$P(25) = 150($ _____ $) - ($ _____ $)^2$ $= \$$ _____ $P(20) = 150($ _____ $) - ($ _____ $)^2$ $= \$$ _____ $\$$ _____ $- \$$ _____ $= \$$ _____
Step 4: Am I finished? You're not done yet! The question asks how much more profit *per unit* the company makes, so divide by the number of units.	$\$$ _____ $\div$ _____ $= \$$ _____ Choice _____ is correct.

14. For the piecewise function $f(x)$ defined below, what is the value of $f(-3)$?

$$f(x) = \begin{cases} x^2 + 1, & \text{if } x \le 0 \\ \dfrac{2x}{3} - 1, & \text{if } 0 < x \le 3 \\ 4 - x, & \text{if } x > 3 \end{cases}$$

F. −3

G. 7

H. 10

J. −3 and 7

K. −3, 7, and 10

Use the following scaffolding as your map through the question. If you aren't sure where to start, fill in the blanks in the table as you work from top to bottom.

Strategic Thinking	Math Scratchwork
Step 1: What is the question? You need to find the value of $f(-3)$.	
Step 2: What information am I given? You're given a function defined in three pieces.	
Step 3: What can I do with the information? First, you need to decide which piece of the domain the input value fits within. Compare −3 to each description of x-values (after the "if" in each statement). All that's left to do is plug −3 into the piece you selected.	−3 is < _____ so use the: Circle one: top / middle / bottom function. $f(-3) =$ _____ = _____
Step 4: Am I finished? Is your answer 10? Super!	Choice _____ is correct.

Math

15. The graph of a function $h(x)$ is found by translating the graph of the function $g(x)$ up 4 units and left 3 units. If $g(x) = (x - 1)^2$, then $h(x) = ?$

   A. x^2

   B. $(x - 3)^2 + 4$

   C. $(x + 2)^2 + 4$

   D. $(x + 3)^2 + 4$

   E. $(x + 4)^2 - 3$

Use the following scaffolding as your map through the question. If you aren't sure where to start, fill in the blanks in the table as you work from top to bottom.

Strategic Thinking	Math Scratchwork
Step 1: What is the question? You're asked to find the expression that represents $h(x)$.	
Step 2: What information am I given? You're given an original function and two translations.	original function: _____ shift up _____ units shift left _____ units
Step 3: What can I do with the information? Work with one translation at a time. How does the vertical translation affect the original function? Now the horizontal translation—don't forget that horizontal shifts are opposite of what they look like. Finally, simplify the quantity inside the parentheses.	up 4 units → $(x - 1)^2$ _____ _____ left 3 units → $(x - 1$ _____ _____$)^2 + 4$ $h(x) =$ _____
Step 4: Am I finished? Does your final function look like this: $h(x) = (x + 2)^2 + 4$? If so, you're spot on!	Choice _____ is correct.

16. If $\log_2 M = a$ and $\log_2 N = b$, then $\log_2 (MN)^3 = ?$

   F. $3(a + b)$

   G. $a + b$

   H. $9ab$

   J. $3ab$

   K. ab

Use the following scaffolding as your map through the question. If you aren't sure where to start, fill in the blanks in the table as you work from top to bottom.

Strategic Thinking	Math Scratchwork
Step 1: What is the question? You need to find the expression that represents the value of $\log_2 (MN)^3$.	
Step 2: What information am I given? You are given "values" for the individual logarithms. (You'll need these later.)	$\log_2 M = $ _____ $\log_2 N = $ _____
Step 3: What can I do with the information? The given expression involves two different operations: It has an exponent and a product. You need to rewrite it so that it only involves $\log_2 M$ and $\log_2 N$. Jot down the two properties of logs that you'll need. Apply the two rules to the given expression. Finally, substitute the values given for the individual logarithms and look for a match among the answer choices.	exponent rule: $\log_b x^y = $ _____ product rule: $\log_b (xy) = $ _____ $\log_2 (MN)^3 = $ ___ (_____ + _____) $= $ ___ (___ + ___)
Step 4: Am I finished? Hopefully, you got $3(a + b)$. Did you?	*Choice* _____ *is correct.*

17. Four numbers are in a sequence with 8 as its first term and 36 as its last term. The first three numbers form an arithmetic sequence with a common difference of −7. The last three numbers form a geometric sequence. What is the common ratio of the last three terms of the sequence?

A. −10

B. −6

C. 0

D. 10

E. 32

Use the following scaffolding as your map through the question. If you aren't sure where to start, fill in the blanks in the table as you work from top to bottom.

Strategic Thinking	Math Scratchwork
Step 1: What is the question? You need to find the common ratio of the last three terms.	
Step 2: What information am I given? You know the first term and the last term and the number of terms in all. You're also told that the first three terms form an arithmetic sequence and you know what the common difference is.	first term = _____ ; last term = _____ number of terms = _____ common difference = _____
Step 3: What can I do with the information? Set up the sequence using blanks in place of the numbers you don't know. Use the given common difference to find the second and third terms. To find the common ratio (for the last three terms only), divide the fourth term by the third term.	8, _____ , _____ , 36 second term: 8 + (_____) = _____ third term: _____ + (_____) = _____ 36 ÷ _____ = _____ The common ratio is _____ .
Step 4: Am I finished? Did you get −6? Awesome!	Choice _____ is correct.

18. The graph below shows $f(x) = \cos x$. What is the value of $\cos 90° + \cos 180°$?

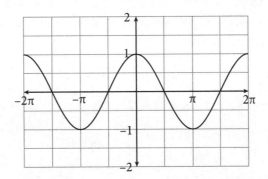

    F.   −2

    G.   −1

    H.   0

    J.   1

    K.   2

Use the following scaffolding as your map through the question. If you aren't sure where to start, fill in the blanks in the table as you work from top to bottom.

Strategic Thinking	Math Scratchwork
Step 1: What is the question? You need to find the value of $\cos 90° + \cos 180°$.	
Step 2: What information am I given? You're given the graph of $f(x) = \cos x$.	
Step 3: What can I do with the information? The values along the horizontal axis (the angle measures) are given in radians, but the angle measures in the question are given in degrees, so convert the degrees to radians to match the graph. Next, evaluate each of angles. Finally, add the two values.	$90° = 90° \times \dfrac{\square}{\square} = \underline{\hspace{1cm}}$ $180° = 180° \times \dfrac{\square}{\square} = \underline{\hspace{1cm}}$ $\cos \underline{\hspace{1cm}} = \underline{\hspace{1cm}}$ $\cos \underline{\hspace{1cm}} = \underline{\hspace{1cm}}$ $\underline{\hspace{1cm}} + \underline{\hspace{1cm}} = \underline{\hspace{1cm}}$
Step 4: Am I finished? Did you get −1? Good work!	*Choice* _____ *is correct.*

Math

Now that you've seen the variety of ways in which the ACT can test you on Functions, try the following questions to check your understanding. Give yourself 4 minutes to answer these 4 questions. Make sure you use the Kaplan Method for ACT Math as often as you can. Remember, you want to emphasize speed and efficiency in addition to simply getting the correct answer.

19. For the function $g(x) = 3x^2 - 5x - 7$, what is the value of $g(-2)$?

   A. −29

   B. −9

   C. −5

   D. 15

   E. 39

20. The graph of a quadratic function $f(x)$ is shown here. Which of the following represents the domain and range of the function?

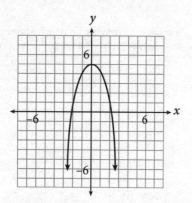

   F. Domain: $f(x) \geq 5$; Range: all real numbers

   G. Domain: $f(x) \leq 5$; Range: all real numbers

   H. Domain: all real numbers; Range: $f(x) \geq 5$

   J. Domain: all real numbers; Range: $f(x) \leq 5$

   K. Domain: all real numbers; Range: all real numbers

21. If $\log_7 7^{\frac{3}{2}} = x$, then x is between which of the following pairs of consecutive integers?

   A. 1 and 2

   B. 3 and 4

   C. 5 and 6

   D. 7 and 8

   E. 18 and 19

22. On her first day of ACT prep, Winnie answered 12 math questions. Her goal was to answer 2 more math questions on each successive day than she answered the day before. If Winnie met but did not exceed her goal, how many math questions had she answered in all after prepping for exactly 30 days?

   F. 360

   G. 420

   H. 1,050

   J. 1,230

   K. 1,590

Answers and Explanations are provided at the end of the book.

ON YOUR OWN

The following questions provide an opportunity to practice the concepts and strategic thinking covered in this chapter.

1. If $f(x) = 3\sqrt{x^2 + 3x + 4}$, what is the value of $f(4)$?

   A. 4

   B. $3\sqrt{2}$

   C. $4\sqrt{2}$

   D. 12

   E. $12\sqrt{2}$

2. Doctors use the function shown below to calculate the concentration, in parts per million, of a certain drug in a patient's bloodstream after t hours. How many more parts per million of the drug are in the bloodstream after 20 hours than after 10 hours?

$$c(t) = -0.05t^2 + 2t + 2$$

   F. 5

   G. 7

   H. 12

   J. 17

   K. 22

3. If $f(x) = -4x + 1$ and $g(x) = \sqrt{x} + 2.5$, what is the value of $f\left(g\left(\dfrac{1}{4}\right)\right)$?

   A. −11

   B. −2

   C. 0

   D. 2.5

   E. 3

4. If $f(x) = x^2 + 1$ and $g(x) = 3x + 1$, which of the following expressions represents $f(g(x))$?

   F. $3x^2 + 2$

   G. $3x^2 + 4$

   H. $9x^2 + 2$

   J. $9x^2 + 3x + 4$

   K. $9x^2 + 6x + 2$

   > Use the following information to answer questions 5–6.

   The graph that follows shows $h(x)$, which represents a portion of a polynomial function.

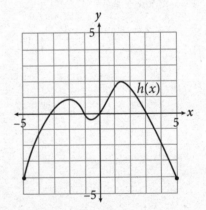

5. What is the range of $h(x)$?

   A. All real numbers

   B. All real numbers greater than or equal to −5

   C. All real numbers greater than or equal to −4

   D. All real numbers between and including −5 and 5

   E. All real numbers between and including −4 and 2

6. Given that $-5 \leq x \leq 5$, for how many values of x does $h(x) = 0$?

   F. 0

   G. 1

   H. 2

   J. 3

   K. 4

   _____

7. For what value(s) of x does the function

   $R(x) = \dfrac{3x}{x^2 - 16}$ have a vertical asymptote?

   A. $x = 0$

   B. $x = 0$ and $x = 3$

   C. $x = 4$

   D. $x = -4$ and $x = 4$

   E. $x = -4, x = 0,$ and $x = 4$

8. Which of the following piecewise functions could have been used to generate the graph below?

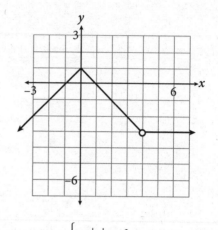

   F. $g(x) = \begin{cases} -|x|, & \text{if } x \leq 4 \\ -3, & \text{if } x > 4 \end{cases}$

   G. $g(x) = \begin{cases} -|x|, & \text{if } x < 4 \\ x - 3, & \text{if } x > 4 \end{cases}$

   H. $g(x) = \begin{cases} -|x| + 1, & \text{if } x < 4 \\ -3x, & \text{if } x > 4 \end{cases}$

   J. $g(x) = \begin{cases} -|x| + 1, & \text{if } x < 4 \\ -3, & \text{if } x > 4 \end{cases}$

   K. $g(x) = \begin{cases} -|x + 3| - 1, & \text{if } x < 4 \\ -3, & \text{if } x > 4 \end{cases}$

9. If a function is given by the rule $a \downarrow b = \sqrt[b]{a}$, then $64 \downarrow 3 = ?$

   A. 4

   B. 8

   C. $8\sqrt{3}$

   D. 16

   E. $21.\overline{3}$

10. If $\log_5 (25x) = 2$, then $x = ?$

    F.   0

    G.   1

    H.   2

    J.   5

    K.   625

11. What three numbers should be placed in the blanks below so that the difference between consecutive numbers is the same?

    12, ___ , ___ , ___ , 32

    A.   16, 22, 28

    B.   17, 22, 27

    C.   20, 22, 30

    D.   22, 24, 30

    E.   23, 29, 31

12. If the first and second terms of a geometric sequence are 3 and 12, what is the expression for the value of the 24th term of the sequence?

    F. $a_{24} = 3^4 \times 12$

    G. $a_{24} = 3^4 \times 23$

    H. $a_{24} = 4^3 \times 12$

    J. $a_{24} = 4^{23} \times 3$

    K. $a_{24} = 4^{24} \times 3$

13. What is the amplitude of the function $f(x) = 2 \cos(4x - \pi)$?

    A. $\dfrac{1}{4}$

    B. $\dfrac{1}{2}$

    C.   2

    D.   4

    E.   8

14. If $\cos G = 0.5$, which of the following would also equal 0.5 ?

    F. $1 - \sin G$

    G. $1 - \tan G$

    H. $1 - \dfrac{1}{\sin G}$

    J. $1 - \dfrac{1}{\sec G}$

    K. $1 - \dfrac{1}{\csc G}$

15. Which trigonometric function could be represented by the graph below?

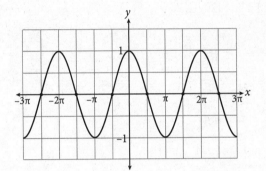

    A. $g(x) = \sin(x - \pi)$

    B. $g(x) = \sin(x + \pi)$

    C. $g(x) = \sin(x + 2\pi)$

    D. $g(x) = \sin\left(x - \dfrac{\pi}{2}\right)$

    E. $g(x) = \sin\left(x + \dfrac{\pi}{2}\right)$

16. If $h(x) = 3x - 1$, what is the value of $h(5) - h(2)$?

    F.   3

    G.   8

    H.   9

    J.   12

    K.   14

17. If $f(x) = x^2 + 3x - 5$, what is the value of $f(x + h)$?

   A. $x^2 + 3x - 5 - h$

   B. $x^2 + 3x - 5 + h$

   C. $x^2 + 3x - 5 + 2h$

   D. $x^2h^2 + 2xh + 3x + 3h - 5$

   E. $x^2 + 2xh + 3x + h^2 + 3h - 5$

18. If $a(x) = \sqrt{x^2 + 7}$ and $b(x) = x^3 - 7$, then what is the value of $\dfrac{a(3)}{b(2)}$?

   F. $\dfrac{\sqrt{11}}{20}$

   G. $\dfrac{1}{4}$

   H. $\sqrt{11}$

   J. 4

   K. $4\sqrt{11}$

19. Several values for the functions $g(x)$ and $h(x)$ are shown in the tables that follow. What is the value of $g(h(3))$?

x	$g(x)$
-6	-3
-3	-2
0	-1
3	0
6	1

x	$h(x)$
0	6
1	-4
2	2
3	0
4	-2

   A. -1

   B. 0

   C. 1

   D. 3

   E. 6

20. The graph below shows two functions, $f(x)$ and $g(x)$. Which of the following statements is true?

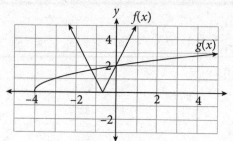

   F. $f(0) = -4$

   G. $g(2) = 0$

   H. $f(x) > g(x)$ for all values of x

   J. $(0,2)$ is a solution for $f(x) = g(x)$

   K. $f(x) = 0$ has exactly two solutions

21. Which of the following correctly describes the range of the function $h(x) = 4x^2 - 9$?

   A. All real numbers

   B. All real numbers greater than $-\dfrac{3}{2}$

   C. All real numbers greater than or equal to -9

   D. All real numbers between $-\dfrac{3}{2}$ and $\dfrac{3}{2}$

   E. All real numbers between and including -9 and 9

22. For the piecewise function $f(x)$ defined below, what is the value of $f(6)$?

$$f(x) = \begin{cases} x^2 + 5, & \text{if } x \leq 0 \\ 2x - 9, & \text{if } 0 < x \leq 6 \\ 4 + x, & \text{if } x > 6 \end{cases}$$

   F. 3

   G. 10

   H. 41

   J. 3 and 10

   K. 3, 10, and 41

23. Which of the following piecewise functions could have been used to generate the graph below?

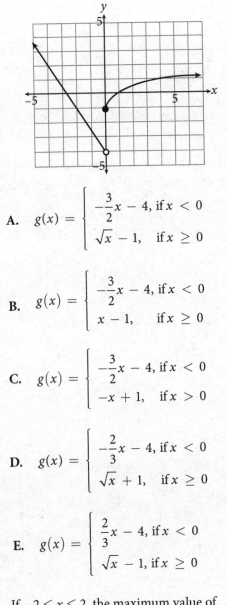

A. $g(x) = \begin{cases} -\dfrac{3}{2}x - 4, & \text{if } x < 0 \\ \sqrt{x} - 1, & \text{if } x \geq 0 \end{cases}$

B. $g(x) = \begin{cases} -\dfrac{3}{2}x - 4, & \text{if } x < 0 \\ x - 1, & \text{if } x \geq 0 \end{cases}$

C. $g(x) = \begin{cases} -\dfrac{3}{2}x - 4, & \text{if } x < 0 \\ -x + 1, & \text{if } x > 0 \end{cases}$

D. $g(x) = \begin{cases} -\dfrac{2}{3}x - 4, & \text{if } x < 0 \\ \sqrt{x} + 1, & \text{if } x \geq 0 \end{cases}$

E. $g(x) = \begin{cases} \dfrac{2}{3}x - 4, & \text{if } x < 0 \\ \sqrt{x} - 1, & \text{if } x \geq 0 \end{cases}$

24. If $-2 \leq x \leq 2$, the maximum value of $f(x) = 1 - x^2$ is which of the following?

F. 2

G. 1

H. 0

J. -1

K. -2

25. The graph below shows Aaron's distance from home over a one-hour period, during which time he first went to the library to return some books, then went to the post office, and then returned home. Based on the graph, which of the following statements could be true?

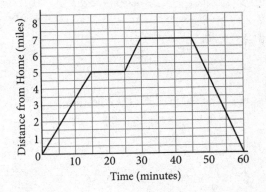

A. The post office is about 5 miles from Aaron's house.

B. Aaron traveled a total of 7 miles from the time he left home until he returned.

C. The post office is 7 miles farther from Aaron's house than the library is.

D. Aaron spent 10 minutes at the library and 15 minutes at the post office.

E. Aaron spent more time at his destinations than he spent traveling to and from his destinations.

26. The factorial function given by $n!$ means the product $n(n - 1)(n - 2) \dots (1)$. What is the value of $\dfrac{6!}{2!3!}$?

F. 1

G. 6

H. 15

J. 30

K. 60

27. What value of x satisfies the equation $\log_2 x = -3$?

    A. -8

    B. $-\dfrac{1}{8}$

    C. $\dfrac{1}{8}$

    D. 8

    E. 9

28. For what value of x is the equation $\log_2 x + \log_2 (8x) = 5$ true?

    F. 2

    G. $\dfrac{32}{9}$

    H. 4

    J. 8

    K. 32

29. If the first four terms of an arithmetic sequence are 25, 21, 17, and 13 respectively, what is the 20th term of the sequence?

    A. -55

    B. -51

    C. -47

    D. -43

    E. -39

30. If the fifth and sixth terms of a geometric sequence are 3 and 1 respectively, what is the first term of the sequence?

    F. 27

    G. -5

    H. $\dfrac{1}{27}$

    J. 11

    K. 243

31. A finite arithmetic sequence has five terms, and the first term is 2. What is the difference between the mean and the median of the five terms?

    A. 0

    B. 1

    C. 2

    D. 4

    E. Cannot be determined from the given information

32. In the figure below, if point P is located on the unit circle, then $x + y$ is approximately equal to which of the following values?

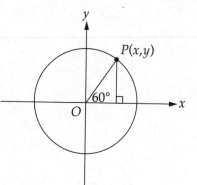

    F. 0.37

    G. 0.50

    H. 0.78

    J. 0.87

    K. 1.37

Math

33. The graph of $g(x) = \cos(3x)$ is shown below. Which of the following lists represents the values of x for which $g(x) = 0$?

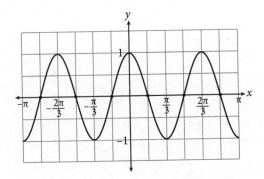

  A. $-180°, -120°, -60°, 60°, 120°, 180°$

  B. $-165°, -105°, -45°, 45°, 105°, 165°$

  C. $-150°, -90°, -30°, 30°, 90°, 150°$

  D. $-120°, -80°, -40°, 40°, 80°, 120°$

  E. $-105°, -90°, -75°, 75°, 90°, 105°$

34. If $x > 0$, $a = x \cos\theta$, and $b = x \sin\theta$, then $\sqrt{a^2 + b^2} = ?$

  F. 1

  G. x

  H. $2x$

  J. $x(\cos\theta + \sin\theta)$

  K. $x \cos\theta \sin\theta$

35. Which of the following is equivalent to
$$\frac{\tan\theta\cos^2\theta + \tan\theta\sin^2\theta}{\sin\theta} \; ?$$

  A. $\cos\theta$

  B. $\sin\theta$

  C. $\csc\theta$

  D. $\sec\theta$

  E. $\tan\theta$

Answers and Explanations are provided at the end of the book.

CHAPTER 13

Geometry

CHAPTER OBJECTIVES

By the end of this chapter, you will be able to:

1. Graph linear equations and inequalities on a coordinate plane and identify key features of the graph (such as intercepts and slope)

2. Use the Midpoint and Distance formulas

3. Answer questions involving parabolas, circles, and ellipses in the coordinate plane

4. Reflect points over an axis or over another line

5. Use the Pythagorean theorem, Pythagorean triplets, and special right triangles to answer questions involving triangles

6. Use relationships among angles, arcs, and distances in a circle

7. Compute the area and perimeter of polygons and composite figures

8. Compute the area and circumference of circles

9. Solve problems using surface area and volume formulas

10. Use scale factors to determine the magnitude of a size change

11. Answer questions involving right triangle trigonometry

SMARTPOINTS

Point Value	SmartPoints Category
5 Points	Geometry

Geometry includes coordinate, plane, and solid geometry, as well as some basic right-triangle trigonometry. Geometry questions make up about 12–15% of the Math test. These questions test your ability to graph equations and inequalities in the coordinate plane and to solve problems related to lines, angles, and figures. Triangles—specifically right triangles—and circles are the two most commonly tested shapes, but you can expect to see a variety of polygons, including complex 2-D and simple 3-D shapes. The test will also ask questions that require knowledge of the Midpoint and Distance formulas and occasionally the graphs of simple shapes such as triangles and circles in the coordinate plane.

COORDINATE GEOMETRY

Of the highly tested SmartPoints areas, coordinate geometry questions have the narrowest scope. Though they can ask about anything and everything related to an (x,y) coordinate plane, they most commonly ask about straight lines. Thus, being adept at working with slope (and slope-intercept form specifically) can allow you to master a good portion of the Geometry category quickly.

Also note that the ACT does not test parabolas extensively. Most questions involving quadratics are best solved using algebra, as opposed to coordinate geometry strategies. Similarly, graphs of circles and triangles are best solved using plane geometry strategies, which will be covered in the second half of this chapter.

Linear Equations and Inequalities in the Coordinate Plane

Two-variable equations have an independent variable (input) and a dependent variable (output). The dependent variable (often y), depends on the independent variable (often x). For example, in the equation $y = 3x + 4$, x is the independent variable; any y-value depends on what you plug in for x. You can construct a table of values for the equation, which can then be plotted in the coordinate plane.

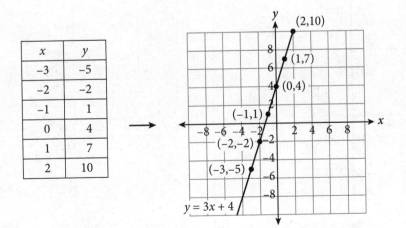

x	y
−3	−5
−2	−2
−1	1
0	4
1	7
2	10

A more efficient approach to graphing lines is to plot the y-intercept and then use the slope to "rise" and "run" to the next point. Let's review some concepts related to lines:

- The **graph** of an equation is the set of all its **solutions**. Each point on the line makes the equation true.

- The **slope** of a line is the ratio of the change in *y*-values over the change in *x*-values (rise over run, or the slant of the line). To find the slope of a line from its graph, identify two points that lie on the line and use the slope formula: $m = \dfrac{y_2 - y_1}{x_2 - x_1}$. You can also count the "rise" and the "run" if the line intersects the grid lines in convenient places.

- A **horizontal line** has a slope of 0, and a **vertical line** has an undefined slope.

- An ***x*-intercept** is a point at which the graph crosses (or intercepts) the *x*-axis. The coordinates of an *x*-intercept take the form (*x*,0). A ***y*-intercept** is a point at which the graph crosses (or intercepts) the *y*-axis. The coordinates of a *y*-intercept take the form (0,*y*).

- To **plot a line** using slope-intercept form, $y = mx + b$, plot the *y*-intercept (*b*) on the *y*-axis and then use the slope (*m*) to find another point. When *m* is written in fraction form, the numerator is the distance up (positive) or down (negative), and the denominator is the distance to the right.

- The solution set for a **linear inequality** is the **half-plane** below (< or ≤) or above (> or ≥) the line. The **boundary** line is a dashed line when it is a strict inequality (< or >) and a solid line when it is ≤ or ≥.

> ✔ **Note**
>
> In a real-world scenario, the **average rate of change** is the same as the slope of the equation that is used to model the scenario.

Take a look at the following examples to review how to graph linear equations and inequalities in the coordinate plane.

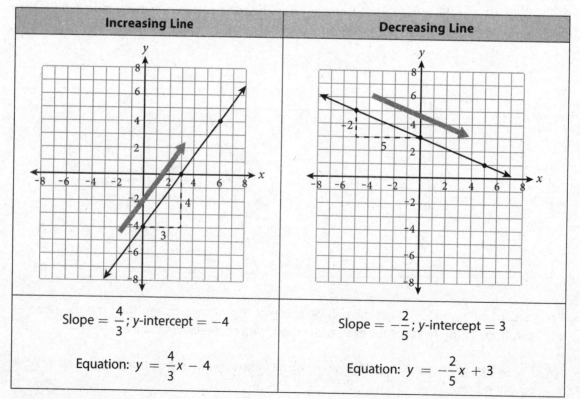

Increasing Line	Decreasing Line
Slope = $\dfrac{4}{3}$; *y*-intercept = −4	Slope = $-\dfrac{2}{5}$; *y*-intercept = 3
Equation: $y = \dfrac{4}{3}x - 4$	Equation: $y = -\dfrac{2}{5}x + 3$

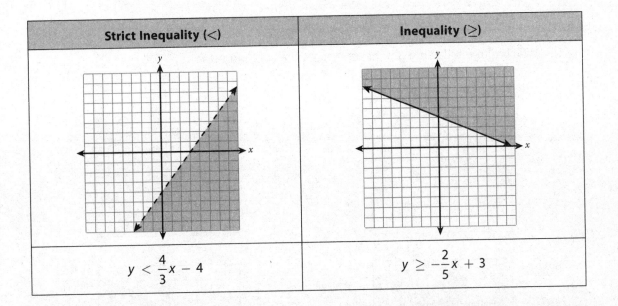

Strict Inequality ($<$)	Inequality ($\geq$)
$y < \dfrac{4}{3}x - 4$	$y \geq -\dfrac{2}{5}x + 3$

✔ **Expert Tip**

If you're not sure which way to shade when graphing an inequality, choose a test point, such as (0,0), and test it in the inequality. If the result is a true statement, then the half plane that contains the test point should be shaded. If the result is a false statement, then the half plane that contains the test point should not be shaded.

Parallel and Perpendicular Lines

Lines that are parallel to each other have the same slope, and lines that are perpendicular to each other have negative-reciprocal slopes.

In the figure below, the two parallel lines both have slope = 2, and the line that's perpendicular to them has slope = $-\dfrac{1}{2}$.

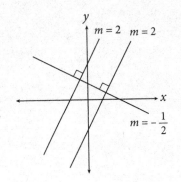

Math

Let's practice before moving on. Take a look at the next question about an inequality.

1.   Which of the following graphs represents the solution set for $5x - 10y > 6$?

A.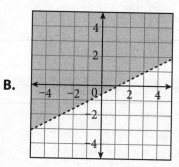

D.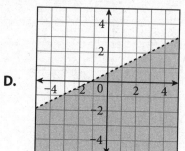

B.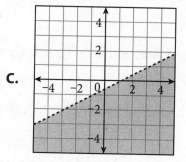

E.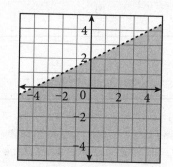

C.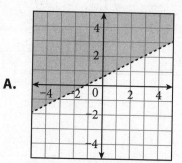

Work through the Kaplan Method for ACT Math step-by-step to answer this question. The following table shows Kaplan's strategic thinking on the left, along with suggested math scratchwork on the right.

Math

Strategic Thinking	Math Scratchwork
Step 1: What is the question? Your goal is to find the graph that matches the given inequality.	
Step 2: What information am I given? You're given a linear inequality written in standard form.	$5x - 10y > 6$
Step 3: What can I do with the information? It's risky to eliminate choices right away because the inequality is not in slope-intercept form. Rearrange the inequality, remembering to flip the inequality symbol in the final step because you're dividing by -10.	$5x - 10y > 6$ $-10y > -5x + 6$ $\dfrac{-10y}{-10} < \dfrac{-5x}{-10} + \dfrac{6}{-10}$ $y < \dfrac{1}{2}x - \dfrac{3}{5}$
The inequality in slope-intercept form indicates a negative y-intercept, so you can eliminate A, D, and E. The "less than" symbol indicates that the shading should be below the dashed line, meaning (C) must be correct.	negative y-intercept, so boundary line crosses y-axis below the origin < symbol, so shade below the boundary line
Alternatively, you can plug a point (such as the origin) into the inequality. When plugged into the inequality, the origin should not be in the solution set.	$0 \not< \dfrac{1}{2}(0) - \dfrac{3}{5} \rightarrow 0 \not< -\dfrac{3}{5}$ Do not shade half-plane containing $(0,0)$.
Step 4: Am I finished? You found the correct graph, so you're all done.	Choice (C) is correct.

Midpoint and Distance

Two formulas that you'll certainly need to know for Test Day are the Midpoint and Distance formulas.

- **Midpoint formula:** The midpoint of a line segment bounded by the points (x_1,y_1) and (x_2,y_2) is $M = \left(\dfrac{x_1 + x_2}{2}, \dfrac{y_1 + y_2}{2} \right)$.

- **Distance formula:** The distance between two points (x_1,y_1) and (x_2,y_2) is $D = \sqrt{(x_2 - x_1)^2 + (y_2 - y_1)^2}$.

Math

For the Midpoint formula, keep in mind that you're forming two new values, a new value for x and a new value for y. You're trying to find the x-value that falls exactly halfway between the two given x's and the y-value that falls halfway between the given y's. Thus, you're simply finding the average of the given x's and the average of the given y's.

The Distance formula is a derivation of the Pythagorean theorem, which we'll discuss in detail later in this chapter. As a quick reminder, the Pythagorean theorem is $a^2 + b^2 = c^2$. For the Distance formula, you are looking for the value of c. To isolate c, take the square root of the other side of the equation. Think of a as the distance along the x-axis (subtracting the second x from the first). Think of b as the distance along the y-axis (subtracting the second y from the first). If you're looking at a diagonal line and have found its distance along the x-axis and distance along the y-axis, you've formed a right triangle, with the line you're looking for as the hypotenuse. Simply square a and b, add them together, and take the square root. And there you have the Distance formula.

Let's give a distance question a try.

2. Point P (−3,5) and point Q (0,1) are points on the (x,y) coordinate plane. What is the distance between points P and Q ?

    F.   4

    G.   5

    H.   6

    J.   7

    K.   8

Work through the Kaplan Method for ACT Math step-by-step to answer this question. The following table shows Kaplan's strategic thinking on the left, along with suggested math scratchwork on the right.

Strategic Thinking	Math Scratchwork
Step 1: What is the question?	
You're asked to find the distance between points P and Q.	
Step 2: What information am I given?	
You are given the coordinates of the two points.	$P(−3,5)$ and $Q(0,1)$

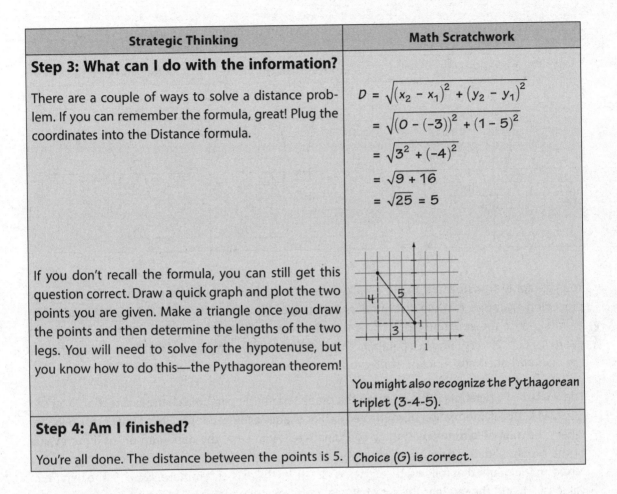

Strategic Thinking	Math Scratchwork
Step 3: What can I do with the information?	
There are a couple of ways to solve a distance problem. If you can remember the formula, great! Plug the coordinates into the Distance formula.	$D = \sqrt{(x_2 - x_1)^2 + (y_2 - y_1)^2}$ $= \sqrt{(0 - (-3))^2 + (1 - 5)^2}$ $= \sqrt{3^2 + (-4)^2}$ $= \sqrt{9 + 16}$ $= \sqrt{25} = 5$
If you don't recall the formula, you can still get this question correct. Draw a quick graph and plot the two points you are given. Make a triangle once you draw the points and then determine the lengths of the two legs. You will need to solve for the hypotenuse, but you know how to do this—the Pythagorean theorem!	You might also recognize the Pythagorean triplet (3-4-5).
Step 4: Am I finished?	
You're all done. The distance between the points is 5.	Choice (G) is correct.

Parabolas, Circles, and Ellipses

The only curved graphs you're likely to encounter on the ACT (other than graphs of functions) are parabolas, circles, and possibly ellipses. Like slope-intercept questions, these questions are essentially algebraic and are often just a matter of recalling and applying the appropriate equation. Let's review.

Parabolas in the Coordinate Plane

A **parabola** is the graph of a quadratic equation, such as $y = x^2$. The graph is a symmetric U-shaped graph that opens either up or down. To determine whether a parabola will open up or down, examine the coefficient of the squared term. If the coefficient is positive, the parabola will open up; if the coefficient is negative, it will open down.

A parabola can have 0, 1, or 2 *x*-intercepts, as shown in the following examples:

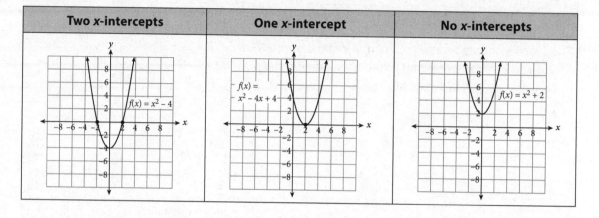

Two *x*-intercepts	One *x*-intercept	No *x*-intercepts

You can apply **transformations** to parabolas just as you can to any other function. Notice in the preceding examples that the first graph is the standard quadratic function $f(x) = x^2$ shifted down 4 units (hence the equation $f(x) = x^2 - 4$). If you were to factor the second equation, you would get $f(x) = (x - 2)^2$, resulting in a parabola that is shifted to the right 2 units. Finally, the third graph is the standard quadratic function shifted up 2 units, which matches its equation of $f(x) = x^2 + 2$.

The **vertex** of a parabola is the point on the graph where the parabola changes direction. You can glean all kinds of information from the vertex. For example, the *x*-coordinate of the vertex tells you where the **axis of symmetry** is; the *y*-coordinate tells you what the minimum or maximum value of the graph is (depending on whether the parabola opens up or down) and, consequently, the range. In the graph that follows, the vertex is $(3, -4)$, so the axis of symmetry is $x = 3$, the minimum value is -4, and the range is the set of all real numbers such that $y \geq -4$.

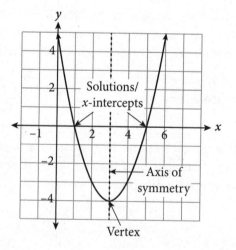

Solutions/
x-intercepts

Axis of symmetry

Vertex

Math

In the preceding graph, notice that the *x*-intercepts, 1 and 5, which are equidistant from the axis of symmetry, are labeled as **solutions**. This means the factored form of the equation looks like $y = a(x - 1)(x - 5)$. To find the value of *a*, you could plug in any other point, such as the vertex, and solve for *a* like this:

$$y = a(x - 1)(x - 5)$$
$$-4 = a(3 - 1)(3 - 5)$$
$$-4 = -4a$$
$$1 = a$$

Thus, the equation of the parabola shown in the graph is $y = (x - 1)(x - 5)$ or $y = x^2 - 6x + 5$.

Circles and Ellipses in the Coordinate Plane

The equation of a **circle** in the coordinate plane is $(x - h)^2 + (y - k)^2 = r^2$, where *r* is the radius of the circle and (h,k) is its center. A circle centered at the origin, $(0,0)$, has equation $x^2 + y^2 = r^2$.

The equation of an **ellipse** is $\dfrac{(x - h)^2}{a^2} + \dfrac{(y - k)^2}{b^2} = 1$, where *a* represents half of the length of the horizontal axis and *b* represents half of the length of the vertical axis. An ellipse looks like an oval (one axis is longer than the other). The longer axis is called the **major axis,** and the shorter axis is called the **minor axis.**

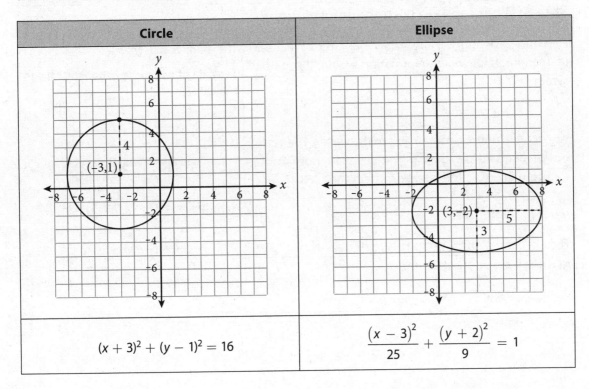

Circle	Ellipse
$(x + 3)^2 + (y - 1)^2 = 16$	$\dfrac{(x - 3)^2}{25} + \dfrac{(y + 2)^2}{9} = 1$

These equations are extremely lightly tested. If you see a question on either, there will only be one.

Take some time now to explore the following question to test your new wealth of knowledge.

3. If the axis of symmetry of the graph given by the equation $y = (x + 3)^2 + 1$ is $x = p$, then what is the value of p?

A. −3

B. −1

C. 1

D. 2

E. 3

Work through the Kaplan Method for ACT Math step-by-step to answer this question. The following table shows Kaplan's strategic thinking on the left, along with suggested math scratchwork on the right.

Strategic Thinking	Math Scratchwork
Step 1: What is the question?	
You need to find the value of p.	
Step 2: What information am I given?	
You're given a quadratic equation, and you're given the equation for the axis of symmetry.	$y = (x + 3)^2 + 1$ axis of symmetry: $x = p$
Step 3: What can I do with the information?	
First, think about the graph. What shape is it? What part of the graph provides information about the axis of symmetry?	The graph is a parabola. The axis of symmetry passes through the vertex.
You need to find the coordinates of the vertex. The vertex of the standard parabola, $y = x^2$, is (0,0). How do the transformations to the equation affect the vertex?	$(x + 3)$ translates vertex left 3 + 1 on the end translates vertex up 1 New vertex = $(0 - 3, 0 + 1) = (-3,1)$
The x-coordinate of the vertex tells you the axis of symmetry.	axis of symmetry: $x = -3$, so $p = -3$
Step 4: Am I finished?	
You found that $p = -3$, so your work is done.	Choice (A) is correct.

Reflecting Points Over an Axis or Over Another Line

You've seen translations in action several times (in this chapter and the Functions chapter). Now let's take a closer look at reflections.

There are lots of rules to describe how the coordinates of a point change when the point is **reflected over a line**. However, there is no need to memorize these rules. The best way to answer a question about reflections is to visualize the situation (or draw a quick sketch). Two general rules to remember are these:

- If a point is reflected **over an axis**, or over any other horizontal or vertical line, then only one coordinate of the point changes.

- If a point is reflected **over the line $y = x$**, then both coordinates change (unless the point happens to lie on the line $y = x$).

Take a look at these reflections applied to the point (3,2):

Over the *axes*	Over other lines	Over the line $y = x$

✔ **Expert Tip**

When a point is reflected over the line $y = x$, the coordinates simply change places: The x-coordinate becomes the y-coordinate, and the y-coordinate becomes the x-coordinate.

Math

Let's take a moment to reflect on reflections:

4. If the reflection of point P (6,2) is P' (6,8), over which line was point P reflected?

F. x-axis

G. y-axis

H. $y = x$

J. $y = 5$

K. $x = 5$

Work through the Kaplan Method for ACT Math step-by-step to answer this question. The following table shows Kaplan's strategic thinking on the left, along with suggested math scratchwork on the right.

Strategic Thinking	Math Scratchwork
Step 1: What is the question?	
You need to determine over which line point P was reflected to get point P'.	
Step 2: What information am I given?	
You are given the coordinates of both points.	P (6,2) → P' (6,8)
Step 3: What can I do with the information?	
Process of elimination is the best approach. You don't have to draw each reflection—just try to picture it in your head. Try the axes first.	x-axis: flips down 2 units below axis, x-value stays the same = (6,–2) ✗ y-axis: flips across 6 units to the left of the axis, y-value stays the same = (–6,2) ✗
Reflection over the line $y = x$ is easy to eliminate: The coordinates of the point don't change places.	over $y = x$ would be (2,6) ✗
Next up is the line $y = 5$. Picture the line: It's a horizontal line 5 units above the x-axis.	$y = 5$: P is 3 units below the line, so it flips 3 units above the line. On the line would be (6,5), so P' = (6,5 + 3) = (6,8). ✔
Step 4: Am I finished?	
There is no need to check K. You've found the correct line.	Choice (J) is correct.

PLANE AND SOLID GEOMETRY

We'll turn our attention to plane and solid geometry for the rest of this chapter. You saw a bit of plane geometry in the Essential Skills chapter, but now it's time to dig a little deeper.

To solve complex plane geometry questions, keep these two important steps in mind:

1) Find familiar shapes.

2) Transfer information within those shapes.

We'll work on each of those steps individually, discussing each shape you'll need to know in turn and how to use your knowledge of those shapes to find information and transfer them throughout.

Then, we'll combine those steps to see how these fundamental pieces of knowledge can help you solve even the most complicated plane geometry question.

Two-Dimensional Shapes

Perimeter and area are basic properties that all two-dimensional shapes have. The **perimeter** of a polygon can easily be calculated by adding the lengths of all its sides. **Area** is the amount of two-dimensional space a shape occupies. The most common shapes for which you'll need these two properties on Test Day are triangles, parallelograms, and circles.

- The area (A) of a **triangle** is given by $A = \frac{1}{2}bh$, where b is the base of the triangle and h is its height. The base and height are always perpendicular. Any side of a triangle can be used as the base; just make sure you use its corresponding height (the longest perpendicular line you can draw within the triangle). You can use a right triangle's two legs as the base and height, but in non-right triangles, if the height is not given, you'll need to draw it in (from the vertex of the angle opposite the base down to the base itself at a right angle) and compute it.

- **Parallelograms** are quadrilaterals with two pairs of parallel sides. Rectangles and squares are subsets of parallelograms. You can find the area of a parallelogram using $A = bh$. As with triangles, you can use any side of a parallelogram as the base; in addition, the height is still perpendicular to the base. Use the side perpendicular to the base as the height for a rectangle or square; for any other parallelogram, the height (or enough information to find it) will be given.

- A **trapezoid** is a quadrilateral with only one set of parallel sides. Those parallel sides form the two bases. To find the area, average those bases and multiply by the height.

- A **circle's** perimeter is known as its circumference (C) and is found using $C = 2\pi r$, where r is the radius (distance from the center of the circle to its edge). Area is given by $A = \pi r^2$. The strange symbol is the lowercase Greek letter pi (π, pronounced "pie"), which is approximately 3.14.

We'll cover these shapes in more detail as we move through the chapter, but first, let's review some important vocabulary.

Symmetry, Congruence, and Similarity

A shape is said to have **symmetry** when it can be split by a line (called an *axis of symmetry*) into two identical parts. Consider folding a shape along a line: If all sides and vertices align once the shape is folded in half, the shape is symmetrical about that line. Some shapes have no axis of symmetry, some have one, some have multiple axes, and still others can have an infinite number of axes of symmetry (e.g., a circle).

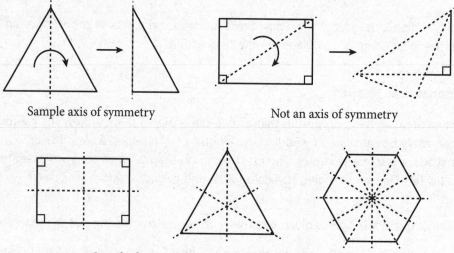

Sample axis of symmetry   Not an axis of symmetry

Sample shapes with corresponding axes of symmetry

Congruence simply means identical. Angles, lines, and shapes can be congruent. Congruence is indicated by using tick marks: Everything with the same number of tick marks is congruent.

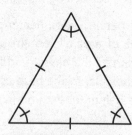

Equilateral triangle:
3 congruent sides,
3 congruent angles

Isosceles triangle:
2 congruent sides,
2 congruent angles

Similarity between shapes indicates that they have identical angles and proportional sides. Think of taking a shape and stretching or shrinking each side by the same ratio. The resulting shape will have the same angles as the original. While the sides will not be identical, they will be proportional.

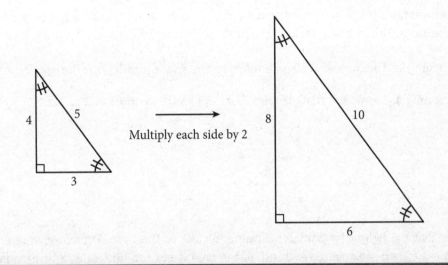

Multiply each side by 2

> ✔ **Note**
>
> Be sure to review these terms and concepts before Test Day, because solving at least a few of the Geometry questions on the ACT will involve them (directly or indirectly).

Triangles, Triangles, and More Triangles

Most plane geometry questions are about closed figures: polygons and circles. And the test maker's favorite closed figure by far is the three-sided polygon, that is, the triangle. All three-sided polygons are interesting because they share so many characteristics, and certain special three-sided polygons—equilateral, isosceles, and right triangles—are interesting because of their special characteristics.

Let's look at some facts about triangles and some useful theorems.

A **triangle** is a closed figure with three angles and three straight sides. The sum of the measures of the angles in a triangle is 180°.

Triangle Inequality Theorem: The length of any side of a triangle is less than the sum of the lengths of the other two sides and greater than their positive difference.

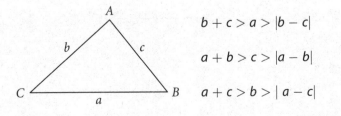

$$b + c > a > |b - c|$$

$$a + b > c > |a - b|$$

$$a + c > b > |a - c|$$

For example, if two sides of a triangle are 8 and 5, the third side has to be greater than the difference, 3, and less than the sum, 13. The third side must fall between those two values in order to form a triangle.

Angle relationships: If the lengths of two sides of a triangle are unequal, the greater angle lies opposite the longer side and vice versa. In the previous figure, if $m\angle A > m\angle B > m\angle C$, then $a > b > c$.

Area of a triangle: The area of a triangle refers to the space it takes up. The area of a triangle is $\frac{1}{2} \times$ base $\times$ height. Consider a triangle with a base of length 4 and an altitude of 3:

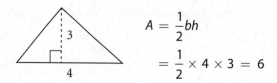

$$A = \frac{1}{2}bh$$
$$= \frac{1}{2} \times 4 \times 3 = 6$$

Remember that the height (or altitude) is perpendicular to the base. Therefore, when two sides of a triangle are perpendicular to each other, the area is easy to find. In a right triangle, we call the two sides that form the 90° angle the legs. Then the area is one-half the product of the legs.

In the triangle shown next, you could treat the hypotenuse as the base, because that's how the figure is drawn. If you did this, you would need to know the distance from the hypotenuse to the opposite vertex in order to determine the area of the triangle. A more straightforward method is to notice that this is a right triangle with legs of lengths 6 and 8, which allows us to use the legs as the base and the height:

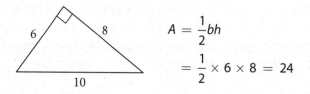

$$A = \frac{1}{2}bh$$
$$= \frac{1}{2} \times 6 \times 8 = 24$$

Perimeter of a triangle: The perimeter of a triangle is the distance around the triangle. In other words, the perimeter is equal to the sum of the lengths of the sides.

In the following triangle, the sides have lengths 5, 6, and 8. Therefore, the perimeter is $5 + 6 + 8$, or 19.

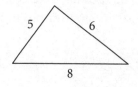

There are three **basic types of triangles**: isosceles, equilateral, and scalene. You will not be tested directly on these types—that is, asked to identify which triangle is which type—but knowing the rules of all three will help you find relevant information quickly. Note that unless you can determine (either because of information provided in the question stem or as you solve for the sides and angles) lengths, angles, or relationships, you cannot tell from the drawing what kind of triangle you are looking at. Figures are not necessarily drawn to scale.

An **isosceles triangle** is a triangle that has at least two sides of equal length. The two equal sides are called the legs, and the third side is called the base. Because the two legs have the same length, the two angles opposite the legs must have the same measure. In the figure shown here, $\overline{PQ} = \overline{PR}$ and $m\angle R = m\angle Q$.

An **equilateral triangle** is a triangle that has three equal sides. Because all the sides are equal, all the angles are also equal. All three angles in an equilateral triangle measure 60°, regardless of the lengths of the sides. All equilateral triangles are also isosceles, but not all isosceles triangles are equilateral.

A **scalene triangle** has three sides all of different lengths and three angles all of different measures. The rules to remember are that the angles will still add up to 180°, the largest angle will be opposite the longest side, and the smallest angle will be opposite the shortest side.

Triangles are **similar** if they have the same shape (that is, corresponding angles with the same measure). For instance, any two triangles whose angles measure 30°, 60°, and 90° are similar, regardless of side length. While the lengths are different, corresponding sides are in the same ratio. The **ratio of the perimeters** of similar triangles is the same as the ratio of the side lengths.

Example: What is the perimeter of $\triangle DEF$?

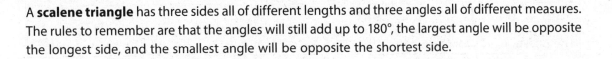

Each triangle has an $x°$ angle, a $y°$ angle, and a $z°$ angle, so they are similar, and corresponding sides are in the same ratio. $\overline{BC}$ and $\overline{EF}$ are corresponding sides—each is opposite the $x°$ angle. Because $\overline{EF}$ is twice the length of $\overline{BC}$, each side of $\triangle DEF$ will be twice the length of its corresponding side in $\triangle ABC$, and thus the perimeter of $\triangle DEF$ will be twice the perimeter of $\triangle ABC$. This means the perimeter is $2(2 + 3 + 4) = 2(9) = 18$.

The **ratio of the areas** of two similar triangles is the square of the ratio of their corresponding lengths. In the previous example, because each side of $\triangle DEF$ is twice the length of its corresponding side in $\triangle ABC$, the area of $\triangle DEF$ must be $2^2 = 4$ times the area of $\triangle ABC$.

Try your hand at these typical ACT problems that test your knowledge of triangle basics. Then we'll move on to right triangles.

5. In isosceles triangle ABC, $\overline{AB}$ and $\overline{BC}$ are congruent. If $m\angle CAB = 27°$, what is the measure of $\angle ABC$?

    A.   27°

    B.   54°

    C.   90°

    D.   126°

    E.   153°

Work through the Kaplan Method for ACT Math step-by-step to answer this question. The following table shows Kaplan's strategic thinking on the left, along with suggested math scratchwork on the right.

Strategic Thinking	Math Scratchwork
Step 1: What is the question? The question asks for the measure of $\angle ABC$.	
Step 2: What information am I given? You know that $\overline{AB}$ and $\overline{BC}$ are congruent lines of $\triangle ABC$ and that $m\angle CAB = 27°$.	
Step 3: What can I do with the information? Sketch out $\triangle ABC$. Because $\overline{AB}$ and $\overline{BC}$ are congruent, $m\angle BCA$ must also equal 27°.	
The sum of the measures of the interior angles of a triangle is 180°; therefore, subtract 2(27°) from 180°.	$m\angle ABC = 180° - 54° = 126°$
Step 4: Am I finished? You found the measure of $\angle ABC$, so your work is done.	Choice (D) is correct.

6. In the figure shown here, △ABC is similar to △DEF. ∠A corresponds to ∠D, ∠B corresponds to ∠E, and ∠C corresponds to ∠F. If the given lengths are of the same unit of measure, what is the value of *x* ?

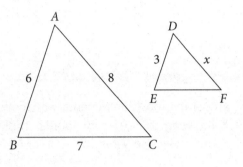

F. 3

G. 3.5

H. 4

J. 5

K. 6

Work through the Kaplan Method for ACT Math step-by-step to answer this question. The following table shows Kaplan's strategic thinking on the left, along with suggested math scratchwork on the right.

Strategic Thinking	Math Scratchwork
Step 1: What is the question?	
You need to find the value of *x*.	
Step 2: What information am I given?	
You're told that the triangles are similar, and you're given a figure with side lengths labeled.	△ABC is similar to △DEF.
Step 3: What can I do with the information?	
In similar triangles, corresponding sides are proportional. *DE* corresponds to *AB*, and *DF* corresponds to *AC*. Use this relationship to set up a proportion.	$\dfrac{AB}{DE} = \dfrac{AC}{DF}$ $\dfrac{6}{3} = \dfrac{8}{x}$
Cross-multiply to solve for *x*.	$6x = 3 \times 8$ $6x = 24$ $x = 4$
Step 4: Am I finished?	
You found the value of *x*, so you're all set.	Choice (H) is correct.

Math

Right Triangles

A **right triangle** has one interior angle of 90°. The longest side, which lies opposite the right angle, is called the **hypotenuse**. The other two sides are called the **legs**. Right triangles have several properties that are frequently tested on the ACT, including the Pythagorean theorem and triplets, which are discussed next.

The Pythagorean Theorem, Pythagorean Triplets, and Special Right Triangles

The Pythagorean theorem is one of the most fundamental equations in geometry, and it will be of great use to you on the ACT. Knowing common Pythagorean triplets and special right triangle ratios that originate from this formula will also serve you well on Test Day.

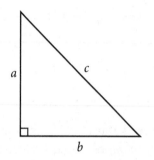

The **Pythagorean theorem** is an important triangle topic that you are probably familiar with already. If you know the lengths of any two sides of a right triangle, you can use the Pythagorean theorem to find the missing side. The equation is expressed as $a^2 + b^2 = c^2$, where a and b are the shorter sides of the triangle (called legs) and c is the hypotenuse, which is always across from the right angle of the triangle.

> ✔ **Note**
>
> The Pythagorean theorem can only be applied to right triangles.

Consider an example: A right triangle has a leg of length 9 and a hypotenuse of length 14. To find the missing leg, plug the known values into the Pythagorean theorem: $9^2 + b^2 = 14^2$. This simplifies to $81 + b^2 = 196$, which becomes $b^2 = 115$. Take the square root of both sides to get $b = \sqrt{115}$. The length of the missing leg is $\sqrt{115}$, or approximately 10.7.

> ✔ **Note**
>
> Wait to simplify radicals until you have your final answer. Leave answers in radical form unless a question says otherwise or the answer choices are written as decimals.

Because time is at such a premium on the ACT, time-saving strategies are invaluable, and there are two that will come in handy on triangle questions. The first is knowing common **Pythagorean**

triplets, which are right triangles that happen to have integer sides. These triangles show up *very* frequently on the ACT. The two most common are 3-4-5 and 5-12-13. Multiples of these lengths (e.g., 6-8-10 and 10-24-26) can also pop up, so watch out for them as well. The beauty of these triplets is that if you see any two sides, you can automatically fill in the third without having to resort to the time-consuming Pythagorean theorem.

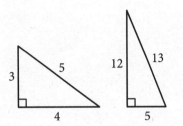

The second time-saving strategy involves recognizing **special right triangles**. Like Pythagorean triplets, special right triangles involve a ratio comparing the lengths of a right triangle's legs and hypotenuse, but with these triangles, you only need to know the length of one side in order to calculate the other two. These triangles are defined by their angles.

The ratio of the sides of a **45°-45°-90°** triangle is $x:x:x\sqrt{2}$, where x is the length of each leg and $x\sqrt{2}$ is the length of the hypotenuse.

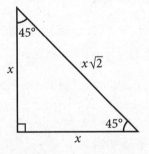

The ratio of the sides of a **30°-60°-90°** triangle is $x:x\sqrt{3}:2x$, where x is the shorter leg, $x\sqrt{3}$ is the longer leg, and $2x$ is the hypotenuse.

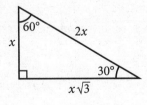

While the Pythagorean theorem can always be used to solve right triangle questions, it is not always the most efficient way to proceed. Further, many students make errors when simplifying radicals and exponents. Pythagorean triplets and special right triangles allow you to save time and avoid those mistakes. Use them whenever possible!

Ready to try a right triangle question or two? Let's go!

7. During a hiking trip, Keesha and Dwayne decide to climb a mountain using two different routes to the top. Keesha takes the hiking route that travels 5 miles south, 6 miles east, 7 miles south, and 2 miles west to the summit; Dwayne uses the climbing route that starts at the same point as the hiking route but goes directly from there to the summit. About how many miles in all will the two hike on the way to the summit?

A. 12.65

B. 29.42

C. 32.65

D. 33.42

E. 34.00

Work through the Kaplan Method for ACT Math step-by-step to answer this question. The following table shows Kaplan's strategic thinking on the left, along with suggested math scratchwork on the right.

Strategic Thinking	Math Scratchwork
Step 1: What is the question? You're asked to find the number of miles Keesha and Dwayne will hike on their way to the summit.	
Step 2: What information am I given? You're given descriptions of the hikers' paths to the summit.	
Step 3: What can I do with the information? Draw a diagram of Keesha and Dwayne's routes to the summit to visualize the situation. After drawing and labeling the diagram with the information given, look for a way to uncover a right triangle by drawing in additional lines. Then, fill in the lengths of any new segments you drew.	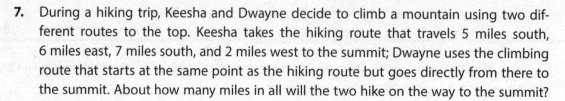
Use the Pythagorean theorem to calculate the distance Dwayne hikes.	$c^2 = (5 + 7)^2 + 4^2$ $c^2 = 144 + 16$ $c^2 = 160$ $c = \sqrt{160} = 4\sqrt{10} \approx 12.65$
Step 4: Am I finished? You're not done yet! The question asks you to find the total distance the two hikers travel.	Keesha: $5 + 6 + 7 + 2 = 20$ mi. Total: $12.65 + 20 = 32.65$ mi. Choice (C) is correct.

8. If the area of △*ABC* shown below is $8\sqrt{3}$ square centimeters, what is the length of $\overline{AB}$ in centimeters?

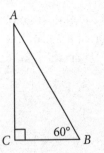

Note: Figure not drawn to scale.

F. 4

G. 6

H. 6.5

J. 7

K. 8

Work through the Kaplan Method for ACT Math step-by-step to answer this question. The following table shows Kaplan's strategic thinking on the left, along with suggested math scratchwork on the right.

Strategic Thinking	Math Scratchwork
Step 1: What is the question? You need to find the length of $\overline{AB}$.	
Step 2: What information am I given? You're given the area of the triangle and a diagram showing that the triangle is a right triangle with one acute angle equal to 60°.	area = $8\sqrt{3}$ square cm m∠ABC = 60°

Math

Strategic Thinking	Math Scratchwork
Step 3: What can I do with the information?	
Because the measure of one angle of the right triangle is 60°, the other must be 30°. The sides of a 30°-60°-90° triangle are in the ratio $x:x\sqrt{3}:2x$, so label the triangle accordingly.	
The area of a triangle is $A = \dfrac{1}{2}bh$, and you're told that the area of this triangle is $8\sqrt{3}$. Substitute this for A and use the side lengths from the ratio. Then solve for x.	$8\sqrt{3} = \dfrac{1}{2}(x)(x\sqrt{3})$ $8 = \dfrac{1}{2}x^2$ $16 = x^2$ $\pm 4 = x$
Length must be positive, so the value of x is 4.	$x = 4$
Step 4: Am I finished?	
You're not done yet! You solved for x, which is the length of $\overline{CB}$. The question asks for the length of $\overline{AB}$, which is twice $\overline{CB}$, so the correct answer is 8.	*Choice (K) is correct.*

Circles

A **circle** is the set of all points in a plane that are the same distance from a certain point. This point is called the focus and lies at the center of the circle. A circle is labeled by its center point: Circle *O* means the circle with center point *O*. Two circles of different size with the same center are **concentric** circles.

Circles have lots of interesting parts, as shown in the figure that follows. Let's review.

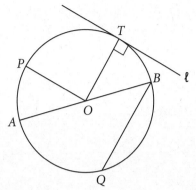

The **diameter** of a circle is a line segment that connects two points on the circle and passes through the center of the circle. In circle O, $\overline{AB}$ is a diameter.

The **radius** of a circle is a line segment from the center of the circle to any point on the circle. The radius of a circle is one-half the length of its diameter. In circle O, $\overline{OA}$, $\overline{OB}$, $\overline{OP}$, and $\overline{OT}$ are all radii.

A **chord** is a line segment joining two points on the circle. In circle O, $\overline{QB}$ and $\overline{AB}$ are chords. The longest chord in a circle is a diameter.

A **central angle** is an angle formed by two radii. $\angle AOP$, $\angle POB$, and $\angle BOA$ are three of circle O's central angles.

A line outside the circle that touches only one point on the circumference of the circle is a **tangent**. A line drawn tangent to a circle is perpendicular to the radius at the point of tangency, meaning it forms a right angle. Line ℓ is tangent to circle O at point T.

The distance around a circle is its **circumference**. The number π (pi) is the ratio of a circle's circumference to its diameter. The value of π is usually approximated as 3.14. For the ACT, it is generally sufficient to remember that pi is a little more than 3. Because π equals the ratio of the circumference to the diameter, a formula for the circumference is $C = \pi d = 2\pi r$.

The **area** of a circle is given by the formula $\text{Area} = \pi r^2$.

Those are the basics of circles! Know those and you will be ready for ACT circle questions.

Try a couple of sample questions involving these concepts. Then we'll look more closely at central angles and how they can make circle problems more complex by asking about arcs and sectors.

9. What is the area, in square inches, of a circle that has a circumference of 8π inches?

   A. 4π

   B. 8π

   C. 16π

   D. 32π

   E. 64π

Math

Work through the Kaplan Method for ACT Math step-by-step to answer this question. The following table shows Kaplan's strategic thinking on the left, along with suggested math scratchwork on the right.

Strategic Thinking	Math Scratchwork
Step 1: What is the question? You need to find the area of the circle.	
Step 2: What information am I given? You're given the circumference of the circle.	$C = 8\pi$ inches
Step 3: What can I do with the information? As with most circle questions, the first thing you need to do is find the radius. Use the given circumference and the circumference formula to find r. Now you can use that to find the area.	$C = 2\pi r$ $8\pi = 2\pi r$ $4 = r$ $A = \pi r^2 = \pi(4)^2 = 16\pi$
Step 4: Am I finished? You found the area, 16π, so you're done.	Choice (C) is correct.

Now, put on your thinking cap! The next question is a tough one.

10. The semicircle below has a radius of r inches, and chord $\overline{YZ}$ is parallel to diameter $\overline{WX}$. If the length of $\overline{YZ}$ is 25% shorter than the length of $\overline{WX}$, what is the shortest distance between $\overline{YZ}$ and $\overline{WX}$ in terms of r?

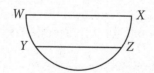

Note: Figure not drawn to scale.

F. $\dfrac{1}{4}\pi r$

G. $\dfrac{3}{4}\pi r$

H. $\dfrac{5}{4}\pi r$

J. $\dfrac{\sqrt{2}}{4} r$

K. $\dfrac{\sqrt{7}}{4} r$

Work through the Kaplan Method for ACT Math step-by-step to answer this question. The following table shows Kaplan's strategic thinking on the left, along with suggested math scratchwork on the right.

Strategic Thinking	Math Scratchwork
Step 1: What is the question? You need to determine the shortest distance between the two chords in terms of r.	
Step 2: What information am I given? You're told that $\overline{WX}$ is the diameter and that $\overline{YZ}$ is 25% smaller than $\overline{WX}$.	
Step 3: What can I do with the information? One of the simplest ways to uncover information in tough geometry questions is to draw additional lines. Start with an additional radius (call it r) that extends from the center of the diameter of the semicircle to $\overline{YZ}$. Then add a line that represents the shortest distance between the two chords, which will create a right triangle. You know that YZ is 25% shorter than WX, so $YZ = \frac{3}{4}WX$. Now, because the radius is half the diameter, $r = \frac{1}{2}WX$, and consequently, $\frac{3}{4}r = \frac{1}{2}YZ$. You now have two of the three sides of the right triangle and can solve for the third using the Pythagorean theorem.	$$YZ = \frac{3}{4}WX$$ $$r = \frac{1}{2}WX \rightarrow \frac{3}{4}r = \frac{1}{2}YZ$$ $$\left(\frac{3}{4}r\right)^2 + x^2 = r^2$$ $$\frac{9}{16}r^2 + x^2 = r^2$$ $$x^2 = \left(\frac{16}{16} - \frac{9}{16}\right)r^2$$ $$x^2 = \frac{7}{16}r^2$$ $$x = \pm\frac{\sqrt{7}}{4}r$$
Step 4: Am I finished? A distance can't be negative, so (K) is the correct answer.	*Choice (K) is correct.*

Arc Length and Sectors

An **arc** is a portion of the circumference of a circle. In the figure shown, *AB* is an arc of the circle, with the same degree measure as central angle *AOB*. The shorter distance between *A* and *B* along the circle is called the **minor arc**, while the longer distance *AXB* is the **major arc**. An arc that is exactly half the circumference of the circle is called a **semicircle** (meaning half a circle).

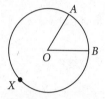

The **length of an arc** is the same fraction of a circle's circumference as its degree measure is of the degree measure of the circle (360°). For an arc with a central angle measuring *n* degrees, the following applies:

$$\text{Arc length} = \frac{n}{360} \times (\text{circumference})$$

$$= \frac{n}{360} \times 2\pi r$$

For example, the radius of circle *O* below is 6, so its circumference is $2\pi r = 2 \times \pi \times 6 = 12\pi$. Because ∠*AOC* measures 60°, the length of the arc is $\frac{60}{360} = \frac{1}{6}$ the circumference, or 2π.

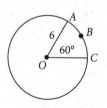

A **sector** is a portion of a circle bounded by two radii and an arc. In the circle shown with center *O*, *OAB* is a sector. To determine the area of a sector of a circle, use the same method you used to find the length of an arc. Determine what fraction of 360° is in the degree measure of the central angle of the sector and then multiply that fraction by the area of the circle. In a sector for which the central angle measures *n* degrees, the following applies:

$$\text{Area of sector} = \frac{n}{360} \times (\text{Area of circle})$$

$$= \frac{n}{360} \times \pi r^2$$

For example, the 60° "slice" of circle O shown below is $\frac{60}{360} = \frac{1}{6}$ of the circle, so sector AOC has

an area of $\frac{1}{6} \times \pi r^2 = \frac{1}{6} \times \pi \times 6^2 = \frac{1}{6} \times 36\pi = 6\pi$.

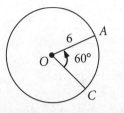

> ✔ **Note**
>
> An alternate way to answer questions involving arc lengths and sectors is to recognize that these are all part-to-whole ratios you can set in proportion to each other.
>
> $$\frac{\text{Central angle}}{360 \text{ (full circle)}} = \frac{\text{Sector area}}{\text{Area of the circle}} = \frac{\text{Arc length}}{\text{Circumference}}$$
>
> All three ratios are equal to each other. Any two can be used in a proportion to find one missing piece.

Try a sample question.

11. In the figure below, O is the center of the circle, and the ratio of the area of sector OABC to the area of sector OCDA is 3 to 5. What is the value of x ?

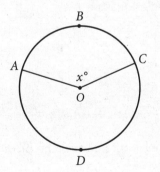

A. 120°

B. 135°

C. 144°

D. 150°

E. 216°

Work through the Kaplan Method for ACT Math step-by-step to answer this question. The following table shows Kaplan's strategic thinking on the left, along with suggested math scratchwork on the right.

Strategic Thinking	Math Scratchwork
Step 1: What is the question? You need to find the value of x.	
Step 2: What information am I given? You're given a circle that is divided into two sectors. You're also given the ratio of the areas of the sectors.	area $OABC$ to area $OCDA$ = 3:5
Step 3: What can I do with the information? Because the only angle measure you know is the whole circle (360°), you need to rewrite the given part-to-part ratio as a part-to-whole ratio. Now use what you now about the parts of a circle: The ratio between the interior angle of a sector and 360° is the same as the ratio between the area of a sector and the area of the whole circle. This means you can use the part-to-whole ratio from the areas to find the missing angle measure by setting up a proportion.	$OABC:OCDA = 3:5$ $OABC:$whole circle = 3:(5 + 3) = 3:8 $\dfrac{\text{area of sector}}{\text{area of whole } \bigcirc} = \dfrac{\text{central } \angle \text{ measure}}{\text{full circle (360°)}}$ $\dfrac{3}{8} = \dfrac{x}{360}$ $360(3) = 8x$ $1{,}080 = 8x$ $135 = x$
Step 4: Am I finished? Well done! You found the value of x.	Choice (B) is correct.

Note that you could also use Backsolving to answer the previous question if you're not sure how to set up the ratios.

Other Polygons and Complex Two-Dimensional Shapes

A **polygon** is any closed figure whose sides are straight line segments. As with any closed figure, the perimeter of a polygon is the sum of the lengths of its sides.

A **vertex** of a polygon is the point where two adjacent sides meet. A **diagonal** of a polygon is a line segment connecting two nonadjacent vertices.

A **regular polygon** has sides of equal length and interior angles of equal measure.

Interior and exterior angles: A polygon can be divided into triangles by drawing diagonals from any given vertex to all other nonadjacent vertices. For instance, the following pentagon can be divided into three triangles. Because the sum of the interior angles of each triangle is 180°, the sum of the interior angles of a pentagon is $3 \times 180° = 540°$.

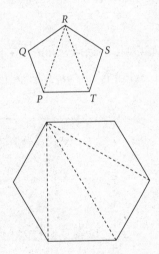

Now, suppose the hexagon shown above is a regular hexagon, and you want to find the measure of each interior angle. Because this is a *regular* hexagon, all angles are equal, so each is equal to one-sixth the sum of the angles. Because we can draw four triangles in a six-sided figure, the sum of the interior angles is $4 \times 180° = 720°$. Therefore, each interior angle measures $\frac{720}{6} = 120°$.

> **✔ Note**
>
> The formula to represent the total measure of an *n*-sided polygon's interior angles is $180(n - 2)$.

Math

Complex Two-Dimensional Shapes

Let's walk through examples of how the ACT can ask you to combine your knowledge of shapes and angles to find information within figures that are themselves unrecognizable. These figures can always be broken down into simpler shapes we've already reviewed.

We're getting into complex plane geometry questions now, so remember the two steps discussed earlier:

1) Find familiar shapes.

2) Transfer information.

Those familiar shapes will be triangles, quadrilaterals, and circles. You can use the rules we discussed about each to transfer information from one to the next within a complex figure and find the value you need. Let's give one a try.

12. In the figure shown here, *ABCD* is a square, and $\overline{AB}$ is a diameter of the circle centered at *O*. If $\overline{AD}$ is 10 units long, what is the area, in square units, of the shaded region?

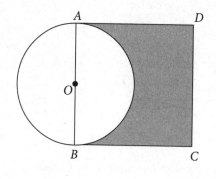

F. $100 - 50\pi$

G. $100 - 25\pi$

H. $100 - \dfrac{25}{2}\pi$

J. $100 - 10\pi$

K. $100 - \dfrac{5}{2}\pi$

Work through the Kaplan Method for ACT Math step-by-step to answer this question. The following table shows Kaplan's strategic thinking on the left, along with suggested math scratchwork on the right.

Strategic Thinking	Math Scratchwork
Step 1: What is the question? You're looking for the area of the shaded region.	
Step 2: What information am I given? You're given a figure and told that $\overline{AB}$ is a diameter of the circle and that $\overline{AD}$ (one side of the square) is 10 units long.	
Step 3: What can I do with the information? First, decide what area you're actually looking for. Describe it in words first, then apply the correct formulas. Finally, fill in the dimensions given in the question stem: The side of the square is 10 units, and the radius of the circle is half the diameter (which is another side of the square), or half of 10 = 5.	shaded region = whole square − semicircle $A_{shaded} = s^2 - \dfrac{1}{2}\pi r^2$ $A_{shaded} = 10^2 - \dfrac{1}{2}\pi(5)^2$ $= 100 - \dfrac{1}{2}(25\pi)$ $= 100 - \dfrac{25}{2}\pi$
Step 4: Am I finished? Yes, stop! Look back at the answer choices before you waste time trying to simplify. You already have a match.	Choice (H) is correct.

Math

Three-Dimensional Shapes

Fortunately, the ACT only tests regular, uniform three-dimensional figures. You won't see any crazy 3-D combinations like you just worked with on a 2-D plane. Questions with 3-D figures can get complex, but they still involve finding those familiar 2-D shapes and using them to transfer information.

The following is a diagram showing the basic anatomy of a 3-D shape.

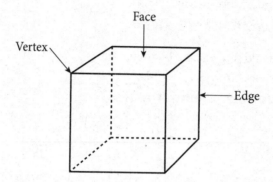

A **face** (or **surface**) is a 2-D shape that acts as one of the sides of the solid. Two faces meet at a line segment called an **edge**, and three faces meet at a single point called a **vertex**.

Keep reading for more on types of 3-D shapes and questions you could be asked about them.

The only formulas to remember are **volume** and **surface area**. The only 3-D shapes to memorize are rectangular solids and right cylinders. If a question involves any other shape, the formula will be provided in the question stem.

Volume is the amount of 3-D space occupied by a solid. This is analogous to the area of a 2-D shape like a triangle or circle. You can find the volume of many 3-D shapes by finding the area of the base and multiplying it by the height. We've highlighted the base area components of the formulas in the following table using parentheses.

Rectangular Solid	Cube	Right Cylinder
$(l \times w) \times h$	$(s \times s) \times s = s^3$	$(\pi \times r^2) \times h$

Surface area is the sum of the areas of all the faces of a solid. You might liken this to determining the amount of wrapping paper needed to cover all faces of a solid.

To calculate the surface area of a solid, simply find the area of each face using your 2-D geometry skills, then add them all together.

> ✔ **Note**
>
> You won't be expected to know the surface area formulas for right pyramids, right cones, and spheres; they'll be provided if you need them. However, you could be asked to find the surface area of a prism, in which case you'll be given enough information to find the area of each surface of the solid.

If you're ready to test your knowledge of 3-D shapes, check out the next two questions.

13. Hailee bought several right cylindrical candles as party favors and plans to wrap them such that the gift paper wraps around the candle exactly once with no overlap. She wants to leave an extra three inches of wrapping paper past each end of the candles so she can tie both ends with a bit of ribbon. If each candle has a diameter of 4 inches and is 8 inches tall, how many square inches of wrapping paper will Hailee need to wrap one candle?

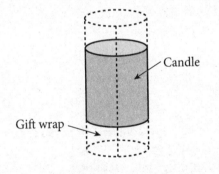

Candle

Gift wrap

A. 32π

B. 40π

C. 44π

D. 56π

E. 64π

Work through the Kaplan Method for ACT Math step-by-step to answer this question. The following table shows Kaplan's strategic thinking on the left, along with suggested math scratchwork on the right.

Strategic Thinking	Math Scratchwork
Step 1: What is the question? You need to find the amount of wrapping paper needed to wrap one candle.	
Step 2: What information am I given? You're given a figure and the dimensions of the candle. You're also told that there will be extra paper on each end.	cylinder with diameter = 4 inches and height = 8 inches extra 3 inches on each end
Step 3: What can I do with the information? Covering a 3-D shape (with gift wrap here) implies surface area, but be careful: One piece of gift wrap is not identical to the surface area of one of the candles because the circular top and bottom will not be covered exactly. Draw a sketch to visualize the situation.	
The gift wrap will be in the shape of a rectangle. The question states that Hailee will leave extra gift wrap at both ends, so remember to take this into account. The rectangle length shares an edge with the circular top of the candle; therefore, the length is equal to the top's circumference.	C is rect. length, h is rect. width $d = 4$ in. $\rightarrow C = \pi d = 4\pi$ in. $h = 8$ in. gift wrap for one candle: area = $l \times w$ $= 4\pi$ in. $\times$ (3 in. + 8 in. + 3 in.) $= 56\pi$ in.^{2}
Step 4: Am I finished? Nicely done! You've found the amount of gift wrap Hailee needs for one candle.	Choice (D) is correct.

14. If the solid shown here is half of a cube, what is its volume?

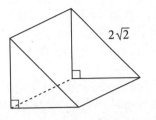

$2\sqrt{2}$

F. 4

G. $4\sqrt{2}$

H. 8

J. $8\sqrt{2}$

K. 12

Work through the Kaplan Method for ACT Math step-by-step to answer this question. The following table shows Kaplan's strategic thinking on the left, along with suggested math scratchwork on the right.

Strategic Thinking	Math Scratchwork
Step 1: What is the question? You need to find the volume of the solid.	
Step 2: What information am I given? You're told that the solid is half a cube, and you're given the length of one part.	
Step 3: What can I do with the information? Use your complex figure tactics. You know the shape is half a cube, so the perpendicular edges are equal and form the legs of a 45°-45°-90° triangle. Divide the hypotenuse by $\sqrt{2}$ to get the lengths of the legs (and the edges of the half cube).	45°-45°-90° Δ → x:x:x $\sqrt{2}$ hypotenuse is $2\sqrt{2}$, so x = 2 2 $2\sqrt{2}$ 2 2
Find the volume of the whole cube and then divide by 2.	$V_{\text{whole cube}} = s^3 = (2)^3 = 8$ half that = 4
Step 4: Am I finished? You found the volume of the solid. Job well done!	Choice (F) is correct.

Math

Right Triangle Trig and SOHCAHTOA

You've already seen some trig questions in the Functions chapter. Those questions were related to trigonometric functions, their graphs, and trig identities. The Geometry category includes questions specifically related to right triangle trig and SOHCAHTOA.

You probably remember learning the acronym SOHCAHTOA, a mnemonic device for the sine, cosine, and tangent ratios. Check out the triangle and the table beneath for a summary of the ratios and what each equals for angle *A* in triangle *CAB*.

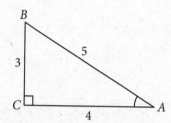

Sine (sin)	Cosine (cos)	Tangent (tan)
$\dfrac{\text{opposite}}{\text{hypotenuse}}$	$\dfrac{\text{adjacent}}{\text{hypotenuse}}$	$\dfrac{\text{opposite}}{\text{adjacent}}$
$\dfrac{3}{5}$	$\dfrac{4}{5}$	$\dfrac{3}{4}$

✔ **Note**

Related note: $\tan A = \dfrac{\sin A}{\cos A}$.

Let's try a couple of questions so you can get comfortable with how the ACT will test your knowledge of trigonometry. You can expect to see three or four trig questions on Test Day, about half of which will involve right triangles.

15. In the following figure, a surfboard is propped up against a rectangular box. If the board is 7 feet long, which of the following is closest to the height, in feet, of the box? (Note: sin 23° ≈ 0.3907, cos 23° ≈ 0.9205)

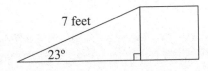

A. 2.7

B. 3.0

C. 4.3

D. 5.6

E. 6.4

Work through the Kaplan Method for ACT Math step-by-step to answer this question. The following table shows Kaplan's strategic thinking on the left, along with suggested math scratchwork on the right.

Strategic Thinking	Math Scratchwork
Step 1: What is the question?	
You need to find the height of the box.	
Step 2: What information am I given?	
You're given a figure that includes a right triangle and an angle measure. You're also given the length of the surf board.	$m\angle$ between ground and board = 23° length of board (hypotenuse of $\triangle$) = 7
You're also given two trig values, which you may or may not need.	sin 23° ≈ 0.3907 cos 23° ≈ 0.9205
Step 3: What can I do with the information?	
Let x equal the height of the triangle (which is also the height of the box). Now, look at the triangle. You know the length of the hypotenuse, and you're looking for the side opposite the given angle. This tells you which trig function to use.	know hypotenuse, want opposite use sine $\sin 23° = \dfrac{opp}{hyp} = \dfrac{x}{7}$
The question states that sin 23° ≈ 0.3907. Add this information to the ratio and solve for x.	$\sin 23° = \dfrac{x}{7}$ $0.3907 \approx \dfrac{x}{7}$ $0.3907 \times 7 \approx x$ $2.7349 \approx x$
Step 4: Am I finished?	
All done. The height of the box is the value of x.	Choice (A) is correct.

Math

16. Given any right triangle, if $\tan x = \dfrac{7}{24}$, then what is the value of $\sin x$?

  F. $\dfrac{7}{25}$

  G. $\dfrac{24}{25}$

  H. $\dfrac{25}{24}$

  J. $\dfrac{24}{7}$

  K. $\dfrac{25}{7}$

Work through the Kaplan Method for ACT Math step-by-step to answer this question. The following table shows Kaplan's strategic thinking on the left, along with suggested math scratchwork on the right.

Strategic Thinking	Math Scratchwork
Step 1: What is the question?	
You need to find the value of $\sin x$.	
Step 2: What information am I given?	
You're given the value of $\tan x$.	$\tan x = \dfrac{7}{24}$
Step 3: What can I do with the information?	
If $\tan x = \dfrac{7}{24}$, then the sides that are opposite and adjacent to angle x must be 7 and 24, respectively. Draw a diagram to reflect this.	$\tan x = \dfrac{opp}{adj}$, $\sin x = \dfrac{opp}{hyp}$
Because $\sin x = \dfrac{opp}{hyp}$, you'll need to find the length of the hypotenuse using the Pythagorean theorem. Once you calculate this, plug that value into the sine ratio.	$7^2 + 24^2 = hyp^2$ $49 + 576 = hyp^2$ $625 = hyp^2$ $25 = hyp$
Step 4: Am I finished?	
The value of $\sin x$ is $\dfrac{7}{25}$. Well done!	Choice (F) is correct.

Now you'll have a chance to try a few test-like questions in a scaffolded way. We've provided some guidance, but you'll need to fill in the missing parts of the explanation or the step-by-step math to get to the correct answer. Don't worry—after going through the worked examples at the beginning of this section, these questions should be completely doable.

17. The graph that follows shows the average cost of a certain kind of surgery followed by a hospital stay in Virginia. The hospital charges for the surgery itself plus all the costs associated with recovery care for each night the patient remains in the hospital. Based on the graph, what is the average cost per night spent in the hospital?

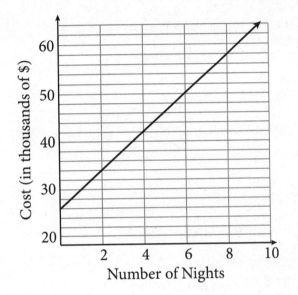

A. $ 2,600

B. $ 4,000

C. $ 6,600

D. $ 8,000

E. $26,000

Use the following scaffolding as your map through the question. If you aren't sure where to start, fill in the blanks in the table as you work from top to bottom.

Strategic Thinking	Math Scratchwork
Step 1: What is the question? The question asks for the average cost per night spent in the hospital.	
Step 2: What information am I given? You are given a graph of a line that models the cost from 0 to 10 nights.	
Step 3: What can I do with the information? The cost per night is the same as the unit rate, which is represented by the slope of the line. Use the grid lines and the axis labels to identify two points on the line. Next, use the slope formula to find the slope between the two points.	y-intercept: (0, _____) another point: (_____ , _____) $\dfrac{y_2 - y_1}{x_2 - x_1} = \dfrac{\rule{2cm}{0.4pt}-}{\rule{2cm}{0.4pt}-}$ $= \rule{2cm}{0.4pt}$ $= \rule{2cm}{0.4pt}$
Step 4: Am I finished? Did you get a unit rate of $4,000 per night? If so, you're absolutely right!	*Choice* _____ *is correct.*

18. If a parabola is given by the equation $y = (x - 2)^2 - 5$, which of the following statements is true?

    F. The graph of y is increasing over the entire domain.

    G. The graph of y is decreasing over the entire domain.

    H. The graph of y is increasing for $x < 2$ and decreasing for $x > 2$.

    J. The graph of y is decreasing for $x < 2$ and increasing for $x > 2$.

    K. The graph of y is decreasing for $x < 5$ and increasing for $x > 5$.

Use the following scaffolding as your map through the question. If you aren't sure where to start, fill in the blanks in the table as you work from top to bottom.

Strategic Thinking	Math Scratchwork
Step 1: What is the question? You need to determine which statement is true.	
Step 2: What information am I given? You don't have a lot to go on—just an equation.	$y = (x - 2)^2 - 5$
Step 3: What can I do with the information? You could graph the equation in your graphing calculator, or you can use what you know about the parent function (x^2) and transformations.	The parent function is a _____, which has a _____ shape. The vertex of the parent is (___ , ___).
What kind of transformations have been applied to the parent function?	_____ 2 units _____ 5 units
What is the vertex of this parabola? Use the vertex and the direction in which the parabola opens to describe the graph in terms of increasing (going up) and decreasing (going down). Translate this information into math.	vertex at (___ , ___) graph _____ to the left of ____ graph _____ to the right of ____ _____ when $x <$ ____ _____ when $x >$ ____
Step 4: Am I finished? Is your answer (J)? That's super!	Choice _____ is correct.

Note that you could eliminate F and G as soon as you realize that the equation's graph is a parabola (which is a U shape).

19. Marge has a rectangular orchard that she would like to divide into two triangular fields—one for planting orange trees and one for planting grapefruit trees—by building a fence from one corner of the field to the opposite corner. If the area of the field is 540 square feet and the length of the field is 36 feet, how many feet of fence will Marge need to create the divider?

    A. 39
    B. 51
    C. 60
    D. 81
    E. 102

Use the following scaffolding as your map through the question. If you aren't sure where to start, fill in the blanks in the table as you work from top to bottom.

Strategic Thinking	Math Scratchwork
Step 1: What is the question? You need to find the length of the fence.	
Step 2: What information am I given? You're told that the orchard is rectangular and that Marge will split it diagonally into two triangles. You're also given some dimensions. Jot those down.	$A =$ _____ $l =$ _____
Step 3: What can I do with the information? Draw a figure to visualize the situation. Sketch a rectangle and label what you know. The area of a rectangle is the product of its length and width. Because you know the length and the area, you can find the width.	 36 $A = l \times w$ _____ = _____ × w $w =$ _____ ÷ _____ = _____
Add the width to the diagram. The diagonal of the rectangle is also the hypotenuse of a right triangle, so you can use the Pythagorean theorem.	$c^2 = a^2 + b^2$ $c^2 = $ _____^{2} + _____^{2} $c^2 = $ _____ $c = \sqrt{\underline{}} = $ _____
Step 4: Am I finished? Did you get 39? Perfect!	Choice _____ is correct.

20. What is the volume, in cubic inches, of the cylinder shown here?

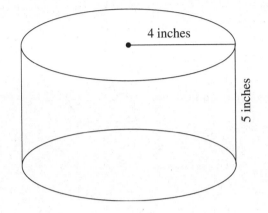

4 inches

5 inches

    F.   20π

    G.   40π

    H.   60π

    J.   80π

    K. 100π

Use the following scaffolding as your map through the question. If you aren't sure where to start, fill in the blanks in the table as you work from top to bottom.

Strategic Thinking	Math Scratchwork
Step 1: What is the question? Find the volume of the cylinder.	
Step 2: What information am I given? You're given a figure that includes a couple of dimensions. Jot those down.	$r =$ _____ $h =$ _____
Step 3: What can I do with the information? The volume of a cylinder is the area of its base (a circle) times its height. Jot down the formula and fill in the dimensions. Then simplify (but leave the π because the answer choices all have it).	$V =$ ____ × ____^{2} × h $V =$ ____ × ____^{2} × ____ $V =$ ____ π
Step 4: Am I finished? Did you come up with 80π? Superb!	Choice _____ is correct.

Math

21. In the figure that follows, a wooden plank is shown with its dimensions in inches. If Marcus wants to spray-paint every surface of the plank, how much paint, in square inches, will Marcus need?

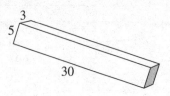

   A.   38

   B.   76

   C.   240

   D.   450

   E.   510

Use the following scaffolding as your map through the question. If you aren't sure where to start, fill in the blanks in the table as you work from top to bottom.

Strategic Thinking	Math Scratchwork
Step 1: What is the question? You need to determine the amount of paint Marcus needs.	
Step 2: What information am I given? You're given a figure (a rectangular prism) with several dimensions. Jot those down.	$l = \underline{\hspace{1cm}}$ $w = \underline{\hspace{1cm}}$ $h = \underline{\hspace{1cm}}$
Step 3: What can I do with the information? The amount of paint needed to cover all the surface is the same as the total surface area of the solid. Add the areas of all six faces to find the surface area.	area of 2 ends = 2(___ × ___) area of front/back = 2(___ × ___) area of bottom/top = 2(___ × ___) Total area = _____ square inches
Step 4: Am I finished? Did the total equal 510? That's right!	Choice _____ is correct.

22. Which of the following expressions represents the length of $\overline{VX}$ shown in the figure below?

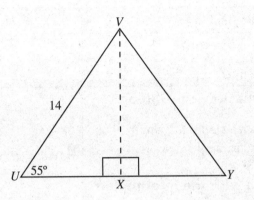

   F. 14 sin 55°

   G. 14 cos 55°

   H. 14 tan 55°

   J. $\dfrac{14}{\sin 55°}$

   K. $\dfrac{14}{\cos 55°}$

Math

Use the following scaffolding as your map through the question. If you aren't sure where to start, fill in the blanks in the table as you work from top to bottom.

Strategic Thinking	Math Scratchwork
Step 1: What is the question? You need to find the length of $\overline{VX}$.	
Step 2: What information am I given? You're given a figure, which includes the length of one side of a right triangle and an angle measure.	$\overline{UV} = $ _____ , $\overline{VX} = ?$ $m\angle VUX = $ _____
Step 3: What can I do with the information? The triangle is a right triangle, but you only have one side length, and the angle given is not a special angle, so you'll need to use trig (SOHCAHTOA). Look at the figure: As it relates to the given angle, which side do you know? Which side do you need? Which trig function involves these two sides? Use the definition (SOHCAHTOA) to set up a ratio. Then cross-multiply to solve for *VX*.	*Circle one:* Know: opposite / adjacent / hypotenuse *Circle one:* Need: opposite / adjacent / hypotenuse _____ _____ 55° = _____ _____ 55° = _____ VX = _____
Step 4: Am I finished? Did you get 14 sin 55°? Super!	Choice _____ is correct.

Now that you've seen the variety of ways in which the ACT can test you on Geometry, try the following questions to check your understanding. Give yourself 5 minutes to answer these 4 questions. Make sure you use the Kaplan Method for ACT Math as often as you can. Remember, you want to emphasize speed and efficiency in addition to simply getting the correct answer.

23. In the figure below, at which point does $\overline{XZ}$ intersect with its perpendicular bisector?

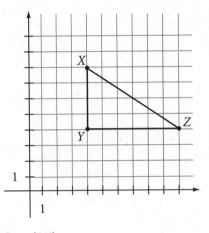

A. (5,6)

B. (6,6)

C. (6,7)

D. (7,6)

E. (7,7)

24. Square *QRST* is inscribed inside square *ABCD*. If *SR* = 5, what is the area of triangle *QAT* ?

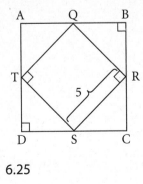

F. 6.25

G. 5

H. 4.50

J. 3.125

K. 3

25. The opening of a perfectly circular sewer tunnel has a circumference of 8π. The tunnel has a volume of 2,048π cubic feet. How many feet long is the tunnel?

A. 44

B. 62

C. 84

D. 128

E. 156

26. To determine the height *h* of a pole, Allison stands *b* feet from the base of the pole and measures the angle of elevation from the base of the pole to be θ, as shown in the figure below. Which of the following illustrates the relationship between *h* and *b* ?

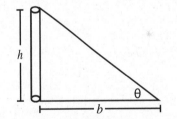

F. $\cos \theta = \dfrac{h}{b}$

G. $\cos \theta = \dfrac{b}{h}$

H. $\cos \theta = \dfrac{b}{b + h}$

J. $\cos \theta = \dfrac{b}{\sqrt{b^2 + h^2}}$

K. $\cos \theta = \dfrac{\sqrt{b^2 + h^2}}{b}$

Answers and Explanations are provided at the end of the book.

ON YOUR OWN

The following questions provide an opportunity to practice the concepts and strategic thinking covered in this chapter.

1. What is the slope of the line shown on the coordinate plane below?

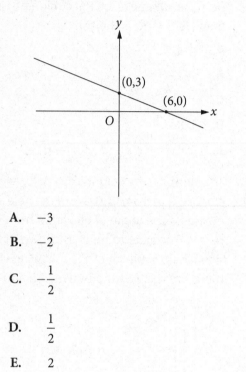

   A. -3

   B. -2

   C. $-\dfrac{1}{2}$

   D. $\dfrac{1}{2}$

   E. 2

2. The solution to which inequality is represented in the graph shown?

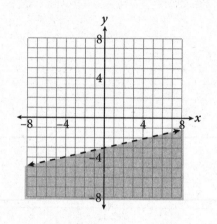

   F. $x - 4y > 12$

   G. $x - 4y < 12$

   H. $x + 4y > -12$

   J. $x + 4y > -12$

   K. $4x + y < -3$

3. The graph below shows the cost of installing a pressure-treated wood fence. The company charges a flat installation fee plus a cost per linear foot of fencing. Based on the graph, how much does one linear foot of this particular wood cost?

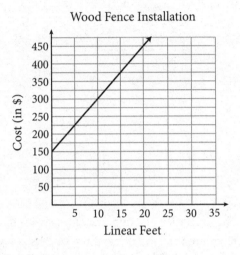

Wood Fence Installation

A. $ 4

B. $ 5

C. $ 15

D. $ 75

E. $150

4. What is the length of a line segment with endpoints $(3,-6)$ and $(-2,6)$?

F. 1

G. 5

H. 10

J. 12

K. 13

5. Given point $A(-3,-8)$, if the midpoint of segment AB is $(1,-5)$, what are the coordinates of point B ?

A. $(5,-2)$

B. $(4,-2)$

C. $(-1,-6.5)$

D. $(-2,-2)$

E. $(-1,-1.5)$

6. What is the area of the shaded sector of the circle shown in the figure below?

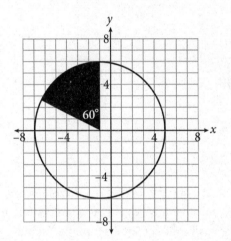

F. 2π

G. 6π

H. 8π

J. 12π

K. 36π

7. If triangle *ABC* shown below is reflected over line *l*, what will be the coordinates of the reflection of point *B* ?

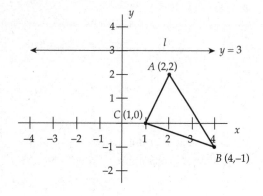

A. (4,1)

B. (4,4)

C. (4,6)

D. (4,7)

E. (4,8)

8. Which of the following equations describes the set of all points (*x*,*y*) in the coordinate plane that are a distance of 5 units from the point $(-3,4)$?

F. $(x+3)+(y-4)=5$

G. $(x-3)+(y+4)=5$

H. $(x+3)^2+(y-4)^2=5$

J. $(x+3)^2+(y-4)^2=25$

K. $(x-3)^2+(y+4)^2=25$

9. What is the value of $b - c$ in the figure below given the equalities stated here?

$$\overline{LM} = \overline{MN} = \overline{NO} = \overline{OL} = \overline{LN}$$

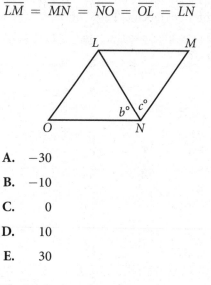

A. -30

B. -10

C. 0

D. 10

E. 30

10. The longer leg of a right triangle is twice the length of the shorter leg. If the lengths of both legs are whole numbers, which of the following could be the length of the hypotenuse?

F. $\sqrt{45}$

G. $\sqrt{48}$

H. $\sqrt{54}$

J. $\sqrt{63}$

K. $\sqrt{67}$

11. The ramp shown in the figure below is placed at a 30° angle with the ground, 8 feet from the bottom step in front of the building. About how long, in inches, is the ramp? (There are 12 inches in 1 foot.)

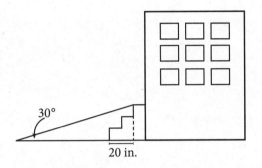

Note: Figure not drawn to scale.

A. 67

B. 84

C. 116

D. 128

E. 134

12. In the figure below, the shaded region is a square with an area of 12 square units, inscribed inside equilateral triangle *ABC*. What is the perimeter of triangle *ABC*?

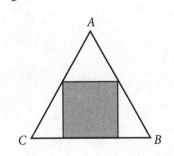

F. $18\sqrt{3}$

G. $4 + \sqrt{3}$

H. $4 + 6\sqrt{3}$

J. $8 + 6\sqrt{3}$

K. $12 + 6\sqrt{3}$

13. Mark's rectangular flowerbed is twice as long as it is wide. He wants to build a rectangular vegetable garden that is twice as long and twice as wide as the flowerbed. The area of the vegetable garden will be how many times as large as the area of the flowerbed?

A. 2

B. 3

C. 4

D. 6

E. 8

14. A circle with radius 5 is inscribed in a square. What is the difference between the area of the square and the area of the circle?

F. 25π

G. 50π

H. $50 - 25\pi$

J. $100 - 25\pi$

K. 100

15. In the figure shown below, chord *FG* has a length of 12 units and triangle *GOH* has an area of 24 square units. What is the area in square units of the circle centered at *O*?

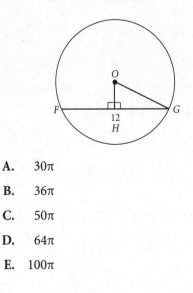

A. 30π

B. 36π

C. 50π

D. 64π

E. 100π

16. Circle O (not shown) has a radius of 5 and $m\angle AOB = 45°$. What is the length of arc AB ?

    F. $\dfrac{4\pi}{5}$

    G. 3

    H. $\dfrac{5\pi}{4}$

    J. 5

    K. $\dfrac{25\pi}{8}$

17. The figure below shows a vertical cross section of a bulldozer shovel used for moving large volumes of sand. The shovel is 40 inches wide (not shown) and 35 inches long. The bottom is horizontal for 25 inches and then slopes up, and the sides are vertical. What is the volume of sand, in cubic inches, that is required to fill the shovel to a depth, as shown, of 15 inches on the deep side and 10 inches on the shallow side?

    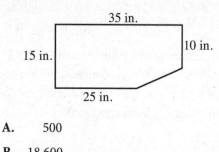

    A.   500

    B.   18,600

    C.   20,000

    D.   21,000

    E.   24,000

18. In the figure below, point C is the center of the circle and the measure of angle D is 37°. Which of the following expresses the length of the radius?

    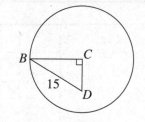

    F.   15 sin 53°

    G.   15 sin 37°

    H.   15 cos 37°

    J.   15 tan 53°

    K.   15 tan 37°

19. If $0° < \theta < 90°$ and $\cos\theta = \dfrac{5\sqrt{2}}{8}$, then $\tan\theta = ?$

    A. $\dfrac{8}{5\sqrt{2}}$

    B. $\dfrac{\sqrt{7}}{5}$

    C. $\dfrac{\sqrt{14}}{8}$

    D. $\dfrac{5}{\sqrt{7}}$

    E. $\dfrac{8}{\sqrt{14}}$

20. The table below shows several points through which the graph of a parabola passes. One of the x-intercepts for the graph is given in the table. What is the other x-intercept for the graph?

x	1	2	3	4	5	6
y	3.5	0	-2.5	-4	-4.5	-4

   F. $(-2,0)$

   G. $(5,0)$

   H. $(8,0)$

   J. $(10,0)$

   K.   Cannot be determined from the given information

21. Points $A\left(\sqrt{2},4\right)$, $B\left(6, -\sqrt{3}\ \right)$, and C are collinear. If B is the midpoint of line segment AC, what are the approximate (x,y) coordinates of point C?

   A. $(3.71,1.13)$

   B. $(3.71,5.73)$

   C. $(7.41,-7.46)$

   D. $(10.59,-7.46)$

   E. $(10.59,5.73)$

22. In the standard (x,y) coordinate plane, if the distance between $(a,2)$ and $(16,a)$ is 10 units, which of the following could be the value of a?

   F.   10

   G.   6

   H. -6

   J. -8

   K. -10

23. Bob and his wife Linda both leave their house at 7:30 AM to commute to work. Bob drives 60 mph and goes north for half an hour, then east for 1 hour. Linda drives 50 mph and goes east for 1 hour, then north for half an hour. Which of the following is an expression for the number of miles apart Bob and Linda are at 9:00 AM, when they each arrive at work?

   A. $3(60 - 50)$

   B. $\sqrt{(60 - 50)^2 + (25 - 30)^2}$

   C. $\sqrt{(60 - 50)^2 + (25 + 30)^2}$

   D. $\sqrt{(60 + 50)^2 + (25 - 30)^2}$

   E. $\sqrt{(3 - 60)^2 + (3 - 30)^2}$

24. What is the greatest possible number of points of intersection between a parabola and a circle when graphed in the coordinate plane?

   F.   1

   G.   2

   H.   3

   J.   4

   K.   6

Math

25. If the distance from $-a$ to b in the figure shown is 10, which of the following could be the factored form of the graph's equation?

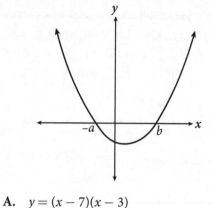

    A. $y = (x - 7)(x - 3)$

    B. $y = (x - 7)(x + 3)$

    C. $y = (x - 8)(x - 2)$

    D. $y = (x - 1)(x + 10)$

    E. $y = (x + 10)(x + 1)$

26. Which of the following is the equation of the largest circle that can be inscribed in the ellipse with equation $\dfrac{(x - 3)^2}{16} + \dfrac{(y + 2)^2}{25} = 1$?

    F. $(x - 3)^2 + (y + 2)^2 = 400$

    G. $(x - 3)^2 + (y + 2)^2 = 25$

    H. $(x - 3)^2 + (y + 2)^2 = 16$

    J. $x^2 + y^2 = 25$

    K. $x^2 + y^2 = 16$

27. $\triangle PQR$ has side lengths a, b, and c, as shown in the figure below. A dotted line segment, d, originates at point P and is perpendicular to $\overline{QR}$. What is the ratio of the length of d to the length of $\overline{PQ}$?

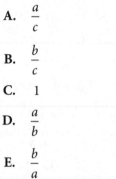

    A. $\dfrac{a}{c}$

    B. $\dfrac{b}{c}$

    C. 1

    D. $\dfrac{a}{b}$

    E. $\dfrac{b}{a}$

28. For the area of a square to triple, the new side lengths must be the old side lengths multiplied by which of the following?

    F. $\sqrt{3}$

    G. 3

    H. 9

    J. $\sqrt{27}$

    K. 27

29. A certain rectangle is $(x + 3)$ units long and $(x + 7)$ units wide. If a square with sides of length x is removed from the interior of the rectangle, which of the following is an expression for the remaining area?

    A. 10

    B. 21

    C. $2x + 10$

    D. $10x + 21$

    E. $x^2 + 10x + 21$

30. In the figure shown here, $\overline{BE}$ is perpendicular to $\overline{AD}$, and the lengths of $\overline{AB}$, $\overline{BC}$, $\overline{CD}$, and $\overline{BE}$ are given in inches. What is the area, in square inches, of trapezoid $ABCD$?

    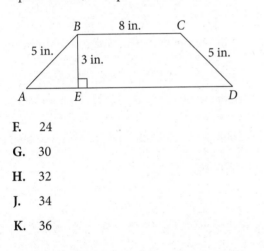

    F. 24

    G. 30

    H. 32

    J. 34

    K. 36

31. A geometer uses the following formula to estimate the area A of the shaded portion of a circle, as shown in the following figure, when only the height h and the length of the chord c are known:

    $$A = \frac{2ch}{3} + \frac{h^3}{2c}$$

    What is the geometer's estimate of the area, in square inches, of the shaded region if the height is 2 inches and the length of the chord is 6 inches?

    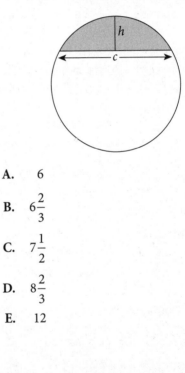

    A. 6

    B. $6\dfrac{2}{3}$

    C. $7\dfrac{1}{2}$

    D. $8\dfrac{2}{3}$

    E. 12

32. In the circle centered at O in the figure shown below, the measure of $\angle AOB$ is 40°. If $\overline{OA}$ is 9 units long, how many units long is minor arc AB ?

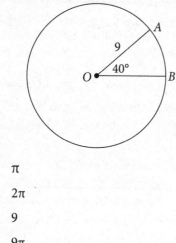

F. π

G. 2π

H. 9

J. 9π

K. 40

33. A rectangular prism has three faces with areas of 28, 20, and 35 square centimeters. What is the volume of this solid?

A. 83 cubic cm

B. 140 cubic cm

C. 166 cubic cm

D. 196 cubic cm

E. 19,600 cubic cm

34. If a sphere of radius 3 is inscribed in a cube such that it is tangent to all six faces of the cube, the volume contained outside the sphere and inside the cube is approximately:

F. 97 cubic units.

G. 103 cubic units.

H. 115 cubic units.

J. 109 cubic units.

K. 121 cubic units.

35. A rectangular box with an open top is constructed from cardboard to have a square base of area x^2 and height h. If the volume of this box is 50 cubic units, how many square units of cardboard, in terms of x, are needed to build the box?

A. $5x^2$

B. $6x^2$

C. $\dfrac{200}{x} + x^2$

D. $\dfrac{200}{x} + 2x^2$

E. $\dfrac{250}{x} + 2x^2$

36. The radius of right circular cone A is $\dfrac{1}{5}$ of the radius of right circular cone B, and the height of right circular cone A is $\dfrac{1}{4}$ of the height of right circular cone B. What is the ratio of the volume of cone A to the volume of cone B ? (The volume of a right circular cone is given by the formula $V = \dfrac{1}{3}\pi r^2 h$.)

F. $\dfrac{1}{16}$

G. $\dfrac{1}{25}$

H. $\dfrac{1}{64}$

J. $\dfrac{1}{80}$

K. $\dfrac{1}{100}$

37. Earth makes one complete rotation about its axis every 24 hours, at a fairly constant rate. Through how many degrees would Quito, Ecuador, which lies on the Earth's equator, rotate from 12:00 noon on January 1 to 3:00 PM on January 2 ?

    A. 340°

    B. 370°

    C. 385°

    D. 405°

    E. 415°

38. Elizabeth wants to determine the height of a flagpole. She stands 100 feet from the base of the flagpole and measures the angle of elevation to be 40°, as shown in the figure below. Which of the following is the best approximation of the height of the flagpole, in feet?

    Note: sin 40° ≈ 0.643
    cos 40° ≈ 0.766
    tan 40° ≈ 0.839

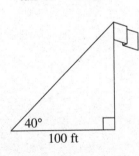

    F.   40

    G.   50

    H.   64

    J.   77

    K.   84

39. If $0° < \theta < 90°$ and $\sin \theta = \dfrac{\sqrt{11}}{2\sqrt{3}}$, then what is the value of $\cos \theta$?

    A. $\dfrac{1}{2\sqrt{3}}$

    B. $\dfrac{1}{\sqrt{11}}$

    C. $\dfrac{2\sqrt{3}}{\sqrt{11}}$

    D. $2\sqrt{3}$

    E. $\sqrt{11}$

40. Bob is a glass collector. The figure below is one of the triangular glass fragments that Bob collected. Which of the following expressions is the value of Z ? (Note: The law of sines states that for a triangle with sides of lengths a, b, and c and opposite angles of measure A, B, and C, respectively, $\dfrac{\sin A}{a} = \dfrac{\sin B}{b} = \dfrac{\sin C}{c}$).

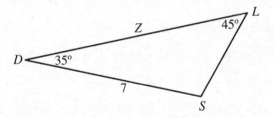

    F. $\dfrac{7 \sin 35°}{\sin 45°}$

    G. $\dfrac{7 \sin 35°}{\sin 100°}$

    H. $\dfrac{7 \sin 45°}{\sin 100°}$

    J. $\dfrac{7 \sin 100°}{\sin 35°}$

    K. $\dfrac{7 \sin 100°}{\sin 45°}$

Answers and Explanations are provided at the end of the book.

CHAPTER 14

Statistics and Probability

CHAPTER OBJECTIVES

By the end of this chapter, you will be able to:

1. Analyze data sets using descriptive statistics (mean, median, and mode)

2. Analyze, manipulate, and draw conclusions based on information displayed in tables and graphs, including two-way frequency tables

3. Calculate simple, conditional, and joint probabilities

4. Use probability distributions to answer questions and calculate expected value

5. Apply counting techniques, including finding combinations and permutations

SMARTPOINTS

Point Value	SmartPoints Category
4 Points	Statistics and Probability

STATISTICS AND PROBABILITY

Statistics and Probability questions make up about 8–12% of the Math test. These questions test your ability to interpret and/or use data presented in a variety of forms. Common questions include finding or using averages and describing or analyzing the center or spread of a set of data.

You'll also have to calculate simple and conditional probabilities that are based on a description of a scenario, data presented in a two-way table or other type of chart or graph, or a probability distribution function. Finally, you'll see questions involving counting techniques, such as combinations and permutations.

You already practiced questions involving measures of center (mean, median, and mode) in the Essential Skills chapter, so let's begin this chapter with a review of measures of spread (how the data in a set varies).

Variability

The **variability** (spread) of a set of data can be described using range and standard deviation. Variability is a representation of how much the data varies.

- The **range** of a data set is the difference between the highest and lowest values.

- The **standard deviation** of a data set is a measure of how far a typical data point is from the mean (how spread out the numbers are). A low standard deviation means most values in the set are fairly close to the mean; a high standard deviation means there is much more spread in the data set. The symbol for standard deviation is σ.

To **find the standard deviation** of a data set, follow these steps:

Step 1: Find the mean of the data.

Step 2: For each data point, subtract the mean and then square the result.

Step 3: Find the average of all the squared results.

Step 4: Take the square root of the result from Step 3.

Chances are that you won't have to calculate the standard deviation of a data set on Test Day, but it's a good idea to practice doing so now, just in case.

Math

1. Ian bowled 5 games during a bowling tournament. The table below shows his scores. What is the approximate standard deviation of Ian's scores?

Game 1	Game 2	Game 3	Game 4	Game 5
110	160	140	130	110

   A.   19

   B.   26

   C.   31

   D.   50

   E.   130

Work through the Kaplan Method for ACT Math step-by-step to answer this question. The following table shows Kaplan's strategic thinking on the left, along with suggested math scratchwork on the right.

Strategic Thinking	Math Scratchwork
Step 1: What is the question? You need to find the standard deviation of Ian's scores.	
Step 2: What information am I given? You're given a table with 5 scores.	110, 160, 140, 130, 110
Step 3: What can I do with the information? Perform one step at a time. First, find the mean of the data (the average).	$\dfrac{110 + 160 + 140 + 130 + 110}{5}$ $= \dfrac{650}{5} = 130$
Next, subtract the mean from each data point and square the result.	$110 - 130 = -20 \rightarrow (-20)^2 = 400$ $160 - 130 = 30 \rightarrow (30)^2 = 900$ $140 - 130 = 10 \rightarrow (10)^2 = 100$ $130 - 130 = 0 \rightarrow (0)^2 = 0$ $110 - 130 = -20 \rightarrow (-20)^2 = 400$
Then, find the average of all the squared results.	$\dfrac{400 + 900 + 100 + 0 + 400}{5}$ $= \dfrac{1,800}{5} = 360$
Finally, take the square root of the average found in the previous step.	$\sqrt{360} \approx 18.97$, or about 19

Strategic Thinking	Math Scratchwork
Step 4: Am I finished? Nicely done! You've found the standard deviation of Ian's scores.	*Choice (A) is correct.*

> ✔ **Note**
>
> If your calculator includes a standard deviation function, it may be worth the time invested to learn how to use it before Test Day.

Shape

On Test Day, you might also be asked to analyze the **shape** of data. The shape of a data set can be either **symmetric** (also referred to as a *normal* distribution) or **skewed** (asymmetric). Many data sets have a head, where a lot of data points are clustered in one area, and tails, where the number of data points slowly decreases to 0. Examining the tails will help you describe the shape of a data set. A data set is skewed in the direction of its longer tail.

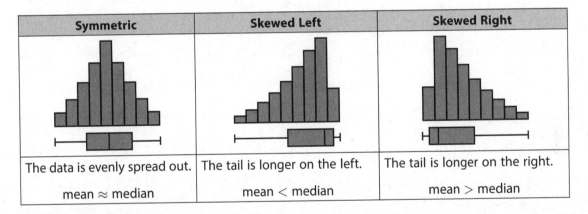

Symmetric	Skewed Left	Skewed Right
The data is evenly spread out.	The tail is longer on the left.	The tail is longer on the right.
mean ≈ median	mean < median	mean > median

Data Representations

It is essential that you be able to read and interpret data presented in a variety of forms. These include tables or charts, bar graphs, circle graphs, line graphs, and even graphs that use small icons to model data (you probably saw these when you first started learning about statistics in elementary or middle school). Let's quickly review each form:

- **Tables** or **charts** display information in rows and columns.

- **Bar graphs** display numerical values of variables represented by the height or length of rectangles of equal width. Bar graphs can be vertical or horizontal.

- **Circle graphs** (also called pie graphs) represent data as parts of a circle where relative percentages dictate the portions of the circle.

- **Line graphs** display how data changes, usually over time.

- **Pictographs** use small icons to represent data. Pictographs always include a key (or legend) that tells how much or how many of something each icon represents.

> ✔ **Expert Tip**
>
> When displaying data in a circle graph, you'll need to find the measures of the central angles for each sector of the circle. To do this, multiply each percent by 360°. For example, a sector that represents 35% of the data should have a central angle that measures approximately 0.35(360°) = 126°. When you're done, the percentages should sum to 100%, and the angle measures should sum to 360°.

Here is an easy question to begin with.

2. Lunenburg County has 4 public parks. The pictograph below shows the number of trees in each park. What is the average number of trees per park in Lunenburg County?

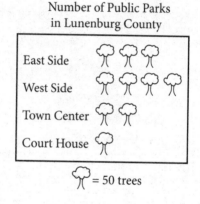

Number of Public Parks
in Lunenburg County

= 50 trees

    F.   50

    G.   75

    H.   125

    J.   150

    K.   200

Work through the Kaplan Method for ACT Math step-by-step to answer this question. The following table shows Kaplan's strategic thinking on the left, along with suggested math scratchwork on the right.

Strategic Thinking	Math Scratchwork
Step 1: What is the question? You're asked for the the average number of trees per park in Lunenburg County.	
Step 2: What information am I given? You're told the number of parks, and you're given a pictograph with a key.	4 parks 1 tree icon = 50 trees
Step 3: What can I do with the information? A data display question about an average is essentially the same as any other question about averages. Start by finding the total number of trees. To save time, count the total number of tree icons and multiply by 50 rather than finding the number in each area separately. As usual, the next step is to divide by the number of data values. Here, you're finding the average number *per park*, so the number of data values is 4.	$(3 + 4 + 2 + 1) \times 50$ $= 10 \times 50$ $= 500$ $500 \div 4 = 125$ trees per park
Step 4: Am I finished? You found the average number of trees per park, 125, so your job is done.	Choice (H) is correct.

Math

Let's try one more before moving on to probability.

3. The circle graph below shows the distribution of registered voters in a certain district in Florida by party and by age. If there are 18,400 voters in the district, what is the ratio of Republicans to Independents?

A. 3:1

B. 7:2

C. 22:3

D. 22:6

E. 23:6

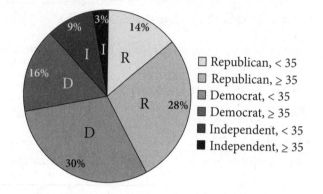

☐ Republican, < 35
☐ Republican, ≥ 35
☐ Democrat, < 35
◼ Democrat, ≥ 35
◼ Independent, < 35
◼ Independent, ≥ 35

Work through the Kaplan Method for ACT Math step-by-step to answer this question. The following table shows Kaplan's strategic thinking on the left, along with suggested math scratchwork on the right.

Strategic Thinking	Math Scratchwork
Step 1: What is the question? You're asked for the ratio of Republicans to Independents.	
Step 2: What information am I given? You're given a circle graph with percentages and a key. You're also told there are 18,400 voters in the district.	
Step 3: What can I do with the information? Because the numbers in the circle graph are given as percentages, the ratio will be the same no matter how many voters there are in the district. All you need to do is compare Republicans to Independents. The question does not specify an age range, so add both together for each party affiliation. Now write the ratio in the order requested.	Republican: 14 + 28 = 42 Independent: 9 + 3 = 12 Republicans:Independents 42:12, which reduces to 7:2
Step 4: Am I finished? You found the correct ratio, so you're done.	Choice (B) is correct.

Probability and Two-Way Tables

In the Essential Skills chapter, you answered some basic probability questions. Let's expand on that knowledge now.

Probability is a fraction or decimal comparing the number of desired outcomes to the number of total possible outcomes. Here's the formula:

$$\text{Probability} = \frac{\text{number of desired outcomes}}{\text{number of possible outcomes}}$$

For instance, if you have a full deck of playing cards and want to know the probability of drawing an ace, you would compute $\frac{\text{\# aces}}{\text{\# cards}} = \frac{4}{52} = \frac{1}{13} \approx 0.077$. To find the probability that an event will *not* happen, subtract the probability that the event will happen from 1. In the ace example, this would be:

$$1 - \frac{\text{\# aces}}{\text{\# cards}} = 1 - \frac{4}{52} = \frac{48}{52} = \frac{12}{13} \approx 0.923$$

You can also find the probability for a series of events. If you're asked for the probability of drawing an ace without replacement (the card does not go back in the deck) followed by a red nine, multiply the probability of the first event by that of the second:

$$\frac{\text{\# aces}}{\text{\# cards}} \times \frac{\text{\# red nines}}{\text{\# cards} - 1} = \frac{4}{52} \times \frac{2}{51} = \frac{8}{2,652} \approx 0.003$$

✔ Note

"With replacement" means the item chosen, in this case a card, is returned to the original group (here, the deck). The number of possible outcomes in the denominator will stay constant. "Without replacement" indicates the item is not returned; the number of possible outcomes will change to reflect the new possible outcome count.

A **two-way table** contains data on two variables. This type of table can be used to make comparisons and determine whether relationships exist between the variables. You might see this data referred to as bivariate (two-variable) data.

If you're worried about having to learn a new topic, you need not be. You've likely encountered two-way tables in the past and just not known their formal name—if you've ever generated a spreadsheet, two-way tables should look familiar.

Using a two-way table, you can find the probability that a randomly selected data value (be it a person, object, etc.) will fit a certain profile. In addition, you might be asked to calculate a **conditional probability**. Conditional probability questions are easy to spot, as the word *given* is often present, and they usually boil down to identifying the relevant row(s) and/or column(s).

The following is a two-way table summarizing the responses to a survey on water preference.

	Bottled	Carbonated	Tap	Total
Female	325	267	295	887
Male	304	210	289	803
Total	629	477	584	1,690

If asked for the probability of randomly selecting a female who prefers bottled water from all the participants, you would calculate it using the same general formula as before:

$$\frac{\text{\# female, bottled}}{\text{\# possible outcomes}} = \frac{325}{1,690} = \frac{5}{26} \approx 0.192$$

If asked for the probability of randomly selecting a female for a follow-up survey, given that the chosen participant prefers bottled water, the setup is a little different. The clause starting with "given" indicates the number of possible outcomes is the total participants who prefer bottled water, which is 629, not the grand total of 1,690. The calculation is now this:

$$\frac{\text{\# female, bottled}}{\text{\# bottled}} = \frac{325}{629} \approx 0.517$$

Conversely, if you need to find the probability of selecting someone who prefers bottled water for a follow-up survey, given that the chosen participant is female, the new number of possible outcomes is the female participant total (887). The calculation becomes this:

$$\frac{\text{\# female, bottled}}{\text{\# females}} = \frac{325}{887} \approx 0.366$$

Take a look at the next two questions about a two-way table.

> Use the following information to answer questions 4–5.

The following table shows the number of infants born in a certain hospital in August 2016. The table categorizes the births by gender and whether the infant was below, above, or within the healthy weight range, as defined by the World Health Organization.

	Below Range	Within Range	Above Range	Total
Male	1	56	10	67
Female	8	48	5	61
Total	9	104	15	128

4. Approximately what percent of the infants born at this hospital in August 2016 were below the healthy weight range?

   F. 7%

   G. 8%

   H. 9%

   J. 12%

   K. 15%

Work through the Kaplan Method for ACT Math step-by-step to answer this question. The following table shows Kaplan's strategic thinking on the left, along with suggested math scratchwork on the right.

Strategic Thinking	Math Scratchwork
Step 1: What is the question? You're asked for the percent of infants who were below the healthy range.	
Step 2: What information am I given? You're given data displayed in a two-way table.	
Step 3: What can I do with the information? Identify the relevant row(s) and/or column(s). Keep in mind that the question does not specify male or female. Find the percent.	% below range = total below range (9) ÷ total born (128) 9 ÷ 128 ≈ 0.0703 = about 7%
Step 4: Am I finished? The percent born below the healthy range is 7%, so you have your answer.	Choice (F) is correct.

5. A neonatal care company conducted a study on the female infants born at this hospital in August 2016 who were either below or above the healthy weight range. If an infant is randomly selected from females born at this hospital in August 2016, what is the probability that the infant is one of those who were included in the study?

A. $\dfrac{5}{128}$

B. $\dfrac{5}{61}$

C. $\dfrac{13}{128}$

D. $\dfrac{13}{61}$

E. $\dfrac{61}{128}$

Work through the Kaplan Method for ACT Math step-by-step to answer this question. The following table shows Kaplan's strategic thinking on the left, along with suggested math scratchwork on the right.

Strategic Thinking	Math Scratchwork
Step 1: What is the question? You need to find the probability that a randomly selected female will be either below or above the healthy weight range.	
Step 2: What information am I given? You're given data displayed in a two-way table.	
Step 3: What can I do with the information? As before, identify the relevant row(s) and or column(s). Now use the probability formula.	*female, below range = 8* *female, above range = 5* *total # female = 61* $\text{Probability} = \dfrac{\# \ desired \ outcomes}{\# \ possible \ outcomes}$ $= \dfrac{8 + 5}{61} = \dfrac{13}{61}$
Step 4: Am I finished? You found the desired probability. Nice work!	*Choice (D) is correct.*

Probability Distribution Tables

A **probability distribution table** correlates each possible outcome of an experiment with its probability of occurrence. It is simply a way of organizing probabilities in a table rather than describing them verbally.

Suppose you flip a coin two times. The possible outcomes, referred to as the **sample space** of the experiment, would be HH, HT, TH, and TT. Now suppose a different experiment involves the number of heads, X, that are possible on two flips of a coin: The sample space of this experiment is 0, 1, and 2. The table below, which associates each outcome (the number of heads) with its probability, is an example of a probability distribution.

X	Probability $P(X = x)$
0	0.25
1	0.50
2	0.25

✔ **Expert Tip**

If all possible outcomes are listed in a probability distribution, then the sum of all the probabilities is 1.

You can use a probability distribution table to answer probability questions by reading the table carefully. Let's try one.

6. A number cube is referred to as "loaded" if it is weighted in such a way that some numbers are rolled more often than others. The table below shows the probability distribution for rolling the number X on a certain loaded number cube. What is the probability of rolling a number less than 4 ?

    F. 0.083
    G. 0.249
    H. 0.333
    J. 0.500
    K. 0.918

X	Probability $P(X = x)$
1	0.083
2	0.083
3	0.083
4	0.083
5	0.168
6	0.500

Math

Work through the Kaplan Method for ACT Math step-by-step to answer this question. The following table shows Kaplan's strategic thinking on the left, along with suggested math scratchwork on the right.

Strategic Thinking	Math Scratchwork
Step 1: What is the question? You need to find the probability of rolling a number that is less than 4.	
Step 2: What information am I given? You are given a probability distribution table.	
Step 3: What can I do with the information? First, translate English to math. Now use the table to calculate the probability.	"less than 4" → 1, 2, or 3 $P(X < 4) = P(1) + P(2) + P(3)$ $= 0.083 + 0.083 + 0.083$ $= 0.249$
Step 4: Am I finished? The probability you're looking for is 0.249.	Choice (G) is correct.

Expected Value

The **expected value** of an experiment is the weighted average over the long run (a long-term measure of center). In plain English, that simply means based on the calculated probabilities, what do you expect the outcome to be?

If you encounter an expected value question on Test Day, you can bet it will be associated with a probability distribution table. This is good news! Calculating expected value from a probability distribution table is very straightforward: Simply multiply each outcome by its corresponding probability and add the results. The formula for finding the expected value when there are i possible outcomes is:

$$E(X) = x_1 p_1 + x_2 p_2 + x_3 p_3 + \ldots + x_i p_i$$

The formula itself looks much more daunting than the actual process, so let's give one a try to put your mind at ease.

7. Dr. Lee has taught 1,520 university students over the past 10 years. The grade points (0–4) earned by past students and their corresponding probabilities are recorded in the table below. Based on this probability distribution, what is the expected number of grade points that a randomly selected student in his class this semester can expect to earn?

Grade Points	Probability
4	0.20
3	0.35
2	0.30
1	0.10
0	0.05

- **A.** 1.85
- **B.** 2.0
- **C.** 2.25
- **D.** 2.55
- **E.** 3

Work through the Kaplan Method for ACT Math step-by-step to answer this question. The following table shows Kaplan's strategic thinking on the left, along with suggested math scratchwork on the right.

Strategic Thinking	Math Scratchwork
Step 1: What is the question? You're asked to find the expected number of grade points that a student in Mr. Lee's class will earn.	
Step 2: What information am I given? You're given the number of students Mr. Lee has taught and a probability distribution table related to grade points earned in the past.	number of students = 1,520
Step 3: What can I do with the information? Expected value questions are very straightforward. First, multiply each outcome by its corresponding probability. (The number of students Mr. Lee taught in the past is not relevant to the actual calculation.)	$4(0.20) = 0.8$ $3(0.35) = 1.05$ $2(0.30) = 0.6$ $1(0.10) = 0.1$ $0(0.05) = 0$
All that's left to do is add the results.	$0.8 + 1.05 + 0.6 + 0.1 = 2.55$
Step 4: Am I finished? The expected value is 2.55. All done!	Choice (D) is correct.

✔ **Expert Tip**

Expected value is an easy concept to master, so be sure to review it before Test Day.

Counting Techniques

Counting techniques are used to find how many arrangements of something are possible. Sometimes counting the number of ways an event E can occur or the total number of possible outcomes can be fairly complicated, depending on whether repeats are allowed, whether the events are independent or dependent, and whether you're taking the whole group or just part of the group. Let's explore three different (but related) counting techniques.

The Fundamental Counting Principle

When dealing with groups of numbers, keep in mind the **Fundamental Counting Principle**: If an event has m possible outcomes, and another independent event has n possible outcomes, then there are mn ways for the two events to occur together (multiply). You'll know to use this principle when you see phrases like "how many different" or "how many distinct." Here's a good general strategy to follow:

Step 1: Draw a blank to represent each position.

Step 2: Fill in the number of possibilities for each position.

Step 3: Multiply.

Let's see this in action before moving on to more sophisticated techniques.

8. Jake has 4 types of cheese and 5 types of crackers to make a snack. How many different ways can Jake combine one piece of cheese and one cracker to make his snack?

F. 4

G. 5

H. 9

J. 20

K. 25

Work through the Kaplan Method for ACT Math step-by-step to answer this question. The following table shows Kaplan's strategic thinking on the left, along with suggested math scratchwork on the right.

Strategic Thinking	Math Scratchwork
Step 1: What is the question? You need to determine how many different snacks Jake can make.	
Step 2: What information am I given? You're told how many types of each item he has to choose from and that he'll select one of each.	cheese = 4 crackers = 5
Step 3: What can I do with the information? Start by drawing blanks to represent each item to be included in the snack. Fill in the number of possibilities for each item. Then multiply.	_____ _____ cheese cracker _4_ × _5_ = 20
Step 4: Am I finished? Yep, that's it. He can make 20 different snacks.	Choice (J) is correct.

Math

Permutations and Combinations

Permutations and combinations are a bit more complex. Sometimes, the most difficult task is deciding which of these applies to a given question. The difference is this:

Permutations are *sequences* in which order matters.

Combinations are *groups* in which order does not matter.

A computer password would be an example of a permutation—even if you have the right numbers, letters, and/or special characters, it doesn't work if they're out of order. Choosing from a selection of ice cream flavors would be an example of a combination—the order in which you choose doesn't change the end result.

Let's discuss permutations first, as they can often be calculated using a form of the Fundamental Counting Principle. The primary difference is that a permutation might involve dependent events and you may have to adjust the numbers as you fill in the blanks.

There are also three formulas for calculating permutations, depending on the situation. You'll need to decide when to use the Fundamental Counting Principle and when to use one of the formulas.

- The number of permutations of **n distinct objects** is $n! = n(n-1)(n-2) \ldots (3)(2)(1)$. The notation $n!$ is referred to as n factorial.

- The number of permutations of **n objects**, a of which are **indistinguishable**, b of which are indistinguishable, etc., is $\dfrac{n!}{a! \times b! \times \ldots}$.

- The number of permutations of **n objects taken r at a time** is $_nP_r = \dfrac{n!}{(n-r)!}$.

The best way to learn when, and how, to apply these formulas is to practice, so let's try a couple.

9. Jose is going to randomly choose a 5-character computer password consisting of, first, 2 letters, then 2 numbers, and then 1 special symbol (there are 8 special symbols to choose from). Which of the following expressions gives the number of different pass-words Jose can choose?

   A. $26^2 + 10^2 + 8$

   B. $26^2 \cdot 10^2 \cdot 8$

   C. $2(26!) + 2(10!) + 8!$

   D. $(2 \cdot 26)! + (2 \cdot 10)! + 8!$

   E. $(26 + 10 + 8)!$

Work through the Kaplan Method for ACT Math step-by-step to answer this question. The following table shows Kaplan's strategic thinking on the left, along with suggested math scratchwork on the right.

Strategic Thinking	Math Scratchwork
Step 1: What is the question? You need to determine the number of different passwords Jose can choose.	
Step 2: What information am I given? You're given the number of characters in the password and the types of options Jose will choose from.	5 characters 2 letters, 2 numbers, 1 special symbol
Step 3: What can I do with the information? The question stem contains the phrase "number of different," so use the Fundamental Counting Principle. Start by drawing blanks to represent each character to be included in the password. Fill in each blank with the number of possible choices. The question doesn't say that numbers or letters can't be repeated, so keep that in mind. Before you multiply, check the answer choices. The numbers aren't multiplied out, so just rewrite your answer to match.	__ __ __ __ __ lett. lett. num. num. special <u>26</u> <u>26</u> <u>10</u> <u>10</u> <u>8</u> $26^2 \cdot 10^2 \cdot 8$
Step 4: Am I finished? There's a perfect match among the answer choices, so your job is done.	Choice (B) is correct.

One more permutation question for good measure—this one's tougher and does require knowing the appropriate formula. The good news is that there will be at most one of these questions on the ACT.

10. Which of the following expressions gives the number of distinct permutations of the letters in the word HOMEWORK ?

   F. $8!(2!)$

   G. $8!$

   H. $\dfrac{8!}{2!}$

   J. $\dfrac{8!}{6!}$

   K. $\dfrac{8!}{(2!)(6!)}$

Work through the Kaplan Method for ACT Math step-by-step to answer this question. The following table shows Kaplan's strategic thinking on the left, along with suggested math scratchwork on the right.

Strategic Thinking	Math Scratchwork
Step 1: What is the question? You need to find the number of distinct permutations of the letters in HOMEWORK.	
Step 2: What information am I given? You're told this is a permutation question!	
Step 3: What can I do with the information? Distinct permutations are permutations without repetition, meaning you have to account for "indistinguishable" outcomes (the O and the O). Use the formula for n objects, a of which are indistinguishable.	$\dfrac{n!}{a!}$ $n = 8$ letters $a = 2$ indistinguishable (the two Os)
The answer choices aren't simplified, so fill in the values and you're all set.	$\dfrac{8!}{2!}$
Step 4: Am I finished? You found the correct expression. Great!	Choice (H) is correct.

If you encounter a **combinations** question on Test Day, the good news is that there is only one formula to remember. The first step, however, is to determine that the question indeed involves a combination (a group in which order doesn't matter). Here's the formula for finding the number of combinations of **n objects taken r at a time**:

$$_nC_r = \frac{n!}{r!(n-r)!}$$

Let's see how you would apply this formula.

11. A club with 24 members is forming a 3-person committee to plan a fund-raiser. Which expression gives the number of different 3-person committees that can be formed?

    A. $\dfrac{24}{3}$

    B. $\dfrac{24!}{3!(21!)}$

    C. $\dfrac{24!}{21!}$

    D. $\dfrac{24!}{3!}$

    E. $24!$

Work through the Kaplan Method for ACT Math step-by-step to answer this question. The following table shows Kaplan's strategic thinking on the left, along with suggested math scratchwork on the right.

Strategic Thinking	Math Scratchwork
Step 1: What is the question? You need to find the expression that represents the number of different 3-person committees that can be formed.	
Step 2: What information am I given? You're given the number of people in the club and the number of people who will be on the committee.	24 people in club 3-person committee
Step 3: What can I do with the information? The big clue here is that a *group* is being formed, so this is a combination question. Use the formula for a combination of n objects taken r at a time.	$_nC_r = \dfrac{n!}{r!(n-r)!}$ $n = 24, r = 3$
Fill in the numbers, simplify just a bit, and look for a match.	$_{24}C_3 = \dfrac{24!}{3!(24-3)!} = \dfrac{24!}{3!(21!)}$
Step 4: Am I finished? You've identified the correct expression, so your work here is done.	Choice (B) is correct.

Math

Unions and Intersections of Sets

Let's review one final quick topic to finish off this chapter.

The **union** of sets (∪) is what you get when you combine two sets. It includes all elements in either or both sets.

Example: What is the union of sets $A = \{1, 2, 3, 4, 5\}$ and $B = \{2, 4, 6, 8, 10\}$?

To find the union, simply list everything from both sets once (don't repeat any numbers): $A \cup B = \{1, 2, 3, 4, 5, 6, 8, 10\}$.

The **intersection** of sets (∩) is what you get when you overlap two sets. It includes only elements *common* to the sets.

Example: What is the intersection of sets $A = \{1, 2, 3, 4, 5\}$ and $B = \{2, 4, 6, 8, 10\}$?

To find the intersection, simply list the numbers that appear in both: $A \cap B = \{2, 4\}$.

You might also see sets organized in Venn diagrams. Sets A and B from the previous examples would look like this:

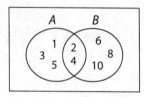

Ready to wrap up your math review? Let's try one final question together.

12. How many whole numbers less than 10 are also prime numbers?

    F. 2

    G. 3

    H. 4

    J. 7

    K. 9

Work through the Kaplan Method for ACT Math step-by-step to answer this question. The following table shows Kaplan's strategic thinking on the left, along with suggested math scratchwork on the right.

Strategic Thinking	Math Scratchwork
Step 1: What is the question? You're asked for a count of whole numbers less than 10 that are also prime.	
Step 2: What information am I given? You have two sets of numbers to consider.	Set A = whole numbers < 10 Set B = prime numbers
Step 3: What can I do with the information? The words "are also" tell you that you're looking for an intersection of the two sets. You can make a list or draw a Venn diagram. Count how many numbers are in the overlapping region of the diagram.	 There are 4 numbers in the overlap.
Step 4: Am I finished? There are 4 numbers less than 10 that are prime numbers. That's your answer.	Choice (H) is correct.

Now you'll have a chance to try a few test-like questions in a scaffolded way. We've provided some guidance, but you'll need to fill in the missing parts of the explanation or the step-by-step math to get to the correct answer. Don't worry—after going through the worked examples at the beginning of this section, these questions should be completely doable.

13. Carin's test grades in AP Statistics this semester were rather inconsistent: 100, 85, 55, 95, and 75. What is the standard deviation of Carin's test grades?

   A. 12

   B. 15

   C. 16

   D. 19

   E. 24

Use the following scaffolding as your map through the question. If you aren't sure where to start, fill in the blanks in the table as you work from top to bottom.

Strategic Thinking	Math Scratchwork
Step 1: What is the question? You're asked to calculate the standard deviation of Carin's grades.	
Step 2: What information am I given? You're given the five test grades.	100, 85, 55, 95, 75
Step 3: What can I do with the information? Follow the steps for finding standard deviation. First, find the mean of the grades (the average). Next, for each data point, subtract the mean and square the result.	mean = _____ $(100 - \underline{\quad})^2 = \underline{\qquad}$ $(85 - \underline{\quad})^2 = \underline{\qquad}$ $(55 - \underline{\quad})^2 = \underline{\qquad}$ $(95 - \underline{\quad})^2 = \underline{\qquad}$ $(75 - \underline{\quad})^2 = \underline{\qquad}$
Next, find the average of all the squared results. Finally, take the square root of the number from the previous step.	average = _____ standard deviation = _____
Step 4: Am I finished? Was the result of all your hard work 16? Nice job!	Choice _____ is correct.

14. Michael works for a landscaping company and is spreading fertilizer on all the lawns in a neighborhood. The figure below shows the layout of the neighborhood and the times that Michael started the lawns at two of the houses. Each lawn in the neighborhood is approximately the same size and takes the same amount of time to fertilize. About how many minutes should it take Michael to fertilize all the lawns in the neighborhood?

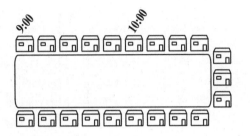

F. 180

G. 210

H. 224

J. 252

K. 280

Use the following scaffolding as your map through the question. If you aren't sure where to start, fill in the blanks in the table as you work from top to bottom.

Strategic Thinking	Math Scratchwork
Step 1: What is the question? You need to determine how many minutes it should take Michael to fertilize all the lawns.	
Step 2: What information am I given? You're given a diagram of the neighborhood and a start time for two houses. You're also told that each lawn takes about the same amount of time.	start house _____ at _____ start house _____ at _____
Step 3: What can I do with the information? First, determine how long it took Michael to complete one lawn (his rate in minutes). Then, count the number of houses in the diagram and multiply by the rate.	_____ houses in _____ minutes rate of _____ minutes per house _____ houses x _____ min/house = _____ minutes
Step 4: Am I finished? Is your answer 252 minutes? Great job!	Choice _____ is correct.

Math

15. A rodent geneticist studied a sample of 200 mice to see how many offspring they had per birth. The results of the study are recorded in the bar graph below. What percent of the mice in the sample had a litter of seven or more pups?

A. 18%

B. 22%

C. 26%

D. 38%

E. 44%

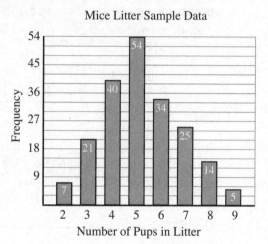

Mice Litter Sample Data

Use the following scaffolding as your map through the question. If you aren't sure where to start, fill in the blanks in the table as you work from top to bottom.

Strategic Thinking	Math Scratchwork
Step 1: What is the question? You need to find the percent of the mice in the sample that had a litter of seven or more pups.	
Step 2: What information am I given? You're given the total number of mice in the sample, and you're given a bar graph showing the distribution of pup numbers.	total number in sample = _____
Step 3: What can I do with the information? First, identify the bars on the graph that you'll need (seven or more pups). Then jot down the heights of those bars, because they represent the number of mice that birthed that many pups. To find the percent, complete the statement. Now divide, simplify, and multiply by 100%.	7 pups = _____ 8 pups = _____ 9 pups = _____ _____ out of _____ mice had 7 or more pups $\dfrac{}{} = \dfrac{}{100} \times 100\% = \_\_\_\_\_\%$
Step 4: Am I finished? Did you come up with 22%? Awesome!	Choice _____ is correct.

16. For each month over the past 24 months, a research team counted the number of bald eagles that returned to a particular reservation feeding area. The number of returning eagles and their corresponding probabilities are shown in the probability distribution table below. There was no distinguishable pattern based on the season of the year.

Based on this distribution, which of the following is the closest to the number of bald eagles that the research team should expect to see return to the feeding area next month?

F. 1

G. 2

H. 3

J. 4

K. 5

Number of Returning Eagles	Probability
0	0.02
1	0.08
2	0.15
3	0.28
4	0.25
5	0.22

Use the following scaffolding as your map through the question. If you aren't sure where to start, fill in the blanks in the table as you work from top to bottom.

Strategic Thinking	Math Scratchwork
Step 1: What is the question? Find the expected number of returning bald eagles.	
Step 2: What information am I given? You're given a probability distribution table.	
Step 3: What can I do with the information? Multiply each number of returning bald eagles by the corresponding probability.	____ × ____ = ____ ____ × ____ = ____ ____ × ____ = ____ ____ × ____ = ____ ____ × ____ = ____ ____ × ____ = ____
Find the sum and round to find the closest value.	total = ____ closest value is
Step 4: Am I finished? Did you get 3? Way to go!	Choice ____ is correct.

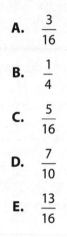

Math

17. A fair coin is flipped five times. What is the probability that at least four of the five flips will be heads?

A. $\frac{3}{16}$

B. $\frac{1}{4}$

C. $\frac{5}{16}$

D. $\frac{7}{10}$

E. $\frac{13}{16}$

Use the following scaffolding as your map through the question. If you aren't sure where to start, fill in the blanks in the table as you work from top to bottom.

Strategic Thinking	Math Scratchwork
Step 1: What is the question? You need to find the probability that at least four of the five flips will be heads.	
Step 2: What information am I given? You know that the coin is fair and how many times it will be flipped.	____ flips
Step 3: What can I do with the information? Jot down the probability formula. First, find the number of favorable outcomes. Because at least four of the five flips must be heads, simply writing out all the desired outcomes won't take much time. To find the number of total possible outcomes, use the Fundamental Counting Principle. How many possible outcomes are there on a single flip? How many flips are there? Now fill in the probability formula and reduce your answer.	probability = $\dfrac{\text{\# _____ outcomes}}{\text{\# _____ outcomes}}$ _____ , _____ _____ , _____ _____ , _____ # poss. outcomes: = ___ · ___ · ___ · ___ · ___ = ___ $P = \dfrac{\quad}{\quad} = \dfrac{\quad}{\quad}$
Step 4: Am I finished? Did you get $\dfrac{3}{16}$? Excellent work!	*Choice _____ is correct.*

18. How many different ways are there to assign three students to five desks, with no more than one person to a desk?

   F. 8

   G. 15

   H. 30

   J. 60

   K. 120

Use the following scaffolding as your map through the question. If you aren't sure where to start, fill in the blanks in the table as you work from top to bottom.

Strategic Thinking	Math Scratchwork
Step 1: What is the question? You're looking for the number of different ways to assign three students to five desks.	
Step 2: What information am I given? You're given the number of students and the number of available desks.	3 students 5 desks
Step 3: What can I do with the information? First, determine whether order matters. Imagine the five desks in a row: Is Charlie, then Sam, then Katy a different arrangement from Sam, then Charlie, then Katy? Now that you know what type of question it is, draw blanks to represent the three students and then fill in the number of options for which desk each student could be assigned. Finally, multiply.	Order does / does not matter, so this is a _____ question. ____ · ____ · ____ = ____ ways to arrange 3 students
Step 4: Am I finished? Did you get 60 ways? Perfect!	Choice _____ is correct.

Now that you've seen the variety of ways in which the ACT can test you on Statistics and Probability, try the following questions to check your understanding. Give yourself 5 minutes to answer these 4 questions. Make sure you use the Kaplan Method for ACT Math as often as you can. Remember, you want to emphasize speed and efficiency in addition to simply getting the correct answer.

19. In a company of 50 people, the 30 males have an average age of 42, and the 20 females have an average age of 37. To the nearest year, what is the average age of the company's workforce?

    A. 39

    B. 40

    C. 41

    D. 42

    E. 43

20. A survey is conducted regarding a proposed change in the attendance policy at a law school. The table below categorizes the results of the survey by year of the student (1L, 2L, or 3L) and whether they are for, against, or undecided about the new policy. What fraction of all 1Ls and 2Ls are against the new policy?

	For	Against	Undecided	Total
1L	32	16	10	58
2L	24	12	28	64
3L	17	25	13	55
Total	73	53	51	177

    F. $\dfrac{28}{177}$

    G. $\dfrac{14}{61}$

    H. $\dfrac{24}{61}$

    J. $\dfrac{28}{53}$

    K. $\dfrac{122}{177}$

21. How many positive four-digit integers have 3 as their hundreds digit and 5 or 9 as their ones digit?

    A. 180

    B. 190

    C. 200

    D. 210

    E. 220

22. In 3 fair coin tosses, what is the probability of obtaining at least 2 heads? (Note: In a fair coin toss, the 2 outcomes, heads and tails, are equally likely.)

    F. $\dfrac{1}{8}$

    G. $\dfrac{3}{8}$

    H. $\dfrac{1}{2}$

    J. $\dfrac{2}{3}$

    K. $\dfrac{7}{8}$

Answers and Explanations are provided at the end of the book.

ON YOUR OWN

The following questions provide an opportunity to practice the concepts and strategic thinking covered in this chapter.

1. Mary's goal is to collect 200 cans of food during a food drive. During her first four days, she averaged 10 cans per day. With 10 days remaining, Mary must average how many cans per day to meet her goal?

   A. 12

   B. 14

   C. 16

   D. 18

   E. 20

2. A cooking class has 20 spaces available for each daily session. Data showed that 19 people attended the first session, 17 people attended the second session, and 15 people attended each of the remaining sessions. If the average number of attendees was exactly 16 per class session, how many total sessions of the cooking class were there?

   F. 3

   G. 4

   H. 6

   J. 11

   K. Cannot be determined from the given information

3. Mr. Foster took the students in his driver's education class to the Department of Motor Vehicles to take their driver's license test. The number of questions missed by each student is recorded in the bar graph below. Which of the following statements must be true?

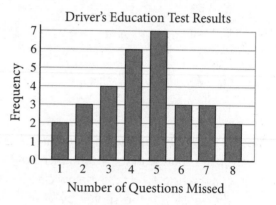

Driver's Education Test Results

   A. More than half of the students missed 5 or more questions.

   B. The mean number of questions missed was between 4 and 5.

   C. More students missed 3 questions than any other number of questions.

   D. Thirty-six students from Mr. Foster's class took the driver's license test that day.

   E. Two of Mr. Foster's students will have to retake the driver's license test before they can get their licenses.

4. The line plot below represents the amount of water carried by all of the campers on a backpacking trip, in gallons.

Water Record

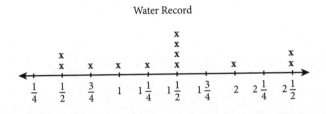

When the campers arrive at their campsite, they distribute the water equally among themselves. How many gallons of water should each camper receive?

F. $\dfrac{3}{4}$

G. $\dfrac{5}{6}$

H. $1\dfrac{1}{12}$

J. $1\dfrac{5}{12}$

K. $1\dfrac{1}{2}$

5. Jordan owns a small car dealership. He plans to display the number of different types of vehicles on his car lot in a circle graph. The vehicle count is shown in the table that follows. What should the angle measure of the largest section of the circle graph be?

Vehicle Type	Number on Lot
Subcompact	64
Compact	30
Midsize	61
Fullsize	58
Luxury	35
SUV	44
Truck	28
TOTAL	320

A. 60°

B. 64°

C. 68°

D. 72°

E. 80°

6. The table below gives the frequency of grades in certain grade intervals for 25 test grades in an AP Statistics class. Which interval contains the median of the grades?

Grade Interval	Frequency
A (91−100)	5
B (81−90)	7
C (71−80)	7
D (61−70)	4
F (60 and below)	2

F. A (91−100)

G. B (81−90)

H. C (71−80)

J. D (61−70)

K. F (60 and below)

Use the following information to answer questions 7–8.

The probability distribution of the discrete random variable X is shown in the table below.

X	Probability $P(X = x)$
0	$\frac{1}{5}$
1	$\frac{1}{10}$
2	$\frac{3}{10}$
3	$\frac{3}{20}$
4	$\frac{1}{4}$

7. If a computer program uses this distribution to randomly generate a value for X, what is the probability that the value will be odd?

   A. $\frac{3}{200}$

   B. $\frac{3}{20}$

   C. $\frac{1}{5}$

   D. $\frac{1}{4}$

   E. $\frac{2}{5}$

8. Based on the probability distribution, what is the expected value of X ?

   F. $\frac{3}{20}$

   G. 1

   H. 2

   J. $2\frac{1}{10}$

   K. $2\frac{3}{20}$

9. Alicia is playing a game in which she draws marbles from a box. There are 50 marbles, numbered 01 through 50. Alicia draws one marble from the box and sets it aside, then draws a second marble. If both marbles have the same units digit, then Alicia wins. If the first marble she draws is numbered 25, what is the probability that Alicia will win on her next draw?

   A. $\frac{1}{50}$

   B. $\frac{1}{49}$

   C. $\frac{2}{25}$

   D. $\frac{4}{49}$

   E. $\frac{9}{49}$

10. License plates in a certain state consist of 6 alphanumeric characters (letters A−Z and numbers 0−9) with the constraint that the letters I and O cannot be used. Which of the following expressions gives the number of distinct license plates that are possible assuming that repetition of both letters and numbers is allowed?

    F. $24^3 + 10^3$

    G. $24^3 \cdot 10^3$

    H. 34^6

    J. 6^{34}

    K. $34!$

11. What is the average of the expressions $2x + 5$, $5x − 6$, and $−4x + 2$?

    A. $x - \dfrac{1}{3}$

    B. $x + \dfrac{1}{4}$

    C. $x + \dfrac{1}{3}$

    D. $3x + 3$

    E. $3x − 3$

12. Brooks scored an average of 30 points per game on his basketball team. The numbers of points he scored in each game are shown below.

Game	1	2	3	4	5	6
Points	28	31	20	42	32	?

How many points did Brooks score in Game 6 ?

    F. 24

    G. 27

    H. 30

    J. 31

    K. 33

13. The table below displays Jamie's income for each of the years 1989–1994. Which of the years 1990–1994 shows the greatest percent increase over the previous year?

Year	Income
1989	$20,000
1990	$25,000
1991	$30,000
1992	$33,000
1993	$36,000
1994	$44,000

    A. 1990

    B. 1991

    C. 1992

    D. 1993

    E. 1994

Use the following information to answer questions 14–16.

Phase I clinical trials are run to determine the safety of an investigational drug. Dr. Gibbons is overseeing a treatment-resistant influenza Phase I trial with 400 healthy participants: Half are given the drug, and half are given an inert pill. The circle graph below shows a distribution of the severity of common side effects.

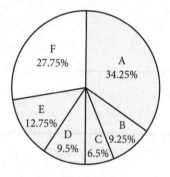

A: inert, mild or no side effects
B: inert, moderate side effects
C: inert, severe side effects
D: drug, mild or no side effects
E: drug, moderate side effects
F: drug, severe side effects

14. What percent of the participants experienced severe side effects?

F. 6.50%

G. 21.25%

H. 27.75%

J. 34.25%

K. 65.75%

15. How many more participants experienced mild or no side effects than severe side effects?

A. 10

B. 38

C. 42

D. 50

E. 64

16. What percent of the participants who experienced severe side effects were given the drug?

F. 28%

G. 50%

H. 75%

J. 81%

K. 90%

_____

17. At a district-wide student government convention, 1 female and 1 male will be selected to lead the discussions for the day. If there are 90 females and 125 males at the convention, how many different 2-person combinations of 1 female and 1 male are possible?

A. 35

B. 215

C. 430

D. 5,625

E. 11,250

18. Which of the following expressions gives the number of distinct permutations of the letters in STATISTICS ?

F. 10!(3!)

G. 10!

H. $\dfrac{10!}{3!}$

J. $\dfrac{10!}{5!}$

K. $\dfrac{10!}{(3!)(3!)(2!)}$

19. Two marbles are randomly chosen from a bag that contains 3 red marbles, 2 blue marbles, and 7 green marbles. After the first marble is chosen, it is not replaced in the bag. What is the probability of picking two green marbles?

    A. $\dfrac{7}{22}$

    B. $\dfrac{49}{144}$

    C. $\dfrac{6}{11}$

    D. $\dfrac{7}{12}$

    E. $\dfrac{149}{132}$

20. A local high school is raffling off a college scholarship to the students in its junior class. If a girl has a 0.55 chance of winning the scholarship and 154 of the juniors are girls, how many of the juniors are boys? (Assume that every junior has an equal chance to win.)

    F. 85

    G. 126

    H. 154

    J. 161

    K. 280

21. For the first 5 passes attempted in a football game, the table below gives the probability, $P(x)$, that a certain quarterback completes x passes. What is the probability that this quarterback will complete at least 1 pass in the first 5 passes he attempts?

x Completed Passes	$P(x)$
0	0.0219
1	0.0432
2	0.3118
3	0.5288
4	0.0822
5	0.0121

    A. 0.0432

    B. 0.0651

    C. 0.5288

    D. 0.9349

    E. 0.9781

22. A scientist was studying a meadow and the birds that lived in the meadow. He kept a count of the birds that appeared in the meadow by tagging them so that the individual birds could be distinguished from one another. There are only three types of birds that live in the meadow: buntings, larks, and sparrows. He found that the ratio of buntings to total birds in the meadow was 35:176, while the ratio of larks to total birds was 5:11. If the scientist randomly chooses one individual bird that he had previously counted, which type of bird is he most likely to choose?

    F. Bunting

    G. Lark

    H. Sparrow

    J. All bird types are equally likely.

    K. Cannot be determined from the given information

23. Jamal has a suitcase that contains 10 white socks (and no other socks). He wants to add enough black socks so that the probability of randomly selecting a white sock is $\frac{1}{5}$. How many black socks should Jamal add to the suitcase?

    A. 30

    B. 35

    C. 40

    D. 45

    E. 50

24. The histogram that follows shows the number of vehicles that a car rental agency currently has available to rent, categorized by fuel efficiency ratings. If a customer randomly selects one of the available cars, what is the probability that he will get a car that has a fuel efficiency rating of at least 25 miles per gallon?

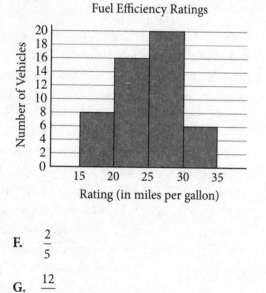

Fuel Efficiency Ratings

    F. $\frac{2}{5}$

    G. $\frac{12}{25}$

    H. $\frac{13}{25}$

    J. $\frac{10}{13}$

    K. $\frac{21}{25}$

25. A certain baseball stadium has 12,000 seats. Based on several previous years' attendance rates, the owners of the stadium constructed the table below showing the daily attendance rates and their probabilities of occurring for the coming baseball season. Based on the probability distribution in the table, what is the expected number of seats that will be occupied on any given day during the coming baseball season?

Attendance Rate	Probability
0.40	0.15
0.50	0.25
0.60	0.35
0.70	0.15
0.80	0.10

    A. 5,400

    B. 6,240

    C. 6,960

    D. 7,080

    E. 7,200

Answers and Explanations are provided at the end of the book.

READING INTRODUCTION

BY THE END OF THIS UNIT, YOU WILL BE ABLE TO:

1. Identify the format and timing of the ACT Reading test

2. Apply tips and strategies to the ACT Reading test

CHAPTER 15

ACT Reading

CHAPTER OBJECTIVES

By the end of this chapter, you will be able to:

1. Identify the four types of passages on the ACT Reading test

2. Identify the seven ACT Reading question types

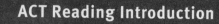

INSIDE THE ACT READING TEST

The Reading test is 35 minutes long and includes 40 questions. The test is comprised of four sections, each with either one long passage or two short passages. This means you only have 8–9 minutes to spend on each section. Each section will have 10 multiple-choice questions based on the text. You should spend 3–4 minutes mapping the passage(s) and 4–6 minutes answering the questions. Feel free to skip around within a section and answer the easy questions first. Just make sure to keep track of time so you get to all the questions. The Kaplan Method for ACT Reading will help you answer the questions strategically within the time allowed.

THE FORMAT

ACT Reading Passages

The three Reading passages and one paired passage set will each be in one of four genres, and these genres will always appear in the same order: Literary Narrative (including prose fiction), Social Studies, Humanities, and the Natural Sciences. The paired passages will discuss the same or related topics. Always note the genre as you begin reading a passage; your approach will vary slightly according to passage type. Being aware of the genre will also make it easier to identify the passage's central idea, thesis, or theme.

TEST DAY DIRECTIONS AND FORMAT

Although the exact wording might vary, here's what the Reading directions could look like:

> **Directions:** The Reading Test includes multiple passages. Each passage includes multiple questions. After reading each passage, choose the best answer and fill in the corresponding bubble on your answer sheet. You may review the passages as often as necessary.

If you would like to read through the exact wording you will see on Test Day, visit the test maker's website and download the Preparing for the ACT guide.

QUESTION TYPES

ACT Reading questions fall into two general categories: questions that ask about specifically stated information and questions that ask you to make inferences based on the author's intended purpose.

OUTSIDE KNOWLEDGE

No outside knowledge is required. The answers to every question can be found in the passage.

THE INSIDE SCOOP

As noted in the section on test format, the ACT Reading test always has the same four passage types in the same order. You can expect to see—in order—Literary Narrative (including prose fiction), Social Science, Humanities, and Natural Science passages. Each passage is about 800 words, and the pair of two shorter passages add up to about 800 words. They are written at the same level of complexity as typical college textbooks and readings.

Paired Passages deal with the same topic or related topics. Some questions ask about only one of the passages, while others ask you to consider both. The passage or passages each question addresses will be clearly labeled. The Paired Passages constitute one of the four sections of the Reading test, and the questions on these passages will make up about 25% of your Reading score.

The nonfiction passages (Social Science, Humanities, and Natural Science) are written with a clear purpose that you are expected to understand. You'll need to comprehend the author's use of structure as well as specific facts relayed in these essays.

The Prose Fiction passage asks you to focus more on the thoughts, feelings, and motivations of fictional characters, even when these are not explicitly stated in the passage.

The questions *do not* get harder as you proceed through the test.

TIMING

Take a few seconds at the beginning of the Reading test to flip through the four passages, gauging the difficulty of each. Start with the one that best suits your strengths and interests.

Plan to spend 8–9 minutes on each passage. That way, when time is called, you will have looked at all 40 Reading questions and at least gridded in a guess for every question.

Have an organized approach. We recommend that you start with the passage type in which you consistently answer the greatest number of questions correctly. Next tackle your second and third best passage types, leaving your least favorite for last. That way you grab as many points as possible at the beginning, and if you start to run out of time toward the end, you won't be sacrificing points you usually earn on the easier passages.

WHEN YOU'RE RUNNING OUT OF TIME

If you have less than five minutes left for the last passage, do the following:

1. Look for questions with specific line references and answer those.

2. Refer to the cited location in the passage and answer the question as best you can, based on what you see there.

3. Make sure you have gridded in an answer for every question before time is called.

SCORING

You will receive a Reading subject score—from 1 to 36—for the entire Reading subject test. This score will be averaged into your ACT Composite Score, equally weighted with your scores on the other three major subject tests. You will also receive three other scores based on specific Reading knowledge and concepts. These are called reporting categories and consist of:

- Key Ideas and Details
- Craft and Structure
- Integration of Knowledge and Ideas

QUICK TIPS

Mind-Set

- **Know where the passage is going.** Read the passage actively, paying attention to structural clues and key words and sentences to predict and evaluate what the passage is "doing." The easiest way to do this is to create a passage map.

- **Conquer the questions.** Look up the answers directly in the passage; don't be tempted by the choices or your memory.

- **Start with your strengths.** There's no reason to tackle these passages in the order given. Which subject interests you the most? Do you want to do that one first or last? Do you prefer fiction? Science stuff? Passages about people? Get yourself on a roll by starting with the passage that will most help you build confidence and bank your time.

SPECIAL STRATEGIES

Paired Passages

If you are tackling a set of paired passages, you will want to follow the Kaplan Method for Paired Passages in which you divide and conquer. Here are the steps:

Step 1: Actively read Passage A, then answer its questions
Step 2: Actively read Passage B, then answer its questions
Step 3: Answer questions about both passages

The ACT will make clear which questions relate to Passage A, Passage B, and both Passages A and B, which is very helpful. By concentrating on one passage at a time before you tackle questions that discuss both, you can avoid trap answer choices that refer to the wrong passage.

Prose Fiction Passages

Pay attention to the characters, especially the main character, and who gets the most (or best) lines. Read between the lines to determine unspoken emotions and attitudes. Ask yourself:

- **Who are these people?** What are they like? How do the characters relate to each other?

- **What is their state of mind?** Are they angry, sad, reflective, excited?

- **What's going on?** What's happening on the surface? What's happening beneath the surface?

- **What is the author's attitude toward the characters?** What words indicate a particular tone? Do any phrases suggest the author is either approving of or critical of one of the characters?

Reading

Nonfiction Passages

- **Don't be intimidated by technical vocabulary.** The Natural Science passage may take you into strange territory, but remember: this is the Reading test, not the Science test. Everything you need to know will be covered in the passages. If you find a difficult term, odds are the definition will be given to you in context (or else it simply might not matter what the word means).

- **Don't be thrown by unfamiliar topics.** You can get most questions right even if you don't fully understand the passage. Remember, you can find all the answers in the passage.

SMARTPOINTS BREAKDOWN

By studying the information released by the ACT, Kaplan has been able to determine how often certain topics are likely to show up on the test and, therefore, how many points these topics are worth on Test Day. If you master a given topic, you can expect to earn the corresponding number of SmartPoints on Test Day.

Here is a brief overview of what exactly to expect on the ACT Reading test.

KEY IDEAS AND DETAILS—21 POINTS

Key Ideas and Details questions make up 55–60% of the Reading test. The questions in this category require you to determine a text's central ideas and themes, draw logical inferences, and summarize information accurately.

Global—2 Points

The test will require you to identify an author's central idea and purpose. Some concepts you will be tested on include, but are not limited to:

- Choosing a correct summary of the passage as a whole
- Identifying key information within a passage

Inference—5 Points

The test will present Narrow and Broad Inference questions. Some concepts you will be tested on include, but are not limited to:

- Understanding relationships
- Drawing logical inferences and conclusions

Detail—14 Points

The test will require you to locate key details the author includes in a passage. Some concepts you will be tested on include, but are not limited to:

- Identifying key information within a passage
- Locating specific evidence an author provides

CRAFT AND STRUCTURE—11 POINTS

Craft and Structure questions make up 25–30% of the Reading test. The questions in this category require an understanding of the author's word choice, text structure, and perspective.

Vocab-in-Context—3 Points

The test will require you to determine word and phrase meanings. Some concepts you will be tested on include, but are not limited to:

- Determining the meaning of a word in context
- Identifying the meaning of a phrase in context

Function—4 Points

The test will require you to demonstrate an understanding of the text structure. You'll need to identify the purpose of portions of a passage. Some concepts you will be tested on include, but are not limited to:

- Analyzing text structure
- Determining the purpose of portions of a passage

Writer's View—4 Points

The test will require you to demonstrate an understanding of an author's perspective. You'll need to identify the author's point of view and differentiate among various perspectives. Some concepts you will be tested on include, but are not limited to:

- Identifying the author's point of view
- Distinguishing among multiple perspectives

INTEGRATION OF KNOWLEDGE AND IDEAS—4 POINTS

Knowledge of Language questions make up 13–18% of the Reading test. The questions in this category are called Synthesis questions, and they require you to understand authors' claims and use facts to make connections between different texts. Some concepts you will be tested on include, but are not limited to:

- Analyzing how authors construct arguments
- Evaluating reasoning and evidence from multiple sources
- Making connections between two short paired passages

UNIT EIGHT

ACT READING

BY THE END OF THIS UNIT, YOU WILL BE ABLE TO:

1. Identify Reading test question types and apply the appropriate strategies to answer questions correctly

2. Apply the Kaplan Method for ACT Reading

CHAPTER 16

The Kaplan Method for ACT Reading & Global and Inference Questions

CHAPTER OBJECTIVES

By the end of this chapter, you will be able to:

1. Identify and avoid the five wrong answer traps on the ACT Reading Test

2. Create a Passage Map using the Kaplan Method for ACT Reading, identifying key words and central ideas across passage types

3. Use a Passage Map to predict an answer and find its match among the answer choices

4. Identify central ideas and themes of a passage to answer questions about them

5. Identify and answer Global questions

6. Identify and answer Inference questions

SMARTPOINTS

Point Value	SmartPoints Category
Point Builder	The Kaplan Method for ACT Reading
2 Points	Global
5 Points	Inference

THE KAPLAN METHOD FOR ACT READING

It is imperative that you use the Kaplan Method for ACT Reading for every passage on the Reading test. Doing so ensures that you spend your time efficiently and maximize your opportunity to earn points. The Method will help you focus on important information as you read, anticipate possible questions, avoid excessive rereading of the passage, and—most importantly—answer more questions correctly.

The Kaplan Method for ACT Reading has three steps:

> **Step 1: Read actively**
> **Step 2: Examine the question stem**
> **Step 3: Predict and answer**

Let's take a closer look at each step.

Step 1: Read Actively

Active reading means that as you read the passage, you are asking questions and taking notes—both integral to acing the ACT Reading test.

You should ask questions such as:

- Why did the author write this word/detail/sentence/paragraph?

- Is the author taking a side? If so, what side is the author taking?

- What are the tone and purpose of the passage?

Be sure to:

- Identify the passage type (Literary Narrative/Prose Fiction, Social Studies, Humanities, or Natural Sciences)

- Note the main idea of each paragraph

Step 2: Examine the Question Stem

This means you should:

- Identify key words and line references in the question stem

- Apply question type strategies as necessary

Step 3: Predict and Answer

This means you should:

- Predict an answer before looking at the answer choices, also known as "predict before you peek"

- Select the best match

Predicting before you peek helps you:

- Know precisely what you are looking for in the answer choices

- Avoid weighing each answer choice equally, which saves time

- Eliminate the possibility of falling into wrong answer traps

Wrong Answer Traps

Wrong Answer Trap	Description
Distortion	The answer slightly alters details from a passage so they are no longer correct.
Extreme	The answer is too extreme to reflect the author's purpose.
Misused Detail	The answer is a true statement from the passage, but it doesn't answer the question.
Opposite	The answer contradicts the information in the passage.
Out-of-Scope	The answer includes information that is not in the passage

PASSAGE MAPPING

Step 1 of the Kaplan Method for ACT Reading dictates that you must take notes as you read the passage. We call these notes a Passage Map because they guide you through the passage and lead you to the correct answers.

Be sure to pay attention to and take note of the following as you map the passage:

- The "why" or the central idea of the passage—in other words, the thesis statement

- Transitions or changes in direction in a passage's logic

- The author's opinions and other opinions the author cites

- The author's tone and purpose

> ✔ **Note**
>
> A Passage Map should not replace the occasional underline or circle—it is important that you underline, circle, and take notes to create the most effective Passage Map.

While passage mapping may seem time-consuming at first, with practice it will become second nature by Test Day. Your overall ACT Reading test timing will actually improve because you'll spend less time searching the passage for answers to the questions.

Passage Types

Your approach to passage mapping will vary based on the passage type.

Passage Type(s)	Approach
Prose Fiction (includes **Literary Narrative**)	• Note the author's central ideas and themes • Note characters' personalities, opinions, and relationships with each other
Social Studies & Humanities	• Identify the author's thesis (often explicitly stated in the first paragraph) • Note the main idea of each paragraph
Natural Science	• Identify the author's thesis • Note the main idea of each paragraph • Don't let technical scientific terms intimidate you; no outside science knowledge is needed • Note the definitions of scientific terms that are provided within the passage text (or passage introduction)

> ✔ **Expert Tip**
>
> The ACT Reading test is an open-book test! The answer is always in the passage.

Reading

GLOBAL QUESTIONS

Global questions require you to identify both explicit and implicit themes in a text. As you go through ACT Reading passages, pay attention to the big picture—the author's central idea and purpose—and you will be able to answer Global questions with little to no rereading of the passage. To fully understand the central ideas of a passage, you must synthesize the various points the author makes with his or her thesis statement.

Global questions may ask you to choose a correct summary of the passage as a whole or to identify key information and ideas within the passage. When presented with this type of Global question, you can use your Passage Map, which is essentially a brief summary of what you have read.

On Test Day

The introductory section before an ACT Reading passage can be very helpful in determining the author's central ideas and themes. Make sure you take the time on Test Day to read this information and orient yourself to the passage.

You can recognize Global questions because they typically do not reference line numbers or even individual paragraphs. To confidently answer Global questions, you need to not only identify the central idea or theme of the passage but also avoid choosing answers that summarize secondary or supplementary points.

> ✔ **Note**
>
> Social Studies, Humanities, and Natural Sciences passages on the ACT Reading test are just well-written essays or article excerpts. You can normally find the thesis statement of a well-written piece at the end of the introductory paragraph.
>
> Note that there is a slight difference among the passage types. Social Studies, Humanities, and Natural Science passages are nonfiction and will have a definite central idea and thesis statement; Literary Narrative passages are usually fiction and will have a central theme but no thesis statement.

INFERENCE QUESTIONS

Inference questions ask about something that must be true based on the passage but that is not directly stated in the passage. To answer these questions efficiently and effectively, you must use your Passage Map and also fully utilize Step 3 of the Kaplan Method for ACT Reading: Predict and answer.

Narrow Inferences

Narrow inferences refer to specific parts of the passage. To answer these questions, look for clues indicating how the author connects relevant details within that part of the passage. Then, make a prediction.

Narrow Inference questions often use phrasing such as:

- *In lines xx–xx, the author **implies** that . . .*

- *The author's claim (line x) strongly **suggests** that . . .*

- *Based on the information in the second paragraph (lines xx–xx), it can be reasonably **inferred** that . . .*

Broad Inferences

Broad inferences ask what can be inferred from the passage as a whole or with what type of statements the author would generally agree. To answer these questions, consider how the author's point of view limits the range of what could be true.

Broad Inference questions often use phrasing such as:

- *The author strongly **suggests** that . . .*

- *It can be reasonably **inferred** that . . .*

- *The author most strongly **implies** that . . .*

✔ Expert Tip

An inference is NOT an opinion. It is a conclusion drawn from facts in the passage.

Work through the Kaplan Method for ACT Reading step-by-step to answer the questions that accompany the following Reading passage excerpt. The table below the excerpt contains two columns. The column on the right features the strategic thinking a test expert employs when approaching passages and related questions. Pay attention to how a test expert varies the approach to answer different question types.

Strategic Thinking
Step 1: Read actively
Read the passage and the notes provided. Remember, a well-crafted Passage Map should summarize the central idea of each paragraph as well as important topics or themes. Use your Passage Map to help you answer each question.

Reading

NATURAL SCIENCE: The following passage is excerpted from "The Transformer" by John W. Coltman. Reprinted with permission. (© 1988 by Scientific American, Inc.)

¶1: Transformer: function, importance to power systems

The transformer is an essential component of modern electric power systems. Simply put, it can convert electricity with a low current and a high voltage into electricity with a high current and a
5 low voltage (and vice versa) with almost no loss of energy. The conversion is important because electric power is transmitted most efficiently at high voltages but is best generated and used at low voltages. Were it not for transformers, the distance
10 separating generators from consumers would have to be minimized; many households and industries would require their own power stations, and electricity would be a much less practical form of energy.

¶2: Important in other electronics

15 In addition to its role in electric power systems, the transformer is an integral component of many things that run on electricity. Desk lamps, battery chargers, toy trains, and television sets all rely on transformers to cut or boost voltage. In its
20 multiplicity of applications, the transformer can range from tiny assemblies the size of a pea to behemoths weighing 500 tons or more. This article will focus on the transformers in power systems, but the principles that govern the function of
25 electrical transformers are the same regardless of size or application.

¶3: Discovery – Faraday; development

The English physicist Michael Faraday discovered the basic action of the transformer during his pioneering investigations of electricity in 1831. Some
30 50 years later, the advent of a practical transformer, containing all the essential elements of the modern instrument, revolutionized the infant electric lighting industry. By the turn of the century, alternating-current power systems had been universally adopted,
35 and the transformer had assumed a key role in electrical transmission and distribution.

Yet the transformer's tale does not end in 1900. Today's transformers can handle 500 times the power and 15 times the voltage of their turn-
40 of-the-century ancestors; the weight per unit of power has dropped by a factor of 10, and efficiency typically exceeds 99 percent. The advances reflect the marriage of theoretical inquiry and engineering that first elucidated and then exploited the
45 phenomena governing transformer action.

¶4: Current use; very efficient b/c inquiry + engineering

Faraday's investigations were inspired by the Danish physicist Hans Christian Oersted, who had shown in 1820 that an electric current flowing through a conducting material creates a
50 magnetic field around the conductor. At the time, Oersted's discovery was considered remarkable, since electricity and magnetism were thought to be separate and unrelated forces. If an electric current could generate a magnetic field, it seemed likely that
55 a magnetic field could give rise to an electric current.

¶5: Pre-Faraday, Oersted

In 1831, Faraday demonstrated that in order for a magnetic field to induce a current in a conductor, the field must be changing. Faraday caused the strength of the field to fluctuate by making and
60 breaking the electric circuit generating the field; the same effect can be achieved with a current whose direction alternates in time. This fascinating interaction of electricity and magnetism came to be known as electromagnetic induction.

¶6: Faraday; changing field = current

Reading

Questions	Strategic Thinking
1. It can be inferred from the passage that: **A.** Faraday was the first to show how an electric current can produce a magnetic field. **B.** Oersted was the first to utilize transformers in a practical application, by using them to power electric lights. **C.** Oersted coined the term "electromagnetic induction." **D.** Faraday showed that, when a magnetic field is changing, it can produce an electric current in a conducting material.	**Step 2: Examine the question stem** The key words in this question stem are "inferred from the passage." This is a broad Inference question, so it is best answered through the process of elimination and with support from the passage. **Step 3: Predict and answer** Notice that two choices start with "Faraday" and two start with "Oersted," and both are discussed in Paragraphs 5 and 6. Eliminate A and B, which contain false information. There is no evidence to support the claim made in C. Line 57 mentions the magnetic field and provides support for the correct answer, (D).
2. The passage strongly implies that advances in the efficiency of the transformer are: **F.** based solely on Faraday's discovery of electromagnetic induction. **G.** attributable to a combination of engineering and theoretical study. **H.** most likely at a peak that cannot be surpassed. **J.** found in transformers that weigh 500 tons or more.	**Step 2: Examine the question stem** The question's specific reference to "advances in the efficiency of the transformer" indicates that this is a narrow Inference question. The Passage Map note for Paragraph 4 mentions efficiency, so use that to make your prediction. **Step 3: Predict and answer** The Passage Map note for Paragraph 4 is "Current use; very powerful b/c inquiry + engineering." Choice (G) matches this prediction.
3. The main purpose of the passage is to: **A.** explain how electric power systems work. **B.** discuss the development and importance of the transformer. **C.** describe types of currents and voltages. **D.** explain reactions to Faraday's discovery and investigations.	**Step 2: Examine the question stem** The key phrase *main purpose* indicates that this is a Global question. Find the answer by using the entire Passage Map to summarize the central idea and purpose of the passage. **Step 3: Predict and answer** Paragraph 1 states that transformers are important to power systems, and the rest of the passage supports this idea. Choice (B) matches this prediction.

Reading

You have seen the ways in which the ACT tests you on Global and Inference questions in Reading passages and how an ACT expert approaches these types of questions. You will use the Kaplan Method for ACT Reading and the strategies discussed in this chapter to complete this section. Strategic thinking questions have been included to guide you. Use your answers to the strategic thinking questions to select the correct answer, just as you will on Test Day.

Strategic Thinking
Step 1: Read actively
The passage below is partially mapped. Read the passage and the first part of the Passage Map. Then, complete the Passage Map on your own. Remember to focus on the central ideas of each paragraph as well as the central idea of the overall passage. Use your Passage Map as a reference when you're answering questions.

HUMANITIES: The following passage is excerpted from a study of modern architecture.

Fallingwater, a small country house constructed in 1936, stands as perhaps the greatest residential building achievement of the American architect Frank Lloyd Wright. In designing the dwelling

5 for the Pittsburgh millionaire Edgar J. Kaufmann, Wright was confronted with an unusually challenging site beside a waterfall deep in a Pennsylvania ravine. However, Wright viewed this difficult location not as an obstacle, but as a unique

10 opportunity to put his architectural ideas into concrete form. In the end, Wright was able to turn Fallingwater into an artistic link between untamed nature and domestic tranquility, and a masterpiece in his brilliant career.

15 Edgar J. Kaufmann had originally planned for his house to sit at the bottom of the waterfall, where there was ample flat land on which to build. But Wright proposed a more daring response to the site. The architect convinced Kaufmann to build his

20 house at the top of the waterfall, on a small stone precipice. Wright further proposed extending the living room of the house out over the rushing water and making use of modern building techniques so that no vertical supports would be needed to hold

25 up the room. Rather than allowing the environment to determine the placement and shape of the house, Wright sought to construct a home that actually confronted and interacted with the landscape.

In one sense, Fallingwater can be viewed as a

30 showcase for unconventional building tactics. In designing the living room, for example, Wright made brilliant use of a technique called the "cantilever," in which steel rods are laid inside a shelf of concrete, eliminating the need for external

35 supports. But Fallingwater also contains a great many traditional and natural building materials. The boulders that form the foundation for the house also extend up through the floor and form part of the fireplace. A staircase in the living room

40 extends down to an enclosed bathing pool at the top of the waterfall. To Wright, the ideal dwelling in this spot was not simply a modern extravaganza or a direct extension of natural surroundings; rather, it was a little of both.

45 Critics have taken a wide range of approaches to understanding this unique building. Some have postulated that the house exalts the artist's triumph over untamed nature. Others have compared Wright's building to a cave, providing a

50 psychological and physical safe haven from a harsh,

¶1: FLW: Notable architectural achievement, Fallingwater

¶2: Choosing site and techniques

¶3:

¶4:

violent world. Edgar Kaufmann Jr., the patron's son, may have summed up Fallingwater best when he said, "Wright understood that people were creatures of nature; hence, an architecture which conformed
55 to nature would conform to what was basic in people.... Sociability and privacy are both available,

as are the comforts of home and the adventures of the seasons." This, then, is Frank Lloyd Wright's achievement in Fallingwater, a home that connects
60 the human and the natural for the invigoration and exaltation of both.

Questions	Strategic Thinking
4. The passage suggests that Edgar J. Kaufmann's original plans for the site were: **F.** conservative. **G.** daring. **H.** idealistic. **J.** architecturally unsound.	**Step 2: Examine the question stem** The phrase "The passage suggests" indicates this is a broad Inference question, so use the entire Passage Map. **Step 3: Predict and answer** Look for where the passage discusses the *original plans*. Lines 15–21 mention that Kaufmann originally wanted to build the house on flatter land, but Wright convinced him otherwise. Which answer choice matches this prediction? _____
5. Critics' comparisons of Fallingwater to a cave (lines 48–51) suggest that the house conveys a sense of: **A.** warmth. **B.** darkness. **C.** claustrophobia. **D.** security.	**Step 2: Examine the question stem** This is a narrow Inference question. What are the key words and phrases in the question stem? _____ _____ **Step 3: Predict and answer** The line references should lead you to a discussion of the critics' interpretation of the house. What clues indicate the feelings associated with their cave imagery? _____ _____ Which answer choice matches this prediction? _____

Questions	Strategic Thinking
6. The main purpose of the passage is to show how Wright designed Kaufmann's home to be: **F.** representative of its owner's wealth and position. **G.** as durable as current construction techniques would allow. **H.** impressive, yet in harmony with its surroundings. **J.** a symbol of the human triumph over the natural landscape.	**Step 2: Examine the question stem** This is a Global question. What are the key words and phrases in the question stem? _____ _____ **Step 3: Predict and answer** Review the entire Passage Map. The end of Paragraph 3 has a description of the two ideals that Wright wished to incorporate. Which answer choice matches this prediction? _____

Answers and Explanations are provided at the end of the book.

Now try a test-like ACT Reading passage and question set on your own. Give yourself 7 minutes to read the passage and answer the questions.

NATURAL SCIENCE: This passage is excerpted from a textbook about the solar system and discusses research that examines the possibility of life on Mars.

When the first of the two Viking landers touched down on Martian soil on July 20, 1976, and began to send camera images back to Earth, the scientists at the Jet Propulsion Laboratory could not suppress
5 a certain nervous anticipation. Like people who hold a ticket to a lottery, they had a one-in-a-million chance of winning. The first photographs that arrived, however, did not contain any evidence of life. What was revealed was merely a barren
10 landscape littered with rocks and boulders. The view resembled nothing so much as a flat section of desert. In fact, the winning entry in a contest at J.P.L. for the photograph most accurately predicting what Mars would look like was a snapshot taken from a
15 particularly arid section of the Mojave Desert.

The scientists were soon ready to turn their attention from visible life to microorganisms. The twin Viking landers carried experiments designed to detect organic compounds. Researchers thought
20 it possible that life had developed on early Mars just as it is thought to have developed on Earth, through the gradual chemical evolution of complex organic molecules. To detect biological activity, Martian soil samples were treated with various nutrients
25 that would produce characteristic by-products if life forms were active in the soil. The results from all three experiments were inconclusive. The fourth experiment heated a soil sample to look for signs of organic material but found none—an unexpected
30 result because organic compounds were thought to have been present due to the steady bombardment of the Martian surface by meteorites.

The absence of organic materials, some scientists speculated, was the result of intense ultraviolet
35 radiation penetrating the atmosphere of Mars and destroying organic compounds in the soil. Although Mars' atmosphere was at one time rich in carbon dioxide and thus thick enough to protect its surface from the harmful rays of the sun, the
40 carbon dioxide had gradually left the atmosphere and been converted into rocks. This means that even if life had gotten a start on early Mars, it could not have survived the exposure to ultraviolet radiation that occurred when the atmosphere
45 thinned. Mars never developed a protective layer of ozone as Earth did.

Despite the disappointing Viking results, there are those who still keep open the possibility of life on Mars. They point out that the Viking data
50 cannot be considered the final word on Martian life because the two landers only sampled limited—and uninteresting—sites. The Viking landing sites were not chosen for what they might tell of the planet's biology. They were chosen primarily because they
55 appeared to be safe for landing a spacecraft. The landing sites were on parts of the Martian plains that appeared relatively featureless according to orbital photographs.

The type of terrain that these researchers suggest
60 may be a possible hiding place for active life has an Earthly parallel: the ice-free region of southern Victoria Land, Antarctica, where the temperatures in some dry valleys average below zero. Organisms known as endoliths, a form of blue-green algae that has adapted
65 to this harsh environment, were found living inside certain translucent, porous rocks in these Antarctic valleys. The argument based on this discovery is that if life did exist on early Mars, it is possible that it escaped worsening conditions by similarly seeking
70 refuge in rocks. Skeptics object, however, that Mars in its present state is simply too dry, even compared with Antarctic valleys, to sustain any life whatsoever.

Should Mars eventually prove barren of life, as some suspect, then this finding would have
75 a significant impact on the current view of the chemical origins of life. It could be much more difficult to get life started on a planet than scientists thought before the Viking landings.

7. The passage suggests that an important difference between Mars and Earth is that, unlike Earth, Mars:

   A. accumulated organic compounds in its soil.

   B. lies in the path of harmful rays of ultraviolet radiation.

   C. once possessed an atmosphere rich in carbon dioxide.

   D. could not sustain any life that developed.

8. The main point of the second paragraph (lines 16–32) is that:

   F. scientists were disappointed by the inconclusive results of their experiments.

   G. theories about how life developed on Earth were shown to be flawed.

   H. there was no experimental confirmation that life exists on Mars.

   J. meteorite bombardment of the Martian surface is less constant than scientists predicted.

9. The researchers' argument that life may exist in Martian rocks rests on the idea that:

   A. life evolved in the same way on two different planets.

   B. organisms usually adopt identical survival strategies in similar environments.

   C. life developed in the form of a blue-green algae on Mars.

   D. organisms that survived in Antarctica could survive on Mars.

Answers and Explanations are provided at the end of the book.

ON YOUR OWN

The following questions provide an opportunity to practice the concepts and strategic thinking covered in this chapter. While many of the questions pertain to Global and Inference questions, some touch on other concepts tested on the Reading test to ensure that your practice is test-like, with a variety of question types per passage.

SOCIAL STUDIES: The following passage was adapted from a speech given by a prominent city planner.

The North American suburb is an architectural and civic phenomenon distinct from suburban areas in any other part of the world. It was a response to the need, especially keen after World
5 War II, to "get away" from the city and all the noise, pollution, and general nastiness that went along with it. Cities were where the factories were, and factories before modern pollution and safety standards were horrific things to behold. Of those
10 who could get out, many did.

Suburban communities, however, were not sufficient by themselves to support life. The people who lived in them needed to work, shop, and socialize, and most of the active part of their lives
15 remained fixed in urban centers. Therefore, suburbs were clustered around their parent cities, with all the suburban inhabitants commuting daily to the city center for work and play.

All of this seems perfectly logical and inevitable.
20 The suburb should be the perfect halfway point between city and country—away from the noise, congestion, and pollution, but not so far away that there's no access to culture, to income, to all the exciting benefits of urban life. In reality, though, few
25 suburbs have actually approached this ideal. Some critics have charged that, as suburbs have grown to the size of sprawling towns themselves, they are revealed as communities somehow devoid of community necessities. They lack local stores, community centers,
30 and places for kids to hang out; instead, they offer parking lots, chain stores, and strip malls.

The structure of the modern suburb, while offering a respite from city pollution, has created

health and environmental risks of its own. Because
35 of the separation of living and commercial spaces imposed by many suburban zoning laws, the city dweller's fond experience of walking down the block to the neighborhood café may be rare or entirely alien to a suburbanite. Should a suburb
40 dweller, on a Saturday morning, desire a change of scenery and a cup of coffee, she must get in her car and drive some distance. In fact, nearly everything, aside from the other houses and the occasional neighborhood park, requires an automobile trip.
45 (No facet of suburban life better represents this car culture than the gridlock of the rush-hour commute.) All of this driving comes at the cost of pollution and a lack of daily exercise. Of course, America has had a long love affair with the car,
50 and any city planner who thinks he can single-handedly change that is in for a rude surprise. Surely, though, we must begin to balance the appeal and freedom of the car with ecological and civic responsibility.

55 Some have charged that America doesn't need any more of these bland developments, that these projects line construction companies' pockets without contributing much to the value and diversity of American culture. I, however, see the
60 problem of suburbs as one of degree rather than kind. We don't need to abandon suburbs altogether; we instead need to more knowingly pursue that ideal of the best of city and country. I haven't given up yet on the possibility of injecting the suburbs
65 with public spaces that we can be proud of, that are rewarding to the human spirit. Suburbs could be fascinating and beautiful places; we need only exercise our power to determine the nature of the places in which we live.

1. The main purpose of the passage is to:

   A. bemoan the detrimental effect suburbs have had on individual quality of life.

   B. discourage the suburb dweller's dependence on the automobile.

   C. encourage a different, more effective vision of the place of suburbs in communities.

   D. call for a return to the type of suburb that prevailed before World War II.

2. The discussion of factories in the first paragraph implies that:

   F. the author believes people were foolish to move to suburbs.

   G. many people moved to the suburbs to find safer, more rewarding jobs.

   H. the author regards factories as less objectionable now than in the past.

   J. suburban driving actually creates similar levels of pollution.

3. The observation "All of this seems perfectly logical and inevitable" (line 19) implies that suburbs:

   A. fill an important need for those who work in the city.

   B. are devoid of community necessities.

   C. should become more diverse.

   D. are examples of good city planning.

4. In line 25, "this ideal" is best understood as:

   F. a community that can fulfill residents' needs and desires within its own boundaries.

   G. a diverse and interesting space with easy access to the city.

   H. a suburb that is culturally similar to its parent city.

   J. a neighborhood entirely made up of private residences.

5. The passage suggests that "many suburban zoning laws" (line 36):

   A. ban parks from suburban neighborhoods.

   B. make it difficult to sustain successful businesses.

   C. contribute to adverse environmental effects.

   D. address environmental concerns at the cost of cultural diversity.

6. In line 39, "alien" most nearly means:

   F. extraterrestrial.

   G. unheard of.

   H. from another country.

   J. puzzling.

7. According to Paragraph 4, city planners need to consider:

   A. accepting suburban residents' reluctance to give up driving.

   B. minimizing every boundary between residential and retail spaces.

   C. placing more coffee shops and restaurants across the street from houses.

   D. moving the local parks to safer and more accessible neighborhoods.

8. The discussion in the final paragraph implies that the author:

   F. blames poor city planning for the existence of the suburb.

   G. thinks today's suburbs are actually fascinating and beautiful.

   H. believes most people take too little interest in their surroundings.

   J. is optimistic about the possibilities for the American suburb.

9. According to the passage, if people want to *get away* (line 5) from urban life, one of the considerations regarding suburbs would be:

   A. quieter, cleaner housing options.

   B. structural advantages that inspire most people to walk and jog in their own neighborhoods.

   C. a variety of activities that allow residents to meet other suburban families.

   D. local employment opportunities.

10. Based on the passage, the author would regard the changes in modern suburbs over the years as:

    F. beneficial, due to the abundance of recreational and retail locations within walking distance.

    G. minimal, since the suburbs that developed after World War II had the same features.

    H. alarming, since modern suburbs have serious pollution problems that the older suburbs never faced.

    J. disappointing, since today's suburbs often place residents even farther away from stores and community centers.

HUMANITIES: This passage explores the relationship between the immigrant experience and one person's career choice.

My grandfather was born in a turbulent time in Russia. His non-communist lineage made him unwelcome before he had left the womb. His father, an officer in the Russian army, was considered an enemy of the com-
5 munist Bolsheviks, so my grandfather lived less than a year in what was his native Moscow and spent most of his younger years moving across Asia. Despite this, he had pride in being Russian, associated with Russians throughout his life, and would frequently quiz
10 me on Russian history. This all in tribute to a country that ended up under different rule during the time his mother was pregnant with him.

As a child, exiled to Siberia, my grandfather heard his father tell of the greatness that existed
15 within the country that had forced the family into exile. It was known that, first with his parents, and later as an adult, my grandfather was going to have to seek a new place to call home. Despite this foregone conclusion, Russia was still romanticized,
20 and my grandfather learned to treat the country with reverence. This was in contrast to the sentiments found in other recently exiled Russians, who would not simply lament the actions taken by the country, but disparage all eight million
25 square miles. In my family's search for a place to settle, attempting to forge a consistent identity was nearly impossible, as no one knew whether the next location would hold for a month, let alone a year. All hoped for an unattainable "new Moscow."

30 The first long-term refuge was found, ironically, in China, which would have its own communist revolution. After several years of relative stability, the revolution precipitated the move to the United States. Upon arrival in San Francisco, my
35 grandfather, along with my grandmother and their young son, my father, found other Russian immigrants who were also new to the country. "*Ya amerikanets*," people would say, and despite the fact that they were recent immigrants who
40 associated primarily with those of shared ethnicity and circumstance, they would play the role they desired and repeat "*ya amerikanets*"—"I am American." They would share many stories about their native land, but did not repeat "*ya russkiy*,"
45 because being Russian went without saying. While it was clear that this would be the last country my grandfather would reside in, and that he wished to become more American, it was perhaps the most confusing of times. It was less of a problem
50 of acclimating to an adopted setting; the problem was dealing with a permanent setting at all. The only consistency throughout the first thirty years of my grandfather's life was the knowledge that

every "home" was temporary, and now this was
55 no longer the case. I often wonder if his successful
career in the real estate business had anything to
do with what must have been a rare transformation
of circumstance.

Not only was my grandfather interested in
60 real estate, he was ardent about the importance of
ownership, a naturally discordant view to that of
the then Soviet Union. Thus, selling homes became
a purpose in addition to an occupation.

Part of his success in real estate was owed to
65 strategic compromise. Considering American
sentiments regarding Russia during the Cold War,
there were times that he was sure he lost certain
house sales due to his last name and accent.
However, to those willing to listen, he found
70 advantages in informing people that he was an
exiled Russian and ardently disagreed with the
communist government. He would also point out
his pride in being a new American and allow a
potential buyer to degrade Russia without blinking.

75 Fortunately, the 1950s were a time of settling
across the country, and this made real estate a
very lucrative profession. It wasn't just this that
attracted my grandfather, though; he also saw it as
an opportunity to give tiny parts of the country to
80 other people—returning the favor, in a way.

Yet, it always seemed that something vital
still rested in the opposite hemisphere. Once
communism fell, he began returning to Russia
yearly, and while he and my grandmother never
85 showed the family pictures from Russia the way
they would from the various cruise ships they
traveled on, it could be deduced that returning to
Russia was analogous to an adopted child traveling
to meet his or her birth parents: the journey is one
90 of personal necessity rather than pleasure, and the
encounter is one that elucidates one's very existence.
In selling real estate, my grandfather had worked to
make this unnecessary. I believe that he wished for
people to keep those houses and pass them down to
95 later generations, giving the space a sort of familial
permanence rather than a fleeting stay.

For most, the thought of real estate agents
conjures up images of smiling advertisements
on benches and buses and the skill of selling
100 something so important. Many are wary of
salespeople in general, questioning the practice
of convincing people something is in their best
interest when the salesperson stands to personally
benefit. My grandfather did financially benefit from
105 sales, but there was more to it; his realization of the
American dream only made him want to be a part
of others reaching for the same thing, whether their
native home was around the block or thousands of
miles away.

11. One of the main points the author attempts to convey in the passage is that:

    A. immigrants would often rather live in their native land.

    B. American-born people tend not to be able to understand how displacement affects immigrants.

    C. immigrants who acclimate well to America still may have indelible ties to their native land.

    D. immigrants are often shocked by the stability offered to them in America.

12. Based on the first three paragraphs, which of the following best describes the movements of the author's grandfather, prior to his emigration to America?

    F. He grew up primarily in Siberia and then moved to China during the Russian Revolution.

    G. He grew up in Moscow, was exiled as an adult, and rapidly moved through Asia.

    H. He was born in Moscow, moved rapidly through Asia, and settled for a while in communist China.

    J. He was born in Moscow, was exiled to Siberia with his family, and moved frequently before settling for a somewhat longer period in China.

13. The author's grandfather's *purpose* (line 64) and desire to return *the favor* (line 81) are best described as:

    A. providing others with a sense of pride in being American.

    B. shedding light on injustices carried out by other countries.

    C. facilitating a stable situation for others.

    D. providing well for his family.

14. Which of the following actions contradicts a general attitude held by the author's grandfather?

    F. "He would also point out his pride in being a new American, and allow a potential buyer to degrade Russia without blinking" (lines 73–75).

    G. "They would share many stories about their native land, but did not repeat '*ya russkiy*,' because being Russian went without saying" (lines 44–46).

    H. "He was ardent about the importance of ownership, a naturally discordant view to that of the then Soviet Union" (lines 61–63).

    J. "Once communism fell, he began returning to Russia yearly" (lines 83–85).

15. The author classifies a *new Moscow* as *unattainable* (line 30) because:

    A. the family believed Moscow to be the most desirable city in the world.

    B. it was unlikely that communism would fall shortly after the revolution.

    C. cities in other countries are entirely unlike those in Russia.

    D. it would not be possible to find a new home that could still be considered a native home.

16. It can be inferred that when the author refers to Russians playing *the role* (lines 42–43), he most likely means that the Russians were:

    F. convincing themselves that they were ready to acclimate.

    G. joking with each other.

    H. naïve about the way Americans tend to act with each other.

    J. still hopeful that they would see Russia again.

17. The *strategic compromise* applied by the author's grandfather (line 66) would most likely involve:

    A. agreeing with the potential buyer, no matter what.

    B. ignoring offensive statements.

    C. acting as American as possible.

    D. always defending America in international disputes.

18. According to the passage, the grandfather's trip back to his native Russia provided him with:

    F. a greater understanding of the inner workings of his native land.

    G. greater motivation to sell homes in America.

    H. a greater sense of personal understanding.

    J. a necessary visit with estranged family members.

19. According to the first paragraph, the author's grandfather's birth happened:

    A. during the communist revolution.

    B. under communist rule.

    C. prior to the communist revolution.

    D. after the fall of communism.

20. When the author states that his grandfather "worked to make this unnecessary" (lines 93–94), he is suggesting that his grandfather's occupation could potentially:

    F. help his grandfather feel more connected to America through his success.

    G. facilitate a transaction that could give others a sense of belonging.

    H. sell houses that would bring stability to young families.

    J. help others realize the American dream.

Answers and Explanations are provided at the end of the book.

Reading

CHAPTER 17

Detail and Vocab-in-Context Questions

CHAPTER OBJECTIVES

By the end of this chapter, you will be able to:

1. Identify and answer Detail questions that ask for explicit information within the passage

2. Identify and answer Vocab-in-Context questions that ask how words or phrases are used within the passage

SMARTPOINTS

Point Value	SmartPoints Category
14 Points	Detail
3 Points	Vocab-in-Context

DETAIL QUESTIONS

Detail questions are the most abundant question type on the ACT Reading test. They ask you to track down a piece of information explicitly stated in the passage, so you will not have to make any inferences as you answer these. Remember that you will not (and should not!) remember every detail from your reading of the passage. Your Passage Map can help you find the *location* of the detail in question; then review the passage text directly to answer Detail questions.

You can recognize Detail questions because they will often use phrases like "According to the passage/author," "The author states," or "The passage makes clear." These questions will almost never have wording such as "The author suggests" or "The author implies," which indicate an Inference question.

To answer Detail questions successfully:

- Use line references or specific phrasing in the question to find the relevant section of the passage

- Quickly skim through the relevant section to find specific evidence for your prediction; you should be able to put your finger on the exact information required to answer the question

- Rephrase the evidence in the passage in your own words to make a prediction and find a match among the answer choices

Avoid these major wrong answer traps when answering Detail questions:

- Misused details—details that are directly from the passage but are unrelated to or do not answer the question

- Distortions—details from the passage that are altered to be partially incorrect

VOCAB-IN-CONTEXT QUESTIONS

Vocab-in-Context questions ask you to understand how the author uses a certain word or phrase, based on clues you see around it. These questions are easy to recognize, as they will almost always be phrased "As it is used in line _____ , the word _____ most nearly means . . . ."

To answer Vocab-in-Context questions successfully:

- Use the line reference to find the word or phrase in the passage

- Skim through the surrounding lines, pretending there is a blank space in place of the word or phrase

- While keeping in mind the purpose of the overall passage and paragraph, use the surrounding context to come up with your own replacement for the word or phrase. Then find the closest match among the answer choices

Avoid this major wrong answer trap when answering Vocab-in-Context questions:

- Thinking of the primary definition of the word or phrase—its most common meaning. For example, *celebrated* commonly means "commemorated via a social event," but when used in the phrase "the author was celebrated for his work," it means "acknowledged."

Work through the Kaplan Method for ACT Reading step-by-step to answer the questions that accompany the following Reading passage excerpt. The table below the excerpt contains two columns. The column on the right features the strategic thinking a test expert employs when approaching passages and related questions. Pay attention to how a test experts varies the approach to answer different question types.

Strategic Thinking
Step 1: Read actively
Read the passage and the notes provided. Remember, a well-crafted Passage Map should summarize the central idea of each paragraph as well as important topics or themes. Use your Passage Map to help you answer each question.

SOCIAL SCIENCE: The following passage is adapted from *The Heart of Man* by Erich Fromm (© 1964 by Erich Fromm. Reprinted with permission of HarperCollins Publishers).

¶1: Differences in violence types, motivations

The distinction among various types of violence is based on the distinction between their respective unconscious motivations. Only the understanding of the unconscious dynamics of behavior permits
5 us to understand the behavior itself, its roots, its course, and the energy with which it is charged.

¶2: Playful viol. = to display skill

The most normal and non-pathological form of violence is playful violence. We find it in those forms in which violence is exercised in the pursuit
10 of displaying skill, not in the pursuit of destruction, not motivated by hate or destructiveness. Examples of this playful violence can be found in many instances, from the war games of primitive tribes to the Zen Buddhist art of sword fighting. In all such
15 games of fighting, it is not the aim to kill; even if the outcome is the death of the opponent it is, as it were, the opponent's fault for having "stood in the wrong spot." In reality, one would often find unconscious aggression and destructiveness hidden

20 behind the explicit logic of the game. But even this being so, the main motivation in this type of violence is the display of skill, not destructiveness.

Of much greater practical significance than playful violence is reactive violence. By reactive
25 violence, I am referring to violence that is employed in the defense of life, freedom, dignity, property— one's own or that of others. It is rooted in fear, and for this very reason it is probably the most frequent form of violence: The fear can be real or
30 imagined, conscious or unconscious. This type of violence is in the service of life, not of death; its aim is preservation, not destruction. It is not entirely the outcome of irrational passions, but, to some extent, of rational calculation; hence it also implies
35 a certain proportionality between end and means. It has been argued that from a higher spiritual plane, killing—even in defense—is never morally right. But most of those who hold this conviction admit that violence in the defense of life is of a different
40 nature than violence which aims at destructiveness for its own sake.

¶3: Reactive viol. = to defend; based on fear

4: Reactive
ol. can be
aused by
rustration;
o meet a
eed

Another aspect of reactive violence is the kind of violence that is produced by frustration. We find aggressive behavior in animals, children, and adults 45 when a wish or a need is frustrated. Such aggressive behavior constitutes an attempt, although often a futile one, to attain the frustrated aim through the use of violence. It is clearly an aggression in the service of life, and not one for the sake of 50 destruction. Since frustration of needs and desires has been an almost universal occurrence in most societies even to the present day, there is no reason to be surprised that violence and aggression are constantly produced and exhibited.

Questions	Strategic Thinking
1. What does the author state that war games of primitive tribes and the Zen Buddhist art of sword fighting have in common? **A.** They use violence primarily to exhibit skills. **B.** They are motivated by a wish to destroy. **C.** Their primary aim is to preserve, rather than destroy, life. **D.** They typically lead to death of the participants.	**Step 2: Examine the question stem** This is a Detail question because it uses the phrase "What does the author state." The other key phrases in the question stem are "war games of primitive tribes" and "Zen Buddhist art of sword fighting." These are specific examples of playful violence, which the Passage Map indicates can be found in Paragraph 2. **Step 3: Predict and answer** Skimming the text around the examples, you can put your finger on evidence the author provides about playful violence; it is "exercised in the pursuit of displaying skill . . . not motivated by hate or destructiveness" (lines 9–11). Choice (A) matches this prediction. Choices B and D are distortions, and C is a misused detail.

Questions	Strategic Thinking
2. According to the passage, people who react violently when frustrated: **F.** have replaced constructive motives with destructive ones. **G.** are reliving frustrating experiences from their childhood. **H.** want to take revenge on the source of their frustration. **J.** do so in order to achieve a desired goal.	**Step 2: Examine the question stem** The phrase "According to the passage" tells you this is a Detail question, and another key phrase is "react violently when frustrated." Based on your Passage Map, frustration is discussed in paragraph 4. **Step 3: Predict and answer** Skimming through the first few sentences of paragraph 4, you will find evidence that violence in response to frustration occurs because a person is trying to reach a difficult aim: "such aggressive behavior constitutes an attempt . . . to attain the frustrated aim through the use of violence" (lines 45–48). Choice (J) matches this prediction. The other answer choices are all distortions of what the passage indicates.
3. As it is used in line 33, the phrase *irrational passions* most nearly means: **A.** intense desires. **B.** instinctive emotions. **C.** unreasonable actions. **D.** superficial interests.	**Step 2: Examine the question stem** This is a Vocab-in-Context question because it provides a line reference and uses the phrase "most nearly means." **Step 3: Predict and answer** The context around the phrase *irrational passions* discusses the motivation for reactive violence, suggesting that it results in part from *rational calculation* rather than *irrational passions*. Hence, the phrase means a possible cause of reactive violence that is the opposite of *rational calculation*. A possible replacement for the phrase might be *reactive feelings*. Choice (B) matches this prediction. Choices A and C contain primary meanings that might make sense in a different context, but not within this passage. Choice D does not convey the author's intended meaning.

You have seen the ways in which the ACT tests you on Detail and Vocab-in-Context questions in Reading passages and how an ACT expert approaches these types of questions. You will use the Kaplan Method for ACT Reading and the strategies discussed in this chapter to complete this section. Strategic thinking questions have been included to guide you. Use your answers to the strategic thinking questions to select the correct answer, just as you will on Test Day.

Strategic Thinking

Step 1: Read actively

The passage below is partially mapped. Read the passage and the first part of the Passage Map. Then, complete the Passage Map on your own. Remember to focus on the central ideas of each paragraph as well as the central idea of the overall passage. Use your Passage Map as a reference when you're answering questions.

NATURAL SCIENCE: This passage is adapted from "The Quasar 3C 273," by Thierry Courvoisier and E. Ian Robson. It originally appeared in *Scientific American*, June 1991, Volume 264. Reprinted with permission. (© 1991 by Scientific American, Inc.)

The quasar 3C 273 lies about one-fifth of the way from Earth to the edge of the known universe. Of all the objects in the cosmos, only a few other quasars surpass the energy and activity of 3C 273.
5 On an average day, it is more luminous than 1,000 galaxies, each containing 100 billion stars. During one remarkable day in February 1988, the quasar erupted with a burst of radiation equivalent to lighting up stars the size of our sun at the rate of 10
10 million per second.

By monitoring 3C 273 in all domains of the electromagnetic spectrum and by observing variations in its luminosity, astronomers have begun to understand quasars and the physical
15 processes that power them.

Since quasars were first identified some 28 years ago, astronomers have come to realize that quasars are the cores of extremely active galaxies. Quasars are unmatched in luminosity and hence
20 are the most distant objects that can be detected in the universe. One of the most important discoveries about quasars is that their luminosity can vary greatly over periods of less than a year.

This variability led investigators to the conclusion
25 that the tremendous energy of quasars is radiated from a region many times smaller than the cores of ordinary galaxies.

Quasars are powered by the gravitational energy that is released as gas and dust fall toward the
30 quasars' massive, dense centers. Some of this energy channels particles into beams, blasting material out into the host galaxy at speeds close to that of light. Most of the energy is converted into radiation by a wide range of physical processes, probably
35 occurring at different distances from the core. Yet quasars exhibit many phenomena that cannot be explained, and they remain among the most enigmatic objects in the universe.

On the whole, we know more about 3C 273
40 than any other quasar. It possesses a very wide range of properties, not all of which are shared by all quasars. The wealth of activity displayed by 3C 273, however, is a key to helping astronomers understand the phenomena at work in quasars.

45 The task of observing 3C 273 is as challenging as it is rewarding. After traveling through space for more than a billion years, only a tiny fraction of the radiation from 3C 273 reaches Earth. Capturing this radiation requires frequent observations using
50 a battery of ground-based telescopes and satellite-borne instruments.

Margin notes:

¶1: Quasar very bright

¶2: Scientists studying Qs

¶3: Qs can be seen from far away; brightness varies

¶4: Qs powered by energy; sci. can't explain all

¶5: _____ _____

¶6: _____ _____

The effort began more than a century ago. The object known today as 3C 273 was first recorded on photographic plates as astronomers surveyed
55 the stars in the constellation Virgo. It looked like nothing more than an ordinary, moderately bright star. Then in 1962, Cyril Hazard and his colleagues at Sydney University discovered that the starlike object occupied the same position in the sky as a
60 strong source of radio waves. The radio emitter had been previously identified as 3C 273, which stood for number 273 in the Third Cambridge Catalogue of Radio Sources. Objects such as 3C 273 were subsequently described as quasi-stellar
65 radio sources, or quasars.

¶7:
_____
_____

In 1963, Maarten Schmidt of the Mount Wilson and Palomar Observatories deduced that the quasar 3C 273 was about three billion light-years away from Earth. The implications of this discovery
70 were extraordinary. The quasar was by far the most luminous and distant object ever observed. Soon a few other quasars were identified that seemed to be even farther away and brighter than 3C 273. At the time, many of Schmidt's colleagues had good
75 reason to question these results. Yet as modern astronomers review the evidence collected during the past 28 years, we find little room to doubt that Schmidt was right.

¶8:
_____
_____

Questions	Strategic Thinking
4. As it is used in line 42, the word *wealth* most nearly means: **F.** affluence. **G.** profusion. **H.** assets. **J.** possessions.	**Step 2: Examine the question stem** The phrase "most nearly means" indicates that this is a Vocab-in-Context question. **Step 3: Predict and answer** Based on how it is used in the passage, what does *wealth* mean? _____ Which answer choice matches this prediction? _____

Questions	Strategic Thinking

5. According to the passage, quasars remain a mystery to scientists due to:
 	
  A. scientists' inability to determine how quasar energy is converted to radiation.
 	
  B. the amount of radio waves surrounding quasars.
 	
  C. unexplained phenomena that quasars exhibit.
 	
  D. how difficult it is to observe quasars.
	Step 2: Examine the question stem
	
	What are the key words and phrases in the question stem?
	
	_____
	_____
	
	Step 3: Predict and answer
	
	Review the Passage Map to pinpoint where the passage discusses scientists not understanding quasars. Use this portion of the passage to make a prediction.
	
	_____
	_____
	
	Which answer choice matches this prediction? _____

6. According to the passage, what observation has helped astronomers understand quasars?
 	
  F. Mapping the domains of the electromagnetic spectrum
 	
  G. Measuring the distance from Earth to 3C 273
 	
  H. Determining the frequency of radio waves emitted from 3C 273
 	
  J. Surveying the stars in the constellation Virgo
	Step 2: Examine the question stem
	
	What are the key words and phrases in the question stem?
	
	_____
	_____
	
	Step 3: Predict and answer
	
	Refer to the Passage Map for a reference to astronomers studying quasars.
	
	_____
	_____
	
	Which answer choice matches this prediction? _____

Answers and Explanations are provided at the end of the book.

Now try a test-like ACT Reading passage and question set on your own. Give yourself 9 minutes to read the passage and answer the questions.

SOCIAL SCIENCE: This passage is from a book about neurobiology and linguistics written in the 1990s. It examines theories about whether all human languages share a common underlying structure.

Noam Chomsky's influential theory of Universal Grammar postulates that all humans have an innate, genetic understanding of certain grammatical "rules," which are universal across
5   all languages and absolutely not affected by environment. We are all born, Chomsky says, with a knowledge of "deep structure," basic linguistic constructions that allow us, if not to understand all languages, at least to understand how they are put
10 together. From there, we have only to learn how the options are set in our particular language in order to create an unlimited number of "correct" utterances.

For example, he suggests that structure
15 dependency—a rule that says that sentences are defined by phrase structure, not linear structure—is inherent to all languages, with minor variations. Thus, the meaning of a sentence is really dependent on the meaning of its phrases,
20 rather than each individual word. In addition, the head parameter rule stipulates that each phrase contains a "head" (main) word, and all languages have it in essentially the same position within the phrase. Chomsky's famous sentence "Colorless
25 green ideas sleep furiously" exemplifies this theory of Universal Grammar—while the sentence itself is meaningless, it is easily recognizable as a grammatical sentence that fits a basic, but higher level of organization. "Furiously sleep ideas green
30 colorless," on the other hand, is obviously not grammatical, and it is difficult to discern any kind of meaning in it. For other evidence to support this theory, Chomsky points to our relative ease

in translating one language to another; again,
35 while we may not necessarily recognize individual words in an unfamiliar language, we can certainly recognize and engage with sentences that are grammatical.

This evidence is still fairly theoretical, receiving
40 play mostly in the linguistic sphere. Most researchers seem more concerned with attempting to draw universal parallels across languages than with searching for biological evidence of such phenomena. We might ask: Where exactly are these
45 Universal Grammar constraints located? How and when are they altered by natural evolutionary processes—or do they remain relatively unaltered and nonmutated from generation to generation? As language evolves over time, does Universal
50 Grammar also evolve or stay relatively stable? Other scientists say that Universal Grammar is not nearly as ordered and absolute as Chomsky and other linguists make it out to be and suggest that the Universal Grammar theory is the result of our
55 flawed human tendency to impose order where there is none. Still others suggest that by ignoring the role of environment in language development, Chomsky completely discredits the possible important effect our surroundings could have on
60 language development.

A few researchers are beginning to suggest that, rather than focusing on explaining linguistic similarities among various languages, we instead acknowledge the evolutionary roots of
65 language and look specifically for neurobiological explanations. Claiming that the humanistic exploration of Universal Grammar is too abstract, they recommend that we instead view language (and grammar) as a function of the brain. Because

70 language is so unbelievably complex, offering
several definitions and associations contained
within a single word, any single connection
between, say, two languages causes those myriad
associations to become oversimplified and sterile.

75 For example, simply pointing out the position of
a sentence's subject in Turkish versus that same
subject position in English as an illustration
of the existence of Universal Grammar merely
acknowledges that single linguistic association

80 without taking into account any social
circumstances that may cause the mind to modify
that grammar. In short, say these scientists, not
until we create a better marriage between biology
and linguistics—and a better understanding of the

85 human brain—can we even begin to address the
complexities of human language development.

7. According to the passage, Chomsky
   claimed that an "innate, genetic
   understanding" (line 3):

   A. allows humans to understand all
      languages.

   B. allows humans to understand all
      language structure.

   C. allows humans to easily speak in
      multiple languages.

   D. explains that grammar is a natural
      function of the human brain.

8. The passage states that the structure rule
   applies to:

   F. linear structure.

   G. grammatical structure.

   H. phrase structure.

   J. head word.

9. As it is used in line 37, the word *engage* most
   nearly means:

   A. promise.

   B. attract.

   C. undertake.

   D. participate.

10. As it is used in line 74, the word *sterile* most
    nearly means:

    F. sanitary.

    G. meaningless.

    H. barren.

    J. musty.

Answers and Explanations are provided at the end
of the book.

ON YOUR OWN

The following questions provide an opportunity to practice the concepts and strategic thinking covered in this chapter. While many of the questions pertain to Detail and Vocab-in-Context, some touch on other concepts on the Reading test to ensure that your practice is test-like, with a variety of question types per passage.

NATURAL SCIENCE: The following passage is excerpted from "Earth's Ozone Shield Under Threat," by France Bequette (© *UNESCO Courier*, June 1992, Vol. 45, Issue 6, p. 26).

The ozone layer, the tenuous layer of gas that surrounds our planet between 12 and 45 kilometers above our surface, is being rapidly depleted. Seasonally occurring holes have appeared in it over
5 the poles, and, more recently, over the temperate regions of the Northern Hemisphere. The threat is a serious one since the ozone layer traps almost all incoming ultraviolet radiation, which is harmful to all living organisms—humans, animals, and plants.

10 Even though the ozone layer is 25 kilometers thick, the atmosphere in it is very tenuous, and the total amount of ozone, compared with other atmospheric gases, is quite small. If all of the ozone in a vertical column reaching up through the atmo-
15 sphere were to be compressed to sea-level pressure, it would form a layer only a few millimeters thick.

Detailed study of the ozone layer began comparatively recently, the earliest observations being made in 1930 by the English scientist Sydney
20 Chapman. These initial observations were taken up by the World Meteorological Organization (WMO), which established the Dobson network of one hundred observation stations. Since 1983, on the initiative of the WMO and the United Nations
25 Environment Programme (UNEP), seven of these stations have been entrusted with the task of making long-term forecasts of the likely evolution of our precious shield.

In 1958, the researchers who permanently
30 monitor the ozone content of the layer above the South Pole began to observe several seasonal variations. From June, there was a slight reduction in ozone content that reached a minimum in October. In November, there was a sudden increase
35 in the ozone content. The fluctuations appeared to result from the natural phenomena of wind effects and temperature change.

However, although the October minimum remained constant until 1979, the total ozone
40 content over the pole was steadily diminishing until, in 1985, public opinion was finally roused by reports of a "hole" in the ozone layer and observations were intensified. The culprits responsible for the hole had already been
45 identified as being supersonic aircraft, such as the Concorde (although these have now been exonerated), and the notorious compounds known as chlorofluorocarbons, or CFCs. Synthesized in 1928 by chemists working at General Motors in
50 the United States, CFCs are compounds of atoms of carbon, chlorine, and fluorine. Having the advantage of being nonflammable, nontoxic, and non-corrosive, they came into widespread use in the 1950s. They are widely used in refrigerators;
55 air conditioners; the "bubbles" in the foam plastic used, for example, in car seats; and as insulation in buildings.

In 1989, CFCs represented a market valued at over $1 billion and a labor force of 1.6 million.
60 Of the twenty-five countries producing CFCs, the

United States, France, the United Kingdom, Japan, and Germany accounted for three-quarters of the total world production of some 1.2 million tons.

These figures give some idea of the importance
65 of the economic interests that are at stake in any decision to ban the industrial use of CFCs. But, with CFCs incriminated by scientists, the question arose as to whether we were prepared to take the risk of seeing an increase in the number of cases of
70 skin cancer, eye ailments such as cataracts, or even a lowering of the human immune-defense system, all effects that would follow further depletion of the ozone layer.

The Montreal Protocol was the first world
75 agreement aimed at halting the production of CFCs. As more evidence emerged concerning the seriousness of the threat, it became apparent that the protocol was not stringent enough and, year by year, its severity was increased until, in 1990
80 in London, seventy countries agreed to stop all production of CFCs by the year 2000.

Unfortunately, even if the entire world were to agree today to halt all production and use of CFCs, this would not provide an immediate solution
85 to the problem. A single molecule of chlorine can destroy from 10,000 to 100,000 molecules of ozone. Furthermore, CFCs have a life span of between 75 and 400 years, and they take 10 years to reach the ozone layer. In other words, what we
90 are experiencing now results from CFCs emitted 10 years ago.

Industrialists are now urgently searching for substitute products. Some, such as propane, are too dangerous because they are flammable;
95 others, the HCFCs, might prove to be toxic and to contribute to the greenhouse effect (i.e., to the process of global warming). Nevertheless, nobody can say that the situation will not right itself, whether in the short term or long term, if we
100 ourselves lend a hand.

1. As it is used in line 1, the word *tenuous* most nearly means:

   A. strong.

   B. insubstantial.

   C. hazy.

   D. delicate.

2. The main purpose of this passage is to:

   F. inform scientists of the harm done by CFCs.

   G. explain the purpose of the ozone layer.

   H. encourage people to stop using CFCs before dire consequences are incurred.

   J. explain the importance and vulnerability of the ozone layer.

3. Why does the author refer to the ozone layer as a *precious shield* in line 28?

   A. It traps chlorofluorocarbons.

   B. It prevents ultraviolet rays from entering the atmosphere.

   C. It protects the human immune system.

   D. It prevents the greenhouse effect.

4. The description of the ozone layer's size in Paragraph 2 serves to:

   F. highlight how vulnerable the ozone layer is.

   G. emphasize how thick the ozone layer is.

   H. show the limitations of standard measurements.

   J. compare and contrast the ozone with other atmospheric gases.

5. As it is used in line 41, the word *roused* most nearly means:

    A. woken.

    B. electrified.

    C. stimulated.

    D. angered.

6. Why does the author discuss the market value and labor force costs of CFC production?

    F. To argue for why CFCs are important and should be produced

    G. To explain why halting production of CFCs is so difficult

    H. To point out that economic health is more important than the ozone layer

    J. To argue that the United States has produced more ozone-damaging CFCs than have other countries

7. Why does the author mention skin cancer, cataracts, and lowered human immune systems?

    A. To provide evidence that the depleted ozone layer is responsible for higher incidents of these ailments

    B. To provide evidence that not addressing the hole in the ozone will have severe consequences

    C. To emphasize that healing the ozone layer will stop increases in these ailments

    D. To scare scientists into halting production of CFCs

8. What is one reason cited by the author that CFCs caused damage even after they were no longer produced by countries that agreed to the Montreal Protocol?

    F. Too many other countries still relied on them.

    G. The products that contain CFCs were still being used.

    H. It takes ten years for CFCs to reach the ozone layer.

    J. There are no replacement products for CFCs.

9. According to the information presented in the passage, in approximately what year did CFCs stop reaching the ozone?

    A. 1992

    B. 2000

    C. 2010

    D. Never

10. According to the passage, which property that is an advantage of CFCs is NOT a property that is a disadvantage of CFCs substitutes?

    F. Flammability

    G. Toxicity

    H. Corrosiveness

    J. Sustainability

SOCIAL SCIENCE: This passage is adapted from an essay written by an art critic for general audiences. It discusses a small art movement in the 1980s and 1990s when children of immigrants to Western nations traveled in large numbers to their parents' lands of origin.

The political upheavals of the twentieth century created masses of displaced people who had to flee their countries of birth for refuge in faraway lands. These people and their children were then
5 caught in limbo between their native cultures in the developing world and their adopted ones in the West, creating not only crises of identity but also pangs of nostalgia. This "rust of memory," as one author termed it, frequently led to a general sense
10 of confusion and displacement. As the children of these immigrants later matured, many traveled in search of their identity. This gave rise to a small but interesting art movement, as the travelers documented their journeys through journals, films,
15 and other media. Taken as a group, these works form a fascinating picture of the struggle to define one's self, as well as the role of place and culture in this struggle.

Ironically, much of the longing expressed by
20 these individuals was for a motherland most of them never knew. Many were either born in their adopted lands or immigrated there early in life. One critic has explained this paradox by pointing to the shared memory and experience of close-
25 knit immigrant and expatriate groups, which can act to project a coherent imagined identity for the lost homeland. Authentic or not, the halcyon images recounted by elders fuel the idealization of a motherland so often experienced by immigrants
30 and their children.

By the 1980s and 1990s, several regional conflicts in Southern Asia, Eastern Europe, and Latin America had quieted, and many of these areas had become at least comparatively politically stable.
35 Many who had lived in exile found opportunities for return visits and even repatriation. Travel for these individuals was not a tour of new places but instead a journey toward a physical and spiritual homecoming, and their true destination was an
40 imagined, idealized land rather than a specific physical locale.

Because of the deeply personal nature of these trips, many people documented their journeys through a variety of art forms such as
45 video journals, documentary films, novels, and even web pages. (New digital technology that was inexpensive, portable, and powerful made these modern travelogues especially feasible.) In examining these documents, one cannot
50 help but notice a consistent theme. So many of these individuals were shocked to find not the unspoiled and exotic lands of their parents' gilded descriptions, but rather countries that had decayed through years of strife. Furthermore, many of
55 these individuals had become so westernized that they found it difficult to relate to their ancestral countrymen, who in turn felt no kinship with the children of those who had fled long ago.

Not all of these travelogues are great art.
60 Many are clumsy and overly earnest. Some are downright boring. In all of them, though, there is something compelling, even heartbreaking. In them, we are confronted with an evident sense of disappointment, a frustration with the complex
65 and often unpleasant nature of reality. These travelers were searching for answers, and found instead only questions. How lucky we are that they chronicled these journeys so that we can share in this mystery.

11. The primary purpose of the passage is to:

    A. evaluate the journalistic quality of documentaries made by immigrants about their journeys.

    B. contrast immigrant travel with non-immigrant travel in the 1980s and 1990s.

    C. describe changes in travel opportunities created by political change.

    D. examine the causes and results of a minor art movement.

12. In the context of the passage, the primary function of the discussion of a paradox in lines 19–27 is to:

    F. explain why children of immigrants tended to share a particular view of their families' homelands.

    G. illustrate the marked contrast between the viewpoints of children and their elders.

    H. provide a detailed explanation of how group mind-sets can develop.

    J. warn about the dangers of maintaining unrealistic viewpoints.

13. According to the passage, the main reason that some immigrants traveled back to the developing world in the 1980s and 1990s was to:

    A. seek an identity through a physical and emotional homecoming.

    B. seek the companionship of like-minded people.

    C. research and produce films, novels, and other works of art.

    D. satisfy a desire for freedom and adventure.

14. The author states that the creation of the works of art discussed in the passage was directly facilitated by:

    F. the considerable artistic skill of the artists.

    G. the lifting of press restrictions in the native countries.

    H. new media technologies.

    J. the stable political environment of the native countries.

15. According to the passage, many of the travelers to their homelands decided to create artwork about their journeys because:

    A. the inherent danger of such journeys led to exciting recollections.

    B. the journeys inspired self-reflection.

    C. the political environments of the homelands led the travelers to activism.

    D. the elders longed to hear about the homelands of their childhoods.

16. As it is used in line 52, the word *gilded* most nearly means:

    F. overlaid with gold.

    G. distorted deliberately in order to deceive.

    H. given an unnecessarily ornamented appearance.

    J. given a falsely attractive appearance.

17. As it is used in line 53, the word *decayed* most nearly means:

    A. disappointed.

    B. rotten.

    C. deteriorated.

    D. spoiled.

18. Which of the following describes the author's attitude about the art inspired by the travels described in the passage?

    F. It is fortunate that society can be impacted by the artists' reflections.

    G. It is unfortunate that art critics must endure its boring recollections.

    H. It is ironic that beautiful art could be inspired by nations struggling with political turmoil.

    J. It is disturbing that the creators of the artwork were out of touch with the people of their homelands.

19. As it is used in line 60, the word *clumsy* most nearly means:

    A. lacking in grace.

    B. socially unacceptable.

    C. physically unwieldy.

    D. awkwardly done.

20. The author finds the artwork discussed in the passage most noteworthy for its:

    F. technical sophistication.

    G. political impact.

    H. personal revelations.

    J. widespread appreciation.

Answers and Explanations are provided at the end of the book.

CHAPTER 18

Function and Writer's View Questions

CHAPTER OBJECTIVES

By the end of this chapter, you will be able to:

1. Determine why the author uses a certain word, phrase, or other feature in a given passage

2. Determine the author's purpose and point of view in a given passage

3. Recognize and answer Function questions

4. Recognize and answer Writer's View questions

SMARTPOINTS

Point Value	SmartPoints Category
4 Points	Function Questions
4 Points	Writer's View Questions

FUNCTION QUESTIONS

Function questions ask about why the author did something in the passage. They can ask about the purpose of any of the following:

- a word

- a sentence

- a paragraph

- a detail

- a quote

- punctuation

You can identify Function questions because they use phrasing such as "in order to," "serves to," "is meant to," or "functions to." Function questions may also ask about the main purpose of a specific paragraph.

To answer Function questions effectively, you need to understand the author's reason for including the cited feature. To do this, it's helpful to put yourself in the author's place. Take note of any transition words, and read around the cited text to get context and an understanding of the author's reasoning. Another useful strategy is to rephrase the original question as "Why did the author include xxx?"

WRITER'S VIEW QUESTIONS

Writer's View questions ask about part of the passage from the writer's perspective. You can spot them because they reference the author's or narrator's belief, attitude, or point of view.

To answer Writer's View questions effectively, use the author's tone and purpose to understand the author's intention in writing the text. Consider the author's opinion about the subject, situation, or character described in the question stem.

Work through the Kaplan Method for ACT Reading step-by-step to answer the questions that accompany the following Reading passage excerpt. The table below the excerpt contains two columns. The column on the right features the strategic thinking a test expert employs when approaching passages and related questions. Pay attention to how a test expert varies the approach to answer different question types.

Reading

Strategic Thinking

Step 1: Read actively

Read the passage and the notes provided. Remember, a well-crafted Passage Map should summarize the central idea of each paragraph as well as important topics or themes. Use your Passage Map to help you answer each question.

HUMANITIES: The passage below is an excerpt from *American Houses* by Philip Langdon (© 1987 by Philip Langdon).

People carry in their minds a picture of what constitutes an "American house." For most of us, it is and has long been a freestanding dwelling that rises from its own piece of land. Whether that
5 piece of land is a 40-foot-wide lot on a city street or an expanse of farmland stretching off toward the horizon is almost irrelevant; what matters is that the house stands as an individual object, separate from the walls of its neighbors. This may not be the
10 sort of dwelling in which every American actually lives—millions inhabit apartment buildings and blocks of row houses—yet the detached house holds such an allure for the imagination that it remains a national ideal, in good times and bad, in
15 periods both of dense urban development and of outward suburban dispersal. So deeply embedded in the country's consciousness is the ideal of a freestanding dwelling that even young children, when asked to draw a house, will unhesitatingly
20 make a sketch of a family-sized dwelling with a pitched roof on top, a few windows in its facade, and a prominent front door.

Some of the details that embellish this notion of the American house have, of course, changed
25 greatly with the passage of time. In the 1850s, when the landscape of architect Andrew Jackson Downing exerted a major influence on residential design, the image of an American house would have included verandas and vestibules, parlors
30 and pantries. In the 1920s, a decade enchanted

by "Old English" architecture but also gripped by a concern for cleanliness, it often summoned up a picturesque, even quaint, exterior with arched doorways and a steeply pitched roof, yet with a
35 shiny white-surfaced kitchen and bathroom within. In the 1960s, the prevailing vision was of a house that had substituted a back patio or deck for the front porch and had added a "family room" as a casual, unceremonious alternative to the formality
40 of the living room.

Despite such modifications, the governing ideal remained constant in its essentials—an individual residence enclosing a comfortable amount of space beneath the slopes of its roof and enjoying
45 dominion over a certain amount of land beyond its walls. Gradually, too, the American house was accompanied by a standard arrangement of its grounds. In the front grew a neatly kept lawn, setting a scene that possessed a measure of
50 dignity and repose. To the rear, a more informal yard provided a space for relaxation and outdoor recreation. Side yards acted as buffers against the noise and nosiness of neighbors, while at the same time making each household feel more
55 autonomous.

This was by no means a perfect or universal way to provide shelter, but it did satisfy many of the needs of millions of people. From East Coast to West, vast numbers of houses were built
60 in accordance with the common image of the American house—dwellings set apart from one another in a pattern that suited, above all, the interests of families.

¶1: American house = free-standing, very embedded in minds

¶2: Details change over time; examples 1850–1960

¶3: Essentials are constant; outdoor aspects

¶4: Satisfied needs, very popular

Today much of this arrangement has lost
65 its important reason for being: the traditional
family—a working husband, a wife who stays home,
and their not-yet-grown children—until recently
the predominant form of American household, now
makes up a minority of America's population. As
70 the population and the workforce have dramatically
changed, the house has been pressed to adapt.
Detached dwellings accounted for 80 percent
of the newly constructed private housing in the

United States as late as 1975; a decade later,
75 the proportion had steadily diminished to 62
percent. Instead of an "American house," it has
become more accurate to speak in the plural:
"American houses." The nation has entered a
period in which many houses are distinguished
80 less by their lingering similarities than by how
they diverge both from one another and from
homes of the past.

65: Today,
house is
changing with
changing
families

Reading

Questions	Strategic Thinking
1. The author uses the example of the child's sketch (lines 18–22) in order to: **A.** emphasize the simplicity of design in the typical American house. **B.** show the connection between the traditional family and the traditional American house. **C.** support the idea that the ideal of the American house pervades American society. **D.** indicate that the desire for the American house begins at a very early age.	**Step 2: Examine the question stem** The phrase "in order to" indicates that this is a Function question. The question stem references an example and provides a location. **Step 3: Predict and answer** The first paragraph establishes the idea that the concept of the typical American house is deeply embedded in people's minds. The example of the child's sketch is then introduced with the phrase "So deeply embedded in the country's consciousness is the ideal…." Predict that the child's sketch example is given as further evidence for the image people have about houses. Choice (C) matches this prediction.
2. The main purpose of the second paragraph is to: **F.** emphasize how much the American sense of style has changed since the 1850s. **G.** indicate that the architectural details of American houses have changed over time. **H.** argue that architectural trends inevitably change over time. **J.** show the influence of one important nineteenth-century American architect on subsequent generations.	**Step 2: Examine the question stem** The question asks about the function of a paragraph. Use your Passage Map note for the second paragraph to make a prediction. **Step 3: Predict and answer** The Passage Map note for Paragraph 2 is "Details change over time; examples 1850–1960." Choice (G) matches this information.

Reading

Questions	Strategic Thinking
3. The author's attitude toward the main subject of the passage can best be described as: **A.** bored indifference. **B.** awestruck exuberance. **C.** amused nostalgia. **D.** academic interest.	**Step 2: Examine the question stem** The phrase "The author's attitude" indicates that this is a Writer's View question. The question asks you to determine the author's attitude toward the passage's main subject. **Step 3: Predict and answer** Determine the author's tone. Throughout the paragraph, the author demonstrates an objective, interested tone toward the subject. Choice (D) matches this prediction.
4. The statistics in lines 72–76 indicate the author's belief that: **F.** the changing nature of the American population has resulted in a change in house construction trends. **G.** fewer Americans are interested in owning a home of their own than in the past. **H.** most families can no longer afford to buy a detached home. **J.** the change in the structure of American families has led to a reduced interest in traditional American design.	**Step 2: Examine the question stem** The question asks what the statistics in the final paragraph reveal about the author's belief, and it provides a location in the passage. **Step 3: Predict and answer** The topic of the last paragraph and the statistics included indicate the author's belief that the change in the American population has resulted in a lower percentage of detached houses being built. Choice (F) matches this prediction.

You have seen the ways in which the ACT tests you on Function and Writer's View questions in Reading passages and how an ACT expert approaches these types of questions. You will use the Kaplan Method for ACT Reading and the strategies discussed in this chapter to complete this section. Strategic thinking questions have been included to guide you. Use your answers to the strategic thinking questions to select the correct answer, just as you will on Test Day.

Strategic Thinking
Step 1: Read actively The passage below is partially mapped. Read the passage and the first part of the Passage Map. Then, complete the Passage Map on your own. Remember to focus on the central ideas of each paragraph as well as the central idea of the overall passage. Use your Passage Map as a reference when you're answering questions.

SOCIAL STUDIES: The following passage is adapted from an article in a travel journal on tourism in Mexico.

¶1: Tourist towns not "typical" Mexico; terrain dictates difference

Before tourism became a mainstay of the economy, the value of terrain in Mexico was defined by the arability of the land. To many Americans, tropical tourist-oriented beach towns
5 such as Acapulco and Puerto Vallarta characterize Mexico. These may be the most common sorts of destinations for foreign travelers but certainly are not the most representative areas of the country itself. These cities, and others like them, are set up
10 to be attractive to the tourist trade, for better or worse. But the land and culture are vastly different from those of the *altiplano*, or high plain. The function and appearance of each type of terrain dictate this divergence.

¶2: Beach areas require specialization but aren't representative

15 A tropical beach is a specialized area, and not only because it cannot be found outside of specific longitude measurements. Any living thing must be highly specialized in order to survive there or else must acclimate quickly. This is the least livable area:
20 the closer a land dweller moves to the ocean, the fewer the resources necessary to sustain life, and vice versa. Specialized areas in nature are analogous to the settlements of indigenous people untouched by modern society in forbidding environments.
25 Surroundings dictate the life of a consumer—human or otherwise—and, through adaptation,

one is nearly defined by the other. In sharp contrast is the tourist in the tropics, who has likely settled upon a destination by how different it looks from
30 home. The beach towns often contain earmarks of earlier civilizations but do not characterize the history or culture of the portions of the country inhabited for their function rather than their beauty.

35 Mexico's beach towns import resources to accommodate a great number of people, but the terrain itself generally lacks certain basic human necessities: soil suitable for plant cultivation and sufficient reserves of drinking water, both of
40 which occur naturally in the temperate and fertile *altiplano* region. A traveler in Acapulco would learn no more about the foundations of Mexican agriculture than a visitor to Yellowstone Park would learn about New York City. While the tourist often
45 delights in the year-round heat and humidity of the coast, the Mayan people, the first known to flourish in coastal Mexico, are considered to have been brilliant in their eschewing of the natural hazards and barrenness of tropical coasts rather than
50 reveling in this environment. The Mayans relied on the discovery and utilization of *cenotes*, natural springs that provided fresh water. Without a *cenote* nearby, the Mayans would not settle in a locale, no matter how picturesque.

¶3:
_____
_____

55 The tropical coast is uniformly regulated by the ocean, but the *altiplano* is a tapestry of microclimates and varies from one mile to the next. The coast extends laterally, breaking only for the mouth of a river or the edge of a mountain range, 60 where cliffs are slowly eroding into future beaches. The *altiplano,* on the other hand, expands in all directions and gradually fades into the mountains. The coast presents a border; the *altiplano* is expansive and indefinite. The difference is akin to 65 that between a gymnasium and an open market. A gymnasium is set up to provide a basic range of functions, and because of this, a person familiar with one gymnasium will find similar equipment and be able to obtain a similar experience at 70 another. The gymnasium is equipped to sustain its patrons for a short period of time. It presents a widely understood and repeatable experience to visitors. Any great variance would do customers a disservice. The market, conversely, represents the 75 surroundings through products and vendors. When

there are avocados at a market, there are avocados in fields nearby. If one product is found in a disproportionately large number of vendors' stands, it is likely well suited for cultivation or popular with 80 local consumers. The local residents set the tone for both what is available and what is popular. A different market keeps only the conventions of the seller and buyer; the local residents and agricultural terrain dictate price, product, and appearance. 85 The traveler's preferences are not addressed. An unseasoned cut of meat may not be available, and its replacement may include an array of flavors completely new to a foreign palate. A desired apple could be a rare and exotic indulgence and may give 90 way to the ubiquitous guava.

The best way to experience foreign lands, therefore, is the least recognizable way, through areas defined by local culture rather than by tourists, avoiding both the prepared environments 95 and the artificial familiarity that defines them.

¶4: _____ _____

¶5: _____ _____

Questions	Strategic Thinking
5. The reference to the Mayans in lines 46–54 mainly serves to: **A.** glorify the indigenous people of the *altiplano.* **B.** contrast their experiences on the coast with those of tourists. **C.** contrast their society with that of current locals. **D.** lament the lack of cultural knowledge on the part of tourists.	**Step 2: Examine the question stem** The key words and clues in this question stem are *Mayans* and *serves to.* Look at your Passage Map. Which parts are relevant? _____ _____ **Step 3: Predict and answer** The selection compares the Mayans' means of survival with what tourists find desirable. You can predict that the subject of the Mayans is used to illustrate the differences between what they looked for on the coast with what tourists look for. Which answer choice matches this prediction? _____

Questions	Strategic Thinking

6. The comparison between a gymnasium and an open market in Paragraph 4 is meant to:
 	
  F. contrast tourists who visit the coast with those who visit the *altiplano*.
 	
  G. show that inland areas are better equipped than beach towns to accommodate the needs of visitors.
 	
  H. emphasize that beach resorts are set up to cater to visitors in a way that the *altiplano* is not.
 	
  J. indicate that consumer goods are less available on the coast than inland.
	Step 2: Examine the question stem
	
	The key words and clues in this question stem are *comparison* and *is meant to*. What does your Passage Map indicate about the purpose of Paragraph 4?
	
	_____
	
	_____
	
	Step 3: Predict and answer
	
	This paragraph contrasts the specialized nature of the beach resorts with the more varied qualities of the *altiplano*. What can you predict?
	
	_____
	
	_____
	
	Which answer choice matches this prediction?
	
	_____

7. Which of the following most closely matches the author's view of tourist-oriented beach towns?
 	
  A. They are representative of their surroundings.
 	
  B. They are difficult to navigate.
 	
  C. They lack sufficient supplies to accommodate visitors.
 	
  D. They offer little insight into the culture of the country as a whole.
	Step 2: Examine the question stem
	
	The clue words here are "author's view of tourist-oriented beach towns." What parts of your Passage Map are relevant?
	
	_____
	
	_____
	
	Step 3: Predict and answer
	
	What can you predict?
	
	_____
	
	_____
	
	Which answer choice matches your prediction?
	
	_____

Questions	Strategic Thinking
8. The author most likely believes that the regions outside of tourist-oriented beach towns are: **F.** inaccessible to the average tourist. **G.** too varied in nature to provide any useful understanding of Mexico's culture. **H.** not welcoming to tourists. **J.** more representative of Mexico's culture than are the beach towns.	**Step 2: Examine the question stem** What are the clues and key words in the question stem? _____ _____ What parts of your Passage Map are relevant? _____ _____ **Step 3: Predict and answer** What can you predict? _____ _____ Which answer choice matches your prediction? _____

Answers and Explanations are provided at the end of the book.

Now try a test-like ACT Reading passage and question set on your own. Give yourself 5 minutes to read the passage and answer the questions.

PROSE FICTION: The following passage is a work of fiction based on the real experiences of Wilma Mankiller, the first female principal chief of the Cherokee Nation.

During an interview for a literary magazine, I was asked why my autobiography, titled *Mankiller: A Chief and Her People,* contained so much history of the Cherokee, history that occurred almost five
5 centuries before I was born. That answer is a very simple one for me to give, but may be difficult to understand. The person that I am has been defined by my people and their experiences, whether it was a week ago or centuries ago. When I ran for
10 Deputy Chief in 1985, I ran as a Cherokee, not as a Cherokee woman. I was shocked by how much my gender played a role in the election, because it never once entered my mind when I made the decision to run. My decision to run for office was
15 founded on the desire to help my people recognize their own strength and realize they had the power to rebuild their lives and their communities because they had been able to accomplish these goals in the past.

20 I am proud to be a Cherokee and I am proud of my people, both past and present. Everything that has happened in our past has affected our present and will affect our future. But one theme remains constant: survival. Our history has been
25 full of obstacles and hardships, yet we persevere. In the late 1830s, the Cherokee were forced to relocate from their homelands throughout the Southeast to Indian Territory in what later became Oklahoma. We were stripped of our land, our
30 homes, and our possessions and then forced to walk to the new territory. Many others may have simply succumbed to the hardships and ceased to exist. Instead, we rebuilt our tribe and our community with a new constitution, a new tribal
35 government including our own judicial system,

businesses, schools for both girls and boys, and even newspapers printed in both Cherokee and English. This renewal occurred within seven years of our arrival in Indian Territory. These
40 accomplishments alone show the limitless tenacity of the Cherokee People.

It becomes even more clear when the story continues and the history of the early 1900s includes the destruction of everything we had
45 rebuilt in the previous fifty years. Our schools and our courts were closed down. Our sovereignty was stripped away. From 1906 to 1971 we could not even elect our own tribal leaders. But the Cherokees did what we had always done; we
50 survived. This second rebirth took much longer than the first, but we found the strength to do what had been done before. You may wonder why I use "we" when I speak of Cherokee history. Again, I return to the idea that as a Cherokee, my tribe's
55 history has defined me, just as it has defined all Cherokee.

In fact, some of my personal experiences parallel the experiences of my ancestors. In 1956, my parents, siblings, and I were moved to California
60 as part of the Bureau of Indian Affairs relocation program. We were moved away from our family, our tribe, and our community in an effort to improve our lives. Unlike the forced removal of the 1830s, the program was voluntary, but it had
65 the same effect on the tribe as a whole. It divided us and showed us that the federal government believed we could not improve our lives without aid. But just as my ancestors survived the hardships, so did my family. We found a new community
70 at the San Francisco Indian Center. We found a place where we belonged and where we could find strength in sharing experiences with other Native Americans.

Reading

In 1977, I began working for the Cherokee
75 Nation as an economic stimulus coordinator. I was
charged with the task of getting university training
in environmental science and health for as many
Cherokee students as possible so that they could
return to their communities and provide service
80 for their people. All around me, I saw a rebuilt
Cherokee government working hard to restore the
tribe to its earlier glory. One project in particular
was a shining example of how the Cherokee are
capable of finding and implementing our own
85 solutions—the Bell Project. Bell was a small rural
community where violence was a method of
solving problems, where indoor plumbing was a
luxury, and where many houses were on the brink
of falling down. We entered the community and
90 asked them what needed to be done and what their
dreams for the future included. We asked them to
define the problems, then worked with them to
decide how they could rebuild their community.
As a community, they decided to build a water
95 system, rehabilitate twenty of their existing houses,
and build twenty-five new ones. They would
provide volunteer labor while we would provide
the materials and technical resources by soliciting
financial support for the project.

9. The author introduces the San Francisco
   Indian Center in lines 70–73 in order to:

   A. show where her family found a
      community after their relocation to
      California.

   B. illustrate the size of the San Francisco
      Native American community.

   C. describe how the government helped
      the author's family after their
      relocation.

   D. emphasize the need for community
      centers outside of the Indian tribal
      lands.

10. The author mentions the forced relocation of the
    Cherokee in lines 26–31 in order to:

    F. provide an example of an insurmountable
       obstacle faced by her people.

    G. describe a personal experience that
       defined her identity as a Cherokee.

    H. emphasize the Cherokee people's
       perseverance in the face of hardships.

    J. indicate the motivation behind the Bell
       Project.

11. With which of the following claims would the
    author most likely agree?

    A. More women should run in government
       elections.

    B. Education is vital to community-
       rebuilding efforts.

    C. Maintaining traditional cultural values is
       important.

    D. The Cherokee people should look to their
       history for inspiration.

12. Which of the following best describes the
    author's attitude toward the Bureau of Indian
    Affairs relocation program described in lines
    58–68?

    F. resigned

    G. dismayed

    H. inspired

    J. agreeable

Answers and Explanations are provided at the end
of the book.

ON YOUR OWN

The following questions provide an opportunity to practice the concepts and strategic thinking covered in this chapter. While many of the questions pertain to Function and Writer's View, some touch on other concepts tested on the Reading test to ensure that your practice is test-like, with a variety of question types per passage.

SOCIAL SCIENCE: This passage is adapted from an entry on the War of 1812 from *The Columbia Encyclopedia*, Sixth Edition (Copyright © 2004 Columbia University Press).

In 1806, Great Britain instituted a partial blockade of the European coast. The French emperor, Napoleon I, retaliated with a blockade of the British Isles. Napoleon's Continental System was
5 intended to exclude British goods or goods cleared through Britain from countries under French control. British orders in council threatened the American merchant fleet with confiscation of goods by one side or the other. Although the French
10 subjected American ships to considerable arbitrary treatment, the difficulties with England were more apparent. The conscription of sailors alleged to be British from U.S. vessels was a particularly great source of anti-British feeling.

15 Despite the infringement of U.S. rights, President Thomas Jefferson hoped to achieve a peaceful settlement with the British. Toward this end, he supported a total embargo on trade in the hope that economic pressure would force the
20 belligerents to negotiate with the United States. The Non-Importation Act of 1806 was followed by the Embargo Act of 1807. Difficulty of enforcement and economic conditions that rendered England and the Continent more or less independent of America
25 made the embargo ineffective, and in 1809, it was replaced by the Non-Intercourse Act. This in turn was superseded by Macon's Bill No. 2. Macon's Bill repealed the trade restrictions against Britain and France under the condition that if one country

30 withdrew its offensive decrees or orders, non-intercourse would be reimposed with the other.

In reality, it was not so much the infringement of neutral rights that occasioned the actual outbreak of hostilities as the desire of the
35 frontiersmen for free land, which could only be obtained at the expense of the Native Americans and the British. Moreover, the West suspected the British, with some justification, of attempting to prevent American expansion and of encouraging
40 and arming the Native Americans. Matters came to a head after the battle of Tippecanoe in 1811; the radical Western group believed that the British had supported the Native American confederacy, and they dreamed of expelling the British from Canada.
45 Their militancy was supported by Southerners who wished to obtain West Florida from the Spanish, who were allies of Great Britain.

War was declared June 18, 1812. It was not until hostilities had begun that Madison discovered
50 how woefully inadequate American preparations for war were. The rash hopes of the "war hawks," who expected to take Canada at a blow, were soon dashed. The force under Gen. William Hull, far from gaining glory, disgracefully surrendered
55 at Detroit to a smaller Canadian force under Isaac Brock. On the Niagara River, an American expedition was repulsed after a successful attack on Queenston Heights, because the militia leader Stephen Van Rensselaer refused to cross the New
60 York state boundary.

The first months of 1814 held gloomy prospects for the Americans. The finances of the government were somewhat restored in 1813, but there was no guarantee of future supplies. New England, never
65 sympathetic with the war, now became openly hostile, and the question of secession was taken up by the Hartford Convention. Moreover, with Napoleon checked in Europe, Britain could devote more time and effort to the war in America.

70   In July 1814, the American forces along the Niagara River, now under Gen. Jacob Brown, maintained their own in engagements at Chippawa and Lundy's Lane. Shortly afterward, Sir George Prevost led a large army into New York down
75 the west side of Lake Champlain and seriously threatened the Hudson Valley. But when his accompanying fleet was defeated near Plattsburgh by Capt. Thomas Macdonough, he was forced to retreat to Canada. In August, a British expedition to
80 Chesapeake Bay won an easy victory at Bladensburg and took Washington, burning the Capitol and the White House. The victorious British, however, were halted at Fort McHenry before Baltimore.

The final action of the war took place after
85 the signing of the treaty, when Andrew Jackson decisively defeated the British at New Orleans on January 8, 1815. This victory, although it came after the technical end of the war, was important in restoring American confidence. The peace treaty
90 failed to deal with the matters of neutral rights and conscription that were the visible causes of the conflict, but the war did quicken the growth of American nationalism.

1. It can be reasonably inferred from the passage that the Americans:

    A. bravely won an undisputed victory in the face of mounting adversity.

    B. were barely saved from certain defeat at the hands of Andrew Jackson at New Orleans.

    C. could not have withstood another such conflict immediately following the War of 1812.

    D. were in reality ill-prepared to assert their rights and desires against the British in the early 1800s.

2. The author believes that the conflict between the British and the Americans:

    F. was a sham started by the Americans to help Napoleon conquer the Continent.

    G. began as a result of the British drive to acquire more territory.

    H. arose from the opposing and antagonistic goals of two growing nations.

    J. detracted from the welfare of Native Americans.

3. One of the functions of the first sentence of Paragraph 3 (lines 32–37) is to:

    A. indicate the overrepresentation of the interests of frontiersmen in Washington.

    B. introduce the author's assertion that each nation held some blame in starting the war.

    C. explain why the British are primarily responsible for the War of 1812.

    D. foreshadow the downfall of the arrogant "war hawks."

4. Based on the information provided in the second paragraph (lines 15–31), which of the following statements best reflects the reasoning of the Americans in passing legislation in reaction to the French and British?

    F. The legislation represented an emphatically hostile reaction to the policies of the Europeans.

    G. American legislators grudgingly acquiesced to the will of the British and French.

    H. The Americans attempted several legislative solutions before resorting to physical conflict.

    J. The legislation attempted to pit the British and French against each other for American benefit.

5. The function of Paragraph 4 (lines 48–60) in relation to the passage as a whole is to:

    A. foreshadow the ineffectiveness of the peace treaties signed when the war ended.

    B. introduce the ensuing difficulties suffered by the Americans.

    C. describe how smaller, better trained forces can defeat larger armies.

    D. introduce General William Hull as an important figure in history.

6. The author describes the defeat of the British at New Orleans (lines 84–89) in order to:

    F. show how the War of 1812 had detracted from America's self-confidence.

    G. demonstrate how the victory catapulted Andrew Jackson to lasting fame.

    H. contend that wars do not always end when participating countries agree to end them.

    J. posit that the reasons behind warfare will not always be addressed by a treaty.

7. The use of the phrase *arbitrary treatment* (lines 10–11) to describe the actions of the French toward the Americans indicates the author's belief that:

    A. the French treatment of American interests was mostly justified.

    B. the French were secretly helping the Americans.

    C. the British were more consciously antagonistic to American interests.

    D. conscription may not have violated Americans' rights.

8. According to Paragraph 3 (lines 32–47), one of the reasons for the outbreak of the War of 1812 was:

    F. conflict over territorial expansion.

    G. the British maltreatment of Native Americans.

    H. deteriorating relations with the Spanish, who were allied with Britain.

    J. conscription of American sailors into the British and French navies.

9. The passage states that the United States passed the Non-Importation and Non-Intercourse Acts because its leadership:

    A. feared the reprisals of the British navy.

    B. wanted to find a diplomatic solution.

    C. thought the British would be threatened into respecting the rights of the Americans.

    D. wished to gain revenge on its foes through embargoes.

Reading

10. The author describes American preparations for war as *woefully inadequate* (line 50) in order to:

   F. underscore the reversal of expectations represented by the American defeats.

   G. highlight the later genius that Andrew Jackson displayed in New Orleans.

   H. point out the wisdom of the "war hawks."

   J. suggest that the British should have been more aggressive toward the Americans.

The following passage was adapted from the article "Land Art: Here Today, Gone Tomorrow?" by Helen Stoilas (© 2008 by *The Art Newspaper*).

Humans have always bent their imagination to aesthetically reshape the world around them. However, a particular problem for early artists seems to have been finding ways to make
5 artwork last. It was not an easy task to create artwork with natural and often perishable materials. Despite these difficulties, countless examples of ancient art fill museums through the world, from the cave drawings in Lascaux to Egyptian
10 hieroglyphics to Greek sculpture. However, a contemporary movement called land art, which embraces this difficulty, has increased in popularity around the world. Land art is defined as art that either naturally deteriorates or is deliberately
15 dismantled after it is constructed.

Land or earth art was first developed during the mid-1960s as a backlash in the art community against the progressive seclusion of art from the real world. Artists like Alan Sonfist sought to
20 incorporate nature in their work as well as return to the fundamental principles upon which they believed art was based. The pioneers of land art rejected the museum and art gallery as the rightful settings for creative work. They sought to remove
25 the "plastic" influences and what they viewed as

the corrosive influence on pure aesthetics. Thus, land art began with a mission to create three-dimensional works set in and wrought from the natural world.

30 Above all, land artists utilize simple materials. More specifically than other minimalist artists, land artists use natural media such as rocks, soil, sand, wood, water, and even plant matter in the creation of their masterpieces. Land art icon Robert
35 Smithson's work *Spiral Jetty* was constructed using nothing more than stones, mud, algae, and water. Created in the Great Salt Lake in 1970 during a severe drought, *Spiral Jetty* was a 1,500-meter spiral of rocks that projected from the lakeshore and was
40 allowed to deteriorate *in situ*. The Jetty was covered by the lake within a few years and remained underwater until 2004 when, to the delight of contemporary artists, another drought revealed the 30-year-old sculpture.

45 Another feature of land art is its massive scale. Since land art makes extensive use of landscape, entire vistas can be said to be part of a work. The sheer size of land art thus requires collaboration between the artist and engineers as well as the
50 employment of laborers and volunteers to complete a project. Australian artist Andrew Rogers's piece *Rhythms of Life* was constructed in twelve different sites around the world, making the work the largest piece of aesthetic art in the world—a feat
55 reminiscent of Christo and Jeanne-Claude's 1991 *Umbrellas* project, which placed massive blue and yellow umbrellas in selected stretches of the Japanese countryside and the California mountains. Christo, however, denies the label of "land artist,"
60 claiming that his and his wife's work neither rejects gallery art nor eschews the use of synthetic building materials.

Despite semantic differences, Christo and Jeanne-Claude's work is similar to those of
65 land artists in that both are short-lived. Land art is extensively photographed during exhibition but afterward exists only on film or in memory. Some

critics and art lovers decry limiting public access
to a work of art by sheer brevity. Because land art
70 often requires substantial funding to be created,
allowing the finished product to fall into ruin or
even purposefully dismantling it is considered by
their critics to be a waste of resources. Land artists
counter such indictments by pointing out that
75 they only borrow the elements of nature to produce
their work and once a piece has been exhibited,
they feel justified in returning the materials to
their rightful owner. Moreover, land artworks that
capture the imagination can live on in memory and
80 appear even greater to the public consciousness
than they really were. As Christo once stated, "Do
you know that I don't have any artworks that exist?
They all go away when they're finished . . . giving
my works an almost legendary character. I think it
85 takes much greater courage to create things to be
gone than to create things that will remain."

11. The author views the creation of artwork
    designed to last through time as:

    A. misguided.

    B. challenging.

    C. essential.

    D. noble.

12. According to the passage, why did ancient
    artists have a difficult time creating lasting
    artworks?

    F. Such works were not popular among
    land artists of the time.

    G. The media available to ancient artists
    were prone to decay.

    H. Patrons refused to pay the necessary
    expense for such work.

    J. The elements of nature succumbed to
    man-made endeavors.

13. According to the passage, the land art
    movement:

    A. originated with the creation of *Spiral Jetty*
    by Robert Smithson.

    B. began as a backlash against the creation
    of permanent artworks.

    C. was primarily motivated by a desire to
    use natural materials in art.

    D. was a negative reaction to attributes of
    modern art during the 1960s.

14. The passage states all of the following about
    Spiral Jetty EXCEPT:

    F. it was constructed on the shore of a body
    of water.

    G. it was systematically dismantled after
    exhibition.

    H. it could not be viewed for long periods of
    time.

    J. Robert Smithson chose to allow the work
    to fall into neglect.

15. The author mentions *Rhythms of Life* in lines
    51–54 in order to:

    A. provide an example of how large land
    artworks can be.

    B. compare *Rhythms of Life* to the
    Umbrellas project.

    C. emphasize the diminutive scale of land
    artworks.

    D. describe the largest work of aesthetic art
    in human history.

16. The main purpose of the last paragraph is to:

 F. examine the implications of creating artworks that exist for a brief period of time.

 G. refute criticism of land art and the work of Christo and Jeanne-Claude.

 H. analyze the difference between land art and Christo and Jeanne-Claude's work.

 J. provide examples of legendary pieces of land art.

17. The author quotes Christo (lines 81–86) in order to:

 A. argue that none of the preeminent works in modern art still exist.

 B. demonstrate that when Christo and Jeanne-Claude dismantle their artwork, they exhibit a courage entirely lacking in land artists.

 C. show that the destruction of a piece of artwork can enhance that work's reputation in the minds of critics and admirers.

 D. provide information about how artists care very little about wasting natural resources when they allow their artwork to be destroyed.

18. According to the passage, what happens to the building materials of land artwork after it is taken apart?

 F. They are recycled.

 G. They are replaced in nature.

 H. They are given to a new owner.

 J. They are used in future art.

19. Based on the passage, the author would most likely agree with which of the following statements?

 A. *Rhythms of Life* is unsurpassed in popularity within the art world.

 B. Christo and Jeanne-Claude are not land artists because they refuse to use synthetic materials.

 C. All land artists require generous levels of funding in order to create their artwork.

 D. The reemergence of *Spiral Jetty* from the Great Salt Lake does not pass without notice in the art world.

20. The author's attitude toward land art can best be described as:

 F. dismissive.

 G. skeptical.

 H. zealous.

 J. supportive.

Answers and Explanations are provided at the end of the book.

CHAPTER 19

Paired Passages

CHAPTER OBJECTIVES

By the end of this chapter, you will be able to:

1. Apply the Kaplan Method for Paired Passages

2. Synthesize, compare, and contrast information from two different but related passages

SMARTPOINTS

Point Value	SmartPoints Category
Point Builder	The Kaplan Method for Paired Passages
4 Points	Synthesis

PAIRED PASSAGES

The ACT Reading test includes three long passages and one paired passage set consisting of two shorter passages. These paired passages are on a similar topic, but they present different information or points of view. Some questions for paired passages ask about only one of the passages, while other questions ask about both passages. The key to success with paired passages is to keep straight who said what. To help you accomplish that task, Kaplan has a specific Method for approaching paired passages.

The Kaplan Method for Paired Passages has three steps:

> **Step 1: Actively read Passage A, then answer its questions**
>
> **Step 2: Actively read Passage B, then answer its questions**
>
> **Step 3: Answer questions about both passages**

These steps are to be used along with the Kaplan Method for ACT Reading (Read actively; Examine the question stem; Predict and answer).

By reading Passage A and answering its questions before moving on to Passage B, you avoid falling into wrong answer traps that reference the text of Passage B. Furthermore, by addressing each passage individually, you will have a better sense of the central idea and purpose of each passage. This will help you answer questions that ask you to synthesize information about both passages.

> ✔ **Note**
>
> Even though the individual passages are shorter in a paired passage set, you should still map them. Overall, there is too much information to remember effectively in your head. Your Passage Maps will save you time by helping you locate key details.

Fortunately, questions in a paired passage set that ask about only one of the passages will be no different from questions you've seen and answered about single passages. Use the same strategies you've been using to answer these questions.

SYNTHESIS QUESTIONS

Several questions in a paired passage set will be Synthesis questions. These questions will ask you about both passages. You may be asked to identify similarities or differences between the passages or how the author of one passage might respond to a point made by the author of the other passage.

Work through the Kaplan Method for Paired Passages step-by-step to answer the questions that accompany the following excerpts from a Reading paired passage set. The tables below the excerpts contain two columns. The column on the right features the strategic thinking a test expert employs when approaching passages and related questions. Pay attention to how a test expert varies the approach to answer different question types.

Reading

Strategic Thinking
Step 1: Read actively
Read the passage and the notes provided. Remember, a well-crafted Passage Map should summarize the central idea of each paragraph as well as important topics or themes. Use your Passage Map to help you answer each question.

NATURAL SCIENCE: The following passages describe commercial fish farming.

Passage A

When commercial fish farming—a technique that essentially applies the breeding structures used for raising animals on land to the ocean—was first introduced, it was seen as a creative alternative
5 to the depletion of the world's large finfish and shellfish populations through conventional harvesting methods. New research, however, is beginning to reign in this initial enthusiasm. Production of farmed food fish was about 60
10 million tons by 2010, no doubt a significant contribution to the world's fish supplies. Yet the cost of this production includes millions of tons of smaller wild fish used as feed, an amount that, if perpetuated, could soon virtually wipe out both the
15 world's supply of small fish and the potential of fish farming.

¶1: Fish farms were alt. to conventional; now realize dangers of wild fish loss

Questions	Strategic Thinking
Question 1 asks about Passage A.	**Step 2: Examine the question stem**
1. The first sentence of Passage A indicates that fish farming was initially considered to be: **A.** a complicated technique. **B.** an innovative method. **C.** a simple improvement on a successful process. **D.** environmentally safe.	This question asks about a detail in the passage. Return to the first sentence to make a prediction. **Step 3: Predict and answer** The referenced sentence says fish farming was seen as a *creative alternative* (line 4). This prediction matches (B).

Passage B

Our seemingly insatiable appetite for seafood delicacies like smoked salmon, king prawns, and grilled sea bass has inevitably contributed to a sharp
20 reduction in ocean fish populations. As a growing number of commercial boats found themselves frequently returning to shore with empty nets, it became clear that supply was starting to run significantly short of an ever-increasing demand.

¶1: High demand → depleted fish pop.; commercial fish farms help

25 But then came a potential solution in the form of a tried and true method of food production: farming. Today, while traditional ocean fisheries remain in decline, commercial fish farming is booming—and presently premium fish remain on menus across
30 the world. Through ingenuity and flexible thinking, a seemingly doomed resource was made more sustainable.

Reading

Questions	Strategic Thinking
Question 2 asks about Passage B.	**Step 2: Examine the question stem**
2. As it is used in line 19, the word *sharp* most nearly means: **F.** piercing. **G.** intense **H.** abrupt. **J.** appreciable.	Vocab-in-Context questions almost always test secondary meanings. Watch out for answer choices that do not make sense in the context. **Step 3: Predict and answer** The following sentence says that fish supplies were *significantly short* (line 24), so predict that *sharp* means *noticeable*. Choice (J) is a match.

Questions	Strategic Thinking
Questions 3 and 4 ask about both passages.	**Step 2: Examine the question stem**
3. Both passages raise which of the following questions regarding commercial fish farming? **A.** Will fish farming ultimately help or harm wild fish populations? **B.** Is commercial fish farming a sustainable means of food production? **C.** What will happen when wild fish supplies are fully depleted? **D.** Can commercial fish farming meet the growing demand for premium fish?	Because you are asked about both passages, watch out for answer choices that are only half correct. **Step 3: Predict and answer** Passage A refers to *New research* (line 7) that sheds doubt on the initial enthusiasm for fish farming and that the cost of production could *wipe out* (line 14) this industry's potential. Passage B refers to fish farming as a *potential solution* (line 25) and asserts at the end that this method is *more sustainable* (lines 31–32). Both passages express an opinion about the long-term prospects of fish farming, so the correct answer is (B). The effects on wild fish are only discussed in Passage A, so A and C are incorrect. Only Passage B discusses the demand for premium fish, so D is incorrect.

Questions	Strategic Thinking
4. The passages differ in their evaluations of commercial fish farming in that Passage A focuses on: **F.** the relationship between farmed and wild fish populations, whereas Passage B addresses the discrepancy between fish supplies and demand. **G.** statistics to make an argument, whereas Passage B relies more on general predictions. **H.** the results of various research studies, whereas Passage B relies primarily on data obtained from fisheries. **J.** the application of land-based farming techniques to the ocean, whereas Passage B considers fish farming as a distinct approach.	**Step 2: Examine the question stem** Because commercial fish farming is the main topic of each passage, this is a Global question. **Step 3: Predict and answer** When asked a Global question, restate what each passage is about and use that as your prediction. Passage A describes the effect of fish farming on wild fish, and Passage B describes the supply and demand of premium seafood. This prediction matches (F).

You have seen the ways in which the ACT tests you on Paired Passages questions and how an ACT expert approaches these types of questions. You will use the Kaplan Method for Paired Passages and the strategies discussed in this chapter to complete this section. Strategic thinking questions have been included to guide you. Use your answers to the strategic thinking questions to select the correct answer, just as you will on Test Day.

Strategic Thinking
Step 1: Read actively
The passage below is partially mapped. Read the passage and the first part of the Passage Map. Then, complete the Passage Map on your own. Remember to focus on the central ideas of each paragraph as well as the central idea of the overall passage. Use your Passage Map as a reference when you're answering questions.

SOCIAL STUDIES: The following passages describe urbanization, which is the growth of cities.

Passage A

Throughout most of world history, humans have lived a rural lifestyle wedded to the surrounding land and natural resources. In 1800, for example, only 3 percent of the world's population resided in
5 urban areas. Even a century later, that figure had risen to just 14 percent, although 12 of the world's cities at that time had each swelled to more than a million inhabitants. In recent decades, however, the trend toward greater urbanization has accelerated.
10 Today, roughly half of the world's population lives in cities, and this number will only increase as less-developed nations continue to experience the same causes of urbanization that altered the developed world a century ago.

Passage B

15 While the ways in which a city can grow—the excess of births and immigrations over deaths and out-migrations—are not difficult to understand at the most basic level, determining precisely how such ratios have interacted in specific situations
20 is a more complicated process. During the early twentieth century in the world's most developed nations, urbanization was most directly the result of massive migrations spurred by the creation of new job opportunities in city factories. These
25 jobs arose in cities with extremely unsanitary and disease-ridden conditions, but they were jobs nonetheless. Conversely, urbanization in most less-developed countries in recent years has occurred largely because of falling death rates resulting from
30 improvements in health services.

¶1: Recent urbanization rate ↑, will continue to ↑

¶1: _____ _____

Questions	Strategic Thinking

Question 5 asks about Passage A.
 	
5. As it is used in line 2, the phrase *wedded to* most nearly means:
  A. affectionately united with.
  B. mutually beneficial for.
  C. strongly committed to.
  D. unfortunately dependent upon.
	Step 2: Examine the question stem
	
	The key words indicate that this is a Vocab-in-Context question.
	
	Step 3: Predict and answer
	
	Return to the cited line and treat the phrase as a blank to be filled in. In context, *wedded to* means something like *tied to*, with a neutral tone.
	
	Which answer choice matches this prediction? _____

Question 6 asks about Passage B.
 	
6. Which of the following most nearly captures the meaning implied by the phrase "they were jobs nonetheless" (lines 26–27)?
  F. Few people were concerned about disease.
  G. Those who were employed could avoid disease.
  H. Job growth created unsanitary conditions.
  J. Employment was judged more important than health.
	Step 2: Examine the question stem
	
	The key word *implied* indicates that this is an Inference question. Use the cited lines to make a prediction.
	
	Step 3: Predict and answer
	
	_____
	
	_____

Reading

Questions	Strategic Thinking
Questions 7 and 8 ask about both passages.	**Step 2: Examine the question stem**
7. How would the author of Passage B most likely respond to the assertion made in Passage A that less-developed nations will "experience the same causes of urbanization that altered the developed world" (lines 12–14)?	The key words *most likely* signal that this is an Inference question. Determine how Author B feels about the issue before using the cited lines to make a prediction.
A. The cities in less-developed nations are actually growing due to different factors.	**Step 3: Predict and answer**
B. The world has changed significantly since the urbanization of the developed nations.	_____
C. Most developed nations were not burdened by unsanitary conditions.	_____
D. It is unrealistic to expect less-developed nations to urbanize to the same extent as developed nations.	
8. Which statement best describes how the authors of the two passages differ in their views on urbanization trends?	**Step 2: Examine the question stem**
F. The author of Passage A ties a lack of rural land to urbanization, whereas the author of Passage B focuses on working conditions.	_____ _____
G. The author of Passage A is decidedly opinionated on the merits of urbanization, whereas the author of Passage B remains objective.	**Step 3: Predict and answer** _____
H. The author of Passage A relies upon specific statistics, whereas the author of Passage B cites conclusions that are more general.	_____
J. The author of Passage A encourages the urbanization of less-developed nations, whereas the author of Passage B is more wary.	

Answers and Explanations are provided at the end of the book.

Now try a test-like ACT Reading paired passage and question set on your own. Give yourself 5 minutes to read the passages and answer the questions.

SOCIAL SCIENCE: The following passages discuss political advertising.

Passage A

Often, the winner of an election is the candidate who best masters the art of the political advertisement. Most voters have a stake in the issues of the day but cannot make sense of the rules
5 and rhetoric of the real processes of government. The thirty-second commercial on prime-time television therefore plays a crucial part in the political process, making sense out of technical political jargon. Those who wish to speak for an
10 electorate must make their case to that electorate, and the political advertisement is the most direct and effective way to achieve that goal.

Passage B

We can find no greater evidence of indifference to democracy's inner workings than the political
15 commercial. Sandwiched between advertisements for microwave meals and new cars, the political ad suggests that government, too, is a product that, once purchased, will offer us the same convenience and value as any other good or service. The less
20 we have to worry about and examine the crucial issues of the day, the thinking goes, the better our interests have been served. Yet the electorate's disciplined—and often inconvenient—examination of government is the act from which representative
25 government derives its greatest strength. The messages that bombard us with competing political factions blunt our power before a single ballot has been cast.

Question 9 asks about Passage A.

9. Which of the following best summarizes the central point of Passage A?

   A. The political commercial confuses voters with heavy reliance on political jargon.

   B. The political commercial is one of many methods used to influence voters.

   C. The political commercial performs a function that is vital to democracy.

   D. The political commercial ensures the participation of every voter in the real processes of government.

Question 10 asks about Passage B.

10. The author of Passage B mentions "microwave meals and new cars" in line 16 because they:

   F. offer valid comparisons to the services provided by government.

   G. illustrate the electorate's unwillingness to examine government in a disciplined fashion.

   H. serve as examples of consumer products that use advertising to influence buyers.

   J. represent ways in which political commercials empower voters.

Questions 11 and 12 ask about both passages.

11. The author of Passage B suggests that voters should see the "rules and rhetoric of the real processes of government," mentioned in Passage A (lines 4–5), as:

A. essential realities that should be examined and understood.

B. worthy subject matter for more effective political ads.

C. examples of a preoccupation with superficialities.

D. inferior to real participation in government by the public.

12. The authors of both passages agree on the significance of:

F. the political commercial as the most effective way to motivate voters.

G. the failure of advertising to influence the political climate.

H. the political commercial as a major factor in shaping the behavior of voters.

J. the disciplined scrutiny of government by voters.

Answers and Explanations are provided at the end of the book.

ON YOUR OWN

The following questions provide an opportunity to practice the concepts and strategic thinking covered in this chapter. While many of the questions pertain to Synthesis, some touch on other concepts tested on the Reading Test to ensure that your practice is test-like, with a variety of question types per passage.

LITERARY NARRATIVE: Passage A is adapted from the essay "The Language Barrier or Silence" by Joseph Fellows. Passage B is adapted from the essay "The First and Last Time" by Randy Benson.

Passage A by Joseph Fellows

I hadn't slept the night before I left, nor could I even doze on the plane. Piqued and red-eyed is not how I had envisioned my first day abroad. I had also hoped to have a little bit of the German
5 language under my belt before mingling with locals.

Unfortunately, the absurdly unpredictable nature of the *der/die/das* articles frustrated me so much that I never really got past the general salutations and simple, commonly used phrases. I was therefore
10 stubbornly determined to get as much mileage out of *Danke* and *Bitte* as I could. Every German person in Tegel Airport must have thought me incredibly gracious but dim-witted. I tried saying *Freut mich, Sie kennenzulernen* (nice to meet you) to the cab
15 driver that I hailed, and after three tries, each receiving a quizzical stare in return, I gave up and simply told him my destination in English. I then squeezed myself into the tiny Peugeot; evidently, SUVs are not fashionable in Europe.

20 The bed-and-breakfast I had booked was nice— very quaint, but obviously a tourist spot. The owner was a scowling old woman who said little and waddled around, pointing and grunting, rightfully assuming I was linguistically stunted. Thoroughly
25 intimidated by the locals and their language, I decided to take a walk through historic Berlin in hopes of bonding with the nature and architecture, rather than the people. I was immediately glad that I did.

30 Despite being exhausted and surly, I found myself awestruck and humbled by the ubiquitous artistry of the city. Despite knowing little about World War II and having been born forty years after, I was profoundly affected by my first view of
35 the Kaiser Wilhelm Gedächtniskirche (Memorial Church), with its crushed steeple and bomb-ravaged stone walls, existing in jarring juxtaposition to the surrounding modern architecture.

Further east near the Berlin Zoo, I found a lovely
40 park along the murky water of the Landwehrkanal, and eventually, I came to a massive traffic circle. In the midst of this automotive maelstrom of Berlin rush hour stood the magnificent Siegessäule (Victory Column). The immaculate craftsmanship
45 against the verdant horizon and cerulean sky— there are no words in any language to describe it. So I sat on a stone bench, smiled contentedly, and said nothing.

Passage B by Randy Benson

My room was gray and windowless, with a
50 cement floor painted blood-red. The mattress had no sheets, but I was too disoriented to care. Bad way to start the semester. Why had I picked up with Greg, anyway?

After we stored our bags in a locker at Termini,
55 Greg marched me to a trattoria where we feasted on pasta, fish, veal, salad, cheese, and fruit. After the meal, Greg took me on a bistro-and-basilica tour. "C'mon, Paisan'. I'm gonna show you how to do Rome right."

60 After two churches and two restaurants, I said to Greg, "I understand loving the food here. But what's your thing with churches?"

Reading

Reading

Greg looked at me like I had a trinity of heads. "I know you're not really that clueless, Paisan'. Quit
65 being such a middle-class American sophomore and ask me a real question, like 'Gee, Greg, that bone church we just went through makes me wonder whatever would possess a herd of Capuchin monks to make artistic masterpieces out of their
70 own skeletal remains.'"

Actually, the thought of the bone church made the hunk of Fontinella cheese I'd just wolfed down twist in my stomach. "No. I don't wanna talk about the bones. I wanna know why you're dragging me
75 through churches. Is it just a scenic way to pace ourselves between bistros?"

"You mean to tell me, Paisan', that you really got nothing out of St. Peter's?"

I wasn't going to admit it to Greg, but St. Peter's
80 really was kind of awesome. Made my jaw drop, actually.

"Eh. It's a big church. Who cares?"

"You should, Paisan'. This is Rome, man. The Republic. The Empire. The Church. In a place like
85 this, I shouldn't have to agitate you into an outburst of culture. Up 'til now, everything about life has numbed you. This place is gonna wake up your soul." At this, he pushed another hunk of Fontinella at me, and I had no confidence that it would sit any better
90 than the last after one more church full of bones.

After seven more churches and three more bistros, we finally ground to a halt at the Cafe Montespiné. The locals gawked at the Americani and engaged Greg in conversations that mixed
95 French, Greek, Italian, and Martian. We dragged ourselves out of Montespiné at four-thirty in the morning, with half of our new-found friends still acting like the night was just starting.

Which is why I woke up this morning, bleary-
100 eyed, in the previous night's clothes, my head heavy as a crushed Italian moon-rock breakfast roll. Maybe not the best way to start the semester. But I have to admit—it was quite a start.

Questions 1–3 ask about Passage A.

1. The author includes the interaction with the cab driver (lines 13–19) in order to:

    A. explain how the narrator got from the airport to the bed-and-breakfast.

    B. provide an example of the narrator's aggravation with the German language.

    C. show the affinity that the narrator has for the German language.

    D. explain how to greet someone unfamiliar in German.

2. In the third paragraph of Passage A (lines 20–29), the narrator's decision to go for a walk is prompted by:

    F. his insecurity that had developed as a result of his difficulty with the German language.

    G. his anger toward the owner of the bed-and-breakfast.

    H. his eagerness to sightsee and experience the culture of the city.

    J. his stubborn determination to succeed at speaking the German language.

3. The narrator states that "there are no words" (line 46) to describe the view at the Siegessäule because the narrator:

    A. can't speak German well enough to translate the description thoroughly.

    B. is too frustrated with the German language to take the time to depict the scene's beauty.

    C. feels that any explanation of the beauty of the scene could not do it justice.

    D. chose to sit quietly on the stone bench rather than say anything.

Questions 4–6 ask about Passage B.

4. The last paragraph of Passage B (lines 99–104) summarizes:

   F. the narrator's transition from sleep to regret for staying out the previous night.

   G. the narrator's transition from sleep to a celebratory embrace of new life circumstances.

   H. the narrator's recognition of the previous night as a unique way to begin the stay in Rome.

   J. the narrator's return to a reality made much happier by the absence of Greg.

5. In Passage B, the narrator's descriptions of Greg suggest that the narrator sees Greg as:

   A. too daring and bold to be a traveling companion in the future.

   B. compelling enough to follow and see what happens next.

   C. too numb to experience any pleasure in Rome.

   D. a religious fanatic.

6. In Passage B, the author uses line 79 ("I wasn't going to admit it to Greg") in order to:

   F. illustrate the narrator's unwillingness to follow Greg's scheme.

   G. argue that admiration of Roman churches is a more privately held matter.

   H. call attention to the jaw-dropping nature of St. Peter's.

   J. suggest the favorable influence that Greg's tour is having on the narrator.

Questions 7–10 ask about both passages.

7. Compared to Passage B's narrator, Passage A's narrator spends more time discussing:

   A. the history of the city he is visiting.

   B. his interactions with the local people.

   C. the various religious landmarks he encounters.

   D. his inability to speak the foreign language fluently.

8. Which of the following statements best summarizes the similarity or difference of the tone of the two passages?

   F. Passage A is impersonal and historical, while Passage B is thoughtfully nostalgic.

   G. Passage A is animated and comical, while Passage B is serious and introspective.

   H. Both passages begin with a sense of trepidation but end with an air of equability and calm.

   J. Both passages begin humorously and end on a note of introspection.

9. While Passage A straightforwardly recounts the narrator's experiences abroad, Passage B is more:

   A. colloquial.

   B. informative.

   C. didactic.

   D. impersonal.

10. Which of the following best describes the narrators' reactions to the architecture in the cities they visited?

F. Passage A's narrator appreciates the architecture, while Passage B's narrator is indifferent.

G. Passage A's narrator does not notice the architecture, while Passage B's narrator is wholly captivated by it.

H. Passage A's narrator and Passage B's narrator both begin by appreciating the architecture and then grow tired of it.

J. Passage A's narrator finds peace by looking at the architecture, while Passage B's narrator has a more complicated response to it.

SOCIAL SCIENCE: In Passage A, an eminent historian recalls his university education. In Passage B, a journalist compares the history books she read when she was younger with the history currently taught in schools.

Passage A

When I studied ancient history at this university many years ago, I had as a special subject "Greece in the Period of the Persian Wars." I collected fifteen or twenty volumes on my shelves and took it for
5 granted that there, recorded in these volumes, I had all the facts relating to my subject. Let us assume—it was very nearly true—that those volumes contained all the facts about it that were then known, or could be known. It never occurred to me
10 to inquire by what accident or process of attrition that minute selection of facts, out of all the myriad facts that must have once been known to somebody, had survived to become the facts of history. I suspect that even today one of the fascinations of
15 ancient and medieval history is that it gives us the illusion of having all the facts at our disposal within a manageable compass: the nagging distinction between the facts of history and other facts about the past vanishes because the few known facts are
20 all facts of history.

Today, historians are more skeptical, of course, and more apt to acknowledge that our picture of Greece in the fifth century BCE is defective, not because so many details have been accidentally lost,
25 but because it is, by and large, the picture formed by a tiny group of people in the city of Athens. We know a lot about what fifth-century Greece looked like to an Athenian citizen, but hardly anything about what it looked like to a Spartan, a Corinthian,
30 or a Theban. In the same way, when I read in a modern history of the Middle Ages that the people of the Middle Ages were deeply concerned with religion, I wonder how we know this and whether it is true. What we know as the facts of medieval
35 history have almost all been selected for us by generations of chroniclers who were professionally occupied in the theory and practice of religion and who therefore thought it supremely important, and recorded everything related to it and not
40 much else. The picture of the Russian peasant as devoutly religious was destroyed by the revolution of 1917. The picture of medieval man as devoutly religious, whether true or not, is indestructible, because nearly all the known facts about him were
45 preselected for us by people who believed it, and a mass of other facts, in which we might have found evidence to the contrary, has been lost beyond recall.

Passage B

Ideologically speaking, the history books of
50 the fifties were immutable, seamless. Inside their covers, America was perfect: the greatest nation in the world and the embodiment of democracy, freedom, and technological progress. For them, the country never changed in any important way:
55 its values and its political institutions remained constant from the time of the American Revolution. To my generation—the children of the fifties—these texts seemed perfect just because they were so self-contained. Their orthodoxy, it seemed, left no
60 handholds for attack, no lodging for decay. Who, after all, would dispute the wonders of technology

or the superiority of the English colonists over
the Spanish? There was, it seemed, no point in
comparing these visions with reality, since they
65 were the public truth and were thus quite irrelevant
to what anyone privately believed.

Now the texts have changed, however, and with
them changed the country that American children
are growing up into. The society that was once
70 uniform is now a patchwork of rich and poor, old
and young, men and women, blacks, whites, Asians,
Hispanics, and Native Americans. The system that
ran so smoothly by means of the Constitution
under the guidance of benevolent presidents is now
75 a rattletrap affair. The past is no highway to the
present; it is a collection of issues and events that do
not fit together and that lead in no single direction.
The word "progress" has been replaced by the word
"change": children, the modern texts insist, should
80 learn history so that they can adapt to the rapid
changes taking place around them. The present,
which was once portrayed in the concluding
chapters as a peaceful haven of scientific advances
and presidential inaugurations, is now a tangle of
85 problems, and some of the books illustrate these
problems dramatically.

The surprise that adults feel in seeing the
changes in history texts must come from the
lingering hope that there is, somewhere out there,
90 an objective truth. We know that each historian, to
some degree, creates the world anew and that all
history, to some degree, is contemporary history,
but beyond this knowledge there is still a hope for
some reliable authority, for some fixed stars in the
95 universe.

We may know that journalists cannot be wholly
unbiased and that "balance" is an imaginary point
between two extremes, and yet we hope that our
nightly news anchor will tell us the truth of things.
100 In the same way, we hope that our history will not
change—that we learned the truth of things as
children.

Questions 11–13 ask about Passage A.

11. As it is used in line 17, the word *nagging* most
nearly means:

A. carping.

B. complaining.

C. irritating.

D. manageable.

12. According to Passage A, today our picture of
ancient Greece is defective primarily because:

F. the population of ancient Greece was too
small to make generalizations about.

G. a mass of facts that would shed further
light on ancient Greece has been lost.

H. earlier historians did not distinguish
between the facts of history and other
facts.

J. we only know ancient Greek history from
the viewpoint of one group.

13. In the second paragraph of Passage A, the
author most likely refers to "generations of
chroniclers" (line 36) in order to:

A. compare the methods of historians during
different periods.

B. illustrate one of the fascinations of
studying medieval history.

C. support the theory that medieval people
were devoutly religious.

D. explain the basis of a prevailing
interpretation.

Questions 14–16 ask about Passage B.

14. As it is used in line 56, the word *constant* most nearly means:

    F. regular.

    G. unaltered.

    H. faithful.

    J. unremitting.

15. The primary purpose of the second paragraph (lines 67–86) is to:

    A. emphasize the extent to which history texts have changed.

    B. describe the social problems facing children in the United States.

    C. highlight the influence of each U.S. president on the course of history.

    D. make the point that history books should be relevant to current events.

16. It can reasonably be inferred from Passage B that the phrase "fixed stars in the universe" (lines 94–95) refers to:

    F. journalistic insight.

    G. scientific evaluation.

    H. original interpretation.

    J. indisputable facts.

Questions 17–20 ask about both passages.

17. Both Passage A and Passage B are primarily concerned with the:

    A. inaccuracy of many ancient history books.

    B. phenomenon of changing perspectives on history.

    C. relationship between history and journalism.

    D. relevance of studying history today.

18. The author of Passage A would most likely react to Passage B's characterization of American history expressed in the history books of the 1950s (lines 49–66) by:

    F. comparing public opinion with the private beliefs of individuals.

    G. questioning the source of facts that support this interpretation.

    H. scrutinizing a large sample of textbooks for alternate viewpoints.

    J. looking for similar characteristics in the history of the Middle Ages.

19. How would the author of Passage B most likely respond to the characterization of the "picture of medieval man" as "indestructible" in Passage A (lines 42–43)?

    A. A more objective picture will develop when other facts emerge.

    B. Only children believe that certain historical facts are unchanging.

    C. This interpretation should be adapted to meet the needs of children today.

    D. Such a stable picture is desirable to many people.

20. Both authors indicate that, when they were younger, they:

    F. accepted rather uncritically the history presented to them.

    G. were attracted to subjects that were easy to understand.

    H. were better able to adjust to the rapid pace of social change.

    J. often questioned the reliability of their source material.

Answers and Explanations are provided at the end of the book.

SCIENCE INTRODUCTION

BY THE END OF THIS UNIT, YOU WILL BE ABLE TO:

1. Identify the format and timing of the ACT Science test

2. Identify ACT Science passage and question types

CHAPTER 20

ACT Science

CHAPTER OBJECTIVES

By the end of this chapter, you will be able to:

1. Identify the structure of the ACT Science test

2. Identify the three ACT Science passage types

3. Identify the three ACT Science question types

INSIDE THE ACT SCIENCE TEST

The Science test is 35 minutes long and includes 40 questions. The test consists of 6 passages, each accompanied by 6–8 questions. This means you'll have less than 6 minutes per passage and question set. Assuming that it takes you only a couple of minutes on average to read each passage, you'll have about 30–40 seconds per question. Of course, some passages and questions take longer to work through than others.

THE FORMAT

ACT Science Passages

Passages in the ACT Science test are taken from a variety of natural science subjects that you are expected to have studied in high school. These include topics in:

- Earth and Space Science—astronomy, geology, meteorology, etc.
- Biology—botany, genetics, zoology, etc.
- Chemistry—acids/bases, kinetics/equilibria, organic chemistry, etc.
- Physics—electromagnetism, mechanics, thermodynamics, etc.

While the text of Science passages is considerably shorter than what is found in the English and Reading tests, most Science passages are accompanied by graphs, tables, and/or diagrams, which you will have to interpret and analyze to answer some questions.

ACT Science Questions

ACT Science test questions follow the same basic multiple-choice format: each question is attached to the passage that precedes it and features four possible answers. Based on the particular question posed, answer choices can vary considerably in appearance—from words, phrases, and sentences to numbers, measurements, and graphs.

TEST DAY DIRECTIONS AND FORMAT

Although the exact wording might vary, here's what the Science directions could look like:

Directions: The Science Test includes multiple passages. Each passage includes multiple questions. After reading each passage, choose the best answer and fill in the corresponding bubble on your answer sheet. You may review the passages as often as necessary.

You may NOT use a calculator on this test.

If you would like to read through the exact wording you will see on Test Day, visit the test maker's website and download the Preparing for the ACT guide.

There isn't much to these directions—they could be attached to just about any passage-based multiple-choice test. Thus, there's no need to waste your time reading them on Test Day; make the most of your limited time by jumping into the first passage right away.

PASSAGE TYPES

Passages in ACT Science fall into three basic types:

- Data Representation
- Research Summaries
- Conflicting Viewpoints

Data Representation passages tend to be light on text but heavy on data presented in graphs or tables. Research Summaries passages tend to contain more text, largely consisting of descriptions of multiple experimental procedures, and often feature their own graphs or tables filled with results. Conflicting Viewpoints passages contain accounts of two or more competing theories on a particular phenomenon, typically featuring more text and fewer figures than the other two passage types.

While the order varies in any given ACT Science test, you can always expect to see 3 Research Summaries passages (accounting for 45–55% of the questions), 2 Data Representation passages (accounting for 30–40% of the questions), and 1 Conflicting Viewpoints passage (accounting for 15–20% of the questions).

Each passage type has a corresponding Kaplan Method, specifically designed to handle that kind of passage and the questions that accompany it. See Chapter 21 for Data Representation, Chapter 22 for Research Summaries, and Chapter 23 for Conflicting Viewpoints.

QUESTION TYPES

Questions in ACT Science are also divided into three types:

- Interpretation of Data
- Scientific Investigation
- Evaluation of Models, Inferences, and Experimental Results

Interpretation of Data questions require you to work with the information presented in graphs, tables, and other figures. Scientific Investigation questions test your understanding of the scientific method and experimental design. Evaluation of Models questions depend upon your ability to make judgments about theories, data, and other scientific information.

Any type of passage can contain any type of question but the frequency of question types remains relatively constant across different administrations of the ACT Science test. Interpretation of Data questions make up 45–55% of the test, or 18–22 questions out of 40. Evaluation of Models questions account for 25–35%, or 10–14 questions. Scientific Investigation questions account for 20–30%, or 8–12 questions.

Interpretation of Data questions are the most common type in Data Representation passages, so they are featured in Chapter 21. (Note, however, that Interpretation of Data questions are also often found with Research Summaries, which typically contain graphs or tables of results.) Scientific Investigation questions are usually found in Research Summaries passages, so they are covered in Chapter 22. Finally, Evaluation of Models questions are the most prevalent question type in Conflicting Viewpoints passages, so they are discussed in Chapter 23.

OUTSIDE KNOWLEDGE

The ACT Science test is first and foremost a test of your scientific reasoning ability, not a test of your knowledge of scientific content. Nevertheless, you are expected to have some outside knowledge of the natural sciences. While you won't need to understand advanced concepts or memorize equations, you will need to have knowledge of basic scientific concepts and terminology to answer some of the questions.

If you've completed high school courses in biology, chemistry, earth/space science, and physics, then you should already know everything you'll need to know for Test Day. In fact, you can still do quite well on the ACT Science test even if you've never taken or you're still in the process of taking one or more of these courses. On Test Day, if you run across a question that requires knowledge you don't have, just skip over it. Spend your time instead working on the vast majority of questions that don't require outside knowledge.

THE INSIDE SCOOP

The ACT Science test relies upon your capacity to think like a scientist: to work with data in a variety of presentations, to understand the design of scientific experiments, to evaluate theories in the light of empirical evidence, and to engage in other kinds of scientific problem-solving.

Science questions are not ordered by difficulty, so they do *not* get harder as you continue working on a passage or as you move from one passage to the next.

TIMING

Plan to spend no more than about 6 minutes per passage. Six passages in 35 minutes means you have an average of exactly 5 minutes and 50 seconds to complete each passage and its 6–8 questions. The timing on the ACT Science test is definitely tight, so be sure to keep yourself moving. Even the lengthiest passages should take you no more than about 3 minutes to read and mark up—whenever possible, try to finish reading in 2 minutes or less to maximize the time you can spend on the questions, where the points are.

Never spend more than a minute on a question. In the ACT Science test, there are more questions (40) than there are minutes (35) to work with, so even if you didn't have passages to read, your average time working on a question would still have to be less than a minute. While there will be quick and easy questions that allow you to spend more time on some of the harder questions, if you find yourself getting close to about a minute working on a problem without an answer immediately in sight, it's time to guess and move on. Aim for completing most questions in 30 seconds or less.

Be organized in your approach. You should generally try to work on the passages and questions in the order they appear, because you're unlikely to have much time remaining at the end to return to previous passages and questions. (Conflicting Viewpoints passages are an exception to the rule of answering questions in order, as explained in the Kaplan Method for these passages in Chapter 23.) Be sure to grid in your answers regularly, either at the end of every page or two or immediately after each question. Don't wait until the very end or you may run out of time.

WHEN YOU'RE RUNNING OUT OF TIME

If you find yourself significantly behind on time with multiple passages remaining, you can still make the most of your score by being a bit more selective about how you work on the passages. Say that you have 3 passages remaining, but only 12 minutes left in the section, and the next passage coming up seems harder than any that you've seen so far. If you ever find yourself in such a situation, your best bet is to skip reading the passage entirely and just enter random guesses for all of that passage's questions. Then you can work on the last two passages as you normally would. Just make sure to enter an answer for every question before time expires.

No one wants to deal with tough choices like guessing through an entire passage, so a better approach is to avoid this type of time crunch entirely by being more aggressive with your guessing whenever you start to fall behind in your pacing. Don't forget that every question is worth the same amount in ACT Science, so it simply doesn't pay to use large amounts of time on a single hard question, even if you get it right.

SCORING

Like the other required sections of the ACT, the Science test is scored on a scale from 1 to 36. This score also accounts for one-quarter of the ACT Composite Score, which is the average of your English, Math, Reading, and Science scores. Unlike the other tests that make up the ACT, however, the Science test does not contain subscores.

Science

QUICK TIPS

Mind-Set

- **Mark up the passages.** ACT Science questions may seem to come in many varieties, but they are ultimately predictable. With enough practice and the right strategies (like those provided in Chapters 21, 22, and 23), you can learn what questions to expect as you read through a passage. By marking up the passage—underlining key portions of the text and taking brief notes on highly testable material like patterns in data and controls in experiments—you can prepare yourself to answer its questions more quickly.

- **Focus on getting the points.** Remember that your goal is to answer as many Science questions correctly as possible. There are no points awarded simply for making your way through a tough passage. That doesn't mean you should rush through the passages as quickly as possible—that can actually cost you time when you find yourself having to reread more while working on questions—but it does mean that you should read and mark up each passage efficiently. In addition, because hard questions are worth as much as easy ones, you should never take too long on any one question. Know when to give up and make an educated guess, so you can spend your time getting points elsewhere.

- **Don't be afraid to guess.** When you encounter an especially tough problem that you think would take you too long to answer, it's usually better to make a random guess than to leave it blank and expect to come back later. You have a 0% chance of getting a Science question right if you leave it blank but a 25% chance of getting it right with a blind guess. Don't worry if you find yourself guessing on a lot of questions, because you can miss quite a few on the Science test and still get a great score. Keep in mind that the average ACT test taker gets only about half of the Science questions correct!

SPECIAL STRATEGIES: IF YOU GET STUCK ...

If you have the time to spend on a tough problem, but aren't sure where to begin, consider the following strategies:

- **Make a prediction first.** Avoid looking at the answer choices when you first start working on a question. Instead, take everything you can from the question stem, including clues about the parts of the passage that are relevant, and approach the question as though it were open-ended rather than multiple-choice. Even if you can't home in on the exact answer, you can often develop some expectations about what the correct response would have to look like. If you know what to expect before looking at the answer choices, you'll be far less likely to fall into a trap.

- **Eliminate answers that contradict the passage.** If you can't figure out what to predict, narrow down the possibilities by ruling out definite wrong answers. If an answer choice comes into conflict with scientific information from the text or with data from the passage's graphs and tables, it is almost certainly incorrect. In addition, sometimes you can eliminate answer choices that contradict a key piece of information from the question stem itself; in other cases, you can even use common sense and basic logic to rule out choices that are implausible. Using process of elimination like this will either reveal the one answer that must be correct or at least increase your odds of guessing correctly among the remaining options.

- **Don't overthink it.** Remember that the science on the ACT Science test remains relatively basic. Most relationships in data will be relatively simple linear ones, either direct or inverse—so don't strain your brain looking for something more complex when you don't need to. In addition, you'll never have to bring in advanced scientific concepts or equations, nor will you need to perform elaborate calculations since you aren't allowed to use a calculator. If it seems like answering a question will require advanced knowledge or a complex calculation, you're most likely overthinking it.

SMARTPOINTS BREAKDOWN

By studying the information released by the ACT, Kaplan has been able to determine how often certain topics are likely to show up on the test, and therefore how many points these topics are worth on Test Day. If you master a given topic, you can expect to earn the corresponding number of SmartPoints on Test Day.

Here is a brief overview of what exactly to expect and how much of it you should be expecting.

INTERPRETATION OF DATA—17 POINTS

Approximately 45–55% of the questions on the Science test are Interpretation of Data questions. These questions test skills such as the following:

- Recognizing data, variables, units and other information in figures
- Understanding scientific terms and other scientific information from texts
- Determining relationships between variables
- Synthesizing data from multiple figures
- Constructing figures from given information
- Interpolating and extrapolating data
- Analyzing information in the light of new data

SCIENTIFIC INVESTIGATION—9 POINTS

Approximately 20–30% of Science test questions fall into the Scientific Investigation category. Scientific Investigation questions test skills such as the following:

- Understanding descriptions of experiments, equipment used in experiments, and experimental methods
- Recognizing controls and other aspects of experimental design
- Finding similarities and differences in multiple experiments
- Predicting experimental results
- Identifying hypotheses and methods for testing them
- Evaluating precision and accuracy in experiments

EVALUATION OF MODELS, INFERENCES, AND EXPERIMENTAL RESULTS—10 POINTS

Approximately 25–35% of Science test questions belong to the final SmartPoints category, typically shortened to Evaluation of Models. These questions test skills such as the following:

- Identifying basic claims, assumptions, and implications of theories
- Evaluating the consistency of information with a theory
- Finding similarities and differences in multiple theories
- Identifying what would strengthen or weaken a theory
- Determining the effect of new information on a theory
- Making predictions based on theories

UNIT TEN

SCIENCE

BY THE END OF THIS UNIT, YOU WILL BE ABLE TO:

1. Apply the Kaplan Methods for ACT Science

2. Identify Science test passage and question types and apply the appropriate strategies to answer questions correctly

CHAPTER 21

Data Representation

CHAPTER OBJECTIVES

By the end of this chapter, you will be able to:

1. Evaluate and interpret data presented in charts, tables, and graphs

2. Analyze information presented in diagrams

3. Synthesize information from multiple charts, tables, graphs, and diagrams

SMARTPOINTS

Point Value	SmartPoints Category
Point Builder	Data Representation
17 Points	Interpretation of Data

Data Representation passages present information in charts, tables, graphs, and diagrams. They tend to contain more figures than any of the other passage types but are the shortest in terms of text. You can expect to encounter exactly two of these passages on Test Day.

Approximately 45–55% of the questions on the ACT Science test involve Interpretation of Data, which is the most common category of question on Data Representation passages. Interpretation of Data involves:

- Understanding basic scientific terminology and finding information in the text
- Identifying features of figures (headings, units, axis labels, etc.)
- Determining how the value of one variable changes as the value of another changes
- Identifying mathematical relationships between data (linear, exponential, etc.)
- Reading values from figures with two or three variables
- Interpolating and extrapolating from data points
- Translating information into a table, graph, or diagram
- Comparing or combining data
- Analyzing given information when presented with new information

These skills will be discussed in further detail throughout this chapter.

THE KAPLAN METHOD FOR DATA REPRESENTATION

Students who approach Data Representation passages in a systematic way will be rewarded on Test Day. Applying the same basic steps to Data Representation passages will help you spend your time efficiently and maximize the number of points you earn.

The Kaplan Method for Data Representation consists of three steps:

Step 1: Actively read the passage
- Underline keywords
- Underline key phrases

Step 2: Examine the figures provided
- Locate variables in the figures
- Identify trends and patterns

Step 3: Find support for the answer in the passage
- Identify keywords in the question stem
- Locate the corresponding data in the passage
- Make a prediction and match it to the correct answer

Let's examine each of these steps in more detail.

Step 1: Actively read the passage

This means you should:

- Read the passage for the central idea before looking at the questions

- NOT spend time trying to understand everything or be intimidated by technical terminology

- Underline keywords such as terms or variables that are defined, italicized, or usable as reference points for finding information (for example, "mass" or "Method 1")

- Underline key phrases that describe the contents of the passage, define a term or variable, or explain a concept to help you find support for answers in the passage (for example, "acceleration is the rate of change of velocity per unit of time")

Step 2: Examine the figures provided

This means you should:

- Locate variables in the figures and, if applicable, identify whether the variables are independent or dependent (note: not all Data Representation passages present experiments involving independent and dependent variables)

  - Independent variables are what scientists intentionally manipulate; they are usually plotted on the x-axis of a graph

  - Dependent variables are what scientists observe and measure; they are usually plotted on the y-axis of a graph

  - In general, researchers try to determine if a change in the independent variable produces a change in the dependent variable (for example, a biologist might change the concentration of a disinfectant used to clean equipment—the independent variable—to determine if it changes the number of colonies that survive cleaning—the dependent variable)

  - Remember that, unlike in algebra, variables in experiments do NOT have to have numerical values (for example, in an experiment on pollination, a flower's color or the species of bee could be the independent variable)

- Locate units of measurement, which also are a clue to what is being investigated—time in seconds, height in meters, weight in pounds, volume in cubic centimeters, etc.

- Identify trends, which indicate the general direction in which the data are changing (for example, the dependent variable decreases when the independent variable increases)

- Identify a pattern within trends, which indicates a recognizable sequence in the data (for example, the dependent variable increases by 5 units when the independent variable increases by 1 unit)

Science

Step 3: Find support for the answer in the passage

This means you should:

- Identify information in the question like variables, units, or figure headings to help you home in on the specific parts of the passage that apply to the question (for example, "mass," "kg," or "Figure 1")

- Locate the corresponding data in the passage and circle the parts of the figure or text that relate directly to the question

- Based on what you discover in the passage, formulate a prediction about what the correct answer should say

- Match your prediction to the correct answer choice

EVALUATE AND INTERPRET DATA IN FIGURES

Some Interpretation of Data questions will ask you to evaluate and interpret data in charts, tables, and graphs, which will require you to examine and make sense of the data by forming conclusions from the collected information.

These questions are best approached by looking back at the passage, because the answers rely on information in the text or figures and rarely require any additional knowledge of the topic. Clues in the question should lead you to the relevant parts of the passage. Use table headings and figure keys to help you locate information. If you are running short on time, these questions are usually faster to answer than other question types; they are an opportunity for quick points on Test Day.

At first glance, figures in Data Representation passages may seem overwhelming. For instance, graphs may contain multiple axes (a left axis and a right axis with separate units) and multiple curves that correspond to one of the two sides, and tables may contain multiple rows and columns of information. When presented with a complex figure:

- Focus on the relevant information and block out the rest

- Check the figure key or table headings to ensure you are referring to the correct variable(s)

- Circle relevant points to avoid distractions when comparing data from multiple curves in a graph or multiple rows/columns in a table

Below is an example of a complex table that you saw on Practice Test A.

Table 1				
Material	Resistivity (mV-cm)	Length (cm)	Cross-sectional area (mm²)	Resistance (mV)
Au	2.44	1.0	5.26	46.4
Au	2.44	1.0	1.31	186.3
Au	2.44	2.0	5.26	92.8
Au	2.44	2.0	1.31	372.5
Al	2.83	1.0	5.26	53.8
Al	2.83	1.0	1.31	216.0
Al	2.83	2.0	5.26	107.6
Al	2.83	2.0	1.31	432.1
W	5.51	1.0	5.26	104.8
W	5.51	1.0	1.31	420.6
W	5.51	2.0	5.26	209.5
W	5.51	2.0	1.31	841.2
Fe	10.00	1.0	5.26	190.1
Fe	10.00	1.0	1.31	763.4
Fe	10.00	2.0	5.26	380.2
Fe	10.00	2.0	1.31	1,526.7

Identifying Trends

An important skill on the ACT Science test is determining trends; that is, how one variable changes in response to another. Some Interpretation of Data questions will ask you to evaluate the relationship between variables.

A linear relationship is one where a change in one variable will cause a corresponding change in the other variable; the variables may be directly or inversely related. When plotted on a graph, the data form a straight line.

- If, as one variable increases, the other also increases (or, as one variable decreases, the other decreases), the relationship is direct (positive slope).

- If, as one variable increases, the other decreases or vice versa, the relationship is inverse (negative slope).

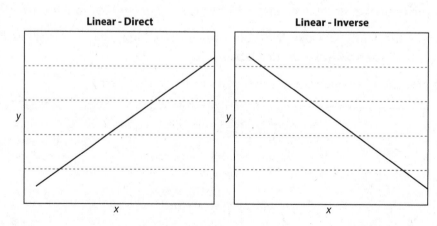

An exponential relationship is a more complex relationship you might see on the ACT Science test. Exponential relationships also can be direct or inverse. For example:

- If, as one variable doubles, the other quadruples, the relationship is direct.

- If, as one variable halves, the other quadruples, the relationship is inverse.

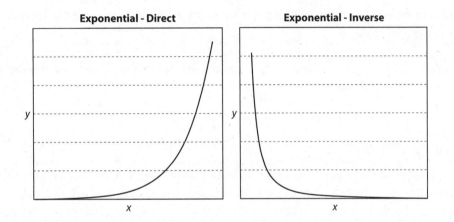

For data in a scatterplot, a general trend can be determined by looking at the line of best fit, which is the line that most closely matches the pattern in the data. This line should pass through the center of the data points and may pass through some of the points, none of the points, or all of the points.

- If the line of best fit increases, the variables are positively correlated.

- If the line of best fit decreases, the variables are negatively correlated.

- If the line of best fit neither increases nor decreases, the variables are not correlated.

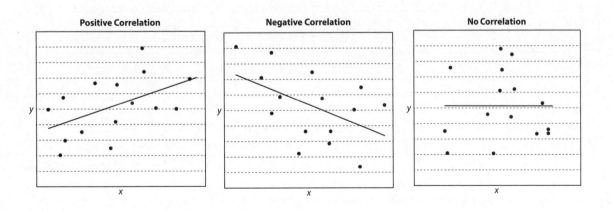

Data in tables may not always be in ascending or descending order. To identify the relationship between variables, use your pencil to reorder the data for one variable from least to greatest or vice versa. Then, match the data of the other variable to the reordered data to identify the trend.

Determining Values

When you read from a graph or table, do not eyeball the value. Instead, use your pencil to track what you are looking for:

- In a graph, find the value of a data point by tracing or drawing a line up from the *x*-axis and over to the *y*-axis or vice versa.

- In a table, circle data to keep your eyes from reading the wrong row or column.

To locate the answer, you can also use units to help you determine where to look in the passage.

Some Interpretation of Data questions will ask you to interpolate or extrapolate values. *Interpolation* means estimating a value between known data points, whereas *extrapolation* means estimating a value outside the known range. When questions ask you to extrapolate or predict the value of a data point that is beyond the range of the presented data, assume the data trend continues on the table or graph. For instance, if the trend of the data in a graph is increasing linearly, assume it will continue to increase linearly.

Let's look at an example. Table 2 shows how much energy a person uses when walking at 3 miles per hour.

Table 2	
Minutes walking (min)	Energy used (Cal)
2	10
4	20
6	30
8	40
10	50

To determine how much energy a person uses when walking at 3 mph for 5 min, you need to interpolate. The amount of energy used would fall in between 20 and 30 Cal, most likely about 25 Cal. To determine how much energy a person uses when walking for 12 min, you need to extrapolate. According to the pattern, there is a 10 Cal increase for every 2 min increase in walking time, so the amount of energy used would be approximately 60 Cal.

Translating Data

Some Interpretation of Data questions will ask you to translate information into a graph or table. When asked to identify the correct figure that matches the presented data, check the trend of the data—is it increasing, decreasing, or constant? Match the shape of the trend to the answer choices; then check specific values at a given point to find the correct answer.

For example, consider the following graphs:

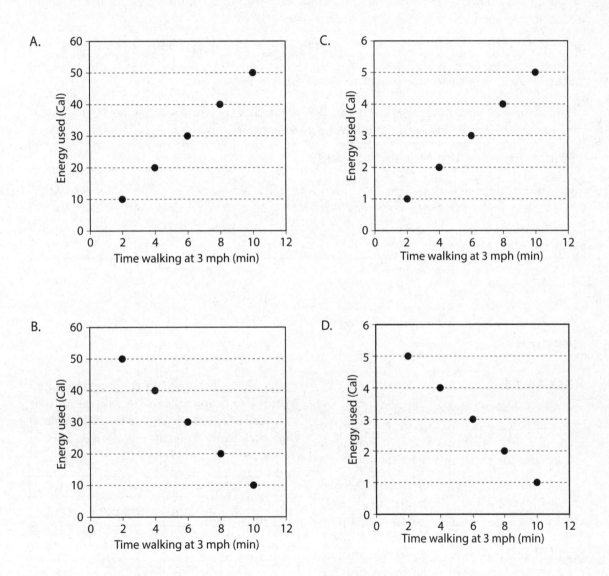

Science

To determine which graph matches the data in Table 2, first look at the trend of the data. As minutes walking increases, energy used also increases, so the relationship is direct. Next, match the shape of the trend to the answer choices. Choices B and D show a decreasing trend, so eliminate them. Then, check a point from the table on the remaining figures. Walking for 2 min will use 10 Cal. This point can be found in the graph for (A), so (A) is the correct answer.

Now take a look at the following Data Representation passage to practice evaluating and interpreting data. The strategic thinking presented below explains what an expert test taker would do while following the Kaplan Method for Data Representation step-by-step, giving you some guidance about how to approach these passages on Test Day.

Strategic Thinking
Step 1: Actively read the passage
Read the passage and note the keywords and key phrases that have been underlined. Remember to read for the central idea and not get distracted by technical terminology.
Step 2: Examine the figures provided
The independent variable is the initial speed with units mi/hr and ft/sec. The dependent variables are D, S, and T from Method 1 and D from Method 2, all of which have ft as units. Initial speed and D are directly related because as initial speed increases, D also increases for both Method 1 and Method 2.

Questions 1–5 are based on the following passage.

Passage I

A snowmobile's underline(total braking distance, D), is the distance a snowmobile travels from the moment a driver first sees a "stop" signal until the snowmobile comes to a complete stop.

Students used underline(2 methods) to calculate D. Based on equations in physics, underline(Method 1) calculated D using S and T. S is the underline(distance traveled) after a driver sees a "stop" signal but underline(before) a driver begins the underline(braking) process. A driver reaction time of 0.8 sec was assumed. $\underline{T}$ is the average underline(distance traveled after) the brakes are applied. Based on the hypothesis that D is the distance the snowmobile would have traveled over 2 sec if the brakes had not been applied, underline(Method 2) maintains that $\underline{D \text{ is}}$ underline(simply the initial speed in ft/sec multiplied by 2 sec). Table 1 shows the results of both methods with various initial speeds, and Figure 1 graphs D from both methods versus initial speed.

Table 1					
Initial speed (mi/hr)	Initial speed (ft/sec)	Method 1			Method 2
		S (ft)	T (ft)	D (ft)	D (ft)
25	37	29	28	57	73
35	51	41	75	116	102
45	66	53	144	197	132
55	81	65	245	310	162

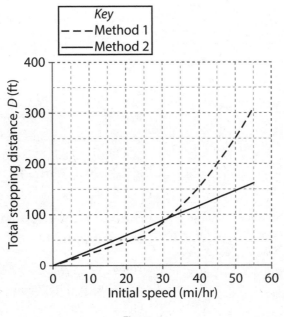

Figure 1

Now look at questions for Passage I. The left column contains questions similar to those you'll see on the ACT Science test on Test Day. The right column features the strategic thinking a test expert employs when approaching the passage and question presented.

Questions	Strategic Thinking
1. Based on Table 1, what is the approximate value of *D* according to Method 1 when the initial speed is 58 ft/sec ? **A.** 70 ft **B.** 150 ft **C.** 250 ft **D.** 320 ft	**Step 3: Find support for the answer in the passage** Pay attention to units in the question stem: initial speed is in ft/sec (column 2) and not mi/hr (column 1). 58 ft/sec is not listed in Table 1, so you need to interpolate, or read between known data points: 51 ft/sec and 66 ft/sec. At 51 ft/sec, *D* from Method 1 is 116 ft, and at 66 ft/sec, *D* from Method 1 is 197 ft. Therefore, *D* at 58 ft/sec should fall between 116 and 197 ft. The only choice within that range is 150 ft. The correct answer is (B). Watch out for choice D, which gives a value that you might estimate if you looked at the mi/hr column instead of the ft/sec column.

Science

Questions	Strategic Thinking
2. According to Figure 1, at which of the following initial speeds is the value of *D* from Method 1 equal to that from Method 2 ? F. 20 mi/hr G. 30 mi/hr H. 40 mi/hr J. 50 mi/hr	**Step 3: Find support for the answer in the passage** The value of *D* from Method 1 is equal to that from Method 2 where the two lines intersect on Figure 1. Draw a line down from where the two lines cross to the *x*-axis to find the corresponding initial speed of 30 mi/hr. The correct answer is (G).
3. According to either Table 1 or Figure 1, if a snowmobile is traveling at an initial speed of 75 mi/hr, what will its *D* be according to Method 2 ? A. Less than 100 ft B. Between 100 and 200 ft C. Between 200 and 300 ft D. Greater than 300 ft	**Step 3: Find support for the answer in the passage** Since 75 mi/hr is beyond the range of the presented data, you need to extrapolate. Either continue the straight line that represents Method 2 to 75 mi/hr on Figure 1 or use Table 1 to estimate *D*. Choice D might be tempting if you were looking at Method 1 instead of Method 2. The straight line from Figure 1, if extended, gives a *D* of about 225 ft. Looking at Table 1, you can see that each 10 mi/hr increase in initial speed increases *D* by about 30 ft. Hence, an initial speed of 75 mi/hr would have a *D* that's about 60 ft greater than the *D* at 55 mi/hr: 60 ft + 162 ft = 222 ft. Either way, the answer lies between 200 and 300 ft, so the correct answer is (C).
4. *S* for an initial speed of 25 mi/hr, compared to *S* for an initial speed of 55 mi/hr, is approximately: F. ¼ as large. G. ½ as large. H. 2 times as large. J. 4 times as large.	**Step 3: Find support for the answer in the passage** Circle 25 mi/hr and 55 mi/hr on Table 1 to compare them. According to Table 1, *S* for an initial speed of 25 mi/hr is 29 ft. *S* for an initial speed of 55 mi/hr is 65 ft. Since 29 is less than 65, eliminate H and J (which would make 29 larger than 65). 29 is about half of 65. The correct answer is (G).

Questions	Strategic Thinking

5. Which of the following graphs best represents the relationship between the distances traveled before and after the brakes were applied?

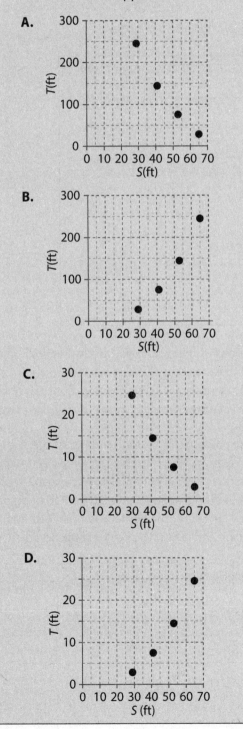

A.

B.

C.

D.

Step 3: Find support for the answer in the passage

The distance traveled before the driver begins the braking process is S, and the distance traveled after the brakes were applied is T. According to Table 1, as the values for S increase, the values for T also increase. Hence, the relationship is direct. Eliminate choices A and C, which show an inverse relationship. Check values from Table 1 on the remaining two graphs. According to the table, for $S = 29$, $T = 28$. Choice (B) plots the data as given in the table, so the correct answer is (B). Choice D has the appropriate shape, but the vertical axis is incorrect (it runs from 0 to 30 ft, rather than 0 to 300 ft).

Science

ANALYZE INFORMATION PRESENTED IN DIAGRAMS

Diagrams in Data Representation passages generally show qualitative or simple quantitative data. For instance, diagrams may present science concepts with blocks or circles connected by lines and arrows to indicate relationships between components. Analyzing information presented in diagrams means breaking down the diagram—identifying the separate components and their interactions.

For example, the following diagram shows the layers of the Earth's atmosphere:

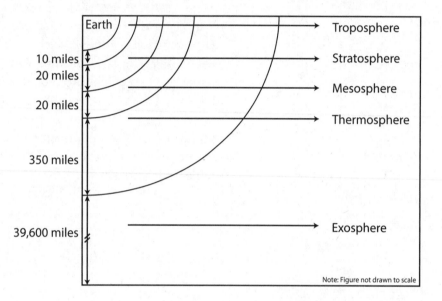

To answer Interpretation of Data questions about diagrams, make sure you understand all of the ways that the different components in a diagram relate to each other. Use only what the diagram and supporting paragraphs tell you. For example, according to the diagram above, the troposphere is closest to Earth and the thinnest layer whereas the exosphere is farthest from Earth and the thickest layer.

Let's look at the following Data Representation passage and question set. After the passage, the left column contains test-like questions. The right column features the strategic thinking a test expert might employ when approaching the passage and question presented. Remember to use the Kaplan Method for Data Representation for every Data Representation passage on the ACT, whether practicing, completing homework, working on a Practice Test, or taking the actual exam on Test Day. Its steps are applicable to every Data Representation passage and reflect the best test-taking practices.

Strategic Thinking
Step 1: Actively read the passage
Read the passage and note the keywords and key phrases that have been underlined. Remember to read for the central idea.
Step 2: Examine the figures provided
The boxes represent components in the Earth's carbon cycle, and the arrows represent processes in the cycle that connect the components.

Questions 6–8 are based on the following passage.

Passage II

The <u>utilization</u> and <u>replenishment</u> of Earth's <u>carbon</u> supply is a <u>cyclic process</u> involving all <u>living</u> matter. This cycle is shown in Diagram 1.

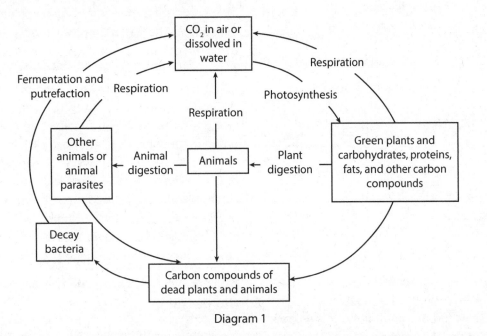

Diagram 1

Questions	Strategic Thinking
6. Which of the following statements is (are) consistent with the carbon cycle as presented in the diagram? I. Both plant and animal respiration contribute CO_2 to Earth's atmosphere. II. A non-plant-eating animal does not participate in the carbon cycle. III. All CO_2 is released into the air by respiration. F. I only G. II only H. I and II only J. I and III only	**Step 3: Find support for the answer in the passage** Statement I is clearly true: there are arrows labeled *respiration* going from the green plants, animals, and other animals or animal parasites boxes back to the CO_2 box. Eliminate G. Statement II is false because the diagram shows that the carbon in animals can move to other animals through the process of *animal digestion*—an animal that only eats other animals is participating in the carbon cycle when it digests its prey. Eliminate H. Statement III is not true because some CO_2 is released into the air by fermentation and putrefaction. Eliminate J. Since only statement I is true, (F) is correct.

Questions	Strategic Thinking
7. The elimination of which of the following would be most likely to cause Earth's carbon cycle to come to a complete halt? **A.** Animals **B.** Animal digestion **C.** Decay bacteria **D.** Green plants	**Step 3: Find support for the answer in the passage** According to Diagram 1, the only way that CO_2 in the atmosphere can reenter the carbon cycle is through photosynthesis, in which it is taken up by green plants. Therefore, if green plants were eliminated, the carbon cycle would probably come to a complete stop. Choice (D) is the correct answer. Choice A is incorrect because animals are not the only source of CO_2. Green plants emit it through respiration, decay bacteria through fermentation and putrefaction, and animal parasites though respiration. Choice B is incorrect because animal digestion is one of many sources of CO_2 in the air. Without animal digestion, the carbon cycle would still continue because other processes add CO_2 to the air. Choice C is incorrect for the same reasons. Decay bacteria are one of many sources for atmospheric CO_2.
8. What effect would a sudden drop in the amount of Earth's decay bacteria have on the amount of carbon dioxide in the atmosphere? **F.** The CO_2 level would drop to a life-threatening level since the bacteria are the sole source of CO_2. **G.** The CO_2 level would rise because the bacteria usually consume CO_2. **H.** The CO_2 level would decrease slightly because the bacteria are not the only source of CO_2. **J.** The CO_2 level would increase slightly due to an imbalance in the carbon cycle.	**Step 3: Find support for the answer in the passage** Remember that the answer is in Diagram 1. Decay bacteria get carbon from the carbon compounds of dead plants and animals and add to the supply of carbon dioxide (CO_2) in air and water through fermentation and putrefaction. Since there is no other way to get carbon from dead plants and animals back to CO_2, you know that a drop in decay bacteria will reduce the amount of carbon available for forming CO_2. The CO_2 level will not be greatly affected, though, because there are other sources of carbon for CO_2. The correct answer is (H). Choice F is incorrect because decay bacteria are not the sole source of CO_2. Choice G is incorrect because the bacteria emit CO_2; they don't consume it. Choice J is incorrect because decay bacteria emit CO_2. If they were eliminated from the cycle, it is unlikely that the amount of CO_2 would increase.

SYNTHESIZE INFORMATION FROM MULTIPLE FIGURES

More difficult Interpretation of Data questions often require you to synthesize information from multiple figures. Synthesizing information means combining or piecing together a number of elements into a coherent whole. These questions are a little more complicated and require more steps. Focus on taking one step at a time and these questions will become more manageable.

For example, you may need to use information found in one figure to look up information from another figure, or you may need to combine data by performing simple mathematical operations like adding, subtracting, multiplying, and/or dividing. You will also need to apply patterns in the data to new variables in order to determine how they will behave. Use clues in the question stem to determine where to look first.

Let's look at an example. Figure 1 shows the percentage of 30 samples of bacterial colonies in a scratch that survived 48 hours after cleaning with 25 or 250 ppm chlorine for 5 min. Figure 2 shows the average log reduction of the 30 samples after cleaning with 25 or 250 ppm chlorine for 5 min.

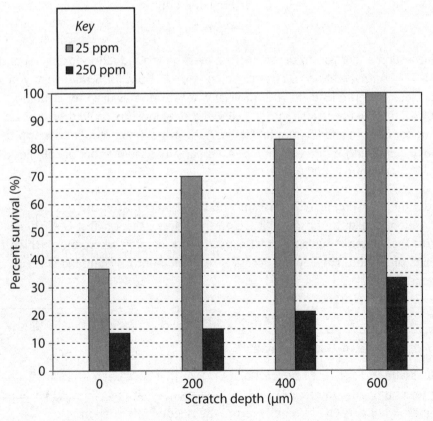

Figure 1

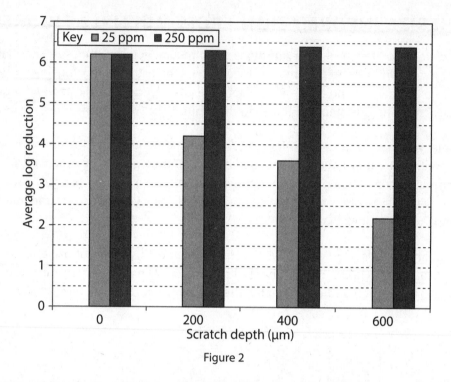

Figure 2

Suppose a question asked you to determine the average log reduction for bacterial colonies in a scratch with 70% survival 48 hours after cleaning with 25 ppm for 5 min. First, you would need to find what scratch depth leads to 70% survival when 25 ppm is used for cleaning. According to Figure 1, 70% of the 200 μm scratch samples survived cleaning. You could then look up the average log reduction for 200 μm and 25 ppm on Figure 2; the average log reduction is approximately 4.2. (In case you're wondering, a log reduction of 4.2 means that the number of colonies decreased by a factor of $10^{4.2}$, or about 16,000.)

Now consider the following test-like passage and question set. After the passage, the left column contains questions similar to those you'll see on the Science test on Test Day. The column on the right features the strategic thinking a test expert might employ when approaching the passage and questions presented. The key to success is to implement a systematic strategy, like the one the expert uses here.

Strategic Thinking
Step 1: Actively read the passage
Read the passage and note the keywords and phrases that have been underlined. Remember to read for the central idea. You do not need to figure out what any technical vocabulary means unless a question directs you to; simply locate the needed information.
Step 2: Examine the figures provided
Figures 1 and 2 show an inverse relationship between time and N/N_0 for the two isotopes, and Figure 3 shows an inverse relationship between time and radiation energy. ^{234}Th takes more time to decay.

Questions 9–11 are based on the following passage.

Passage III

Physicists and medical technicians can detect the amount of radiation emitted by unstable isotopes as they spontaneously decay into other elements. The half-life of these radioactive isotopes is the amount of time necessary for one-half of the initial number of their nuclei to decay.

The decay curves of two radioactive thorium isotopes (^{231}Th and ^{234}Th) are graphed below as functions of the ratio of N, the number of nuclei remaining after a given time period, to N_0, the initial number of nuclei. The results are recorded in Figure 1 and Figure 2, respectively.

In order to study the correlation between isotope decay and radiation, the technicians also measured and recorded the amount of radiation emitted (measured in megaelectronvolts, or MeV) as 1-g samples of the 2 isotopes decayed. The results are recorded in Figure 3.

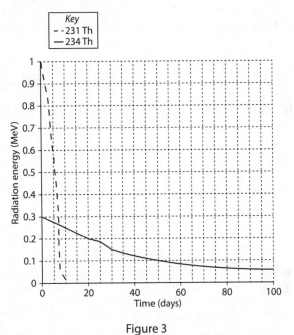

Figure 3

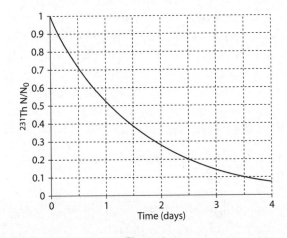

Figure 1

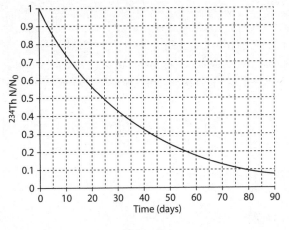

Figure 2

Questions	Strategic Thinking
9. According to Figures 1 and 2, the half-life of ^{234}Th is approximately how many times more than the half-life of ^{231}Th ? **A.** 1 **B.** 12 **C.** 24 **D.** 48	**Step 3: Find support for the answer in the passage** Don't forget to check the passage for terms and definitions. In the introduction to the passage, the *half-life* of an isotope is defined as the amount of time needed for one-half of the initial number of nuclei to decay. To figure out the half-life of ^{231}Th, look at the first graph. When half of the nuclei have decayed, the N/N_0 ratio will be ½ or 0.5. (Think about it this way: if you started with 100 nuclei and half decayed, you'd have 50 left. That's an N/N_0 ratio of 50/100 or 0.5.) Draw a horizontal line across the graph from 0.5 on the y-axis. Where that line intersects the curve, draw a vertical line down to the x-axis. This line intersects the x-axis slightly above 1.0, which means the amount of time it takes for half of the nuclei to decay is about 1 day. Repeat the process to determine the half-life for ^{234}Th. Its half-life is about 24 days. Thus, the half-life of ^{234}Th is approximately 24 times the half-life of ^{231}Th. The correct answer is (C).
10. Based on the figures, as the ratio of remaining nuclei to initial number of nuclei for ^{231}Th decreases, radiation energy: **F.** decreases. **G.** increases. **H.** decreases, then increases. **J.** increases, then decreases.	**Step 3: Find support for the answer in the passage** Ask yourself, where is the information you need? According to Figure 1, as the ratio of remaining nuclei to initial number of nuclei (N/N_0) for ^{231}Th decreases, time increases. According to Figure 3, as time increases, radiation energy for ^{231}Th decreases. Thus, as the ratio of remaining nuclei to initial number of nuclei for ^{231}Th decreases, radiation energy decreases. In other words, the relationship is direct. The correct answer is (F).

Questions	Strategic Thinking
11. If a decaying sample of ^{234}Th that initially weighed 1 g is emitting 0.2 MeV of radiation per day, what is the ratio of its remaining nuclei to its initial number of nuclei? **A.** 0.4 **B.** 0.55 **C.** 0.8 **D.** 1.0	**Step 3: Find support for the answer in the passage** There are lots of chances to make mistakes on questions that ask you to jump back and forth between figures, so pay extra attention. You can get the ratio N/N_0 from Figure 2. Because the question stem gives you the energy released by the sample, which is only mentioned in Figure 3, you'll need to use that first to figure out the age of the sample. Draw a line from 0.2 MeV on Figure 3 across to where it intersects the line corresponding to ^{234}Th. Be sure you don't confuse it with the line corresponding to ^{231}Th. Your line should intersect the plot at about 20 days, so the sample is 20 days old. Now, go to Figure 2. Draw a vertical line up from 20 days on the *x*-axis to where it intersects the graph. Draw a horizontal line from this point to the *y*-axis. It falls between 0.5 and 0.6. Choice (B) is a perfect match. Choice A is too low, while C and D are far too high.

You have seen the ways in which the ACT tests you with Data Representation passages and Interpretation of Data questions, as well as the way an ACT expert might approach these passages and questions.

Now, use the Kaplan Method for Data Representation to answer the five questions that accompany the following Science passage. Part of the test-like passage has been annotated already. Your first step is to complete marking up the passage. Strategic thinking questions have been included to guide you—some of the answers have been filled in, but you will have to fill in the answers to others.

Use your answers to the strategic thinking questions to select the correct answer, just as you would on Test Day.

Strategic Thinking
Step 1: Actively read the passage
The passage below is partially annotated. Continue marking up the remainder of the passage. Remember to focus on the central idea and underline keywords and key phrases. Use the marked-up passage as a reference when you're answering questions.
Step 2: Examine the figures provided
What are the variables and units? What are the trends and patterns in the data?
_____
_____
_____

Questions 12–16 are based on the following passage.

Passage IV

The <u>force of gravity</u> on an object <u>is calculated by multiplying</u> the object's mass, <u>*m*, by</u> the gravitational acceleration, *g*. A block with mass *m* was attached to the bottom of a spring of length *L*, which was hung from a ceiling. <u>At equilibrium</u> the magnitude of the <u>downward force</u> on the block caused by gravity <u>equals</u> the magnitude of the <u>upward restoring force</u> of the spring. The <u>restoring force is determined by multiplying</u> <u>*x*,</u> the spring's displacement from its original position, <u>by a constant, *k*,</u> which represents the spring's stiffness. The magnitude of the force, *F*, is calculated from the following formula:

$$F = mg = kx$$

Pulling and releasing the block will cause it to oscillate up and down from the equilibrium position (see Diagram 1). Starting at the equilibrium position, a spring completes one cycle of periodic motion when it goes up, then down, and then returns back to the equilibrium position. The time to complete one cycle is called the period of oscillation, *T*.

To examine the effect of *g* on *x*, *x* was calculated for a spring with *k* = 50 N/m and *L* = 2 cm for different *m* on the surface of Earth, Titan (Saturn's largest moon), and Jupiter (see Figure 1). The gravitational acceleration at each surface is shown in Table 1. For the same spring on Earth, Figure 2 shows *T* plotted against *m*. In Figure 3, *T* and *k* as a function of *L* are graphed for a spring with *m* = 500 g.

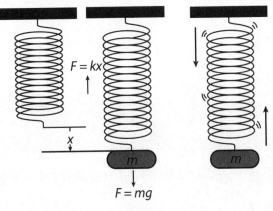

Diagram 1

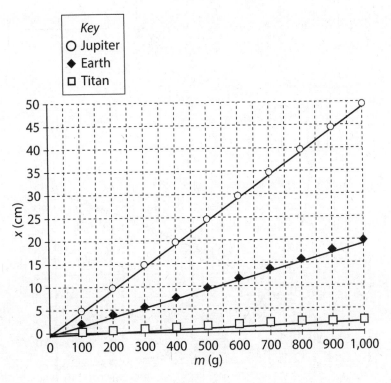

Figure 1

Table 1	
Planet or moon	Gravitational acceleration at surface (m/sec²)
Jupiter	24.9
Earth	9.8
Titan	1.4

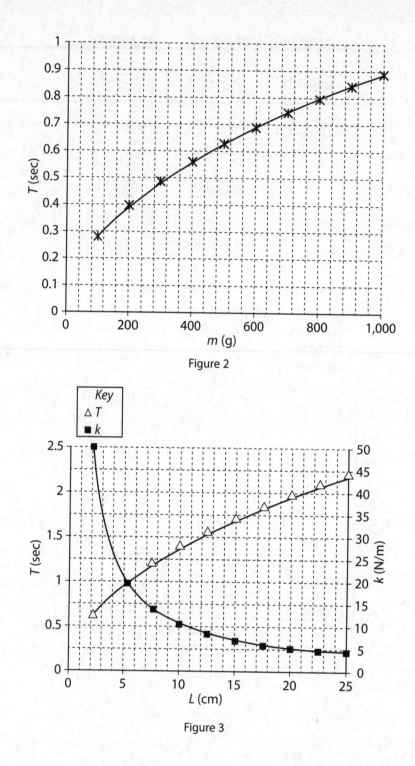

Figure 2

Figure 3

Science

Questions	Strategic Thinking
12. Based on Figure 1, on the surface of Earth what is the expected displacement of the spring with a block of 0.8 kg attached? **F.** 2 cm **G.** 10 cm **H.** 15 cm **J.** 40 cm	**Step 3: Find support for the answer in the passage** *What are the keywords in the question stem?* The keywords in the question stem are *Figure 1*, *Earth*, and *0.8 kg*. *Where can you find the corresponding data in the passage?* The keywords are clues to where you should look for the answer. On Figure 1, draw a vertical line up from 800 g, which equals 0.8 kg, to Earth's line. Then draw a horizontal line to the *y*-axis to determine the expected displacement. *Which answer choice matches?* _____
13. Based on Figure 2, a spring with $k = 50$ N/m and $L = 2$ cm has a period of oscillation of 1 sec on Earth when the mass of the attached block is approximately: **A.** 5 g. **B.** 20 g. **C.** 400 g. **D.** 1,300 g.	**Step 3: Find support for the answer in the passage** *What are the keywords in the question stem?* The keywords in the question stem are *Figure 2* and *1 sec*. *Where can you find the corresponding data in the passage?* According to Figure 2, the relationship between the period of oscillation of a spring on Earth and mass is direct. As *m* increases, *T* also increases. Extending the trend of the data on Figure 2, you need to extrapolate to find *m* at a *T* of 1 sec. *Which answer choice matches?* _____

Science

Questions	Strategic Thinking
14. According to the information in the passage, which statement best describes the relationship between gravitational acceleration and a spring's displacement? **F.** As gravitational acceleration increases, displacement increases. **G.** As gravitational acceleration increases, displacement decreases. **H.** As gravitational acceleration increases, displacement stays the same. **J.** There is no relationship between gravitational acceleration and displacement.	**Step 3: Find support for the answer in the passage** *What are the keywords in the question stem?* The keywords in the question stem are *relationship, gravitational acceleration,* and *displacement.* *Where can you find the corresponding data in the passage?* _____ _____ _____ *Which answer choice matches?* _____
15. Suppose the spring in Figure 1 has a displacement of 10 cm on Jupiter's surface. For the spring to have the same displacement on Earth's surface, *m* would have to be approximately: **A.** 2.5 times greater than that on Jupiter's surface. **B.** 2.5 times less than that on Jupiter's surface. **C.** 250 times greater than that on Jupiter's surface. **D.** 250 times less than that on Jupiter's surface.	**Step 3: Find support for the answer in the passage** *What are the keywords in the question stem?* _____ _____ *Where can you find the corresponding data in the passage?* _____ _____ _____ *Which answer choice matches?* _____

Questions	Strategic Thinking

16. Based on the data, what would be the expected displacement of a spring with $L = 20$ cm and $m = 500$ g on the surface of Jupiter?
 	
  F.   0.25 cm
  G.   2.5 cm
  H.   25   cm
  J.   250   cm
	Step 3: Find support for the answer in the passage
	
	What are the keywords in the question stem?
	
	_____
	
	_____
	
	Where can you find the corresponding data in the passage?
	
	_____
	
	_____
	
	_____
	
	Which answer choice matches? _____

Science

Now try some test-like Data Representation passages on your own. The following passages provide an opportunity to practice the concepts and strategic thinking covered in this chapter. Give yourself 12 minutes to read the passages and answer the questions.

Questions 17–21 are based on the following passage.

Passage V

Blue-green algae are actually not algae but photosynthesizing bacteria. They are often blue or green in color but can also be red or pink. In large numbers, they appear as a thick, slimy coating on aquatic rocks and plants. They are capable of smothering plants and may release toxins that are harmful to fish. Some varieties of red tide (discoloration of seawater from algal bloom) are caused by blue-green algae.

Like other bacteria, blue-green algae reproduce through a process wherein one cell divides completely to form two distinct cells. The average time for a colony of blue-green algae to divide and for its population to double is called the *generation time*. Table 1 shows the generation time for different varieties of blue-green algae. The temperatures and salts used to grow each species are listed.

Table 1			
Algae	Growth medium	Temperature (°C)	Generation time (min)
Aphanothece gelatinosa	Na_3PO_4	30	42
Arthrospira fusiformis	K_2SiO_3	30	103
Chroococcus submarinus	NH_4NO_3	30	231
Dactylococcopsis salina	Na_3PO_4	38	259
Geitlerinema carotinosum	NH_4NO_3	38	39
Gloeothece rupestris	K_2SiO_3	38	61
Kalagnymene spiralis	Na_3PO_4	38	131
Merismopedia glauca	NH_4NO_3	38	751
Rhabdoderma rubrum	NH_4NO_3	38	225
Synechococcus leopoliensis	Na_3PO_4	30	458
Synechococcus vulcanus	K_2SiO_3	30	321
Thermo-synechococcus vulcanus	K_2SiO_3	38	56

Because blue-green algae cannot travel in search of necessary nutrients, the population density of a colony also affects its generation time. Figure 1 shows the generation time of a colony of *Dactylococcopsis salina* as a function of its population per square centimeter at 38°C.

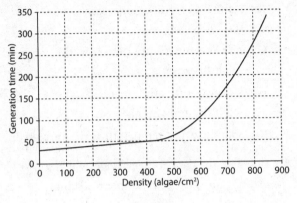

Figure 1

17. Based on the data presented in Table 1, if *Arthrospira fusiformis* was placed in a petri dish containing potassium silicate (K_2SiO_3) at 30°C, its generation time would most likely be:

    A. less than 50 min.

    B. between 50 and 70 min.

    C. between 70 and 90 min.

    D. greater than 90 min.

18. Based on Figure 1, if a colony of *Dactylococcopsis salina* covered a pond floor with a density of 400 algae per square centimeter, approximately how long would its generation time most likely be?

    F. 20 min

    G. 50 min

    H. 100 min

    J. 200 min

19. Based on the data recorded in Table 1, which of the following blue-green algae growing in the presence of ammonium nitrate (NH_4NO_3) takes the longest amount of time to double its population?

    A. *Merismopedia glauca*

    B. *Geitlerinema carotinosum*

    C. *Chroococcus submarinus*

    D. *Rhabdoderma rubrum*

20. Twelve tanks of water were enriched with sodium phosphate (Na_3PO_4). One of the varieties of blue-green algae from Table 1 was introduced into each tank, and the water was heated to 38°C. If the population in each tank almost doubled in 2 hours, which of the following algae was most likely introduced?

    F. *Geitlerinema carotinosum*

    G. *Kalagnymene spiralis*

    H. *Rhabdoderma rubrum*

    J. *Dactylococcopsis salina*

21. According to the information in Figure 1, what was the approximate population density, in algae/cm², of the colony of *Dactylococcopsis salina* that was studied in Table 1 ?

    A. 100

    B. 300

    C. 800

    D. 1,000

Science

Questions 22–26 are based on the following passage.

Passage VI

The extent to which a solute will dissolve in a given solvent is dependent on several factors, including conditions of temperature and pressure and the electrochemical natures of the solute and solvent.

Students measured the solubilities in distilled water of several pairs of common sodium (Na) and potassium (K) salts at various temperatures. The pairs were NaCl and KCl, $NaNO_3$ and KNO_3, and $NaClO_3$ and $KClO_3$. All measurements were conducted at 1 atmosphere of pressure. After pooling and averaging all the data, the students plotted solubility curves to produce Figure 1.

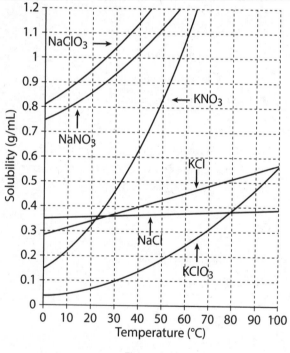

Figure 1

22. For the salts given, which of the following conclusions can be drawn concerning the relationship between solubility and temperature?

   F. As the temperature increases, the solubility increases.

   G. As the temperature increases, the solubility decreases.

   H. As the temperature increases, the solubility remains the same.

   J. Solubility and temperature are unrelated.

23. Based on the data in the passage, which solute exhibits the greatest variation in solubility between 0°C and 60°C ?

   A. KNO_3

   B. NaCl

   C. KCl

   D. $KClO_3$

24. How does the solubility data for NaCl and KCl differ from the data for the two other pairs of salts?

   F. For the other two pairs, the K salt is always more soluble than the Na salt.

   G. For the other two pairs, the Na salt is always more soluble than the K salt.

   H. The Na salts are usually not soluble in water.

   J. The K salts are usually not soluble in water.

25. For which of the following salts would it be possible to dissolve more than 0.65 g/mL at 55°C ?

    A. Any of the Na salts

    B. Any of the K salts

    C. Either of the NO_3 salts

    D. Either of the ClO_3 salts

26. According to the data, how many more grams of KNO_3 in 1 L of distilled water are dissolved at 50°C and normal atmospheric pressure than of $KClO_3$ in 1 L of distilled water?

    F. 0.18 g

    G. 0.66 g

    H. 180 g

    J. 660 g

Answers and Explanations are provided at the end of the book.

ON YOUR OWN

The following questions provide an opportunity to practice the concepts and strategic thinking covered in this chapter.

Questions 1–7 are based on the following passage.

Passage I

Gravitational acceleration, g, is the acceleration of an object due to gravity. The conventional standard value of g at the Earth's surface is exactly 9.80665 m/sec². Students wished to study variations in g at various latitudes and altitudes. They measured the gravitational acceleration of a 5 kg block in a vacuum as a function of (north) latitude at sea level and of altitude at 15°N latitude. The results are plotted in Figure 1. Table 1 shows the gravitational acceleration at various locations.

Table 1	
Location	g (m/sec²)
Anchorage	9.826
Chicago	9.804
Denver	9.798
Helsinki	9.825
Kandy	9.775
Kuala Lumpur	9.776
London	9.816
Mexico City	9.776
Oslo	9.825
Singapore	9.776
Washington D.C.	9.801

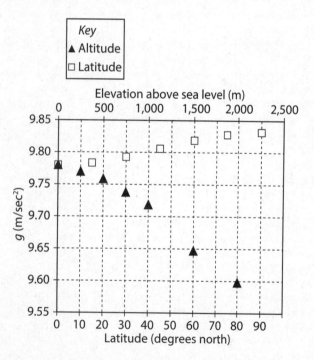

Figure 1

1. The gravitational acceleration when the block is 500 meters above sea level is approximately:

   A. 9.60 m/s².

   B. 9.65 m/s².

   C. 9.76 m/s².

   D. 9.80 m/s².

2. According to Figure 1, as altitude increases, gravitational acceleration:

   F. increases.

   G. decreases.

   H. increases, then decreases.

   J. decreases, then increases.

3. Based on the results, at approximately what latitude is the gravitational acceleration of a 5 kg block in a vacuum 9.81 m/s² at sea level?

   A.   0°N

   B.   20°N

   C.   50°N

   D.   90°N

4. Based on the information given in the passage, assuming the following cities are located at sea level, which is closest to the equator?

   F.   Singapore

   G.   Anchorage

   H.   London

   J.   Oslo

5. Chicago, Denver, and Washington D.C. are all located near 40°N. According to the data, which of the following correctly ranks the 3 locations from *highest to lowest* elevation above sea level?

   A.   Chicago, Washington D.C., Denver

   B.   Washington D.C., Denver, Chicago

   C.   Denver, Chicago, Washington D.C.

   D.   Denver, Washington D.C., Chicago

6. If gravitational acceleration for latitudes south of the equator were added to Figure 1, the curve would look like a parabola with the minimum *g* at 0°. What would be the approximate gravitational acceleration for Buenos Aires, which is located at latitude 35°S at sea level?

   F.   9.73 m/s²

   G.   9.78 m/s²

   H.   9.80 m/s²

   J.   9.83 m/s²

7. How would the results of the study be affected if the gravitational acceleration at various altitudes had been measured at the North Pole instead of at 15°N latitude? For a given altitude, gravitational acceleration measured at the North Pole:

   A.   would be higher.

   B.   would be lower.

   C.   would be the same.

   D.   could not be determined.

Questions 8–14 are based on the following passage.

Passage II

Most natural substances can occur in any of three phases (states of matter): solid, liquid, or gas. A phase diagram indicates what phase (or phases) a substance can be found in at varying temperatures and pressures. The molecular structure of a substance determines the conditions under which it will experience a phase change, such as freezing or boiling. Solid lines in a phase diagram represent these phase changes, when two phases exist in equilibrium as the substance transitions from one phase to another. The *triple point* is the temperature and pressure at which all three phases of a substance exist in equilibrium. Figure 1 presents a phase diagram for water (H_2O), while Figure 2 presents a phase diagram for carbon dioxide (CO_2).

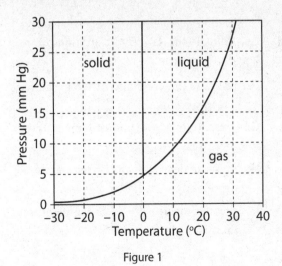

Figure 1

Science

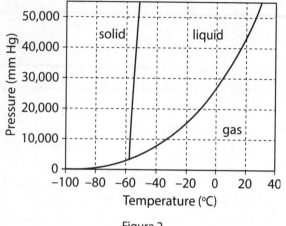

Figure 2

8. Based on Figure 2, CO_2 exists in the liquid phase between what two temperatures?

F. −100°C to −57°C

G. −57°C to 31°C

H. 31°C to 57°C

J. 57°C to 100°C

9. Based on the information in the figures, at 13°C and 28 mm Hg, H_2O and CO_2 exist in which phases?

	H₂O	CO₂
A.	solid	liquid
B.	liquid	liquid
C.	gas	gas
D.	liquid	gas

10. According to the data, H_2O transitions from liquid to gas when:

F. pressure increases and/or temperature decreases.

G. pressure increases and/or temperature increases.

H. pressure decreases and/or temperature decreases.

J. pressure decreases and/or temperature increases.

11. Based on the data, approximately what is the freezing point of CO_2 at 70,000 mm Hg ?

A. −100°C

B. −50°C

C. −30°C

D. 0°C

12. Based on Figure 1, at a pressure greater than 5 mm Hg, when temperature decreases, H_2O can transition directly from:

F. solid to liquid.

G. solid to gas.

H. liquid to gas.

J. liquid to solid.

13. According to Figure 2, the triple point of CO_2 is at approximately what temperature and pressure?

	temperature	pressure
A.	−55°C	4,000 mm Hg
B.	0°C	5 mm Hg
C.	5°C	0 mm Hg
D.	4000°C	−55 mm Hg

14. Based on the data, compared to the temperature at which CO_2 melts, the temperature at which H_2O melts is:

F. lower.

G. equal.

H. higher.

J. higher at some pressures and lower at other pressures.

Answers and Explanations are provided at the end of the book.

CHAPTER 22

Research Summaries

CHAPTER OBJECTIVES

By the end of this chapter, you will be able to:

1. Recognize the scientific method and identify the key components of experiments, including hypotheses, controls, and independent and dependent variables

2. Interpret information from two or more related experiments

3. Evaluate and interpret the design and procedures of two or more related experiments

4. Predict how additional information affects experimental design or results

SMARTPOINTS

Point Value	SmartPoints Category
Point Builder	Research Summaries
9 Points	Scientific Investigation

Research Summaries typically consist of an introductory paragraph or two providing background information about a scientific phenomenon and perhaps also some details on an experimental setup. This will be followed by a series of experiments, differentiated with helpful labels like "Study 1" and "Experiment 2." The paragraphs under each of these headings will offer details on the experiment, typically focusing on its method, and will usually be accompanied by a graph or table that indicates the experiment's results. You can expect half (three) of the passages on Test Day to be Research Summaries.

These passages often feature Interpretation of Data questions that ask about the results of the experiments, but they will also frequently test you on aspects of the scientific method and experimental design, questions that fall into the Scientific Investigation category. Approximately 20–30% of the questions in the ACT Science test are Scientific Investigation questions, which appear more often with Research Summaries than with any other passage type. These questions involve:

- Understanding experimental tools and procedures

- Understanding experimental design by identifying variables and controls

- Analyzing experimental designs and results

- Extending experiments to predict results of additional trials

- Identifying the expected impact of modifying an experiment's design

These skills will be discussed in further detail throughout this chapter.

THE KAPLAN METHOD FOR RESEARCH SUMMARIES

Since the ACT is a standardized test, students who approach each passage type in a consistent way will be rewarded on Test Day. Applying the same basic steps to each Research Summaries passage will help ensure that you understand the design of each experiment and can interpret the data from those experiments accurately and efficiently.

The Kaplan Method for Research Summaries consists of three steps:

Step 1: Actively read the passage

- Underline the purpose and/or hypothesis

- Identify key components of the experiments

- Look for similarities and differences among experiments

Step 2: Examine the figures provided

- Locate variables in the figures

- Identify trends and patterns

- Look for relationships among variables

Step 3: Find support for the answer in the passage

- Identify keywords in the question stem

- Locate the corresponding data in the passage

- Make a prediction and match it to the correct answer

Step 1: Actively read the passage

This means you should:

- Read with your pencil

- Locate and underline the purpose and/or hypothesis of the experiments

  - Look for information telling you *what* the researchers are investigating

  - Often the purpose will begin with the word "to" (for example, "to determine," "to evaluate," "to examine")

  - The purpose is often to test a particular hypothesis

- Identify key components of experiments

  - Independent variables

  - Dependent variables

  - Controls

- Look for similarities and differences among experimental methods, the step-by-step procedures explaining *how* each experiment was conducted (for example, in Experiment 1 scientists measured the pH of acidic substances and in Experiment 2 they measured the pH of basic substances at the same temperature)

- NOT spend time trying to understand all the technical details

- Locate the results of the experiments

  - They will often be provided in tables, charts, or graphs, but they can also be given to you in paragraph form

Step 2: Examine the figures provided

This means that, before you look at the questions, you should:

- Locate variables in the figures

  - In many cases you will have just one independent variable and one dependent variable for each experiment, but you could have more than one of either

  - Identify which variables change and note their units

- Identify trends and patterns

  - Look for direct or inverse relationships

  - Identify patterns within the trends, such as specific mathematical relationships (for example, the dependent variable doubles whenever the independent variable doubles)

  - Note: not all data will have a clear trend or pattern

- Identify relationships among variables (for example, cause-and-effect relationships, such as when a change in an independent variable causes a change in a dependent variable)

Step 3: Find support for the answer in the passage

This means you should:

- Identify keywords in the question stem to help you locate where to go in the passage to find support for your answer

- Locate the corresponding data or other relevant information in the passage

  - Results will usually be found in the tables or figures provided, while other experimental details (hypotheses, methods, controls, etc.) will often be found in the text of the passage

  - Form an idea and make a prediction about the correct answer—this will help to focus your thinking and assist you in avoiding trap answers

- Match your predicted answer to an answer choice

RECOGNIZE THE SCIENTIFIC METHOD AND KEY ASPECTS OF EXPERIMENTS

The scientific method is the process by which both scientists and students engage in systematic investigations of natural phenomena. This method covers everything involved in the practice of science, from deciding what to investigate to designing an experiment to publishing the results. Some Scientific Investigation questions will test your ability to understand the scientific method, in other words, how well you can think like a scientist.

While there are some differences of opinion about what exactly the scientific method is (and even about whether there is just one scientific method that applies equally to all the diverse sciences that exist in the world today), for the ACT Science test, you can think of the scientific method as the following set of steps:

1. Ask a question based on observations and initial research

2. Formulate a hypothesis that answers the question

3. Design an experiment to test the hypothesis

4. Conduct the experiment and record data

5. Analyze the data and draw conclusions

6. Communicate the results

Before you can begin to identify the scientific method in ACT passages, you must understand what these steps actually involve. The following example will help to demonstrate:

Example	Scientific Method
Dave is **fascinated** by how his friend Rose, who works at a restaurant, is able to hold and carry hot plates that he can't stand to touch. He wonders to himself, why can some people tolerate more heat than others? He does some **research** on the subject, learns about sensory adaptation, and receives permission to run a small experiment with laboratory mice. His **hypothesis** is that laboratory mice exposed to uncomfortably hot surfaces over a period of time will eventually stop responding negatively to those hot surfaces.	**Observation and Research:** All scientific investigation begins by noticing a phenomenon that is interesting and posing a question about it. **Hypothesis:** Based on initial observations and research, scientists form hypotheses. A hypothesis is an attempt to explain a particular observation and often indicates the independent and dependent variables.
To ensure that he tests only the effect of heat exposure, Dave **designs** the following experiment. He splits the mice into two groups: one (the **experimental group**) whose cage floor is made hot for one minute every hour, and the other (the **control group**) whose cage is left alone but who otherwise live identically to the experimental group. At the end of one week, Dave exposes all mice (in both groups) to a hot surface and monitors their reactions. He **records data** on their reactions and repeats the process for several more weeks.	**Experimental Design:** A good experimental design will isolate the effect of one or more independent variables (manipulated quantities—exposure to heat in Dave's experiment) on one or more dependent variables (measured quantities—reaction to a hot surface in Dave's experiment). **Control:** A control is a kind of baseline within an experiment that allows for effective comparison. Dave uses a control group that lives in almost identical circumstances to his experimental group: the only difference between them is the independent variable, so Dave knows that any difference in reaction can be attributed to exposure to a hot floor.
Upon **analysis of the data**, Dave immediately recognizes that mice in the experimental group react less visibly to the hot surface, and some seem not to be affected at all. He therefore **concludes** that his hypothesis was correct, and that his friend Rose is in some ways like the mice in the experimental group: acclimated to hot surfaces.	**Analysis and Conclusion:** Once data is obtained, scientists will look at that data and interpret it. Using trends in the results, scientists can conclude whether or not their hypothesis is supported. As a final step, scientists will often publish their results to share them with the scientific community.

Experiments on the ACT won't highlight each step of the scientific method for you, but a thorough understanding of the scientific method will make it easier to answer Scientific Investigation questions on Test Day!

Many Research Summaries passages rely on your ability to use your knowledge of the scientific method to find the key components (hypotheses, independent and dependent variables, and controls) of each experiment. Finding these components can make it easier to recognize the purpose of an experiment, understand its methods, and interpret its results. This will help you to answer Scientific Investigation questions about experimental design (for example, which variable is deliberately manipulated or how you might change the method of an experiment to achieve a particular outcome).

INTERPRET THE RESULTS OF EXPERIMENTS

Like on Data Representation passages, Interpretation of Data questions on Research Summaries passages will ask you to interpret data such as results from a given experiment. Step 2 of the Kaplan Method for Research Summaries will help you locate many of these answers quickly and efficiently.

When you are presented with a question asking you to interpret experimental results, expect to go back to where you noted the major trends and any tables or graphs that were provided.

Any time you are asked to locate information in charts and graphs you need to ask yourself two questions: what is the figure showing and what are the units of measurement? Knowing the units of measurement is especially important to be sure you know what is being measured.

Additionally, you will also be asked to piece together data and information from multiple sources. For example, a question might ask you to combine information from two or more figures.

Take a look at the following Research Summaries passage and question set to practice interpreting experimental results. After the passage, the left column contains test-like questions. The right column features the strategic thinking a test expert might employ when approaching the passage and question presented. The Kaplan Method for Research Summaries is demonstrated consistently throughout.

Strategic Thinking
Step 1: Actively read the passage
Read the passage and note the purpose, hypothesis, and key components (for example, variables) that have been underlined. Remember to look for differences among the experiments and to identify possible relationships, such as cause-and-effect.
Step 2: Examine the figures provided
In Table 1, the variables are collision rating on the Torino scale and collision strength. In Figure 1, there are two independent variables. The first is the size of the asteroid (measured in multiples of 100,000 kg); the second is the humidity—Experiment 1, the bottom curve, is measured at 86% humidity, while Experiment 2, the top curve, is measured at 12% humidity. As the size of the asteroid increases, the collision rating also increases. For all asteroid sizes, Experiment 2 has a higher collision rating than Experiment 1.

Questions 1–3 are based on the following passage.

Passage I

Astronomers <u>want to know the effects of atmospheric conditions on the impact of an asteroid-to-Earth collision</u>. The most common <u>hypothesis is that the presence of moisture in Earth's atmosphere significantly reduces the hazardous effects of such a collision</u>. One researcher decided to create a laboratory model of Earth. The researcher has the ability to control the amount of moisture surrounding the model. She has also created models of asteroids at various sizes. The researcher measures the potential impact of such collisions on the Torino scale, which rates collisions on a scale from 0 to 10. The potential effects associated with such impacts are described in Table 1.

Table 1	
Collision rating (Torino scale)	Strength of collision
0	A collision capable of little destruction
1 to 3	A collision capable of localized destruction
4 to 6	A collision capable of regional destruction
7 to 10	A collision capable of global catastrophe

Experiment 1

The researcher simulated collisions on the Earth model with asteroid models that have <u>masses ranging from 100,000 kg to 1,000,000 kg</u>. The <u>moisture level</u> of the model Earth's atmosphere was <u>86%</u>. The effects of the collisions were recorded.

Experiment 2

The researcher simulated collisions on the Earth model with asteroid models using the <u>same range of masses</u> as in Experiment 1. The moisture level of the model Earth's atmosphere in this experiment was adjusted to <u>12%</u>. The effects of the collisions were recorded. The results of both experiments are shown in Figure 1.

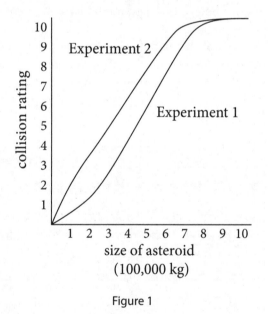

Figure 1

Questions	Strategic Thinking
1. If the asteroid that killed the dinosaurs rated a 9 on the Torino scale, and if Earth's atmospheric moisture level at that time was approximately 86%, then how large was the asteroid that impacted Earth, according to the research discussed in the passage? **A.** 200,000 kg **B.** 500,000 kg **C.** 700,000 kg **D.** 1,000,000 kg	**Step 3: Find support for the answer in the passage** This question is asking you to apply the results from the experiments to a natural phenomenon that occurred in the past. Experiment 1 used a moisture level of 86%, so its results are the relevant ones. Draw a horizontal line from 9 on the *y*-axis to find where it intersects with the curve for Experiment 1. Draw a vertical line down from that point to find the size of the asteroid. The line intersects the *x*-axis at about 700,000 kg, so choice (C) is correct.
2. In an additional simulation of an asteroid-to-Earth collision, a 400,000 kg asteroid received a collision rating of 4. The amount of moisture in the atmosphere was most likely closest to: **F.** 0% **G.** 12% **H.** 86% **J.** 100%	**Step 3: Find support for the answer in the passage** As with the previous question, you'll need to work with Figure 1. Draw a horizontal line across from a collision rating of 4 on the *y*-axis and a vertical line up from a size of 400,000 kg on the *x*-axis and see where they intersect. The two lines intersect on the curve for Experiment 1. According to the passage, this experiment used a moisture level of 86%. Thus, (H) is correct.
3. What would be the result, according to the Torino scale, of a 500,000 kg asteroid colliding with Earth at an atmospheric moisture level of 12% ? **A.** A collision capable of little destruction **B.** A collision capable of localized destruction **C.** A collision capable of regional destruction **D.** A collision capable of global catastrophe	**Step 3: Find support for the answer in the passage** The text in the answer choices comes from Table 1, so you'll need to use it together with Figure 1 to find an answer. Draw a vertical line up from 500,000 kg on the *x*-axis until it intersects with the curve from Experiment 2, which used a 12% moisture level. From the point of intersection, draw a line over to the *y*-axis to find a collision rating of 8. According to Table 1, a collision rating of 7 or higher corresponds to a *global catastrophe*, so choice (D) is correct.

EVALUATE EXPERIMENTAL DESIGN

You are guaranteed to see Scientific Investigation questions asking you to identify the similarities and differences among experiments on the ACT Science test. These questions are pretty straightforward. For example, the methods of Experiment 2 might state "the scientists repeated Experiment 1 but at a temperature of 45°C." If you look back at the methods for Experiment 1, you might find that the scientists ran that experiment at 15°C. Sometimes looking at figures or tables of results can also help you identify differences.

Some of the more difficult Scientific Investigation questions you will see on Test Day require you to evaluate the design of experiments. They will ask you to think like a scientist and understand why experiments were conducted the way they were. Recognizing the components of experiments outlined previously will help you to make such evaluations.

Whenever you evaluate an experiment's design, the major question to ask yourself is the following: Did the researchers properly regulate the experimental conditions so that the only differences among subjects are due to changes in independent variables? If so, then it is safe to conclude that a change in an independent variable was the direct cause of a change in a dependent variable. However, if the researchers are unable to limit differences to changes in independent variables, then it is quite possible that some other difference is affecting the results.

For example, suppose that a researcher wants to test the effect of temperature on the growth of a particular plant. She creates two groups of these plants, one grown in a controlled environment at 20°C and the other in a different controlled environment at 30°C. If the only difference between the two environments is temperature, then the researcher can safely conclude that any change in average growth is due to the change in temperature. But, if the 30°C environment is also exposed to significantly more sunlight than the 20°C environment, then it would be impossible for her to tell whether a change in average growth is due to temperature, sunlight, or the combination of the two.

PREDICT THE IMPACT OF NEW INFORMATION ON EXPERIMENTS

Some Scientific Investigation questions will require you to predict the results of a new experiment or to predict the experimental conditions that would produce a certain result. For example, a question might ask how the solubility of a salt would be affected if an additional trial was conducted at a higher temperature, or one might ask for the conditions that would lead to an increase in solubility. To answer these types of questions, you should look at the existing data and see if they contain any trends that suggest what to expect in the new circumstances.

Some of the more challenging Scientific Investigation questions will ask you to identify a new experiment to conduct to learn more about the phenomenon being investigated. To answer them, you should generally avoid answer choices that investigate variables already tested in the passage's experiments, as well as answer choices that stray too far from the topic. Questions like these are more likely to draw on some outside knowledge of the topic, but there may be clues in the passage, such as in the introductory paragraph, that can assist you.

Sometimes, Scientific Investigation questions following a Research Summaries passage will introduce new information in the form of text in the question stem or a new table or graph. The key to these questions is not to get lost in the details, but to look for similarities between the new information and what was already revealed in the experiments.

For example, questions might ask you if new information supports or weakens the hypothesis from the passage or even whether the experimental results from the passage support/weaken a new hypothesis. When answering these questions, figure out how the new information relates to what's given in the passage and find an answer choice that properly expresses this relationship. Other questions in this vein might present a problem (like contamination of a substance) that could arise in one of the steps of an experimental procedure and ask you to identify the effect the problem causes or even a possible solution.

Now consider the following test-like passage and question set. After the passage, the left column contains questions similar to those you'll see on the Science test on Test Day. The column on the right features the strategic thinking a test expert might employ when approaching the passage and questions presented.

Strategic Thinking
Step 1: Actively read the passage
Read the passage and note the purpose and key components that have been underlined. Remember to look for similarities and differences between the experiments and identify possible relationships among variables.
Step 2: Examine the figures provided
In Table 1, the independent variable is temperature and the dependent variable is moles O_2 absorbed/hr. For the skin, as temperature increases, O_2 increases then decreases, whereas for the lungs, as temperature increases, O_2 simply increases. In Table 2, the independent variable again is temperature but the dependent variable is moles CO_2 eliminated/hr. For the skin, as temperature increases, CO_2 consistently increases, whereas for the lungs, as temperature increases, CO_2 increases then decreases slightly.

Questions 4–7 are based on the following passage.

Passage II

The Brazilian tree frog (*Hyla faber*) exchanges gases through both its skin and lungs. The exchange rate depends on the temperature of the frogs' environment. A pair of experiments was performed to investigate this dependence.

Experiment 1

Fifty frogs were placed in a controlled atmosphere that, with the exception of temperature, was designed to simulate their native habitat. The temperature was varied from 5°C to 25°C, and equilibrium was attained before each successive temperature change. The amount of oxygen absorbed by the frogs' lungs and skin per hour was measured, and the results for all the frogs were averaged. These results are shown in Table 1.

Table 1		
	Moles O_2 absorbed/hr	
Temperature (°C)	Skin	Lungs
5	15.4	8.3
10	22.7	35.1
15	43.6	64.9
20	42.1	73.5
25	40.4	78.7

Experiment 2

The same frogs were placed under the same conditions as in Experiment 1. For this experiment, the amount of carbon dioxide eliminated through the skin and lungs was measured. The results were averaged and are shown below in Table 2.

Table 2		
	Moles CO_2 eliminated/hr	
Temperature (°C)	Skin	Lungs
5	18.9	2.1
10	43.8	12.7
15	79.2	21.3
20	91.6	21.9
25	96.5	21.4

Questions	Strategic Thinking
4. Which of the following factors did the researchers intentionally vary? **F.** The number of frogs studied **G.** The humidity of the frogs' simulated habitat **H.** The temperature of the frogs' simulated habitat **J.** The amount of oxygen in the frogs' simulated habitat	**Step 3: Find support for the answer in the passage** The phrase *intentionally vary* indicates that this question is asking for the independent variable. The passage explains that, for both experiments, "temperature was varied from 5°C to 25°C," so choice (H) is correct. Choice F is incorrect because the passage states that the number of frogs studied was constant (50 total). Choice G is incorrect because the passage does not mention humidity. Watch out for J, which is a common trap for these kinds of questions. The amount of oxygen that the frogs *absorbed* (not the amount in the habitat) varied according to temperature, but that was the dependent variable in Experiment 1, not the independent variable.
5. Experiment 1 and Experiment 2 differed in that Experiment 2: **A.** used a different species of tree frog. **B.** studied a broader range of temperatures. **C.** measured oxygen absorption through the skin only. **D.** measured carbon dioxide elimination.	**Step 3: Find support for the answer in the passage** According to the description of Experiment 2, the frogs studied and the conditions of the habitat were the same as in Experiment 1. The only difference was that "the amount of carbon dioxide eliminated through the skin and lungs was measured" instead of the amount of oxygen absorbed. Choice (D) is thus correct.

Science

Questions	Strategic Thinking
6. Which of the following best explains why the researchers allowed the temperature in the simulated habitat to achieve equilibrium before each temperature change? The researchers wanted to allow: **F.** time for additional oxygen to be removed from the habitat. **G.** time for the frogs to adjust their gas exchange rate to the new temperature. **H.** time for the researchers to increase or decrease carbon dioxide levels in the habitat. **J.** time for the habitat's humidity level to adjust with the new temperature.	**Step 3: Find support for the answer in the passage** Keep in mind the purpose of the experiment when trying to answer a question about its design. According to the first paragraph of the passage, the researchers were interested in investigating the dependence of the frogs' gas exchange rate on the temperature of their environment. The description of the first experiment also indicates that the researchers simulated the frogs' native habitat "with the exception of temperature." Thus, the researchers did not remove oxygen from the habitat or modify its carbon dioxide levels, meaning F and H can be eliminated. Similarly, there is no suggestion in the passage that the humidity level changed, so J is also incorrect. This leaves only (G). And indeed, to achieve their stated purpose, the researchers had to allow the frogs' rate of gas exchange to adjust to each new temperature. Otherwise, the data they collected would not actually demonstrate a connection between the independent variable and the dependent variable. Choice (G) is correct.
7. Which of the following best explains why the frogs were placed in a controlled atmosphere designed to simulate their native habitat? **A.** The researchers wanted to manipulate some variables but leave other elements as they were naturally. **B.** The researchers wanted to exclude natural predators from the frogs' environment. **C.** The researchers wanted to be able to control the frogs' food supply. **D.** The researchers wanted to be able to control the frogs' oxygen intake.	**Step 3: Find support for the answer in the passage** According to the introduction of the passage, the researchers wanted to investigate the dependence of gas exchange on temperature in the Brazilian tree frog. If the researchers had constructed an artificial environment that greatly differed from the frogs' natural habitat, then it would be impossible to tell whether temperature alone was responsible for changes in oxygen absorption and carbon dioxide elimination, or whether there was some other environmental difference or combination of differences that caused these changes. Making sure that the only differences are in the independent variable ensures more accurate results. Choice (A) is correct. Choices B and C are incorrect because predators and food supply are never discussed in the passage and have no discernible impact on gas exchange. Choice D is incorrect because oxygen intake was not directly controlled by the experimenters; rather, it was one of the dependent variables that they measured.

You have seen the ways in which the ACT tests you with Research Summaries passages and Scientific Investigation questions, as well as the way an ACT expert might approach these passages and questions.

Now, use the Kaplan Method for Research Summaries to answer the six questions that accompany the following Science passage. Part of the test-like passage has been annotated already. Your first step is to complete marking up the passage. Strategic thinking questions have been included to guide you—some of the answers have been filled in, but you will have to fill in the answers to others.

Use your answers to the strategic thinking questions to select the correct answer, just as you would on Test Day.

Strategic Thinking
Step 1: Actively read the passage
The passage below is partially annotated. The hypothesis of the research group has been underlined in the introductory paragraph, and key variables have been noted in the methods of Experiment 1. Continue taking notes on the methods of Experiment 2. Remember to look for differences between the two experiments. Use your notes as a reference when you're answering questions.
Step 2: Examine the figures provided
What are the variables and units? What are the trends and patterns in the data?   _____   _____   _____

Questions 8–13 are based on the following passage.

Passage III

Humans can experience toxic symptoms when concentrations of mercury (Hg) in the blood exceed 200 parts per billion (ppb). Frequent consumption of foods high in Hg content contributes to high Hg levels in the blood. On average, higher Hg concentrations are observed in people whose diets include relatively extreme amounts of certain types of seafood. A research group proposed that <u>sea creatures that live in colder waters acquire greater amounts of Hg than those that reside in warmer waters</u>. The researchers performed the following experiments to examine this hypothesis.

Experiment 1

Samples of several species of consumable sea life caught in the <u>cold waters of the northern Atlantic Ocean</u> were chemically prepared and analyzed using a cold vapor atomic fluorescence spectrometer (CVAFS), a device that indicates the relative concentrations of various elements and compounds found within a biological sample. <u>Comparisons</u> of the spectra taken from the seafood samples with those taken from <u>samples of known Hg levels</u> were made to determine the exact concentrations in parts per billion (ppb). <u>Identical volumes of tissue from eight different</u>

specimens for each of four different species were tested, and the results are shown in Table 1, including the average concentrations found for each species. Note that the specimen numbers are assigned arbitrarily.

Table 1				
	Hg concentration in cold water species (ppb)			
Specimen	Cod	Crab	Swordfish	Shark
1	160	138	871	859
2	123	143	905	820
3	139	152	902	839
4	116	177	881	851
5	130	133	875	818
6	134	148	880	836
7	151	147	910	847
8	109	168	894	825
Average	133	151	890	837

Experiment 2

The same four species, this time caught in the warmer waters of the Gulf of Mexico, were examined using the procedure from Experiment 1. The results are shown in Table 2.

Table 2				
	Hg concentration in warm water species (ppb)			
Specimen	Cod	Crab	Swordfish	Shark
1	98	113	851	812
2	110	122	856	795
3	102	143	845	821
4	105	128	861	803
5	94	115	849	798
6	112	136	852	809
7	100	129	853	815
8	117	116	837	776
Average	105	125	851	804

Questions	Strategic Thinking
8. Given that the shark and the swordfish are both larger, predatory animals, and the cod and the crab are smaller, nonpredatory animals, do the results of Experiment 2 support the hypothesis that the tissue of larger predatory species exhibits higher levels of Hg than does the tissue of smaller nonpredatory species? **F.** Yes; the highest concentration of Hg was found in the shark. **G.** Yes; both the swordfish and the shark had higher Hg concentrations than the cod and the crab. **H.** No; the lowest concentration of Hg was in the cod. **J.** No; both the cod and the crab had lower Hg concentrations than the swordfish and the shark.	**Step 3: Find support for the answer in the passage** *What are the keywords in the question stem?* The keywords in the question stem are *Experiment 2* and "larger predatory species exhibits higher levels of Hg." *Where can you find the corresponding data in the passage?* The keywords are clues to where you should look for the answer. The results for Experiment 2 are found in Table 2. Identify which columns correspond to the larger animals (shark and swordfish) and which columns correspond to the smaller animals (cod and crab). Then, compare the average Hg concentration values for shark and swordfish to those for cod and crab. The values for the larger animals are higher than those for the smaller animals. So, the hypothesis in the question stem is supported by the results in Experiment 2. *Which answer choice matches?* _____

Questions	Strategic Thinking

9. Which of the following is an independent variable in Experiment 2 ?
 	
  A. The volume of tissue tested
 	
  B. The method by which the marine organisms were caught
 	
  C. The species of marine organism tested
 	
  D. The method of sample analysis
	Step 3: Find support for the answer in the passage
	
	What are the keywords in the question stem?
	
	The keywords in the question stem are *intentionally varied* and *Experiment 2.*
	
	Where can you find the corresponding information in the passage?
	
	Independent variables are factors that are intentionally varied within an experiment. Refer back to the methods of Experiment 2. The only independent variable was the species.
	
	Which answer choice matches? _____

10. Based on the results of the experiments and the data in the table below, sharks caught in which of the following locations would most likely possess the largest concentrations of Hg in February?	**Step 3: Find support for the answer in the passage** *What are the keywords in the question stem?* The keywords in the question stem are *locations* and "largest concentration of Hg." *Where can you find the corresponding information in the passage?* To identify which location would contain sharks with the largest Hg concentration, you need to refer to Step 2 where you identified the relationship between water temperature and Hg concentration. Since the relationship between water temperature and Hg concentration is inverse, sharks at the coldest location will have the largest Hg concentration. *Which answer choice matches?* _____

Table for question 10:

Location	Average water temperature (°F) for February
Northern Atlantic Ocean	33
Gulf of Mexico	70
Northern Pacific Ocean	46
Tampa Bay	72

  F. Northern Atlantic Ocean

  G. Northern Pacific Ocean

  H. Gulf of Mexico

  J. Tampa Bay

Questions	Strategic Thinking
11. A researcher, when using CVAFS, was concerned that lead (Pb) in the tissue samples might be interfering with the detection of Hg. Which of the following procedures would best help the researcher explore this trouble? **A.** Flooding the sample with a large concentration of Pb before using the CVAFS **B.** Using the CVAFS to examine a nonbiological sample **C.** Analyzing tissue from additional species **D.** Testing a sample with known concentrations of Hg and Pb	**Step 3: Find support for the answer in the passage** *What are the keywords in the question stem?* The keywords in the question stem are *Pb* and "interfering with the detection of Hg." *Where can you find the corresponding information in the passage?* _____ _____ *Which answer choice matches?* _____
12. Based on the results of the experiments, which of the following specimens would be most likely to have the highest Hg concentration if additional CVAFS analyses were conducted? **F.** A crab caught in cold water **G.** A swordfish caught in cold water **H.** A cod caught in warm water **J.** A swordfish caught in warm water	**Step 3: Find support for the answer in the passage** *What are the keywords in the question stem?* _____ _____ *Where can you find the corresponding data in the passage?* _____ _____ *Which answer choice matches?* _____

Science

Questions	Strategic Thinking
13. How might the results of the experiments be affected if the chemical preparation described in Experiment 1 increased the volume of the samples without adding any additional mercury? The measured concentrations of Hg would be: **A.** the same as the actual concentrations for both cold-water and warm-water specimens. **B.** higher than the actual concentrations for both cold-water and warm-water specimens. **C.** lower than the actual concentrations for cold-water specimens but higher than the actual concentrations for warm-water specimens. **D.** lower than the actual concentrations for both cold-water and warm-water specimens.	**Step 3: Find support for the answer in the passage** *What are the keywords in the question stem?* _____ _____ *Where can you find the corresponding information in the passage?* _____ _____ *Which answer choice matches?* _____

Now try some test-like Research Summaries passages on your own. The following passages provide an opportunity to practice the concepts and strategic thinking covered in this chapter. Give yourself 12 minutes to read the passages and answer the questions.

Questions 14–19 are based on the following passage.

Passage IV

A solution is a mixture composed of a solute (usually solid or gas) dissolved in a solvent (usually liquid). Solutions that can conduct an electrical current are called electrolytes. Electrolytes dissociate into ions, whereas nonelectrolytes do not. Nonelectrolytes cannot conduct an electric current. Researchers hypothesize that as the concentration of dissolved salts or acids increases, there are more ions and the conductivity increases, and that an increase in temperature also increases conductivity. The conductivity of solutions can be measured by passing a small alternating current between two electrodes. The basic units for conductivity measurement are siemens per meter (S/m).

The researchers conducted the following experiments to determine whether increasing the solute in a solution or increasing the temperature of the solution would increase the solution's conductivity.

Experiment 1

Researchers mixed 5 solutions, each containing 10.0 grams (g) of solute dissolved in 100 milliliters (mL) of pure water at 20°C. The conductivity of each solution was then measured in millisiemens per centimeter (mS/cm). The water was also tested for conductivity without the addition of solute. The results of Experiment 1 are shown in Table 1.

Table 1	
Solute	Conductivity measurement (mS/cm)
Water (H_2O)	0.0
Sodium chloride (NaCl)	73.6
Sucrose ($C_{12}H_{22}O_{11}$)	0.0
Potassium iodide (KI)	119.2
Magnesium chloride ($MgCl_2$)	102.8
Formic acid (HCOOH)	3.6

Experiment 2

The researchers repeated Experiment 1, this time tripling the amount of solute in each solution to 30.0 g. The solute was again dissolved in 100 mL of water at 20°C. The results of Experiment 2 are shown in Table 2.

Table 2	
Solute	Conductivity measurement (mS/cm)
Water (H_2O)	0.0
Sodium chloride (NaCl)	129.7
Sucrose ($C_{12}H_{22}O_{11}$)	0.0
Potassium iodide (KI)	371.8
Magnesium chloride ($MgCl_2$)	93.3
Formic acid (HCOOH)	4.8

Experiment 3

Experiment 2 was repeated with 30.0 g of solute dissolved in 100 mL of water. This time, however, researchers heated the water to 70°C. The results of Experiment 3 are shown in Table 3.

Table 3	
Solute	Conductivity measurement (mS/cm)
Water (H_2O)	0.0
Sodium chloride (NaCl)	349.2
Sucrose ($C_{12}H_{22}O_{11}$)	0.0
Potassium iodide (KI)	1000.9
Magnesium chloride ($MgCl_2$)	251.1
Formic acid (HCOOH)	13.0

14. Increasing the amount of solute in a solution increases the conductivity of the solution in each of the following solutes EXCEPT for:

    F. NaCl.

    G. $C_{12}H_{22}O_{11}$.

    H. KI.

    J. HCOOH.

15. On the basis of the results of each of the three experiments, which of the following solutions of NaCl should conduct the most electricity?

    A. 10 g in 100 mL of H_2O at 10°C

    B. 20 g in 100 mL of H_2O at 20°C

    C. 20 g in 100 mL of H_2O at 70°C

    D. 30 g in 100 mL of H_2O at 80°C

16. Suppose that when a solute reaches saturation, the conductivity of the solution decreases. Which of the following solutes most likely reached saturation during the experiments described by the passage?

    F. NaCl

    G. KI

    H. $MgCl_2$

    J. HCOOH

17. If Experiment 2 were repeated, only this time with the water heated to 50°C, the conductivity of the electrolyte solutions would most likely:

    A. increase.

    B. increase, except for $MgCl_2$.

    C. decrease.

    D. decrease, except for $MgCl_2$.

18. Which of the following objectives best explains why H_2O alone was tested in all three experiments?

    F. To determine the amount of conductivity that could be attributed to H_2O

    G. To test whether H_2O was the solute or the solvent

    H. To test whether H_2O would dissolve all of the salts equally

    J. To prove that H_2O conducts electricity well

19. Based on the results of all three experiments, which effect would be most appropriate to test next to learn more about conductivity in a solution?

    A. How temperature influences conductivity

    B. How solute color influences conductivity

    C. How different solvents influence conductivity

    D. How water influences conductivity

Science

Questions 20–25 are based on the following passage.

Passage V

Ground-level ozone gas is a major component of urban smog. It is not emitted directly as a pollutant but is formed through a complex set of chemical reactions involving hydrocarbons, nitrogen oxides, and sunlight. The rate of ozone production increases with sunlight intensity and temperature and therefore peaks during hot summer afternoons. The hydrocarbons and nitrogen oxides from which ozone is formed come primarily from engines that burn fossil fuels. Students at an urban high school hypothesized that their school buses emit more hydrocarbons when the engines idle than they do when the drivers turn off the engines and then restart them. The students performed a series of experiments to test their hypothesis.

Experiment 1

Students connected a collection bag to the exhaust pipe of one of their school buses. The bus's engine was started, and the exhaust was captured by the collection bag. A syringe was then used to extract a 5-mL sample of the exhaust. The exhaust was injected into a gas chromatograph, which separates mixtures of gases into their individual components. Students compared the exhaust to mixtures of known hydrocarbon concentration samples to determine what percentage of the sample (by volume) was composed of hydrocarbons. The bus was started, and samples of the exhaust were collected and extracted at 30-second intervals. Exhaust samples from two other buses were also collected. The results are reproduced below in Table 1.

Table 1			
	Percentage of hydrocarbons in the exhaust		
Time after starting (sec)	Bus 1 1994 Model X	Bus 2 1992 Model X	Bus 3 2006 Model X
30	10.3	9.0	5.4
60	11.2	9.8	4.9
90	12.0	13.2	6.0
120	10.5	22.9	4.9
150	9.6	21.0	4.5
180	9.5	20.1	4.2
210	9.4	19.2	4.2
240	9.3	19.2	3.8

Experiment 2

The exhaust of the buses was collected and tested again after the buses had been allowed to idle for 15 minutes, using the same procedure as Experiment 1. The results are reproduced below in Table 2.

Table 2			
	Percentage of hydrocarbons in the exhaust		
Time after starting (min)	Bus 1 1994 Model X	Bus 2 1992 Model X	Bus 3 2006 Model X
15.0	5.5	6.1	1.8
15.5	5.5	6.1	1.8
16.0	5.4	6.2	1.8
16.5	5.4	6.2	1.8
17.0	5.4	6.1	1.8
17.5	5.4	6.1	1.8
18.0	5.3	6.1	1.8
18.5	5.3	6.1	1.8

20. Several students in the class also hypothesized that, at any given time, the exhaust of newer buses contains a lower percentage of hydrocarbons on average than the exhaust of older buses. Do the results of Experiment 1 support this hypothesis?

    F. Yes; the highest percentage of hydrocarbons was found in the exhaust of the 2006 bus.

    G. Yes; the lowest percentage of hydrocarbons was found in the exhaust of the 2006 bus.

    H. No; the highest percentage of hydrocarbons was found in the exhaust of the 1992 bus.

    J. No; the lowest percentage of hydrocarbons was found in the exhaust of the 1992 bus.

21. Which of the following factors did the students vary in Experiment 1 ?

    A. The time of day at which the samples were taken

    B. The instruments used to collect the exhaust samples

    C. The age of the buses tested

    D. The amount of exhaust used in the gas chromatograph

22. Many states require that buses undergo emissions testing to pass an annual inspection. If the goal of the test is to determine peak hydrocarbon emissions, then, based on the results of the students' experiments, how long after starting the bus should the exhaust be sampled?

    F. Less than 75 seconds

    G. Between 75 and 150 seconds

    H. Between 150 and 240 seconds

    J. Greater than 15 minutes

23. The main purpose of Experiment 2 was to:

    A. determine the percentage of nitrogen oxides in a bus's exhaust.

    B. calibrate the gas chromatograph.

    C. determine the percentage of hydrocarbons in the exhaust of an idling bus.

    D. test the effectiveness of the exhaust collection bag.

24. Which of the following best explains why the students collected exhaust samples in a collection bag?

    F. To keep air and other gases from contaminating the exhaust samples

    G. To allow outside air and gases to mix with the exhaust samples equally

    H. To capture only the hydrocarbons in the exhaust

    J. To filter out sediments from the exhaust

25. One student was concerned that the school's gas chromatograph was unable to distinguish between the hydrocarbons and the carbon monoxide in a bus's exhaust. Which of the following procedures could the student follow to investigate this possibility?

   A. Adding hydrocarbons to the bag before collecting exhaust

   B. Testing a sample of exhaust from a teacher's car

   C. Testing a sample of pure oxygen in the gas chromatograph

   D. Testing a sample with known volumes of hydrocarbons and carbon monoxide

Answers and Explanations are provided at the end of the book.

ON YOUR OWN

The following questions provide an opportunity to practice the concepts and strategic thinking covered in this chapter.

Questions 1–7 are based on the following passage.

Passage I

As part of an ecological impact study, factors affecting the rate of algae growth were investigated by measuring the relative amounts of algal blooms produced under various conditions.

Experiment 1

The two basins of Lake Eight were separated by an impermeable partition (see Diagram 1). The experimenters varied the temperatures in different regions of each basin. Basin A was fertilized with phosphorus, carbon, and nitrogen, whereas basin B received only carbon and nitrogen. Two months after fertilization, the number of algal blooms per square meter of surface area of water was measured, yielding the data in Table 1.

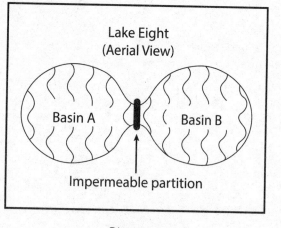

Diagram 1

Table 1			
Basin	Additives	Temperature (°C)	Algal blooms per square meter
Basin A	phosphorus, carbon, and nitrogen	10	0.18
		25	0.48
		35	0.56
Basin B	carbon and nitrogen	10	0.04
		25	0.07
		35	0.08

Experiment 2

For Experiment 2, the conditions of the first experiment were repeated one year later, but sodium bicarbonate ($NaHCO_3$)—which reacts with water to produce carbon dioxide (CO_2)—replaced phosphorus, yielding the data in Table 2.

Table 2			
Basin	Additives	Temperature (°C)	Algal blooms per square meter
Basin A	sodium bicarbonate, carbon, and nitrogen	10	0.26
		25	0.56
		35	0.78
Basin B	carbon and nitrogen	10	0.04
		25	0.07
		35	0.08

1. Which of the following was an independent variable in Experiment 1 ?

    A. The surface area of the basin

    B. The rate of algae growth

    C. The number of algal blooms produced per square meter

    D. The temperature of the water

2. Suppose scientists wanted to conduct a new study using a different lake. Based on the results presented in the passage, which of the following additives would most likely result in the greatest production of blooms in the new study?

    F. Carbon, nitrogen, and sodium bicarbonate

    G. Carbon, nitrogen, and phosphorus

    H. Carbon and nitrogen

    J. Carbon and hydrogen

3. According to the data, what effect does raising the temperature of the water have on the rate of algae production?

    A. It always increases the rate of production.

    B. It always decreases the rate of production.

    C. It increases the rate of production for some additives and decreases the rate of production for other additives.

    D. It has no effect on the rate of production.

4. If carbon, nitrogen, and sodium bicarbonate were added to a basin at 40°C, after 2 months the average number of algal blooms in 1 square meter of surface area would most likely be approximately:

    F. 0.25.

    G. 0.51.

    H. 0.91.

    J. 2.50.

5. From the results of Experiment 2, it can be inferred that carbon dioxide:

    A. promotes algae growth.

    B. inhibits algae growth.

    C. does not affect algae growth.

    D. promotes algae growth only at certain temperatures.

6. Extensive algal blooms cause pollution problems. Detergents are one of the major sources of phosphorus in fresh water. To reduce the pollution associated with algal blooms, it would be most useful to:

    F. increase the amount of detergent present in fresh water.

    G. decrease the amount of detergent present in fresh water.

    H. replace the phosphorus in detergents with sodium bicarbonate.

    J. balance the phosphorus added to detergents with equal amounts of sodium bicarbonate.

7. Why did the experimenters modify the fertilizers added to Basin A between the two experiments without changing those added to Basin B ? Most likely, the experimenters:

    A. wanted to use the same control for both experiments.

    B. wanted to test variations in the amount of fertilizer used.

    C. wanted to confirm the results from Experiment 1.

    D. did not have another fertilizer to test.

Questions 8–14 are based on the following passage.

Passage II

Many proteins undergo denaturation upon heating. A denatured protein is unfolded and can no longer perform its normal biological functions. Denaturation usually occurs over a temperature range. Some proteins can fold back (renature) into their original conformation when the temperature is decreased. A series of experiments was performed to determine the denaturation and renaturation behavior of 3 different proteins.

Experiment 1

Fifteen separate 15-mL samples of each of the proteins ribonuclease (RNase), carboxypeptidase (Case), and hexokinase (Hase) were heated slowly from 20°C to 160°C and cooled slowly back to 20°C. After every 5°C increase in temperature, 0.002 mL of each sample was removed and chemically analyzed to determine the temperature at which denaturation occurred. After every 5°C decrease in temperature, 0.002 mL of each sample was removed and analyzed to determine the temperature at which renaturation occurred. The results of the experiment are shown in Table 1.

	Table 1		
Protein	Approximate molecular weight (amu)	Denaturation temperature range (°C)	Renaturation temperature range (°C)
RNase	13,700	135–145	110–135
Case	35,000	150–155	60–140
Hase	100,000	85–95	–

Experiment 2

Solubility is also a measure of protein denaturation. A protein can be considered fully denatured when its solubility drops to zero. Each 0.002 mL sample of ribonuclease, carboxypeptidase, and hexokinase was dissolved in 10 mL of ethyl alcohol, and its solubility was measured. The solubility measurements were taken in 5°C increments as the samples were heated from 20°C to 160°C and again as they were cooled from 160°C to 20°C. The results are shown in Figure 1 and Figure 2.

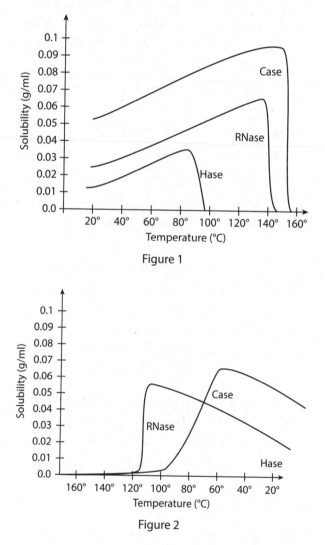

Figure 1

Figure 2

8. If the protein RNase were heated from 40°C to 150°C and then cooled back to 40°C, which of the following plots would its solubility curve most likely resemble?

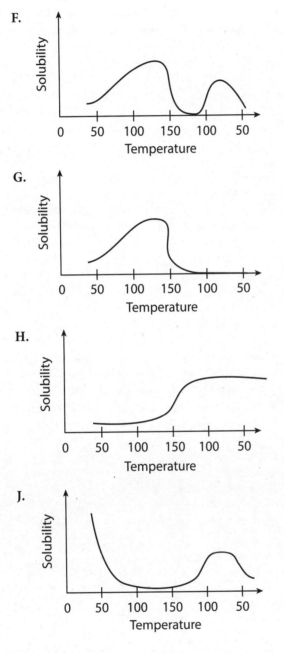

F.

G.

H.

J.

9. According to Figure 1, what would most likely be the solubility of Case in 10 mL of ethyl alcohol at 0°C ?

A. 0.055 g/mL

B. 0.045 g/mL

C. 0.015 g/mL

D. 0.000 g/mL

10. According to Table 1, Hase renatured within what temperature range?

F. 85–95°C

G. 60–140°C

H. 110–135°C

J. Hase did not renature.

11. Based on Table 1 and Figure 1, the maximum of the solubility curves for each of the three proteins corresponds to:

A. denaturation molecular weight.

B. renaturation molecular weight.

C. denaturation temperature range.

D. renaturation temperature range.

12. A student hypothesized that a higher molecular weight yields a higher average denaturation temperature. Do the results of Experiment 1 support this hypothesis?

F. Yes, because RNase had the highest molecular weight and highest average denaturation temperature.

G. Yes, because Case had the highest molecular weight and the highest average denaturation temperature.

H. No, because higher molecular weights actually correspond to lower average denaturation temperatures.

J. No, because there is no correlation between molecular weight and average denaturation temperature.

13. Which of the following best explains why the peak solubility of Case was lower after going through the process of denaturation and rena-turation?

    A. Part of the renatured protein formed a precipitate.

    B. The samples before denaturation and after renaturation were taken from different parts of the solution.

    C. Only a fraction of denatured protein renatured back into its native, active form.

    D. There were contaminants in the samples that lowered solubility.

14. A fourth protein, ovalbumin, denaturates between 115°C and 130°C and renaturates between 70°C and 100°C. Based on the results from the passage, if the procedures of Experiment 2 were repeated with ovalbumin, its solubility curve would most likely peak at about:

    F. 85°C.

    G. 95°C.

    H. 105°C.

    J. 115°C.

Answers and Explanations are provided at the end of the book.

CHAPTER 23

Conflicting Viewpoints

CHAPTER OBJECTIVES

By the end of this chapter, you will be able to:

1. Identify a theory's central claims and implications

2. Determine the similarities and differences among related theories

3. Determine whether given information is consistent with a theory

4. Identify what strengthens or weakens theories

SMARTPOINTS

Point Value	SmartPoints Category
Point Builder	Conflicting Viewpoints
10 Points	Evaluation of Models, Inferences, and Experimental Results

Conflicting Viewpoints passages present theories about a particular phenomenon and require you to understand, compare, and evaluate them. Generally, the introductory paragraph(s) will define key terms and provide background information about the phenomenon. Then each viewpoint (often a "scientist" or "student") will offer in a paragraph or two a theory to explain the phenomenon. These passages may occasionally include figures that illustrate the phenomenon or the theories.

Conflicting Viewpoints passages are most similar to those on the Reading test, typically containing more text and fewer figures than Data Representation and Research Summaries passages. Thus, if you prefer reading, you'll probably want to jump at the chance to work on the Conflicting Viewpoints passage (there will always be exactly one in the Science test) when you encounter it on Test Day.

The most common category of question on Conflicting Viewpoints passages is Evaluation of Models, Inferences, and Experimental Results. These questions are also found in conjunction with the other two types of passages and constitute approximately 25–35% of the questions on the ACT Science test. Evaluation of Models questions involve:

- Finding basic information and identifying key assumptions in theories
- Identifying strengths and weaknesses of theories
- Identifying similarities and differences among theories
- Determining which theories are supported or weakened by new information
- Determining which hypothesis, prediction, or conclusion is consistent or inconsistent with a theory or other piece of information from the passage

These skills will be discussed in further detail throughout this chapter.

THE KAPLAN METHOD FOR CONFLICTING VIEWPOINTS

The Kaplan Method for Conflicting Viewpoints uses a divide-and-conquer strategy to help you attack the passage. Rather than processing the theories and questions all at once, this method breaks up the passage into smaller, more manageable portions to help you keep straight who said what. Students who use the Kaplan Method for Conflicting Viewpoints spend their time more efficiently and maximize their opportunity to earn points.

The Kaplan Method for Conflicting Viewpoints consists of three steps:

Step 1: Read the introductory paragraph(s) and the 1st viewpoint, then search for questions that ask only about the 1st viewpoint and answer them

Step 2: Read the 2nd viewpoint, then search for questions that ask only about the 2nd viewpoint and answer them; if there are additional viewpoints, repeat this process with each of them

Step 3: Answer questions that ask about multiple viewpoints and any other remaining questions

Let's examine each of these steps in more detail.

Step 1: Read the introductory paragraph(s) and the 1st viewpoint, then search for questions that ask only about the 1st viewpoint and answer them

This means you should:

- Identify the phenomenon presented in the introduction, which contains general information about the phenomenon

- Identify the 1st viewpoint's central claim, and underline it when you find it (often but not always, it is the first sentence of the paragraph(s) on that viewpoint)

- Underline keywords and key phrases that can be used as reference points for finding support when answering questions

- NOT be distracted by jargon or technical terms because answering questions, not reading the passage, earns you points

- Skip to the questions that relate only to the 1st viewpoint and answer them to minimize your opportunities to confuse the two (or three, or four) viewpoints

  - Come back later to a question about the 1st viewpoint if you cannot answer it without reading the other viewpoint(s)

Step 2: Read the 2nd viewpoint, then search for questions that ask only about the 2nd viewpoint and answer them; if there are additional viewpoints, repeat this process with each of them

This means you should:

- Identify and underline the 2nd viewpoint's central claim

- Underline keywords and key phrases in the 2nd viewpoint

- Skip to the questions that relate only to the 2nd viewpoint and answer them

- If applicable, repeat for each additional viewpoint

  - Read and answer questions that ask only about that additional viewpoint

Step 3: Answer questions that ask about multiple viewpoints and any other remaining questions

This means you should:

- Go back to the remaining unanswered questions and answer them

- NOT spend too much time on any one question

Science

IDENTIFY A THEORY'S CENTRAL CLAIMS AND IMPLICATIONS

Some Evaluation of Models questions that accompany a Conflicting Viewpoints passage will simply test your ability to identify central claims or implications of a viewpoint. The central claims are the main points that sum up the theory. They are explicitly stated in the passage, whereas implications are what can be inferred from the theory.

Questions about a theory's claims are typically straightforward because they ask about only one viewpoint. They refer to details of that viewpoint that are spelled out explicitly in the passage. To find the answer, use clues in the question stem to go back to the relevant part of the passage.

To avoid trap answers, predict an answer before reading the answer choices. Sometimes, such as when a question stem is short on clues, it's more efficient to use process of elimination, evaluating each answer choice individually. However, in such cases you should at a minimum try to set expectations about what would allow a choice to be eliminated. For instance, wrong answer choices in these questions will often do one of the following:

- State the exact opposite of what is true

- Use keywords that are from the passage but aren't relevant to the question at hand

- Be outside the scope of the passage

- Draw on information from other viewpoints (this is why dealing with one viewpoint at a time, as in the Kaplan Method for Conflicting Viewpoints, is to your advantage)

Other Evaluation of Models questions will ask you to identify implications based on the theories. For example, suppose a passage presented four viewpoints about gene replication in bacteria. A question might ask you to infer the order in which the genes would be copied according to each viewpoint. While the passage won't state this outright, it will give you all the information necessary to deduce the order. Confusion tends to be the biggest source of error on these sorts of questions, so make sure you keep straight who said what by following the Kaplan Method for Conflicting Viewpoints.

FIND SIMILARITIES AND DIFFERENCES

Some Evaluation of Models questions will ask you to identify similarities or differences among theories. These questions are typically among the easier questions in the passage, so answer them immediately after you answer the questions that deal with just one viewpoint at a time. For instance, a question might ask you to identify points of agreement or disagreement among theories. Information mentioned in the introductory paragraph(s) or explicitly stated in multiple theories should generally be regarded as points of agreement, while details included in one theory but not in the other(s) should be treated as points of disagreement.

Take a look at the following Conflicting Viewpoints passage to practice identifying claims and implications and determining similarities and differences among theories. You will see the Kaplan Method for Conflicting Viewpoints followed step-by-step. After the passage, the left column contains test-like questions. The right column features the strategic thinking a test expert might employ when approaching the passage and question presented.

Strategic Thinking
Step 1: Read the introductory paragraph(s) and the 1st viewpoint, then search for questions that ask only about the 1st viewpoint and answer them
Read the passage and note the key phrases and main points that have been underlined. Remember to read for the central claim and do not get distracted by jargon and technical terms. Answer Question 3 first, which asks about the 1st viewpoint.
Step 2: Read the 2nd viewpoint, then search for questions that ask only about the 2nd viewpoint and answer them; if there are additional viewpoints, repeat this process with each of them
Read for the central claim and note the underlined key phrases and main points. Answer Question 2, which asks about the 2nd viewpoint.
Step 3: Answer questions that ask about multiple viewpoints and any other remaining questions
Answer the remaining Question 1, which asks about both the 1st and 2nd viewpoints.

Questions 1–3 are based on the following passage.

Passage I

Schizophrenia is a mental disorder that severely impacts the way 2.5 million Americans think, feel, and act. It is a disorder that makes it difficult for a person to tell the difference between real and imagined experiences or to behave normally in social situations. Two researchers discuss possible causes of schizophrenia.

Researcher 1

Schizophrenia is an organic disorder. Mounting pharmacological evidence suggests that schizophrenia is somehow related to hyperactivity of the dopaminergic system. The cause of the hyperactivity has yet to be determined. Some leading possibilities are a simple overrelease of dopamine (a neurotransmitter), overreaction to a dopaminergic stimulus by nerve receptors, overactivity in a related system, underactivity in an antagonist system, or a defect in a feedback mechanism. Antipsychotic drugs used in the treatment of schizophrenia are known to block dopamine receptors. Patients using these drugs sometimes develop side effects identical to Parkinson's disease, which is primarily a state of dopamine deficiency. Radioisotope studies clearly show that such antipsychotics bind to dopamine receptors in the brain and that the degree of binding correlates quite strongly with the anti-schizophrenic efficacy of the drug.

Researcher 2

There is as yet no clear-cut evidence that all schizophrenics produce increased levels of dopamine, let alone that such levels are the causative agent of schizophrenia. If schizophrenia were caused by hyperactivity of the dopaminergic system, one would expect schizophrenics to display increased levels of homovanillic acid and decreased levels of serum prolactin. Such is not the case, however. Moreover, dopamine blockers effectively relieve most states of agitation and psychosis, whether or not the patient shows signs of schizophrenia. Schizophrenia is not an organic ailment but an emotional disorder. It is caused by childhood exposure to chronically dysfunctional communications within the family. One or both parents habitually emit double-bind messages (communications with multiple, conflicting levels of meaning that the child can neither accept nor reject). The child is mystified both by the constant injection of hidden meaning into seemingly routine messages and by the denial that such hidden meanings exist. The cognitive problems of many schizophrenics strongly resemble their families' transactional patterns of illogic and denial.

Questions	Strategic Thinking
1. Both researchers would agree that: **A.** some of the symptoms of schizophrenia can be treated with drugs. **B.** some of the symptoms of schizophrenia are similar to those of Parkinson's disease. **C.** schizophrenia is caused by imbalances in neurotransmitters. **D.** schizophrenia is caused by early childhood exposure to dysfunctional communications.	Since this question asks about both viewpoints, come back to this question during Step 3, after answering all questions that ask about just one viewpoint. Because the researchers disagree about what causes schizophrenia, you should immediately rule out C and D, which discuss the causes of the illness. Researcher 2 does not mention Parkinson's disease, so B cannot be correct either. Both researchers do mention that drugs have been effective in the treatment of schizophrenia's symptoms, so (A) is correct.

Questions	Strategic Thinking
2. Which of the following actions would Researcher 2 suggest to prevent schizophrenia in an individual? **F.** Blocking the dopaminergic receptors **G.** Suppressing the release of dopamine **H.** Facilitating effective family communication **J.** Giving the individual regular blood transfusions	Skip this question until after you've answered the question related to the 1st viewpoint and read the 2nd viewpoint. Anything Researcher 2 suggests to prevent schizophrenia can be inferred from the hypothesis—that schizophrenia is caused by early childhood exposure to double-bind communications. Only (H) addresses this cause. Choices F, G, and J are more closely related to Researcher 1's biology-based hypothesis, so they can't be correct.
3. Based on Researcher 1's viewpoint, schizophrenia is caused by: **A.** antipsychotic drugs. **B.** an emotional disorder. **C.** dopamine deficiency. **D.** increased levels of dopamine.	After reading the introductory paragraph and the 1st viewpoint, answer this question first. Researcher 1 believes schizophrenia is related to the hyperactivity of the dopaminergic system (increased levels of dopamine), so the correct answer is (D). Since you have not yet read the 2nd viewpoint, you will not fall for trap answer B, which is Researcher 2's viewpoint. Choices A and C would treat or prevent schizophrenia, according to Scientist 1.

DETERMINE WHETHER INFORMATION IS CONSISTENT WITH A THEORY

Another Evaluation of Models question type will ask you to identify evidence, hypotheses, conclusions, or predictions that are consistent (or, less often, inconsistent) with a particular viewpoint or another piece of passage information. To be consistent means that the new information agrees with the information from the passage; in other words, both could be true at the same time. On the other hand, to be inconsistent means that the new information conflicts with the relevant parts of the passage; both could not be true at the same time. When answering these questions, make sure you understand exactly what each theory states and how the new information relates to the theories—does it agree or conflict?

IDENTIFY WHAT STRENGTHENS OR WEAKENS THEORIES

Evaluation of Models questions can also test your ability to understand the reasoning and evidence that backs up theories. It's common to see at least one question with a Conflicting Viewpoints passage that asks about strengthening or weakening. You will be asked either to determine whether new information in the question stem strengthens/weakens one or more of the viewpoints or to identify a piece of strengthening/weakening evidence among the answer choices.

Information that strengthens a theory makes the theory more likely to be true, while information that weakens a theory makes it less likely to be true. The information does not have to prove a viewpoint true in order to strengthen it, nor does it have to prove it false to weaken it. Your job is simply to judge whether the information adds to or detracts from any part of the theory. Remember that questions require little outside knowledge, so you will generally be provided with all the information you need to answer them. Refer back to the passage and reread the relevant parts if necessary to understand exactly what each theory is saying and how it relates to the new information.

In many of the cases you'll encounter on Test Day, a theory is not strengthened simply by refuting the competing theory or theories but only by positive evidence in favor of the theory itself. Likewise, a theory is generally not weakened simply by evidence for a competing theory but only by information that directly challenges the theory itself. Of course, there are exceptions to these rules, such as when two theories take diametrically opposed positions on a particular issue.

Consider the following Conflicting Viewpoints passage and question set. After the passage, the left column contains questions similar to those you'll see on the ACT Science test on Test Day. The right column features the strategic thinking a test expert might employ when approaching the passage and question presented. Once again, pay special attention to how the expert uses the Kaplan Method for Conflicting Viewpoints.

Strategic Thinking
Step 1: Read the introductory paragraph(s) and the 1st viewpoint, then search for questions that ask only about the 1st viewpoint and answer them Read the passage and note the key phrases and main points that have been underlined. Remember to read for the central claim and do not dwell on the technical details. Answer Questions 6 and 8 first, which ask about the 1st viewpoint.
Step 2: Read the 2nd viewpoint, then search for questions that ask only about the 2nd viewpoint and answer them; if there are additional viewpoints, repeat this process with each of them Read for the central claim and note the underlined key phrases and main points. Answer Question 5, which asks about the 2nd viewpoint.
Step 3: Answer questions that ask about multiple viewpoints and any other remaining questions Answer Questions 4, 7, and 9, which ask about both the 1st and 2nd viewpoints.

Science

Questions 4–9 are based on the following passage.

Passage II

At the deepest part of a breath, when the lungs have the greatest force, the lungs fill up the rib cage and then lift the ribs. The ribs lift the spine, and the force is transferred from the top of the spine to a bone of the skull called the occipital bone. The result is a yawn. Yawning has been associated with drowsiness or weariness, as well as acute myocardial infarction and aortic dissection. However, the reasons why humans yawn remain unconfirmed. Two students offer their own hypotheses on the functions of yawning.

Student 1

Yawning is the human body's way of crying out for more oxygen in the bloodstream. Most yawns occur when a person is tired or bored. At such times, the body is not functioning at its optimal level and requires an increase in oxygen to return to normal activities. The respiratory system responds to this need by inducing a yawn. The deep breath of a yawn provides a sudden increase in the amount of oxygen in the blood and simultaneously rids the body of the excess carbon dioxide that has accumulated because of oxygen deficiency.

Student 2

Recent studies have shown that the number of times a person yawns is not affected by the amount of oxygen in the air he or she breathes. Oxygen-rich, oxygen-depleted, and normal air all lead to the same average number of yawns in a given time period. Respiration, therefore, is not the primary function of yawning. Both yawning and stretching most commonly occur during periods of tiredness. Thus, it is far more likely that yawning is actually a stretching mechanism. Particularly striking support for this theory is found in the behavior of people who are paralyzed on one side of their bodies from a stroke. It has been observed that such people can stretch limbs on the otherwise paralyzed sides of their bodies when they yawn.

Questions	Strategic Thinking
4. Suppose there is a correlation between the amount of oxygen in the air and the number of times a person yawns in a day. If true, this would strengthen the view of: F. Student 1, who argues respiration is a function of yawning. G. Student 1, who argues stretching is a function of yawning. H. Student 2, who argues respiration is a function of yawning. J. Student 2, who argues stretching is a function of yawning.	Since this question asks about both viewpoints, skip it until Step 3, after you've answered all the questions that ask about a single viewpoint. How does the new information in the question stem relate to each student's viewpoint? Student 1 argues that the amount of oxygen in the air affects the number of times a person yawns, and Student 2 argues that yawning is a stretching mechanism. Choices G and H can be eliminated, because they assign the students to the wrong explanations. You should also eliminate J, because the new information is not related to stretching but respiration. The correct answer is (F).

Questions	Strategic Thinking
5. According to Student 2, the best evidence that yawning is associated with stretching is that: **A.** individuals who are paralyzed on one side can stretch their mobile side by yawning. **B.** individuals who are paralyzed on one side can stretch limbs on both sides by yawning. **C.** most yawns occur when a person lacks oxygen in the bloodstream. **D.** most people yawn regardless of whether or not they are tired.	Come back to this question during Step 2, after you've answered questions related to the 1st viewpoint. Student 2 says "yawning is actually a stretching mechanism." To see the evidence for this, recall that Student 2 points to studies showing that "people who are paralyzed…can stretch limbs on the otherwise paralyzed sides of their bodies when they yawn." This matches (B). Choice A might be tempting because it starts off right, so be sure you are reading carefully. Choice C would support Student 1's viewpoint. Choice D is incorrect because Student 2 does not cite it as the *best evidence*.
6. Student 1 states that yawning is a body's way of bringing more oxygen into the bloodstream. Which of the following, if true, would weaken this statement? **F.** A person's blood oxygen levels neither increase nor decrease after a yawn. **G.** A person's blood oxygen levels always increase after a yawn. **H.** A person's blood carbon dioxide levels always decrease after a yawn. **J.** A person's muscles are insufficiently stretched by a yawn.	Since this question asks about the 1st viewpoint, answer this question first during Step 1. Then look for other questions that ask about the 1st viewpoint. To counter a statement, you should ask yourself which answer choice would make it less likely to be true. If a person's oxygen levels don't change after a yawn, then it can't be that yawns function to increase the amount of oxygen in the blood. Choice (F) is correct. Choice G is incorrect because it supports, not counters, the statement. Choice H is incorrect because you're told that an increase in oxygen flushes out excess carbon dioxide. A decrease in carbon dioxide, then, would support the statement. Choice J is irrelevant to the statement, but instead concerns Student 2's hypothesis.

Questions	Strategic Thinking
7. Student 1 and Student 2 would agree that: **A.** yawns are caused by tiredness or boredom. **B.** yawns are caused by acute myocardial infarction and aortic dissection. **C.** the primary cause of yawns is biological, not social. **D.** yawns are caused by a need to stretch.	Since this question asks about both viewpoints, come back to it in Step 3, after answering questions about only one viewpoint. Start by looking at the answer choices, because the question stem offers few clues. Choice D should be eliminated, because this is the viewpoint of Student 2 only. You can also eliminate A because, while both students agree that yawns occur during periods of tiredness or boredom, neither describes this as the cause of yawns. Choice B misstates what is said in the introduction (the introduction says *associated with,* not *caused by*). Choice (C) accurately reflects that both students agree the cause is biological in nature. You may have heard from other sources the theory that yawning is a social phenomenon (for example, one person yawns when they see another yawn), but that theory is not addressed in the passage.
8. According to Student 1, which of the following would keep a person from yawning? **F.** Increasing the amount of carbon dioxide in the bloodstream **G.** Stretching throughout the day **H.** Reducing pressure on the lungs **J.** Increasing the amount of oxygen in the bloodstream	This question also asks about the 1st viewpoint, so answer it before moving on to Step 2 of the Method. Student 1's main argument is that a lack of oxygen in the bloodstream leads to an increase in the number of yawns. Thus, (J) is consistent with the theory and is the correct answer. Choice F would likely increase the need to yawn, based on Student 1's explanation. Choice G is related to Student 2, not Student 1, while H distorts information from the introductory paragraph.

Questions	Strategic Thinking
9. A sleep center study found that individuals who had been awake for more than 24 hours yawned 1.5 times more frequently than those who had been awake for fewer than 12 hours. What conclusion would each student draw from this information? **A.** Student 1 would conclude that a lack of sleep caused an increased need to stretch; Student 2 would conclude that a lack of sleep caused an increased need for oxygen. **B.** Student 1 would conclude that a lack of sleep caused an increased need for oxygen; Student 2 would conclude that a lack of sleep caused an increased need to stretch. **C.** Both students would agree that a lack of sleep caused an increased need for oxygen. **D.** Both students would agree that a lack of sleep caused an increased need to stretch.	This question asks about both viewpoints, so skip this question until you've answered the other questions. Save time on this question by eliminating an answer choice as soon as you see something false in it. To determine which statement is consistent with the theories and the new information, think about what each viewpoint suggests. Choice A reverses the students' viewpoints: Student 2 connected yawning to stretching, and Student 1 connected yawning to oxygen deprivation. Choice (B) is consistent with the theories and therefore the correct answer: Student 1 would likely conclude that a lack of sleep caused an increased need for oxygen, while Student 2 would likely conclude that a lack of sleep caused an increased need to stretch. Choice C is wrong about Student 2: only Student 1 would consider the need for oxygen. Choice D is wrong about Student 1: only Student 2 would consider the need to stretch.

You have seen the ways in which the ACT tests you with Conflicting Viewpoints passages and Evaluation of Models questions, as well as the way an ACT expert might approach these passages and questions.

Now, use the Kaplan Method for Conflicting Viewpoints to answer the seven questions that accompany the following Science passage. Part of the test-like passage has been annotated already. Your first step is to complete marking up the passage. Strategic thinking questions have been included to guide you—some of the answers have been filled in, but you will have to fill in the answers to others.

Use your answers to the strategic thinking questions to select the correct answer, just as you would on Test Day.

Strategic Thinking
Step 1: Read the introductory paragraph(s) and the 1st viewpoint, then search for questions that ask only about the 1st viewpoint and answer them
The passage below is partially annotated. The introductory paragraph and 1st viewpoint have already been marked up. After you read it, move on to the questions and answer all those that ask only about the 1st viewpoint, which includes only Question 14.
Step 2: Read the 2nd viewpoint, then search for questions that ask only about the 2nd viewpoint and answer them; if there are additional viewpoints, repeat this process with each of them
Finish marking up the passage by underlining the central claim and key phrases in the 2nd viewpoint.
Which questions ask only about the 2nd viewpoint?
_____
Step 3: Answer questions that ask about multiple viewpoints and any other remaining questions
Which questions ask about multiple viewpoints?
_____

Questions 10–16 are based on the following passage.

Passage III

When the Voyager 2 spacecraft passed near Triton, the largest moon of Neptune, the pictures it transmitted of the surface became a source of controversy. Two scientists present <u>possible explanations of Triton's surface features</u>.

Scientist 1

The images of Triton seem to indicate <u>recent volcanic activity</u>, probably from <u>millions or tens of millions of years ago</u>. We can see no large-scale blemishes from around 4 billion years ago, when, shortly after the formation of our solar system, swarms of planetoids struck elsewhere. <u>Many features are clearly visible that appear to be recently formed lava lakes</u>, similar to the ice-lava lakes found on Jupiter's moon Ganymede. <u>Other features resemble the icy slush</u> found flowing from fractures on Uranus's Ariel. There even seems to be <u>ongoing volcanic activity</u>; this would <u>explain the dark streaks seen in several places on the surface</u>. We know that Triton's surface is covered with a thick layer of methane and nitrogen ice. It would take only a relatively small amount of internal heat to boil nitrogen to drive a nitrogen volcano. It can't be ruled out that <u>Triton has a source of internal heat</u>, like the <u>radioactive decay</u> within Earth, that <u>supplies sufficient energy for volcanic reactions</u>.

Scientist 2

The surface features we have observed on Triton can all be explained without assuming any volcanism within the last 4 billion years. Undoubtedly, Triton was molten for some time past the earliest days of the solar system. Its unusual orbit—it revolves in the direction opposite to the planet's rotation—indicates that it was captured by Neptune. The original orbit must have been highly elliptical and the gravitational stresses enormous, leading to frictional heating. But Triton has been settled into its current circular orbit for billions of years. Closer examination of the Voyager 2 images, particularly the higher-resolution pictures, shows many small craters on Triton due to the impact of small meteorites over a long period of time. What appear as lava lakes and volcanic-flows from fractures are most likely the result of the glacier-like movement of the methane-nitrogen polar ice caps. The dark streaks are probably the result of methane-nitrogen "snowfall." Finally, Triton's size—much smaller than that of Earth—rules out the possibility of internal heating.

Questions	Strategic Thinking
10. Scientists 1 and 2 would be most likely to agree that: **F.** volcanic activity has occurred on Triton within the last million years. **G.** Triton may be internally heated by natural radioactive decay. **H.** nitrogen and methane snowfalls cause dark streaks on Triton. **J.** the surface of Triton contains methane and nitrogen ice.	*What are the keywords in the question stem?* The keywords in the question stem are *Scientists 1 and 2* and *agree*. *When should you answer this question?* Since this question asks about both viewpoints, answer it during Step 3. *Although the scientists have very different theories, what do they have in common?* _____ _____ _____ *Which answer choice reflects the agreement?* _____
11. Scientist 2 points out that many small craters have been seen on Triton, particularly in the higher-resolution images, in order to: **A.** contradict Scientist 1's claim that there are no signs of planetoids having struck Triton. **B.** provide evidence of recent volcanic activity on the surface of Triton. **C.** demonstrate that some of Triton's surface features have evolved over a long period of time. **D.** emphasize that Scientist 1's view is based on lower-resolution images of Triton.	*What are the keywords in the question stem?* The keywords in the question stem are *Scientist 2* and *small craters*. *When should you answer this question?* Since this question asks about the 2nd viewpoint, answer it during Step 2. *Where can you find the corresponding information in the passage?* Go back to the passage and reread the part where Scientist 2 discusses higher-resolution images. *Which answer choice matches the viewpoint?* _____

Science

Questions	Strategic Thinking

12. Which of the following instruments, if included in a future mission to Triton, would supply additional information likely to resolve the controversy between Scientists 1 and 2 ?
 	
    I. A mass spectrometer capable of chemically analyzing Triton's surface
 	
    II. An infrared sensor able to determine surface and subsurface temperatures
 	
    III. A subatomic particle detector that could determine core radioactivity
 	
  F. I and II only
  G. I and III only
  H. II and III only
  J. I, II, and III
	What are the keywords in the question stem?
	
	The keywords in the question stem are *Scientists 1 and 2* and *resolve the controversy.*
	
	When should you answer this question?
	
	Come back to this question that asks about both viewpoints during Step 3.
	
	Which items would provide evidence that could resolve the controversy over whether there is volcanic activity on Triton?
	
	_____
	
	_____
	
	Which answer choice contains exactly those items?
	_____

13. Scientists 1 and 2 disagree about:
  A. the presence of dark streaks visible in images of Triton.
  B. the physical processes responsible for features seen in images of Triton.
  C. the chemical composition of the surface of Triton.
  D. the origin of Triton.
	What are the keywords in the question stem?
	
	_____
	
	_____
	
	When should you answer this question?
	
	_____
	
	What is the biggest difference between the theories of Scientist 1 and Scientist 2?
	
	_____
	
	_____
	
	_____
	
	Which answer choice reflects the disagreement?
	_____

Science

Questions	Strategic Thinking
14. Which of the following discoveries would most conclusively support the viewpoint of Scientist 1 ? **F.** Triton's surface has the same composition as Ganymede's and Ariel's. **G.** The apparent small craters seen in the high resolution pictures of Triton were introduced by faulty image processing. **H.** Further inspection of images from Triton reveals an erupting volcano. **J.** Triton is shown not to have been captured by Neptune but to have originated together with Neptune.	*What are the keywords in the question stem?* The keywords in the question stem are *Scientist 1* and *support*. *When should you answer this question?* Since this question asks about Scientist 1 only, you should answer it during Step 1. *What does the viewpoint state about the source of the surface features on Triton?* According to Scientist 1, a number of features on Triton arise from volcanic activity. *Which answer choice provides evidence of an active volcano on Triton?* _____
15. New research suggests that slow radioactive decay may persist in a body much smaller than Earth for up to 10 billion years. This information, if true, supports the viewpoint of: **A.** Scientist 1 only. **B.** Scientist 2 only. **C.** both Scientist 1 and Scientist 2. **D.** neither Scientist 1 nor Scientist 2.	*What are the keywords in the question stem?* _____ _____ *When should you answer this question?* _____ *Does the new information strengthen either, neither, or both of the viewpoints from the passage?* _____ _____ *Which answer choice matches?* _____

Questions	Strategic Thinking

16. Based on Scientist 2's description of Triton's orbit, what must be true about a typical moon?
 	
  F. Most moons travel in circular orbits.
 	
  G. Most moons are less than 10,000 km from the planets they orbit.
 	
  H. Most moons are much smaller than the planets they orbit.
 	
  J. Most moons revolve in the direction of their planet's rotation.
	What are the keywords in the question stem?
	
	_____
	
	_____
	
	When should you answer this question?
	
	_____
	
	Where can you find the corresponding information in the passage?
	
	_____
	
	_____
	
	Which answer choice is consistent with the viewpoint? _____

Science

Now try some test-like Conflicting Viewpoints passages on your own. The following passages provide an opportunity to practice the concepts and strategic thinking covered in this chapter. Give yourself 12 minutes to read the passages and answer the questions.

Questions 17–23 are based on the following passage.

Passage IV

Two scientists present various grounds for classifying the giant panda (*Ailuropoda melanoleuca*) as a raccoon or as a bear.

Scientist 1

Although the giant panda superficially resembles bears (*Ursidae*), many of its anatomical, behavioral, and genetic characteristics are closer to those of raccoons (*Procyonidae*). The bones and teeth of *Ailuropoda melanoleuca*, for example, are very similar in structure to those of the raccoon. While male bears can be up to 100% larger than females of the same species, male giant pandas and raccoons differ very little in size from females of their species. Like the raccoon, the giant panda has a friendly greeting that consists of bleating and barking. When intimidated, both animals cover their eyes with their front paws. Most bears do not exhibit these behaviors. Finally, *Ailuropoda melanoleuca* and *Procyonidae* have 21 and 19 pairs of chromosomes, respectively, while *Ursidae* have 36 pairs.

Scientist 2

Giant pandas should be classified as *Ursidae*. Research studies have shown that the ancestors of *Ailuropoda melanoleuca* had about 40 chromosomal pairs; geneticists theorize that the reduction occurred when the chromosomes underwent head-to-head fusion. Other research has shown that the DNA of the giant panda is far more similar to that of the *Ursidae* than to that of any other family. Furthermore, giant pandas and other bears are not only of similar size, but also have very similar body proportions and walk with the same pigeon-toed gait. Giant pandas display aggressive behavior in the same manner as do other bears, by swatting and trying to grab adversaries with their forepaws.

17. According to Scientist 2, the giant panda should be classified as a bear because:

   A. there is little disparity in the size of male and female giant pandas.

   B. the greeting rituals of the giant panda resemble those of bears.

   C. both bears and giant pandas are herbivorous.

   D. the DNA of giant pandas is similar to that of bears.

18. Scientist 1 and Scientist 2 would most likely agree on which of the following points?

   F. Giant pandas should be classified in a separate family.

   G. The giant panda should not be classified as a raccoon.

   H. Raccoons and bears are physically and behaviorally very similar.

   J. Animals should be classified into families based on physical, behavioral, and genetic traits.

19. According to Scientist 1, which of the following is the giant panda most likely to do when frightened?

   A. Bleat and bark

   B. Cover its eyes with its paws

   C. Swat and grab with its forepaws

   D. Walk away pigeon-toed

20. Based on the passage, which of the following characteristics would support the classification of a mammal as a member of the *Ursidae* family?

    I. 36 pairs of chromosomes and DNA similar to that of many bear species

    II. Raccoon-like markings and 19 pairs of chromosomes

    III. 62% greater average size among males than among females

    F. I only

    G. II only

    H. I and III only

    J. II and III only

21. Which of the following, if true, would provide additional support for the hypothesis of Scientist 2 ?

    A. The blood proteins of giant pandas are very similar to those of several bear species.

    B. Giant pandas and raccoons have similar markings, including dark rings around their eyes.

    C. Giant pandas have 21 pairs of chromosomes, while raccoons have only 19 pairs.

    D. There is little difference in size between male and female giant pandas.

22. Suppose that giant pandas have scent-releasing glands. This fact could be used to support the viewpoint of:

    F. Scientist 1, if it were shown that raccoons also have scent-releasing glands.

    G. Scientist 2, if it were shown that bears do not have scent-releasing glands.

    H. Scientist 1, if it were shown that raccoons have a poor sense of smell.

    J. Scientist 2, if it were shown that bears urinate to lay down their scent.

23. Which of the following claims could Scientist 1 use as an effective counter against Scientist 2's claims about the behavior of giant pandas and bears?

    A. The giant panda walks with a pigeon-toed gait.

    B. Unlike most bears but like raccoons, an aggressive giant panda bobs its head up and down.

    C. The giant panda swats and grabs at its adversaries.

    D. Unlike most bears, the giant panda has only 19 pairs of chromosomes.

Questions 24–30 are based on the following passage.

Passage V

Gastric ulcers are sores that form on the lining of the stomach. Normally, the gastric mucosa, a thick mucous membrane layer, protects the stomach from digestive juices, which contain hydrochloric acid and an enzyme called pepsin. The gastric mucosa also removes hydrogen ions and secretes bicarbonate ions to maintain a neutral environment in the mucosal layer. Ulcers form when the gastric mucosa is reduced and/or damaged, enabling digestive juices to eat away at the exposed stomach lining tissues. Three scientists discuss possible causes of gastric ulcers.

Scientist 1

Lifestyle habits are the most common etiological factors of gastric ulcers. People who drink caffeinated and carbonated beverages and eat spicy and acidic foods are more likely to develop ulcers. This type of diet leads to hyperacidity in the stomach, which damages the gastric mucosa. Stress, especially prolonged physical and emotional stress, can also cause gastric ulcers. It has been shown that people in stressful situations experience increased gastric acidity, necrosis of mucosal cells, and changes in the mucous barrier.

Scientist 2

There is no clear evidence that diet and stress cause gastric ulcers. Lifestyle habits may aggravate existing ulcers, but the causative agent is the bacterium *Helicobacter pylori* (*H. pylori*). Studies have found that people with gastric ulcers test positive for *H. pylori*. The bacterium lives and grows on the stomach lining tissues, disrupting the mucus barrier and increasing the amount of digestive juices produced. This causes ulcers to form on the underlying tissue. When people with gastric ulcers were administered only acid-suppressing drugs, 80% experienced recurrence of ulcers, whereas only 6% of those treated solely with antibiotics for *H. pylori* infection experienced recurrence.

Scientist 3

Over half of the world's population is infected with *H. pylori*, but not all of those infected with *H. pylori* will develop an ulcer. The bacterium, as well as consuming caffeine and spicy foods, may contribute to the development of ulcers but not to the underlying cause. The major cause of ulcers is nonsteroidal anti-inflammatory drugs (NSAIDs) such as ibuprofen and aspirin. NSAIDs decrease inflammation, which is caused by prostaglandins, a natural chemical in the body. However, certain prostaglandins promote the secretion of mucus and bicarbonate ions. Thus, chronic use of NSAIDs disrupts the production of prostaglandins in the stomach and leads to an increase in gastric acid and decrease in mucus. This imbalance causes the formation of ulcers.

24. What would Scientists 1 and 2 each suggest as treatment for gastric ulcers?

   F. Scientist 1 would suggest antacids, and Scientist 2 would suggest antibiotics.

   G. Scientist 1 would suggest antibiotics, and Scientist 2 would suggest antacids.

   H. Scientist 1 would suggest antacids, and Scientist 2 would suggest NSAIDs.

   J. Scientist 1 would suggest NSAIDs, and Scientist 2 would suggest antibiotics.

25. According to the passage, the gastric mucosa does all of the following EXCEPT:

   A. protect the stomach lining.

   B. remove hydrogen ions.

   C. promote necrosis of cells.

   D. secrete bicarbonate ions.

26. Scientist 3 would predict that an increase in gastric ulcers is due to:

 F. increased intake of acidic foods.

 G. increased growth of *H. pylori* on stomach lining tissue.

 H. decreased levels of prostaglandins in the stomach.

 J. decreased use of NSAIDs.

27. Which of the following discoveries, if accurate, would strengthen the viewpoint of Scientist 1 but weaken the viewpoint of Scientist 2 ?

 A. Emotional stress causes a decrease in the number of ulcers that test negative for *H. pylori*.

 B. Emotional stress causes a decrease in the number of ulcers that test positive for *H. pylori*.

 C. Emotional stress causes an increase in the number of ulcers that test negative for *H. pylori*.

 D. Emotional stress causes an increase in the number of ulcers that test positive for *H. pylori*.

28. Which of the following statements would all three scientists most likely agree on?

 F. Consuming NSAIDs causes gastric ulcers.

 G. Taking antibiotics increases prostaglandins secretion.

 H. Taking antacids effectively treats gastric ulcers.

 J. Consuming caffeinated drinks and spicy foods aggravates existing gastric ulcers.

29. Suppose a person 65 years old with arthritis developed a gastric ulcer. Which of the following statements is most consistent with the information in the passage?

 A. Scientist 1 would conclude the person chronically uses NSAIDs.

 B. Scientist 2 would conclude the person experiences chronic stress.

 C. Scientist 3 would conclude the person is infected with *H. pylori*.

 D. Scientist 3 would conclude the person chronically uses NSAIDs.

30. Which of the following arguments could Scientist 1 use to counter Scientist 2's evidence that acid-suppressing drugs are ineffective treatments for ulcers?

 F. *H. pylori* were not completely eliminated by the acid-suppressing drugs.

 G. The way the acid-suppressing drugs were administered in the study led to significant increases in stress.

 H. The patients in the study were also taking NSAIDs along with the acid-suppressing drugs.

 J. The acid-suppressing drugs neutralized the digestive juices in the stomach.

Answers and Explanations are provided at the end of the book.

ON YOUR OWN

The following questions provide an opportunity to practice the concepts and strategic thinking covered in this chapter.

Questions 1–7 are based on the following passage.

Passage I

Will the universe continue to expand, or will it eventually collapse? The answer to this question depends on the average density of the matter in the universe. If it is greater than a certain critical density (6×10^{-27} kg/m^3), then the universe is "closed" and it will eventually stop expanding and begin contracting. If the average density is less than this critical value, then the universe is "open" and the expansion will continue indefinitely. Two scientists present their views on this issue.

Scientist 1

Astronomers can estimate the average density of the universe by tabulating all the detectable matter over a large volume of the universe. The mass of galaxies, intergalactic stars, and gas has been determined from luminosity (brightness) measurements. From these measurements, the average density of the universe was calculated to be only 3×10^{-28} kg/m^3 or 5% of the critical value. Therefore, the universe is open and will continue to expand.

Scientist 2

There is a great deal more mass in the universe than has been detected. Observations of the motions of stars in other galaxies indicate that the force of gravity is greater than the total mass of the detected matter in those galaxies could possibly exert. The missing mass must be non-luminous matter that cannot be detected by luminosity measurements.

Taking this "dark" matter into consideration, the average density of the universe does exceed the critical value. Therefore, the universe must be closed—it will eventually stop expanding and collapse.

1. Scientist 1 and Scientist 2 disagree on the point that:

    A. the universe will be closed if its actual density is greater than the critical density.

    B. luminosity measurements are related to brightness.

    C. some of the matter in the universe has not been detected.

    D. luminosity measurements can be used to calculate the universe's density accurately.

2. Both scientists make the assumption that:

    F. the universe is currently static.

    G. the universe is currently contracting.

    H. the universe is currently expanding.

    J. the critical density cannot be determined.

3. Scientist 2 believes that the missing mass in the universe:

    A. does not exist.

    B. will never be detected.

    C. is made up of non-luminous matter.

    D. is made up of an alien form of matter.

4. According to Scientist 1, the average density of the universe can be determined by:

    I. measuring luminosities.

    II. studying the motions of planets in other galaxies.

    III. determining the mass of non-luminous matter.

    F. I only

    G. II only

    H. I and III only

    J. II and III only

5. To support her hypothesis, Scientist 2 could attempt to:

    A. find a way to measure the mass of non-luminous matter in a large portion of the universe.

    B. show that the universe's average density is exactly 27% of the critical value.

    C. determine the origin of the universe.

    D. develop a method for measuring the temperature at which galaxies come together.

6. Suppose that new measurements were taken, leading to a new scientific consensus that the average density of matter in the universe is greater than the critical density. Which of the following statements could most reasonably be inferred from this new information and the information from the passage?

    F. The new density must come entirely from non-luminous matter.

    G. The new mass accounts for at least 95% of the density of the universe.

    H. The motions of the stars in other galaxies is inconsistent with the new information.

    J. The universe should be considered open.

7. The evidence presented by Scientist 1 supports which of the following conclusions?

    A. The universe is much closer to the critical density than current calculations indicate.

    B. The critical density of the universe is about 20 times greater than its actual density.

    C. The total mass of stars cannot be determined from their brightness.

    D. Non-luminous matter accounts for about 5% of the total mass of the universe.

Questions 8–14 are based on the following passage.

Passage II

The first prokaryotes (single-celled organisms with no nucleus) appeared two billion years before the first eukaryotes (organisms whose cells contain a nucleus). Most bacteria are prokaryotes, while most complex organisms consist of eukaryotic cells. Eukaryotic cells contain mitochondria, rod-shaped energy-producing organelles. Different from other organelles in the cell, mitochondria are surrounded by two membranes, contain their own DNA, and divide independently from the host cell. Two scientists discuss the evolutionary origin of mitochondria-containing eukaryotes.

Scientist 1

Mitochondria-containing eukaryotes developed from an endosymbiotic relationship between two types of prokaryotes. Early prokaryotes were anaerobic, meaning they did not require oxygen to survive. There was virtually no free oxygen in Earth's atmosphere until prokaryotes began releasing oxygen as a metabolic by-product. As the oxygen levels in the atmosphere rose, some prokaryotes evolved into aerobes to utilize the free oxygen. Since anaerobic prokaryotes could not metabolize oxygen, they engulfed the aerobic prokaryotes. This endosymbiotic relationship resulted in the aerobes gaining a secure environment and a continuous food supply and the anaerobes gaining the ability to survive in an oxygen-rich environment. Over time, the symbiotic partners lost their independence, and the aerobic prokaryotes evolved into mitochondria. For that reason, mitochondrial DNA differs both genetically and structurally from the DNA in the eukaryotic cell's nucleus.

Scientist 2

The DNA, ribosomal proteins, and membranes of mitochondria structurally differ from those of bacteria. Therefore, mitochondria could not have evolved from the endosymbiosis of two prokaryotes. It is far more likely that eukaryotes first developed directly from a single prokaryote and then the mitochondria developed from the membrane of the cell. Although mitochondria, like prokaryotes, synthesize several of the enzymes necessary for their own function, most mitochondrial proteins are controlled by genes in the nucleus of the eukaryotic cell and are synthesized outside of the mitochondria. Moreover, the key components of mitochondrial DNA replication are more eukaryotic in nature than prokaryotic, indicating mitochondria originated inside the eukaryotic cell.

8. Scientist 1 and Scientist 2 would mostly likely agree that mitochondria:

   F. originated from the membrane of a eukaryotic cell.

   G. originated from aerobic prokaryotes.

   H. contain their own DNA.

   J. cannot self-replicate.

9. According to Scientist 1, an endosymbiotic relationship arose between two prokaryotes because:

   A. aerobic bacteria were not able to utilize free oxygen.

   B. anaerobic bacteria did not require oxygen to survive.

   C. mitochondria use oxygen to generate energy.

   D. the Earth's atmosphere became oxygen-rich.

10. Scientist 1 states that the best evidence that mitochondria evolved from bacteria is that:

    F. mitochondrial DNA is structurally different from DNA in the eukaryotic nucleus.

    G. ribosomal proteins of mitochondria and bacteria are different.

    H. eukaryotes developed directly from a single bacterium.

    J. mitochondria have a single outer membrane.

11. Mitochondrial DNA molecules are circular, having the same structure as prokaryotic DNA. This information, if true, strengthens the viewpoint of:

    A. Scientist 1 only.

    B. Scientist 2 only.

    C. both Scientist 1 and Scientist 2.

    D. neither Scientist 1 nor Scientist 2.

Science

12. Scientist 2 emphasizes the differences between mitochondria and bacteria in order to:

    F. demonstrate the prokaryotic nature of mitochondria.

    G. illustrate the superior aerobic capacity of mitochondria.

    H. prove that bacteria are genetically less complex than mitochondria.

    J. argue that mitochondria could not have evolved from aerobic prokaryotes.

13. Suppose a study shows that mitochondria divide by binary fission, much like bacteria. This study could be used to support the viewpoint of:

    A. Scientist 1, who states mitochondria originated from aerobic eukaryotes.

    B. Scientist 1, who states mitochondria originated from aerobic prokaryotes.

    C. Scientist 2, who states mitochondria originated from an endosymbiotic relationship between prokaryotes.

    D. Scientist 2, who states mitochondria originated from the membrane of eukaryotes.

14. Which of the following arguments could Scientist 1 use to respond effectively to Scientist 2's claim that most mitochondrial proteins originate from outside the mitochondria?

    F. As a result of endosymbiosis, all proteins in a eukaryotic cell are synthesized from genes in the nucleus.

    G. After the two organisms became one, many genes coding for mitochondrial proteins were transferred to the nucleus.

    H. Two billion years ago, prokaryotes evolved to eukaryotes.

    J. Mitochondria do not have the genes to synthesize their own proteins.

Answers and Explanations are provided at the end of the book.

ACT WRITING

BY THE END OF THIS UNIT, YOU WILL BE ABLE TO:

1. Apply the Kaplan Method for ACT Writing

2. Use the Kaplan Template for the ACT Essay to create an effective outline

CHAPTER 24

ACT Writing Introduction

CHAPTER OBJECTIVES

By the end of this chapter, you will be able to:

1. Identify the structure and format of the ACT Writing test

2. Recognize the standard components of ACT Writing prompts

SHOULD I TAKE THE ACT WRITING TEST?

The Writing test is optional. If you don't want to spend 40 minutes writing an essay, you certainly don't have to. You are free to leave after the final multiple-choice section of the test.

However, just because you can leave without completing the ACT Writing test doesn't mean that you should. If you can state with 100% certainty that the colleges to which you are applying do not require the ACT Writing test, feel free to omit it on Test Day. However, if you are unsure, or don't yet have a finalized list of colleges, Kaplan recommends you complete the ACT Writing test for two reasons:

First, consider the fact that the ACT is not an exam you can take in bits and pieces. If you want to take the ACT Writing test at a later date, you'll have to sit through the entire ACT again. That can translate to a lot of unnecessary stress during your senior year.

Second, while the ACT Writing test can be challenging, it is also standardized. That means you can learn how to write a high-scoring essay by putting in time, effort, and practice. This chapter is a great place to start.

INSIDE THE ACT WRITING TEST

The Writing test is 40 minutes long and includes one prompt. You will use that time to read the prompt and then plan, write, and proofread your response.

The ACT Writing test is designed to gauge your ability to compose a clear and logical argument and effectively present that argument in written form.

The writing prompt will present a specific, complex issue and three perspectives on it. You are asked to analyze those multiple perspectives and to arrive at a point of view on the issue. Then you must state your point of view clearly, support it with clear and relevant examples, and compare it to at least one other perspective.

THE FORMAT

Although a different issue will be presented on each ACT Writing test, the Writing test directions, prompt format, and essay task will always be the same. This means that, by becoming familiar with the expectations ahead of time, you will save yourself valuable time on Test Day. When other students will be busy wading through the directions and figuring out what to do, you will be able to jump right into reading through the issues and perspectives. The predictable format also means that with preparation and practice, you can achieve success on the ACT Writing test.

TEST DAY DIRECTIONS AND FORMAT

Familiarize yourself with the directions ahead of time so you will not need to spend time reading them on Test Day. Although the exact wording might vary, here's what the Writing directions could look like:

Directions: The essay is used to evaluate your writing skills. You will have **40 minutes** to review the prompt and plan and write an essay in English. Before you begin, read everything in this test booklet carefully to make sure you understand the task.

Your essay will be judged based on the evidence it provides of your ability to do the following:

- Assert your own perspective on a complex issue and evaluate the relationship between your perspective and at least one other perspective

- Use reasoning and evidence to refine and justify your ideas

- Present your ideas in an organized way

- Convey your ideas effectively using standard written English

Write your essay on the lined essay pages in the answer booklet. All writing on those lined pages will be scored. Use the unlined pages in the test booklet to plan your essay. Your work on these unlined pages will not be scored.

Put your pencil down as soon as time is called.

Writing

The next page in your test booklet will contain the actual **writing prompt** for the specific issue you will be asked to analyze on Test Day. Remember, although the issue will be different on each test, the format of the prompt will be the same:

- The prompt will contain a **paragraph** that summarizes the issue in question. Read this paragraph carefully, marking key words and important ideas. Pay special attention to any questions that are raised, which are usually at the end of the paragraph.

- After the introductory paragraph, there will be three boxes that summarize **three viewpoints** about the issue.

- After the three boxes will be a large box containing the **essay task**. The task will always be the same, so again, familiarize yourself with it before Test Day.

If you would like to read through the exact wording you will see on Test Day, visit the test maker's website and download the Preparing for the ACT guide.

American History Curriculum

Educators and curriculum designers continuously debate the best way to teach American history to high school students. Whether students are reading historical interpretations or primary source documents, teachers often put the most emphasis on memorizing important names and dates. Although history is generally regarded as a compilation of facts, should high school students be expected to learn more about history than general information regarding famous people and events? Given the richness of American history, it is worthwhile to explore best practices in presenting the story of the United States to students.

Read and carefully consider these perspectives. Each suggests a particular way of teaching American history.

Perspective One	Perspective Two	Perspective Three
It is important to focus on a nation's prominent historical leaders when studying history. Leaders are representative of the nation as a whole, so studying historical figures provides a full perspective.	The clearest lens through which to view a nation's history is the welfare of its entire population. It is only through an examination of the ways in which society has been affected by historical events that students will truly understand a nation's foundation.	In order to learn the story of America, students need to know what happened, when, and who influenced those events. Becoming familiar with and being tested on important dates and events is the most effective way to study history. Students need to know what happened in years past in order to plan for the future.

Writing

Essay Task

Write a clear, well-reasoned essay evaluating multiple perspectives on the most effective way to teach American history to high school students. In your essay, be sure to:

- Assert your own perspective on the issue and evaluate the relationship between your perspective and at least one other perspective

- Use reasoning and evidence to refine and justify your ideas

- Present your ideas in an organized way

- Convey your ideas effectively using standard written English

Your perspective may be fully, somewhat, or not at all in agreement with one or more of the three perspectives in the prompt.

Your test booklet will also include **planning your essay** pages that provide prewriting questions and space for notes. It is helpful to review these prewriting questions ahead of time, but since you will already be familiar with the essay task, don't spend too much time reading the Planning Your Essay questions on Test Day; rather, after carefully reading the essay prompt, begin your planning of the essay according to the Kaplan Method for ACT Writing. Remember that anything you write on these pages will not be scored.

Planning Your Essay

These pages are not scored.

Use the space below to brainstorm and plan your essay. Consider the following as you think about the prompt:

- Strengths and weaknesses of the three perspectives in the prompt

  ○ What observations do they offer, and what do they overlook?

  ○ Why are they persuasive or why are they not persuasive?

- Your own background and identity

  ○ What is your perspective on this issue, and what are its strengths and weaknesses?

  ○ What evidence will you use in your essay?

Again, if you would like to read through the exact wording you will see on Test Day, visit the test maker's website and download the Preparing for the ACT guide.

OUTSIDE KNOWLEDGE

No outside knowledge is required. However, you may choose to strengthen your essay with examples from history, science, literature, or even your own experiences.

THE INSIDE SCOOP

The essay is argument based, not fact based. That is, you're being tested on what you can effectively argue, not what you know about the topic. Does this mean true examples aren't relevant? Yes and no—you will not be scored based on whether your examples are true or not, but you will be scored based on whether you use examples effectively. In an essay about being active in your community, for example, if you attribute the quote "Ask not what your country can do for you; ask what you can do for your country" to Ronald Reagan, you will be factually wrong, but you will be using an effective piece of evidence anyway. So you will get credit for effective use of information, even though the quote was said by John F. Kennedy.

TIMING

With only 40 minutes for the Writing test, efficient use of time is critical. Divide your time as follows:

- **8 minutes:** Read the prompt and plan your essay

- **30 minutes:** Produce (write) your essay, sticking to the plan

- **2 minutes:** Proofread and correct any errors

WHEN YOU'RE RUNNING OUT OF TIME

On the Writing test, you won't be able to guess on the last few questions when you're running out of time, as you can on the other tests. Thus, practice the timing carefully to avoid losing coherence toward the end. If you do start running out of time, don't write a second body paragraph. Instead, take the time to write a thorough final body paragraph and a clear conclusion paragraph. The conclusion is a necessary component of your essay, and its exclusion will cost you more than a strong body paragraph will gain you. Even when you're rushed, try to allow 1 to 2 minutes to proofread for errors that affect clarity.

SCORING

Your essay will be scored according to four domains: **Ideas and Analysis**, **Development and Support**, **Organization**, and **Language Use and Conventions**. (Notice that these correspond with the four bulleted items in the Essay Task.) What is significant for you, prep-wise, is to make sure you can write an essay that is well developed in each of these four domain areas in order to maximize your Writing test score. You will learn more about what is expected in each of these domains in Chapter 25.

Two trained readers score your essay on a scale of 1–6 for each of the four Writing test domains; those scores are added to arrive at your four Writing domain scores (each from 2 to 12). You will also receive an overall Writing test score ranging from 2 to 12, which is determined by a rounded average of the four domain scores. Essays can receive a zero if they are entirely off-topic, left blank, illegible, or written in a language other than English. If there's a difference of more than 1 point between the two readers' scores (for example, one reader gives the essay a 3 and the other a 5), your essay will be read by a third reader.

Statistically speaking, there will be few essays that score 12 out of 12 for all four Writing test domains. If each grader gives your essay a 4 or 5 for each of the four domains (making your subscores 8–10), that will place you within the upper range of those taking the exam.

QUICK TIPS

- **Brainstorm potential examples ahead of time.** Sometime before Test Day, refresh your memory about school subjects, current events, personal experiences, and activities—anything. By doing so, you strengthen mental connections to those ideas and details, making it easier to use them as specific, relevant support for your thesis on Test Day. Again, the important thing to remember is that real-world evidence is far more powerful than hypothetical stances. Saying "This is right because I believe it" will never be as strong as saying "This is right—here is some evidence."

- **Practice!** Students commonly run into issues with timing on Test Day, so it is imperative to practice the timing ahead of time so you feel comfortable when it counts. Practicing will also help you commit the Method and Template to memory so the process is second nature on Test Day. Remember, no matter what issue is raised in the prompt, the directions and task will always be the same. To prepare effectively, read sample essays and practice both planning essay prompts (Steps 1 and 2 of the Method) and writing complete essays (Steps 1–4) multiple times before Test Day. Doing so will enable you to approach the ACT Writing test with confidence.

CHAPTER 25

ACT Writing in Depth

CHAPTER OBJECTIVES

By the end of this chapter, you will be able to:

1. Understand the four domains by which your essay will be evaluated

2. Apply the Kaplan Method for ACT Writing to produce a clear analysis of the perspectives provided

3. Apply the Kaplan Template for the ACT Essay to a test-like prompt

SMARTPOINTS

Point Value	SmartPoints Category
Point Builder	The Kaplan Method for ACT Writing

THE KAPLAN METHOD FOR ACT WRITING

The Kaplan Method for ACT Writing is the method you will use to boost your score on the Writing test. Use the Kaplan Method for ACT Writing for every ACT Writing test prompt you encounter, whether you are practicing, completing your homework, working on a Practice Test, or taking the actual exam on Test Day.

The Kaplan Method for ACT Writing has four steps:

Step 1: Prompt (3 minutes)

Step 2: Plan (5 minutes)

Step 3: Produce (30 minutes)

Step 4: Proofread (2 minutes)

Let's take a closer look at each step.

Step 1: Prompt (3 Minutes)

- **Read the prompt.** Read about the issue and be sure you clearly understand each of the three core arguments. Getting a high score requires clearly responding to at least one of the three perspectives.

- **Choose a position.** Once you've determined what each perspective is arguing, pick a position on the issue. There is no right or wrong answer, and you can partially or fully agree or disagree with the perspectives provided. You should plan a thesis that you can best defend with evidence and examples, whether it's what you personally believe or not. Be aware that multiple sides can be effectively defended; there's no "easy" or "right" side. The essay graders do not care what position you choose, only that you explain and support it effectively.

- **Understanding the issue and addressing the Essay Task are essential to earning a high score.** Do not hurry too quickly through this step: make sure you clearly understand the issue, each of the three perspectives, and which position you are going to argue. You cannot get a high score if you misunderstand the issue and do not address the Essay Task.

Step 2: Plan (5 Minutes)

- **Allow up to 8 minutes for Steps 1 and 2.** You must strategically plan your essay before you write. Most students skip this step on Test Day! Take this time to plan so you know what you're trying to accomplish and can put forth your best first draft.

Writing

- **Use the Kaplan Template for the ACT Essay.** The template will serve as your guide to efficiently plan your essay. In general, the template will help you structure an introduction paragraph, three body paragraphs (two supporting your own perspective and a third explaining how your thesis compares/contrasts with another perspective), and a short concluding paragraph.

- **Write a thesis.** Begin by stating your thesis. Since you already decided upon a stance during Step 1, now compose a sentence that clearly states your position.

- **Brainstorm examples.** Then, start brainstorming examples and reasoning that you can use to support your own position, as well as to support (or refute) at least one of the three perspectives provided in the prompt. Choose the best specific, relevant examples: you'll use these to support your own perspective and argue against competing perspectives.

> ✔ **Expert Tip**
>
> **If you find you have better supporting evidence for a different position from the one you originally thought you would take, just change your position.**

Step 3: Produce (30 Minutes)

- **Write your essay.** Write your draft, sticking closely to your plan. You're not scored on how many words or paragraphs you write but on the strength of your content, evidence, and organization.

- **Write paragraphs with transitions.** Using about 30 minutes, you should aim to produce five well-developed paragraphs with topic sentences and supporting details. Include transition words as you write your essay: do everything you can to make your essay organization and ideas understandable for your readers.

- **Include both an introductory and a concluding paragraph.** Be sure to include an introductory paragraph stating your position and a concluding paragraph that summarizes your position because without those two framing components, you're missing fundamental ingredients your essay needs to earn a high score.

- **Be neat.** As you produce your essay, write as neatly as possible; words that cannot be read cannot be scored.

- **Don't sweat the small stuff.** Finally, do not get caught up in small details or technicalities: do your best and keep writing. It is much more important to write an essay with complete ideas than a technically perfect, but inadequately developed, essay. Even the top-scoring essays contain minor errors. The essay graders understand you are writing a first draft under timed conditions.

Step 4: Proofread (2 Minutes)

- **Check your work.** Always leave yourself the last couple of minutes to review your work; this time spent proofreading is definitely to your benefit. Very few of us can avoid the occasional confused sentence or omitted word when we write under pressure, and a missed word can affect the meaning of a sentence. Again, graders can only score what they read, not what you might mean. Therefore, always quickly review your essay to be sure your ideas are clearly stated.

✔ **Expert Tip**

Use a caret ^ or an asterisk * to insert a word or words, write a backward ¶ to create a new paragraph, and cross out words with one line. Your goal is to stay organized so graders can easily read your essay.

Writing

ACT WRITING SCORING RUBRIC

To effectively prepare for the ACT Writing test, it is important to understand what components are needed for a high-scoring essay. The ACT essay readers will be looking for proficiency in four areas (domains).

The four separate score domains for ACT Writing are Ideas and Analysis, Development and Support, Organization, and Language Use and Conventions. Each of your essay's two readers will assign each domain a score on a scale from 1 to 6. Added together, these individual scores determine your score for each domain on a scale from 2 to 12. The readers use a rubric similar to the following to determine each domain score.

6	5	4
Ideas and Analysis		
• Includes a comprehensive, detailed, and insightful thesis • Establishes thorough context for analysis of the issue and its perspectives • Evaluates implications, intricacies, and/or assumptions	• Includes a detailed, insightful thesis • Establishes effective context for analysis of the issue and its perspectives • Discusses implications, intricacies, and/or assumptions	• Includes a detailed thesis • Establishes adequate context for analysis of the issue and its perspectives • Identifies implications, intricacies, and/or assumptions
Development and Support		
• Provides additional insight and context • Skillfully provides relevant reasoning and significant evidence to support claims • Explores the significance and complexity of the argument • Skillfully analyzes potential counterarguments to strengthen the essay's claims	• Provides additional understanding • Effectively reasons and supports the thesis with evidence • Discusses the significance and complexity of the argument • Analyzes potential counterarguments to give context to the essay's claims	• Provides additional clarity • Adequately reasons and supports the argument • Identifies the significance of the argument • Acknowledges potential counterarguments to the essay's claims

6	5	4
Organization		
• Demonstrates a skillful structure • Focuses on a well-defined main idea throughout the essay • Includes transitions that skillfully connect and deepen understanding between ideas	• Demonstrates an effective structure • Focuses on a main idea • Includes transitions that effectively connect ideas	• Demonstrates an adequate structure • Reflects a main idea • Includes transitions that adequately connect ideas
Language Use and Conventions		
• Features skillful, precise, appropriate word choice that strengthens the argument • Consistently includes varied sentence structure • May include a few minor errors in grammar that do not distract from clarity or readability	• Features precise, appropriate word choice that serves the argument • Often includes varied sentence structure • May include minor errors in grammar that do not distract from clarity or readability	• Features appropriate word choice for the argument • Sometimes includes varied sentence structure • Includes minor errors in grammar that rarely distract from clarity or readability

3	2	1
Ideas and Analysis		
• Includes a thesis • Establishes some context for analysis of the issue and its perspectives • May mention implications, intricacies, and/or assumptions	• Does not include a clear thesis • Does not provide context for analysis of the issue and its perspectives • Does not discuss implications, intricacies, and/or assumptions	• Does not include a thesis • Does not provide context for analysis of the issue and its perspectives • Does not identify implications, intricacies, and/or assumptions

Writing

3	2	1
Development and Support		
• Provides general information • Reasons and supports the argument in a redundant or inexact way • Mentions potential counterarguments to the essay's claims	• Weakly provides information • Inadequately reasons and supports the argument • Ignores potential counterarguments to the essay's claims	• Lacks development • Does not reason or support the argument
Organization		
• Demonstrates a basic structure • Contains a main idea • Includes transitions that sometimes connect ideas	• Demonstrates a simplistic structure • May not reflect a main idea • Does not use transitions that adequately connect ideas	• Demonstrates a confusing structure • Does not reflect a main idea • Does not use transitions that adequately connect ideas
Language Use and Conventions		
• Features basic word choice that does not detract from the argument • Rarely includes varied sentence structure • Includes errors in grammar that somewhat distract from clarity and readability	• Features unclear word choice that detracts from the argument • Often includes unclear sentence structure • Includes errors in grammar that distract from clarity and readability	• Features confusing word choice • Often includes unclear, confusing sentence structure • Includes numerous errors in grammar that distract from clarity and readability

KAPLAN TEMPLATE FOR THE ACT ESSAY

¶1: Introductory paragraph

- **Introductory statement**
- **Thesis**

¶2: 1st body paragraph

- Describe your **thesis**
- Provide **1st example/reasoning:** include specific, relevant information

¶3: 2nd body paragraph

- Continue supporting your **thesis**
- Provide **2nd example/reasoning:** include specific, relevant information

—**Time valve:** *If you are running out of time, don't write a 2nd body paragraph. Instead, take the time to write a thorough 3rd body paragraph and a clear conclusion paragraph.*—

¶4: 3rd body paragraph

- Explain how your thesis compares and contrasts with **Perspectives One, Two, and/or Three**
- **Strengths/Weaknesses** of the perspective(s)
  - Insights offered / Insights not considered
  - Persuasive / Not persuasive
- **Example or Reasoning:** provide specific, relevant information

✔ **Expert Tip**

The goal of your 4th paragraph (the 3rd body paragraph) is to evaluate and critique at least one perspective provided, and it is often easiest to discuss a perspective that mostly clearly *contrasts* with your thesis.

¶5: Conclusion paragraph

- Recap your **thesis**
- Recap how your thesis compares and contrasts with **Perspectives One, Two, and/or Three**

Look at the test-like prompt that follows. Notice what kinds of notes an ACT expert takes in the margins of the passage. Then, look at how the ACT expert creates an outline using the Kaplan Template for the ACT Essay.

Prompt	Strategic Thinking
### American History Curriculum Educators and curriculum designers continuously debate the best way to teach American history to high school students. Whether students are reading historical interpretations or primary source documents, teachers often put the most emphasis on memorizing important names and dates. Although history is generally regarded as a compilation of facts, should high school students be expected to learn more about history than general information regarding famous people and events? Given the richness of American history, it is worthwhile to explore best practices in presenting the story of the United States to students.	*debate on how to teach US history* *2 methods, but emphasis on facts* *key question = students just learn facts?*

Prompt	Strategic Thinking
Read and carefully consider these perspectives. Each suggests a particular way of teaching American history.	

Perspective One	Perspective Two	Perspective Three	
It is important to focus on a nation's prominent historical leaders when studying history. Leaders are representative of the nation as a whole, so studying historical figures provides a full perspective.	The clearest lens through which to view a nation's history is the welfare of its entire population. It is only through an examination of the ways in which society has been affected by historical events that students will truly understand a nation's foundation.	In order to learn the story of America, students need to know what happened, when, and who influenced those events. Becoming familiar with and being tested on important dates and events is the most effective way to study history. Students need to know what happened in years past in order to plan for the future.	*P1: focus on leaders b/c rep everyone* *P2: focus on how events impact society* *P3: focus on dates/events to prep for future*

Essay Task

Write a clear, well-reasoned essay evaluating multiple perspectives the most effective way to teach American history to high school students. In your essay, be sure to:

- Assert your own perspective on the issue and evaluate the relationship between your perspective and at least one other perspective

- Use reasoning and evidence to refine and justify your ideas

- Present your ideas in an organized way

- Convey your ideas effectively using standard written English

Your perspective may be fully, somewhat, or not at all in agreement with one or more of the three perspectives in the prompt.

Planning Your Essay

These pages are not scored.

Use the space below to brainstorm and plan your essay. Consider the following as you think about the prompt:

- Strengths and weaknesses of the three perspectives in the prompt

  ○ What observations do they offer, and what do they overlook?

  ○ Why are they persuasive or why are they not persuasive?

- Your own background and identity

  ○ What is your perspective on this issue, and what are its strengths and weaknesses?

  ○ What evidence will you use in your essay?

Now that you've seen what kinds of notes a test expert takes when reading a prompt, look at how the Kaplan Template for the ACT Essay helps create an extremely useful outline. In the following abbreviated outline, note which position the test expert will defend and how that viewpoint is related to the three perspectives in the prompt.

¶1: Introductory paragraph

- **Introductory statement** <u>understanding Am history = important part of well-rounded edu.</u>

- **Thesis** <u>best approach = examine how imp. leaders affect dev. of entire population</u>

¶2: 1st body paragraph

- Describe your **thesis** <u>examining the development of the entire population = best understanding</u>

- Provide **1st example/reasoning**: include specific, relevant information <u>Lincoln signed EP, but discrimination continued</u>

Now, look at how the Kaplan Template for the ACT Essay translates into the first two paragraphs of a high-scoring student response.

A good understanding of American history is an important part of a well-rounded education. History enables us to understand how and why our culture and political systems came about. Just as scientific discoveries build one upon the other, our knowledge of social systems improves when we understand their foundations through the study of history. Because of this importance, teachers look for the best way to teach history. Three of these methods include focusing on the lives of important leaders, concentrating on the welfare of the society as a whole, and focusing on the important events and dates. Since simple memorization of dates and events does not lead to a deeper understanding of the development of our culture or social systems, history should be taught by examining the development of the entire population, as shaped by the lives and decisions of important leaders.

The best comprehension of history comes through examining the development or progress of the entire population. While great changes are inspired or instigated by great leaders, these changes must be perpetuated by the population as a whole if they are to be effective. My grandparents and teachers have told me that, when they were growing up, there were "White Only" restrooms and water fountains. Even as recently as 50 years ago, some Americans were subjected to open discrimination, despite the Emancipation Proclamation and the efforts of Abraham Lincoln. What is most important for Americans to understand through the study of history is how our society and culture have developed since Lincoln's bold decision. We have moved from enslaving persons of African descent, through enshrining discrimination in law, to electing Barack Obama, a president of African descent, twice by the votes of a majority of the population. Understanding the dynamics and developments that led to this remarkable turnaround are the most important aspects of history, and support the idea that the optimal teaching of history is done through analysis of the welfare of the entire population of a nation, as shaped by the decisions of its leaders.

You have seen the kinds of notes ACT experts take and the strategic thinking questions they ask while planning their responses to the ACT Writing test prompt.

Continuing to work with the American History Curriculum prompt, use the Kaplan Template for the ACT Essay to plan additional body paragraphs for the response. Plan a paragraph that presents a second example or reasoning in support of your thesis. Then plan your third body paragraph, in which you compare or contrast your thesis with one of the perspectives in the prompt. Finish with a short conclusion. Give yourself 5 minutes to plan the paragraphs using the template.

¶3: 2nd body paragraph

Continue supporting your **thesis**

_____
_____
_____

Provide **2nd example/reasoning:** include specific, relevant information

_____
_____
_____

¶4: 3rd body paragraph

Explain how your thesis compares and contrasts with **Perspectives One, Two, and/or Three**

_____
_____
_____

Strengths/Weaknesses of the perspective(s)

- Insights offered / Insights not considered
- Persuasive / Not persuasive

_____
_____
_____

Example or Reasoning: provide specific, relevant information

_____
_____
_____

¶5: Conclusion paragraph

Recap your **thesis**

_____

_____

_____

Recap how your thesis compares and contrasts with **Perspectives One, Two, and/or Three**

_____

_____

_____

Remember that everyone's plans will vary slightly, but every paragraph template should include an analysis of the issue along with a supporting example or reasoning. If you're stuck, review the sample paragraph templates in the Answers & Explanations for this chapter, which are provided at the end of the book.

Now, use your ¶4 (the last body paragraph) notes on the American History Curriculum prompt to write a full body paragraph. Give yourself 8 minutes to write the paragraph.

_____

_____

_____

_____

_____

_____

_____

_____

_____

_____

_____

_____

_____

_____

_____

_____

_____

_____

_____

_____

_____

_____

_____

_____

_____

_____

_____

See the Answers and Explanations, which are provided at the end of the book, for high-scoring examples of Paragraphs 3, 4 and 5.

ON YOUR OWN

The following prompts provide an opportunity to practice the concepts and strategic thinking covered in this chapter. See the Answers and Explanations, which are provided at the end of the book, for sample student essays.

Prompt 1

Education Technology

Education technology (ed tech) companies gather data about the elementary through high school students who use their products. Some for-profit and not-for-profit ed tech providers have pledged to protect student data so that it is not sold to outside companies that may target students with advertisements, or compile profiles that could be harmful for students later in life. However, student data is extremely valuable in helping both for-profit and not-for-profit companies develop effective educational software that records student progress and adapts lessons to meet individual needs. While schools have a responsibility to protect students, some argue that all ed tech companies should be allowed to buy student data to develop better educational products, even if the data is used for commercial purposes. As ed tech continues to evolve, it is important to develop policies that both protect and benefit students.

Read and carefully consider these perspectives. Each suggests a particular way of thinking about sharing student data.

Perspective One	Perspective Two	Perspective Three
Information gathered about anyone under the age of 18 should be wholly protected. Even though student data may aid in ed tech advancements, the activities of minors should not be accessed by any entity other than the provider, and the data should not be sold to third parties. It is better to save students from possible harm than to take a risk, even if the goal is to foster innovation.	There is a clear distinction between educational initiatives and for-profit strategies. Student data should exclusively be available to not-for-profit ed tech developers who provide software at little or no cost to students and educators.	Using software that tracks student progress in real time relies on continuous access to student data. Therefore, there is no reason to expect that the very data that provides immediate adaptation for students will be inaccessible to ed tech companies—whether for-profit or not.

Essay Task

Write a clear, well-reasoned essay evaluating multiple perspectives on sharing student data. In your essay, be sure to:

- Assert your own perspective on the issue and evaluate the relationship between your perspective and at least one other perspective

- Use reasoning and evidence to refine and justify your ideas

- Present your ideas in an organized way

- Convey your ideas effectively using standard written English

Your perspective may be fully, somewhat, or not at all in agreement with one or more of the three perspectives in the prompt.

Planning Your Essay

These pages are not scored.

Use the space below to brainstorm and plan your essay. Consider the following as you think about the prompt:

- Strengths and weaknesses of the three perspectives in the prompt

  ○ What observations do they offer, and what do they overlook?

  ○ Why are they persuasive or why are they not persuasive?

- Your own background and identity

  ○ What is your perspective on this issue, and what are its strengths and weaknesses?

  ○ What evidence will you use in your essay?

Prompt 2

Writing

College Tuition

As the cost of college continues to rise, some states are creating programs that provide free or reduced tuition for students who are accepted into community colleges and state universities. While these programs require considerable amounts of taxpayer money, proponents argue that a more educated population benefits the entire nation. Should states continue to fund these programs despite the exorbitant cost? Considering that affording college costs is a major factor in students' decision to pursue higher education, it is prudent for politicians and educators to explore this issue.

Read and carefully consider these perspectives. Each suggests a particular approach to alleviating the burden of college tuition for students.

Perspective One	Perspective Two	Perspective Three
While attending college is expensive, studies show that it is worth the investment by students. As long as students have access to low-interest loans they can pay off later, when they are gainfully employed, states have no obligation to help students pay for college.	Money that is currently funding reduced or free tuition should instead be spent on programs that aid college graduates in securing employment that will allow them to make loan payments. Students will have more incentive to graduate if they know they will be able to get a job, and repaying their student loans teaches both responsibility and proper fiscal planning.	Despite the cost to taxpayers, in-state college tuition should be free or greatly reduced for all students who receive acceptance letters. Providing affordable education will help more students attend and complete college, which betters society as a whole.

Essay Task

Write a clear, well-reasoned essay evaluating multiple perspectives on college tuition. In your essay, be sure to:

- Assert your own perspective on the issue and evaluate the relationship between your perspective and at least one other perspective
- Use reasoning and evidence to refine and justify your ideas
- Present your ideas in an organized way
- Convey your ideas effectively using standard written English

Your perspective may be fully, somewhat, or not at all in agreement with one or more of the three perspectives in the prompt.

Planning Your Essay

These pages are not scored.

Use the space below to brainstorm and plan your essay. Consider the following as you think about the prompt:

- Strengths and weaknesses of the three perspectives in the prompt
  - What observations do they offer, and what do they overlook?
  - Why are they persuasive or why are they not persuasive?
- Your own background and identity
  - What is your perspective on this issue, and what are its strengths and weaknesses?
  - What evidence will you use in your essay?

REVIEW

CHAPTER 26

Putting It All Together

ENGLISH

THE KAPLAN METHOD FOR ENGLISH

> **Step 1: Read the passage and identify the issue**
>
> **Step 2: Eliminate answer choices that do not address the issue**
>
> **Step 3: Plug in the remaining answer choices and select the most correct, concise, and relevant one**

Let's take a closer look at each step.

Step 1: Read the passage and identify the issue

Rather than reading the whole passage and then answering all of the questions, you can answer questions as you read because they are mostly embedded in the text itself.

When you see a number, stop reading and look at the question. If you can answer it with what you've read so far, do so. If you need more information, keep reading until you have enough context to answer the question.

Step 2: Eliminate answer choices that do not address the issue

Eliminating answer choices that do not address the issue increases your odds of getting the correct answer by removing obviously incorrect answer choices.

Step 3: Plug in the remaining answer choices and select the most correct, concise, and relevant one

Correct, **concise**, and **relevant** means that the answer choice you select:

- Makes sense when read with the correction
- Is as short as possible while retaining the information in the text
- Relates well to the passage overall

Correct answers do NOT:

- Change the intended meaning of the original sentence, paragraph, or passage

- Introduce new grammatical errors

MATH

THE KAPLAN METHOD FOR MATH

Step 1: What is the question?

Step 2: What information am I given?

Step 3: What can I do with the information?

Step 4: Am I finished?

Step 1: What is the question?

First, focus on the *question stem* (the part before the answer choices) and make sure you understand the question. ACT Math questions can have complicated phrasing, and if you don't know *precisely* what you're looking for, you aren't likely to find it. So first, locate the end goal—the objective—and circle it. Do you need to solve for x? Find an odd number? Maybe it's a story problem and you need to find how many adults were admitted to an exhibit, or the number of girls in a classroom. If it is a word problem and you get lost, break the question into pieces and make sure you come away with a clear understanding of what you're looking for. What is the end objective of your work? Again, *circle the question*, or objective as stated in the question stem, when you've found it.

Step 2: What information am I given?

Look through the question stem again and *underline the pieces of information provided*. Ask yourself whether you have everything you'll need to solve the problem or there are intermediary steps you'll have to take. By underlining everything, you'll have a place to start, even if you're lost, as the ACT rarely provides information you don't need to solve the problem. Then, examine the format of the answer choices. This can help you determine your strategy. For example, you may think you need to solve for x in an equation, but then you see that all of the answers are given *in terms of x*, so you don't actually need to find x, you just need to come up with a different expression. Additionally, if you are given information in fractions and see answers in decimals, you'll know you need to convert from one to the other at some point.

Step 3: What can I do with the information?

Now that you've gathered the information, it's time to answer the question. Decide on a plan of attack:

- **Straightforward math.** Do you know how to answer the question using your math skills? Go for it!

- **Picking numbers.** Are there variables in the answer choices? If so, is there a way to pick some easy-to-use numbers you can plug in for the variable to help you get to the right answer?

- **Backsolving.** Are there numbers in the answer choices? What is the question asking for? Is there a way to use the answer choices to get to the right answer?

- **Guess strategically.** If you're really not sure, you can guess—you don't lose points for incorrect answers on the ACT. Try to eliminate as many incorrect choices as you can before guessing. Also, mark the question in your booklet so you can return to it at the end of the Math test and try again. If you still can't answer the question, bubble in your Letter of the Day.

A Letter of the Day is an answer choice letter that you choose before Test Day to select for all questions you guess on. You'll need to select one letter from A, B, C, D, E and one from F, G, H, J, K.

Step 4: Am I finished?

In Step 1, you circled the objective. Check what you circled now. Is that what you found? Have you fully answered the question? Some questions may require several steps, and you may miss the last step if you don't check before you select. The ACT will frequently offer tempting answer choices for students who don't recheck the question. For example, you may need to find the area of a circle and you've only determined the radius—and the radius might be an answer choice! Because you will have identified and marked the question in Step 1, double-checking that you're finished should take only a few seconds, and it can make a real difference on Test Day. If you're stuck, circle the problem in your test book and come back later—always get through the easy questions first.

POINT BUILDERS

Picking Numbers

Step 1: Pick a simple number to stand in for the variables, making sure it follows the criteria stated in the question stem. Does the number have to be even or odd? Positive or negative? Be careful when using 0 and 1, as they behave differently than most other numbers, but always pick easy-to-use numbers.

Step 2: Solve the *question* using the number(s) you picked.

Step 3: Test each of the *answer choices* using the number(s) you picked, eliminating those that give you a result that is different from the one you're looking for.

Step 4: If more than one choice remains, pick a different set of numbers and repeat steps 1–3.

Backsolving

Because you can know for certain that one of the answer choices is correct (as opposed to a fill-in-the-blank test), with some ACT Math problems, it may actually be easier to try out each answer choice until you find the one that works, rather than attempt to solve the problem and then look among the choices for the answer. This approach is called Backsolving.

Review

When Backsolving, always start with the middle answer choice. The numerical answer choices on the ACT are always either in ascending or descending order. If you solve for the one in the middle and it comes out too big, you can eliminate it *and the two larger numbers*, and the same if it's too small. So trying *one* answer choice can eliminate *three* options.

READING COMPREHENSION

THE KAPLAN METHOD FOR READING COMPREHENSION

Step 1: Read actively

Step 2: Examine the question stem

Step 3: Predict and answer

Step 1: Read actively

Active reading means that as you read the passage, you are asking questions and taking notes—both integral to acing the ACT Reading test.

You should ask questions such as:

- Why did the author write this word/detail/sentence/paragraph?

- Is the author taking a side? If so, what side is the author taking?

- What are the tone and purpose of the passage?

Be sure to:

- Identify the passage type (Literary Narrative/Prose Fiction, Social Studies, Humanities, or Natural Sciences)

- Note the main idea of each paragraph

Step 2: Examine the question stem

This means you should:

- Identify key words and line references in the question stem

- Apply question type strategies as necessary

Step 3: Predict and answer

This means you should:

- Predict an answer before looking at the answer choices, also known as "predict before you peek"

- Select the best match

Predicting before you peek helps you:

- Know precisely what you are looking for in the answer choices

- Avoid weighing each answer choice equally, saving time

- Eliminate the possibility of falling into wrong answer traps

WRONG ANSWER TRAPS

Wrong Answer Trap	Description
Distortion	The answer slightly alters details from a passage so they are no longer correct.
Extreme	The answer is too extreme to reflect the author's purpose.
Misused Detail	The answer is a true statement from the passage, but it doesn't answer the question.
Opposite	The answer contradicts the information in the passage.
Out-of-Scope	The answer includes information that is not in the passage.

PASSAGE TYPES

Your approach to Passage Mapping will vary based on the passage type.

Passage Type(s)	Approach
Prose Fiction	• Note the author's central ideas and themes • Note characters' personalities, opinions, and relationships with each other
Social Studies & Humanities	• Identify the author's thesis (often explicitly stated in the first paragraph) • Note the main idea of each paragraph
Natural Science	• Identify the author's thesis • Note the main idea of each paragraph • Don't let technical scientific terms intimidate you; no outside science knowledge is needed • Note the definitions of scientific terms that are provided within the passage text (or passage introduction)

THE KAPLAN METHOD FOR PAIRED PASSAGES

Step 1: Actively read Passage A, then answer its questions

Step 2: Actively read Passage B, then answer its questions

Step 3: Answer questions about both passages

SCIENCE

THE KAPLAN METHOD FOR DATA REPRESENTATION

Step 1: Actively read the passage

- Underline keywords

- Underline key phrases

Step 2: Examine the figures provided

- Locate variables in the figures

- Identify trends and patterns

Step 3: Find support for the answer in the passage

- Identify keywords in the question stem

- Locate the corresponding data in the passage

- Make a prediction and match it to the correct answer

Step 1: Actively read the passage

This means you should:

- Read the passage for the central idea before looking at the questions

- NOT spend time trying to understand everything or be intimidated by technical terminology

- Underline keywords such as terms or variables that are defined, italicized, or usable as reference points for finding information (for example, "mass" or "Method 1")

- Underline key phrases that describe the contents of the passage, define a term or variable, or explain a concept to help you find support for answers in the passage (for example, "acceleration is the rate of change of velocity per unit of time")

Step 2: Examine the figures provided

This means you should:

- Locate variables in the figures and, if applicable, identify whether the variables are independent or dependent (note: not all Data Representation passages present experiments involving independent and dependent variables)

  - Independent variables are what scientists intentionally manipulate; they are usually plotted on the *x*-axis of a graph

  - Dependent variables are what scientists observe and measure; they are usually plotted on the *y*-axis of a graph

- In general, researchers try to determine if a change in the independent variable produces a change in the dependent variable (for example, a biologist might change the concentration of a disinfectant used to clean equipment—the independent variable—to determine if it changes the number of colonies that survive cleaning—the dependent variable)

  - Remember that, unlike in algebra, variables in experiments do NOT have to have numerical values (for example, in an experiment on pollination, a flower's color or the species of bee could be the independent variable)

- Locate units of measurement, which also are a clue to what is being investigated—time in seconds, height in meters, weight in pounds, volume in cubic centimeters, etc.

- Identify trends, which indicate the general direction in which the data are changing (for example, the dependent variable decreases when the independent variable increases)

- Identify a pattern within trends, which indicates a recognizable sequence in the data (for example, the dependent variable increases by 5 units when the independent variable increases by 1 unit)

Step 3: Find support for the answer in the passage

This means you should:

- Identify information in the question like variables, units, or figure headings to help you hone in on the specific parts of the passage that apply to the question (for example, "mass," "kg," or "Figure 1")

- Locate the corresponding data in the passage and circle the parts of the figure or text that relate directly to the question

- Based on what you discover in the passage, formulate a prediction about what the correct answer should say

- Match your prediction to the correct answer choice

THE KAPLAN METHOD FOR RESEARCH SUMMARIES

Step 1: Actively read the passage

- Underline the purpose and/or hypothesis
- Identify key components of the experiments
- Look for similarities and differences among experiments

Step 2: Examine the figures provided

- Locate variables in the figures
- Identify trends and patterns
- Look for relationships among variables

Review

Step 3: Find support for the answer in the passage

- Identify keywords in the question stem

- Locate the corresponding data in the passage

- Make a prediction and match it to the correct answer

Step 1: Actively read the passage

This means you should:

- Read with your pencil

- Locate and underline the purpose and/or hypothesis of the experiments

  - Look for information telling you *what* the researchers are investigating

  - Often the purpose will begin with the word "to" (for example, "to determine," "to evaluate," "to examine")

  - The purpose is often to test a particular hypothesis

- Identify key components of experiments

  - Independent variables

  - Dependent variables

  - Controls

- Look for similarities and differences among experimental methods, the step-by-step procedures explaining *how* each experiment was conducted (for example, in Experiment 1 scientists measured the pH of acidic substances and in Experiment 2 they measured the pH of basic substances at the same temperature)

- NOT spend time trying to understand all the technical details

- Locate the results of the experiments

  - They will often be provided in tables, charts, or graphs, but they can also be given to you in paragraph form

Step 2: Examine the figures provided

This means that, before you look at the questions, you should:

- Locate variables in the figures

  - In many cases you will have just one independent variable and one dependent variable for each experiment, but you could have more than one of either

  - Identify which variables change and note their units

- Identify trends and patterns
  - Look for direct or inverse relationships
  - Identify patterns within the trends, such as specific mathematical relationships (for example, the dependent variable doubles whenever the independent variable doubles)
  - Note: not all data will have a clear trend or pattern
- Identify relationships among variables (for example, cause-and-effect relationships, such as when a change in an independent variable causes a change in a dependent variable)

Step 3: Find support for the answer in the passage

This means you should:

- Identify keywords in the question stem to help you locate where to go in the passage to find support for your answer
- Locate the corresponding data or other relevant information in the passage
  - Results will usually be found in the tables or figures provided, while other experimental details (hypotheses, methods, controls, etc.) will often be found in the text of the passage
  - Form an idea and make a prediction about the correct answer—this will help to focus your thinking and assist you in avoiding trap answers
- Match your predicted answer to an answer choice

THE KAPLAN METHOD FOR CONFLICTING VIEWPOINTS

Step 1: Read the introductory paragraph(s) and the 1st viewpoint, then search for questions that ask only about the 1st viewpoint and answer them

Step 2: Read the 2nd viewpoint, then search for questions that ask only about the 2nd viewpoint and answer them; if there are additional viewpoints, repeat this process with each of them

Step 3: Answer questions that ask about multiple viewpoints and any other remaining questions

Step 1: Read the introductory paragraph(s) and the 1st viewpoint, then search for questions that ask only about the 1st viewpoint and answer them

This means you should:

- Identify the phenomenon presented in the introduction, which contains general information about the phenomenon

Review

- Identify the 1st viewpoint's central claim, and underline it when you find it (often but not always, it is the first sentence of the paragraph(s) on that viewpoint)

- Underline keywords and key phrases that can be used as reference points for finding support when answering questions

- NOT be distracted by jargon or technical terms because answering questions, not reading the passage, earns you points

- Skip to the questions that relate only to the 1st viewpoint and answer them to minimize your opportunities to confuse the two (or three, or four) viewpoints

  - Come back later to a question about the 1st viewpoint if you cannot answer it without reading the other viewpoint(s)

Step 2: Read the 2nd viewpoint, then search for questions that ask only about the 2nd viewpoint and answer them; if there are additional viewpoints, repeat this process with each of them

This means you should:

- Identify and underline the 2nd viewpoint's central claim

- Underline keywords and key phrases in the 2nd viewpoint

- Skip to the questions that relate only to the 2nd viewpoint and answer them

- If applicable, repeat for each additional viewpoint

  - Read and answer questions that ask only about that additional viewpoint

Step 3: Answer questions that ask about multiple viewpoints and any other remaining questions

This means you should:

- Go back to the remaining unanswered questions and answer them

- NOT spend too much time on any one question

WRITING

THE KAPLAN METHOD FOR ACT WRITING

Step 1: Prompt (3 minutes)

Step 2: Plan (5 minutes)

Step 3: Produce (30 minutes)

Step 4: Proofread (2 minutes)

Step 1: Prompt (3 Minutes)

- **Read the prompt.** Read about the issue and be sure you clearly understand each of the three core arguments. You cannot get a high score without clearly responding to at least one of the three perspectives.

- **Choose a position.** Once you've determined what each perspective is arguing, pick a position on the issue. There is no right or wrong answer, and you can partially or fully agree or disagree with the perspectives provided. You should plan a thesis that you can best defend with evidence and examples, whether it's what you personally believe or not. Be aware that multiple sides can be effectively defended; there's no "easy" or "right" side. The essay graders do not care what position you choose, only that you explain and support it effectively.

- **Don't rush!** Do not hurry too quickly through this step: make sure you clearly understand the issue, each of the three perspectives, and which position you are going to argue. You cannot get a high score if you misunderstand the issue and do not address the Essay Task.

Step 2: Plan (5 Minutes)

- **Allow up to 8 minutes for Steps 1 and 2.** You must strategically plan your essay before you write. Most students skip this step on Test Day! Take this time to plan so you know what you're trying to accomplish and can put forth your best first draft.

- **Use the Kaplan Essay Template.** The Kaplan Essay Template (explained in detail below) will serve as your guide to efficiently plan your essay. In general, the template will help you structure an introduction paragraph, three body paragraphs (two supporting your own perspective and a third explaining how your thesis compares/contrasts with another perspective), and a short concluding paragraph.

- **Write a thesis.** Begin by stating your thesis. Since you already decided upon a stance during Step 1, now compose a sentence that clearly states your position.

- **Brainstorm examples.** Then, start brainstorming examples and reasoning that you can use to support your own position, as well as to support (or refute) at least one of the three perspectives provided in the prompt. Choose the best specific, relevant examples: you'll use these to support your own perspective and argue against competing perspectives.

Step 3: Produce (30 Minutes)

- **Write your essay.** Write your draft, sticking closely to your plan. You're not scored on how many words or paragraphs you write but on the strength of your content, evidence, and organization.

- **Write paragraphs with transitions.** In about 30 minutes, you should aim to produce five well-developed paragraphs with topic sentences and supporting details. Include transition words as you write your essay: do everything you can to make your essay organization and ideas understandable for your readers.

- **Include both an introductory and a concluding paragraph.** Be sure to include an introductory paragraph stating your position and a concluding paragraph that summarizes your position, because without those two framing components, you're missing fundamental ingredients your essay needs to earn a high score.

- **Be neat.** As you produce your essay, write as neatly as possible—words that cannot be read cannot be scored.

- **Don't sweat the small stuff.** Finally, do not get caught up in small details or technicalities: do your best and keep writing. It is much more important to write an essay with complete ideas than a technically perfect, but inadequately developed, essay. Even the top-scoring essays contain minor errors. The essay graders understand you are writing a first draft under timed conditions.

Step 4: Proofread (2 Minutes)

- **Check your work.** Always leave yourself the last couple of minutes to review your work—this time spent proofreading is definitely to your benefit. Very few of us can avoid the occasional confused sentence or omitted word when we write under pressure, and a missed word can affect the meaning of a sentence. Again, graders can only score what they read, not what you might mean. Therefore, always quickly review your essay to be sure your ideas are clearly stated.

COUNTDOWN TO TEST DAY

The Week Before the Test

- Finish up any required homework assignments, including online quizzes.

- Focus your additional practice on the question types and/or subject areas in which you usually score highest. Now is the time to sharpen your best skills, not cram new information.

- Make sure you are registered for the test. Remember, Kaplan cannot register you. If you missed the registration deadlines, you can request Waitlist Status on the test maker's website, act.org.

- Confirm the location of your test site. Never been there before? Make a practice run to make sure you know exactly how long it will take to get from your home to your test site. Build in extra time in case you hit traffic on the morning of the test.

- Get a great night's sleep the two days before the test.

The Day Before the Test

- Review the Kaplan Methods and Strategies, as well as the ReKap pages.

- Put new batteries in your calculator.

- Pack your backpack or bag for Test Day with the following items:

  - Photo ID

  - Registration slip or printout

  - Directions to your test site location

  - Five or more sharpened no. 2 pencils (no mechanical pencils)

  - Pencil sharpener

  - Eraser

  - Calculator

  - Extra batteries

  - Nonprohibited timepiece

  - Tissues

  - Prepackaged snacks, like granola bars

  - Bottled water, juice, or sports drink

  - Sweatshirt, sweater, or jacket

The Night Before the Test

- No studying!

- Do something relaxing that will take your mind off the test, such as watching a movie or playing video games with friends.

- Set your alarm to wake up early enough so that you won't feel rushed.

- Go to bed early, but not too much earlier than you usually do. You want to fall asleep quickly, not spend hours tossing and turning.

The Morning of the Test

- Dress comfortably and in layers. You need to be prepared for any temperature.

- Eat a filling breakfast, but don't stray far from your usual routine. If you normally aren't a breakfast eater, don't eat a huge meal, but make sure you have something substantial.

- Read something over breakfast. You need to warm up your brain so you don't go into the test cold. Read a few pages of a newspaper, magazine, or novel.

- Get to your test site early. There is likely to be some confusion about where to go and how to sign in, so allow yourself plenty of time, even if you are taking the test at your own school.

- Leave your cell phone at home or in your car's glovebox. Many test sites do not allow them in the building.

- While you're waiting to sign in or be seated, read more of what you read over breakfast to stay in reading mode.

During the Test

- Be calm and confident. You're ready for this!

- Remember that while the ACT is an almost three-hour marathon (or three-and-a-half if you opt to do the essay), it is also a series of shorter sections. Focus on the section you're working on at that moment; don't think about previous or upcoming sections.

- Use the Kaplan Methods and Strategies as often as you can.

- Don't linger too long on any one question. Mark it and come back to it later.

- Can't figure out an answer? Try to eliminate some choices and guess strategically. Remember, there is no penalty for an incorrect answer, so even if you can't eliminate any choices, you should take a guess.

- There will be plenty of questions you CAN answer, so spend your time on those first!

- Maintain good posture throughout the test. It will help you stay alert.

- If you find yourself losing concentration, getting frustrated, or stressing about the time, stop for 30 seconds. Close your eyes, put your pencil down, take a few deep breaths, and relax your shoulders. You'll be much more productive after taking a few moments to relax.

- Use your breaks effectively. During the breaks, go to the restroom, eat your snacks, and get your energy up for the next section.

After the Test

- Congratulate yourself! Also, reward yourself by doing something fun. You've earned it.

- If you got sick during the test or if something else happened that might have negatively affected your score, you can cancel your scores by the Wednesday following your test date. Request a score cancellation form from your test proctor, or visit the test maker's website for more information (act.org). If you have questions about whether you should cancel your scores, call 1-800-KAP-TEST.

- Your scores will be available online approximately three to four weeks after your test and will be mailed to you in approximately six weeks.

- Email your instructor or tutor with your ACT scores. We want to hear how you did!

Review

PRACTICE TEST

HOW TO SCORE YOUR PRACTICE TEST

The ACT is scored differently from most tests that you take at school. Your ACT score on a test section is not reported as the total number of questions you answered correctly, nor does it directly represent the percentage of questions you answered correctly. Instead, the test makers add up all of your correct answers in a section to get what's called your raw score. They then use a conversion chart, or scale, that matches up a particular raw score with what's called a scaled score. The scaled score is the number that gets reported as your score for that ACT subject test.

You gain one point for every question you answer correctly. You lose no points for answering a question wrong OR for leaving a question blank. This means you should ALWAYS answer EVERY question on the ACT—even if you have to guess.

SCORE TRACKER

1. **Figure out your raw score for each subject test.** Refer to the answer key to determine how many questions you answered correctly. Enter the results below:

RAW SCORES

English: ☐

Math: ☐

Reading: ☐

Science: ☐

2. **Covert your raw scores to scaled scores for each subject test.** Locate your raw score for each subject test in the following table. The score in the far left column indicates your estimated scaled score if this were an actual ACT. Enter your scaled scores in the boxes that follow the table.

SCALED SCORE	RAW SCORES			
	English	Mathematics	Reading	Science
36	75	60	40	40
35	74	–	–	–
34	73	59	39	39
33	72	58	–	–
32	71	57	38	38
31	70	55–56	37	37
30	69	53–54	36	36
29	68	50–52	35	35
28	67	48–49	34	34
27	65–66	45–47	33	33
26	63–64	43–44	32	32
25	61–62	40–42	31	30–31
24	58–60	38–39	30	28–29
23	56–57	35–37	29	26–27
22	53–55	33–34	28	24–25
21	49–52	31–32	27	21–23
20	46–48	28–30	25–26	19–20
19	44–45	26–27	23–24	17–18
18	41–43	23–25	21–22	16
17	39–40	20–22	19–20	15
16	36–38	17–19	17–18	14
15	34–35	15–16	15–16	13
14	30–33	13–14	14	12
13	28–29	11–12	12–13	11
12	25–27	9–10	10–11	10
11	23–24	8	9	9
10	20–22	7	8	8
9	17–19	6	7	7
8	14–16	5	6	6
7	12–13	4	5	5
6	9–11	3	4	4
5	7–8	2	3	3
4	4–6	–	2	2
3	3	1	1	1
2	2	–	–	–
1	0–1	0	0	0

SCALED SCORES

English: ☐

Math: ☐

Reading: ☐

Science: ☐

3. **Calculate your estimated Composite score.** Simply add together your scaled scores for each subject test and divide by four.

ACT Practice Test
ANSWER SHEET

ENGLISH TEST

1. (A)(B)(C)(D) 11. (A)(B)(C)(D) 21. (A)(B)(C)(D) 31. (A)(B)(C)(D) 41. (A)(B)(C)(D) 51. (A)(B)(C)(D) 61. (A)(B)(C)(D) 71. (A)(B)(C)(D)
2. (F)(G)(H)(J) 12. (F)(G)(H)(J) 22. (F)(G)(H)(J) 32. (F)(G)(H)(J) 42. (F)(G)(H)(J) 52. (F)(G)(H)(J) 62. (F)(G)(H)(J) 72. (F)(G)(H)(J)
3. (A)(B)(C)(D) 13. (A)(B)(C)(D) 23. (A)(B)(C)(D) 33. (A)(B)(C)(D) 43. (A)(B)(C)(D) 53. (A)(B)(C)(D) 63. (A)(B)(C)(D) 73. (A)(B)(C)(D)
4. (F)(G)(H)(J) 14. (F)(G)(H)(J) 24. (F)(G)(H)(J) 34. (F)(G)(H)(J) 44. (F)(G)(H)(J) 54. (F)(G)(H)(J) 64. (F)(G)(H)(J) 74. (F)(G)(H)(J)
5. (A)(B)(C)(D) 15. (A)(B)(C)(D) 25. (A)(B)(C)(D) 35. (A)(B)(C)(D) 45. (A)(B)(C)(D) 55. (A)(B)(C)(D) 65. (A)(B)(C)(D) 75. (A)(B)(C)(D)
6. (F)(G)(H)(J) 16. (F)(G)(H)(J) 26. (F)(G)(H)(J) 36. (F)(G)(H)(J) 46. (F)(G)(H)(J) 56. (F)(G)(H)(J) 66. (F)(G)(H)(J)
7. (A)(B)(C)(D) 17. (A)(B)(C)(D) 27. (A)(B)(C)(D) 37. (A)(B)(C)(D) 47. (A)(B)(C)(D) 57. (A)(B)(C)(D) 67. (A)(B)(C)(D)
8. (F)(G)(H)(J) 18. (F)(G)(H)(J) 28. (F)(G)(H)(J) 38. (F)(G)(H)(J) 48. (F)(G)(H)(J) 58. (F)(G)(H)(J) 68. (F)(G)(H)(J)
9. (A)(B)(C)(D) 19. (A)(B)(C)(D) 29. (A)(B)(C)(D) 39. (A)(B)(C)(D) 49. (A)(B)(C)(D) 59. (A)(B)(C)(D) 69. (A)(B)(C)(D)
10. (F)(G)(H)(J) 20. (F)(G)(H)(J) 30. (F)(G)(H)(J) 40. (F)(G)(H)(J) 50. (F)(G)(H)(J) 60. (F)(G)(H)(J) 70. (F)(G)(H)(J)

MATHEMATICS TEST

1. (A)(B)(C)(D)(E) 11. (A)(B)(C)(D)(E) 21. (A)(B)(C)(D)(E) 31. (A)(B)(C)(D)(E) 41. (A)(B)(C)(D)(E) 51. (A)(B)(C)(D)(E)
2. (F)(G)(H)(J)(K) 12. (F)(G)(H)(J)(K) 22. (F)(G)(H)(J)(K) 32. (F)(G)(H)(J)(K) 42. (F)(G)(H)(J)(K) 52. (F)(G)(H)(J)(K)
3. (A)(B)(C)(D)(E) 13. (A)(B)(C)(D)(E) 23. (A)(B)(C)(D)(E) 33. (A)(B)(C)(D)(E) 43. (A)(B)(C)(D)(E) 53. (A)(B)(C)(D)(E)
4. (F)(G)(H)(J)(K) 14. (F)(G)(H)(J)(K) 24. (F)(G)(H)(J)(K) 34. (F)(G)(H)(J)(K) 44. (F)(G)(H)(J)(K) 54. (F)(G)(H)(J)(K)
5. (A)(B)(C)(D)(E) 15. (A)(B)(C)(D)(E) 25. (A)(B)(C)(D)(E) 35. (A)(B)(C)(D)(E) 45. (A)(B)(C)(D)(E) 55. (A)(B)(C)(D)(E)
6. (F)(G)(H)(J)(K) 16. (F)(G)(H)(J)(K) 26. (F)(G)(H)(J)(K) 36. (F)(G)(H)(J)(K) 46. (F)(G)(H)(J)(K) 56. (F)(G)(H)(J)(K)
7. (A)(B)(C)(D)(E) 17. (A)(B)(C)(D)(E) 27. (A)(B)(C)(D)(E) 37. (A)(B)(C)(D)(E) 47. (A)(B)(C)(D)(E) 57. (A)(B)(C)(D)(E)
8. (F)(G)(H)(J)(K) 18. (F)(G)(H)(J)(K) 28. (F)(G)(H)(J)(K) 38. (F)(G)(H)(J)(K) 48. (F)(G)(H)(J)(K) 58. (F)(G)(H)(J)(K)
9. (A)(B)(C)(D)(E) 19. (A)(B)(C)(D)(E) 29. (A)(B)(C)(D)(E) 39. (A)(B)(C)(D)(E) 49. (A)(B)(C)(D)(E) 59. (A)(B)(C)(D)(E)
10. (F)(G)(H)(J)(K) 20. (F)(G)(H)(J)(K) 30. (F)(G)(H)(J)(K) 40. (F)(G)(H)(J)(K) 50. (F)(G)(H)(J)(K) 60. (F)(G)(H)(J)(K)

READING TEST

1. (A)(B)(C)(D) 6. (F)(G)(H)(J) 11. (A)(B)(C)(D) 16. (F)(G)(H)(J) 21. (A)(B)(C)(D) 26. (F)(G)(H)(J) 31. (A)(B)(C)(D) 36. (F)(G)(H)(J)
2. (F)(G)(H)(J) 7. (A)(B)(C)(D) 12. (F)(G)(H)(J) 17. (A)(B)(C)(D) 22. (F)(G)(H)(J) 27. (A)(B)(C)(D) 32. (F)(G)(H)(J) 37. (A)(B)(C)(D)
3. (A)(B)(C)(D) 8. (F)(G)(H)(J) 13. (A)(B)(C)(D) 18. (F)(G)(H)(J) 23. (A)(B)(C)(D) 28. (F)(G)(H)(J) 33. (A)(B)(C)(D) 38. (F)(G)(H)(J)
4. (F)(G)(H)(J) 9. (A)(B)(C)(D) 14. (F)(G)(H)(J) 19. (A)(B)(C)(D) 24. (F)(G)(H)(J) 29. (A)(B)(C)(D) 34. (F)(G)(H)(J) 39. (A)(B)(C)(D)
5. (A)(B)(C)(D) 10. (F)(G)(H)(J) 15. (A)(B)(C)(D) 20. (F)(G)(H)(J) 25. (A)(B)(C)(D) 30. (F)(G)(H)(J) 35. (A)(B)(C)(D) 40. (F)(G)(H)(J)

SCIENCE TEST

1. (A)(B)(C)(D) 6. (F)(G)(H)(J) 11. (A)(B)(C)(D) 16. (F)(G)(H)(J) 21. (A)(B)(C)(D) 26. (F)(G)(H)(J) 31. (A)(B)(C)(D) 36. (F)(G)(H)(J)
2. (F)(G)(H)(J) 7. (A)(B)(C)(D) 12. (F)(G)(H)(J) 17. (A)(B)(C)(D) 22. (F)(G)(H)(J) 27. (A)(B)(C)(D) 32. (F)(G)(H)(J) 37. (A)(B)(C)(D)
3. (A)(B)(C)(D) 8. (F)(G)(H)(J) 13. (A)(B)(C)(D) 18. (F)(G)(H)(J) 23. (A)(B)(C)(D) 28. (F)(G)(H)(J) 33. (A)(B)(C)(D) 38. (F)(G)(H)(J)
4. (F)(G)(H)(J) 9. (A)(B)(C)(D) 14. (F)(G)(H)(J) 19. (A)(B)(C)(D) 24. (F)(G)(H)(J) 29. (A)(B)(C)(D) 34. (F)(G)(H)(J) 39. (A)(B)(C)(D)
5. (A)(B)(C)(D) 10. (F)(G)(H)(J) 15. (A)(B)(C)(D) 20. (F)(G)(H)(J) 25. (A)(B)(C)(D) 30. (F)(G)(H)(J) 35. (A)(B)(C)(D) 40. (F)(G)(H)(J)

Practice Test

ENGLISH TEST

45 Minutes—75 Questions

Directions: Each passage has certain words and phrases that are underlined and numbered. The questions in the right column will provide alternatives for the underlined segments. Most questions require you to choose the answer that makes the sentence grammatically correct, concise, and relevant. If the word or phrase in the passage is already the correct, concise, and relevant choice, select Choice A, NO CHANGE. Some questions will ask a question about the underlined segment. When a question is presented, choose the best answer.

Some questions will ask about part or all of the passage. These questions do not refer to a specific underlined segment. Instead, these questions will accompany a number in a box.

For each question, choose your answer and fill in the corresponding bubble on your answer sheet. Read the passage once before you answer the questions. You will often need to read several sentences beyond the underlined portion to be able to choose the correct answer. Be sure to read enough to answer each question.

Passage I

My Old-Fashioned Father

My father, though he is only in his early 50s, is stuck in his old-fashioned <u>ways. He has a</u> general
₁
mistrust of any innovation or technology that he

can't immediately grasp, and he always <u>tells us, that</u> if
₂
something isn't broken, then you shouldn't fix it.

He <u>has run</u> a small grocery store in town, and if you
₃
were to look at a snapshot of his back office taken

1. **A.** NO CHANGE
   B. ways he has a
   C. ways having a
   D. ways, and still has a

2. **F.** NO CHANGE
   G. tells us, that,
   H. tells us that,
   J. tells us that

3. **A.** NO CHANGE
   B. was running
   C. runs
   D. ran

GO ON TO THE NEXT PAGE

when he opened the store in 1975, you would <u>see that</u>
<u>not much has changed since</u>. He is the most disorgan-
ized person I know and still uses a pencil and paper to

keep track of his <u>inventory.</u> His small office is about to
burst with all the various documents, notes, and receipts

he has accumulated over the <u>years, his filing cabinets</u>
have long since been filled up. The centerpiece of all the
clutter is his ancient typewriter, which isn't even electric.
In the past few years, Father's search for replacement
typewriter ribbons has become an increasingly difficult
task, because they are no longer being produced. He is
perpetually tracking down the few remaining places that
still have these antiquated ribbons in their dusty inven-
tories. When people ask him why he doesn't upgrade
his equipment, he tells them, "Electric typewriters won't
work in a blackout. All I need is a candle and some
paper, and I'm fine." Little does Father <u>know, however,</u>
<u>is that</u> the "upgrade" people are speaking of is not to an
electric typewriter but to a computer.

4. **F.** NO CHANGE
   G. not be likely to see very much that has changed since
   H. be able to see right away that not very much has changed since
   J. not change very much

5. Assuming that all are true, which of the following additions to the word "inventory" is most relevant in context?
   A. inventory of canned and dry goods.
   B. inventory, refusing to consider a more current method.
   C. inventory, which he writes down by hand.
   D. inventory of goods on the shelves and in the storeroom.

6. **F.** NO CHANGE
   G. years; his filing cabinets
   H. years, and besides that, his filing cabinets
   J. years and since his filing cabinets

7. **A.** NO CHANGE
   B. know, besides, that
   C. know, however, that
   D. know, beyond that,

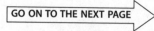

[1] Hoping to bring Father out of the dark ages, <u>my sister, and I</u> bought him a brand new computer for his
[8]
fiftieth birthday. [2] We offered to help him to transfer all of his records onto it and to teach him how to use it. [3] <u>Eagerly,</u> we told him about all the new spreadsheet
[9]
programs that would help simplify his recordkeeping

and organize his <u>accounts; and</u> emphasized the advan-
[10]
tage of not having to completely retype any document when he found a typo. [4] Rather than offering us a look of joy for the life-changing gift we had presented him, however, he again brought up the blackout scenario. [5] To Father, this is a concrete argument, although our town hasn't had a blackout in five years, and that one only lasted an hour or two. [11] [12]

My father's state-of-the-art computer now serves as a very expensive bulletin board for the hundreds of adhesive notes he uses to keep himself organized.

8. **F.** NO CHANGE
    G. me and my sister
    H. my sister and I
    J. my sister and I,

9. **A.** NO CHANGE
    B. On the other hand,
    C. In addition
    D. Rather,

10. **F.** NO CHANGE
    G. accounts and
    H. accounts and,
    J. accounts, we

11. The purpose of including this fact about the town's blackout history is to:
    A. make the father appear delusional.
    B. suggest that the father's reasons not to update his technology are ill-founded.
    C. add an interesting detail to set the scene.
    D. foreshadow an event that occurs later in the story.

12. The author wants to include the following statement in this paragraph:

    We expected it to save him a lot of time and effort.

    The most logical placement for this sentence would be:
    F. before Sentence 1.
    G. after Sentence 1.
    H. after Sentence 4.
    J. after Sentence 5.

GO ON TO THE NEXT PAGE

Sooner than later, we fully expect it will completely dis-
            13
appear under the mounting files and papers in the

back office. In the depths of that disorganized office, the
                        14
computer will join the cell phone my mom gave him
                        14
a few years ago. Interestingly enough, every once in a
    14
while, that completely forgotten cell phone will ring

from under the heavy clutter of the past. 15

13. **A.** NO CHANGE
    B. Sooner rather than later
    C. Sooner or later
    D. As soon as later

14. **F.** NO CHANGE
    G. Deep in the disorganization of that office's, the computer will join the cell phone my mom gave him a few years back.
    H. In the disorganized depths of the office, the computer will soon be joined by the cell phone my mom gave him a few years ago.
    J. The computer will join the cell phone my mom gave him a few years back in the disorganized depths of that office.

15. Which of the following would provide the most appropriate conclusion for the passage?
    A. It's hard to say what else might be lost in there.
    B. We tell my father it's a reminder that he can't hide from the future forever.
    C. We have no idea who might be calling.
    D. Maybe one day I will try to find it and answer it.

GO ON TO THE NEXT PAGE

Passage II

Breaking Baseball's Color Barrier

A quick perusal of any modern major league baseball team will reveal a roster of players of multiple ethnicities <u>from the farthest</u> reaches of the globe.
16
Second only to soccer, baseball has evolved into a global

sport and <u>a symbol among races for equality</u>.
17
Its diversity today presents a stark contrast to the state of the sport just sixty years ago. As late as the 1940s, there existed an unwritten rule in baseball that prevented all but white players <u>to participate</u> in
18
the major leagues. This rule was known as the "color barrier" or "color line." The color line in baseball actually predated the birth of the major leagues. Prior to the official formation of any league of professional baseball teams, there existed an organization of amateur baseball clubs known as the National Association of Baseball Players, <u>which was the precursor to today's</u>
19
<u>National League.</u> On December 11, 1868, the governing
19
body of this association had unanimously adopted a rule

16. F. NO CHANGE
G. from the most far
H. from the most farthest
J. from farther

17. A. NO CHANGE
B. among races for equality a symbol
C. a symbol for equality among races
D. for equality among races a symbol

18. F. NO CHANGE
G. to be able to participate
H. from participating
J. to participation

19. Is the underlined portion relevant here?

A. Yes, because it helps familiarize the reader with the range of baseball associations that once existed.

B. Yes, because it helps clarify the development the author traces.

C. No, because the names of the organizations are not important.

D. No, because it is inconsistent with the style of the essay to provide specific historical data.

GO ON TO THE NEXT PAGE

that effectively barred any team that <u>had, any "colored</u>
                                                20
<u>persons"</u> on its roster. However, when baseball started to
20

organize into leagues <u>by</u> professional teams in the early
                                   21
1880s, the National Association of Baseball Players'

decree no longer had any weight, especially in the newly

formed American Association. <u>For a brief period in</u>
                                  22
<u>those early years, a few African Americans played side</u>
                                22
<u>by side with white players on major league diamonds.</u>
                                22

[1] Most baseball historians believe that the first

African American to play in the major leagues was

Moses "Fleet" Walker. [2] <u>Walker was a catcher</u> for the
                                       23
Toledo Blue Stockings of the American Association

between 1884 and 1889. [3] During that time, a few

other African Americans, <u>including</u> Walker's brother
                                  24

Weldy, <u>would be joining him</u> on the Blue Stockings.
                         25
[4] Unfortunately, this respite from segregation did not

last for very long; as Jim Crow laws took their hold on

the nation, many of the most popular white ballplayers

20. F. NO CHANGE
   G. had any, "colored persons"
   H. had any "colored persons"
   J. had any "colored persons,"

21. A. NO CHANGE
   B. of
   C. from
   D. about

22. The writer is considering deleting the under-lined portion. Should the writer make this deletion?

   F. Yes, because the information is not relevant to the topic of the paragraph.

   G. Yes, because the information contradicts the first sentence of the paragraph.

   H. No, because the information shows that white players did not object to integration.

   J. No, because the statement provides a smooth transition to the specific information about early African American players in the next paragraph.

23. A. NO CHANGE
   B. Walker, being a catcher
   C. Walker, a catcher
   D. Walker who was a catcher

24. F. NO CHANGE
   G. that included
   H. who would include
   J. including among them

25. A. NO CHANGE
   B. joined him
   C. were to join him
   D. will join him

GO ON TO THE NEXT PAGE

Practice Test

started to refuse to take the field with their African American teammates. [5] By the 1890s, the color barrier had fully returned to baseball, where it would endure for more than half a century. 26

Jackie Robinson would become the first African American to cross the color line <u>at the time when</u> he debuted for the Brooklyn Dodgers in 1947. For Robinson's landmark achievements on and off the diamond, he will <u>forever be recognized as</u> a hero of the civil rights movement and a sports icon. <u>His response to</u> the prejudices of American society during the 1940s and 1950s opened the door for the multi-racial and multi-national face of modern baseball, and fans of the sport worldwide will be forever in his debt.

26. Upon reviewing this paragraph, the author discovers that he has neglected to include the following information:

> A handful of African Americans played for other teams as well.

This sentence would be most logically placed after:

F. Sentence 1.
G. Sentence 2.
H. Sentence 3.
J. Sentence 4.

27. A. NO CHANGE
    B. when
    C. while
    D. when the time came that

28. F. NO CHANGE
    G. one day be recognized
    H. forever recognize
    J. be admired by a lot of people for being

29. Which choice best maintains the essay's positive tone while emphasizing the unique role that Robinson played?

A. NO CHANGE
B. The path that he blazed through
C. The stance he took against
D. His collaboration in the face of

GO ON TO THE NEXT PAGE

Practice Test

Question 30 asks about the essay as a whole.

30. Suppose the writer had been assigned to develop a brief essay on the history of baseball. Would this essay successfully fulfill that goal?

    F. Yes, because it covers events in baseball over a period of more than a century.

    G. Yes, because it mentions key figures in baseball history.

    H. No, because people played baseball before 1868.

    J. No, because the focus of this essay is on one particular aspect of baseball history.

GO ON TO THE NEXT PAGE

Passage III

The Bear Mountain Bridge

When the gleaming Bear Mountain Bridge officially opened to traffic on Thanksgiving Day in <u>1924, it</u>
31
was known as the Harriman Bridge, after Edward H. Harriman, wealthy philanthropist and patriarch of the family most influential in the bridge's construction. Before <u>they were</u> constructed, there were no bridges
32
spanning the Hudson River south of Albany. By the early 1920s, the ferry services used to transport people back and forth across the river had become woefully inadequate. In February of 1922, in an effort to alleviate some of the burden on the ferries and create a permanent link across the Hudson, the New York State Legislature <u>had authorized</u> a group of private investors,
33
led by Mary Harriman, to build a bridge. The group,

known as the Bear Mountain Hudson Bridge Company (BMHBC), was allotted thirty years to <u>build, construct,</u>
34
<u>and maintain</u> the structure, at which time the span
34
would be handed over to New York State.

The BMHBC invested almost $4,500,000 into the suspension bridge and hired the world-renowned design team <u>of Howard Baird and George Hodge</u> as
35

31. A. NO CHANGE
    B. 1924; it
    C. 1924. It
    D. 1924 and it

32. F. NO CHANGE
    G. the bridges were
    H. it was
    J. it were

33. A. NO CHANGE
    B. authorized
    C. was authorized
    D. would authorize

34. F. NO CHANGE
    G. build and construct and maintain
    H. construct and maintain
    J. construct, and maintain

35. A. NO CHANGE
    B. of Howard Baird, and George Hodge
    C. of Howard Baird and, George Hodge
    D. of, Howard Baird and George Hodge

GO ON TO THE NEXT PAGE

Practice Test

architects. 36 Baird and Hodge enlisted the help of John

36. The purpose of including the cost of the bridge is to:

    F. provide a piece of information critical to the point of the essay.

    G. insert a necessary transition between the second and third paragraphs.

    H. add a detail contributing to the reader's understanding of the magnitude of the project.

    J. provide an explanation of how the group raised money to invest in the bridge.

A. Roebling and Sons, <u>who were</u> instrumental in the

37
steel work of the Brooklyn Bridge and would later work on the Golden Gate and George Washington Bridges.

    Amazingly, the bridge took only twenty months and eleven days to complete, and not one life was lost. 38 It was a technological marvel and would stand as a model for the suspension bridges of the future. At the time of the Harriman Bridge's completion, it was, at 2,257 feet,

37. **A.** NO CHANGE

    B. who was

    C. a company

    D. a company that had been

38. If the writer were to delete the preceding sentence, the essay would lose primarily:

    F. information about how long the project had been expected to take.

    G. a warning about the dangers of large-scale construction projects.

    H. crucial information about the duration of the project.

    J. a necessary transition between Paragraphs 3 and 4.

the longest single-span steel suspension bridge in the world. <u>Therefore, the</u> two main cables used in the

39
suspension were 18 inches in diameter, and each contained 7,752 individual steel wires wrapped in 37 thick strands. If completely unraveled, the single wires in both

39. **A.** NO CHANGE

    B. Nonetheless, the

    C. At the same time, the

    D. The

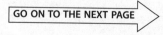

GO ON TO THE NEXT PAGE

cables would be 7,377 miles <u>longer</u>. The bridge links
40
Bear Mountain on the western bank of the Hudson

to Anthony's Nose on the eastern <u>side, it lies</u> so precisely
41
on an east-west plane that one can check a compass by

it. It carries Routes 6 and 202 across the Hudson and is

the point of river crossing for the Appalachian Trail.

In an attempt to recoup some of its investment after

the bridge <u>opened, the BMHBC charged</u> an exorbitant
42
toll of eighty cents per crossing. Even with the high

toll, however, it operated at a loss for thirteen of its first

sixteen years. Finally it was acquired, more than ten

years earlier than planned, by the New York State Bridge

Authority. The bridge was renamed the Bear Mountain

Bridge. <u>Moreover</u>, the Bear Mountain Bridge sees
43

<u>more than</u> six million vehicles cross its concrete decks
44
each year.

40. **F.** NO CHANGE
G. long
H. in total length
J. lengthy

41. **A.** NO CHANGE
B. side, lies
C. side, lying
D. side; and it lies

42. **F.** NO CHANGE
G. opened the BMHBC charged
H. opened: the BMHBC charged
J. opened; the BMHBC charged

43. **A.** NO CHANGE
B. In contrast
C. Besides that fact
D. Today

44. **F.** NO CHANGE
G. over
H. even more than
J. a higher amount than

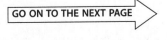
GO ON TO THE NEXT PAGE

Question 45 asks about the essay as a whole.

45. Suppose the author had been assigned to write a brief history of bridge building in the United States. Would this essay successfully fulfill that requirement?

A. Yes, because it provides information on the entire process from the initial funding through the opening of the bridge.

B. Yes, because Bear Mountain Bridge is historically significant.

C. No, because it focuses on only one bridge.

D. No, because the essay is primarily concerned with the financial aspects of building and maintaining the bridge.

GO ON TO THE NEXT PAGE

Passage IV

The Dream of the American West

As the sun <u>was slowly rising</u> over the Atlantic Ocean
46
and painted New York harbor a spectacular fiery orange,

I started my old Toyota's engine. At this early hour, there

was still some semblance of the night's tranquility left

on the city sidewalks, but I knew that, as the minutes

ticked by, <u>the streets would flood with humanity.</u>
47

I smiled <u>with</u> the thought that soon all the wonderful
48
chaos of New York City would be disappearing behind

me as I <u>embarked on my trip to the other side of</u> the
49
country.

<u>As the morning sun climbed into the sky,</u>
50

46. **F.** NO CHANGE
   G. rising slowly
   H. rose slowly
   J. continued to rise

47. The author wants to contrast the statement
   about the quiet of the night streets with a related
   detail about the daytime activity. Assuming that
   all of the choices are true, which of the following
   best accomplishes that goal?
   A. NO CHANGE
   B. some people might appear.
   C. everything would be different.
   D. the tranquility would be unbroken.

48. **F.** NO CHANGE
   G. along with
   H. at
   J. all because of

49. **A.** NO CHANGE
   B. embarked on this journey across
   C. traveled to the other side of
   D. traveled across

50. Which of the following alternatives to the
   underlined portion would NOT be acceptable?
   F. At sunrise,
   G. Watching the morning sun climb into the
     sky,
   H. The morning sun climbed into the sky,
   J. As the sun rose,

GO ON TO THE NEXT PAGE

Practice Test

I shuddered with excitement <u>to think that my final stop</u>
⁵¹
<u>would be in California, where the sun itself ends its</u>
⁵¹
<u>journey across America.</u> Like the sun, however, I still
⁵¹
had quite a journey before me.

I had been planning this road trip across the United
States for as long as I could remember. In my life, I had
been fortunate enough to see some of the most beautiful
countries in the world. However, it had always bothered
me that although I'd stood in the shadow of the <u>Eiffel</u>
⁵²
<u>Tower, marveled in the desert heat at the Pyramids</u>
⁵²
<u>of Giza,</u> I'd never seen any of the wonders of my own
⁵²
country, except those found in my hometown of New
York City. All of that was about to change.

<u>As I left the city, the tall buildings began to give way</u>
⁵³
<u>to smaller ones, then to transform into the quaint rows of</u>
⁵³
<u>houses that clustered in the crowded suburbs.</u> Trees and
⁵³
grass, then the yellow-green of cornfields and the golden

wash of wheat were slowly <u>replacing the familiar mazes</u>
⁵⁴
<u>of cement and steel.</u> My world no longer stretched
⁵⁴

---

51. The writer is considering revising this sentence
by deleting the underlined portion. If she did so,
the paragraph would primarily lose:

  A. information about the reasons for the
writer's trip.

  B. information about the writer's destination.

  C. a description of the writer's planned
route.

  D. a comparison between the sunrise in New
York and the sunset in California.

52. **F.** NO CHANGE

  G. Eiffel Tower and had marveled in the
desert heat at the Pyramids of Giza,

  H. Eiffel Tower and marveled in the desert
heat at the Pyramids of Giza

  J. Eiffel Tower, and had marveled, in the desert heat, at the Pyramids of Giza

53. Given that all are true, which of the following
provides the most effective transition between
the third paragraph and the description of the
Midwest in the fourth paragraph?

  A. NO CHANGE

  B. In fact, there were changes on the horizon
almost immediately.

  C. My excitement hadn't diminished.

  D. I realized that people who lived in other
areas might feel the same way about
visiting New York.

54. Assuming that all are true, which of the following provides information most relevant to the
main focus of the paragraph?

  F. NO CHANGE

  G. appearing before me

  H. racing past my window

  J. becoming monotonous

GO ON TO THE NEXT PAGE ⟹

Practice Test

vertically toward <u>the sky, it now spread</u> horizontally
₅₅
toward eternity. For two days, I pushed through the
wind-whipped farmlands of Mid-America, hypnotized
by the beauty of the undulating yet unbroken lines. At
night, the breeze from my car would stir the wheat fields
to dance beneath the moon, and the silos hid in the
shadows, quietly imposing their <u>simply</u> serenity upon
₅₆
everything.

55. **A.** NO CHANGE
    B. the sky but it now spread
    C. the sky; it now spread
    D. the sky spreading

56. **F.** NO CHANGE
    G. simple
    H. simplest
    J. simpler

Then, as the <u>night's shadows</u> gave way to light, there
₅₇

57. **A.** NO CHANGE
    B. nights shadows
    C. shadows from the night
    D. night shadow

seemed to be a great force rising to meet the <u>sun as it</u>
₅₈
<u>made its reappearance.</u>
₅₈

58. **F.** NO CHANGE
    G. sun as it reappeared
    H. reappearing sun
    J. sun as it was also rising

<u>Still,</u> I had no idea what I was looking at. Then, there
₅₉

59. **A.** NO CHANGE
    B. Even so,
    C. At first,
    D. Eventually,

was no <u>mistaking it</u>. The unbroken lines of Mid-America
₆₀
had given way to the jagged and majestic heights of the
Rockies and the gateway to the American West.

60. **F.** NO CHANGE
    G. mistake to be made
    H. chance to mistake it
    J. having made a mistake

GO ON TO THE NEXT PAGE

Practice Test

Passage V

Traveling at the Speed of Sound

The term "supersonic" refers to anything that travels faster than the speed of sound. When the last of the supersonic Concorde passenger planes made its final trip across the Atlantic in <u>November of 2003, an interesting</u> chapter in history was finally closed. The fleet of supersonic Concorde SSTs, or

61

61

"Supersonic Transports," <u>they were</u> jointly operated by Air France and British Airways, had been making

62

the intercontinental trip across the Atlantic for almost thirty years. These amazing machines cruised at Mach 2, more than twice the speed of sound. They flew <u>to a height</u> almost twice that of standard passenger

63

airplanes. The Concorde routinely made the trip from New York to London in less than three hours and was much more expensive than normal transatlantic flights. <u>Furthermore,</u> the majority of the passengers

64

who traveled on the Concorde were celebrities or the extremely wealthy, it also attracted ordinary people who simply wanted to know how it felt to travel faster than the speed of sound. Some would save money for years just to gain that knowledge.

What is the speed of sound? Many people are surprised to learn that there is no fixed answer to this question. The speed <u>that</u> sound travels through a given

65

medium depends on a number of factors. To understand

61. A. NO CHANGE
   B. November, of 2003 an interesting
   C. November of 2003 an interesting
   D. November of 2003; an interesting

62. F. NO CHANGE
   G. those were
   H. which were
   J. which being

63. A. NO CHANGE
   B. at an altitude
   C. toward an altitude
   D. very high

64. F. NO CHANGE
   G. Despite
   H. Though
   J. Along with

65. A. NO CHANGE
   B. to which
   C. at which
   D. where

GO ON TO THE NEXT PAGE ⟶

Practice Test

the speed of sound, we must first understand what a "sound" really is. 66

The standard dictionary definition of sound is "a vibration or disturbance transmitted, like waves through water, through a material medium such as a gas." Our

ears are able to pick up those sound waves and <u>convert</u>
                                                    67
them into what we hear. This means that the speed at

which sound travels through gas <u>directly depends on</u>
                                         68
<u>what gas it is traveling through, and the temperature</u>
                    68
<u>and pressure of the gas.</u> When discussing aircraft
            68
breaking the speed of sound, that gas medium, of

course, is air. As air temperature and pressure decrease

<u>with altitude,</u> so does the speed of sound. An airplane
      69
flying at the speed of sound at sea level is traveling

66. The purpose of this paragraph, as it relates to the surrounding paragraphs, is primarily to:

F. provide an example of the main idea before continuing discussion of that idea.

G. transition from a discussion of certain aircraft to the science behind them.

H. present a counterargument to the main thesis before refuting that counterargument.

J. transition from the general topic of aircraft to a story about specific airplanes.

67. Which of the following alternatives to the underlined portion would be the LEAST acceptable?

A. change

B. translate

C. alter

D. transform

68. F. NO CHANGE

G. depends directly on the type, temperature, and pressure of the gas it is traveling through

H. directly depends on what gas it is and also on the temperature and pressure of that gas

J. depends directly on the type, temperature, and pressure of the gas

69. A. NO CHANGE

B. with height

C. with a drop in altitude

D. at higher altitudes

GO ON TO THE NEXT PAGE

Practice Test

roughly at 761 mph; <u>however</u> when that same plane
70
climbs to 20,000 feet, the speed of sound is only about

707 mph. This is why the Concorde's cruising altitude

was so much higher than that of a regular passenger

aircraft; <u>planes can reach supersonic speeds more easily</u>
71
<u>at higher altitudes.</u>
71

70. **F.** NO CHANGE

    G. however,

    H. and so,

    J. even so

71. Given that all are true, which of the following provides the most logical conclusion for this sentence?

    A. NO CHANGE

    B. they're much faster

    C. they use much more fuel than regular aircraft

    D. they're rarely visible because they fly above the cloud cover

        In the years since the Concorde <u>has been</u>
72
decommissioned, only fighter pilots and astronauts

have been able to experience the sensation of

breaking "the sound barrier." <u>But that is all about</u>
73
<u>to change very soon.</u> Newer and faster supersonic
73
passenger planes are being developed that will

be technologically superior to the Concorde

and much cheaper to operate. <u>Now,</u> supersonic
74
passenger travel will be available not only to the rich

and famous, <u>but also be for</u> the masses so they, too, can
75
experience life at supersonic speeds.

72. **F.** NO CHANGE

    G. came to be

    H. was

    J. had been

73. **A.** NO CHANGE

    B. Soon, however, that is about to change.

    C. Soon, however, that will change.

    D. That is about to change soon.

74. **F.** NO CHANGE

    G. Nearby,

    H. Soon,

    J. Upcoming,

75. **A.** NO CHANGE

    B. but also be available to

    C. but also to

    D. but for

IF YOU FINISH BEFORE TIME IS CALLED, YOU MAY CHECK YOUR WORK ON THIS SECTION ONLY. DO NOT TURN TO ANY OTHER SECTION IN THE TEST. **STOP**

MATHEMATICS TEST

60 Minutes—60 Questions

Directions: Choose the correct solution to each question and fill in the corresponding bubble on your answer sheet.

Do not continue to spend time on questions if you get stuck. Solve as many questions as you can before returning to any if time permits.

You may use a calculator on this test for any question you choose. However, some questions may be better solved without a calculator.

Note: Unless otherwise stated, you can assume:

1.   Figures are NOT necessarily drawn to scale.

2.   Geometric figures are two dimensional.

3.   The word *line* indicates a straight line.

4.   The word *average* indicates arithmetic mean.

1.   The eighth grade girls' basketball team played a total of 13 games this season. If they scored a total of 364 points, what was the mean (average) score per game?

A.   13

B.   16

C.   20

D.   28

E.   32

2.   When $4\frac{3}{7}$ is written as an improper fraction in simplest form, what is the numerator of the fraction?

F.   12

G.   21

H.   27

J.   28

K.   31

3.   If $4x + 18 = 38$, then $x = $?

A.   3

B.   4.5

C.   5

D.   14

E.   20

4.   John weighs 1.5 times as much as Ellen. If John weighs 144 pounds, how many pounds does Ellen weigh?

F.   84

G.   96

H.   104

J.   164

K.   216

GO ON TO THE NEXT PAGE

5. What positive number when divided by its reciprocal gives a result of $\dfrac{9}{16}$?

   A. $\dfrac{3}{16}$

   B. $\dfrac{3}{4}$

   C. $\dfrac{4}{3}$

   D. $\dfrac{16}{9}$

   E. $\dfrac{16}{3}$

6. If $\sqrt[3]{x} = \dfrac{1}{4}$, then $x = ?$

   F. $\dfrac{1}{256}$

   G. $\dfrac{1}{64}$

   H. $\dfrac{1}{12}$

   J. $\dfrac{1}{\sqrt[3]{4}}$

   K. 64

7. If $x^2 + 14 = 63$, then x could be which of the following?

   A. 4.5

   B. 7

   C. 14

   D. 24.5

   E. 49

8. Two vectors are given by $\mathbf{v}_1 = \langle 7, -3 \rangle$ and $\mathbf{v}_2 = \langle a, b \rangle$. If $\mathbf{v}_1 + \mathbf{v}_2 = \langle 5, 5 \rangle$, then what is the value of a ?

   F. -2

   G. 2

   H. 5

   J. 8

   K. 12

9. Based on past graduations, a university estimates that 6% of the graduating class will not attend the graduation ceremony. Based on this estimate, if there are 1,250 graduates, how many will not attend the ceremony?

   A. 75

   B. 140

   C. 220

   D. 350

   E. 425

10. $5.2^3 + 6.8^2 = ?$

   F. 46.24

   G. 94.872

   H. 120.534

   J. 140.608

   K. 186.848

GO ON TO THE NEXT PAGE

Practice Test

11. Lexi uses her debit card to make a purchase totaling $40. When she records the debit in her checkbook register, she accidentally adds $40 to her balance rather than subtracting it, which results in an inaccurate total. Because of her error, Lexi's checkbook register shows:

    A. $80 less than it should.

    B. $40 less than it should.

    C. $20 more than it should.

    D. $40 more than it should.

    E. $80 more than it should.

12. $3^3 \div 9 + (6^2 - 12) \div 4 = ?$

    F. 3

    G. 6.75

    H. 9

    J. 12

    K. 15

13. If bananas cost $0.24 and oranges cost $0.38, what is the total cost of x bananas and y oranges?

    A. $(x + y)(\$0.24 + \$0.38)$

    B. $\$0.24x + \$0.38y$

    C. $\$0.62(x + y)$

    D. $\dfrac{\$0.24}{x} + \dfrac{\$0.38}{y}$

    E. $\$0.38x + \$0.24y$

14. In the following figure, all of the small triangles are the same size. What percent of the entire figure is shaded?

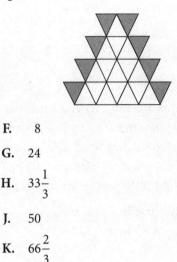

    F. 8

    G. 24

    H. $33\dfrac{1}{3}$

    J. 50

    K. $66\dfrac{2}{3}$

15. In a high school senior class, the ratio of girls to boys is 5:3. If there are a total of 168 students in the senior class, how many girls are there?

    A. 63

    B. 100

    C. 105

    D. 147

    E. 152

16. On her first three geometry tests, Sarah scored an 89, a 93, and an 84. If there are four tests total and Sarah needs at least a 90 average for the four, what is the lowest score she can receive on the final test?

    F. 86

    G. 90

    H. 92

    J. 94

    K. 96

GO ON TO THE NEXT PAGE

Practice Test

17. What is the solution set of $3x - 11 \geq 22$?

   A. $x \geq -11$

   B. $x < -3$

   C. $x \geq 0$

   D. $x > 3$

   E. $x \geq 11$

18. Dillon is going to randomly pick a domino from a pile of dominos that are all facing downward. Of the dominos in the pile, 48 have an even number of dots on them. He randomly picks a single domino. If the probability that he picks a domino with an even number of dots is $\frac{3}{4}$, how many dominos are in the pile?

   F. 36

   G. 48

   H. 56

   J. 64

   K. 72

19. What is the value of $3x - 8y$ when $x = 4$ and $y = -\frac{1}{2}$?

   A. -4

   B. 8

   C. 12

   D. 16

   E. 28

20. Court reporters type every word spoken during trials and hearings so that there is a written record of what transpired. Suppose a certain court reporter can type 3.75 words per second, and a trial transcript contains 25 pages with an average of 675 words per page. If this court reporter typed the transcript at his typical rate, how long was he actively typing?

   F. 1 hour, 15 minutes

   G. 1 hour, 40 minutes

   H. 2 hours, 10 minutes

   J. 2 hours, 30 minutes

   K. 3 hours

21. In the following figure, lines m and l are parallel and the measure of $\angle a$ is 68°. What is the measure of $\angle f$?

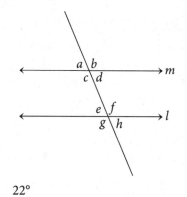

   A. 22°

   B. 68°

   C. 80°

   D. 112°

   E. 292°

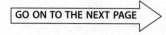
GO ON TO THE NEXT PAGE

Practice Test

22. On a map, the scale is the ratio of the distance shown on the map to the actual distance. A geography teacher has a map on her wall with a scale of 1 inch:100 miles. She uses the school's copier to shrink the large wall map down to the size of a piece of paper to hand out to each of her students. To do this, she makes the map $\frac{1}{4}$ of its original size. Suppose on the students' maps, the distance between two cities is 2.5 inches. How many actual miles apart are those cities?

F. 25

G. 250

H. 800

J. 1,000

K. 1,200

23. A piece of letter-sized paper is $8\frac{1}{2}$ inches wide and 11 inches long. Suppose you want to cut strips of paper that are $\frac{5}{8}$ of an inch wide and 11 inches long. What is the maximum number of strips of paper you could make from 1 piece of letter-sized paper?

A. 5

B. 6

C. 12

D. 13

E. 14

24. In the following figure, $\overline{MN}$ and $\overline{PQ}$ are parallel. Point A lies on $\overline{MN}$, and points B and C lie on $\overline{PQ}$. If $AB = AC$ and $\angle MAB$ has a measure of 55°, what is the measure of $\angle ACB$?

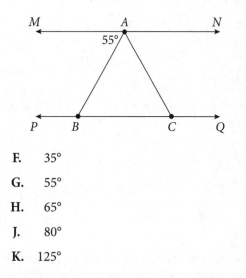

F. 35°

G. 55°

H. 65°

J. 80°

K. 125°

25. What is the slope of the line that passes through the points $(-10,0)$ and $(0,-6)$?

A. $-\frac{5}{3}$

B. $-\frac{3}{5}$

C. $\frac{3}{5}$

D. $\frac{5}{3}$

E. 0

26. For all x, $(x + 4)(x - 4) + (2x + 2)(x - 2) = $?

F. $x^2 - 2x - 20$

G. $3x^2 - 12$

H. $3x^2 - 2x - 20$

J. $3x^2 + 2x - 20$

K. $3x^2 + 2x + 20$

GO ON TO THE NEXT PAGE

Practice Test

27. What is the length of a line segment with endpoints $(3, -6)$ and $(-2, 6)$?

    A. 1
    B. 5
    C. 10
    D. 13
    E. 15

28. If 60 percent of h is 80, what is 30 percent of h ?

    F. 30
    G. 40
    H. 50
    J. 60
    K. 70

29. Set A contains 7 consecutive even integers. If the average of Set A's integers is 46, which of the following is the smallest integer of Set A ?

    A. 36
    B. 38
    C. 40
    D. 42
    E. 44

30. Which of the following statements describes the total of the first n terms of the arithmetic sequence below?

    $$1, 3, 5, 7, 9, \ldots$$

    F. The total is always equal to 25 regardless of n.
    G. The total is always equal to $2n$.
    H. The total is always equal to $3n$.
    J. The total is always equal to n^2.
    K. There is no consistent pattern for the total.

31. Which of the following matrices is equal to the matrix product $\begin{bmatrix} -2 & 0 \\ 1 & -3 \end{bmatrix} \cdot \begin{bmatrix} 2 \\ 2 \end{bmatrix}$?

    A. $\begin{bmatrix} -4 & 0 \\ 2 & -6 \end{bmatrix}$

    B. $\begin{bmatrix} -4 & 2 \\ 2 & -6 \end{bmatrix}$

    C. $\begin{bmatrix} 0 & 0 \\ 0 & 0 \end{bmatrix}$

    D. $\begin{bmatrix} -4 \\ -4 \end{bmatrix}$

    E. $\begin{bmatrix} -4 \\ -6 \end{bmatrix}$

32. A playground is $(x + 7)$ units long and $(x + 3)$ units wide. If a square of side length x is sectioned off from the playground to make a sandpit, which of the following could be the remaining area of the playground?

    F. $x^2 + 10x + 21$
    G. $10x + 21$
    H. $2x + 10$
    J. $21x$
    K. 21

33. Assume m and n are nonzero integers such that $m > 0$ and $n < 0$. Which of the following *must* be negative?

    A. $-n^m$
    B. $-mn$
    C. m^n
    D. $-n - m$
    E. $n - m$

GO ON TO THE NEXT PAGE

Practice Test

34. The point $(-3,-2)$ is the midpoint of the line segment in the standard (x,y) coordinate plane with endpoints $(1,9)$ and (m,n). Which of the following is (m,n) ?

F. $(-7,-13)$

G. $(-2,7)$

H. $(-1,3.5)$

J. $(2,5.5)$

K. $(5,20)$

35. If $f(x) = 16x^2 - 20x$, what is the value of $f(3)$?

A. -12

B. 36

C. 84

D. 144

E. 372

36. What is the length of side AC in triangle ABC graphed on the following coordinate plane?

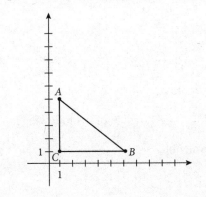

F. 3

G. 4

H. 5

J. 6

K. 7

37. If $f(x) = \dfrac{1}{3}x + 13$ and $g(x) = 3x^2 + 6x + 12$, which expression represents $f(g(x))$?

A. $x^2 + 12x + 4$

B. $\dfrac{x^2}{3} + 2x + 194$

C. $x^2 + 2x + 17$

D. $x^2 + 2x + 25$

E. $x^2 + 2x + 54$

38. What is the equation of a line that is perpendicular to the line $y = \dfrac{2}{3}x + 5$ and contains the point $(4,-3)$?

F. $y = \dfrac{2}{3}x + 4$

G. $y = -\dfrac{2}{3}x + 3$

H. $y = -\dfrac{3}{2}x + 3$

J. $y = -\dfrac{3}{2}x - 9$

K. $y = -\dfrac{3}{2}x + 9$

39. The formula for converting a Fahrenheit temperature reading to Celsius is $C = \dfrac{5}{9}(F - 32)$, where C is the reading in degrees Celsius and F is the reading in degrees Fahrenheit. Which of the following is the Fahrenheit equivalent to a reading of 95° Celsius?

A. 35°F

B. 53°F

C. 63°F

D. 203°F

E. 207°F

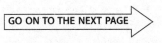

GO ON TO THE NEXT PAGE

Practice Test

40. When 3 times x is increased by 5, the result is less than 11. Which of the following is a graph of the real numbers x for which the previous statement is true?

F.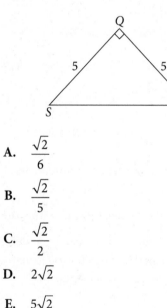

G.

H.

J.

K.

41. In the following triangle, what is the value of $\cos R$?

A. $\dfrac{\sqrt{2}}{6}$

B. $\dfrac{\sqrt{2}}{5}$

C. $\dfrac{\sqrt{2}}{2}$

D. $2\sqrt{2}$

E. $5\sqrt{2}$

42. Marvin has two saltwater fish tanks in his home. One has tangs and angelfish in a ratio of 5 to 2. The second tank has tangs and puffers in a ratio of 2 to 3. Marvin wants to put a tank in his office with angelfish and puffers using the same ratio he has at home to make it easier to buy food for them in bulk. What ratio of angelfish to puffers should he use?

F. 2:3

G. 2:5

H. 5:2

J. 5:7

K. 4:15

43. The volume of a sphere is given by the formula $V = \dfrac{4}{3}\pi r^3$, where r is the radius of the sphere. What is the volume, in cubic inches, of a sphere that has a diameter of 6 inches?

A. 3π

B. 9π

C. 27π

D. 36π

E. 288π

44. For all $x \neq -1$, which of the following is equivalent to $\dfrac{x^2 - 5x - 6}{x + 1} + x + 1$?

F. $x - 5$

G. $2x - 5$

H. $x^2 - 5x - 6$

J. $\dfrac{2x - 5}{x + 1}$

K. $\dfrac{x^2 - 4x - 5}{x + 1}$

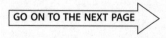

GO ON TO THE NEXT PAGE

45. Which of the following expressions is the greatest monomial factor of $60a^3b + 45a^2b^2$?

A. $15a^2b$

B. $15a^3b^2$

C. $15a^5b^3$

D. $180a^3b^2$

E. $180a^5b^3$

Use the following information to answer questions 46–47.

The population of fish in a certain pond from 1985 to 1995 is shown in the graph below.

Population of the Pond

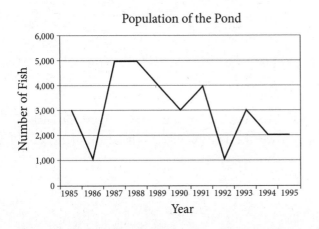

46. Which of the following best describes the percent change in the population from 1985 to 1995 ?

F. 33.33% increase

G. 33.33% decrease

H. 50% decrease

J. 333.33% increase

K. 333.33% decrease

47. Which of the following years contains the median population for the data?

A. 1986

B. 1989

C. 1990

D. 1991

E. 1995

---

48. The table below shows the results of a study identifying the number of males and females with and without college degrees who were unemployed or employed at the time of the study. If one person from the study is chosen at random, what is the probability that that person is an employed person with a college degree?

	Unemployed	Employed	Totals
Female Degree	12	188	200
Female No Degree	44	156	200
Male Degree	23	177	200
Male No Degree	41	159	200
Totals	120	680	800

F. $\dfrac{73}{160}$

G. $\dfrac{10}{17}$

H. $\dfrac{73}{136}$

J. $\dfrac{17}{20}$

K. $\dfrac{73}{80}$

GO ON TO THE NEXT PAGE

49. Which of the following expressions gives the number of distinct permutations of the letters in GEOMETRY ?

A. $8!(2!)$

B. $8!$

C. $\dfrac{8!}{2!}$

D. $\dfrac{8!}{6!}$

E. $\dfrac{8!}{(6!)(2!)}$

50. The graph below represents the solution set to which inequality, assuming each grid line represents 1 unit?

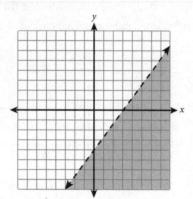

F. $y < -\dfrac{4}{3}x - 4$

G. $y > -\dfrac{3}{4}x - 4$

H. $y < \dfrac{3}{4}x - 4$

J. $y < \dfrac{4}{3}x - 4$

K. $y > \dfrac{4}{3}x - 4$

51. A function h is defined by $h(x,y,z) = 4xy^2 - yz^3$. What is the value of $h(2,-1,3)$?

A. -35

B. -19

C. -1

D. 19

E. 35

52. The radius of a circle is increased so that the radius of the new circle is triple that of the original circle. How many times larger is the area of the new circle than that of the original circle?

F. $\dfrac{1}{3}$

G. 3

H. 6

J. 6π

K. 9

53. The function $f(x) = 0.5\sin(2x)$ is graphed below over the domain $[0,2\pi]$. What is the period of the function?

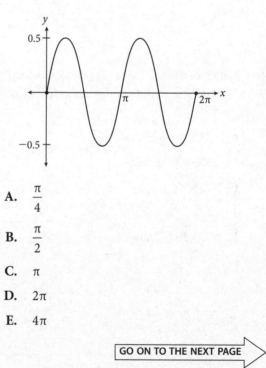

A. $\dfrac{\pi}{4}$

B. $\dfrac{\pi}{2}$

C. π

D. 2π

E. 4π

GO ON TO THE NEXT PAGE

Practice Test

54. For what value of x is the equation
$\sqrt[3]{4x - 12} + 25 = 27$ true?

F. -5

G. -1

H. -2.5

J. 5

K. 6.5

55. The chord shown in the figure is 8 units long. If the chord is 3 units from the center of the circle, what is the area of the circle?

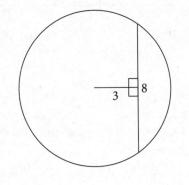

A. 9π

B. 16π

C. 18π

D. 25π

E. 28π

56. If $f(x) = 3^{3x + 3}$ and $g(x) = 27^{\left(\frac{2}{3}x - \frac{1}{3}\right)}$, for what value of x, if any, does the graph of $f(x)$ intersect the graph of $g(x)$?

F. -4

G. $-\dfrac{7}{4}$

H. $-\dfrac{10}{7}$

J. 2

K. The graphs do not intersect.

57. What value of x satisfies the equation $\log_3 (5x - 40) - \log_3 5 = 2$?

A. 17

B. 9

C. 1

D. -9

E. -17

58. A finite arithmetic sequence has five terms. The first term is 4. What is the difference between the mean and the median of the five terms?

F. 0

G. 1

H. 2

J. 4

K. 5

GO ON TO THE NEXT PAGE

Practice Test

59. In the following triangle, if cos ∠BAC = 0.6 and the hypotenuse of the triangle is 15, what is the length of side BC ?

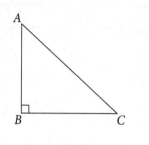

A. 3

B. 5

C. 10

D. 12

E. 15

60. The table below shows several points that lie on the graph of a parabola. Based on the data in the table, what is the value of y when $x = -4$?

x	y
−2	3
0	−3
2	−5
4	−3
6	3
8	13

F. −13

G. −5

H. 5

J. 13

K. Cannot be determined from the given information

IF YOU FINISH BEFORE TIME IS CALLED, YOU MAY CHECK YOUR WORK ON THIS SECTION ONLY. DO NOT TURN TO ANY OTHER SECTION IN THE TEST. **STOP**

Practice Test

READING TEST

35 Minutes—40 Questions

Directions: The Reading Test includes multiple passages. Each passage includes multiple questions. After reading each passage, choose the best answer and fill in the corresponding bubble on your answer sheet. You may review the passages as often as necessary.

Passage I

PROSE FICTION: This passage is adapted from *The Age of Innocence*, by Edith Wharton (1920).

It was generally agreed in New York that the Countess Olenska had "lost her looks."

She had appeared there first, in Newland Archer's boyhood, as a brilliantly pretty little girl
5 of nine or ten, of whom people said that she "ought to be painted." Her parents had been continental wanderers, and after a roaming babyhood she had lost them both, and been taken in charge by her aunt, Medora Manson, also a wanderer, who was
10 herself returning to New York to "settle down."

Poor Medora, repeatedly widowed, was always coming home to settle down (each time in a less expensive house), and bringing with her a new husband or an adopted child, but after a few
15 months she invariably parted from her husband or quarrelled with her ward, and, having got rid of her house at a loss, set out again on her wanderings. As her mother had been a Rushworth, and her last unhappy marriage had linked her to one of
20 the crazy Chiverses, New York looked indulgently on her eccentricities, but when she returned with her little orphaned niece, whose parents had been popular in spite of their regrettable taste for travel, people thought it a pity that the pretty child should
25 be in such hands.

Everyone was disposed to be kind to little Ellen Mingott, though her dusky red cheeks and tight curls gave her an air of gaiety that seemed unsuitable in a child who should still have been in
30 black for her parents. It was one of the misguided Medora's many peculiarities to flout the unalterable rules that regulated American mourning, and when she stepped from the steamer her family was scandalized to see that the crepe veil she wore for
35 her own brother was seven inches shorter than those of her sisters-in-law, while little Ellen wore a crimson dress and amber beads.

But New York had so long resigned itself to Medora that only a few old ladies shook their
40 heads over Ellen's gaudy clothes, while her other relations fell under the charm of her high spirits. She was a fearless and familiar little thing, who asked disconcerting questions, made precocious comments, and possessed outlandish arts, such
45 as dancing a Spanish shawl dance and singing Neapolitan lovesongs to a guitar. Under the direction of her aunt, the little girl received an expensive but incoherent education, which included "drawing from the model," a thing never
50 dreamed of before, and playing the piano in quintets with professional musicians.

Of course no good could come of this, and when, a few years later, poor Chivers finally died, his widow again pulled up stakes and departed
55 with Ellen, who had grown into a tall bony girl with conspicuous eyes. For some time no more was heard of them; then news came of Ellen's marriage to an immensely rich Polish nobleman of legendary fame. She disappeared, and when a few years later
60 Medora again came back to New York, subdued, impoverished, mourning a third husband, and in quest of a still smaller house, people wondered that her rich niece had not been able to do something for her. Then came the news that Ellen's own

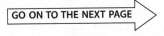

GO ON TO THE NEXT PAGE

65 marriage had ended in disaster, and that she was
herself returning home to seek rest and oblivion
among her kinsfolk.

These things passed through Newland Archer's
mind a week later as he watched the Countess
70 Olenska enter the van der Luyden drawing room
on the evening of the momentous dinner. In the
middle of the room she paused, looking about
her with a grave mouth and smiling eyes, and in
that instant, Newland Archer rejected the general
75 verdict on her looks. It was true that her early
radiance was gone. The red cheeks had paled;
she was thin, worn, a little older-looking than
her age, which must have been nearly thirty. But
there was about her the mysterious authority of
80 beauty, a sureness in the carriage of the head, the
movement of the eyes, which, without being in the
least theatrical, struck him as highly trained and
full of a conscious power. At the same time she was
simpler in manner than most of the ladies present,
85 and many people (as he heard afterward) were
disappointed that her appearance was not more
"stylish"—for stylishness was what New York most
valued. It was, perhaps, Archer reflected, because
her early vivacity had disappeared; because she
90 was so quiet—quiet in her movements, her voice,
and the tones of her voice. New York had expected
something a good deal more resonant in a young
woman with such a history.

1. The author describes which of the following
   practices as undesirable to New York society?

   A. Playing the piano

   B. Performing Spanish shawl dances

   C. Traveling

   D. Adopting children

2. With which of the following would the author
   most likely agree regarding New York society as
   it pertains to Medora?

   F. It is rigid and unaccepting of different
      behavior.

   G. It is usually whimsical, with few solid
      rules.

   H. It is often based on unrealistic
      expectations.

   J. It is snobbish but occasionally accepting of
      less common behavior.

3. It is most reasonable to infer that, after the death
   of Medora's third husband, Ellen did not help
   her aunt primarily because:

   A. Ellen was no longer wealthy, since her
      own marriage had failed.

   B. Medora had become embittered because
      she hadn't heard from Ellen for so long.

   C. Ellen resented the incoherent education
      she received from her aunt.

   D. receiving help from her niece would
      interfere with Medora's desire to be
      eccentric.

GO ON TO THE NEXT PAGE ⇨

4. Based on the characterization of Newland Archer in the last paragraph, he can best be described as:

    F. reflective and nonjudgmental.

    G. likable but withdrawn.

    H. disinterested but fair.

    J. stylish and gregarious.

5. In her descriptions of Medora, the author intends to give the impression that Medora is:

    A. eccentric and peripatetic.

    B. impoverished and resentful.

    C. kind and loyal.

    D. precocious and pretty.

6. As it is used in line 31, the word *flout* most nearly means:

    F. eliminate.

    G. exemplify.

    H. disregard.

    J. float.

7. What does the narrator suggest is a central characteristic of Medora Manson?

    A. Arrogance

    B. Immodesty

    C. Nonconformity

    D. Orthodoxy

8. Which of the following characters learns to do something otherwise unheard of by New York society?

    F. Ellen Mingott

    G. Newland Archer

    H. Medora Manson

    J. Count Olenska

9. The author includes reference to Medora's mother and Medora's marriage to "one of the crazy Chiverses" (lines 19–20) in order to indicate that:

    A. she had an unhappy childhood.

    B. her eccentricities were not surprising.

    C. she was the perfect person to raise Ellen.

    D. she was a wanderer.

10. One can reasonably infer from the passage that on the occasion of the dinner, Newland and Ellen:

    F. had not seen each other for some time.

    G. were interested in becoming romantically involved.

    H. were both disappointed with New York society.

    J. had just met, but were immediately attracted to each other.

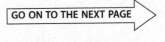
GO ON TO THE NEXT PAGE

Passage II

SOCIAL SCIENCE: The following passage is excerpted from a magazine article discussing scientific research on traditional methods of predicting the timing and character of the Indian monsoon.

Can traditional rules of thumb provide accurate weather forecasts? Researchers in Junagadh, India, are trying to find out. Most farmers in the region grow one crop of peanuts or castor per year. In a
5 wet year, peanuts give the best returns, but if the rains are poor, the more drought-tolerant castor is a better bet. In April and May, before the monsoon comes, farmers decide what to plant, buy the seed, prepare the soil and hope for the best. An accurate
10 forecast would be extremely helpful.

Little wonder, then, that observant farmers have devised traditional ways to predict the monsoon's timing and character. One such rule of thumb involves the blooming of the *Cassia fistula*
15 tree, which is common on roadsides in southern Gujarat. According to an old saying which has been documented as far back as the 8th century, the monsoon begins 45 days after *C. fistula's* flowering peak. Since 1996, Purshottambhai Kanani, an
20 agronomist at Gujarat Agricultural University, has been collecting data to test this rule. He records the flowering dates of trees all over the university's campus and plots a distribution to work out when the flowering peak occurs. While not perfect,
25 *C. fistula* has so far done an admirable job of predicting whether the monsoon will come early or late.

Similarly, with help from local farmers, Dr. Kanani has been investigating a local belief
30 regarding the direction of the wind on the day of Holi, a Hindu festival in spring. The wind direction at certain times on Holi is supposed to indicate the strength of the monsoon that year. Wind from the north or west suggests a good monsoon, whereas
35 wind from the east indicates drought. Each year before Holi, Dr. Kanani sends out postcards to more than 400 farmers in Junagadh and neighbouring districts. The farmers note the wind direction at the specified times, and then send the postcards back.

40 In years of average and above-average monsoons (1994, 1997, 1998, and 2001), the wind on Holi tended to come from the north and west. In the drier years of 1995 and 1996 the majority of farmers reported wind from the east (Dr. Kanani did not
45 conduct the study in 1999 and 2000). As with the *C. fistula* results, the predictions are not especially precise, but the trend is right.

Dr. Kanani first became interested in traditional methods in 1990, when an old saying attributed to
50 a tenth-century sage named Bhadli—that a storm on a particular day meant the monsoon would come 72 days later—proved strikingly correct. This prompted Dr. Kanani to collect other rules from old texts in Gujarati and Sanskrit.

55 Not all of his colleagues approve. Damaru Sahu, a meteorologist at Gujarat Agricultural University and a researcher for India's director-general of meteorology, says that traditional methods are "OK as a hobby." But, he goes on, they cannot be relied
60 upon, and "may not be applicable to this modern age." Yet Dr. Sahu concedes that meteorological science has failed to provide a useful alternative to traditional methods. For the past 13 years, he notes, the director-general for meteorology has
65 predicted "normal monsoon" for the country. Every year, the average rainfall over the whole country is calculated, and this prediction is proved correct. But it is no use at all to farmers who want to know what will happen in their region.

70 Dr. Kanani hopes that his research will put traditional methods on a proper scientific footing. He and his colleagues have even set up a sort of peer-review forum for traditional meteorology. Each spring, he hosts a conference for 100 local
75 traditional forecasters, each of whom presents a monsoon prediction with supporting evidence—the behaviour of a species of bird, strong flowering in a certain plant, or the prevailing wind direction that season. Dr. Kanani records these predictions and
80 publishes them in the local press.

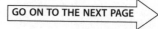

GO ON TO THE NEXT PAGE

He has also started a non-governmental organisation, the Varsha Vigyan Mandal, or Rain Science Association, which has more than 400 members. Its vice-president, Dhansukh
85 Shah, is a scientist at the National Directorate of Meteorology in Pune. By involving such mainstream meteorologists as Dr. Shah in his work, Dr. Kanani hopes to bring his unusual research to the attention of national institutions. They could
90 provide the funding for larger studies that could generate results sufficiently robust to be published in peer-reviewed science journals.

11. According to the passage, all of the following traditional methods of weather prediction have been scientifically tested EXCEPT:

   A. wind direction during the Hindi festival of Holi.

   B. the behavior of certain bird species.

   C. the flowering *Cassia fistula* trees.

   D. a tenth-century prediction connecting storm activity to later monsoons.

12. The author uses the phrase "useful alternative" (line 62) in order to show that:

   F. modern meteorology rarely provides an accurate forecast.

   G. equipment needed for accurate forecasting is too expensive for many in India.

   H. modern meteorology doesn't give as reliable predictions as traditional methods do.

   J. today's science is not yet able to provide specific meteorological forecasts needed by farmers.

13. According to the passage, a good monsoon is associated with winds from the:

   A. north.

   B. south.

   C. east.

   D. southwest.

14. The author's attitude toward traditional methods of weather forecasting may reasonably be described as:

   F. curious as to their development.

   G. cautious hopefulness that they are useful.

   H. skeptical regarding their real scientific value.

   J. regretful of the fad of interest in these methods.

15. According to the passage, which of the discussed methods gives the most advanced prediction of monsoon arrival?

   A. The behavior of the birds

   B. The flowering of the *C. fistula* tree

   C. The wind direction on Holi

   D. Bhadli's prediction based on storms

16. The function of the second paragraph in relation to the passage as a whole is most likely to provide:

   F. a reason that farmers need techniques to predict monsoons earlier.

   G. examples of the inexact nature of predictions made from traditional methods.

   H. an explanation of the ancient saying that the rest of the passage will examine.

   J. an introduction to the modern research of traditional methods.

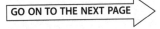

GO ON TO THE NEXT PAGE

17. According to the passage, the purpose of Dr. Kanani's springtime conferences is to:

    A. record the traditional methods of weather prediction before they disappear.

    B. help gain acceptance for traditional methods in the academic community.

    C. publish the methods in the local press.

    D. facilitate the exchange of ideas between farmers from far-flung regions of India.

18. According to the passage, the reason farmers use traditional methods to predict the weather is that:

    F. traditional methods are more accessible to rural populations.

    G. "normal" monsoons can still be very different from each other.

    H. they need to anticipate the local conditions for the coming growing season.

    J. traditional methods get the basic trends right.

19. The author uses the term "admirable job" (line 25) to indicate that:

    A. the flowering of the *C. fistula* tree provides remarkably predictive data on the coming monsoon.

    B. precision isn't everything.

    C. predictions based on the peak of *C. fistula*'s flowering do provide some reliable answers.

    D. sometimes rules of thumb are better than complex formulas.

20. According to Damaru Sahu, traditional weather prediction:

    F. can be curiously accurate.

    G. has a defined place in meteorology.

    H. is useful in some ways despite its lack of scientific foundation.

    J. appeals to an instinct different than the rational brain.

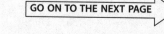

GO ON TO THE NEXT PAGE

Passage III

HUMANITIES: One of the most enjoyable ways to analyze culture is through music. By analyzing musical styles and lyrics, one can explore quintessential characteristics of particular cultures.

Passage A

Country music has its roots in the southern portions of the United States, specifically in the remote and undeveloped backcountry of the central and southern areas of the Appalachian
5 mountain range. Recognized as a distinct cultural region since the late nineteenth century, the area became home to European settlements in the eighteenth century, primarily led by Ulster Scots from Ireland. Early inhabitants have been
10 characterized as fiercely independent, to the point of rudeness and inhospitality. It was in this area that the region's truly indigenous music, now known as country music, was born.

Rooted in spirituals as well as folk music,
15 cowboy songs, and traditional Celtic melodies, country music originated in the 1920s. The motifs are generally ballads and dance tunes, simple in form and accompanied mostly by guitar, banjo, and violin. Though today there are many genres of
20 country music, all have their roots in this mélange of sources.

The term "country" has replaced the original pejorative term, "hillbilly." Hillbillies referred to Appalachian inhabitants who were considered poor,
25 uneducated, isolated, and wary; the name change reflects a more accepting characterization of these mountain dwellers.

Hank Williams put country music on the map nationally, and is credited with the movement of
30 country music from the South to more national prominence. Other early innovators include the Carter family, Ernest Tubb, Woody Guthrie, Loretta Lynn, and Bill Monroe, father of bluegrass music. More recently, Faith Hill, Reba
35 McEntire, and Shania Twain have carried on the tradition.

What might be considered the "home base" of country music is in Nashville, Tennessee, and the legendary music hall, the Grand Ole Opry. Founded
40 in 1925 by George D. Hay, it had its genesis in the pioneer radio station WSM's program *Barn Dance*. Country singers are considered to have reached the pinnacle of the profession if they are asked to become members of the Opry. While noted
45 country music performers and acts take the stage at the Opry numerous times, Elvis Presley performed there only once, in 1954. His act was so poorly received that it was suggested he return to his job as a truck driver.

50 The offshoots and relatives of country music highlight the complexity of this genre. In a move away from its mountain origins, and turning a focus to the West, honky-tonk music became popular in the early twentieth century. Its name is
55 a reference to its roots in honky-tonk bars, where the music was played. Additionally, Western Swing emerged as one of the first genres to blend country and jazz musical styles, which required a great deal of skill and creativity. Some of the most talented
60 and sophisticated musicians performing in any genre were musicians who played in bluegrass string bands, another relative of country music.

Country music has always been an expression of American identity. Its sound, lyrics, and performers
65 are purely American, and though the music now has an international audience, it remains American in its heart and soul.

Passage B

A style of music closely related to country is the similarly indigenous music known as
70 bluegrass, which originated in the Appalachian highland regions extending westwards to the Ozark Mountains in southern Missouri and northern Arkansas. Derived from the music brought over by European settlers of the region,
75 bluegrass is a mixture of Scottish, Welsh, Irish,

GO ON TO THE NEXT PAGE

and English melodic forms, infused, over time, with African-American influences. Indeed, many bluegrass songs, such as "Barbara Allen" and "House Carpenter" preserve their European roots,
80 maintaining the traditional musical style and narratives almost intact. Story-telling ballads, often laments, are common themes. Given the predominance of coal mining in the Appalachian region, it is not surprising that ballads relating to
85 mining tragedies are also common.

Unlike country music, in which musicians commonly play the same melodies together, bluegrass highlights one player at a time, with the others providing accompaniment. This tradition of
90 each musician taking turns with solos, and often improvising, can also be seen in jazz ensembles. Traditional bluegrass music is typically played on instruments such as banjo, guitar, mandolin, bass, harmonica, and Dobro (resonator guitar).
95 Even household objects, including washboards and spoons, have, from time to time, been drafted for use as instruments. Vocals also differ from country music in that, rather than featuring a single voice, bluegrass incorporates baritone and tenor
100 harmonies.

Initially included under the catch-all phrase "folk music," and later referred to as "hillbilly," bluegrass did not come into his own category until the late 1950s, and appeared first in the
105 comprehensive guide, *Music Index*, in 1965. Presumably it was named after Bill Monroe's Blue Grass band, the seminal bluegrass band. A rapid, almost frenetic pace, characterizes bluegrass tempos. Even today, decades after their most
110 active performing era, The Foggy Mountain Boys members Lester Flatt, a bluegrass guitarist and mandolinist, and Earl Scruggs, known for his three-finger banjo picking style, are widely considered the foremost artists on their instruments.
115 Partially because of its pace and complexity, bluegrass has often been recorded for movie soundtracks. "Dueling Banjos," played in the movie *Deliverance*, exemplifies the skill required by the feverish tempo of the genre. The soundtrack for

120 *O Brother, Where Art Thou?* incorporates bluegrass and its musical cousins folk, country, gospel, and blues. Bluegrass festivals are held throughout the country and as far away as the Czech Republic. Interactive, often inviting audience participation, they feature performers
125 such as Dolly Parton and Alison Krauss.

Central to bluegrass music are the themes of the working class—miners, railroad workers, farmers. The phrase "high, lonesome sound" was coined to represent the bluegrass undertones of intensity and cheerlessness,
130 symbolizing the hard-scrabble life of the American worker. As with so much of a nation's traditional music, and for better or worse, bluegrass music reflects America.

Questions 21–23 ask about Passage A.

21. According to the passage, country music originated from all of the following EXCEPT:

   A. Celtic melodies.

   B. spirituals.

   C. jazz.

   D. cowboy songs.

22. Which of the following would be the most logical place to hear the best of country music?

   F. Honky-tonk bars

   G. Ireland

   H. The Appalachian backcountry

   J. The Grand Ole Opry

23. As it is used in line 23, the word *pejorative* most nearly means:

   A. traditional.

   B. accurate.

   C. disparaging.

   D. mountain dwelling.

GO ON TO THE NEXT PAGE

Questions 24–26 ask about Passage B.

24. If a song were a lament with Welsh and African-American derivation, the author of Passage B would classify it as:

   F. bluegrass.

   G. country.

   H. jazz.

   J. hillbilly.

25. According to the passage, the instruments played in bluegrass music are:

   A. both typical and unusual.

   B. derived from African-American influences.

   C. made famous by the piece "Dueling Banjos."

   D. restricted to those used in the Ozarks.

26. In addition to highlighting one player at a time, bluegrass music differs from country music because it often:

   F. features harmonies sung by bass and tenor voices.

   G. features a single voice.

   H. is characterized by musicians commonly playing the same melodies together.

   J. is played on instruments such as the banjo and guitar.

Questions 27–30 ask about both passages.

27. It can be inferred that laments and high, lonesome sounds both reflect:

   A. the influence of Irish music.

   B. the challenges of American life.

   C. songs sung by Shania Twain.

   D. hillbilly music.

28. As it is used in the introductory information, *quintessential* most nearly means:

   F. old-fashioned.

   G. representative.

   H. charming.

   J. unconventional.

29. Passage A states that there were "talented and sophisticated" (lines 59–60) musicians playing bluegrass music. Which sentence in Passage B suggests this claim?

   A. "Central to bluegrass music are the themes of the working class—miners, railroad workers, farmers."

   B. "Partially because of its pace and complexity, bluegrass has often been recorded for movie soundtracks."

   C. "Lester Flatt, a bluegrass guitarist and mandolinist, and Earl Scruggs, known for his three-finger banjo picking style, are widely considered the foremost artists on their instruments."

   D. "A style of music closely related to country is the similarly indigenous music known as bluegrass . . ."

30. It can be inferred that both authors would agree that:

   F. country and bluegrass music are popular genres.

   G. both genres—country and bluegrass—are showcased at the Grand Ole Opry.

   H. music genres can evolve.

   J. country and bluegrass music are gaining in acceptance.

GO ON TO THE NEXT PAGE

Passage IV

NATURAL SCIENCE: The following passage appeared in *Science* magazine as "Pluto: The Planet That Never Was" by Govert Schilling. (© *Science*, Inc., 1999)

Nearly 70 years ago, Pluto became the ninth member of the sun's family of planets, but now it's on the verge of being cast out of that exclusive clan. The International Astronomical Union (IAU)
5 is collecting votes on how to reclassify the icy body: as the first (and largest) of the so-called trans-Neptunian objects, or as the 10,000th entry in the growing list of minor bodies orbiting the sun. In either case, Pluto may officially lose its planetary
10 status, leaving the solar system with only eight planets.

Children's books and planetariums may not acknowledge the loss. And Brian Marsden of the Harvard-Smithsonian Center for Astrophysics
15 in Cambridge, Massachusetts, who launched the discussion six years ago, says no one is trying to demote Pluto. "If anything, we're going to add to Pluto's status," he says, "by giving it the honor of a very special designation."

20 Cold comfort for Pluto, maybe, but its reclassification will at least end a long identity crisis, which began soon after its 1930 discovery at Lowell Observatory in Flagstaff, Arizona, by Clyde Tombaugh, who died in 1997. Pluto turned
25 out to be much smaller than all the other planets (according to recent estimates, its diameter is only 2200 kilometers), and its orbit is strangely elongated. It didn't belong with either the Earth-like rocky planets or the gas giants.

30 A clue to its true nature came in 1992, when David Jewitt of the University of Hawaii, Honolulu, and Jane Luu, then at the University of California, Berkeley, discovered a small, icy object beyond the orbit of Neptune. Provisionally cataloged as
35 1992 QB1, this ice dwarf measures a mere 200 kilometers in diameter. Since then many more trans-Neptunian objects (TNOs) have been detected, some of which move in very Pluto-like orbits around the sun.

40 These "supercomets" populate the Kuiper Belt, named after Dutch-American astronomer Gerard Kuiper, who predicted its existence in the early 1950s. "Pluto fits the picture [of the solar system] much better if it's viewed as a TNO," says Luu, who
45 is now at Leiden University in the Netherlands.

At present, more than 70 TNOs are known, and apparently, Pluto is just the largest member of this new family, which explains why it was found more than 60 years before number two. If astronomers
50 had known about the other TNOs back in the 1930s, Pluto would never have attained the status of a planet, Luu says: "Pluto was lucky."

A couple of months ago, the kinship between Pluto and the TNOs led Richard Binzel of the
55 Massachusetts Institute of Technology to propose that Pluto be made the first entry in a new catalog of TNOs for which precise orbits have been determined. It would then enter the textbooks as something like TN-1 (or TN-0, as some
60 astronomers have suggested).

Marsden agrees that Pluto is a TNO, but he doesn't like the idea of establishing a new catalog of solar system objects, arguing that astronomers already have a perfectly serviceable
65 list of numbered minor bodies (mostly asteroids). "The question is: Do we want to recognize [trans-Neptunian objects] with a different designation?" he asks. He points out that the Centaurs—TNOs that have been nudged well inside Neptune's
70 orbit—have been classified as asteroids and says he sees "no reason for introducing a new designation system for objects of which we have representations in the current [catalog of minor bodies]."

Instead of making Pluto the founding member
75 of a new catalog, Marsden wants to add it to the existing list. "The current number is 9826," he says. "With the current detection rate, we should arrive at number 10,000 somewhere in January or February." He notes that asteroids 1000, 2000,
80 3000, and so on have all been honored by the IAU

GO ON TO THE NEXT PAGE

Practice Test

with special names, including Leonardo and Isaac Newton. "What better way to honor Pluto than to give it this very special number?"

But the prospect of lumping Pluto with the solar
85 system's riffraff outrages supporters of a new TNO category. "It's the most idiotic thing" she's ever heard, says Luu. "Pluto is certainly not an asteroid," she says.

To try to settle the issue, Mike A'Hearn of the
90 University of Maryland, College Park, is collecting e-mail votes from 500 or so members of IAU divisions on the solar system, comets and asteroids, and other relevant topics. "I wanted to arrive at a consensus before Christmas [1998]," he says,
95 "but it may take a while, since the community as a whole doesn't seem to have a consensus." Neither proposal has attracted a majority. Although many people opposed Marsden's proposal, a comparable number were unhappy with Binzel's idea, A'Hearn
100 says, because Pluto would still be an anomaly, being much larger than the other trans-Neptunian objects. A'Hearn says that if no consensus can be reached, Pluto will probably not end up in any catalog at all, making it the ultimate outcast of the
105 solar system.

However the debate settles out, Pluto's career as a planet seems to be ending, and even astronomers are wistful at the prospect. "No one likes to lose a planet," says Luu. A'Hearn agrees. "It will probably
110 always be called the ninth planet" by the general public, he says.

31. According to the passage, regarding the view that Pluto should be categorized as an asteroid, Jane Luu expressed which of the following?

A. Shock

B. Excitement

C. Confusion

D. Forceful opposition

32. It can be inferred that Pluto's original designation as a planet would have never happened if scientists had:

F. understood its size from the beginning.

G. seen the icy core of Pluto sooner.

H. been able to detect the many smaller TNOs when Pluto was discovered.

J. understood the popular misconceptions about Pluto's planethood that would follow.

33. With which of the following statements would the author agree in regard to reclassifying Pluto?

A. It should be classified as a TNO.

B. It should be classified as an IAU.

C. It should remain a planet.

D. Its future classification is unclear.

34. According to the passage, large objects similar to the makeup and orbit of Pluto found nearer to the sun than Neptune are called:

F. Centaurs.

G. IAUs.

H. TNOs.

J. ice dwarves.

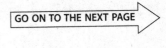
GO ON TO THE NEXT PAGE

35. According to lines 66–73, the central issue in the debate over Pluto is:

   A. whether Pluto is more similar to the rocky planets or the gas giants.

   B. the distance of Pluto from the sun.

   C. whether or not the unique qualities of Pluto warrant the creation of a new classification category for all TNOs.

   D. scientists' conception of Pluto versus the view of the general public.

36. As used in line 64, the term *serviceable* most nearly means:

   F. able to be fixed.

   G. adequate.

   H. beneficial.

   J. durable.

37. One slightly less scientific concern expressed by most of the scientists in the passage is:

   A. the role of the IAU in making classification decisions.

   B. respect for the views of the public.

   C. who gets the credit for Pluto's reclassification.

   D. the preservation of Pluto's fame and importance.

38. According to the passage, what is the major reason for lack of consensus regarding the status of Pluto?

   F. The general population resists the scientific community's belief that Pluto is not a planet.

   G. Pluto seems very different than the other members of any classification.

   H. Pluto's strange orbit makes it asteroid-like, but its surface more closely resembles a planet.

   J. There have been numerous discoveries of other Pluto-like objects nearer to the sun than to Neptune.

39. Details in the passage suggest that Pluto is much different from other planets in:

   A. its distance from the sun and the shape of its orbit.

   B. its size and the shape of its orbit.

   C. the year of its discovery and its size.

   D. its shape and surface composition.

40. Pluto's size accounts for:

   F. its classification as a TNO.

   G. its dissimilarity to asteroids.

   H. its early discovery relative to other TNOs.

   J. its bizarre orbit.

IF YOU FINISH BEFORE TIME IS CALLED, YOU MAY CHECK YOUR WORK ON THIS SECTION ONLY. DO NOT TURN TO ANY OTHER SECTION IN THE TEST. STOP

SCIENCE TEST

35 Minutes—40 Questions

Directions: The Science Test includes multiple passages. Each passage includes multiple questions. After reading each passage, choose the best answer and fill in the corresponding bubble on your answer sheet. You may review the passages as often as necessary.

You may NOT use a calculator on this test.

Passage I

Soil, by volume, consists on average of 45% minerals, 25% water, 25% air, and 5% organic matter (including both living and nonliving organisms). Time and topography shape the composition of soil and cause it to develop into layers known as *horizons*. The soil horizons in a particular area are collectively known as the *soil profile*. The composition of soil varies in each horizon, as do the most common minerals, as can be seen in the soil profile depicted in Diagram 1. Diagram 1 also shows the depth of each horizon and the overall density of the soil.

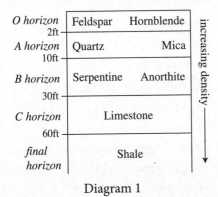

Diagram 1

Table 1 lists the zinc and calcium contents (as percentages) in the minerals that compose soil.

Table 1		
Mineral	Zinc content (%)	Calcium content (%)
Feldspar	35–40	0–10
Hornblende	30–35	10–20
Quartz	25–30	20–30
Mica	20–25	30–40
Serpentine	15–20	40–50
Anorthite	10–15	50–60
Limestone	5–10	60–70
Shale	0–5	70–80

Table 2 shows the average percentage of minerals that compose granite and sandstone, two rock types that are commonly found in soil.

Table 2		
Mineral	Percentage of mineral in:	
	Sandstone	Granite
Feldspar	30	54
Hornblende	2	0
Quartz	50	33
Mica	10	10
Serpentine	0	0
Anorthite	0	0
Limestone	5	0
Shale	0	0
Augite	3	3

GO ON TO THE NEXT PAGE

1. An analysis of an unknown mineral found in soil revealed its zinc content to be 32% and its calcium content to be 12%. Based on the data in Table 1, geologists would most likely classify this mineral as:

   A. hornblende.

   B. anorthite.

   C. serpentine.

   D. mica.

2. Geologists digging down into the A horizon would most likely find which of the following minerals?

   F. Limestone

   G. Shale

   H. Serpentine

   J. Mica

3. Based on the data presented in Diagram 1 and Table 1, which of the following statements best describes the relationship between the zinc content of a mineral and the depth below surface level at which it is dominant? As zinc content increases:

   A. depth increases.

   B. depth decreases.

   C. depth first increases, then decreases.

   D. depth first decreases, then increases.

4. If geologists were to drill 30 feet into the Earth, which of the following minerals would they most likely encounter?

   F. Quartz, mica, and limestone

   G. Feldspar, shale, and serpentine

   H. Feldspar, quartz, and anorthite

   J. Hornblende, limestone, and serpentine

5. If augite is most commonly found in soil in close proximity to the other minerals that make up granite, then augite would most likely be found at a depth of:

   A. less than 10 feet.

   B. between 10 feet and 30 feet.

   C. between 30 feet and 60 feet.

   D. greater than 60 feet.

6. Based on the passage, how is the percentage of zinc content related to the percentage of calcium content in the minerals that make up soil?

   F. The percentage of zinc content increases as the percentage of calcium content increases.

   G. The percentage of zinc content increases as the percentage of calcium content decreases.

   H. Both the percentage of zinc content and the percentage of calcium content remain constant.

   J. There is no discernible relationship between the percentage of zinc content and the percentage of calcium content.

GO ON TO THE NEXT PAGE

Practice Test

Passage II

Students conducted the following studies to determine the melting points of several materials. They attempted to melt the materials by submerging them in a variety of aqueous solutions that were heated to their boiling points. They used the following equation to calculate the boiling points of these solutions:

$$\Delta T_b = K_b \times m \times i,$$

where

ΔT_b = increase in boiling point above pure solvent

K_b = $0.512 \dfrac{°C \times kg}{mol}$

m = molality = $\dfrac{mol\ solute}{kg\ solvent}$

i = number of ions present per molecule of solute

Study 1

In order to prepare various solutions of sodium chloride (NaCl), 100.00 g of H_2O were added to a beaker. A known quantity of NaCl was dissolved into the water and the resulting boiling point of the solution was recorded. This procedure was repeated with different amounts of NaCl as shown in Table 1.

	Table 1		
Solution	Mass of H_2O (g)	Amount of NaCl (mol)	Boiling point (°C)
1	100.00	0	100.00
2	100.00	0.085	100.88
3	100.00	0.171	101.75
4	100.00	0.257	102.63
5	100.00	0.342	103.50

Study 2

In order to prepare various solutions of calcium chloride ($CaCl_2$), 100.00 g of H_2O were added to a beaker. A known quantity of $CaCl_2$ was dissolved into the water and the resulting boiling point of the solution was recorded. This procedure was repeated with different amounts of $CaCl_2$ as shown in Table 2.

	Table 2		
Solution	Mass of H_2O (g)	Amount of $CaCl_2$ (mol)	Boiling point (°C)
6	100.00	0.270	104.15
7	100.00	0.360	105.53
8	100.00	0.450	106.91
9	100.00	0.541	108.29
10	100.00	0.631	109.67

Study 3

Each solution from Studies 1 and 2 was brought to a boil. A small sample of a material was placed in each solution. If the material melted, a "Y" was marked in Table 3. If the material did not melt, an "N" was marked in Table 3. This procedure was repeated for all eight materials.

	Table 3									
	Solution									
Material	1	2	3	4	5	6	7	8	9	10
1	Y	Y	Y	Y	Y	Y	Y	Y	Y	Y
2	N	Y	Y	Y	Y	Y	Y	Y	Y	Y
3	N	N	Y	Y	Y	Y	Y	Y	Y	Y
4	N	N	N	N	Y	Y	Y	Y	Y	Y
5	N	N	N	N	N	Y	Y	Y	Y	Y
6	N	N	N	N	N	N	N	Y	Y	Y
7	N	N	N	N	N	N	N	N	N	Y
8	N	N	N	N	N	N	N	N	N	N

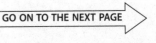

Practice Test

7. Which of the following modifications to Solution 5 of Study 1 would result in an increase in its boiling point?

   I. Increasing the K_b of the solution

   II. Increasing the amount of NaCl

   III. Replacing the NaCl with an equal amount of $CaCl_2$

   A. I only

   B. I and II only

   C. II and III only

   D. I, II, and III

8. In Study 1, what was the boiling point of the solution with 0.171 mol of NaCl?

   F. 100.00°C

   G. 100.88°C

   H. 101.75°C

   J. 109.67°C

9. Based on the results of the studies from the passage, the boiling point of Material 5 is most likely:

   A. less than 102.63°C.

   B. between 102.63°C and 103.50°C.

   C. between 103.50°C and 104.15°C.

   D. greater than 104.15°C.

10. If a sixth solution had been prepared during Study 2 using 0.721 mol $CaCl_2$, its boiling point would most likely be closest to which of the following?

   F. 108.75°C

   G. 111.07°C

   H. 113.72°C

   J. 115.02°C

11. A ninth material was submerged in Solutions 1–6 as in Experiment 3. Which of the following is LEAST likely to be a plausible set of results for this material?

	Solution					
	1	2	3	4	5	6
A.	Y	Y	Y	Y	N	N
B.	Y	Y	Y	Y	Y	Y
C.	N	N	N	N	Y	Y
D.	N	N	N	N	N	N

   A. A

   B. B

   C. C

   D. D

12. Which of the following best explains why the students recorded data for their solutes in mol rather than g or kg?

   F. The H_2O was already measured in kg.

   G. The units for mass are less accurate.

   H. The change in boiling point depends on molality.

   J. The melting points of the various materials do not depend on the masses of the materials.

13. Would the results of Studies 1–3 support the claim that Material 7 has a lower melting point than Material 8?

   A. Yes, because in Solution 10, Material 7 melted and Material 8 did not.

   B. Yes, because in Solution 10, Material 8 melted and Material 7 did not.

   C. No, because the melting point of Material 8 cannot be determined from the data.

   D. No, because the melting point of Material 7 cannot be determined from the data.

GO ON TO THE NEXT PAGE ⟹

Passage III

Engineers designing a roadway needed to test the composition of the soil that would form the roadbed. In order to determine whether their two sampling systems (System A and System B) give sufficiently accurate soil composition measurements, they first conducted a study to compare the two systems.

Soil samples were taken with varying levels of *humidity* (concentration of water). The concentrations of the compounds that form the majority of soil were measured. The results for the sampling systems were compared with data on file with the US Geological Survey (USGS), which compiles extremely accurate data. The engineers' and USGS' results are presented in Table 1 below.

Concentration (mg/L) of:	Level of Humidity				
	10%	25%	45%	65%	80%
Nitrogen (N)					
USGS	105	236	598	781	904
System A	112	342	716	953	1,283
System B	196	408	857	1,296	1,682
Potassium Oxide (K$_2$O)					
USGS	9.4	9.1	8.9	8.7	8.2
System A	9.4	9.0	8.7	8.5	8.0
System B	9.5	9.2	9.0	8.8	8.3
Calcium (Ca)					
USGS	39.8	24.7	11.4	5.0	44.8
System A	42.5	31.4	10.4	8.0	42.9
System B	37.1	23.2	11.6	11.1	45.1
Phosphorus Oxide (P$_2$O$_5$)					
USGS	69.0	71.2	74.8	78.9	122.3
System A	67.9	69.9	72.2	76.7	123.1
System B	74.0	75.6	78.7	82.1	126.3
Zinc (Zn)					
USGS	0.41	0.52	0.64	0.74	0.70
System A	0.67	0.80	0.88	0.97	0.93
System B	0.38	0.48	0.62	0.77	0.73

Table 1

Note: Each system concentration measurement is the average of 5 measurements.

GO ON TO THE NEXT PAGE

14. The hypothesis that increasing humidity increases the concentration of a compound is supported by the results for each of the following EXCEPT:

    F. nitrogen.

    G. potassium oxide.

    H. phosphorus oxide.

    J. zinc.

15. At a humidity level of 25%, it could be concluded that System B LEAST accurately measures the concentration of which of the following compounds, relative to the data on file with the USGS?

    A. N

    B. Ca

    C. K_2O

    D. P_2O_5

16. The engineers hypothesized that the concentration of potassium oxide (K_2O) decreases as the level of humidity increases. This hypothesis is supported by:

    F. the data from the USGS only.

    G. the System A measurements only.

    H. the data from the USGS and the System B measurements only.

    J. the data from the USGS, the System A measurements, and the System B measurements.

17. Do the results in Table 1 support the conclusion that System B is more accurate than System A for measuring the concentration of zinc?

    A. No, because the zinc measurements from System A are consistently higher than the zinc measurements from System B.

    B. No, because the zinc measurements from System A are closer to the data provided by the USGS than the zinc measurements from System B.

    C. Yes, because the zinc measurements from System B are consistently lower than the zinc measurements from System A.

    D. Yes, because the zinc measurements from System B are closer to the data provided by the USGS than the zinc measurements from System A.

GO ON TO THE NEXT PAGE

Practice Test

18. The relationship between humidity level and calcium concentration, as measured by System B, is best represented by which of the following graphs?

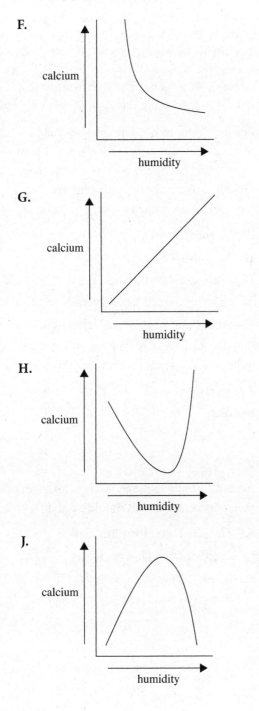

F.

G.

H.

J.

19. After conducting their comparisons, the engineers used System B to test a soil sample at the future road site. They measured the concentrations, in mg/L, of selected compounds in the sample and found that they were: potassium oxide = 9.1, calcium = 17.3, and zinc = 0.57. Based on the data in Table 1, the engineers should predict that the level of humidity is approximately:

A. 16%.

B. 37%.

C. 49%.

D. 57%.

GO ON TO THE NEXT PAGE

Passage IV

Diabetes is a metabolic disorder that causes hyperglycemia (higher-than-normal blood glucose levels). The most common form is type 2 diabetes, which occurs when the body does not produce enough insulin or has a lowered level of response to insulin (insulin resistance). Insulin is a hormone produced in the pancreas that helps regulate blood glucose levels by stimulating cells to absorb and metabolize glucose. Typically occurring in adults, type 2 diabetes has developed in an increasing number of individuals over 45 years old. Three scientists offered hypotheses to explain the cause of type 2 diabetes.

Scientist 1

Studies have shown that the consumption of sugar-sweetened drinks in excess is associated with an increased risk of type 2 diabetes. Thus, the cause of type 2 diabetes is an overconsumption of sugar. When sugar intake is high, the insulin in the body is unable to normalize the increased blood glucose levels. In a study of individuals 18–25 years old who consumed more than the daily recommended amount of sugar, although their insulin levels were normal, their blood glucose levels were significantly elevated. When these individuals received small injections of supplemental insulin once a day, their blood sugar did not return to normal levels.

Scientist 2

Type 2 diabetes primarily occurs as a result of obesity and lack of exercise. Experimental data have shown that diets high in fat but not high in sugar are associated with an increased risk of type 2 diabetes. In a study of healthy young men, those put on a high-fat diet had twice the blood glucose levels compared to those put on a high-carbohydrate diet. Excess fat in the bloodstream breaks down into free radicals that impair insulin action, causing cells to become insulin resistant and blood glucose levels to rise. Studies have also shown that the lack of exercise causes 7% of type 2 diabetes cases. Regular exercise can boost the body's efficiency to regulate blood glucose levels.

Scientist 3

Type 2 diabetes is not caused by lifestyle or diet but inherited. Studies have shown an increased risk of type 2 diabetes in people with a parent or sibling who has type 2 diabetes. More than 36 genes that contribute to the risk of type 2 diabetes have been found. Individuals have about a 15–20% chance of developing type 2 diabetes if one of their parents has it and a roughly 50% chance if both parents have it. The chance of siblings having type 2 diabetes is 25–50%.

20. The liver helps to regulate the amounts of glucose, protein, and fat in the blood. About eighty percent of people with diabetes have buildup of fat in the liver. This information, if true, would strengthen the viewpoint of:

    F. Scientist 1 only.

    G. Scientist 2 only.

    H. both Scientist 1 and Scientist 2.

    J. neither Scientist 1 nor Scientist 2.

21. Scientists 1 and 2 would most likely agree that the occurrence of type 2 diabetes in an individual is associated with the patient's:

    A. lifestyle.

    B. diet.

    C. genetics.

    D. age.

22. According to the passage, adults who have had their pancreas removed should exhibit:

    F. increased blood insulin levels.

    G. decreased blood sugar levels.

    H. increased blood sugar levels.

    J. decreased body fat content.

GO ON TO THE NEXT PAGE

Practice Test

23. Suppose that an individual had an 18% chance of developing type 2 diabetes. Based on the passage, Scientist 3 would most likely predict that this individual has:

    A. a high-sugar diet.

    B. a high-fat diet.

    C. one parent with type 2 diabetes.

    D. two parents with type 2 diabetes.

24. Suppose a 50-year-old patient developed type 2 diabetes. Which of the following statements is most consistent with the information in the passage?

    F. Scientist 1 would conclude that the patient consumes excess fat daily.

    G. Scientist 2 would conclude that the patient has a high-sugar diet.

    H. Scientist 3 would conclude that the patient fails to exercise.

    J. Scientist 3 would conclude that the patient had at least one parent with type 2 diabetes.

25. Which of the following discoveries, if accurate, would support the viewpoint of Scientist 1 ?

    A. High intake of sugar causes insulin resistance.

    B. High intake of fat causes impaired insulin action.

    C. Low intake of sugar causes increased insulin production.

    D. Low intake of sugar causes increased free radical production.

26. Which of the following arguments could Scientist 3 use as an effective counter to Scientist 2's claim that lack of exercise causes 7% of type 2 diabetes cases?

    F. The 7% that lacked exercise also have family histories of type 2 diabetes.

    G. More than 36 genes that contribute to the risk of type 2 diabetes have been found.

    H. The 7% that lacked exercise did not receive insulin injections.

    J. Scientist 2's hypothesis would suggest that more than 7% of type 2 diabetes cases should be due to lack of exercise.

GO ON TO THE NEXT PAGE

Passage V

Human blood is composed of approximately 45% *formed elements*, including blood cells, and 50% plasma. The formed elements of blood are further broken down into red blood cells, white blood cells, and platelets. The mass of a particular blood sample is determined by the ratio of formed elements to plasma; the formed elements weigh approximately 1.10 grams per milliliter (g/mL) and plasma approximately 1.02 g/mL. This ratio varies according to an individual's diet, health, and genetic makeup.

The following studies were performed by a phlebotomist to determine the composition and mass of blood samples from three different individuals, each of whom was required to fast overnight before the samples were taken.

Study 1

A 10-mL blood sample was taken from each of the three patients. The densities of the blood samples were measured using the *oscillator technique*, which determines fluid densities by measuring sound velocity transmission.

Study 2

Each 10-mL blood sample was spun for 20 minutes in a centrifuge to force the heavier formed elements to separate from the plasma. The plasma was then siphoned off and its mass recorded.

Study 3

The formed elements left over from Study 2 were analyzed using the same centrifuge, except this time they were spun at a slower speed for 45 minutes so that the red blood cells, white blood cells, and platelets could separate out. The mass of each element was then recorded. The results of the three studies are shown in Table 1.

			Table 1		
Patient	Plasma (g)	Red blood cells (g)	White blood cells (g)	Platelets (g)	Total density (g/mL)
A	4.54	2.75	1.09	1.32	1.056
B	4.54	2.70	1.08	1.35	1.054
C	4.64	2.65	1.08	1.34	1.050

27. The results of the studies indicate that the blood sample with the lowest density is the sample with the most:

    A. plasma.

    B. red blood cells.

    C. white blood cells.

    D. platelets.

GO ON TO THE NEXT PAGE

28. Which of the following offers the most reasonable explanation for why the phlebotomist required each patient to fast overnight before taking blood samples?

   F. It is more difficult to withdraw blood from patients who have not fasted.

   G. Fasting causes large, temporary changes in the composition of blood.

   H. Fasting ensures that blood samples are not affected by temporary changes caused by consuming different foods.

   J. Blood from patients who have not fasted will not separate when spun in a centrifuge.

29. Which of the following best explains why the amount of plasma, red blood cells, white blood cells, and platelets do not add up to 10.50 g in Patient C ?

   A. Some of the red blood cells might have remained in the plasma, yielding low red blood cell measurements.

   B. Some of the platelets might not have separated from the white blood cells, yielding high white blood cell counts.

   C. The centrifuge might have failed to fully separate the plasma from the formed elements.

   D. There are likely components other than plasma, red and white blood cells, and platelets in blood.

30. Based on the data collected from the studies, it is reasonable to conclude that, as total blood density increases, the mass of red blood cells:

   F. increases only.

   G. increases, then decreases.

   H. decreases only.

   J. decreases, then increases.

31. Suppose that a 10-mL blood sample from a fourth individual contains approximately 5 mL of plasma and approximately 5 mL of formed elements. The mass of this blood sample would most likely be:

   A. less than 10.0 g.

   B. between 10.0 and 12.0 g.

   C. between 12.0 and 14.0 g.

   D. greater than 14.0 g.

32. The phlebotomist varied which of the following techniques between Study 2 and Study 3 ?

   F. The volume of blood taken from each patient

   G. The mass of blood taken from each patient

   H. The instrument used to separate the elements of the blood samples

   J. The amount of time the samples were left in the centrifuge

33. The patient with the greatest mass of red blood cells is:

   A. Patient A.

   B. Patient B.

   C. Patient C.

   D. not possible to determine from the information given.

Practice Test

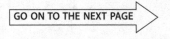

Passage VI

A student performed experiments to determine the relationship between the amount of electrical current carried by a material and the physical dimensions and temperature of a sample of that material. Current is measured in amperes (A) and the resistance to the flow of current is measured in ohms (Ω). Current and resistance are related to voltage, measured in volts (V), by Ohm's law: $V = A \times \Omega$. (Note that Ohm's law can also be written as $V = I \times R$, where V is voltage, I is current, and R is resistance.)

Experiment 1

The student used several lengths of an iron rod with a 1-cm diameter. The rods were heated or cooled to the specified temperatures and used to complete the circuit shown in Diagram 1. The circuit contains a battery and an ammeter, which measures current in milliamperes (mA). The results are presented in Table 1.

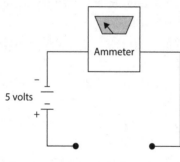

Ammeter

5 volts

Diagram 1

Table 1			
Trial	Length (cm)	Temperature (°C)	Current (mA)
1	16	80	20
2	16	20	40
3	12	80	27
4	12	20	53
5	10	80	32
6	10	20	64
7	8	80	40
8	8	20	80

Experiment 2

The student then repeated the experiment, this time using 1-cm diameter rods made from either iron or copper. The results are presented in Table 2.

Table 2				
Trial	Material	Length (cm)	Temperature (°C)	Current (mA)
9	Iron	16	80	20
10	Copper	16	80	100
11	Iron	16	20	40
12	Copper	16	20	200
13	Iron	12	80	27
14	Copper	12	80	135
15	Iron	12	20	53
16	Copper	12	20	265

34. Based on the experimental results, which of the following most accurately describes the relationships between current and rod length and between current and temperature?

F. Current is directly related to length and inversely related to temperature.

G. Current is inversely related to both length and temperature.

H. Current is inversely related to length and directly related to temperature.

J. Current is directly related to both length and temperature.

35. Based on the information from the passage, which of the following rods would have the highest value for resistance?

A. A 12-cm iron rod at 20°C

B. A 16-cm copper rod at 20°C

C. A 16-cm iron rod at 80°C

D. A 12-cm copper rod at 80°C

GO ON TO THE NEXT PAGE

36. The *conductivity* of a material is a measure of how readily a length of the material allows the passage of an electric current. Conductivity is represented by σ, the Greek letter sigma, with standard units of siemens per meter (S/m). Siemens are equivalent to inverse ohms (that is, $1/\Omega$). Based on this information, which of the following equations accurately describes the relationship between conductivity and resistance?

    F. $\Omega = \dfrac{1}{\sigma}$

    G. $\sigma = \Omega \times m$

    H. $\sigma = \dfrac{1}{\Omega \times m}$

    J. $\Omega = \sigma \times m$

37. If the rod used in Trial 4 of Experiment 1 were heated to a temperature of 50°C, the current it then conducts would most likely be:

    A. less than 27 mA.

    B. between 27 and 53 mA.

    C. between 53 and 80 mA.

    D. greater than 80 mA.

38. What would happen to the results of Experiment 2 if the student replaced the 5-V battery with a 10-V battery instead?

    F. The recorded current values would increase for both the copper and the iron rods.

    G. The recorded current values would increase for the copper rods but decrease for the iron rods.

    H. The recorded current values would decrease for the copper rods but increase for the iron rods.

    J. The recorded current values would decrease for both the copper and the iron rods.

39. Suppose the student took an iron rod of 8 cm and a copper rod of 8 cm, both with a 1-cm diameter, and attached them end to end, creating a composite rod with a length of 16 cm. Based on the results of Experiment 2, at a temperature of 20°C, this composite rod would most likely conduct a current of:

    A. less than 20 mA.

    B. between 20 and 40 mA.

    C. between 40 and 200 mA.

    D. greater than 200 mA.

40. Which of the following variables was NOT directly manipulated by the student in Experiment 2 ?

    F. Material

    G. Length

    H. Temperature

    J. Current

IF YOU FINISH BEFORE TIME IS CALLED, YOU MAY CHECK YOUR WORK ON THIS SECTION ONLY. DO NOT TURN TO ANY OTHER SECTION IN THE TEST.   STOP

Practice Test

WRITING TEST

40 Minutes—1 Question

Directions: The essay is used to evaluate your writing skills. You will have **40 minutes** to review the prompt and plan and write an essay in English. Before you begin, read everything in this test booklet carefully to make sure you understand the task.

Your essay will be judged based on the evidence it provides of your ability to do the following:

- Assert your own perspective on a complex issue and evaluate the relationship between your perspective and at least one other perspective

- Use reasoning and evidence to refine and justify your ideas

- Present your ideas in an organized way

- Convey your ideas effectively using standard written English

Write your essay on the lined essay pages in the answer booklet. All writing on those lined pages will be scored. Use the unlined pages in this test booklet to plan your essay. Your work on these unlined pages will not be scored.

Put your pencil down as soon as time is called.

DO NOT OPEN THIS BOOKLET UNTIL TOLD TO DO SO.

Scientific Research

A great deal of pure research, undertaken without specific goals but generally to further humankind's understanding of itself and its world, is subsidized at least partly, if not fully, by the nation's government to help drive progress and promote outcomes that improve overall quality of life for citizens. Though pure research often involves considerable time, energy, and money without any assurances of positive outcomes, it can result in economic, medical, and technological benefits. However, it can also result in negative, harmful, and perhaps irreversible outcomes, in which case taxpayer dollars can be wasted and society put at risk. Should governments fund research when the outcome is unclear? Given that taxpayers prefer that their dollars be spent efficiently and effectively, it may be unwise to allocate significant funding to endeavors that may not benefit society as a whole.

Read and carefully consider these perspectives. Each discusses government funding of scientific research.

Perspective One	Perspective Two	Perspective Three
Governments should fund as much pure research as they can afford when the intent is to benefit the mass population. Without the government's money, many research projects would have to cease unless alternative funding is secured. Even research without clear, positive consequences should be pursued because the outcome may prove beneficial, and the research can always be paused or stopped entirely if negative repercussions begin to emerge.	Governments should be very cautious and limit efforts to fund research programs with unclear consequences. Rather, these programs should demonstrate their worth and intended results when seeking government money. Governments should evaluate the merit and benefit of each program on a case-by-case basis and fund only those projects that are designed to create—and will likely achieve— clear and acceptable outcomes.	Governments should partner with private contributors to fund research. Private contributors include companies doing research and development as well as nonprofit foundations. These partnerships will distance the government from taking responsibility for any unintended or undesired consequences and relieve the burden on the taxpayer for efforts that do not prove beneficial. Additionally, this approach incentivizes research teams to provide results-based research that can generate private funding, thus increasing the chance that the research will prove useful to multiple entities, including the government.

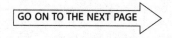
GO ON TO THE NEXT PAGE

Essay Task

Write a clear, well-reasoned essay evaluating multiple perspectives on government funding of scientific research. In your essay, be sure to:

- Assert your own perspective on the issue and evaluate the relationship between your perspective and at least one other perspective

- Use reasoning and evidence to refine and justify your ideas

- Present your ideas in an organized way

- Convey your ideas effectively using standard written English

Your perspective may be fully, somewhat, or not at all in agreement with one or more of the three perspectives in the prompt.

Planning Your Essay

These pages are not scored.

Use the space below to brainstorm and plan your essay. Consider the following as you think about the prompt:

- Strengths and weaknesses of the three perspectives in the prompt

  ○ What observations do they offer, and what do they overlook?

  ○ Why are they persuasive or why are they not persuasive?

- Your own background and identity

  ○ What is your perspective on this issue, and what are its strengths and weaknesses?

  ○ What evidence will you use in your essay?

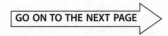

GO ON TO THE NEXT PAGE

_____

_____

_____

_____

_____

_____

_____

_____

_____

_____

_____

_____

_____

_____

_____

_____

_____

_____

_____

_____

_____

IF YOU FINISH BEFORE TIME IS CALLED, YOU MAY CHECK YOUR WORK ON THIS SECTION ONLY. DO NOT TURN TO ANY OTHER SECTION IN THE TEST. **STOP**

Practice Test

ANSWER KEY

ENGLISH TEST

1. **A**	16. **F**	31. **A**	46. **H**	61. **A**
2. **J**	17. **C**	32. **H**	47. **A**	62. **H**
3. **C**	18. **H**	33. **B**	48. **H**	63. **B**
4. **F**	19. **B**	34. **H**	49. **D**	64. **H**
5. **B**	20. **H**	35. **A**	50. **H**	65. **C**
6. **G**	21. **B**	36. **H**	51. **B**	66. **G**
7. **C**	22. **J**	37. **D**	52. **G**	67. **C**
8. **H**	23. **A**	38. **J**	53. **A**	68. **J**
9. **A**	24. **F**	39. **D**	54. **F**	69. **D**
10. **G**	25. **B**	40. **G**	55. **C**	70. **G**
11. **B**	26. **H**	41. **C**	56. **G**	71. **A**
12. **G**	27. **B**	42. **F**	57. **A**	72. **H**
13. **C**	28. **F**	43. **D**	58. **H**	73. **C**
14. **F**	29. **B**	44. **F**	59. **C**	74. **H**
15. **B**	30. **J**	45. **C**	60. **F**	75. **C**

MATHEMATICS TEST

1. **D**	13. **B**	25. **B**	37. **C**	49. **C**
2. **K**	14. **H**	26. **H**	38. **H**	50. **J**
3. **C**	15. **C**	27. **D**	39. **D**	51. **E**
4. **G**	16. **J**	28. **G**	40. **J**	52. **K**
5. **B**	17. **E**	29. **C**	41. **C**	53. **C**
6. **G**	18. **J**	30. **J**	42. **K**	54. **J**
7. **B**	19. **D**	31. **D**	43. **D**	55. **D**
8. **F**	20. **F**	32. **G**	44. **G**	56. **F**
9. **A**	21. **D**	33. **E**	45. **A**	57. **A**
10. **K**	22. **J**	34. **F**	46. **G**	58. **F**
11. **E**	23. **D**	35. **C**	47. **C**	59. **D**
12. **H**	24. **G**	36. **G**	48. **F**	60. **J**

READING TEST

1. C	9. B	17. B	25. A	33. D
2. J	10. F	18. H	26. F	34. F
3. A	11. B	19. C	27. B	35. C
4. F	12. J	20. H	28. G	36. G
5. A	13. A	21. C	29. C	37. D
6. H	14. G	22. J	30. H	38. G
7. C	15. D	23. C	31. D	39. B
8. F	16. J	24. F	32. H	40. H

SCIENCE TEST

1. A	9. C	17. D	25. A	33. A
2. J	10. G	18. H	26. F	34. G
3. B	11. A	19. B	27. A	35. C
4. H	12. H	20. G	28. H	36. H
5. A	13. A	21. B	29. D	37. B
6. G	14. G	22. H	30. F	38. F
7. D	15. A	23. C	31. B	39. C
8. H	16. J	24. J	32. J	40. J

ANSWERS AND EXPLANATIONS

ENGLISH TEST

Passage I

1. A   **Difficulty:** Low

Category: Sentence Structure and Formation

Getting to the Answer: When a period appears in the underlined portion, check to see if each sentence is complete. Here, each sentence is complete and correct; therefore, (A), NO CHANGE, is correct. Choice B creates a run-on sentence. Choices C and D create sentences that are awkward and overly wordy.

2. J   **Difficulty:** Medium

Category: Punctuation

Getting to the Answer: The ACT tests very specific punctuation rules. If punctuation is used in a way not covered by these rules, it will be incorrect. No commas are required in the underlined selection; (J) is correct. Choices F, G, and H all contain unnecessary commas.

3. C   **Difficulty:** Medium

Category: Sentence Structure and Formation

Getting to the Answer: When a verb is underlined, make sure it places the action properly in relation to the other events in the passage. This passage is written primarily in the present tense; *runs*, (C), is the best answer here. Choices A and B use verb tenses that do not make sense in context. The past tense verb in D is inconsistent with the rest of the passage.

4. F   **Difficulty:** Medium

Category: Knowledge of Language / Concision

Getting to the Answer: Very rarely will a correct answer choice be significantly longer than the original selection. The underlined selection is grammatically and logically correct, so check the answer choices for a more concise version. You can eliminate G and H, both of which are

wordier than the original. Choice J may be tempting because it's shorter than the underlined selection, but it changes the meaning of the sentence; the back office, not the reader, is what hasn't changed. Choice (F) is correct.

5. B   **Difficulty:** Medium

Category: Topic Development / Supporting Material

Getting to the Answer: When an English Test question contains a question stem, read it carefully. More than one choice is likely to be both relevant and correct, but only one will satisfy the conditions of the stem. This paragraph deals with the author's father's refusal to give up his old-fashioned ways. Choice (B) is the most consistent choice. Choices A and D describe the items being inventoried, which is irrelevant to the point of the paragraph. Choice C is redundant; since we already know he uses paper and pencil to keep his inventory, it's understood that he's writing it by hand.

6. G   **Difficulty:** Medium

Category: Sentence Structure and Formation

Getting to the Answer: Commas cannot be used to combine independent clauses. Here, the comma connects two independent clauses. Choice (G) correctly replaces the comma with a semicolon. Choice H corrects the run-on error but is unnecessarily wordy. Choice J leaves the meaning of the second clause incomplete.

7. C   **Difficulty:** High

Category: Sentence Structure and Formation

Getting to the Answer: Beware of answer choices that make changes to parts of the selection that contain no error; these choices will rarely be correct. As written, this sentence uses incorrect grammatical structure; the verb *is* is incorrect here, so you should eliminate A. Choice (C) eliminates it without introducing additional errors. Choices B and D correct the sentence's grammatical error, but neither uses the necessary contrast transition to relate this sentence to the one before it.

8. H   **Difficulty:** Low

Category: Punctuation

Getting to the Answer: Commas are used in a series of three or more; they are incorrect in compounds. "My sister and I" is a compound; no comma is needed, so F is incorrect. Choice (H) corrects the error without adding any new ones. Choice G uses the incorrect pronoun case; because you wouldn't say "me bought him a brand new computer," *me* is incorrect in the compound as well. Choice J incorrectly separates the sentence's subject and its predicate verb with a comma.

9. A   **Difficulty:** High

Category: Organization, Unity, and Cohesion / Transitions

Getting to the Answer: When a transition word or phrase is underlined, make sure it properly relates the ideas it connects. The underlined word is the transition between the offer to help transfer records and the information about other ways the computer could be helpful. The second sentence is a continuation of the first, so you can eliminate B and D, both of which suggest a contrast. Choosing between (A) and C is a little more difficult, but remember that new errors may be introduced in answer choices. *In addition* in C would be acceptable if it were followed by a comma, but as written, it's incorrect. Choice (A) is correct.

10. G   **Difficulty:** Medium

Category: Punctuation

Getting to the Answer: Semicolons can only combine independent clauses. Here, the second clause is not independent, so the semicolon is incorrect; eliminate F. Choice (G) correctly eliminates the semicolon. Choice H incorrectly places a comma after the conjunction. Choice J creates a run-on sentence.

11. B   **Difficulty:** High

Category: Topic Development / Writer's Purpose

Getting to the Answer: When asked about the purpose of particular information, consider the purpose of the larger section. This paragraph describes the father's resistance to technology, which stems in part from his desire to be able to work even in blackout conditions. The information about the town's history shows that blackout

conditions seldom occur, making the father's reason a bad one. Choice (B) reflects this reasoning, and it is correct. Choice A is too extreme; the father's reason may be poor, but that does not make him delusional. Choices C and D do not relate to the purpose of the paragraph.

12. G   **Difficulty:** Medium

Category: Organization, Unity, and Cohesion / Passage Organization

Getting to the Answer: When asked to add new information, read it into the passage at the points suggested to choose its most logical placement. There are three pronouns in this new sentence; clarity requires that it be placed somewhere that these pronouns have logical antecedents. Placing it after Sentence 1, as (G) suggests, gives each pronoun a clear antecedent: *we* is the author and his sister, *him* is their father, and *it* is the computer. Choice F puts the siblings' hopes about how a computer could help their father before the information that they bought him one. Choice H's placement makes the antecedent for *it* Father's *blackout scenario*, which doesn't make sense in context. Placing the new sentence where Choice J suggests gives the pronoun the antecedent *blackout*, which is also illogical.

13. C   **Difficulty:** Medium

Category: Usage

Getting to the Answer: Idiom questions often offer more than one idiomatically correct answer choice; use context to determine which is appropriate. "Sooner than later" is idiomatically incorrect, so you should eliminate A; these are comparison words, but nothing is compared here. Both B and (C) offer proper idioms, but (C) is the one that's appropriate here. Choice D is also incorrect idiomatic usage.

14. F   **Difficulty:** Medium

Category: Sentence Structure and Formation

Getting to the Answer: Remember to read for logic as well as for grammar and usage. The best version of this sentence is the way it is written; (F) is correct. Choice G redundantly uses the possessive *office's* where possession has already been indicated by *of*. Choice H misstates the information in the passage; the writer's father received the cell phone before the computer. Choice J incorrectly indicates that "the disorganized depths of that office" is where the writer's father received his cell phone, not where the cell phone ended up.

15. B   Difficulty: Low

Category: Organization, Unity, and Cohesion / Passage Organization

Getting to the Answer: When asked to add information, consider both subject matter and tone. This essay is about the author's father's resistance to technology. Choice (B) concludes the essay by referencing something stated at the beginning: that the writer's father tries to *hide* from the future. Choices A, C, and D, while relevant to the paragraph, do not provide strong conclusions to a passage about the father's aversion to technology.

Passage II

16. F   Difficulty: Medium

Category: Usage

Getting to the Answer: *More* or *-er* adjectives are used to compare two items; for more than two, use *most* or *-est*. This sentence is correct as written, (F); *farthest* is appropriate when comparing all areas of the globe. Choice G uses *most far*, which is incorrect in context. Choice H combines *most* with the *-est* suffix, which is never correct. Choice J uses *farther*, which indicates a comparison that is not present here.

17. C   Difficulty: Medium

Category: Sentence Structure and Formation

Getting to the Answer: The fact that the underlined portion contains multiple prepositions (*among* and *for*) is a clue to look for a misplaced modifier. It makes the most sense to describe equality as being *among races*, eliminating A and B. Choice D awkwardly places the noun after its modifying phrases, so (C) is correct.

18. H   Difficulty: Medium

Category: Usage

Getting to the Answer: Most ACT idiom questions will hinge on preposition usage. "Prevented . . . to participate" is idiomatically incorrect, so you can eliminate F. The proper idiom in this context is "prevented . . . from

participating," (H). Choices G and J are both idiomatically incorrect.

19. B   Difficulty: Medium

Category: Topic Development / Supporting Material

Getting to the Answer: When you're asked whether a piece of text is relevant, first determine the topic of the paragraph. This paragraph is about the evolution of the *color line* in baseball. Therefore, information that talks about the development of the industry and the shift in authority is relevant to the paragraph; (B) is correct. Choice A is incorrect because, although the text does talk about previous associations, knowing that range doesn't further the purpose of the paragraph. Choices C and D can be eliminated, since they indicate that the information is irrelevant.

20. H   Difficulty: Medium

Category: Punctuation

Getting to the Answer: A verb should not be separated from its object by a comma. As written, this sentence places an incorrect comma between the verb *had* and its object; eliminate F. Choice (H) eliminates the comma without introducing any additional errors. Choices G and J both add incorrect commas.

21. B   Difficulty: Medium

Category: Usage

Getting to the Answer: When a preposition is underlined, you're most likely being tested on idioms. Select the choice that sounds the most correct when read with the following noun phrase—in this case, *professional teams*. Because the leagues are made up *of* professional teams, (B) is correct here. Choices A, C, and D all suggest an incorrect relationship between the leagues and the teams.

22. J   Difficulty: Medium

Category: Topic Development / Supporting Material

Getting to the Answer: Determining whether or not the underlined text should be deleted will help you quickly eliminate two answer choices. If you eliminate the underlined selection, the passage skips abruptly from the decree losing its force to a discussion of specific African American players. The underlined text introduces those players generally, as a result of the decree losing its impact, and therefore provides a necessary transition, as indicated in (J). Choices F and G can be eliminated, since they advocate deleting the selection. The reasoning in H is not supported by the passage.

23. A   Difficulty: Medium

Category: Sentence Structure and Formation

Getting to the Answer: Expect about 25% of your English Test questions to have no error. This sentence is correct as written, (A). Choices B, C, and D all create sentence fragments.

24. F   Difficulty: Medium

Category: Usage

Getting to the Answer: The phrase "including Walker's brother Weldy" is properly used here to modify "a few other African Americans"; no change is needed, so (F) is correct. Choice G is incorrect because no comma is used to introduce a clause beginning with *that*. Choices H and J make the sentence wordier unnecessarily.

25. B   Difficulty: Medium

Category: Sentence Structure and Formation

Getting to the Answer: Use context to determine appropriate verb tense usage. The previous sentence says that Walker *was* a catcher; the introductory phrase in this sentence refers us to the same time period. Only (B) uses a consistent tense. Choices A, C, and D all refer to future actions.

26. H   Difficulty: Medium

Category: Organization, Unity, and Cohesion / Passage Organization

Getting to the Answer: Since NO CHANGE is not presented as an option, you'll need to find the most logical placement for the new sentence. *Other teams* must contrast with teams already mentioned, and the only place that happens is in Sentences 2 and 3. Sentence 2 talks about one player for the Blue Stockings, and Sentence 3 mentions some additional players for the same team. Sentence 4 turns to the time when segregation returned, so the information about African Americans playing for other teams must come before that, between Sentences 3 and 4, (H).

27. B   Difficulty: Low

Category: Knowledge of Language / Concision

Getting to the Answer: When you don't spot an error in grammar or usage, check for errors of style. "At the time when" is a longer way of saying *when*; (B) is correct here. Choice C uses *while*, which indicates a continuing period of time, but this sentence refers to a specific moment when Jackie Robinson crossed the color line. Choice D is even wordier than the original.

28. F   Difficulty: Medium

Category: Knowledge of Language / Precision

Getting to the Answer: Make sure your selection reflects the meaning of the sentence. The best version of this sentence is the way it is written, (F). Choice G changes the meaning of the sentence, implying that Robinson has yet to be recognized as a hero. Choice H also changes the sentence's meaning, indicating that Robinson is doing the recognizing rather than being recognized. Choice J is unnecessarily wordy.

29. B   Difficulty: High

Category: Knowledge of Language / Style and Tone

Getting to the Answer: A question that asks about the essay's tone will likely include only answer choices that are grammatically correct. Be as picky as possible when determining which choice best fits the stated tone and emphasis. Choice A is too neutral, so it should be eliminated. Choice C does not emphasize the uniqueness of Robinson's role; eliminate it. Choice D mentions collaboration, which emphasizes teamwork rather than uniqueness, so it is also incorrect. Someone who blazes a path goes where no one has gone before. Thus, only (B) maintains a positive tone while showing that Robinson played a unique role.

30. J   Difficulty: Medium

Category: Topic Development / Writer's Purpose

Getting to the Answer: This question format appears frequently on the ACT; it's asking for the passage's main idea. This essay is about the color barrier in baseball; it would not fulfill an assignment to write about the history of baseball, so you can eliminate F and G. The fact that baseball was played before 1868, H, is not the reason this

Practice Test

essay does not fulfill an assignment on baseball's history. Choice (J) correctly states the reasoning: the essay focuses only on one aspect of the game.

Passage III

31. A   Difficulty: Medium

Category: Punctuation

Getting to the Answer: An introductory phrase should be separated from the rest of the sentence by a comma. This introductory phrase is set off by a comma; the sentence is correct as written, (A). Choices B and C incorrectly treat the introductory phrase as an independent clause. Choice D incorrectly connects a dependent and an independent clause with the conjunction *and*.

32. H   Difficulty: Medium

Category: Usage

Getting to the Answer: When a pronoun is underlined, check whether it matches its antecedent. The underlined portion refers to the bridge, so the correct answer will be singular; eliminate F and G. Choice J contains a subject-verb agreement error; the singular *it* requires the singular *was*. Choice (H) is correct.

33. B   Difficulty: Medium

Category: Sentence Structure and Formation

Getting to the Answer: Make sure verb tenses make sense within the chronology of the passage. The past perfect is used in this sentence, but this tense is only correct when used to describe one past action completed before another. That is not the case here, so A is incorrect; (B) correctly replaces the verb with its past tense form. Choice C changes the meaning of the sentence (the legislature did the authorizing; it wasn't authorized by someone else) and creates a sentence that is grammatically incorrect. Choice D uses a conditional verb phrase, which is inappropriate in context.

34. H   Difficulty: Low

Category: Knowledge of Language / Concision

Getting to the Answer: When the underlined selection contains a compound, check to see if the words mean the same thing. If so, the correct answer choice will eliminate one of them. *Build* and *construct* mean the same thing, so you can eliminate F and G right away. The only difference between (H) and J is a comma, which is incorrect in a compound; eliminate J.

35. A   Difficulty: Medium

Category: Punctuation

Getting to the Answer: Where the only difference among the answer choices is comma placement, remember your tested rules. This sentence needs NO CHANGE, (A). Choice B incorrectly places a comma between items in a compound. Choice C places a comma after the conjunction in a compound, which is also incorrect. Choice D incorrectly inserts a comma between a preposition and its object.

36. H   Difficulty: Medium

Category: Topic Development / Writer's Purpose

Getting to the Answer: Read the sentence without the material in question to determine what it adds to the paragraph and therefore why it was included. Looking at the paragraph as a whole, you can see that the author mentions the amount of money invested, the prominence of the architects, and the accomplishments of the firm the architects brought in to help. Removing one of these details detracts from that description; (H) is the best choice here. Choice F can be eliminated because this is not the only detail that supports the larger point; in and of itself, it's not critical. Removing this one phrase wouldn't impact the transition, as G suggests. Choice J is a trap. The segment in question does concern finances, but the text only mentions the amount of money invested, not how it was raised.

37. D   Difficulty: High

Category: Usage

Getting to the Answer: On the ACT, *who* will only be correct when used to refer to people. Despite the fact that it's named after a person, "John A. Roebling and Sons" is the name of a company, so *who* isn't appropriate. That eliminates A and B. Choice C might be tempting because it's shorter than (D), but when C is read into the sentence, it creates a grammatical problem: "a company . . . and would later" requires another verb. Choice (D) is correct.

Practice Test

38. J   Difficulty: Medium

Category: Topic Development / Supporting Material

Getting to the Answer: Consider context when you're asked about the role a piece of text plays. A question that asks what would be lost if text were deleted is really just asking for the function of that text. If you read the paragraphs before and after the sentence in question, you'll see that what is missing is a clear transition; (J) is correct. Choice F distorts the meaning of the sentence, which discusses how long the project actually took, not how long it was expected to take. Choice G is out of scope; danger is only mentioned in this one sentence and then only in terms of how few lives were lost constructing the bridge. Choice H overstates the significance of the detail regarding construction time.

39. D   Difficulty: Medium

Category: Organization, Unity, and Cohesion / Transitions

Getting to the Answer: When transition words are underlined, focus on the relationship between the sentences or clauses they combine. The preceding sentence talks about the length of the bridge, and the sentence in which the underlined segment appears goes on to describe the cables in more detail. Since the second isn't a result of the first, you can eliminate A. Choice B inaccurately suggests an inconsistent or contradictory relationship between the sentences. Choice C is illogical; these are facts about the bridge, not events occurring simultaneously. The best choice here is no transition at all, as in (D).

40. G   Difficulty: Low

Category: Usage

Getting to the Answer: When you're tested on Usage, wrong answer choices may have the wrong word in context. They may also be wordy or passive. *Longer* means a comparison: one thing is longer *than* something else. Since this sentence doesn't offer a comparison, *longer* can't be correct. Eliminate F. Choices (G) and H are both grammatically correct in context, but H is unnecessarily wordy. *Lengthy*, in J, is not correct when used to describe a specific length.

41. C   Difficulty: Medium

Category: Sentence Structure and Formation

Getting to the Answer: When the underlined portion contains a comma, check for a run-on. Because the comma separates two independent clauses, A is incorrect. Choice B eliminates the subject of the second clause, so it is incorrect. Choice D incorrectly combines a semicolon and a FANBOYS conjunction. Choice (C) makes the second clause dependent and correctly separates the clauses with a comma. Choice (C) is correct.

42. F   Difficulty: Medium

Category: Punctuation

Getting to the Answer: Introductory phrases and clauses should be set off from the rest of the sentence by a comma. The comma here is used correctly, so no change is needed; (F) is correct. Choice G eliminates the comma, making the sentence difficult to understand. Both the colon in H and the semicolon in J would work only if the first clause were independent, which it is not.

43. D   Difficulty: Medium

Category: Organization, Unity, and Cohesion / Transitions

Getting to the Answer: When a transition word is underlined, check to see what ideas are being connected by the transition. The previous sentence mentions that the bridge was renamed, and the sentence beginning with the underlined portion switches to the present tense to describe the number of vehicles that cross the bridge daily. There is no logical contrast between these ideas, so B and C can be eliminated. Choice A indicates a continuation of the previous thought, but that does not fit the context; eliminate it. Choice (D) is correct, because it transitions from the past-tense description in the previous sentence to the present-tense description of the bridge's daily activity.

44. F   Difficulty: Medium

Category: Usage

Getting to the Answer: This sentence is correct as written, (F). Choice G replaces *more than* with *over*, which, despite its common usage, is actually a preposition that indicates location, not amount. Choice H is unnecessarily wordy. Choice J is also wordy and uses *amount*, which is incorrect for a countable noun like *vehicles*.

45. C   Difficulty: Medium

Category: Topic Development / Writer's Purpose

Getting to the Answer: As you read ACT English passages, develop a sense of the topic or *big idea*, just like you do in Reading; this question format is very common on the ACT. This passage is about one specific bridge, so it would not satisfy the requirement set out in the question stem. You can therefore eliminate A and B right away. Now turn to the reasoning. Choice D misstates the topic of the passage; (C) is correct.

Passage IV

46. H   Difficulty: Medium

Category: Sentence Structure and Formation

Getting to the Answer: Verbs in a compound should be in the same tense. The compound verb in this clause is "was . . . rising . . . and painted." Since the second verb is in the past tense, the first should be as well, so F is incorrect; (H) is correct. Choice G uses the gerund verb form without the necessary helping verb. Choice J is unnecessarily wordy.

47. A   Difficulty: Medium

Category: Topic Development / Writer's Purpose

Getting to the Answer: Read English Test question stems carefully. Often, all of the choices will be relevant and grammatically correct, but only one will fulfill the requirements of the stem. This question stem asks for a detail that shows a contrast between the quiet night streets and the daytime activity. The original text does this best. The verb in B does not convey the difference in the streets at these two times as well as *flood* in (A). Choice C is too general. Choice D does not provide the necessary contrast.

48. H   Difficulty: Medium

Category: Usage

Getting to the Answer: Use your Kaplan resources to familiarize yourself with commonly tested idioms. Although all four answer choices form idioms that would be correct in some contexts, one smiles *at* someone or something; (H) is correct.

49. D   Difficulty: Medium

Category: Knowledge of Language / Concision

Getting to the Answer: When you don't spot an error in grammar or usage, look for errors in style. Choice A is a wordy way of saying *traveled across*, (D). Choices B and C are unnecessarily wordy as well.

50. H   Difficulty: Low

Category: Sentence Structure and Formation

Getting to the Answer: Read question stems carefully. This one asks which answer choice would NOT be acceptable, which means that three of the choices will be correct in context. Choices F, G, and J are appropriate introductory clauses, but (H) is an independent clause, which makes the sentence a run-on.

51. B   Difficulty: Medium

Category: Topic Development / Supporting Material

Getting to the Answer: Use your Reading skills for questions like this one that ask for the function of a detail. The underlined portion tells us that the writer's journey will end in California. Choice (B) is correct. The underlined selection does not mention the reasons for the writer's trip, describe her route, or make any comparisons, so A, C, and D are incorrect.

52. G   Difficulty: Medium

Category: Punctuation

Getting to the Answer: Use commas in a list or series only if there are three or more items. Since the writer only mentions two places she has been, the first comma here is incorrect; eliminate F. Choice (G) corrects this without introducing any additional errors. Choice H eliminates the incorrect comma but removes the one at the end of the selection, which is needed to separate the introductory clause from the rest of the sentence. Choice J does not address the error.

53. A   Difficulty: Medium

Category: Organization, Unity, and Cohesion / Transitions

Getting to the Answer: To identify the most effective transition, you'll need to read both paragraphs. Paragraph 3

is about how the author has traveled to foreign countries but, within the United States, she only knows New York City. Paragraph 4 describes her drive through the Midwest. The text as written takes the reader from New York City (tall buildings) to the less populated areas, leading to the description of the cornfields. Choice (A), NO CHANGE, is the best choice here. Choice B misstates the passage; the cornfields didn't appear *almost immediately*, but gradually. Choice C and D do not provide appropriate transitions between the paragraphs.

54. F   Difficulty: Medium

Category: Topic Development / Supporting Material

Getting to the Answer: When you're asked to identify the *most relevant* choice, use context clues. The paragraph is about the change the author experiences as she drives from New York across the country. That contrast is clear in the passage as written; (F) is the best choice here. Choices G and H do not relate to the paragraph's topic. Choice J is opposite; the writer describes many different settings, which is the opposite of *monotonous*.

55. C   Difficulty: Medium

Category: Sentence Structure and Formation

Getting to the Answer: There are a number of ways to correct a run-on sentence, but only one answer choice will do so without introducing any additional errors. Each of the clauses in this sentence is independent; (C) corrects the run-on by replacing the comma with a semicolon. Choice B omits the comma necessary with the coordinating conjunction *but*. Choice D loses the contrast between the clauses that is present in the original.

56. G   Difficulty: Medium

Category: Usage

Getting to the Answer: When a single adverb is underlined, you are most likely being tested on idioms. Determine what is being modified. The underlined portion modifies the noun *serenity*, so it should be an adjective. Eliminate F. Choices H and J compare this serenity to other states of being, but there is no such comparison in the passage. Choice (G) is correct.

57. A   Difficulty: Medium

Category: Punctuation

Getting to the Answer: Only two apostrophe uses are tested on the ACT: possessive nouns and contractions. The noun here is possessive; the apostrophe is used correctly in (A). Choice B uses the plural *nights* instead of the possessive. Choice C is unnecessarily wordy and uses the idiomatically incorrect "shadows from the night." Choice D changes the meaning of the sentence.

58. H   Difficulty: Medium

Category: Knowledge of Language / Concision

Getting to the Answer: If you don't spot a grammar or usage error, check for errors in style. As written, this sentence is unnecessarily wordy, so F is incorrect; (H) provides the best revision. Choices G and J are still unnecessarily wordy.

59. C   Difficulty: Medium

Category: Organization, Unity, and Cohesion / Transitions

Getting to the Answer: When a transition word or clause is underlined, determine the relationship between the ideas being connected. Look at the relationship between the sentences in this paragraph. The ideas are presented chronologically—that is, in the order in which they happened. Choice (C), *At first*, is the best transition into this series of events. Choices A and B imply contradiction or qualification, which is incorrect in context. Choice D implies that a lot went on prior to the writer's not having any idea what she was looking at, but this is presented as the first in a series of events.

60. F   Difficulty: High

Category: Sentence Structure and Formation

Getting to the Answer: The correct answer will rarely be longer than the original selection. This question requires no change, so (F) is correct. The pronoun's antecedent appears in the previous sentence ("what I was looking at"), and the *-ing* verb form is used correctly. Choices G, H, and J are wordy; additionally, G introduces the passive voice unnecessarily.

Practice Test

Passage V

61. A   Difficulty: Low

Category: Punctuation

Getting to the Answer: Commas are used to combine an independent and a dependent clause. This sentence is correct as written, (A), with the comma properly placed after the introductory clause. Choice B places the comma incorrectly; *of 2003* is part of the introductory clause. Choice C omits the necessary comma. Choice D incorrectly uses a semicolon between a dependent and an independent clause.

62. H   Difficulty: Medium

Category: Sentence Structure and Formation

Getting to the Answer: The underlined portion introduces nonessential information, so it should not form an independent clause. Choices F and G both make the clause an independent one; they should be eliminated. The passage is in the past tense, making the present tense verb in J incorrect. Choice (H) is correct.

63. B   Difficulty: Medium

Category: Knowledge of Language / Precision

Getting to the Answer: Precision questions require you to look at context; frequently, words will have similar meanings but be used differently. *Height* means "the distance from the top to the bottom of something"; *altitude* means "height above sea level." Since *altitude* is correct in this context, you can eliminate A. Choices (B) and C both use *altitude,* but "at an altitude" is the correct idiom here; (B) is correct. Choice D creates a grammatically incorrect sentence.

64. H   Difficulty: High

Category: Organization, Unity, and Cohesion / Transitions

Getting to the Answer: When a transition word is underlined, check the logic of the transition as well as the grammar and punctuation. The sentence contrasts the famous and wealthy passengers with passengers who were ordinary people. Eliminate F and J because they do not express contrast. While G presents a contrast, it is grammatically incorrect. *Despite* creates a dependent clause requiring an *-ing* or *-ed* verb form, which is not

present in the sentence. Choice (H) is correct, both logically and grammatically.

65. C   Difficulty: High

Category: Usage

Getting to the Answer: Words like *that*, which are commonly misused in everyday speech, can make a question more challenging. Sound doesn't travel a speed, it travels *at* a speed; eliminate A. Only (C) makes the correction. Sound doesn't travel *to* a speed, as in B; *where*, D, will only be correct on the ACT when used to indicate location or direction.

66. G   Difficulty: Medium

Category: Topic Development / Writer's Purpose

Getting to the Answer: When asked about the purpose of a paragraph in relation to others, take a few seconds to summarize the paragraph in question, the one before it, and the one after it. The previous paragraph introduced the topic of supersonic aircraft. The paragraph in question transitions to questions of science, which are then discussed in the following paragraph. Choice (G) is correct. The paragraph does not provide an example or a counterargument, making F and H incorrect. The passage does not move from the general topic to a specific story, making J incorrect.

67. C   Difficulty: Medium

Category: Knowledge of Language / Precision

Getting to the Answer: Read English Test question stems carefully. This one asks for the LEAST acceptable alternative, which means that three of the choices will be correct in the sentence. All of the answer choices mean "change," so read each of them into the sentence. "Change them into," "translate them into," and "transform them into" are all appropriate usage, but "alter them into" is not because it changes the meaning. Choice (C) is correct here.

68. J   Difficulty: High

Category: Knowledge of Language / Concision

Getting to the Answer: Look for constructions that repeat words unnecessarily; these will be incorrect on the ACT. The sentence tells us that the speed at which sound travels through gas depends on three things: what kind of gas it is, the temperature, and the pressure; "it is traveling through" is redundant, so F is incorrect. Choice (J) is the most concise answer, and it does not lose any of the meaning of the underlined selection. Choices G and H do not address the error.

69. D   Difficulty: High

Category: Knowledge of Language / Ambiguity

Getting to the Answer: Don't choose the shortest answer if it fails to make the writer's meaning clear. "Air temperature and pressure decrease with altitude" isn't clear; "air temperature" and "pressure" themselves do not have altitude, and we're not told to what the altitude is referring, so A is incorrect. Choice (D) makes the writer's meaning clear; when altitudes are higher, the decrease in temperature and pressure occur. Choice B does not address the error and even compounds it by replacing *altitude* with *height*. Choice C contradicts the facts in the passage; higher, not lower, altitudes have this effect.

70. G   Difficulty: Medium

Category: Punctuation

Getting to the Answer: Beware of answer choices that make unnecessary changes to the sentence. The information provided in the two clauses contrasts, so *however* is correct, but it requires a comma to separate it from the rest of the clause. Eliminate F. Choice (G) is correct. Choice H creates an inappropriate cause-and-effect relationship between the clauses. Choice J does not address the punctuation error.

71. A   Difficulty: Medium

Category: Organization, Unity, and Cohesion / Passage Organization

Getting to the Answer: When you're asked to choose the most logical conclusion, first determine the sentence's function within the paragraph. The first half of this sentence previews a reason that the Concorde cruises at a higher altitude than regular planes, and it ties that reason back to the contrast between the speed of sound at two different altitudes. You need, then, a conclusion to the sentence that both explains why the planes would fly higher and does so in light of the information about altitude in the preceding sentence. The best choice here is (A); the original version of the sentence is the most logical.

Choice B doesn't provide a reason; it simply repeats information that has already been stated. Choice C is out of scope; fuel consumption isn't mentioned in the passage. Choice D is a result of the plane's higher altitude, not its cause.

72. H   Difficulty: High

Category: Sentence Structure and Formation

Getting to the Answer: The use of *since* creates a specific marking point in the past and requires a verb that does the same. You need a simple past verb with *since*; (H) is correct. Choice F uses a tense that indicates an action that is ongoing, but the decommissioning of the Concorde has been completed. Choice G is unnecessarily wordy. The past perfect in J is only correct when used to indicate one past action completed prior to another stated past action, which is not the case here.

73. C   Difficulty: Medium

Category: Knowledge of Language / Concision

Getting to the Answer: The phrases *about to* and *very soon* are redundant, making A, B, and D all incorrect. Furthermore, sentences beginning with coordinating (FANBOYS) conjunctions will not be correct on the ACT, which is an additional error in A. Only (C) correctly removes the redundancy.

74. H   Difficulty: Medium

Category: Organization, Unity, and Cohesion / Transition

Getting to the Answer: When a transition word is underlined, check to see if it makes sense in the context. The sentence discusses upcoming advances to supersonic travel. Choice F places the advances in the present, which does not match the future-tense *will* later in the sentence. Choice G is about location rather than time, which does not fit the context. Choices (H) and J both refer to a future time, but only (H) makes sense in context. The answer must be an adverb in order to describe when the advances will take place, but *Upcoming*, choice J, is an adjective. Choice (H) is therefore correct.

75. C   Difficulty: Medium

Category: Sentence Structure and Formation

Getting to the Answer: Here, the items combined by "not only . . . but also" are "to the rich and famous" and

Practice Test

"be for the masses." These items are correlated in the sentence, but they are not parallel in structure; eliminate A. Choices B and D do not address the error in parallel structure. Choice (C) corrects the error.

MATHEMATICS TEST

1. D   **Difficulty:** Low

Category: Essential Skills / Statistics and Probability

Getting to the Answer: The basketball team scored 364 points in 13 games, so they scored an average of $\frac{364}{13} = 28$ points per game. Choice (D) is correct.

2. K   **Difficulty:** Low

Category: Essential Skills / Numbers and Operations

Getting to the Answer: To convert a mixed number to an improper fraction, you have two options:

Option 1: Rewrite the whole number part using the denominator of the fraction part, then add. Here, the result is $\frac{28}{7} + \frac{3}{7} = \frac{31}{7}$.

Option 2: Use the shortcut rule, which is: Multiply the whole number by the denominator of the fraction and add the numerator, then write the result over the original denominator. Here, you get $4 \times 7 + 3 = 28 + 3 = 31$ over 7, or $\frac{31}{7}$.

Using either method, you arrive at a numerator of 31, which is (K).

3. C   **Difficulty:** Low

Category: Essential Skills / Expressions and Equations

Getting to the Answer: To solve for x, you need to isolate it on one side of the equation. To do this, subtract 18 from both sides, then divide by 4. The result is:

$$4x + 18 = 38$$
$$4x = 20$$
$$x = 5$$

Choice (C) is correct. Note that you could also Backsolve to answer this question, but the algebra is quicker.

4. G   **Difficulty:** Low

Category: Essential Skills / Numbers and Operations

Getting to the Answer: Because John weighs *more* than Ellen, begin by eliminating J and K, as doing so will reduce the chance of a miscalculation error. According to the question, John's 144 pounds represents 1.5 times Ellen's weight. Therefore, Ellen's weight must be $\frac{144}{1.5} = 96$ pounds. Choice (G) is correct.

If you're not sure whether to multiply or divide by 1.5, you could also set up an equation and solve it. Let $J =$ John's weight and $E =$ Ellen's weight. Translating from English to math gives:

$$J = 1.5E$$
$$144 = 1.5E$$
$$\frac{144}{1.5} = E$$
$$E = 96$$

5. B   **Difficulty:** Medium

Category: Essential Skills / Numbers and Operations

Getting to the Answer: To find the reciprocal of a number, swap the numerator and the denominator. You could use algebra to answer the question, but Backsolving is likely to be quicker. As usual, start with C:

The reciprocal of $\frac{4}{3}$ is $\frac{3}{4}$ and $\frac{4}{3} \div \frac{3}{4} = \frac{4}{3} \times \frac{4}{3} = \frac{16}{9}$. This is too big (and it's the flip of what you're looking for), so try (B) next:

The reciprocal of $\frac{3}{4}$ is $\frac{4}{3}$ and $\frac{3}{4} \div \frac{4}{3} = \frac{3}{4} \times \frac{3}{4} = \frac{9}{16}$. Choice (B) is correct.

6. G   **Difficulty:** Medium

Category: Higher Math / Number and Quantity

Getting to the Answer: The inverse operation of cube rooting is cubing, so cube both sides of the equation to solve for x:

$$\sqrt[3]{x} = \frac{1}{4}$$
$$x = \left(\frac{1}{4}\right)^3 = \frac{1}{4} \times \frac{1}{4} \times \frac{1}{4} = \frac{1}{64}$$

That's (G).

7. B   Difficulty: Low

Category: Higher Math / Algebra

Getting to the Answer: Isolate the variable, then solve for x. To do this, subtract 14 from both sides, then take the square root:

$$x^2 + 14 = 63$$
$$x^2 = 49$$
$$x = \pm 7$$

Choice (B) matches the positive value of x.

8. F   Difficulty: Medium

Category: Higher Math / Number and Quantity

Getting to the Answer: Don't let the vector notation scare you. Adding vectors works exactly as you would expect it to: To add two vectors, add the corresponding components. The question only asks about the value of a, so focus on the first entries only: $7 + a = 5$, which gives $a = 5 - 7$, or -2. Choice (F) is correct.

9. A   Difficulty: Low

Category: Essential Skills / Rates, Percents, Proportions, and Unit Conversion

Getting to the Answer: The quickest way to answer this question is to estimate. While you may or may not know 6% of 1,250 off the top of your head, 10% of 1,250 is 125. Because 6% < 10%, the correct answer must be less than 125. Only (A) works.

To solve this the more traditional way, multiply 1,250 by the decimal form of 6%: $1{,}250 \times 0.06 = 75$.

10. K   Difficulty: Low

Category: Essential Skills / Numbers and Operations

Getting to the Answer: When the choices are spaced far apart, estimation is generally the quickest way to the correct answer. To estimate, round 5.2 to 5 and 6.8 to 7. Because $5^3 + 7^2 = 125 + 49 = 174$, the correct answer will be close to 174. That would be (K).

11. E   Difficulty: Low

Category: Higher Math / Number and Quantity

Getting to the Answer: You certainly could reason this question out logically, but it's much easier to just pick a

starting balance, make the error described in the question, and see which answer choice matches. Suppose Lexi starts with a balance of $100. If she accidentally adds $40 to this amount, the incorrect new balance is $140. If she had subtracted instead, the correct balance would have been $60. Thus the incorrect balance is $140 − $60 = $80 more than is should be. Choice (E) is correct.

12. H   Difficulty: Medium

Category: Essential Skills / Numbers and Operations

Getting to the Answer: To answer this question, you'll need to follow the order of operations (PEMDAS).

First, evaluate the parentheses:

$$3^3 \div 9 + (6^2 - 12) \div 4$$
$$= 3^3 \div 9 + (36 - 12) \div 4$$
$$= 3^3 \div 9 + 24 \div 4$$

Next, simplify the exponent:

$$3^3 \div 9 + 24 \div 4 = 27 \div 9 + 24 \div 4.$$

Then, take care of any multiplication and/or division, from left to right: $27 \div 9 + 24 \div 4 = 3 + 6$.

Finally, take care of any addition and/or subtraction, from left to right: $3 + 6 = 9$.

So (H) is correct.

13. B   Difficulty: Low

Category: Essential Skills / Expressions and Equations

Getting to the Answer: Each banana costs $0.24, so the price of x bananas is $0.24x$. Similarly, each orange costs $0.38, so the price of y oranges is $0.38y$. Therefore, the total price of x bananas and y oranges is $0.24x + 0.38y$. That's (B).

14. H   Difficulty: Low

Category: Essential Skills / Rates, Percents, Proportions, and Unit Conversion

Getting to the Answer: To find the percent shaded, divide the number of shaded triangles by the total number of triangles. There are 24 small triangles in all, and 8 of them are shaded: $\frac{8}{24} = \frac{1}{3} = 33\frac{1}{3}\%$. Choice (H) is correct.

Practice Test

15. C   Difficulty: Medium

Category: Essential Skills / Rates, Percents, Proportions, and Unit Conversion

Getting to the Answer: The ratio of girls to boys is 5:3, so the ratio of girls to the total number of seniors is 5:(3 + 5), or 5:8. Call g the number of girls in the senior class. Set up a proportion and cross-multiply to solve for g:

$$\frac{5}{8} = \frac{g}{168}$$
$$8g = 840$$
$$g = 105$$

There are 105 girls in the senior class, which is (C).

16. J   Difficulty: Medium

Category: Essential Skills / Statistics and Probability

Getting to the Answer: When a question about averages involves a missing value (here, the final test score), it often helps to think in terms of the sum instead. For Sarah's exam scores to average at least a 90, they must sum to at least $90 \times 4 = 360$. She already has an 89, a 93, and an 84, so she needs at least $360 - (89 + 93 + 84)$, which gives $360 - 266 = 94$ points on her final test. Choice (J) is correct.

17. E   Difficulty: Low

Category: Essential Skills / Expressions and Equations

Getting to the Answer: Treat inequalities just as you would equations. The only exception is that if you multiply or divide by a negative number, you must flip the inequality symbol.

$$3x - 11 \geq 22$$
$$3x \geq 33$$
$$x \geq 11$$

This matches (E).

18. J   Difficulty: Medium

Category: Essential Skills / Statistics and Probability

Getting to the Answer: Probability is the number of desired outcomes divided by the total number of possible outcomes. Here, you're given the probability $\left(\frac{3}{4}\right)$ and the number of desired outcomes (48). You're looking

for the total number of possible outcomes (the number of dominos in the pile). Let d represent the number of dominos in the pile. Set up an equation using the definition of probability and the given information:

$$P(\text{even \# dots}) = \frac{\text{\# with even \# dots}}{\text{total \# dominos in pile}} = \frac{3}{4}$$
$$\frac{3}{4} = \frac{48}{d}$$
$$3d = 192$$
$$d = 64$$

Choice (J) is correct.

19. D   Difficulty: Low

Category: Essential Skills / Expressions and Equations

Getting to the Answer: This is a straightforward substitution question, so just be careful of the negative signs. Plug in 4 for x and $-\frac{1}{2}$ for y and simplify:

$$3x - 8y$$
$$= 3(4) - 8\left(-\frac{1}{2}\right)$$
$$= 12 - (-4)$$
$$= 12 + 4$$
$$= 16$$

That's (D).

20. F   Difficulty: Medium

Category: Essential Skills / Rates, Percents, Proportions, and Unit Conversion

Getting to the Answer: Whenever multiple rates are given, pay very careful attention to the units. As you read the question, decide how and when you will need to convert units. Use the factor-label method as needed. The answer choices are given in hours and minutes, so start by converting the given typing rate from words per second to words per minute:

$$\frac{3.75 \text{ words}}{1 \text{ second}} \times \frac{60 \text{ seconds}}{1 \text{ minute}} = \frac{225 \text{ words}}{1 \text{ minute}}$$

Next, find the number of words in the 25-page transcript:

$$\frac{675 \text{ words}}{1 \text{ page}} \times 25 \text{ pages} = 16,875 \text{ words}$$

Finally, let m be the number of minutes it takes the court reporter to type the whole transcript. Set up a proportion and solve for m:

$$\frac{225 \text{ words}}{1 \text{ minute}} = \frac{16{,}875 \text{ words}}{m \text{ minutes}}$$

$$225m = 16{,}875$$

$$m = 75$$

Because 75 minutes is not an answer choice, convert it to hours and minutes: 75 minutes = 1 hour, 15 minutes, making (F) the correct answer.

21. D   Difficulty: Low

Category: Essential Skills / Geometry

Getting to the Answer: When two parallel lines are cut by a transversal, half of the angles will be acute and half will be obtuse. Each acute angle will have the same measure as every other acute angle. The same is true of every obtuse angle. Furthermore, the acute angles will be supplementary to the obtuse angles. Based on the information provided, $\angle a$ is an acute angle measuring 68°. Based on the figure, $\angle f$ is an obtuse angle, so $\angle a$ must be supplementary to $\angle f$. Therefore, the measure of $\angle f$ is $180° - 68° = 112°$. Choice (D) is correct.

22. J   Difficulty: Medium

Category: Essential Skills / Rates, Percents, Proportions, and Unit Conversion

Getting to the Answer: If the student copy is $\frac{1}{4}$ the size of the wall map, then 2.5 inches on the student map would be $2.5 \times 4 = 10$ inches on the wall map. Now set up a proportion to find the actual distance between the cities using the scale of the wall map:

$$\frac{1}{100} = \frac{10}{x}$$

$$x = 1{,}000$$

The correct answer is (J).

23. D   Difficulty: Medium

Category: Essential Skills / Numbers and Operations

Getting to the Answer: The piece of paper is $8\frac{1}{2}$ inches wide. To find the number of $\frac{5}{8}$-inch wide strips of paper you can cut, divide:

$$8\frac{1}{2} \div \frac{5}{8} = \frac{17}{2} \div \frac{5}{8}$$

$$= \frac{17}{2} \times \frac{8}{5}$$

$$= \frac{136}{10} = \frac{68}{5} = 13.6$$

Thus, you can make 13 strips of paper that are $\frac{5}{8}$ of an inch wide and 11 inches long, and you will have a small, thin strip of paper left over. Choice (D) is correct.

24. G   Difficulty: Medium

Category: Essential Skills / Geometry

Getting to the Answer: This is a pair of parallel lines cut by a transversal, but this time, there's also a triangle thrown into the mix. Begin with segment AB. This is a transversal, so $\angle MAB$ and $\angle ABC$ are alternate interior angles and $m\angle MAB = m\angle ABC = 55°$. Because triangle ABC is isosceles with $AB = AC$, $m\angle ACB$ is also 55° (base angles of an isosceles triangle have equal measures). Choice (G) is correct.

25. B   Difficulty: Low

Category: Higher Math / Algebra

Getting to the Answer: Use the slope formula to find the slope of the line:

$$m = \frac{y_2 - y_1}{x_2 - x_1}$$

$$= \frac{-6 - 0}{0 - (-10)}$$

$$= -\frac{6}{10}$$

$$= -\frac{3}{5}$$

That's (B).

26. H   Difficulty: Medium

Category: Higher Math / Algebra

Getting to the Answer: This question seems long, but it actually isn't that complicated. FOIL the first pair of binomials, FOIL the second pair, then add the results by combining like terms:

$$(x + 4)(x - 4) = x(x) + x(-4) + 4(x) + 4(-4)$$

$$= x^2 - 4x + 4x - 16$$

$$= x^2 - 16$$

(If you noticed the difference of squares above, that will save you some time.)

$$(2x + 2)(x - 2) = 2x(x) + 2x(-2) + 2(x) + 2(-2)$$
$$= 2x^2 - 4x + 2x - 4$$
$$= 2x^2 - 2x - 4$$

Finally, add the two polynomials by combining like terms:

$$\boxed{x^2} \boxed{- 16} + \boxed{2x^2} - 2x \boxed{- 4} = 3x^2 - 2x - 20$$

Choice (H) is correct.

27. D   Difficulty: Medium

Category: Higher Math / Geometry

Getting to the Answer: To find the distance between two points that don't have either the same x-coordinates or the same y-coordinates, plug the points into the Distance formula and evaluate:

$$\begin{aligned}
\text{Distance} &= \sqrt{(x_2 - x_1)^2 + (y_2 - y_1)^2} \\
&= \sqrt{(-2 - 3)^2 + (6 - (-6))^2} \\
&= \sqrt{(-5)^2 + 12^2} \\
&= \sqrt{25 + 144} \\
&= \sqrt{169} \\
&= 13
\end{aligned}$$

Choice (D) is correct.

28. G   Difficulty: Medium

Category: Essential Skills / Rates, Percents, Proportions, and Unit Conversion

Getting to the Answer: Look for shortcuts; you could write an equation and solve for h, but is there a faster way? Examine the two percents: 30 percent is half of 60 percent, so 30 percent of h will be half of 60 percent of h, or half of 80, which is 40. That's (G).

29. C   Difficulty: Medium

Category: Higher Math / Statistics and Probability

Getting to the Answer: Because the integers in Set A are consecutive, their average must equal their middle term. In a set of 7 integers, the middle one is the fourth term.

To find the smallest term, count backward from 46: 46, 44, 42, 40. That's (C). You can also answer this question by using Backsolving. Start with (C). If 40 is the smallest integer of Set A, then the next six consecutive integers must be 42, 44, 46, 48, 50, and 52. Take the average of these 7 integers:

$$\frac{40 + 42 + 44 + 46 + 48 + 50 + 52}{7} = \frac{322}{7} = 46$$

This matches the condition in the question stem: The average of these consecutive integers equals 46, so (C) must be the correct answer.

30. J   Difficulty: Medium

Category: Higher Math / Functions

Getting to the Answer: Test the sum for 2, then 3, then 4, then 5 terms of the sequence to see if a relationship can be determined. If $n = 2$, the sum is $1 + 3 = 4$. If $n = 3$, the sum is $1 + 3 + 5 = 9$. If $n = 4$, the sum is $1 + 3 + 5 + 7 = 16$. If $n = 5$, the sum is $1 + 3 + 5 + 7 + 9 = 25$. The sum is always equal to the square of n. Therefore, the correct answer is (J).

31. D   Difficulty: Medium

Category: Higher Math / Number and Quantity

Getting to the Answer: To multiply two matrices, the sizes (# of rows by # of columns) must match in a certain way. Here, the size of the first matrix is 2×2 and the size of the second is 2×1. If you multiply a 2×2 matrix by a 2×1 matrix (which is possible because the middle dimensions match), the result will be a 2×1 matrix (the outer dimensions when the sizes are written as a product). This means you can eliminate A, B, and C, which are all 2×2 matrices. To multiply the matrices, multiply each element in the first row of the first matrix by the corresponding element in the second matrix and add the products. Then repeat the process using the second row of the first matrix:

$$\begin{bmatrix} -2 & 0 \\ 1 & -3 \end{bmatrix} \cdot \begin{bmatrix} 2 \\ 2 \end{bmatrix} = \begin{bmatrix} -2(2) + 0(2) \\ 1(2) + (-3)(2) \end{bmatrix} = \begin{bmatrix} -4 \\ -4 \end{bmatrix}$$

Choice (D) is correct.

32. G   **Difficulty:** Medium

Category: Higher Math / Geometry

Getting to the Answer: This is an area question with a twist—you're cutting a piece out of the rectangle. To find the area of the remaining space, you will need to subtract the area of the sandpit from the area of the original playground. Recall that the area of a rectangle is length × width. The dimensions of the original playground are $x + 7$ and $x + 3$, so its area is $(x + 7)(x + 3)$ which FOILS to $x^2 + 10x + 21$. The sandpit is a square with side x, so its area is x^2. Remove the pit from the playground, and the remaining area is $x^2 + 10x + 21 - x^2 = 10x + 21$. Choice (G) is correct.

33. E   **Difficulty:** High

Category: Higher Math / Number and Quantity

Getting to the Answer: Because $m > 0$, m is a positive number; likewise, because $n < 0$, n is a negative number. Consider each answer choice and decide whether the expression must be positive, negative, or could be either depending on the values of m and n. Keep in mind that m and n can be even or odd integers.

A: $-n^m \to$ If m is even, n^m is positive so $-n^m$ is negative. However, when m is odd, n^m is negative, so $-n^m$ is positive. Eliminate this choice.

B: $-mn \to$ Because one number is positive and the other is negative, the product mn must be negative, so $-mn$ must be positive. Eliminate this choice.

C: $m^n \to m$ is positive, so m raised to any exponent will also be positive. A negative exponent simply means to take the reciprocal of the number, not to give the number a negative sign. Eliminate this choice.

D: $-n - m \to -n$ equals $-(-\text{number})$, which is positive, and m is positive, so $-n - m$ is a positive minus a positive. If $m > -n$, then $-n - m$ will be negative. However, if $-n > m$, then $-n - m$ will be positive. Eliminate this choice.

(E): $n - m \to n$ is negative and m is positive, so $n - m$ is a negative minus a positive. This must be negative, so (E) is the correct answer.

34. F   **Difficulty:** Medium

Category: Essential Skills / Geometry

Getting to the Answer: Use the midpoint formula and the given midpoint to solve for m and n:

$$M = \left(\frac{x_1 + x_2}{2}, \frac{y_1 + y_2}{2} \right)$$
$$(-3, -2) = \left(\frac{1 + m}{2}, \frac{9 + n}{2} \right)$$

Once you have the formula set up and all the given information plugged in, separate the coordinates into two equations and solve for the variables:

$$-3 = \frac{1 + m}{2} \quad \text{and} \quad -2 = \frac{9 + n}{2}$$
$$-6 = 1 + m \qquad\qquad -4 = 9 + n$$
$$-7 = m \qquad\qquad\quad -13 = n$$

Thus $(m, n) = (-7, -13)$, which is (F).

35. C   **Difficulty:** Low

Category: Higher Math / Functions

Getting to the Answer: When given a function and a value of x, plug in the number value for each x in the equation and simplify. Make sure you follow the order of operations:

$$f(x) = 16x^2 - 20x$$
$$f(3) = 16(3)^2 - 20(3)$$
$$= 16(9) - 60$$
$$= 144 - 60 = 84$$

Choice (C) is the answer.

36. G   **Difficulty:** Low

Category: Essential Skills / Geometry

Getting to the Answer: To find the length of a line segment on the coordinate plane, you would normally need to use the Distance formula. This requires the coordinates of the segment's two endpoints. Because A (1,5) and C (1,1) have the same x-coordinate, a much faster way is to simply subtract the y-coordinate of C from the y-coordinate of A. The length of segment AC is $5 - 1$, or 4. Choice (G) is correct.

Practice Test

37. C   Difficulty: Medium

Category: Higher Math / Functions

Getting to the Answer: With nested functions, work from the inside out. To answer this question, substitute the entire rule for $g(x)$ for x in the function $f(x)$, then simplify:

$$f(g(x)) = \frac{1}{3}(3x^2 + 6x + 12) + 13$$
$$= x^2 + 2x + 4 + 13$$
$$= x^2 + 2x + 17$$

Choice (C) is correct.

38. H   Difficulty: Medium

Category: Higher Math / Algebra

Getting to the Answer: Perpendicular lines have negative-reciprocal slopes. Because the line in the question has a slope of $\frac{2}{3}$ (the coefficient of x), the line you are looking for must have a slope of $-\frac{3}{2}$. Eliminate F and G. The question also says that this line contains the point $(4, -3)$. Plugging all of this information into the equation of a line, $y = mx + b$, will allow you to find the final missing piece of the equation—the y-intercept:

$$y = mx + b$$
$$-3 = -\frac{3}{2}(4) + b$$
$$-3 = -6 + b$$
$$3 = b$$

With a slope of $-\frac{3}{2}$ and a y-intercept of 3, the line is $y = -\frac{3}{2}x + 3$, which matches (H).

39. D   Difficulty: Medium

Category: Higher Math / Algebra

Getting to the Answer: This looks like a chemistry or physics question, but in fact it's just a "plug in the number and solve for the missing quantity" question. Be sure to plug 95 in for C (not F). To clear the fraction (rather than

distributing it), multiply both sides of the equation by the reciprocal of $\frac{5}{9}$:

$$C = \frac{5}{9}(F - 32)$$
$$95 = \frac{5}{9}(F - 32)$$
$$\frac{9}{5} \times 95 = F - 32$$
$$F - 32 = 171$$
$$F = 171 + 32 = 203$$

Choice (D) is correct.

40. J   Difficulty: Medium

Category: Higher Math / Algebra

Getting to the Answer: First, translate from English to math: "3 times x is increased by 5" translates to $3x + 5$, and "the result is less than 11" translates to < 11. Put these together to write an inequality and then solve for x:

$$3x + 5 < 11$$
$$3x < 6$$
$$x < 2$$

This inequality is graphed with an open circle at 2 (because x cannot equal 2) and shaded to the left, where the numbers are less than 2. Your graph should look like (J).

41. C   Difficulty: Medium

Category: Higher Math / Geometry

Getting to the Answer: Because $QS = QR$, triangle QRS must be a 45°-45°-90° triangle and the hypotenuse is $5\sqrt{2}$. Remember that $\cos = \frac{\text{adjacent}}{\text{hypotenuse}}$. Therefore:

$$\cos R = \frac{5}{5\sqrt{2}}$$
$$= \frac{1}{\sqrt{2}}$$
$$= \frac{1}{\sqrt{2}} \times \frac{\sqrt{2}}{\sqrt{2}} = \frac{\sqrt{2}}{2}$$

Choice (C) is correct.

42. K   Difficulty: High

Category: Essential Skills / Rates, Percents, Proportions, and Unit Conversion

Getting to the Answer: You need to find the ratio of angelfish to puffers. You're given two ratios: tangs to angelfish and tangs to puffers.

Both of the given ratios contain tangs, but the tang amounts (5 and 2) are not the same. To directly compare them, find a common multiple (10). Multiply each ratio by the factor that will make the number of tangs equal to 10:

tangs to angelfish: (5:2) × (2:2) = 10:4

tangs to puffers: (2:3) × (5:5) = 10:15

Now that the number of tangs are the same in both ratios, you can merge the two ratios to compare angelfish to puffers directly: **4**:10:**15**. So the proper ratio of angelfish to puffers is 4:15, which is (K).

43. D   Difficulty: Low

Category: Higher Math / Geometry

Getting to the Answer: This question is testing whether you can substitute into a formula correctly. Because you are told the diameter is 6, you know the radius, r, of the sphere is 3. Plug this value into the formula and simplify:

$$V = \frac{4}{3}\pi(3)^3 = \frac{4}{3}\pi(27) = 36\pi$$

Choice (D) is correct.

44. G   Difficulty: Medium

Category: Higher Math / Algebra

Getting to the Answer: To simplify the given expression, look for factors in the fraction term that will cancel. Use the denominator as a hint as to how to factor the numerator. Be careful—you cannot simply cancel the $x + 1$ in the denominator with the $x + 1$ at the end of the expression.

$$\frac{x^2 - 5x - 6}{x + 1} + x + 1 = \frac{(x + 1)(x - 6)}{x + 1} + x + 1$$
$$= x - 6 + x + 1$$
$$= 2x - 5$$

Choice (G) is correct.

45. A   Difficulty: Medium

Category: Higher Math / Algebra

Getting to the Answer: Don't let the language throw you—*greatest monomial factor* just means the greatest common factor. Look for the largest number that divides evenly into 60 and 45. (Use the answer choices as a hint). The number is 15, so eliminate D and E. Next, look for the highest power of each variable that appears in *both* terms: a^2 and plain b. Thus, the greatest monomial factor is $15a^2b$, which is (A).

46. G   Difficulty: Low

Category: Higher Math / Statistics and Probability

Getting to the Answer: Percent change is calculated by dividing the amount of change by the original amount. In 1985, the population was 3,000; in 1995, the population was 2,000. Thus the amount of change was 1,000. Divide this by the original amount (the 1985 population) to find that the percent change was $1,000 \div 3,000 = 0.3333$, or 33.33%. The population went *down* from 1985 to 1995, so this is a decrease of 33.33%, which is (G).

47. C   Difficulty: Medium

Category: Higher Math / Statistics and Probability

Getting to the Answer: This question requires brute force. You need to list the data value corresponding to each year, order the values from least to greatest, find the median (the middle value), match it to a year in the graph, and then select the correct answer.

85	86	87	88	89	90
3,000	1,000	5,000	5,000	4,000	3,000
91	92	93	94	95	
4,000	1,000	3,000	2,000	2,000	

Order the data, keeping the year labels:

86	92	94	95	85	90
1,000	1,000	2,000	2,000	3,000	3,000
93	89	91	87	88	
3,000	4,000	4,000	5,000	5,000	

The median of this group is the sixth value, or 3,000. The years 1985, 1990, and 1993 all had populations of 3,000. The only one of these years among the answer choices is 1990, which is (C).

48. F   Difficulty: Medium

Category: Higher Math / Statistics and Probability

Getting to the Answer: Identify which pieces of information from the table you need. The question asks for the probability that a randomly chosen person from the study is employed and has a college degree, so you need the total of both females and males with college degrees who are employed compared to all the participants in the study. There are 188 employed females with a college degree and 177 employed males with a college degree for a total of 365 employed people with a college degree out of 800 participants, so the probability is $\frac{365}{800}$, which reduces to $\frac{73}{160}$, (F).

49. C   Difficulty: High

Category: Higher Math / Statistics and Probability

Getting to the Answer: Distinct permutations are permutations without repetition. You need to find the number of unique orderings of the letters GEOMETRY. If all eight letters were different, the number of unique orderings would be 8!. Because the E is repeated, you must divide by 2! to account for the repeated E. The result is $\frac{8!}{2!}$, which is (C).

Note that this process is the same as using the formula for "indistinguishable" outcomes: $\frac{n!}{a! \times b! \times \ldots}$. The number of letters is 8 (so $n = 8$), and there are 2 indistinguishable E's, so $a = 2$ and there is no b.

50. J   Difficulty: Low

Category: Higher Math / Geometry

Getting to the Answer: To match an inequality to its graph, you need to consider three things: the equation of the line, whether the line should be solid or dashed, and the direction of the shading. You can use any, or all, of these things to eliminate choices. Here, the shading is below (or less than) the line, so the inequality symbol should be <. Eliminate G and K. The line is dashed, but all the symbols are strict inequalities, so this doesn't help. The y-intercept of the line is -4 and the line rises 4 units for each 3 units that it runs, so the slope is $\frac{4}{3}$. This means the correct inequality is $y < \frac{4}{3}x - 4$, which is (J).

51. E   Difficulty: Medium

Category: Higher Math / Functions

Getting to the Answer: Occasionally, you may encounter a function that is defined in terms of two or three independent variables. These functions behave just as you would expect them to. As with any function, substitute the given values for the corresponding variables and simplify. Here, $x = 2$, $y = -1$, and $z = 3$.

$$h(x,y,z) = 4xy^2 - yz^3$$
$$h(2,-1,3) = 4(2)(-1)^2 - (-1)(3)^3$$
$$= 4(2)(1) - (-1)(27)$$
$$= 8 + 27$$
$$= 35$$

Choice (E) is correct.

52. K   Difficulty: Medium

Category: Higher Math / Geometry

Getting to the Answer: Write the formula for the area of a circle, using r to represent the radius of the original circle in the question: $A = \pi r^2$. This is the area of the original circle. Then write the formula for the area of the new larger circle, using $3r$ as the radius: $A = \pi(3r)^2 = \pi(9r^2) = 9\pi r^2$.

Now, divide the two areas (area of the new circle by the area of the original circle) to find out how many times larger the area of the new circle is compared to the area of the original circle.

$$\frac{\text{area of new circle}}{\text{area of original circle}} = \frac{9\pi r^2}{\pi r^2} = 9$$

Choice (K) is correct.

53. C   Difficulty: High

Category: Higher Math / Functions

Getting to the Answer: You don't really have to know anything about trig functions to answer this question. You just need to know the definition of *period*: The period of a repeating function is the distance along the x-axis required for the function to complete one full cycle. For a sine curve, this means one full wave (one up "bump" and one down "bump"). Here, that happens between 0 and π, which means the period is π. Choice (C) is correct.

If you happen to know the normal period of sine, which is 2π, you could also set the x term ($2x$) equal to that period and solve for x. You'll get $2x = 2\pi$, which simplifies to $x = \pi$.

54. J   Difficulty: High

Category: Higher Math / Algebra

Getting to the Answer: Solving equations that involve radicals may seem daunting, but they work just like other equations. In fact, they're usually easier to solve than quadratic equations because you don't have to worry about factoring. As a general rule, you need to: 1) isolate the radical part; 2) eliminate the radical by squaring both sides of the equation if the radical is a square root, cubing both sides if it's a cube root, and so on; and 3) isolate the variable. To solve the equation here, the steps are:

$$\sqrt[3]{4x - 12} + 25 = 27$$
$$\sqrt[3]{4x - 12} = 2$$
$$\left(\sqrt[3]{4x - 12}\right)^3 = 2^3$$
$$4x - 12 = 8$$
$$4x = 20$$
$$x = 5$$

Choice (J) is correct. Note that you could also use Back-solving to answer this question.

55. D   Difficulty: Medium

Category: Higher Math / Geometry

Getting to the Answer: The chord is perpendicular to the line segment from the center of the circle, so that line segment must be its perpendicular bisector. This allows you to add the following measures to the figure:

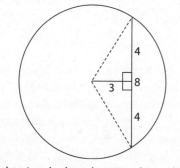

The two right triangles have legs 3 and 4, so they are both 3-4-5 right triangles with hypotenuse 5. This hypotenuse

is also the radius of the circle, so plug that into the area formula to solve:

$$A = \pi r^2$$
$$= \pi(5)^2$$
$$= 25\pi$$

The correct answer is (D).

56. F   Difficulty: High

Category: Higher Math / Functions

Getting to the Answer: Don't let the function notation intimidate you. The graphs of two functions intersect when the function equations are equal. Therefore, you need to set the equations equal to each other and solve for x.

$$f(x) = g(x)$$
$$3^{3x+3} = 27^{\left(\frac{2}{3}x - \frac{1}{3}\right)}$$

When the equations have variables in the exponents, you must rewrite one or both of them so that either the bases are the same or the exponents themselves are the same. In this question, the two bases seem different at first glance but, because 27 is actually 3^3, you can rewrite the equation as:

$$3^{3x+3} = \left(3^3\right)^{\left(\frac{2}{3}x - \frac{1}{3}\right)}$$

This simplifies to $3^{3x+3} = 3^{2x-1}$. Now that the bases are equal, set the exponents equal to each other and solve for x:

$$3x + 3 = 2x - 1$$
$$x + 3 = -1$$
$$x = -4$$

Choice (F) is correct.

57. A   Difficulty: High

Category: Higher Math / Functions

Getting to the Answer: To solve a logarithmic equation, rewrite the equation in exponential form and solve for the variable. To rewrite the equation, use the translation $\log_b y = x$ means $b^x = y$. The left side of the given equation has two logs, so you'll need to

Practice Test

combine them first using properties of logs before you can translate. Don't worry about the right-hand side of the equation just yet.

$$\log_b x - \log_b y = \log_b \left(\frac{x}{y}\right)$$

$$\log_3(5x - 40) - \log_3 5 = \log_3 \left(\frac{5x - 40}{5}\right)$$

$$= \log_3 (x - 8)$$

Now the equation looks like $\log_3 (x - 8) = 2$, which can be rewritten as $3^2 = x - 8$. Simplifying yields $9 = x - 8$, or $17 = x$. Choice (A) is correct.

58. F   Difficulty: High

Category: Higher Math / Functions

Getting to the Answer: Fortunately, "cannot be determined" is not one of the answer choices here, because that would be very tempting. There is in fact enough information to answer this question. You just have to use what you know about arithmetic sequences—specifically, that to get from one term to the next, you add the same number each time. Here, you don't know what that number is, so call it n. The five terms in the sequence are:

4

$4 + n$

$4 + n + n$

$4 + n + n + n$

$4 + n + n + n + n$

These terms are already listed in order, so the median is the middle term, which is $4 + n + n$, or $4 + 2n$. The mean is the sum of all the terms divided by the number of terms: $\frac{20 + 10n}{5} = 4 + 2n$. Thus, the mean and the median have the same value, making the difference between them equal to 0, which is (F).

59. D   Difficulty: High

Category: Higher Math / Geometry

Getting to the Answer: You are given the cosine of $\angle BAC$ and the length of the hypotenuse of the triangle, so begin

by using these and SOHCAHTOA to find the length of the side adjacent to $\angle BAC$ (which is AB):

$$\cos A = \frac{\text{adjacent}}{\text{hypotenuse}}$$

$$0.6 = \frac{AB}{15}$$

$$AB = 0.6(15) = 9$$

So the adjacent side, $\overline{AB}$, is 9, and triangle ABC is a right triangle with a leg length of 9 and a hypotenuse of length 15. Triangle ABC must therefore be a 3-4-5 right triangle (scaled up by a factor of 3), and $\overline{BC}$ must have a length of 12. Choice (D) is correct.

60. J   Difficulty: High

Category: Higher Math / Geometry

Getting to the Answer: The question states that the points lie on the graph of a parabola (which is a nice, symmetric U shape), so use what you know about parabolas to answer the question. Notice that the x-values in the table increase by 2 each time. To find the y-value when $x = -4$, you just need to imagine adding one extra row to the top of the table. Now, think about symmetry—you can see from the points in the table that $(2, -5)$ is the vertex of the parabola. The points $(0, -3)$ and $(4, -3)$ are equidistant from the vertex, as are the points $(-2, 3)$ and $(6, 3)$. This means the point whose x-value is -4 should have the same y-value as the last point in the table $(8, 13)$. So, when $x = -4$, $y = 13$. Choice (J) is correct.

READING TEST

Passage I

Suggested Passage Map notes:

¶1: Countess Olenska (CO) no longer pretty

¶2: CO 1st in NY as little girl adopted by aunt Medora (M)

¶3: M repeatedly widowed, NY accepting of M's eccentricities

¶4: All kind to Ellen (E) [aka CO], M not follow mourning rules

¶5: E was well-liked, fearless child; E's odd edu.

¶6: E married Polish nobleman, ended in disaster

¶7: NY expected CO to be more stylish and vibrant

1. C   Difficulty: Low

Category: Key Ideas and Details / Detail

Getting to the Answer: Remember that the correct answer to Detail questions will be directly stated in the passage. Your notes should guide you as you locate specific references to the details in question. Line 23 mentions Ellen's parents' "regrettable taste for travel" in the context of describing what the people of New York thought. Predict something like "travel." Choice (C) matches this prediction. Choice A is a misused detail; Medora does teach her niece to play the piano, but nothing in the passage suggests that this was undesirable. Choice B is a misused detail; Spanish shawl dances are described as "outlandish," but this is within the context of Medora and Ellen's eccentric, but accepted, behaviors. Choice D is a misused detail; while Medora often adopted children, this is never described as undesirable.

2. J   Difficulty: High

Category: Craft and Structure / Writer's View

Getting to the Answer: Consider how the author writes about New York society. In lines 24–25, she writes that "people thought it a pity that the pretty child [Ellen] should be in such hands," meaning that they did not feel the eccentric Medora was a good influence on Ellen. People call Medora "misguided" (line 30), and the author notes that she scandalized her family by not adhering to the "unalterable rules" of mourning (lines 31–32). All in all, New York society seems to have some rigid and snobbish rules. On the other hand, New Yorkers "looked indulgently on [Medora's] eccentricities" (lines 20–21), and New York "resigned itself to Medora" (lines 38–39). The author's view of New York society as it pertains to Medora seems to be mixed, which matches (J). Choice F doesn't take into account New York society's acceptance of Medora's odd behavior, G is opposite, and H is not mentioned in the passage.

3. A   Difficulty: Medium

Category: Key Ideas and Details / Inference

Getting to the Answer: To answer Inference questions, you will have to go beyond what is directly stated in the passage. However, the correct answer choice will

be supported by evidence from the passage, so make sure you make a prediction that has solid textual support. You can predict, based on lines 56–67, that Ellen was unable to help her aunt because her own marriage to the immensely rich Polish nobleman "had ended in disaster." Choice (A) matches this prediction. Choice B is a distortion; since both Medora and Ellen left New York the amount of their communication over the years is unknown. Choice C is a distortion; while the author tells you that Ellen had an incoherent education, nothing in the passage suggests that she resented this. Choice D is a distortion; though the passage makes it clear that Medora was eccentric, this is in no way related to receiving help from her niece.

4. F   Difficulty: Medium

Category: Key Ideas and Details / Global

Getting to the Answer: Generalization questions require you to synthesize information, sometimes from the entire passage. Predicting an answer is particularly important for questions like this. Make sure you can support your prediction with information in the passage. Lines 68–70 suggest that Newland has spent time thinking about Ellen, and lines 74–93 describe Newland's observations of Ellen. Newland is not disappointed that Ellen is not as "stylish" as others expected (lines 84–87). You can predict that Newland is thoughtful and, unlike many of the other characters in the passage, nonjudgmental. Choice (F) matches this prediction. Choice G is out of scope; it might seem reasonable to conclude that Newland is likable, but the passage does not provide any evidence to directly support this. Also, there is nothing to suggest that he is withdrawn. Choice H is opposite; Newland's observations about Ellen in the last paragraph clearly indicate that he is interested in her. Choice J is a distortion; Newland's observation that Ellen is not as stylish as New York society might expect says nothing about his own stylishness, nor does the author ever describe his level of sociability.

5. A   Difficulty: Medium

Category: Craft and Structure / Writer's View

Getting to the Answer: Wharton writes that Medora has "many peculiarities" (line 31) and that "New York looked indulgently on her eccentricities" (lines 20–21). This matches the first part of answer choice (A). Since you may not know what *peripatetic* means, hold on to (A) while you research the other answers. Though Wharton states that each time Medora returns to New York she looks for a less expensive house, indicating reduced circumstances, this doesn't necessarily mean that Medora is impoverished, and there is no suggestion that she is resentful. Eliminate B. Medora may be kind (she does, after all, take in orphaned Ellen), but *loyal* doesn't describe someone who "invariably parted from her husband or quarrelled with her ward" (lines 15–16), eliminating C. Choice D mixes up Medora with Ellen; these words describe Ellen as a child, so D is incorrect. Choice (A) must be correct, even if you don't know that *peripatetic* means "traveling from place to place."

6. H   Difficulty: Medium

Category: Craft and Structure / Vocab-in-Context

Getting to the Answer: The word *flout* is used in the author's description of Medora wearing a veil considered too short for acceptable mourning and dressing Ellen in a crimson dress and amber beads" (line 37). Both of these are examples of Medora's "misguided . . . many peculiarities" (lines 30–31), which go against accepted New York behavior. Thus (H), *disregard*, is a good match. Choice F is too strong to describe Medora's behavior, as she does partially follow, rather than totally eliminate, the rules of mourning. Choice G is opposite, and while J looks similar to the word *flout*, it doesn't make sense in the passage.

7. C   Difficulty: Medium

Category: Key Ideas and Details / Global

Getting to the Answer: Make sure you have good evidence for your prediction, and the right answer choice will be easy to find. Line 21 mentions Medora's *eccentricities*, line 31 mentions her *peculiarities*, and line 44 mentions the *outlandish arts* that Medora teaches Ellen. From these descriptions, you can predict that Medora is unconventional or eccentric. Choice (C) matches this prediction. Choice A is out of scope; although Medora does not adhere to conventions, as indicated by lines 31–32, there is nothing to suggest that this is attributable to arrogance.

Choice B is a distortion; the description of the short veil that Medora wore to her brother's funeral in lines 34–36 might suggest immodesty, but the author makes clear that this is evidence of Medora's willingness to flout social conventions and never mentions any immodest dress or behavior. Choice D, which means following established practice, is opposite; you are told in lines 31–32 that one of her peculiarities is to "flout the unalterable rules that regulated American mourning."

8. F   Difficulty: Low

Category: Key Ideas and Details / Detail

Getting to the Answer: Detail questions like this one are straightforward, but it can sometimes be difficult to find exactly where in the passage the relevant information comes from. Make sure that you are answering the specific question being asked so that other details don't distract you. Medora teaches Ellen "drawing from the model" (line 49), which is described as "a thing never dreamed of before," so predict Ellen or Countess Olenska. Choice (F) matches your prediction. Choice G is out of scope; Newland is not described as having learned anything at all, let alone something controversial. Choice H is a distortion; Medora teaches Ellen, but the passage does not mention Medora learning anything herself. Choice J is a distortion; Count Olenska is only mentioned indirectly as the rich nobleman whom Medora marries. The passage makes it clear that Ellen is Countess Olenska; don't be fooled by this initially tempting, but incorrect, choice.

9. B   Difficulty: Medium

Category: Craft and Structure / Function

Getting to the Answer: Locate where the author mentions Medora's mother and read the next few lines. The author writes that "her mother had been a Rushworth" (line 18), that Medora married "one of the crazy Chiverses" (lines 19–20), and that because of these two conditions, "New York looked indulgently on her eccentricities" (lines 20–21). In other words, given her mother and her marriage, people were not surprised by Medora's unconventional life, which matches (B). There is no support for A, so it is out of scope. Choice C is opposite; New Yorkers "thought it a pity that the pretty child should be in such hands" (lines 24–25), and D is true but not relevant to Medora's eccentricities.

10. F   **Difficulty:** High

Category: Key Ideas and Details / Inference

Getting to the Answer: Remember that Inference questions will have details in the wrong answer choices that are meant to throw you off. Making a good prediction before reviewing the choices will guard against this. The beginning of the passage (line 4) implies that Newland knew Ellen when he was young. Lines 55–59 state that no one had heard from Ellen for some time, and after a few years, she came back to New York, as Medora had done before her. Predict that at the dinner, Newland and Ellen had not seen one another for an extended period of time. Choice (F) matches your prediction. Choice G is extreme; although Newland is clearly paying attention to Ellen in the last paragraph, there is nothing to suggest that either of them is interested in a romantic relationship. Choice H is extreme; while Ellen's lack of *stylishness* (lines 86–87) might suggest that she is not interested in New York society's conventions, it goes too far to say that she is disappointed. Choice J is opposite; the passage clearly portrays Ellen and Newland's encounter as a re-acquaintance.

Passage II

Suggested Passage Map notes:

¶1: Researchers in Junagadh, India, attempt accurate forecast

¶2: 1st trad. rule: monsoon begins 45 days after *Cassia fistula* tree blooms

¶3: 2nd trad. rule: north or west wind = good monsoon, east = drought

¶4: Trad. rules not exact, but general trend is correct

¶5: Dr. K started in 1990 when old saying was exactly correct

¶6: Meteorologist Sahu disagrees w/ Dr. K

¶7: Dr. K hopes research will show trad. methods are valid; holds conference

¶8: Dr. K started NGO to support further research

11. B   **Difficulty:** Medium

Category: Key Ideas and Details / Detail

Getting to the Answer: More difficult Detail questions can be approached using elimination and careful reading. Remember the EXCEPT. For EXCEPT questions, review the answer choices methodically, eliminating those which fail to meet the conditions of the question stem. The passage deals in some depth with both the flowering of the *C. fistula* tree, C, and the wind during Holi, A, so you can eliminate those first. Paragraph 5 states that Dr. Kanani became interested in traditional methods when a tenth-century rule of thumb "proved strikingly correct," which suggests that D has been tested. In contrast, the bird behavior is merely listed as an example of a rule of thumb uncovered in one of Kanani's conferences, making (B) the correct answer.

12. J   **Difficulty:** Medium

Category: Craft and Structure / Function

Getting to the Answer: Identify the paragraph in which these words appear; it ends with the statement that farmers need more precise forecasts than traditional methods provide. However, science has not developed good alternatives for farmers in different regions. Match this with (J). Choice F is opposite; the author writes that "Every year, the average rainfall over the whole country is calculated, and this prediction is proved correct" (lines 65–67). Choice G isn't mentioned in the passage, and H is a distortion.

13. A   **Difficulty:** Low

Category: Key Ideas and Details / Detail

Getting to the Answer: Your map should tell you that information about the winds observed during the Holi festival is in the third paragraph. In that paragraph, the author states that "the north or west suggests a good monsoon, whereas wind from the east indicates drought" (lines 33–35), which matches (A). Choices B and C are the wrong direction, and D, southwest, is not mentioned.

14. G   **Difficulty:** Medium

Category: Craft and Structure / Writer's View

Getting to the Answer: Inference questions encompassing the whole text will draw on evidence from the entire

Practice Test

passage. A good prediction depends on your ability to synthesize the major ideas from throughout the passage. The passage mentions several traditional methods and their general accuracy. Even the scientific skepticism described in the passage admits a place for traditional methodology. The passage validates traditional methods, so predict that the author finds these methods to be valuable. Choice (G) matches this prediction. Choice F is out of scope; while the author briefly discusses the origins of some methods, she never expresses more interest in the development of the methods. Choice H is a distortion; the skepticism gets relatively little treatment and is followed by a detailed discussion of the progress toward making a real science of traditional methods. Choice J is opposite; the author never casts interest in traditional methods as a fad, and, as noted before, mentions the success of traditional methods more than once.

15. D   **Difficulty:** Low

Category: Key Ideas and Details / Detail

Getting to the Answer: Look to your notes to find specific locations for tested details. According to paragraph 5, Bhadli's storm method offers a 72-day warning. None of the other cited methods provide the same sort of accuracy over such a specific and extended time period, so look for Bhadli's method among the choices. Choice (D) matches this prediction. Choice A is a distortion; while the author mentions bird behavior as a possible predictor discussed at a conference, no information is given about the nature of this prediction. Choice B is a distortion; the flowering of the *Cassia fistula* tree does provide a specific and accurate prediction, but it gives only 45 days' advance warning. Choice C is a distortion; while the passage describes a loose correlation between the character of the monsoon and the wind direction on Holi, this method doesn't predict when the monsoon will arrive.

16. J   **Difficulty:** Low

Category: Craft and Structure / Function

Getting to the Answer: Beware of answer choices that present details that are narrower than the main point of the paragraph or sum up surrounding paragraphs instead of the target of the question. Focus on the overall topic of the paragraph and how it helps build the story or argument in the passage. The passage in general

describes the accuracy of traditional methods of weather prediction. The paragraph provides an example of a traditional method and introduces you to Dr. Kanani and his interest in applying scientific rigor to these methods; this can serve as your prediction. Choice (J) matches this prediction. Choice F is a misused detail; this sums up the first paragraph. Choice G is a misused detail; this accounts only for the last sentence of the cited paragraph. Choice H is a distortion; while the ancient saying is examined in the passage, this choice casts this examination as the central issue.

17. B   **Difficulty:** Low

Category: Key Ideas and Details / Detail

Getting to the Answer: For Detail questions, rely on your notes to direct your research to the relevant part of the passage. The topic sentences of the paragraph, lines 70–73, read: "Dr. Kanani hopes that his research will put traditional methods on a proper scientific footing. He and his colleagues have even set up a sort of peer-review forum." Predict that the conference's goal is this establishment of traditional methods as worthy subjects of scientific inquiry. Choice (B) matches this prediction. Choice A is out of scope; the passage never discusses the disappearance of traditional methods. Choice C is a misused detail; while Dr. Kanani does, in fact, publish the methods in the local press, this is not the objective of the conference. Choice D is out of scope; the passage never mentions the exchange of ideas between geographically distant farmers.

18. H   **Difficulty:** Medium

Category: Key Ideas and Details / Inference

Getting to the Answer: Beware of general answer choices. Attack the question stem, get a good understanding of what it's really asking, and make a solid prediction. The question asks you for the reason farmers predict the weather using traditional methods. What do they hope to accomplish? When the question is rephrased, the answer seems more obvious; predict that the correct choice, according to the first paragraph, will show that they want to know what to plant, so they need to know what's coming. Choice (H) matches this prediction. Choice F is out of scope; the passage never mentions the accessibility of the methods. Choice G is a distortion; while

Practice Test

"'normal' monsoons" are discussed in paragraph 6, this is in reference to modern meteorology, not traditional methods of forecasting. Choice J is a distortion; while traditional methods do get the basics right, the question asks why the farmers are trying to get the basics right in the first place.

19. C   Difficulty: Medium

Category: Craft and Structure / Function

Getting to the Answer: Eliminate answers that are inconsistent with the central concerns of the passage. Reread the specific reference and the surrounding text, which identifies the flowering of *C. fistula* as a monsoon predictor that isn't "perfect," but still of value and interest. Predict that the correct choice will account for both an appreciation of this traditional method and an awareness of its limitations. Choice (C) matches this prediction. Choice A is extreme; while the author feels that the predictive data are useful and noteworthy, calling them "remarkably predictive" goes too far. Choice B is out of scope; the author never attempts to generalize on the relative value of precision. Choice D is out of scope; again, the author neither casts traditional methods as rules of thumb and scientific methods as complex formulas nor attempts to elevate one over the other.

20. H   Difficulty: Low

Category: Key Ideas and Details / Detail

Getting to the Answer: Consult your notes to direct your research to the relevant text. Sahu says in lines 58–61 that traditional prediction may be "OK as a hobby," but "may not be applicable to this modern age." Then he concedes that modern era forecasts are not always helpful to farmers in the way traditional methods claim to be. That some utility exists despite scientific skepticism serves as a good prediction and an accurate paraphrase of his attitude. Choice (H) summarizes Sahu's attitude and matches this prediction. Choice F is opposite; the author identifies Sahu as claiming the methods "cannot be relied upon" (lines 59–60). Choice G is opposite; Sahu rejects traditional methods from the scientific view. Choice J is out of scope; Sahu never mentions the appeal of the methods, only their trustworthiness as predictors.

Passage III

Suggested Passage Map notes:

Passage A

¶1: Country music (C) born in central & southern Appalachians

¶2: Originated in 1920s from multiple sources

¶3: The term "country" replaced "hillbilly"

¶4: Hank Williams 1st to take country national; artists

¶5: Nashville, TN = country home w/ Grand Ole Opry (1925)

¶6: C relatives = honky tonk, Western Swing

¶7: C expresses Am. identity

Passage B

¶1: Bluegrass (B) origin and description

¶2: B diff. from C: highlight 1 musician at a time, diff. instruments, vocal harmonies

¶3: Own category in late 1950s, named after Bill Monroe's band

¶4: Today: movies, festivals

¶5: B themes = working class; reflects Am.

21. C   Difficulty: Medium

Category: Key Ideas and Details / Detail

Getting to the Answer: Use your Passage Map to locate this detail; the second paragraph should include the necessary information. Use the list of the sources of country music ("spirituals as well as folk music, cowboy songs, and traditional Celtic melodies") to make your prediction. Choice (C) is correct because country music is not rooted in jazz. Rather, jazz was combined with country music to create Western Swing. Paragraph 6 states, "Additionally, Western Swing emerged as one of the first genres to blend country and jazz musical styles, which required a great deal of skill and creativity." Choice A is opposite; paragraph 2 describes the many sources of country music with the sentence, "Rooted in spirituals as well as folk music, cowboy songs, and traditional Celtic melodies, country music originated in the 1920s." Choice

Practice Test

B is opposite; spirituals influenced the development of country music. Choice D is opposite; country music is rooted in cowboy songs.

22. J **Difficulty:** Medium

Category: Key Ideas and Details / Detail

Getting to the Answer: The answer to a Detail question is stated in the passage. However, because all answer choices are in the passage, be careful to assess each one in terms of the actual question asked. A look at your notes or a quick scan of the passage should provide enough information to make a prediction about where to find the best country music. Match that prediction to the correct answer. Choice (J) is correct; in paragraph 5, the author writes "Country singers are considered to have reached the pinnacle of the profession if they are asked to become members of the Opry." To hear the best music, it makes sense to go to the place where those at the pinnacle, or top of their field, perform. Choice F is a misused detail; one would hear honky-tonk music, a derivative of country, but not country music itself, in these bars. Choice G is a misused detail; Ireland is the original home of the Ulster Scots, many of whom settled in Appalachia. Choice H is a misused detail; though country music had its origins in the mixture of music created in Appalachia, the author does not state that it is the place to hear the best music.

23. C **Difficulty:** High

Category: Craft and Structure / Vocab-in-Context

Getting to the Answer: As with all Vocab-in-Context questions, use the surrounding clues to define the word in question. The word appears in paragraph 3, where the original term *hillbillies* is used to describe "Appalachian inhabitants who were considered poor, uneducated, isolated, and wary." The more accepting word *country* has replaced *hillbillies*, indicating that *pejorative* is an adjective used to highlight the negative characteristics described in the paragraph. This matches (C), since *disparaging* means "belittling, or bad." Choice A is a synonym for *original* rather than a word that means *negative*. Choice B is out of scope, as the author never expresses that the negative view is accurate, and D refers to where the people live rather than describing the term (i.e., it is not a mountain-dwelling term).

24. F **Difficulty:** Low

Category: Craft and Structure / Writer's View

Getting to the Answer: Both passages introduce several genres of American music, but this question refers to Passage B, so research the passage carefully. In the first paragraph, the author introduces bluegrass music and writes that it is "a mixture of Scottish, Welsh, Irish, and English melodic forms, infused, over time, with African-American influences" (lines 75–77) and that laments "are common themes" (line 82). These are exactly the components of the song in the question, making (F) correct. The other answers refer to Passage A and are described as having different derivations.

25. A **Difficulty:** Medium

Category: Key Ideas and Details / Detail

Getting to the Answer: Locate the paragraph in which bluegrass instruments are described, and match those descriptions with the correct answer choice. Your notes point to only one paragraph in which musical instruments are mentioned. Scan the answer choices, then reread the information in that paragraph to determine which answer choice characterizes the information given. Choice (A) is correct; musical instruments are described in the second paragraph and include typical ones such as "banjo, guitar, mandolin, bass, harmonica, and Dobro (resonator guitar)." But the paragraph goes on to include far less typical ones, such as "household objects, including washboards and spoons," which are not usually considered musical instruments, but are sometimes included in a bluegrass band. Choice B is a misused detail; African-American influences are provided as one more source of the bluegrass genre, but instrumentation is not referenced. Choice C is a misused detail; this is an example of a bluegrass piece used in a movie soundtrack. Choice D is out of scope; the reference to the Ozark mountains concerns the origin of bluegrass and has nothing to do with a description of musical instruments.

26. F **Difficulty:** High

Category: Key Ideas and Details / Detail

Getting to the Answer: The answer to a Detail question is stated in the passage. Locate the paragraph in which the differences between country and bluegrass music

Practice Test

are discussed. Paragraph 2 includes the information you need to answer the question. Be sure to keep straight which details describe each genre of music. Choice (F) is correct. Paragraph 2 details two characteristics of bluegrass music: first, that "bluegrass highlights one player at a time, with the others providing accompaniment," and second, that "bluegrass incorporates baritone and tenor harmonies." Choice G is opposite; country music features a single voice. Choice H is opposite; country musicians commonly play the same melodies together. Choice J is a distortion; which instruments are used is not cited as a difference between the music styles.

27. B   Difficulty: Medium

Category: Key Ideas and Details / Inference

Getting to the Answer: Locate the paragraphs that mention laments and high, lonesome sound, and consider what the author means by including these two details. The reference to *laments* in the first paragraph and the reference to "high, lonesome sound" in the last paragraph are examples of "the hard-scrabble life of the American worker," which matches (B). Choice A is out of scope; the elements mentioned in the question stem do not necessarily reflect Irish music; bluegrass has multiple sources. Choice C is a misused detail; Shania Twain is an example of a country singer and is mentioned in Passage A only. Choice D is a misused detail; though bluegrass was originally called *hillbilly*, this is the name for the genre, not the theme.

28. G   Difficulty: Medium

Category: Craft and Structure / Vocab-in-Context

Getting to the Answer: Vocab-in-Context questions require that you understand the context of a cited word or phrase. Locate the reference, and focus your research on the text immediately preceding and immediately following the word or phrase in question. The introductory paragraph states, "One of the most enjoyable ways to analyze culture is through music." Look for an answer choice that indicates that music can provide specific insight about a culture as a whole. Choice (G) matches this prediction. Choices F, H, and J are distortions; *quintessential* does not mean old-fashioned, charming, or conventional (typical).

29. C   Difficulty: Medium

Category: Integration of Knowledge and Ideas / Synthesis

Getting to the Answer: When asked to use a quote to find support in one paragraph for information in another, be sure to read the quote in the context of the paragraph. First, find the paragraph in which the quote from Passage A appears, then match the quote to one in Passage B. Choice (C) is correct; Flatt and Scruggs are mentioned in Passage B, paragraph 3, in which they are characterized as "the foremost artists on their instruments." The best artists are certainly "talented and sophisticated." Choice A is a misused detail; this quote refers to bluegrass themes, whereas the question asks for one that supports talented and sophisticated musicians. Choice B is out of scope; the "pace and complexity" of the music does not necessarily relate to the skill of the musicians themselves. Choice D is out of scope; the relation between bluegrass and country music refers to the kinship of the genres, not the musicians.

30. H   Difficulty: Medium

Category: Integration of Knowledge and Ideas / Synthesis

Getting to the Answer: When looking for something on which both authors would agree, first determine what each one actually states in the passage, then consider what must be true based on those statements. The evolution, or gradual change, in music, as with anything else, must start from somewhere, so look to the parts of each passage that detail the genesis of the music genres, then consider the progression from there. Choice (H) is correct; both authors detail the various music sources that became either country or bluegrass. In the first passage, the author mentions "folk music, cowboy songs, and traditional Celtic melodies," and in the second passage, the author refers to "Scottish, Welsh, Irish, and English melodic forms, infused, over time, with African-American influences." Both authors affirm that the two music genres are *indigenous*. Thus, it must be true that both country and bluegrass music have evolved from their various roots to become American music, supporting agreement on the fact that music can evolve. Choice F is out of scope; each passage mentions how its particular music genre is popular (as explained in the next sentence in the explanation—the Czech festivals and international growth), but both authors don't describe why *both* genres are popular, only their own. Choice G is a misused detail; the Grand Ole Opry showcases country music only, not bluegrass. Choice J is out of scope; the passages don't each discuss both genres, only their own.

Passage IV

Suggested Passage Map notes:

¶1: 1999, Pluto about to lose planet status

¶2: Marsden says Pluto given special status, not demoted

¶3: Discussion started in 1930, Pluto small & elongated orbit

¶4: 1992 Jewitt and Luu discovered QB1, Luu says Pluto is a TNO

¶5: 70 TNOs are known, Pluto is biggest

¶6: Binzel suggests Pluto be made 1st entry in TNO catalog

¶7: Marsden agrees Pluto is TNO, but doesn't want new way of classifying TNOs

¶8: Marsden wants to give Pluto its own special number in an existing asteroid catalog

¶9: Luu disagrees w/ Marsden

¶10: A'Hearn trying to settle dispute

¶11: General public will still think of Pluto as 9th planet

31. D   Difficulty: Low

Category: Key Ideas and Details / Detail

Getting to the Answer: Luu strongly disagrees with the view that Pluto should be labeled an asteroid (lines 84–88). She goes so far as to use the term *idiotic* in reference to others in her profession, so predict something like *indignation*. Choice (D) matches this prediction. Choice A is a distortion; while *shock* may be an initially tempting choice, it's clear that Luu's surprise stems from her disagreement with the opinion, not her lack of preparation to hear it. Choice B is opposite; *excitement* suggests some degree of positive response, which Luu clearly does not display. Choice C is opposite; Luu quite clearly expresses her feelings on the classification controversy.

32. H   Difficulty: Medium

Category: Key Ideas and Details / Inference

Getting to the Answer: If you get stuck, eliminating answers that have no support in the passage will greatly reduce the number of choices. The passage states that, if astronomers had known about the other TNOs, Pluto would not have been named a planet (lines 49–52). The size of Pluto is indicated as the reason it was discovered before the others. You can infer that a better system of detection would have discovered other TNOs, eliminating Pluto's status as a planet. Account for this in your prediction. Choice (H) matches your prediction. Choice F is a distortion; Pluto's size does indeed make it different from the other planets, but the lack of this knowledge is not cited as the sole reason for its initial classification. Choice G is a distortion; although the icy Pluto is said to belong with neither the *rocky planets* nor the *gas giants* (lines 28–29), this information is included as a way to differentiate Pluto from the planets, and the lack of this knowledge initially is not identified as the reason for Pluto's original classification. Choice J is a distortion; the controversy that would later surround Pluto's initial classification as a planet was never drawn into the discussion of the original classification.

33. D

Category: Craft and Structure / Writer's View

Difficulty: Medium

Getting to the Answer: As interested as the author is in how to describe Pluto, at no point does the author offer a personal opinion. Because of this, you cannot assume that the author would agree with anything other than a neutral statement, as (D) is. The author does not side with those who would call Pluto a TNO, making A incorrect, nor those who argue that it should remain a planet, C. Choice B is a distortion; IAU stands for International Astronomical Union, not a classification.

34. F

Category: Key Ideas and Details / Detail

Difficulty: Low

Getting to the Answer: Your notes on the passage should show the location of key details and terminology so you can quickly find them as you research the question stem.

Neptune is mentioned only a few times; the fourth paragraph mentions Neptune in relation to trans-Neptunian objects, and the seventh paragraph mentions Neptune and Centaurs, one of the answer choices. Sure enough, an examination of the description reveals that Centaurs, a great prediction, are asteroids similar to Pluto "nudged" inside Neptune's orbit. Choice (F) matches this prediction. Choice G is a misused detail; the passage states that IAU stands for International Astronomical Union. Choice H is a misused detail; TNO stands for trans-Neptunian objects, things beyond Neptune. Choice J is a misused detail; the term "ice dwarf" is used in connection with the discovery of a TNO.

35. C   Difficulty: Low

Category: Key Ideas and Details / Inference

Getting to the Answer: Inference questions such as this ask that you interpret the referenced lines, drawing on your reading of the passage as a whole. The quote making up the majority of the referenced lines comes from a scientist who, in the passage, takes a position against creating a new classification. Your prediction should reflect the issue of whether the existing categories are suitable. Choice (C) matches this prediction. Choice A is a misused detail; this is certainly discussed in the passage, but this doesn't pertain to the cited lines or the speaker in question. Choice B is a misused detail; distance from the sun and from Neptune is significant to certain classification schemes, but this is not the central issue in Pluto's specific case. Choice D is a misused detail; that the scientific community and general public have differing opinions is irrelevant to the cited lines.

36. G   Difficulty: High

Category: Craft and Structure / Vocab-in-Context

Getting to the Answer: Vocab-in-Context questions require that you understand the context of a cited word or phrase. Locate the reference and focus your research on the text immediately preceding and immediately following the word or phrase in question. Investigating the word in question contextualizes it within the argument of a scientist who "doesn't like the idea of establishing a new catalog of solar system objects" (lines 62–63) and argues

that "astronomers already have a perfectly serviceable list of numbered minor bodies" (lines 64–65). Predict something like *sufficient* to replace the word in question. Choice (G) matches this prediction. Choice F invokes the most common meaning of the word, which doesn't make sense in context and is usually a trap answer; the scientist does *not* want to change the system. Choices H and J don't work in context, since describing a particular classification system as *beneficial* or *durable* is awkward.

37. D   Difficulty: Low

Category: Key Ideas and Details / Global

Getting to the Answer: Remember that Global questions will attempt to make tempting answer choices out of issues discussed in the passage only briefly. A recurring theme throughout the passage is giving Pluto a "very special designation" (line 19) or honor (line 80), which differs from the predominantly scientific concerns over Pluto's classification discussed elsewhere. Predict an answer that touches on this idea of honoring or distinguishing Pluto in some way. Choice (D) matches this prediction. Choice A is out of scope; the role of the IAU is never discussed by the cited experts. Choice B is a misused detail; the author does relay some information about the ways in which public opinion is unlikely to change, but this is not a significant concern for scientists dealing with deeper issues. Choice C is out of scope; none of the cited scientists seem particularly concerned with being credited for solving the problem.

38. G   Difficulty: Medium

Category: Key Ideas and Details / Detail

Getting to the Answer: The passage ends with a discussion of one scientist's attempt to find consensus about Pluto's status. In this part of the passage, the major ideas are listed. Binzel's idea is rejected because Pluto "would still be an anomaly." Luu forcefully asserts that "Pluto is certainly not an asteroid." Both criticisms are based on the idea that neither category adequately describes Pluto, so predict that the correct answer will focus on the inadequacy of any categorization scheme. Choice (G) matches this prediction. Choice F is a misused detail; the public's recognition of Pluto's controversial status or a potential change in category are not significant issues to scientists. Choice H is a distortion; Pluto's orbit plays little role in the discussion of its classification, and its surface is never mentioned. Choice J is a misused detail; the existence of Pluto-like objects nearer to the sun than Neptune functions as a criticism of only one theory.

39. B   Difficulty: Medium

Category: Key Ideas and Details / Detail

Getting to the Answer: Detail questions will sometimes require a broad approach to information from a variety of locations in the text. Your notes will help you to sort out the specifics. Lines 24–27 discuss Pluto's size in relation to other planets, and lines 27–28 describe its orbit as anomalous. A good prediction will account for both. Choice (B) matches this prediction. Choice A is a misused detail; distance from the sun versus distance from Neptune is significant only in certain classification systems for non-planets. Choice C is out of scope; the year of Pluto's discovery in relation to those of other planets is never discussed. Choice D is out of scope; Pluto's shape is not compared to other planets.

40. H   Difficulty: High

Category: Key Ideas and Details / Detail

Getting to the Answer: Tougher Detail questions will require an investigation of several sections of text. Count on your notes to direct you, even when the search is fairly extensive. Lines 24–27 tell you that Pluto is smaller than other planets, which is why scientists need to reclassify it, yet its large size compared to asteroids and TNOs (lines 101–102) is what keeps many scientists confused about its proper category. Lines 46–49 cite Pluto's size as the exact reason that it was found 60 years before the next body like it. Your prediction should account for this classification difficulty as well as Pluto's early discovery. Choice (H) matches this prediction. Choice F is a distortion; categorizing of Pluto as a TNO is only a proposed solution to the classification problem and takes into consideration issues other than size, most importantly, its relation to Neptune. Choice G is opposite; it is Pluto's relatively small size that potentially allows it the same classification as an asteroid. Choice J is a misused detail; the passage never relates Pluto's size to the nature of the planet's orbit.

SCIENCE TEST

Passage I

1. A   Difficulty: Low

Category: Interpretation of Data

Getting to the Answer: The question stem tells you that you're looking for a mineral composed of 32% zinc and 12% calcium. Table 1 lists the percentages of calcium and zinc in a variety of minerals, so look there for an answer. According to Table 1, hornblende is composed of 30 to 35% zinc and 10 to 20% calcium. Choice (A) is thus correct.

2. J   Difficulty: Low

Category: Interpretation of Data

Getting to the Answer: Diagram 1 presents the most common minerals in each soil horizon. A geologist digging down into the A horizon would encounter mostly quartz and mica. Quartz isn't included as a possible answer, but mica is. Choice (J) is thus correct. Choice F is incorrect because limestone isn't commonly found until the C horizon. Choice G is incorrect because shale isn't common until the final horizon. Choice H is incorrect because serpentine is commonly found in the B horizon.

3. B   Difficulty: Medium

Category: Interpretation of Data

Getting to the Answer: Based on Diagram 1, you can see that the minerals are arranged in Table 1 so that the shallowest are at the top of the table and the deepest are at the bottom. However, as you move down the table, you'll notice that zinc content decreases, which indicates an inverse relationship between depth and zinc content. In other words, as zinc content *increases*, depth *decreases*. Choice (B) is thus correct.

4. H   Difficulty: Low

Category: Interpretation of Data

Getting to the Answer: Based on Diagram 1, the only minerals geologists wouldn't commonly find at a depth of 30 feet or lower (to the bottom of the B Horizon)

Practice Test

are limestone and shale. You can eliminate F, G, and J because each contains one of these minerals. Choice (H), then, is correct.

5. A   Difficulty: Medium

Category: Interpretation of Data

Getting to the Answer: The mineral content of granite is located in Table 2, so start there. Table 2 shows that granite is composed of feldspar, quartz, mica, and augite. If augite is found close to the other minerals in granite, then it should be located at roughly the same depth as feldspar, quartz, and mica. Now use Diagram 1 to find the depths at which those three minerals are most commonly found. Feldspar is found in the O horizon, at a depth of 2 feet or less, while quartz and mica are found in the A horizon, at a depth of 2 to 10 feet. So you should definitely expect to find augite at depths of less than 10 feet, as in (A).

6. G   Difficulty: Low

Category: Interpretation of Data

Getting to the Answer: Zinc content percentage and calcium content percentage are found in Table 1, so examine it for an answer. Moving down the table, zinc content steadily decreases as calcium content steadily increases. The two quantities are inversely related, making (G) correct.

Passage II

7. D   Difficulty: Medium

Category: Scientific Investigation

Getting to the Answer: To answer this question, examine the formula that is provided at the beginning of the passage: $\Delta T_b = K_b \times m \times i$. This equation indicates that the boiling point will increase more if K_b, m, or i is increased. Item I would increase K_b, item II would increase m, and item III would increase i (because $CaCl_2$ splits into 3 ions, while NaCl only splits into 2 ions). Because all three items would increase the boiling point of Solution 5, (D) is correct.

8. H   Difficulty: Low

Category: Interpretation of Data

Getting to the Answer: The results for Study 1 are presented in Table 1. Table 1 shows that for 0.171 mol of NaCl, the boiling point is increased to 101.75°C. Choice (H) is thus correct.

9. C   Difficulty: Medium

Category: Interpretation of Data

Getting to the Answer: This question asks about the melting point of Material 5. Table 3 provides data about when Material 5 melted, indicating that it did not melt in Solution 5, but that it did melt in Solution 6. Therefore, its melting point will be somewhere between the boiling points of those solutions. Table 1 shows that Solution 5 has a boiling point of 103.50°C and Table 2 shows that Solution 6 has a boiling point of 104.15°C, so Material 5's melting point must fall somewhere in between those values. Choice (C) is thus correct.

10. G   Difficulty: Medium

Category: Interpretation of Data

Getting to the Answer: Table 2 provides the boiling points for solutions consisting of various amounts of $CaCl_2$ added to water. The trend seems linear: for each increase of roughly 0.9 mol $CaCl_2$, the boiling point increases by roughly 1.4°C. The highest amount of $CaCl_2$ on the table is 0.631 mol, roughly 0.9 less than the amount in the question stem. Therefore, the increase will be roughly 1.4° higher than 109.67°C, or 111.07°C. Choice (G) is thus correct. Choice F is between the boiling points for Solutions 9 and 10, which is too low. Choices H and J are too high.

11. A   Difficulty: Medium

Category: Scientific Investigation

Getting to the Answer: Table 3 gives an indication of the points at which each material begins to melt. Based on the information from Tables 1 and 2, a higher-numbered solution corresponds to a higher boiling point. It would be highly implausible for a material to melt at a low temperature but not at a higher temperature, which is the trend depicted in (A). The other choices are incorrect because they are all possibilities already revealed in

Study 3's results: B corresponds to the results for Material 1, C to the results for Material 4, and D to the results for Materials 6, 7, and 8.

12. H   Difficulty: High

Category: Scientific Investigation

Getting to the Answer: The equation for boiling point elevation given in the passage indicates that the increase in temperature depends upon the molality of the solution. As noted in the explanation of the equation, molality is defined as moles (mol) of solute over kilograms (kg) of solvent. Thus, the students recorded the moles of a solute, rather than its mass, in order to make the calculation of molality—and the subsequent calculation of change in boiling point—easier. Choice (H) is correct. Choice F makes little sense; measuring the solvent's mass does nothing to prevent measuring the solute's mass. Choice G is a false statement; moles are usually calculated on the basis of mass, so if anything mass measurements are more accurate. Choice J is true but irrelevant to the question.

13. A   Difficulty: Medium

Category: Evaluation of Models, Inferences, and Results

Getting to the Answer: Table 3 shows that Material 7 melted in Solution 10, whereas Material 8 did not. That means that Material 7 must have a melting point of no more than 109.67°C (the boiling point of Solution 10), while Material 8 must have a melting point higher than that temperature. Thus, the results do support the claim that Material 7 has the lower melting point, making (A) correct. Choice B is incorrect because it reverses the results for the materials. Choice C is incorrect because the exact melting point of Material 8 does not need to be determined to support the claim—it only has to be shown to have a higher melting point than Material 7. Choice D is incorrect because the approximate melting point of Material 7 can be determined: it must be between the boiling point temperatures of Solutions 9 and 10.

Passage III

14. G   Difficulty: Medium

Category: Evaluation of Models, Inferences, and Results

Getting to the Answer: According to Table 1, the concentrations of nitrogen, phosphorus oxide, and zinc all

tend to increase as humidity level increases, regardless of which of the three data sources is considered. For potassium oxide, however, the trend is reversed: the concentration decreases as humidity increases. Choice (G) is thus correct.

15. A   Difficulty: Low

Category: Interpretation of Data

Getting to the Answer: To answer this question, compare the System B data to the USGS data at 25% humidity for the 4 compounds given as answer choices. For nitrogen (N), the USGS concentration is 236 mg/L, while System B measures it as 408 mg/L, which is close to double. For calcium (Ca), USGS has 24.7 mg/L and System B has 23.2 mg/L, a much smaller difference, meaning B can be eliminated. For potassium oxide (K_2O), USGS has 9.2 mg/L and System B has 9.1 mg/L, a very small difference, allowing you to eliminate C too. Finally, for phosphorus oxide (P_2O_5), USGS has 71.2 mg/L and System B has 75.6 mg/L, still smaller than the difference seen in nitrogen, meaning D can also be eliminated. Nitrogen shows by far the biggest difference, whether this is calculated in absolute or relative terms, so (A) is correct.

16. J   Difficulty: Low

Category: Evaluation of Models, Inferences, and Results

Getting to the Answer: From Table 1, you can see that the potassium oxide concentration continually decreases from 9.4 mg/L to 8.2 mg/L as humidity increases from 10% to 80% in the USGS data, continually decreases from 9.4 to 8.0 in System A, and continually decreases from 9.5 to 8.3 in System B. Because the data from all 3 sources support the hypothesis that potassium oxide levels decrease with increasing humidity, (J) is correct.

17. D   Difficulty: Medium

Category: Evaluation of Models, Inferences, and Results

Getting to the Answer: The question asks you to determine which system is more accurate, so ultimately you're trying to find the one that is closer to the USGS data, which is described in the passage as "extremely accurate." Looking at the data for zinc, you can see that the measurements from System B are always closer to the data from the USGS than are the measurements from System A. Therefore, you know the answer to the question is yes, allowing you to eliminate A and B. Choice C, though, is incorrect because it gives the wrong reasoning: System B does give lower measurements than System A, but that alone doesn't make it more accurate. The measurements from System B are more accurate because they are closer to the data from the USGS than are the measurements from System A. Choice (D) is thus correct.

18. H   Difficulty: Medium

Category: Interpretation of Data

Getting to the Answer: To answer this question, look at the row in the table that represents calcium concentrations for System B. You can see that the numbers gradually decrease from 10% humidity to 65% humidity, then increase quickly from 65% to 85% humidity. The only graph that shows values decreasing and then rapidly increasing is (H).

19. B   Difficulty: High

Category: Scientific Investigation

Getting to the Answer: Examine the System B data in Table 1 to answer this question. According to the table, a potassium oxide level of 9.1 mg/L falls between the values for 25% humidity (9.2) and 45% humidity (9.0), a calcium level of 17.3 mg/L also falls between the values for 25% (23.2) and 45% (11.6), and a zinc level of 0.57 mg/L likewise falls between the values for 25% (0.48) and 45% (0.62). Therefore, the level of humidity for this sample should almost certainly be some value between 25% and 45%. Only (B) falls within this range.

Passage IV

20. G   Difficulty: Low

Category: Evaluation of Models, Inferences, and Results

Getting to the Answer: What are Scientist 1's and Scientist 2's viewpoints? Scientist 1 believes that type 2 diabetes is caused by excess sugar consumption, and Scientist 2 says that type 2 diabetes is caused by obesity as a result of a high-fat diet and lack of exercise. If new research suggested that 80% of people with diabetes have buildup of fat in the liver, this information would support the view of Scientist 2 only. The correct answer is (G).

21. B   Difficulty: Low

Category: Evaluation of Models, Inferences, and Results

Getting to the Answer: Scientist 1 states that "the cause of type 2 diabetes is an overconsumption of sugar," while Scientist 2 states that "diets high in fat but not high in sugar are associated with an increased risk of type 2 diabetes." Thus, both scientists would mostly likely agree that the occurrence of type 2 diabetes in an individual is associated with the patient's diet. The correct answer is (B). Choice A is only mentioned by Scientist 2, and C is only mentioned by Scientist 3. Age is mentioned in the introductory text, but even though type 2 diabetes is more prevalent in adults, the passage does not suggest that age causes type 2 diabetes, so D is also incorrect.

22. H   Difficulty: Medium

Category: Evaluation of Models, Inferences, and Results

Getting to the Answer: The passage states that type 2 diabetes occurs "when the body does not produce enough insulin," and explains that "Insulin is a hormone produced in the pancreas that helps regulate blood glucose levels." If the pancreas is removed, the body would not produce insulin, and would thus be unable to regulate blood glucose levels, thereby causing type 2 diabetes to develop. None of the answer choices state this explicitly, but (H) gives the major symptom of diabetes that was stated in the introductory paragraph: elevated blood glucose levels (hyperglycemia). Choices F and G are incorrect because they state the opposite of what you should expect. You can also eliminate J because you're given no reason to suspect a link between the pancreas and body fat content.

23. C   Difficulty: Medium

Category: Evaluation of Models, Inferences, and Results

Getting to the Answer: According to Scientist 3, type 2 diabetes is inherited. Eliminate A and B, which correspond to the hypotheses of Scientists 1 and 2, respectively. Scientist 3 states "individuals have about a 15–20% chance of developing type 2 diabetes if one of their parents has it and a roughly 50% chance if both parents have it." 18% falls within the 15–20% range. Therefore, Scientist 3 would probably predict that an individual with an 18% chance of developing type 2 diabetes has one parent with type 2 diabetes. The correct answer is (C).

24. J   Difficulty: Medium

Category: Evaluation of Models, Inferences, and Results

Getting to the Answer: Remember to keep straight who said what. If a 50-year-old developed type 2 diabetes, Scientist 1 would likely conclude the patient has a high-sugar diet, Scientist 2 would likely conclude the patient has a high-fat diet and/or lacks exercise, and Scientist 3 would likely conclude the patient inherited it from one or both parents. The only answer choice that correctly matches one of these predictions is (J).

25. A   Difficulty: High

Category: Evaluation of Models, Inferences, and Results

Getting to the Answer: According to Scientist 1, the elevated blood glucose levels in individuals with normal insulin levels did not return to normal when they received small injections of supplemental insulin. It can thus be inferred that although insulin levels were normal, the body had a lowered response to insulin, indicating insulin resistance. Look for a choice that supports the idea that a high-sugar diet causes or is otherwise related to lowered response to insulin. Choice (A) does just that. Choices B and D are incorrect because they mention fat intake and free radical production, respectively, which were only discussed by Scientist 2. Choice C is incorrect because Scientist 1 discussed the effects of a high-sugar diet, not a low-sugar one.

26. F   Difficulty: High

Category: Evaluation of Models, Inferences, and Results

Getting to the Answer: Scientist 3 believes that "type 2 diabetes is not caused by lifestyle or diet but inherited." To challenge Scientist 2's claim that the lack of exercise causes 7% of type 2 diabetes cases, Scientist 3 would have to explain how the actual cause of the occurrence of type 2 diabetes in these individuals is due to inheritance, rather than lifestyle. Choice (F) does precisely that: if the individuals who didn't exercise also had family histories of diabetes, then Scientist 3 could claim that the patients actually developed diabetes because of their genetics, not their lifestyles. Even though Scientist 3 actually states the information in G, it does not directly address Scientist 2's claim from the question stem. Choice H is incorrect because insulin injections are only discussed by

Scientist 1. Choice J is incorrect because Scientist 2 does not suggest that type 2 diabetes solely results from lack of exercise, but also blames diets high in fat.

Passage V

27. A   Difficulty: Low

Category: Interpretation of Data

Getting to the Answer: To answer this question, turn to the results of the studies in Table 1. According to the table, the lowest-density blood sample is 1.050 g/mL, that of Patient C. Looking at each column, you can see that Patient C has more platelets than Patient A but fewer than Patient B, fewer white blood cells than Patient A, the fewest red blood cells, but the most plasma. Choice (A), then, is correct.

28. H   Difficulty: Medium

Category: Scientific Investigation

Getting to the Answer: According to the passage, the purpose of the studies was "to determine the composition and mass of blood samples." Thus, the phlebotomist has an interest in avoiding anything that could alter the composition or mass of the blood on a temporary basis because it would skew the results of the studies. The passage also states that diet can affect the composition of blood, so it would make sense that the phlebotomist would try to control this factor by requiring the patients to fast. Choice (H) is thus correct. Choice F is incorrect because you're given no reason to suspect that taking blood is easier if a patient has fasted. Choice G is incorrect because if fasting could greatly change the composition of blood, then the phlebotomist would likely have made sure the patients avoided it by eating something beforehand. Choice J is incorrect because you're given no indication in the passage that anything the patient does can affect the ability of blood to separate in a centrifuge.

29. D   Difficulty: High

Category: Scientific Investigation

Getting to the Answer: According to Table 1, Patient C had a density of 1.050 g/mL, which amounts to a 10.50 g mass for a 10-mL sample. However, if you add up the masses of the components listed in Table 1, you get a total of less than 10.50 g (9.71 g, to be specific). The question is asking you to explain this discrepancy. To find the best explanation, consider each of the possibilities offered in the answer choices. Choice A does not offer an adequate explanation, because if some red blood cells remained in the plasma, then they would have been weighed along with the plasma, which means their mass would have been included. Choice B also falls short; the mass of the platelets would have been included when the white blood cells were weighed. Choice C suffers from a similar problem: if some of the formed elements remained in the plasma, their masses would simply be included when the plasma was weighed. By process of elimination, (D) must be correct. And this makes sense because the only components that were weighed were plasma, red blood cells, white blood cells, and platelets. If there were additional components, their masses would not be included in Table 1. This is also consistent with the opening of the passage, which claims that blood is 45% formed elements and 50% plasma, leaving 5% of the blood unaccounted for.

30. F   Difficulty: Low

Category: Interpretation of Data

Getting to the Answer: Go back to Table 1 and look at the columns for total density and red blood cell mass. (Circle each column if you tend to get distracted by the other information.) Reading the table from the bottom up, you can see that, as total density increases, the mass of the red blood cells also increases, (F).

31. B   Difficulty: Medium

Category: Interpretation of Data

Getting to the Answer: The introduction to the passage states that "formed elements weigh approximately 1.10 grams per milliliter (g/mL) and plasma approximately 1.02 g/mL." Here, you have about 5 mL of plasma, so the total mass of plasma is roughly 5 mL × 1.02 g/mL = 5.1 g. You also have about 5 mL of formed elements, so the total mass of formed elements is about 5 mL × 1.10 g/mL = 5.5 g. The total mass of the sample would then be around 5.1 g + 5.5 g = 10.6 g. It may be a bit higher due to elements other than the plasma and formed elements, but the total mass is still likely to be between 10.0 and 12.0 g, as in (B).

32. J   Difficulty: Low

Category: Scientific Investigation

Getting to the Answer: The passage explains that the phlebotomist placed the blood samples in a centrifuge for 20 minutes in Study 2 and at a slower speed for 45 minutes in Study 3. Only (J) captures any element of this difference. Choice F is incorrect because you're told at the beginning of the passage that 10 mL of blood were taken from each patient. Choice G is incorrect because, while the mass of the blood samples did vary from patient to patient, the masses weren't intentionally varied by the phlebotomist from Study 2 to Study 3. Choice H is incorrect because a centrifuge was used in both Studies 2 and 3.

33. A   Difficulty: Low

Category: Interpretation of Data

Getting to the Answer: To answer this question, simply compare the masses in the red blood cell column of Table 1. According to the table, Patient A has a red blood cell mass of 2.75 g, Patient B a mass of 2.70 g, and Patient C a mass of 2.65 g. Because Patient A has the greatest mass of red blood cells, (A) is correct.

Passage VI

34. G   Difficulty: Medium

Category: Interpretation of Data

Getting to the Answer: Since the question asks about length and temperature, the simplest data set to consider is Table 1, because Table 2 includes another variable, type of material. Comparing the odd-numbered trials (all conducted at 80°C) or the even-numbered trials (all conducted at 20°C) shows that the shorter the rod, the higher the current, which is an inverse relationship. Choices F and J can be eliminated. Comparing any trials which hold length of the rod constant while changing the temperature, such as Trials 1 and 2, show that as temperature goes down, current through the rod goes up, which is another inverse relationship. Because both length and temperature are inversely related to current, (G) is correct.

Practice Test

35. C   Difficulty: Medium

Category: Interpretation of Data

Getting to the Answer: The passage states that voltage, current, and resistance are related through Ohm's law, $V = A \times \Omega$, where Ω stands for resistance in ohms and A stands for current in amperes. In the circuit used for these experiments, the voltage is held constant at 5 V, as indicated by the battery in Diagram 1. This means that if current goes up, resistance must have gone down. Conversely, the lowest current will result from the highest resistance. Because each of the rods featured in the answer choices was tested in Experiment 2, to find the rod with the highest resistance, you merely need to find the one with the lowest recorded current in Table 2. The rod in Trial 9 conducted a current of only 20 mA, less than any of the others, so it must have the highest resistance. Choice (C) is thus correct.

36. H   Difficulty: High

Category: Interpretation of Data

Getting to the Answer: According to the question stem, conductivity uses the units of siemens per meter ($\sigma = S/m$) and siemens are equal to inverse ohms ($S = 1/\Omega$). Putting these two equations together, you can see that the units of conductivity are equivalent to inverse ohms divided by meters ($\sigma = [1/\Omega]/m$), which simplifies to $\sigma = 1/(\Omega \times m)$. Choice (H) is thus correct.

37. B   Difficulty: Low

Category: Interpretation of Data

Getting to the Answer: According to Table 1, the rod in Trial 4 conducted 53 mA of electricity at 20°C. A rod of the same length was used in Trial 3, but it was heated to 80°C and conducted only 27 mA. Because 50°C is in between these two values, it is reasonable to assume that the current conducted will fall somewhere between 27 and 53 mA. Choice (B) is therefore correct.

38. F   Difficulty: Medium

Category: Scientific Investigation

Getting to the Answer: The introduction to the passage mentions Ohm's law, $V = I \times R$, which shows that voltage and current are directly related. Because the resistance

values wouldn't change (the same rods would be used), the increase in voltage with the 10-V battery would lead to higher recorded values for current, regardless of the material of the rods. Thus, since both the copper and iron rods would conduct larger currents with a 10-V battery, (F) is correct.

39. C   Difficulty: Medium

Category: Interpretation of Data

Getting to the Answer: According to the results of Experiment 2, copper conducts electricity more effectively than iron. Thus, a 16-cm composite rod that was half-copper and half-iron would be expected to conduct electricity better than a 16-cm iron rod but worse than a 16-cm copper rod. According to Table 2, a 16-cm iron rod at 20°C conducts 40 mA, while a 16-cm copper rod at that temperature conducts 200 mA. Thus, the composite rod should conduct a current of somewhere between 40 and 200 mA, as in (C).

40. J   Difficulty: Low

Category: Scientific Investigation

Getting to the Answer: The variables that are directly manipulated in an experiment are the independent variables, so this question is asking for the one variable that is not an independent variable. In both experiments, the dependent variable—in other words, the variable that was observed and measured—was the current recorded by the ammeter. Thus, current was not directly manipulated by the student, so (J) is correct.

WRITING TEST

LEVEL 6 ESSAY

I fully agree that pure scientific research is vital to increase our understanding of ourselves and our world, and that this research, even without specific goals, can result in important benefits to society. To fund this research, a consortium of government, pharmaceutical companies, and nonprofit agencies should be formed, pooling money but giving no one group entire oversight or responsibility.

Many life-changing discoveries have been found without purposely looking for them. Alexander Fleming did not set out to discover penicilin, but in doing so accidentally saved millions of people from death. Putting a man on the moon did not help people on Earth, but it certainly taught us a lot about our universe. This kind of pure research must continue, and the cost should be shared by the government, drug companies, and nonprofit groups. This type of research can be prohibitively expensive; thus, monies must be drawn from various sources, each contributing as much as possible. No single organization can completely fund ongoing research, especially if there is no stated goal other than to hopefully discover something beneficial. Tax payers, pharmaceutical company investors, and nonprofit group members expect results, which may be long in coming, or, indeed, continually elusive. However, efforts must continue. As Thomas Edison said, "Just because something doesn't do what you planned it to do doesn't mean it's useless."

Consider also that pharmaceutical companies are always searching for new therapeutic drugs. They send scientists out into the field to come back with anything interesting, which is then researched and, if promising, developed into a new drug. Such is the relation between blood sugar and diabetes, leading to the insulin that my diabetic cousin takes; without insulin, he would not survive. If a drug company develops an important drug, it can make millions of dollars from the sale of it, leading to funding more research. Nonprofit organizations also have a stake in pure research, since another accidental discovery could prove to be financially beneficial. Finally, if the government shares the burden of underwriting research, it is not at risk for being fully blamed if the research does not produce positive results. Taxpayers would be more liable to accept a minimal loss in a good cause rather than a major loss in an unsure endeavor. A partnership would ensure continued funding and the funders, as well as all citizens, would benefit from discoveries.

On the other hand, people who say the government should fund only research which has demonstrated its worth do not understand the function of pure research. It is not possible for researchers to say with certainty that they are going to find a cure for cancer. Researchers have to be able to say they are searching for something as yet unknown with the hope that it will be beneficial. And what is a clear and acceptable outcome? If cancer researchers find a cure for diabetes, but not cancer, is that acceptable if it is not the stated intention? A great deal of science is luck and perserverance. According to this perspective, if a researcher wanted government funding to work in the Amazonian rain forest with the general intent of exploring indigenous plants, the government would be unable to fund the project because there is no clearly beneficial objective. But that is exactly how quinine, a now widely used treatment for malaria, was found, and the general exploration was certainly worth funding. Finally, it is unlikely that pure research, no matter who funds it, will result in disaster. Researchers are very careful to prevent this, and even if a disaster did happen, it would not be the fault of whom is funding the research.

It is quite clear that pure research is invaluable, as the examples of penicilin, quinine, and insulin support. It cannot be dependent on the whims, finances, and oversight of any one group but must be a concerted effort among all and for all who may benefit.

SCORE EXPLANATION (6666)

This essay is clearly focused on the prompt, shows complete understanding of the issue, logically assesses the implications of all three perspectives, and puts forth the author's point of view in both the first and fifth paragraphs. This is a cohesive, critical analysis of the perspectives, with a solid, well-supported thesis.

Ideas and Analysis (6)

The argument is driven by strong and clear analysis of each perspective, with good examination of implications. The writer's consistent focus on the benefits of pure research makes the essay cohesive and precise: pure research is worth pursuing and, for economic and oversight reasons, must be funded by a consortium of groups. Keeping this focus, the writer is able to explore each perspective, identify pros and cons, and provide strong support for her point of view. Critical, logical thinking is clearly displayed.

Development and Support (6)

The writer introduces her argument with a strong statement supporting pure research in general, and she immediately follows up with her perspective. That perspective is developed through reference to "life-changing discoveries," the cost of research, specific discussion of drug company research and benefits and what may constitute acceptable risk. Support is strong, referencing Alexander Fleming, penicillin, space exploration, quinine, and insulin, and it includes a relevant quote from Thomas Edison. Reasoning and support are well integrated, and the author never loses sight of the thesis. Both alternatives are discussed. One alternative is discussed in detail, while the other is given only passing, but still with strong consideration ("And what is a clear and acceptable outcome?" "Finally, it is unlikely that pure research, no matter who funds it, will result in disaster"). Development moves from the general to the specific, with excellent support for each point, and a clear and consistent perspective.

Organization (6)

There is a clear and strong introduction and a summary conclusion, both of which expand the specifics of the prompt to the larger issues involved. Each paragraph begins with a topic sentence, and the contrasting view is signaled with the phrase "On the other hand," while the third paragraph is introduced with a creative transition phrase "Consider also." The essay is cohesive and flows well, ideas are well connected, and support is explicit, relevant, and well positioned to enhance the argument.

Language Use (6)

The writing is mostly high-level, with the use of a rhetorical question and words such as *perseverance, accountable, consortium,* and *pharmaceutical*. Several sentences are varied and complex. The grammar and punctuation are mostly correct, though there are some spelling errors (*penicilin, perserverance*). The writer's style is appropriately formal, even with a personal example, and her word choice is effective in characterizing the perspectives and writing a persuasive argument.

LEVEL 4 ESSAY

Pure research is done for the purpose of discovery without a specific goal in mind. Even so, it has produced important breakthroughs such as treatment for Alzheimer's disease, and even the development of the GPS. Though scientific research is vitally important, people disagree about who should pay for it. Some people think that the government should fund the research if the goal is a good one. Others think that the government should only give money to research that can be shown will be helpful. Still others believe that the government and private companies should work together to give scientists the money they need, which is the best way to do it, and the perspective I agree with.

I know the importance of research because my little brother has asthma and requires daily medication. Though I don't know who paid for the research that helped make his meds, I'm quite sure that the research behind it took a long time and cost a great deal of money. Though the government may have enough money to fully fund research like this, it has other responsibilities as well and can't afford to fund research alone, especially if the outcome is unsure. However, with other money from drug companies and nonprofit agencies, research can continue to be funded without any one entity eating into their finances earmarked for other purposes. Even if the research doesn't show results for many years, a group of funders can provide enough money so that scientists can keep working until they discover something helpful and then continue to develop it.

The government can't do everything on its own and companies shouldn't have to work by themselves either. If they team up, lots of research can get done. Asthma is now manageable, but there are plenty of other illnesses that are very deadly. Everybody is hoping for a cure for cancer one day, and scientists need time and money to find one. Groups working together can give those scientists the time and money they need, since no one group is responsible for an immediate, beneifical result from the research it funds. The government and companies should pick an amount of money they want to spend each year on scientific research and give it to a variety of research groups. Then, if any of the groups make a major discovery, they can earn more money and invest it back into ongoing research.

On the other hand, some people think that scientists should have to show the government that their projects will be helpful in order to get money. That would exclude a lot of past and future research that was done purely in the hopes of discovery but without assurances. Louis Pasture wouldn't have gotten money from his government to make penicillin since it was a total accident. Being able to pinpoint the exact purpose and result of pure research is precisely the opposite of what pure research aims to do. Like all important things, research requires time, effort and money. The best way to fund it is to gather a group of government, private, and nonprofit agencies who can pool their resources to let scientists keep working. Some research may fail miserably, but some may change the course of the world. That possibility is surely worth funding.

SCORE EXPLANATION(4444)

The writer provides a minimal discussion of all three perspectives, but fails to fully consider the implications of the other perspectives. She doesn't fully consider counterarguments, but she does provide relevant support for her opinion.

Practice Test

Ideas and Analysis (4)

Ideas are clearly stated, if redundant. The argument centers around "time, effort, and money," with discussion of each taking up most of the essay. Her perspective is analyzed primarily through a personal anecdote about her brother, which is more related to research in general than to pure research. However, the author is consistent in her argument and able to critique another perspective while returning to her own point of view.

Development and Support (4)

The writer begins with a good statement defining pure research, immediately bringing in the examples of Alzheimer's and the GPS, though a brief explanation of their relevance would enhance the support. The first paragraph also introduces all perspectives. However, when the writer states her own opinion at the end of the introduction, she does not do so forcefully. The argument is developed with a personal statement about her brother's asthma, which leads into further discussion of funding. The writer continues this argument in the next paragraph, again referencing asthma and mentioning cancer, though both statements are fleeting and do not offer strong support. One other alternative is discussed in the fourth paragraph, nicely harking back to the definition of pure research (the incorrect reference to Pasteur and penicillin does not affect the support).

Organization (4)

The writer provides a clear introductory paragraph and a good conclusion, and she is able to tie the essay together by returning to the initial definition of pure research at the end of the fourth paragraph with "Being able to pinpoint the exact purpose and result of pure research is precisely the opposite of what pure research aims to do." The first paragraph shows good connection words between perspectives (*Some, Others, Still others*). However, there are few transitions other than the one introducing paragraph 4; better use of transitions would make the essay flow more smoothly. The essay is nonetheless cohesive in its perspective.

Language Use (4)

The writing style is adequate, with some spelling and grammar errors. Word choice could be improved by avoiding very informal words and phrases ("eating into their finances," "total accident," "meds," "plenty of other diseases") and expressing ideas with more high-level vocabulary and complex sentence structure. Less use of contractions would also raise the language to a more appropriately formal essay level.

LEVEL 2 ESSAY

Working with a real goal in mind is the best way to do a project and the goverment has lots of money, so I think the government should pay for research projects but only those which will succeed. I did a school sience project with too other kids but we ended up fighting and not finishing it, which is what would happen if lots of groups got together to fund something.

When my teacher assigns a sience project even though I get to choose which one to do she expects results. The goverment should think the same way because if they don't they will be spending money for something which could be useless. Just like my teacher does when she decides what grade to give my project, the goverment should think about how successful the research might be and save their money for research that will really come up with something important.

Like it says, "to many cooks spoil the broth" which means that when theres a whole group of people, chances are the end result is bad. That goes for the govement partnering with other groups also they should pay for research by themselves but only if it looks like the research will come up with something good.

SCORE EXPLANATION (2222)

Though the author addresses the prompt and takes a side, this essay is very poorly written and supported, and ideas and analysis are weak with little clarity.

Ideas and Analysis (2)

This essay indicates a lack of understanding of the prompt and task, and poor reasoning and writing skills. The author has focused primarily on the issues of money and the negative effects of working with partners, likening the latter to working with others on a science project. She has not analyzed any perspective in depth; instead, ideas are repetitive, with shallow support. The author has not looked beyond her own school experience, thus her argument is weak and analysis of the prompt is superficial.

Development and Support (2)

The author fails to develop her thesis beyond general, poorly supported statements, which repeat her two ideas that working together is detrimental to a project and government money should be spent on projects with demonstrated success. Her support is weak and irrelevant, focusing on a school project, equating it with pure research, and suggesting that the government should determine its funding in the same way that a teacher determines a grade. The saying that opens the third paragraph is a trite platitude, lacking any real analysis. The author's reasoning is inadequate and confused, and she fails to examine the argument logically.

Organization (2)

Though there are three separate paragraphs and the conclusion echoes the first paragraph's perspective, each paragraph is weak and disjointed, with no transition phrases to tie the essay together. Ideas are poorly grouped together; the author repeatedly compares a school project to governmental pure research funding.

Language Use (2)

There are numerous spelling and punctuation errors, word choice is simplistic, and the writing fails to be persuasive. *Government* and *science* are consistently misspelled, and there are several instances of improper pronoun/antecedent agreement. The author misuses the word *too*, omits the apostrophe from *there's*, and follows the missed apostrophe with a run-on sentence. Word choice and sentence structure are rudimentary, and the essay lacks the strength and style of writing which would make it persuasive and engaging.

You can evaluate your essay and the model essay based on the following criteria, covered in the Scoring section of *Inside the ACT Writing Test*:

- Is the author's own perspective clearly stated?
- Does the body of the essay assess and analyze an additional perspective?
- Is the relevance of each paragraph clear?
- Does the author start a new paragraph for each new idea?
- Is each sentence in a paragraph relevant to the point made in that paragraph?
- Are transitions clear?
- Is the essay easy to read?
- Is it engaging?
- Are sentences varied?
- Is vocabulary used effectively?
- Is college-level vocabulary used?

Answers & Explanations

CHAPTER 2

PRACTICE

9. D   Difficulty: Medium

Category: Sentence Structure and Formation

Getting to the Answer: The underlined portion includes a progressive past tense verb phrase, but the surrounding text is written in past tense. Choice A is incorrect as written. Choice B is incorrect because "were to find it" suggests the suffragists would only realize in the future that there was a problem. Choice C is incorrect because it creates a run-on sentence. Choice (D) correctly uses the past tense.

10. H   Difficulty: Medium

Category: Sentence Structure and Formation

Getting to the Answer: Modifying phrases must be correctly placed within sentences. The modifying phrase *in government* should be placed after the verb *participate*. Choices F, G, and J misplace the phrase *in government*. Choice (H) correctly places the phrase after the verb it modifies.

11. C   Difficulty: Medium

Category: Sentence Structure and Formation

Getting to the Answer: Items in a list must have parallel forms in order for the sentence to be grammatically correct. Choices A, B, and D do not include three parallel verb phrases. Choice (C) correctly uses the infinitive verb forms in all three verb phrases.

12. G   Difficulty: High

Category: Sentence Structure and Formation

Getting to the Answer: Semicolons are used to separate two independent clauses. Choices F, H, and J offer dependent clauses, which are grammatically incorrect. Choice (G) correctly places an independent clause after the semicolon.

13. D   Difficulty: Medium

Category: Sentence Structure and Formation

Getting to the Answer: Two independent clauses must be properly combined; otherwise the sentence is a run-on. Choice (D) corrects the run-on by placing the word *While* in front of "early 20th-century women," changing the clause before the comma to a dependent clause. Choices A, B, and C are all run-on sentences.

14. G   Difficulty: Medium

Category: Sentence Structure and Formation

Getting to the Answer: If an underlined segment includes a pronoun, check three things: make sure the pronoun agrees with the antecedent in person as well as number and matches the surrounding text. In this case, the author does not address the audience directly anywhere else in the text, so F is incorrect. Choice H is incorrect because it includes an ambiguous pronoun, and J is incorrect because the author does not use *us* or *we* anywhere else in the text. Choice (G) is the most correct, concise, and relevant option.

PERFORM

15. D   Difficulty: Medium

Category: Sentence Structure and Formation

Getting to the Answer: Incorrect placement of a prepositional phrase can create an illogical sentence. To figure out the correct placement of the underlined prepositional phrase, determine what it describes and then move it to that part of the sentence. In this sentence, the underlined portion logically describes the shop, so (D) is correct. Choice A is illogical, and both B and C are repetitious.

16. F   Difficulty: Low

Category: Sentence Structure and Formation

Getting to the Answer: If a sentence includes two independent clauses, they must be properly combined. The independent clauses can be separated by a coordinating conjunction and a comma as in the original, separated by a semicolon as in G, separated into two sentences as in H, or separated by a dash that emphasizes the second part of the sentence as in J. By omitting punctuation, (F) creates a run-on.

17. D   Difficulty: Medium

Category: Sentence Structure and Formation

Getting to the Answer: The person or thing described by an introductory phrase should be placed as close as possible to its description. In this sentence, the introductory phrase describes the writer, so the first-person pronoun should follow the description. Only (D) correctly orders the sentence. Choices A and B illogically make it sound as though the friends are "not a coffee drinker," and both introduce an agreement error. Choice C creates a sentence fragment.

18. G   Difficulty: Medium

Category: Sentence Structure and Formation

Getting to the Answer: If a pronoun is underlined, make sure it agrees with the antecedent in person and number and matches the surrounding text. The author does not refer to the audience, so F, which refers to *one,* and H, which refers to *you,* are incorrect. The author also does not use the word *we* or *us* anywhere in the text, so J is incorrect. Choice (G) correctly uses the pronoun *I,* which the author uses frequently throughout the text.

19. C   Difficulty: Medium

Category: Sentence Structure and Formation

Getting to the Answer: An *-ing* word without a helping verb isn't a complete verb. As it is written, this is a sentence fragment—without a helping verb such as *were* or *are,* the verb is incomplete. Choice (C) corrects the verb error and inserts the comma necessary to set the descriptive information off from the rest of the sentence. Choice B creates two sentence fragments. Choice D uses the comma correctly but does not address the verb error.

20. F   Difficulty: High

Category: Sentence Structure and Formation

Getting to the Answer: A complicated sentence is not necessarily incorrect. Make sure that your choice does not introduce an error that does not appear in the original.

This sentence is correct as written, so (F) is the correct answer. Choices G, H, and J all use word orders that confuse meaning and create illogical relationships.

21. C   Difficulty: High

Category: Sentence Structure and Formation

Getting to the Answer: Elements within a sentence must be in parallel form. In this sentence, *different groups* wouldn't gather for a single meeting; rather, *different groups* would gather for *small meetings,* which means (C) is correct. Choices A, B, and D are grammatically incorrect.

22. J   Difficulty: Medium

Category: Sentence Structure and Formation

Getting to the Answer: Verb phrases in a list must be in parallel form. As written, the list is not parallel. Choice (J) is the only option includes three verb phrases that are all written in present tense.

ON YOUR OWN

1. C   Difficulty: Medium

Category: Sentence Structure and Formation

Getting to the Answer: Use logic to determine the best word order in context. It is the "parameters of liberal arts study" that "have remained … unchanged over the centuries." Choice (C) provides the most logical word order and is therefore correct.

2. G   Difficulty: Low

Category: Sentence Structure and Formation

Getting to the Answer: The *-ing* verb form cannot serve as the main verb in an independent clause. As written, this sentence is a fragment, so F is incorrect. Choice (G) corrects the fragment. Choices H and J create dependent clauses and thus do not address the error.

3. D   Difficulty: High

Category: Sentence Structure and Formation

Getting to the Answer: As written, the sentence is a run-on, so A is incorrect. Although there are a number

Answers & Explanations

of ways to correct a run-on sentence, only one answer choice will do so without introducing additional errors. Choices B, C, and D all address the run-on error. However, B uses a semicolon while also making the second clause dependent, and the conjunction *so* in C creates a cause-and-effect relationship between the clauses that is inappropriate in context. Only (D) corrects the error and does not introduce new errors.

4. J   Difficulty: Medium

Category: Sentence Structure and Formation

Getting to the Answer: Items in a list must be in parallel form. As written, this list includes four verb phrases, but they are not parallel, so F is incorrect. Only choice (J) includes four parallel verbs in present tense. Choices G and H are not parallel.

5. A   Difficulty: Medium

Category: Sentence Structure and Formation

Getting to the Answer: This sentence is correct as written, so (A) is correct. Choice B incorrectly uses a singular verb form with a plural subject. Choices C and D create sentence fragments.

6. G   Difficulty: Medium

Category: Usage

Getting to the Answer: Adjectives can only modify nouns and pronouns; all other parts of speech are modified by adverbs. This sentence uses an adjective *steady* to modify a verb *increased*, so F is incorrect. Both (G) and H correct the error, but H is unnecessarily wordy. Choice J incorrectly uses the adverb *steadily* to modify the noun *fashion*.

7. A   Difficulty: Medium

Category: Usage

Getting to the Answer: Check underlined verbs and pronouns for agreement errors. Here, both the verb and pronoun are used correctly, so (A) is correct. The infinitive *to give* is idiomatically correct with *sought*, and *their* agrees with its plural antecedent *colleges*. Choices B and D use a singular pronoun with a plural antecedent; C and D do not properly construct the infinitive.

8. F   Difficulty: Medium

Category: Punctuation

Getting to the Answer: Carefully examine the differences involving punctuation. The comma is used correctly here, so choice (F) is correct. Choices G and J misuse the semicolon and the colon, respectively. The second sentence formed by H is a fragment.

9. C   Difficulty: High

Category: Sentence Structure and Formation

Getting to the Answer: Modifying phrases must be correctly placed within sentences. The modifying phrase "behind liberal arts education" should be placed after the noun *philosophy*. Choices A, B, and D misplace the phrase "behind liberal arts education." Choice (C) correctly places the modifying phrase after the noun it modifies.

10. J   Difficulty: Medium

Category: Sentence Structure and Formation

Getting to the Answer: An introductory clause generally modifies the first noun that follows it. As written, this sentence tells us that "courses in computer science and information technology" are "Responding to this concern," so F is incorrect. Choice (J) puts the logical noun phrase, "many colleges and universities," after the modifying clause. Choice G does not address the error. Choice H uses incorrect grammatical structure.

11. B   Difficulty: Medium

Category: Sentence Structure and Formation

Getting to the Answer: The sentence includes a pronoun that doesn't match the surrounding text. The author doesn't use the word *I* anywhere else in the essay, so A is incorrect. The author doesn't doesn't address the audience directly, so C is incorrect. The author doesn't use the word *we* in the essay, so D is incorrect. Choice (B) correctly uses "Many educators" rather than a pronoun.

12. J **Difficulty:** Medium

Category: Knowledge of Language / Concision

Getting to the Answer: When DELETE is among the answer choices, carefully examine the underlined material for relevance. Information about additional degrees offered by liberal arts colleges is irrelevant to this passage and should be deleted, so (J) is correct.

13. C **Difficulty:** Medium

Category: Usage

Getting to the Answer: A verb must agree with its subject noun, which may not be the noun closest to it in the sentence. Although the plural *students* is the closest noun to the verb *remain*, the verb's subject is actually the singular *premise*, so A is incorrect. Choice (C) corrects the agreement error. Choice B creates a run-on sentence. Choice D uses a verb tense that is inappropriate in context.

14. H **Difficulty:** Medium

Category: Topic Development / Supporting Material

Getting to the Answer: Consider where in the essay a reference to "The late 1800s" would fit best. Choice (H) correctly places the sentence between a reference to "the United States since it was a British colony" and mention of "the 20th century." Choices F, G, and J position the sentence in illogical spots within the essay.

15. D **Difficulty:** High

Category: Topic Development / Writer's Purpose

Getting to the Answer: Many Writer's Purpose questions can be answered in two parts. First, answer the "yes" or "no" part of the question; you'll be able to eliminate at least one answer choice. While the author does outline the history of liberal arts, higher education includes numerous majors—everything from biological sciences to hospitality management. Choice (D) is correct.

CHAPTER 3

PRACTICE

7. A   Difficulty: Low

Category: Punctuation

Getting to the Answer: The underlined apostrophe indicates that this is a Punctuation question. The sentence requires a singular possessive noun, so eliminate B and D because they are not possessive nouns. Eliminate C because the passage does not require a plural noun. The correct answer is (A).

8. H   Difficulty: Medium

Category: Punctuation

Getting to the Answer: The underlined segment incorrectly uses a colon. Colons are only tested on the ACT in only one way: to introduce a brief explanation, definition, or list. Eliminate F. Eliminate J because the semicolon neither joins two independent clauses nor separates items containing commas in a series or list. Eliminate G because it does not set off the introductory phrase "In the past." Choice (H) correctly uses a comma to set off the introductory phrase.

9. D   Difficulty: Medium

Category: Punctuation

Getting to the Answer: The underlined portion includes the only dash in this sentence, which does not indicate a hesitation or a break in thought. Eliminate A because either two commas or two dashes are needed to set off a nonessential phrase; using one of each is not correct. Eliminate B because it misuses a colon. Eliminate C because it does not correctly set off the phrase "as if by magic." Choice (D) correctly uses a semicolon to join two independent clauses.

10. J   Difficulty: Medium

Category: Punctuation

Getting to the Answer: The phrase "hoping Mary wouldn't notice" is nonessential information that must be properly punctuated. Eliminate F because it misplaces the comma. Eliminate G because "and gripped the ladder"

is not an independent clause. Eliminate H because it incorrectly includes a colon, which is used to introduce a short phrase, quotation, explanation, example, or list. Choice (J) correctly sets off the nonessential information with two commas.

PERFORM

11. B   Difficulty: Medium

Category: Punctuation

Getting to the Answer: When the underlined portion includes a semicolon, determine whether the sentence has two independent clauses. "During the last five decades of the 20th century" is an introductory phrase and cannot stand on its own, so A is incorrect. Eliminate C, because omitting the comma creates an error. Choice D incorrectly uses a dash—a dash is used either to indicate a hesitation or break in thought or to set off explanatory elements. Choice (B) correctly sets off the introductory phrase with a comma.

12. F   Difficulty: Low

Category: Punctuation

Getting to the Answer: This sentence is correct as written because the list is properly punctuated with commas. Choice G adds an unnecessary comma after *star*. Choice H is incorrect because it omits all punctuation. Choice J misuses a semicolon.

13. C   Difficulty: Medium

Category: Punctuation

Getting to the Answer: Although a parenthetical or nonessential phrase may appear in the beginning, middle, or end of a sentence, punctuation will always separate it from the rest of the sentence. Read the sentence without the first three words to determine if the sentence still makes sense. Because the sentence makes logical sense without the phrase "A multitalented artist," a comma is necessary to correctly set off this nonessential phrase. Eliminate A, which incorrectly uses only one dash. Eliminate B because the semicolon neither joins two independent clauses nor separates items containing commas in a series or list. Choice D is incorrect because it eliminates punctuation altogether. Choice (C) is correct.

14. G   **Difficulty:** Low

Category: Punctuation

Getting to the Answer: Items in a list need to be set off with commas. Although a colon can introduce a list, the colon in F is placed incorrectly. Eliminate H and J, which do not contain the necessary commas to set off the multiple listed items. The correct answer is (G).

15. C   **Difficulty:** Medium

Category: Punctuation

Getting to the Answer: Two commas are needed to set off a nonessential phrase; using one comma is incorrect. Read the sentence without *Maurice* to determine whether the sentence still makes sense. Because the sentence makes logical sense without the brother's name, the commas are necessary to correctly set it off. Eliminate B and D, which misplace a colon. Choice (C) is correct.

16. F   **Difficulty:** Medium

Category: Punctuation

Getting to the Answer: A comma separates an introductory phrase from the rest of the sentence. The introductory phrase *At eight* is followed by a comma, so this sentence is correct as written. Choice G is incorrect because two dashes are used to set off a nonessential phrase; in addition, the dash does not indicate a hesitation or a break in thought in this sentence. Choice H omits the comma. Choice J is incorrect because the semicolon neither joins two independent clauses nor separates items containing commas in a series or list.

17. D   **Difficulty:** Low

Category: Punctuation

Getting to the Answer: The underlined word requires an apostrophe to indicate possession, showing that the *Last Jam* belongs to *Jelly*. The sentence requires a singular possessive noun. Eliminate A, B, and C because they do not contain possessive nouns. The correct answer is (D).

18. H   **Difficulty:** Medium

Category: Punctuation

Getting to the Answer: Determine whether the comma rules apply to the underlined segment. Choice F is incorrect because it interrupts the sentence. Choice G is incorrect because the semicolon neither joins two independent clauses nor separates items containing commas in a series or list. Choice J misuses the colon, which is used to introduce a short phrase, quotation, explanation, example, or list. The sentence does not require punctuation, so (H) is correct.

ON YOUR OWN

1. B   **Difficulty:** Low

Category: Punctuation

Getting to the Answer: Commas set off three or more items in a series or list. Choice A leaves out the comma before *and*, which is necessary on the ACT. Choice C does not include the first comma. Choice D is incorrect because the semicolon neither joins two independent clauses nor separates items containing commas in a series or list. The correct answer is (B).

2. F   **Difficulty:** Medium

Category: Punctuation

Getting to the Answer: Semicolons separate items in a series or list if those items already include commas. The underlined series already includes commas after *appearance* and *use*. Choice G is incorrect because it eliminates the semicolons, which makes the sentence confusing. Choice H incorrectly uses only one semicolon, and Choice J misuses a colon. Choice (F) is correct.

3. D   **Difficulty:** Medium

Category: Punctuation

Getting to the Answer: Parenthetical information includes words or phrases that aren't essential to the sentence structure or content and need to be set off with commas. This information can be explanatory. Choices A and B are incorrect because they do not include commas on both sides of *for example*. Choice C misuses the colon, which is used to introduce a short phrase, quotation, explanation, example, or list. Choice (D) correctly sets off the nonessential phrase *for example*.

4. G **Difficulty:** Medium

Category: Punctuation

Getting to the Answer: The introductory phrase "In the eighteenth century" needs a comma to set it off from the rest of the sentence. Choice F incorrectly uses a colon, and H misuses a dash. Choice J is incorrect because the semicolon does not join two independent clauses; the part before the semicolon is a phrase. The correct answer is (G).

5. D **Difficulty:** Medium

Category: Punctuation

Getting to the Answer: Eliminate both A and B immediately because the word *its'* is not grammatically correct in any circumstance. Choice C correctly uses *it's*, which stands for *it is*, but it changes the meaning of the sentence by using the word *marble*. Choice (D) correctly uses *it's* to stand for *it is* as well as the plural noun *marbles*.

6. F **Difficulty:** Medium

Category: Punctuation

Getting to the Answer: Determine whether any of the tested comma rules apply to the underlined segment. Two commas are used to set off a nonessential phrase, but read the sentence without *in which* to see whether the sentence still makes sense. Choice G is incorrect because commas should not set off any words here. Although *which* often follows a comma, H places the comma incorrectly. Choice J is incorrect because the semicolon neither joins two independent clauses nor separates items containing commas in a series or list. Choice (F) is correct.

7. D **Difficulty:** Low

Category: Punctuation

Getting to the Answer: Commas set off three or more items in a series or list, and the ACT requires a comma before *and*. Choice A is incorrect because the semicolon

neither joins two independent clauses nor separates items containing commas in a series or list. Choice B incorrectly uses a dash, which does not indicate a hesitation or a break in thought in this sentence. Choice C incorrectly leaves out the comma before *and*, which is necessary on the ACT. The correct answer is (D).

8. J **Difficulty:** Low

Category: Punctuation

Getting to the Answer: The underlined portion requires a plural possessive noun because the marbles belong to the *opponents*. Eliminate G, which does not include a possessive noun. Choices F and H both use apostrophes to show possession, but they place the apostrophe on the incorrect noun. The correct answer is (J).

9. B **Difficulty:** Medium

Category: Punctuation

Getting to the Answer: The underlined portion requires a singular possessive noun because the marbles belong to someone. Choice A incorrectly uses the plural possessive. Eliminate C and D because they do not indicate possession. The correct answer is (B).

10. H **Difficulty:** Medium

Category: Punctuation

Getting to the Answer: Although a parenthetical or nonrestrictive phrase may appear in the beginning, middle, or end of a sentence, punctuation will always separate it from the rest of the sentence. Read the sentence without "also known as ringtaw or ringer" to determine whether the sentence still makes sense. Because the sentence makes logical sense without it, the comma is necessary to correctly set off the nonessential phrase. Eliminate F. Choice G is incorrect because the semicolon does not join two independent clauses. Choice J incorrectly uses a colon. Choice (H) is correct.

11. C **Difficulty:** Low

Category: Usage

Getting to the Answer: Pronouns must agree in person and number with their antecedents. The antecedent here is the plural *players*, so the singular *his or her* is incorrect.

Choices B and D use second- and first-person pronouns, respectively, which are also inappropriate with this antecedent. *Their marbles*, in (C), is correct.

12. F   Difficulty: Medium

Category: Usage

Getting to the Answer: The noun closest to a verb in the sentence may not be its subject. Here, the plural *marbles* is the object of the preposition *of*, not the subject of the verb *spans*; the subject is the singular *popularity*, so this sentence is correct as written. Choice G does not agree with the singular subject. The verb form in H creates a grammatically incorrect sentence. Choice J is unnecessarily wordy.

13. B   Difficulty: Medium

Category: Usage

Getting to the Answer: The antecedent of a pronoun may appear in an earlier sentence. The antecedent of *It* is the plural *games* in the previous sentence, so the pronoun should be plural. Eliminate A and D, which use singular pronouns. Choice C uses the wrong verb tense, so it is incorrect. Choice (B) is correct.

14. H   Difficulty: Medium

Category: Usage

Getting to the Answer: The underlined segment contains an idiom, or a phrase that must have a certain combination of words in order to be correct. Choices F, G, and J are all idiomatically incorrect constructions; only the idiom in (H) is correct.

15. A   Difficulty: High

Category: Usage

Getting to the Answer: Some sentences will be correct as written. This sentence contains no error, so (A) is correct. Choice B improperly uses an adjective (*actual*) to modify a verb (*has*). Choices C and D make the sentence unnecessarily wordy, and C incorrectly uses the plural pronoun *they* to refer to the *game*.

Answers & Explanations

CHAPTER 4

PRACTICE

10. G **Difficulty:** Low

Category: Usage

Getting to the Answer: The subject of the sentence, *citizens*, is plural, but the verb phrase *was using* is singular. Eliminate F and J, since they contain singular verb phrases. The verb phrase *are using* is plural, but it is present tense, and the sentence requires past tense. The correct answer is (G).

11. A **Difficulty:** High

Category: Usage

Getting to the Answer: The adjective *most* is in the superlative form, which is used to compare three or more items, and the passage compares "Galloping Gertie" to all other suspension bridges at the time. The sentence is correct as written, so (A) is the correct answer. Choices C and D contain *more*, which is only used to compare two items, and B introduces an unnecessary comma.

12. J **Difficulty:** Medium

Category: Usage

Getting to the Answer: The adjective *relative* modifies the adjective *short*. Only adverbs can modify adjectives, so F and H are incorrect. There is no need for a comma between an adverb and the adjective it modifies, so you can eliminate G. The correct answer is (J).

13. C **Difficulty:** Medium

Category: Usage

Getting to the Answer: The underlined phrase includes the preposition *in*, which indicates this is an idiom question. Choice A is incorrect as written. Eliminate D, since it adds an extra comma and does not address the issue. Plug the remaining prepositions into the sentence to determine which conveys the proper meaning. Choice (C) is correct.

14. G **Difficulty:** Low

Category: Usage

Getting to the Answer: This sentence requires past tense verbs. Eliminate both F and J, which contain present tense verbs. *Was hailed* is past tense, but the added phrase "at the time" in H creates a new issue of redundancy. The correct answer is (G).

15. A **Difficulty:** High

Category: Usage

Getting to the Answer: The underlined segment contains the commonly misused word *effect*, which means "something that is produced by a cause or consequence." Given the context, the sentence is correct as written, so (A) is the correct answer. Choice B includes an incorrect pronoun, and C and D both use the word *affect* (meaning "to act on, to have influence on something").

16. J **Difficulty:** Medium

Category: Usage

Getting to the Answer: The underlined segment contains the plural pronoun *they*, but the antecedent is the singular noun *roadbed*. Eliminate F and G. Eliminate H because it introduces a new issue of incorrect verb tense. The correct answer is (J).

17. D **Difficulty:** Medium

Category: Usage

Getting to the Answer: The word *nickname* requires a singular, gender-neutral pronoun. Eliminate A, because *its'* is never correct, and eliminate B, which uses a plural pronoun. Eliminate C for its use of the contraction *it's*, which means *it is*. Choice (D) is correct.

PERFORM

18. H   **Difficulty:** High

Category: Usage

Getting to the Answer: The underlined segment includes the comparative adjective *earlier*. The comparative form is only used to discuss two items or people, and this sentence is about all examples of basketry. Eliminate F and G. Choice J uses the correct superlative adjective *earliest* but introduces a preposition error. The correct answer is (H).

19. D   **Difficulty:** Low

Category: Usage

Getting to the Answer: The underlined segment contains the adjective *good*. The verb phrase "have been preserved" needs an adverb to modify it. Eliminate A and C. Choice B introduces a verb error. The correct answer is (D).

20. G   **Difficulty:** High

Category: Usage

Getting to the Answer: When a verb is underlined, check to make sure it agrees with its subject in person, number, and tense. While the verb *know* agrees with the subject *Native Americans* in person and number, it is the incorrect tense. Clues such as *ancient* and *early* indicate that the verb needs to be past tense. Choices H and J both create new errors. Choice (G) corrects the verb without introducing new errors.

21. C   **Difficulty:** Medium

Category: Usage

Getting to the Answer: When a verb is underlined, make sure to identify the proper subject. In this sentence, *decoration* is the closest noun to the verb *is*, but the actual subject is the plural noun *materials*. Eliminate A, B, and D since they all contain singular verbs. The correct answer is (C).

22. F   **Difficulty:** High

Category: Usage

Getting to the Answer: The word *many* is often confused with the word *much*. The word *much* refers to items that cannot be quantified, and *many* refers to tangible items that could be counted, such as "palm leaves, tree roots, and grasses." The sentence is correct as written, so (F) is the answer. Choice G uses an unnecessary colon, and both H and J contain the incorrect word *much*.

23. B   **Difficulty:** Medium

Category: Usage

Getting to the Answer: The modifying phrase "quick and gracefully" is not parallel, since it has one adjective and one adverb. Both words need to be adverbs in order to correctly modify the verb *works*. Choices A, C, and D all include incorrect modifiers. The correct answer is (B).

24. F   **Difficulty:** Medium

Category: Usage

Getting to the Answer: The underlined segment contains the singular pronoun *its*, and the antecedent is the singular noun *culture*. The sentence is correct as written, so the answer is (F). Choices G and J include contractions instead of pronouns, and H includes a plural pronoun.

25. D   **Difficulty:** Medium

Category: Usage

Getting to the Answer: The preposition *among* is commonly confused with the preposition *between*. *Among* is used to compare multiple things, but there are only two items in this sentence: *traditional artistry* and *financial security*. Therefore, the word *between* is needed, and (D) is correct. Choices A, B, and C contain incorrect prepositions for the given context.

26. G   **Difficulty:** Medium

Category: Usage

Getting to the Answer: The underlined phrase "a far cry for" is an idiom, but the preposition *for* does not convey the proper meaning, so F is incorrect. Eliminate H, because it introduces a new error. Plug in the remaining choices. Choice (G) is the most correct, concise, and relevant option.

ON YOUR OWN

1. D   **Difficulty:** Low

Category: Usage

Getting to the Answer: The underlined segment contains the pronoun *whom*, which is in the objective case. The sentence requires a subjective pronoun; eliminate A and B. Choice C introduces a verb error. The correct answer is (D).

2. H   **Difficulty:** Medium

Category: Usage

Getting to the Answer:

The contraction *who's* stands for *who is*, which is a present tense verb phrase. The surrounding context indicates a past tense verb is needed. Eliminate F and J. Choice G contains an incomplete verb phrase when plugged into the sentence. Choice (H) is correct.

3. C   **Difficulty:** Medium

Category: Usage

Getting to the Answer: The adjective *greater* is only used when comparing two items or people. The passage compares Shelley's novel to all other horror tales. The superlative adjective form is needed, so A and B are incorrect. Choice D does not make sense when plugged into the sentence. The correct answer is (C).

4. G   **Difficulty:** Medium

Category: Usage

Getting to the Answer: When a list of nouns and pronouns is underlined, make sure that each noun or pronoun matches the verb by itself. "Her had a contest "is not correct, so eliminate F and J. Between the two remaining choices, (G) is the more correct, concise, and relevant option.

5. D   **Difficulty:** Medium

Category: Usage

Getting to the Answer: The underlined verb phrase needs an adverb to modify it, but *whimsical* is an adjective. Eliminate A and B. Choice C contains the correct adverb but introduces redundancy when plugged into the sentence. The correct answer is (D).

6. H   **Difficulty:** Low

Category: Usage

Getting to the Answer: The underlined phrase is an idiom, but the preposition *from* does not convey the proper meaning; eliminate F. Plug the remaining choices into the sentence. Choice (H) conveys the proper meaning for this idiom and is the correct answer.

7. A   **Difficulty:** Low

Category: Sentence Structure and Formation

Getting to the Answer: When a verb is underlined and there are other verbs in the same sentence, check to make sure all of the verbs match in person, number, and tense. *Creates* matches the other verbs, *tells* and *discovers*, so (A) is correct. Choices B, C, and D are not the correct tense.

8. H   **Difficulty:** Medium

Category: Organization, Unity, and Cohesion / Transitions

Getting to the Answer: This sentence calls for a transition phrase that contrasts the monster's *gruesome appearance* with his good nature. The transitions *Similar to* and *Because of* do not convey the proper meaning, so eliminate F and J. Choice G contains a contrasting word, *Although*, but does not fit into the existing sentence structure and creates a fragment. The correct answer is (H).

9. A   **Difficulty:** Medium

Category: Usage

Getting to the Answer: The pronoun *whom* is always in the objective case, and the pronoun *who* is always subjective. The antecedent for *whom* is the *people* the monster has affected, so the objective case is needed. The correct answer is (A). Choice C contains the incorrect subjective pronoun *who*, and B and D introduce new errors into the sentence.

10. J   Difficulty: Low

Category: Sentence Structure and Formation

Getting to the Answer: When a list is underlined, make sure that all items of that list have parallel structure. Choices F and H all contain elements that do not match each other. Choice G adds an unnecessary conjunction. The correct answer is (J).

11. D   Difficulty: High

Category: Usage

Getting to the Answer: The subject of the plural verb *die* is *each*, which requires a singular verb. Eliminate A and C, which contain plural verbs. Choice B includes the singular verb *dies* but introduces a different subject, *both*, which is plural. The correct answer is (D).

12. F   Difficulty: Low

Category: Usage

Getting to the Answer: The verb *provide* matches the subject *other versions*. Choice (F) is the correct answer. Choice H contains the incorrect verb *provides*. Choices G and J introduce new errors into the sentence.

13. C   Difficulty: High

Category: Organization, Unity, and Cohesion / Passage Organization

Getting to the Answer: This paragraph needs a clear topic sentence, followed by further information and examples.

Sentence 2 is the best topic sentence because it provides a transition from the previous paragraph and introduces the main idea of Paragraph 4: the critical acclaim and continued popularity of Frankenstein. Eliminate A and B, which do not start with the correct topic sentence. Choice D is incorrect because Sentence 1 needs to come before Sentences 3 and 4, to set up those examples. The correct answer is (C).

14. H   Difficulty: High

Category: Topic Development / Supporting Material

Getting to the Answer: This sentence's content focuses on the monster's transition from good to evil. Paragraph 2 does not discuss this transformation, so you can eliminate F and G. Choice J would put this sentence too late in Paragraph 3, after the monster has already committed evil acts. Choice (H) is the correct answer.

15. D   Difficulty: High

Category: Topic Development / Writer's Purpose

Getting to the Answer: While the passage does discuss various film adaptations of *Frankenstein*, the essay's focal point is how the classic horror story was created and what it entails. Eliminate A and B. Eliminate C, since the reasoning is not correct; the essay does explore different types of films, even though discussing the films is not the author's main purpose. The correct answer is (D).

CHAPTER 5

PRACTICE

5. C   Difficulty: Low

Category: Organization, Unity, and Cohesion / Transitions

Getting to the Answer: The underlined transition indicates cause and effect, but it does not make sense in the context of the sentence; the sentence needs a contrast transition. Eliminate A and B, since they do not contain contrast transitions and therefore do not reflect the writer's intended meaning. Choice D includes a contrast transition but introduces a grammar error when plugged into the sentence. The correct answer is (C).

6. F   Difficulty: Medium

Category: Organization, Unity, and Cohesion / Transitions

Getting to the Answer: The previous paragraph introduces the new homeland of the Kumeyaay Indians, and the first sentence of the second paragraph introduces Eva Salazar and how she came to learn the traditions of her ancestors. The sentence is in the correct place, and (F) is correct.

7. B   Difficulty: Medium

Category: Organization, Unity, and Cohesion / Transitions

Getting to the Answer: The underlined portion explains the relationship of Eva Salazar to the Kumeyaay. Deleting this would take away a key detail explaining her ties to the native community whose traditions she carries on through her art. Choice (B) is correct. Choice D introduces an idea not discussed in the passage. Choice C is not as clear and relevant as (B).

8. F   Difficulty: Medium

Category: Organization, Unity, and Cohesion / Transitions

Getting to the Answer: Transitions must accurately convey the author's intent. The underlined transition correctly shows a contrast between what Eva is known

for and her other artistic creations. Choice (F) is correct. Choice G is not a contrast transition, and the contrast transitions in H and J do not make sense in the context of the sentence.

9. B   Difficulty: Medium

Category: Organization, Unity, and Cohesion / Transitions

Getting to the Answer: The underlined word indicates that Eva should not be thought of as a master weaver, contradicting the previous statements of the writer; A is incorrect. Eliminate C because it conveys the same incorrect meaning as A. Choice D does not make sense in the context of the sentence. Choice (B) provides a transition that perfectly matches the passage's timeline and the author's intent.

10. H   Difficulty: High

Category: Organization, Unity, and Cohesion / Passage Organization

Getting to the Answer: The passage discusses Eva Salazar's dedication to preserving Kumeyaay traditions. She has done this through learning her craft and passing her knowledge on to more artists. Choice (H) adds the extra information needed to convey the main idea and conclude the passage. Choices F, G, and J all convey accurate information but are not fitting conclusion sentences given the context of this paragraph.

PERFORM

11. B   Difficulty: Medium

Category: Organization, Unity, and Cohesion / Transitions

Getting to the Answer: Transitions must logically convey the writer's purpose. The word *Despite* is a contrast transition, which is the opposite of the writer's intent. The writer's goal is to emphasize how important good manners were for the upper classes. Eliminate A and C because they are contrast transitions. Choice D is incorrect because good manners were important at all times, not just occasionally. Choice (B) is correct; *Especially for* emphasizes the point the writer is making.

12. J   Difficulty: Low

Category: Organization, Unity, and Cohesion / Passage Organization

Getting to the Answer: The best conclusion will most clearly reflect the writer's tone and purpose. Eliminate choices F and G because they are too informal. Choice H matches the writer's tone but does not fulfill the writer's purpose; the writer is discussing marriage, not patriotism. Choice (J) is correct, perfectly matching the writer's tone and purpose.

13. A   Difficulty: Medium

Category: Organization, Unity, and Cohesion / Transitions

Getting to the Answer: This sentence discusses the physical restrictiveness of female fashion during the Victorian Era. The last part of the sentence states that there was just enough room left for women to breathe. The other answer choices make incorrect connections between the physical restriction of the fashion and women's ability to still breathe. Choice (A) is correct. Choices B, C, and D do not convey the writer's intended meaning.

14. J   Difficulty: Medium

Category: Organization, Unity, and Cohesion / Transitions

Getting to the Answer: The preceding sentence discusses the limited educations many women received during the Victorian Era. Then this sentence states that a minority of women were educated more fully. This shift of ideas requires a contrast transition, and the current transition does not serve that purpose. Choices G and H do not provide the appropriate contrast. The correct answer is (J).

15. C   Difficulty: Medium

Category: Organization, Unity, and Cohesion / Transitions

Getting to the Answer: When used to make a point, transitions must correctly convey the writer's intended meaning. The underlined transition indicates a similarity, but given the earlier phrase *not only*, the sentence specifically requires *but also*. Eliminate B and D, which use transition words that do not convey the writer's intended meaning. The correct answer is (C).

16. H   Difficulty: High

Category: Organization, Unity, and Cohesion / Passage Organization

Getting to the Answer: When asked to check for proper passage organization, check the main idea of each paragraph as well as the transition from one paragraph to another. Paragraph 3 discusses men's fashion during the Victorian Era. There is no transition to this either from Paragraph 2 or in the introduction to Paragraph 3. Paragraph 4 begins with a transition to Victorian fashion and goes on to discuss women's fashion. Therefore, Paragraph 3 would be correctly placed after Paragraph 4. The correct answer is (H).

ON YOUR OWN

1. C   Difficulty: High

Category: Sentence Structure and Formation

Getting to the Answer: The passage begins by introducing the time period to be discussed. The following information needs to align with the same tense. *Developed* indicates that the commercialism had already happened rather than being in progress; eliminate A and B. Choice D eliminates the verb and therefore changes the meaning of the sentence. Only (C) correctly describes the premise that the commercialism was a work in progress.

2. G   Difficulty: Low

Category: Punctuation

Getting to the Answer: When there is punctuation present in an underlined portion, check for accuracy. In this case, a comma is needed following the dependent clause "with men working in factories." Eliminate F and H, which use incorrect punctuation for a dependent clause. Eliminate J since it contains no punctuation. The correct answer is (G).

3. C   Difficulty: High

Category: Organization, Unity, and Cohesion / Transitions

Getting to the Answer: As written, the underlined portion indicates a contrast. However, further into the sentence, the passage is discussing the effects of women having more autonomy. The underlined portion should support that point. Eliminate A and D because they incorrectly use contrast transitions. Choices B and C both contain cause-and-effect transitions. Of those two choices, (C) is grammatically correct and completes the sentence.

4. F   Difficulty: Medium

Category: Organization, Unity, and Cohesion / Transitions

Getting to the Answer: The sentence is discussing the fact that women worked at home and still earned money. This was an unusual concept during this time period. The underlined word must demonstrate that contrast but also express the positive aspect of the arrangement conveyed in the passage. The current underlined word serves the appropriate purpose. The correct answer choice is (F). Choices G and H incorrectly use contrast transitions, and J does not convey the sentence's proper meaning.

5. B   Difficulty: Medium

Category: Organization, Unity, and Cohesion / Transitions

Getting to the Answer: The first clause of the sentence introduces shoemaking as another source of income for women. The second clause describes the drawbacks of that job. The transition word needs to link these contrasting ideas. Choices A, C, and D all incorrectly indicate cause and effect. The correct answer is (B).

6. J   Difficulty: Medium

Category: Organization, Unity, and Cohesion / Transitions

Getting to the Answer: When a sentence begins with a transition word, identify what type of transition is needed to link the sentence to the previous one. In this case, the preceding sentence discusses the difficulties women faced as shoemakers. The sentence that follows discusses a change that caused women to have a greater impact in the shoe-making industry. This calls for a contrast transition, which is not supplied by the underlined word; eliminate F. Eliminate G and H, which incorrectly use cause-and-effect transition words. Choice (J) correctly places a contrast transition at the beginning of the sentence.

7. A   Difficulty: Medium

Category: Organization, Unity, and Cohesion / Transitions

Getting to the Answer: This question is another demonstration of a sentence beginning with a transition word. The preceding sentence discusses women's rise in the shoe-making industry. The next sentence goes on to discuss more difficulties of the job. A contrast transition word is required, and the current underlined word fulfills that need. Choice (A) is correct. Choices B, C, and D do not contain the correct type of transition.

8. F   Difficulty: Medium

Category: Organization, Unity, and Cohesion / Passage Organization

Getting to the Answer: When asked to check the order of sentences, determine whether the current placement is correct. Upon reviewing at the flow of ideas in this paragraph, the sentence is already placed in the correct spot. Choice (F) is correct.

9. C   Difficulty: High

Category: Usage

Getting to the Answer: The underlined verb implies that the work is continuing and that women who are working in the present day have the same issues as those in the time period of the passage. Since the issue is not one of the present time, the underlined portion needs to indicate the action took place in the past; eliminate A. Choice B improperly uses the pronoun *that* to refer to women. Choice D uses the incorrect pronoun case *whom*. Choice (C) uses the correct pronoun and verb tense.

10. H   Difficulty: Medium

Category: Organization, Unity, and Cohesion / Transitions

Getting to the Answer: The underlined transition indicates contrast. The preceding sentence discusses a negative side to women working in factories, while this sentence discusses the positive aspects. Eliminate F and J, which contain cause-and-effect transitions. Both G and H use contrast transitions, but (H) is the correct choice given the context of the sentence.

11. A   **Difficulty:** Medium

Category: Usage

Getting to the Answer: To be grammatically correct, the underlined pronoun *which* must join this clause to the previous clause. Therefore, the sentence is correct as written, and the correct answer is (A). Choices B and C are grammatically incorrect, and D changes the meaning of the sentence.

12. J   **Difficulty:** Medium

Category: Punctuation

Getting to the Answer: The underlined portion adds an extra *s* to the word *women*, which is already plural; eliminate F and G. H is incorrect because it omits a word integral to the meaning of the sentence. Choice (J) correctly uses the possessive plural *women's*.

13. C   **Difficulty:** Medium

Category: Usage

Getting to the Answer: The first clause in the sentence includes the word *either*. In order to be idiomatically correct, the word *or* must also be used. Eliminate A and B because they incorrectly use *nor* instead of *or*. Eliminate D because it adds an unnecessary comma. Choice (C) correctly uses *or* and does not introduce any errors.

14. G   **Difficulty:** Low

Category: Usage

Getting to the Answer: When a verb is underlined, make sure it matches the surrounding text. The sentence refers to women in the early 19th century, so a plural past tense verb is required. Eliminate F because it is a singular present tense verb. Eliminate H, which would make a fragment. Choice J is plural, but it is in present tense. Choice (G) is correct.

15. A   **Difficulty:** High

Category: Organization, Unity, and Cohesion / Passage Organization

Getting to the Answer: When asked to to check and potentially rearrange paragraphs in a passage, review the progression of main ideas in the passage to determine whether they are logically placed. Since this paragraph is currently at the end of the passage, it should logically conclude the ideas presented in the passage and not introduce new points. In this case, this paragraph provides the logical conclusion to the passage and is placed correctly. Choice (A) is correct.

Answers & Explanations

CHAPTER 6

PRACTICE

5. B   Difficulty: Medium

Category: Topic Development / Supporting Material

Getting to the Answer: When asked to consider adding a statement, determine the focus of the paragraph in which it would appear. This paragraph discusses Bogart's academic troubles. The proposed statement adds additional information about these troubles, so it should be added; eliminate C and D. Choice A is incorrect because the statement is about academics, not stardom. Choice (B) is correct, because the proposed statement supports the claim that Bogart was a "frequent instigator of trouble."

6. F   Difficulty: Medium

Category: Topic Development / Supporting Material

Getting to the Answer: When considering whether to revise a phrase, determine what, if anything, the revision would add. The proposed revision places greater emphasis on how far Bogart was from fame, which supports the main idea expressed in Paragraph 1; eliminate H and J. Choice G is incorrect because Paragraph 1 has already expressed that Bogart's stardom happened later. Choice (F) correctly describes the role of the proposed revision.

7. C   Difficulty: High

Category: Topic Development / Supporting Material

Getting to the Answer: Transitions should clearly connect adjacent paragraphs. The previous paragraph describes Bogart's life before the theater, ending with a discussion of his time in the navy. The current paragraph describes Bogart's life after the navy, so the transition should reflect this chronological order. The following sentence also refers to *the business*, so the transition sentence should introduce that the business in question is the theater. Eliminate A, because it does not reference Bogart's time in the navy and it abruptly changes the subject. Choice D is similarly abrupt, so it should be eliminated. Choice B does not introduce the subject of the

theater, so it is incorrect. Choice (C) is the best transition because it references Bogart's time in the navy while introducing the subject of the theater.

8. J   Difficulty: High

Category: Topic Development / Supporting Material

Getting to the Answer: When asked what would be lost if a phrase were deleted, consider what the phrase adds to the surrounding text. The second half of the sentence says that Bogart "struggled to find any substantive parts," and the underlined portion supports that claim by citing his inexperience. Eliminate F because the underlined portion is about Bogart's early struggles rather than his success. Eliminate G because the paragraph describes Bogart's life without giving any advice to the reader. Choice H is incorrect because the underlined portion does not provide a specific example of Bogart's inexperience. Choice (J) correctly characterizes the underlined portion and its relationship to the rest of the sentence.

9. C   Difficulty: Low

Category: Topic Development / Supporting Material

Getting to the Answer: When asked to consider adding a sentence, read the surrounding sentences to determine the main point of the paragraph. The paragraph describes Bogart's rise to fame as an actor. The new information in the proposed sentence does not directly pertain to Bogart's career, so it should not be added. Eliminate A and B. The paragraph does not emphasize films, so D is incorrect. Choice (C) accurately expresses the reason not to add the sentence, so it is correct.

10. G   Difficulty: High

Category: Topic Development / Writer's Purpose

Getting to the Answer: To determine an essay's primary purpose, summarize the passage as a whole. The passage describes Bogart's slow rise to fame, detailing the challenges he faced before and during his attempts to become a successful actor. Thus, the passage fulfills the purpose mentioned in the question stem. Eliminate H and J. Choice F is incorrect because the passage does not mention anyone doubting Bogart's talent. Choice (G) is correct because it accurately connects the features of the passage to the stated purpose.

Answers & Explanations

PERFORM

11. D   **Difficulty:** Medium

Category: Topic Development / Supporting Material

Getting to the Answer: When asked to consider adding a sentence, determine what the sentence might contribute to the surrounding context. The paragraph describes the family's reasons for joining a CSA and goes on to describe how a CSA works. While the additional sentence does add details, the details are not relevant to the main point of the paragraph. Eliminate A and B. The additional sentence would distract from the main point even if it included more details, so C is incorrect. Choice (D) states that the sentence distracts from the focus of the paragraph, so this choice is correct.

12. F   **Difficulty:** Medium

Category: Topic Development / Supporting Material

Getting to the Answer: When a question has a question stem, focus more on relevance than on concision, or using the fewest words possible to convey the writer's meaning. The proposed revision adds detail to the original, providing information about the freshness of the produce in the boxes. Eliminate H and J. G is incorrect, because this detail does not clearly emphasize the benefits of the CSA. The correct answer is (F).

13. B   **Difficulty:** Medium

Category: Topic Development / Supporting Material

Getting to the Answer: Think of this question as a matching question. Match the phrase to the answer choice that best describes it. The phrase explains how farmers benefit from the CSA. Choice (B) is the only option that matches this description and is therefore correct. The phrase does not refer to the narrator's family, so A is incorrect. The essay does not mention farmers who do not sell to CSAs, so C is incorrect. Choice D is incorrect because the first paragraph provides a brief explanation of how a CSA works for farmers and customers, making the information relevant.

14. H   **Difficulty:** High

Category: Topic Development / Supporting Material

Getting to the Answer: When asked what would be lost if a phrase were deleted, consider what the phrase adds to the sentence. The phrase describes how the bunch of broccoli relates to the CSA—namely, that it came in one of the CSA boxes. Because the family's experience with the CSA is the main topic of the passage, choice (H) is correct. While the phrase does include a month in which the family participated in the CSA, that is not the primary function of the detail. Thus, F is incorrect. The phrase does not introduce a kind of produce, so G is incorrect. Choice J is incorrect because the main function of the details is to connect the broccoli bunch with the main topic, not to clarify the main topic.

15. B   **Difficulty:** Medium

Category: Topic Development / Supporting Material

Getting to the Answer: The correct answer choice will be clearly connected to the other details in the paragraph or effectively summarize the paragraph. On the ACT, a strong concluding sentence won't introduce a new topic. The paragraph describes how the narrator's family positively reacts to the CSA. Only (B) is connected to this idea, and it is a natural follow-up to the information about the new vegetables the brother has eaten because of the family's CSA membership. The other choices are not connected to the topic of the family's positive experience with new food from the CSA.

16. G   **Difficulty:** Medium

Category: Topic Development / Supporting Material

Getting to the Answer: Use your elimination skills. Once you've determined whether or not to add the proposed sentence, you can immediately eliminate two answer choices. The paragraph describes how the family cooked and baked the overwhelming amount of zucchini they received. This detail is relevant to that idea, so it should be included. Therefore, H and J are incorrect. The family's cooking skills are not a main point in the paragraph, so F is incorrect. The correct answer is (G).

17. A   **Difficulty:** Low

Category: Topic Development / Supporting Material

Getting to the Answer: When asked about revising a phrase, read the sentence with and without the revision. The revised phrase emphasizes the comical lengths to which the family went in using the large amount of zucchini, which is the main point of the paragraph. Thus, the writer should make the revision, and C and D can be eliminated. Choice (A) expresses this reason for making the revision, and it is therefore correct.

18. H   **Difficulty:** Medium

Category: Topic Development / Writer's Purpose

Getting to the Answer: The correct answer to this type of question will be connected to the main idea of the passage, so start by pinpointing the main idea. The main idea of this passage is that one family has enjoyed its experience with a CSA membership but has also experienced some drawbacks. This main idea does not match the much more general, informative purpose given in the question; eliminate F and G. Choice J contradicts the essay, which does provide some information on membership. Choice (H) correctly identifies the focus of the essay.

ON YOUR OWN

1. B   **Difficulty:** Medium

Category: Usage

Getting to the Answer: When a verb is underlined, check whether it agrees with its subject and is in the proper tense. Here, the subject is *a trend*, which is singular. The verb should be in present tense, because the following sentence discusses the speculation using the present tense. Choice (B) is the singular present tense option, so it is correct.

2. J   **Difficulty:** Medium

Category: Topic Development / Supporting Material

Getting to the Answer: When a question asks about revising a phrase, the correct answer should accurately

describe the effect the revision would have on the text. Choices F and G both describe the revision inaccurately. The proposed revision is not easier to understand than the original, so F is incorrect. The original is clearer about the time frame than the revision is, so G is incorrect. There is no such thing as being too concise, so H is incorrect. The original phrase provides a relevant detail about when the change is expected, making (J) the correct choice.

3. D   **Difficulty:** Low

Category: Knowledge of Language / Style and Tone

Getting to the Answer: When asked which choice best maintains a particular tone, eliminate any answer choices that are too neutral or that convey an opposite tone. Choices A and B are too neutral, and C is too negative. Therefore, (D) is correct.

4. J   **Difficulty:** Medium

Category: Organization, Unity, and Cohesion / Transitions

Getting to the Answer: The current paragraph speculates about the future of libraries, and the following paragraph discusses the origin and development of libraries. The transition should connect these topics. Choice F loses the focus on libraries, so it should be eliminated. Choice G connects the past and the future, but it does not provide any reason to begin discussing the history of libraries. Choice H focuses only on the future, so it is not an appropriate transition. Choice (J) connects the topics of the future and the past of libraries, while giving the reader an incentive to want to know more about their history. Choice (J) is correct.

5. A   **Difficulty:** High

Category: Topic Development / Supporting Material

Getting to the Answer: When asked what would be lost if a phrase were deleted, consider what that phrase adds to the paragraph. Because the underlined phrase describes a time, it orients the reader to when the events described in the rest of the sentence take place, helping to situate them within the broader timeline. Choice (A) correctly reflects this role, and it is therefore correct. While the phrase references the seventh century BCE, it does not emphasize this century over others; thus, B is incorrect. The detail does not provide a connection between the King of Assyria and the people of Babylon, so C is incorrect. Choice D is incorrect because the phrase is not an example.

6. G   Difficulty: Medium

Category: Sentence Structure and Formation

Getting to the Answer: The answer choices provide different ways of connecting two halves of a sentence, so check whether the sentence is a run-on. The two halves are independent clauses, so they need to be joined by the proper punctuation: a semicolon, a FANBOYS conjunction and comma, or a period and capital letter. Choice (G) properly connects them with a semicolon. Choices F and H create run-on sentences. Choice J is incorrect because the conjunction *and* must follow a comma when connecting independent clauses.

7. A   Difficulty: High

Category: Topic Development / Supporting Material

Getting to the Answer: A sentence should be added only if it is relevant to the main point of the paragraph and fits well in the context. The additional sentence is relevant to the discussion on the history of libraries, because it helps fill in the timeline of library development. Thus, it should be added. Eliminate C and D. While B may be tempting, the paragraph does not emphasize religious contributions to libraries; it merely mentions that a few of the developments took place in temples. Choice (A) correctly states the reason for adding the sentence.

8. F   Difficulty: Medium

Category: Punctuation

Getting to the Answer: When the answer choices differ only in punctuation, check to see what the punctuation is connecting. Here, it connects essential information in the sentence with the predicate verb. Because no rule requires separating these parts of a sentence with punctuation, no punctuation should be added. Choice (F) is correct.

9. C   Difficulty: Medium

Category: Topic Development / Supporting Material

Getting to the Answer: A transition at the start of a paragraph should flow well with both the preceding paragraph and the sentence that immediately follows it. Because the next sentence lists societal factors that "played a role," the transition sentence should place these factors within the context of the discussion of libraries. Choice (C) is correct because it both introduces the societal changes and continues the timeline of library development from the preceding paragraph.

10. H   Difficulty: Medium

Category: Topic Development / Supporting Material

Getting to the Answer: Look for the answer choice that accurately describes how the sentence in question relates to the surrounding sentences. Because the sentence begins with *However*, we know it is in contrast with the preceding sentence; therefore, F can be eliminated. Choice G is incorrect because the passage establishes the link between Henry VIII's actions and libraries in the sentence after the one in question. The entire paragraph deals with library developments after the thirteenth century, so J is incorrect. The correct answer is (H).

11. D   Difficulty: Low

Category: Topic Development / Supporting Material

Getting to the Answer: Only add sentences that relate to the purpose of the passage. The sentence in question distracts from the purpose of describing the history and development of libraries, so it should not be added. Eliminate A and B. Choice (D) accurately reflects the reason not to add the sentence and is therefore correct.

12. G   Difficulty: Medium

Category: Punctuation

Getting to the Answer: When the answer choices differ only in their punctuation, check what the punctuation is connecting. Here, it connects an introductory phrase with the rest of the sentence, so a comma is needed. Choice (G) is correct.

13. B **Difficulty:** Low

Category: Knowledge of Language / Concision

Getting to the Answer: When one answer choice is much shorter than the others, the question may be testing concision. Given that *consider* and *think about* mean the same thing, A, C, and D are all unnecessarily repetitive. Therefore, (B) is correct.

14. F **Difficulty:** Medium

Category: Organization, Unity, and Cohesion / Transitions

Getting to the Answer: When a transition word is underlined, check that it is appropriate both logically and grammatically. Logically, the connected ideas are in contrast. We may consider questions similar to those considered by English citizens under Henry VIII, but we think about these questions in different ways. Eliminate H and J. Grammatically, the word *despite* can only introduce a noun phrase, so G is incorrect. Choice (F) matches both the logic and the grammar of the sentence, so it is correct.

15. C **Difficulty:** Medium

Category: Topic Development / Writer's Purpose

Getting to the Answer: When asked whether the passage accomplishes a particular purpose, check whether the purpose is too narrow or too broad. While the passage does discuss predictions about the future of libraries, it focuses mostly on the development of libraries throughout the past. Thus, the stated purpose is too narrow. Eliminate A and B. The passage does not emphasize the struggles of libraries, so D is incorrect. The correct answer is (C).

CHAPTER 7

PRACTICE

7. D   **Difficulty:** Medium

Category: Knowledge of Language / Ambiguity

Getting to the Answer: When the underlined portion is a pronoun, check for the antecedent (to what the pronoun refers). In this question, it is unclear to what *them* refers. Choices A and B both contain ambiguous pronouns, so they should be eliminated. Choice C does not make sense in the context, so (D) is correct.

8. G   **Difficulty:** High

Category: Knowledge of Language / Style and Tone

Getting to the Answer: When the answer choices contain pronouns that express different tones, such as *you* or *one*, you are likely being tested on consistent tone. Choices F, H, and J all fit the formal tone of the passage. The question stem says to select the choice that is not acceptable, so eliminate F, H, and J. Because the word *you* is not used in the passage, (G) is unacceptable and is therefore the correct answer.

9. B   **Difficulty:** High

Category: Knowledge of Language / Precision

Getting to the Answer: When the question stem asks which choice best conveys a certain meaning, precision is the issue. While multiple answer choices may seem to fit in the context, only one will convey the intended meaning precisely. Eliminate choices A and D, since they do not indicate a contrast. Choice C, *finally*, does indicate a change, but it alters the original meaning of the sentence. Only (B) accurately conveys contrast, so (B) is correct.

10. J   **Difficulty:** Low

Category: Knowledge of Language / Concision

Getting to the Answer: The words *clear* and *unobstructed* are redundant. Choice H contains forms of these same words, so eliminate both F and H. Choice G, *crystal*, doesn't make sense in context. When the word is used to mean *clear*, it means "clear like a crystal," as in a transparent object that one can see through. However, nothing is being seen through here. Choice (J) is correct.

11. C   **Difficulty:** Medium

Category: Knowledge of Language / Style and Tone

Getting to the Answer: Questions that require you to match the author's purpose in writing are testing your ability to match the tone of the passage. While multiple answer choices may be grammatically correct, you must select the choice that fits best with the author's point of view. Choices A, B, and D all fail to emphasize the symbolic nature of the sweat lodge experience. Choice (C) is therefore correct.

12. J   **Difficulty:** Medium

Category: Knowledge of Language / Concision

Getting to the Answer: When "DELETE the underlined portion" is an option, check whether the underlined portion contributes to the meaning of the passage. Eliminate F and G because *often* means the same thing as *typically*. *Occasionally* contradicts *typically*, so H is incorrect. Because none of the other answer choices add to the meaning of the sentence, (J) is the correct answer.

PERFORM

13. D   **Difficulty:** Low

Category: Knowledge of Language / Concision

Getting to the Answer: The underlined portion uses more words than necessary. Eliminate A and B, which are both too wordy. Eliminate C, which is awkwardly worded. Choice (D) is correct because it expresses the intended meaning concisely and correctly.

14. G   **Difficulty:** Medium

Category: Knowledge of Language / Ambiguity

Getting to the Answer: The underlined portion contains the pronoun *it*, but the antecedent (to what *it* is referring) is unclear. Eliminate F and J, which both contain ambiguous pronouns. Choice H does not convey the proper meaning for the context. The correct answer is (G).

15. C   Difficulty: Medium

Category: Knowledge of Language / Style and Tone

Getting to the Answer: When a pronoun is underlined, check whether it matches the style of the other pronouns in the passage. The author of this passage uses *you* throughout, so *one* does not match the style. Eliminate A and B. Choice D is incorrect for the sentence's meaning. Choice (C) is correct.

16. F   Difficulty: High

Category: Knowledge of Language / Style and Tone

Getting to the Answer: The question stem asks you to match the passage's tone while also conveying a certain meaning. Choices G and H emphasize the benefits of being young, but they do not match the passage's casual language. Choice J is casual, but its meaning is neutral rather than positive. Choice (F) is correct.

17. B   Difficulty: Medium

Category: Knowledge of Language / Ambiguity

Getting to the Answer: The pronoun *it* is ambiguous because several other nouns appear between the true antecedent (the letter) and the pronoun. Thus, eliminate A and D, which are unclear. Because the paragraph mentions several written things, C is also unclear. Choice (B) is correct.

18. F   Difficulty: Medium

Category: Knowledge of Language / Concision

Getting to the Answer: Words in a passage should convey their meaning concisely. Choices G, H, and J use more words than necessary to express the intended meaning. Therefore, (F) is correct.

19. D   Difficulty: Low

Category: Knowledge of Language / Precision

Getting to the Answer: When asked which choice conveys a certain meaning, you are being tested on precision. Choices A and C convey the opposite of the writer's intended meaning, so eliminate them. Choice B awkward and unnecessarily wordy. The correct answer is (D).

20. H   Difficulty: High

Category: Knowledge of Language / Style and Tone

Getting to the Answer: The second-person pronouns *you* and *your* convey a more informal style than the third-person pronouns *one* and *oneself*. When asked about the impact of changing from one set of pronouns to the other, consider the tone of the passage. If *you* were changed to *one*, the passage would lose its sense of personal encouragement to the reader. Choice (H) reflects this loss, so it is correct. The original tone is not primarily humorous, so J is incorrect. The pronoun shift would not result in any gain in friendliness or universal relevance, so F and G are incorrect.

ON YOUR OWN

1. B   Difficulty: Medium

Category: Organization, Unity, and Cohesion / Transitions

Getting to the Answer: When a transition word is underlined, check to see that it makes a logical connection with proper punctuation. The underlined portion connects the idea that Paine is not well known with the claim that many Americans do not know him. These ideas are not in contrast, so eliminate A and C. The second idea is not a result of the first, so D is incorrect. Choice (B) is correct.

2. F   Difficulty: Medium

Category: Knowledge of Language / Precision

Getting to the Answer: This question is testing word choice. The sentence expresses that many people do not remember Paine's historical influence, so the correct choice should reflect that meaning. Eliminate G and J, which do not express the intended meaning. Choice H changes the meaning of the sentence from historical influence to fame, so H is incorrect. Only (F) correctly expresses the intended meaning.

3. C   Difficulty: High

Category: Punctuation

Getting to the Answer: The underlined portion contains an explanatory phrase that must be set off with either commas or dashes on each side. Choice A incorrectly uses a colon. Choices B and D introduce new errors. The correct answer is (C).

4. J   Difficulty: Medium

Category: Knowledge of Language / Concision

Getting to the Answer: The answer choices all express the same meaning, but G and H use more words than necessary. Choice F is also incorrect, since *one* and *true* are redundant in this context. Choice (J) is the most concise and is therefore correct.

5. D   Difficulty: Medium

Category: Sentence Structure and Formation

Getting to the Answer: When the underlined portion contains a comma, check whether the sentence is a run-on. Two independent clauses cannot be separated by either a comma or a dash, so A and B are incorrect. Conjunctions are not needed with semicolons, so C is incorrect. The correct answer is (D) because it combines the two independent clauses with a comma and a FANBOYS conjunction.

6. G   Difficulty: High

Category: Knowledge of Language / Precision

Getting to the Answer: When a question asks which choice best conveys a certain meaning, select the answer choice that conveys that meaning most precisely. While multiple answer choices could make sense in the context, only (G) conveys Paine's increased fame. Choice (G) is therefore correct.

7. C   Difficulty: Medium

Category: Knowledge of Language / Ambiguity

Getting to the Answer: When the underlined portion is a pronoun, make sure the noun to which it refers is clear. *Britain* is the closest noun to *Its*, and before that is *independence*. However, the second half of the sentence makes it clear that *Its* should refer to Paine's book. Eliminate D. Eliminate A and B also, which contain ambiguous pronouns. The correct answer is (C).

8. G   Difficulty: Medium

Category: Knowledge of Language / Precision

Getting to the Answer: Words in a sentence should convey their intended meaning precisely. Choices F and H contain things that can spread, but they do not make sense in the context. Choice J conveys the intended meaning but is redundant (comparing a book to a book), and the spreading discussed here concerns reaching a wide area, not opening up like a book. The correct answer is (G).

9. B   Difficulty: Medium

Category: Knowledge of Language / Ambiguity

Getting to the Answer: The underlined portion contains a pronoun whose antecedent is missing. Choices A and D fail to clarify whose morale is kept up. Paine did not publish a book to increase his own morale, so C can be eliminated. Choice (B) is correct.

10. F   Difficulty: Low

Category: Knowledge of Language / Precision

Getting to the Answer: When the underlined portion is a single word, make sure the word fits in the context. Because Paine lived hundreds of years ago, it does not make sense to say that he is *tasked* or is *helped* with something, so eliminate G and H. Choice J would result in awkward wording. Choice (F) is correct.

11. A   Difficulty: Medium

Category: Knowledge of Language / Style and Tone

Getting to the Answer: Consider both the surrounding details and the author's tone regarding the subject to determine which phrase fits the context of the essay. Throughout, the author advocates more recognition of Paine's achievements. Eliminate choices C and D because they are too neutral to match the author's tone. Choice B is positive in tone, but takes a stance that is too strong for the author's viewpoint in the essay; eliminate B. Choice (A) is correct because it perfectly matches the author's positive tone regarding Paine and accurately describes why Paine's work would be used by Jefferson and Adams.

12. G   Difficulty: High

Category: Topic Development / Supporting Material

Getting to the Answer: When asked whether or not to add a sentence, consider how that sentence might help the paragraph achieve its purpose. The preceding sentence mentions Paine's controversial works; additional information about his being exiled and imprisoned for his writings emphasizes this controversy. Thus, (G) is correct.

13. D   Difficulty: Medium

Category: Usage

Getting to the Answer: The underlined portion contains a comparative modifier, which is only used for two items or people. Because there were more than two Founding Fathers, the superlative form is needed. Thus, eliminate A. Choice B is too wordy, and C changes the intended meaning of the phrase. Choice (D) is correct.

14. H   Difficulty: Low

Category: Knowledge of Language / Concision

Getting to the Answer: The phrase "a whole entire" is redundant. Choices F, G, and J are all too wordy. Choice (H) is correct.

15. A   Difficulty: High

Category: Topic Development / Writer's Purpose

Getting to the Answer: When asked whether a passage accomplishes a particular purpose, consider the scope and tone of the passage. The passage focuses on Paine's influence on the founding of the United States, and the final paragraph says that he deserves recognition. Eliminate B and D, which incorrectly describe the scope of the passage. Although some of Paine's contributions are controversial, the author consistently emphasizes their importance, so eliminate C. Choice (A) reflects the scope and tone of the passage and is therefore correct.

CHAPTER 9

PRACTICE

11. B   Difficulty: Low

Category: Essential Skills / Numbers and Operations

Getting to the Answer: You have two options here. The first is to convert $\frac{3}{4}$ to its decimal form, 0.75, and order the decimals based on place value, but this could get confusing. The other option is to think of each decimal as a fraction in terms of hundredths:

$0.6 = \frac{6}{10} = \frac{60}{100}$, $0.07 = \frac{7}{100}$, and $\frac{3}{4} = \frac{75}{100}$. The fractions can then be ordered based on the size of the numerators:

$\frac{7}{100} < \frac{60}{100} < \frac{75}{100}$, so $0.07 < 0.6 < \frac{3}{4}$. This matches (B).

12. K   Difficulty: Low

Category: Essential Skills / Rates, Percents, Proportions, and Unit Conversion

Getting to the Answer: Questions about map scales almost always involve setting up a proportion. Set up the proportion as $\frac{map}{actual} = \frac{map}{actual}$ and solve by cross-multiplying. Fractions within fractions can be confusing, so write the fractions as decimals in the proportion (because they're easily converted in this question).

$$\frac{0.25}{12} = \frac{3.5}{m}$$
$$0.25m = 3.5(12)$$
$$m = 168$$

Choice (K) is correct.

13. B   Difficulty: Medium

Category: Essential Skills / Rates, Percents, Proportions, and Unit Conversion

Getting to the Answer: Whenever you're working with ratios, pay attention to whether they're part:part or part:whole ratios. Because the ratio of wins to losses was 3:5, the ratio of wins to games was 3:8. Convert this into a percent: $\frac{3}{8} \times 100\% = 37\frac{1}{2}\%$. That's (B).

14. F   Difficulty: High

Category: Essential Skills / Expressions and Equations

Getting to the Answer: Some questions take several steps to solve. First, plug in 8 for x in both the first and second equation. Then, solve the second equation for y. Go back to the first equation and plug in the value of y so that you can solve for a.

$$3x - y = 9$$
$$3(8) - y = 9$$
$$24 - y = 9$$
$$15 = y$$

Then:

$$a(8) + 15 = 23$$
$$8a = 8$$
$$a = 1$$

That's (F).

15. D   Difficulty: Low

Category: Essential Skills / Geometry

Getting to the Answer: Questions like this are simply testing if you remember how many degrees are in a line. Remember that the arc between two points on a line is a half circle, or 180°.

$$20° + 40° + x° = 180°$$
$$x° = 120°$$

Choice (D) is correct.

16. G   Difficulty: Medium

Category: Essential Skills / Statistics and Probability

Getting to the Answer: The probability that two independent events will both occur is the probability of the first times the probability of the second. The probability that the coin will land heads up is $\frac{1}{2}$ (1 desired outcome, heads, over 2 possible outcomes, heads or tails). The probability that the die will land on an even number is also $\frac{1}{2}$ (3 even numbers over 6 possible numbers).

Answers & Explanations

Therefore, the probability that the coin will land on heads and the die will land on an even number is $\frac{1}{2} \times \frac{1}{2} = \frac{1}{4}$. Choice (G) is correct.

PERFORM

17. A   Difficulty: Low

Category: Essential Skills / Numbers and Operations

Getting to the Answer: Although you could take the time to find a common denominator and add the fractions, you're going to have to use your calculator to divide at some point, so you may as well convert the fractions to decimals: $1\frac{1}{2} = 1.5$ and $2\frac{3}{4} = 2.75$. So together, the two dogs eat $1.5 + 2.75 = 4.25$ scoops of dog food per day. This means the bag should last $340 \div 4.25 = 80$ days. Choice (A) is correct.

18. G   Difficulty: Medium

Category: Essential Skills / Rates, Percents, Proportions, and Unit Conversion

Getting to the Answer: The question involves rate (speed), distance, and time, so use the DIRT formula:

$$\text{Distance} = \text{rate} \times \text{time}$$
$$4.62 \times 10^5 = 55,000 \times t$$
$$\frac{4.62 \times 10^5}{55,000} = t$$
$$t = 8.4$$

Choice (G) is correct.

19. D   Difficulty: Medium

Category: Essential Skills / Expressions and Equations

Getting to the Answer: Substitute 3 for each x in the expression. Then use the order of operations (PEMDAS) and the definition of absolute value to simplify. Be careful of all the negative signs.

$$\frac{|5 - 2x| - 13}{-x} = \frac{|5 - 2(3)| - 13}{-(3)}$$
$$= \frac{|5 - 6| - 13}{-3}$$
$$= \frac{|-1| - 13}{-3}$$
$$= \frac{1 - 13}{-3} = \frac{-12}{-3} = 4$$

Choice (D) is correct.

20. K   Difficulty: Medium

Category: Essential Skills / Geometry

Getting to the Answer: The measures of the angles of a triangle sum to 180°. You can use the given ratio to represent the relative sizes of the angles. For example, if x equals one "part," the measures of the angles can be represented by $2x$, $3x$, and $7x$. To find the size of one part, solve the equation $2x + 3x + 7x = 180°$. This simplifies to $12x = 180°$, or $x = 15°$. Be careful—this is not the answer. The question asks for the measure of the largest angle, which is $7(15) = 105°$. Choice (K) is correct.

ON YOUR OWN

1. D   Difficulty: Medium

Category: Essential Skills / Numbers and Operations

Getting to the Answer: Complicated word problems are great situations for Backsolving. The numbers in the answer choices represent the number of people at the conference. Start with the middle answer choice, 60, and see whether each number fits the information in the question stem. If there are 60 participants, then there are $\frac{1}{3}(60) = 20$ anthropologists and $\frac{1}{2}(60) = 30$ biologists. That leaves $60 - 20 - 30 = 10$ chemists, which is not enough. Move to the next higher number: If there are 72 participants, then there are $\frac{1}{3}(72) = 24$ anthropologists and $\frac{1}{2}(72) = 36$ biologists, leaving $72 - 24 - 36 = 12$ chemists. Perfect! Choice (D) is correct.

2. H   Difficulty: Medium

Category: Essential Skills / Numbers and Operations

Getting to the Answer: Variables in the answer choices let you know you can Pick Numbers. Remember, when a question asks about odd or even numbers, you may need to pick one of each.

Pick a value of a that follows the rules in the question stem (meaning it is an integer) and is easy to work with: say, $a = 2$. Then evaluate each answer choice:

Choice F: $2^2 = 4$ Eliminate.
Choice G: $2^2 + 1 = 4 + 1 = 5$ Keep.
Choice H: $2(2)^2 + 1 = 8 + 1 = 9$ Keep.
Choice J: $3(2)^2 + 2 = 12 + 2 = 14$ Eliminate.
Choice K: $4(2)^2 + 4 = 16 + 4 = 20$ Eliminate.

Only G and H are odd when $a = 2$. Because the question asks for the expression that is odd for *any* value of a, try an odd number in the remaining choices. If $a = 3$, then:

Choice G: $3^2 + 1 = 9 + 1 = 10$ Eliminate.
Choice (H): $2(3)^2 + 1 = 18 + 1 = 19$ Correct!

Only (H) is odd for both $a = 2$ and $a = 3$, so it must be correct.

3. A   Difficulty: High

Category: Essential Skills / Numbers and Operations

Getting to the Answer: You could answer this question by solving the two pieces of the inequality separately and then merging the results. However, a quicker approach may be to think strictly in terms of numbers: Make all of the numerators 3 to get $\frac{3}{33} < \frac{3}{n} < \frac{3}{27}$. Now that all the numerators are the same, examine the denominators: This inequality is true for all integer values of n between 27 and 33, which are 28, 29, 30, 31, and 32. That's 5 integer values of n, making (A) the correct answer.

Note: Each question is worth the same amount on the ACT Math test, so don't spend too much time on any one problem. Questions that ask how many different values of something there are tend to be particularly lengthy, so it's a good idea to save them for the end of the test.

4. F   Difficulty: Low

Category: Essential Skills / Numbers and Operations

Getting to the Answer: To find the prime factors of 60, use a prime factorization tree:

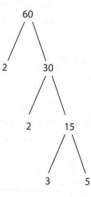

So the prime factorization of 60 is $2 \times 2 \times 3 \times 5$, and the sum of these numbers is $2 + 2 + 3 + 5 = 12$. Choice (F) is correct.

5. D   Difficulty: Low

Category: Essential Skills / Rates, Percents, Proportions, and Unit Conversion

Getting to the Answer: Always be alert to exactly what a ratio is telling you. Is it men to women or women to men? And are you looking for one of these quantities or a total of some sort?

Because the ratio of men to women is 5:3, the ratio of women to committee members is 3:(5 + 3), or 3:8. There are a total of 24 people, so $\frac{3}{8} = \frac{w}{24}$, where w is the number of women on the committee. Cross-multiply to solve the proportion:

$$\frac{3}{8} = \frac{w}{24}$$
$$8w = 24 \times 3$$
$$w = \frac{72}{8} = 9$$

This means (D) is correct. If working through the proportion doesn't go well, notice that all the answer choices are whole numbers, meaning this question can also be solved by Backsolving.

6. J   Difficulty: Medium

Category: Essential Skills / Rates, Percents, Proportions, and Unit Conversion

Getting to the Answer: Converting percent increases and decreases into decimal multipliers will help save time on questions like this one. Be careful—you can't just combine the percents—that is a sure way to make a careless mistake!

If everything in the store is 25% off, then the shirt costs 75% of its original price. The 6% sales tax means that the price must be multiplied by 1.06. Put this all together to find that a shirt originally priced at $22.00 costs ($22.00)(0.75)(1.06) = $17.49, which is (J).

7. A   Difficulty: High

Category: Essential Skills / Rates, Percents, Proportions, and Unit Conversion

Getting to the Answer: Let the units in this question guide you to the solution. The cooking rates of the ovens are given in pounds per hour, but the question asks about the number of ounces each oven can cook in 10 minutes, so use the factor-label method to convert pounds per hour to ounces per minute.

Start by converting pounds to ounces. You are given that 1 pound = 16 ounces, so 3 pounds is 48 ounces and 4.5 pounds is 72 ounces. Now convert the hours to minutes:

Oven at 350°:

$$\frac{48 \text{ oz}}{1 \text{ hr}} \times \frac{1 \text{ hr}}{60 \text{ min}} \times 10 \text{ min} = 8 \text{ oz}$$

Oven at 450°:

$$\frac{72 \text{ oz}}{1 \text{ hr}} \times \frac{1 \text{ hr}}{60 \text{ min}} \times 10 \text{ min} = 12 \text{ oz}$$

In 10 minutes, the oven at 450° can cook 12 − 8 = 4 ounces more than the oven at 350°, making (A) the correct answer.

8. G   Difficulty: Medium

Category: Essential Skills / Expressions and Equations

Getting to the Answer: If x represents the number of whales, "twice as many dolphins as whales" indicates that there are $2x$ dolphins. Therefore, "dolphins and whales combined" is $2x + x$, or $3x$. Because there are eight fewer sharks, you need to subtract 8 from $3x$, making (G) the correct answer.

You can also answer this question by using the Picking Numbers strategy. Pick a small, positive number for the number of whales, like 5. If there are 5 whales and "twice as many dolphins as whales," there must be 10 dolphins. Combine the number of whales and dolphins and subtract 8 from that sum to find the number of sharks: $(5 + 10) − 8 = 15 − 8 = 7$. Plug in 5 for x to determine the answer choice that will give you a final value of 7:

Choice F: $5(5) = 25$ Eliminate.

Choice G: $3(5) − 8 = 15 − 8 = 7$ Keep.

Choice H: $10 + 5 = 15$ Eliminate.

Choice J: $3(5)^2 − 8(5) = 75 − 40 = 35$ Eliminate.

Choice K: $3\sqrt{2(5) − 8} = 3\sqrt{2} \neq 7$ Eliminate.

Choice (G) is the only answer that works.

9. C   Difficulty: Low

Category: Essential Skills / Expressions and Equations

Getting to the Answer: If a question asks for a specific value and there are concrete numbers in the answer choices, you can Backsolve. However, when equations are fairly simple, it's quicker to do the algebra. Just remember that when you're solving an equation, you must do the same thing to both sides. Here, you need to subtract 3 from both sides and then divide both sides by 5:

$$5x + 3 = −17$$
$$5x = −20$$
$$x = −4$$

This matches (C).

10. K   Difficulty: Low

Category: Essential Skills / Expressions and Equations

Getting to the Answer: You solve an inequality the same way you solve an equation. The only difference is this: If you multiply or divide by a negative number, you must reverse the direction of the inequality symbol. To keep things simple, try to move the variable terms in such a way that you don't end up with negatives.

$$-2 − 4x \leq −6x$$
$$-2 + 2x \leq 0$$
$$2x \leq 2$$
$$x \leq 1$$

Choice (K) is correct.

11. C   Difficulty: Low

Category: Essential Skills / Geometry

Getting to the Answer: Just because you see a right triangle, don't assume you need to use the Pythagorean theorem. Here, BC is the horizontal leg of the triangle. The y-coordinates of the endpoints are the same, so you can simply subtract the x-coordinates to find the length: $7 - 1 = 6$ units. Choice (C) is correct.

12. K   Difficulty: Medium

Category: Essential Skills / Geometry

Getting to the Answer: When a transversal crosses parallel lines, the four acute angles formed are all equal, the four obtuse angles formed are all equal, and any angles that are not equal are supplementary. The angle marked x is obtuse, so it's supplementary to the given $40°$ angle: $180 - 40 = 140$, so the answer is (K).

13. B   Difficulty: Low

Category: Essential Skills / Statistics and Probability

Getting to the Answer: Plug the terms into the mean (average) formula and simplify:

$$\text{Average} = \frac{\text{sum of terms}}{\text{number of terms}}$$
$$= \frac{230 + 155 + 320 + 400 + 325}{5}$$
$$= \frac{1{,}430}{5}$$
$$= 286$$

That's (B).

14. K   Difficulty: Medium

Category: Essential Skills / Statistics and Probability

Getting to the Answer: The probability that an event will occur is given by the formula:

$$\text{Probability} = \frac{\text{number of desired outcomes}}{\text{number of possible outcomes}}$$

Here, the number of possible outcomes is 20. To find the number of desired outcomes (multiples of 4), make

a list: 4, 8, 12, 16, 20. There are five desired outcomes, so the probability of randomly selecting a multiple of 4 is $\frac{5}{20} = \frac{1}{4}$. Choice (K) is correct.

15. D   Difficulty: Low

Category: Essential Skills / Statistics and Probability

Getting to the Answer: Make sure you read all the data in the table. The bottom row gives you the total number of vehicles on the lot, so you don't have to add up all the numbers. To save time, rather than adding the numbers of vehicles that are NOT luxury, you can subtract the number that ARE luxury from the total to find that 285 out of 320, or $\frac{285}{320}$ of the vehicles are not luxury. To simplify the fraction, divide the numerator and denominator by 5. The result is $\frac{57}{64}$, which is (D).

16. F   Difficulty: Low

Category: Essential Skills / Numbers and Operations

Getting to the Answer: Always follow the order of operations and be sure to give fractions a common denominator before adding or subtracting them. Per the question stem, don't forget to simplify the fraction before you select your answer.

$$\left(\frac{1}{2} + \frac{1}{6}\right) - \left(\frac{1}{12} + \frac{1}{3}\right) = \left(\frac{6}{12} + \frac{2}{12}\right) - \left(\frac{1}{12} + \frac{4}{12}\right)$$
$$= \left(\frac{8}{12}\right) - \left(\frac{5}{12}\right)$$
$$= \frac{3}{12}$$
$$= \frac{1}{4}$$

The numerator is 1, so (F) is correct.

Answers & Explanations

17. C   Difficulty: Low

Category: Essential Skills / Rates, Percents, Proportions, and Unit Conversion

Getting to the Answer: Cross-multiply to solve the proportion. Be careful when converting the improper fractions into mixed fractions.

$$\frac{2}{9} = \frac{x}{15}$$
$$9x = 15 \cdot 2$$
$$x = \frac{30}{9} = \frac{10}{3} = 3\frac{1}{3}$$

Choice (C) is correct.

18. J   Difficulty: Medium

Category: Essential Skills / Numbers and Operations

Getting to the Answer: Here's another chance to practice Backsolving. As usual, start with the middle answer choice. If Denise answered 38 of the questions correctly and skipped 2, then she answered $60 - 38 - 2 = 20$ questions incorrectly. She gets 2 points for every correct question and loses $\frac{2}{3}$ of a point for every incorrect question, so she would earn

$$38(2) - 20\left(\frac{2}{3}\right) = 76 - \frac{40}{3} = \frac{228}{3} - \frac{40}{3} = \frac{188}{3} = 62\frac{2}{3}$$

points. This is too low, so try the next largest choice, 40. If Denise answered 40 questions correctly, she earned $40(2) - 18\left(\frac{2}{3}\right) = 80 - 12 = 68$ points. This is the number of points you're looking for, so (J) is the correct answer.

19. A   Difficulty: Medium

Category: Essential Skills / Numbers and Operations

Getting to the Answer: Rather than solving an absolute-value inequality here, Backsolving is a much better route. Before you begin, think about the definition of *absolute value*: It is the distance between a number and 0 on the number line. The given inequality is describing temperatures that are less than or equal to 10 units away from 94. You want the temperature that is NOT in the range, or greater than 10 units away. Eyeballing the answer choices should lead you to try 82 first:

$|82 - 94| = |-12| = 12$, which is NOT less than or equal to 10 and is therefore the correct answer. Choose (A).

20. G   Difficulty: Low

Category: Essential Skills / Rates, Percents, Proportions, and Unit Conversion

Getting to the Answer: Write an equation by translating from English to math: The word *of* translates to *times*. Let *n* be the original number and write 125% as 1.25:

$$1.25n = 470$$
$$n = \frac{470}{1.25} = 376$$

Now, find 50% of 376 by multiplying by 0.5. The result is $0.5(376) = 188$, which is (G).

21. B   Difficulty: Medium

Category: Essential Skills / Rates, Percents, Proportions, and Unit Conversion

Getting to the Answer: You aren't given the original price of the television set, so this is a perfect question for Picking Numbers. When Picking Numbers for percents problems, you should start with 100 to make your calculations easier.

Say the original cost is $100. Then Monday's cost is 80% of that, or $100(0.8) = \$80$, and Tuesday's cost is 75% of the new amount, or $80(0.75) = \$60$.

The total amount of the discount is $100 - \$60 = \$40$. Now use the percent change formula:

$$\text{Percent change} = \frac{\$40}{\$100} \cdot 100\% = 40\%$$

Choice (B) is correct.

22. G   Difficulty: Low

Category: Essential Skills / Expressions and Equations

Getting to the Answer: Substitute -2 for *x* in the given expression. Be careful with the negatives and remember to follow the order of operations.

$$14 - 3(x + 3) \rightarrow 14 - 3[(-2) + 3]$$
$$= 14 - 3(1)$$
$$= 11$$

This means (G) is correct.

23. C   Difficulty: Low

Category: Essential Skills / Expressions and Equations

Getting to the Answer: The total cost of the two kinds of items is the cost of the paintbrushes multiplied by the number purchased plus the cost of the canvases multiplied by the number purchased. Because a canvas costs "6 times" the cost of a paintbrush, a canvas costs $6(\$1.50) = \$9$.

Total cost of paintbrushes: $1.50 \times p$ or $1.5p$
Total cost of canvases: $9 \times c$ or $9c$
Sum of both: $9c + 1.5p$

Therefore, (C) is correct.

24. H   Difficulty: Low

Category: Essential Skills / Geometry

Getting to the Answer: To answer questions about angles formed when a transversal cuts parallel lines, figure out which angles are equal and which are supplementary. Remember—when a transversal crosses two parallel lines, all the acute angles are equal and all the obtuse angles are equal. Here, $\angle CRP = \angle ATR$ because CD and AB are parallel. $\angle ATR$ and $\angle ATQ$ are supplementary, so the measure of $\angle ATQ = 180° - 110° = 70°$. Choice (H) is correct.

25. C   Difficulty: Medium

Category: Essential Skills / Geometry

Getting to the Answer: When a line segment is divided in half, it creates two line segments of equal length. Use this definition and the information given in the question stem to determine the lengths of all the line segments. Since G is the midpoint of FH, $GH = FG = 13$. Also, $HK = 18$ and $HJ = JK$, so each is half of HK, and $HJ = JK = 9$. Line segment GJ, then, is made up of $GH + HJ$, which is $13 + 9 = 22$. The answer is (C). Note: Don't be afraid to mark up your test booklet on Test Day to keep all the lengths organized.

26. F   Difficulty: Medium

Category: Essential Skills / Geometry

Getting to the Answer: When the question does not provide a figure, draw one yourself.

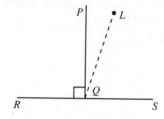

Because lines $\overline{PQ}$ and $\overline{RS}$ are perpendicular, $\angle PQR$ must form a 90°angle. If point L is in the interior of $\angle PQS$, the measure of $\angle LQR$ must be greater than 90°. Only (F) is greater than 90°.

27. B   Difficulty: Medium

Category: Essential Skills / Statistics and Probability

Getting to the Answer: Backsolving is often a great way to solve questions about averages, especially ones that give you the average and ask for a missing number.

The average of a set of terms is the sum of the terms divided by the number of terms. You can either set up an equation involving the missing score or try plugging each of the possible scores into the question stem to see which one works. If you Backsolve, remember to start with the middle number:

Choice C: $\dfrac{150 + 195 + 160 + \boxed{185}}{4} = \dfrac{690}{4} = 172.5$

Too low? Try the next-largest number:

Choice B: $\dfrac{150 + 195 + 160 + \boxed{195}}{4} = \dfrac{700}{4} = 175$

Choice (B) is correct. To answer the question algebraically, call the missing score x and set up the average equation:

$$\dfrac{150 + 195 + 160 + x}{4} = 175$$
$$505 + x = 700$$
$$x = 195$$

28. G   Difficulty: Low

Category: Essential Skills / Statistics and Probability

Getting to the Answer: The probability that an event will occur is given by this formula:

$$\text{Probability} = \frac{\text{number of desired outcomes}}{\text{number of possible outcomes}}$$

In this question, a desired outcome is getting a green marble while a possible outcome is simply getting any marble. There are $8 + 14 + 11 + 6 = 39$ total marbles in the jar. Of these, 6 are green, so the probability of getting a green marble is $\frac{6}{39}$, which simplifies to $\frac{2}{13}$. That's (G).

29. C   Difficulty: Low

Category: Essential Skills / Statistics and Probability

Getting to the Answer: Read the graph and axis labels carefully. The heights of the bars represent the number of trees in the various height ranges. This means the scientist measured $300 + 1,000 + 600 + 200 + 100 + 100 = 2,300$ trees. Choice (C) is correct.

30. G   Difficulty: High

Category: Essential Skills / Statistics and Probability

Getting to the Answer: The median of a set of data is the middle value when the data is written in order. This means that half of the data is less than the median and half is greater. You already know (from the previous question) that there are 2,300 data values, and half of that is 1,150. From left to right, the first bar contains 300 data values and the second bar contains 1,000 more, for a total of 1,300 data values. The middle value for all the data must therefore lie within the interval represented by the second bar, making (G) correct. Note that it is not possible to determine the exact median, only the interval within which it lies.

CHAPTER 10

PRACTICE

10. G Difficulty: Medium

Category: Higher Math / Number and Quantity

Getting to the Answer: To add square roots, the numbers under the radical symbol must be the same. This means you need to simplify each term before you can add. To do this, look for perfect squares that you can remove from the square root. Always simplify the smaller number first, because it will usually give you a hint as to how to factor the larger one.

$$\sqrt{24} = \sqrt{4 \times 6} = \sqrt{4} \times \sqrt{6} = 2\sqrt{6}$$
$$\sqrt{150} = \sqrt{25 \times 6} = \sqrt{25} \times \sqrt{6} = 5\sqrt{6}$$

Now that the numbers under the radicals are the same, you can simply add the coefficients and keep the same radical part.

$$2\sqrt{6} + 5\sqrt{6} = 7\sqrt{6}$$

Choice (G) is correct. Note that you could also use your calculator to find the decimal equivalent of the sum, which is approximately 17.15, and then do the same for each of the answer choices until you find a match.

11. D Difficulty: Medium

Category: Higher Math / Number and Quantity

Getting to the Answer: Scientific notation is defined as a number between 1 and 10 (not including 10) multiplied by a power of 10, so you can eliminate E right away. Use your calculator (or jot the numbers down quickly) to add the numbers: $820,000,000 + 500,000,000 = 1,320,000,000$. Now move the decimal point (which is to the right of the last 0) until it is between the 1 and the 3. To determine the power of 10, count the number of times you moved the decimal, which is 9 times to the left. The sum, $1,320,000,000$, is a very large number, so the exponent on 10 must be positive, making (D) correct.

(Some people forget whether moving the decimal point left or right results in positive powers of 10. It's easier to remember that negative powers of 10 produce tiny decimal numbers, while positive powers produce very large numbers.)

12. H Difficulty: Medium

Category: Higher Math / Number and Quantity

Getting to the Answer: Sometimes, when comparing numbers, it helps to write them in a different format, possibly even an unsimplified form. Here, the answer choices all contain square roots, so rewrite the given inequality using square roots. Write $\frac{4}{5}$ as $\frac{\sqrt{16}}{5}$ and 1 as $\frac{5}{5} = \frac{\sqrt{25}}{5}$. The inequality now reads $\frac{\sqrt{16}}{5} < n < \frac{\sqrt{25}}{5}$, so when written over 5, n must include a square root that is between 16 and 25. Only (H) meets this criterion.

13. A Difficulty: High

Category: Higher Math / Number and Quantity

Getting to the Answer: Start by rationalizing the denominator (getting the i out). To do this, multiply top and bottom by the conjugate of the denominator, $3 + i$. This will require FOILing the denominators and using the given definition of i^2:

$$\frac{1}{3-i} \times \frac{3+i}{3+i} = \frac{3+i}{(3-i)(3+i)}$$
$$= \frac{3+i}{9+3i-3i-i^2}$$
$$= \frac{3+i}{9-(-1)}$$
$$= \frac{3+i}{10}$$

This isn't one of the answer choices, so split the number into its real part and its imaginary part by writing each of the terms in the numerator over 10. The result is $\frac{3}{10} + \frac{1}{10}i$, which matches (A).

Answers & Explanations

14. H Difficulty: Medium

Category: Higher Math / Number and Quantity

Getting to the Answer: Process of elimination is the only way to approach this question—but you don't have to actually multiply the matrices. You just need to check the size combinations. Start by jotting down the sizes under each matrix:

$$A = \begin{bmatrix} 1 & 2 \\ 3 & 4 \end{bmatrix} \quad B = \begin{bmatrix} 5 & 6 & 7 \\ 8 & 9 & 0 \end{bmatrix} \quad C = \begin{bmatrix} 2 \\ 4 \end{bmatrix} \quad D = \begin{bmatrix} 3 & 5 \end{bmatrix}$$
$$\quad\; 2 \times 2 \qquad\quad 2 \times 3 \qquad\quad 2 \times 1 \qquad 1 \times 2$$

Now check each answer choice until you find one that's not possible:

Choice F: AB = 2 × $\boxed{2}$ times $\boxed{2}$ × 3. That works.

Choice G: AC = 2 × $\boxed{2}$ times $\boxed{2}$ × 1. That works.

Choice (H): BC = 2 × $\boxed{3}$ times $\boxed{2}$ × 1. That doesn't work.

The product in (H) is not possible. There is no need to check the others unless you're not sure about your answer.

15. B Difficulty: Medium

Category: Higher Math / Number and Quantity

Getting to the Answer: Even if you're not sure how to perform operations on matrices, you can probably reason out the answer. The number of 18- to 24-year-olds who will utilize the company's health plan more than one time in the next year is 0.3(30) = 9. You can compute the number for each age group, then add them all together. This will give you the same result as multiplying the matrices.

$$[30 \; 20 \; 60 \; 10] \begin{bmatrix} 0.3 \\ 0.5 \\ 0.2 \\ 0.4 \end{bmatrix}$$

$$= 30(0.3) + 20(0.5) + 60(0.2) + 10(0.4)$$
$$= 9 + 10 + 12 + 4 = 35$$

Choice (B) is correct. Note that even though the information is expressed in matrices, you did not need to know how to multiply matrices to answer the question.

16. G Difficulty: Medium

Category: Higher Math / Number and Quantity

Getting to the Answer: Basic vector operations work exactly as you would expect them to. Here, you need to add the corresponding components of **u** and **v**, then multiply each component of the result by $-\frac{1}{2}$:

$$\mathbf{u} + \mathbf{v} = \langle 8 + 4, -24 + 6 \rangle$$
$$= \langle 12, -18 \rangle$$

$$-\frac{1}{2}(\mathbf{u} + \mathbf{v}) = \left\langle -\frac{1}{2} \cdot 12, -\frac{1}{2} \cdot -18 \right\rangle$$
$$= \langle -6, 9 \rangle$$

Choice (G) is correct.

PERFORM

17. C Difficulty: Low

Category: Higher Math / Number and Quantity

Getting to the Answer: The set of real numbers includes rational and irrational numbers. It does not include multiples of $i = \sqrt{-1}$, which are imaginary numbers. Choice (C) simplifies to $\sqrt{-9} = \sqrt{9 \times (-1)} = 3i$, and it is therefore not a real number.

18. H Difficulty: Medium

Category: Higher Math / Number and Quantity

Getting to the Answer: Start by substituting the given values into the expression: $\frac{x + m}{n} \rightarrow \frac{x + 2}{3}$. The expression represents an integer only if the denominator divides evenly into the numerator. In other words, $x + 2$ must be a multiple of 3. Quickly check each of the answer choices, beginning with the first choice: $-1 + 2 = 1$, which is not a multiple of 3; $0 + 2 = 2$, which is not a multiple of 3; $4 + 2 = 6$, which is a multiple of 3. Choice (H) is correct. There is no need to check the remaining choices, but if you're not sure: $6 + 2 = 8$, which is not a multiple of 3; and $12 + 2 = 14$, which is not a multiple of 3.

19. B   Difficulty: Medium

Category: Higher Math / Number and Quantity

Getting to the Answer: Try not to focus too much on the fact that this question involves imaginary numbers. Instead, treat i like any other variable as you simplify the expression, substituting i for $\sqrt{-1}$ and -1 for i^2. Start by looking for common factors that you can divide out of the numerator and denominator.

$$\frac{i^3 + 4i}{\sqrt{-9}} = \frac{i(i^2 + 4)}{\sqrt{9 \times (-1)}}$$

$$= \frac{i(-1 + 4)}{3i}$$

$$= \frac{3i}{3i} = 1$$

Choice (B) is correct.

20. F   Difficulty: High

Category: Higher Math / Number and Quantity

Getting to the Answer: Multiplying matrices is not a quick process, so you may want to skip a question like this on Test Day until you've answered all the easier questions. If you will be using a graphing calculator on Test Day, you may also want to learn how to perform matrix operations on your calculator.

To multiply matrices by hand, use this process:

$$\begin{bmatrix} a & b \\ c & d \end{bmatrix}\begin{bmatrix} e & f \\ g & h \end{bmatrix} = \begin{bmatrix} ae + bg & af + bh \\ ce + dg & cf + dh \end{bmatrix}$$

$$\begin{bmatrix} 1 & 2 \\ 3 & 4 \end{bmatrix}\begin{bmatrix} -1 & -2 \\ -3 & -4 \end{bmatrix} = \begin{bmatrix} 1(-1) + 2(-3) & 1(-2) + 2(-4) \\ 3(-1) + 4(-3) & 3(-2) + 4(-4) \end{bmatrix}$$

$$= \begin{bmatrix} -1 + (-6) & -2 + (-8) \\ -3 + (-12) & -6 + (-16) \end{bmatrix}$$

$$= \begin{bmatrix} -7 & -10 \\ -15 & -22 \end{bmatrix}$$

The question asks for the value of $x + y$, so the correct answer is $-7 + (-10) = -17$, which is (F). Note that to save yourself some time, if you pay careful attention to

what the question is asking, you'll see that you only need to calculate the values in the first row of the product to find the answer.

ON YOUR OWN

1.   E   Difficulty: Medium

Category: Higher Math / Number and Quantity

Getting to the Answer: Questions like this give a lot of students grief. You know there's a rule—and if you could just remember it, you know it would be right—but it's just not coming to mind. Here's a hint: *Think of an easier question testing the same principles.* For example, how would you simplify $x^2 - x$? Most likely, you'd rewrite the expression by factoring out the GCF of the two terms. The result is $x(x - 1)$. Now, apply the same process to $x^{77} - x^{76}$, which can be factored as $x^{76}(x - 1)$. Finally, the rule is no different for 7 than for x. Factoring out the GCF of the two terms gives $7^{76}(7 - 1)$, which is $7^{76}(6)$, or (E).

2.   J   Difficulty: Medium

Category: Higher Math / Number and Quantity

Getting to the Answer: It's more difficult to determine the nature (here, even vs. odd) of a difference of two quantities than of a single quantity, so your first step should be to add the terms together. To do this, find a common denominator:

$$\frac{x}{2} - \frac{x}{6} = \frac{3x}{6} - \frac{x}{6} = \frac{2x}{6} = \frac{x}{3}$$

This form of the expression tells you a lot more. If $\frac{x}{3}$ is an integer, then when x is divided by 3, it must divide evenly. In other words, x is a multiple of 3, which matches (J).

3.   B   Difficulty: Medium

Category: Higher Math / Number and Quantity

Getting to the Answer: Most people find it easier to work with fractions than with numbers that have negative exponents, so start by rewriting the two numbers as fractions. Then find a common denominator and add.

Keep in mind that a negative number raised to an even power returns a positive value, while a negative number raised to an odd power returns a negative value.

$$(-2)^{-3} + (-3)^{-2} = \frac{1}{(-2)^3} + \frac{1}{(-3)^2}$$

$$= \frac{1}{-8} + \frac{1}{9} = \frac{-9}{72} + \frac{8}{72} = -\frac{1}{72}$$

This matches (B).

4. J Difficulty: Medium

Category: Higher Math / Number and Quantity

Getting to the Answer: In most cases, it's easier to rewrite fractional and negative exponents. Remember that a negative exponent means "1 over." Remember, too, that the denominator of a fractional exponent is a root, while the numerator is a power. The given number becomes this:

$$9^{-\frac{3}{2}} = \frac{1}{9^{\frac{3}{2}}} = \frac{1}{\left(\sqrt{9}\right)^3} = \frac{1}{3^3} = \frac{1}{27}$$

Choice (J) is correct.

5. B Difficulty: Medium

Category: Higher Math / Number and Quantity

Getting to the Answer: Just because the quantity contains a variable doesn't mean you can't use your calculator. Take a peek at the answer choices—the coefficients of x are all different, so all you really need to do is find the square root of 0.0016, which is 0.04. This means (B) is correct.

Without using a calculator, you would find the square root like this:

$$\sqrt{0.0016} = \sqrt{\frac{16}{10,000}} = \frac{4}{100} = 0.04$$

6. K Difficulty: Medium

Category: Higher Math / Number and Quantity

Getting to the Answer: Many questions will tell you everything you need to know (even if you've never seen

a complex number). Treat the expression as a binomial, rewrite it as product, and use FOIL to multiply it out. Then substitute −1 for i^2 and simplify as needed:

$$(2i - 3)^2 = (2i - 3)(2i - 3)$$
$$= 2i(2i) + 2i(-3) - 3(2i) - 3(-3)$$
$$= 4i^2 - 6i - 6i + 9$$
$$= 4(-1) - 12i + 9$$
$$= 5 - 12i$$

This matches (K). Note that if you plan to use a graphing calculator on Test Day, you can enter the expression from the question stem into your calculator exactly as it is written, and the calculator will return the correct answer. Most graphing calculators have an i button, and the calculator's programming includes the definition $i^2 = -1$.

7. D Difficulty: High

Category: Higher Math / Number and Quantity

Getting to the Answer: This question is not nearly as complicated as it looks. There is no factoring to be done or rewriting of terms as common powers of i. Instead, jot down the first several powers of i (which repeat in cycles of 4 and which you can use your graphing calculator to find if necessary):

$i^1 = i$	$i^2 = -1$	$i^3 = -i$	$i^4 = 1$
$i^5 = i$	$i^6 = -1$	$i^7 = -i$	$i^8 = 1$
$i^9 = i$	$i^{10} = -1$	$i^{11} = -i$	$i^{12} = 1$

Now take a peek at the answer choices—only even powers of i are involved. What do you notice about the even powers of i in the list above? All the even powers that are multiples of 4 produce a value of 1, while all the even powers that are not multiples of 4 produce a value of −1. Use this pattern to quickly evaluate each of the answer choices: A, B, C, and E each give $-1 + 1 = 0$, while D gives $1 + 1 = 2$. The expression in (D) yields the greatest value and is therefore correct.

8. G Difficulty: High

Category: Higher Math / Number and Quantity

Getting to the Answer: To add matrices of the same size, add corresponding entries (entries that sit in the same spot). Here, you can use the upper-left entries to find x, the upper-right entries to find y, and the lower-right entries to find z as follows:

$$x + 2 = 6 \rightarrow x = 4$$
$$6 + 3y = 12 \rightarrow y = 2$$
$$x + y = z \rightarrow z = 4 + 2 = 6$$

Choice (G) is correct.

9. A Difficulty: Medium

Category: Higher Math / Number and Quantity

Getting to the Answer: To multiply two matrices, the sizes must match in a certain way. Here, the size of the first matrix is 1×3 and the size of the second is 3×1. If you multiply a 1×3 matrix by a 3×1 matrix (which is possible because the middle dimensions match), the result will be a 1×1 matrix. This means you can eliminate D and E. To multiply the matrices, multiply each element in the row matrix by the corresponding element in the column matrix and add the products:

$$\begin{bmatrix} 1 & 2 & 3 \end{bmatrix} \cdot \begin{bmatrix} -1 \\ -2 \\ -3 \end{bmatrix} = 1(-1) + 2(-2) + 3(-3)$$
$$= -1 + (-4) + (-9)$$
$$= -14$$

Choice (A) is correct.

10. G Difficulty: Medium

Category: Higher Math / Number and Quantity

Getting to the Answer: Even if you know absolutely nothing about vectors, answering this question works exactly as you would think. The $-\dfrac{2}{5}$ is called a scalar, and it behaves the same way any number being multiplied by a quantity does: Multiply the scalar by each of the numbers that represent the two components of the vector to get the following:

$$-\frac{2}{5}\mathbf{u} = \left\langle -\frac{2}{5} \cdot 25, \ -\frac{2}{5} \cdot -30 \right\rangle = \langle -10, 12 \rangle$$

This matches (G).

11. A Difficulty: Low

Category: Higher Math / Number and Quantity

Getting to the Answer: This question is a great opportunity to use your calculator, but it can be solved mathematically as well. The square root of a number is the factor of the number that when multiplied by itself gives you the original number.

If you plug the square root of 250 into your calculator, it will come out to approximately 15.81, so the greatest integer smaller than that is 15. To solve this mathematically, you can find the two perfect squares that $\sqrt{250}$ is between: $\sqrt{225}$ and $\sqrt{256}$, or 15 and 16. So, 15 is the greatest integer smaller than $\sqrt{250}$, making (A) the correct answer.

12. J Difficulty: Low

Category: Higher Math / Number and Quantity

Getting to the Answer: When a question asks for something that seems to require hours of calculation, such as the 100th digit after the decimal, use your calculator if possible and look for a pattern instead of using brute calculation. Divide 4 by 11 and see what the first few terms after the decimal are: $\dfrac{4}{11} = 0.363636....$

Every odd term (the first, third, and so on) is 3. Every even term is 6. Because 100 is an even number, the 100th digit after the decimal will be 6. Choice (J) is correct.

13. C Difficulty: Medium

Category: Higher Math / Number and Quantity

Getting to the Answer: When multiplying and dividing numbers written in scientific notation, you can separate the plain numbers from the powers of 10. This allows you to use rules of exponents to simplify the powers of 10.

$$\frac{(3.0 \times 10^4)(8.0 \times 10^9)}{1.2 \times 10^6} = \frac{3 \times 8}{1.2} \times \frac{10^4 \times 10^9}{10^6}$$
$$= \frac{24}{1.2} \times 10^{4+9-6}$$
$$= 20 \times 10^7 = 2.0 \times 10^8$$

This matches (C).

Answers & Explanations

14. G   Difficulty: Medium

Category: Higher Math / Number and Quantity

Getting to the Answer: You could use FOIL right away (just as you would when multiplying two binomials), or you could simplify $\sqrt{8}$ before you FOIL to keep the size of the numbers small. If you happen to notice that the two factors resemble the terms in a difference of squares, you might conclude that the first option will be quicker (because the middle two terms are going to cancel anyway):

$$\left(\sqrt{8} + \sqrt{6}\right)\left(\sqrt{8} - \sqrt{6}\right)$$
$$= 8 - \sqrt{48} + \sqrt{48} - 6$$
$$= 8 - 6 = 2$$

Choice (G) is correct.

15. E   Difficulty: Low

Category: Higher Math / Number and Quantity

Getting to the Answer: A square outside of parentheses means to square every term inside the parentheses.

$$\left(5\sqrt{3}\right)^2 = 5^2\left(\sqrt{3}\right)^2 = 25 \times 3 = 75$$

Choice (E) is correct.

16. F   Difficulty: High

Category: Higher Math / Number and Quantity

Getting to the Answer: This is a great question for Picking Numbers. Take a peek at the answer choices to see that you'll want to pick a value of x that is a perfect square (so you can take the square root). The question states that $x > 1$, and the next perfect square is 4, so let $x = 4$.

Try F: $\dfrac{\sqrt{4}}{4} - 1 = \dfrac{2}{4} - 1 = -\dfrac{1}{2}$, which is less than 0, so keep F.

Try G: $\dfrac{4}{\sqrt{4}} = \dfrac{4}{2} = 2$, which is not less than 1, so eliminate G and K.

Try H: $2\sqrt{4} = 2 \times 2 = 4$, which is equal to *but not less than* 4, so eliminate H.

Try J: $\sqrt{4} + 4 = 2 + 4 = 6$, which is not greater than 4^2, so eliminate J.

Choice (F) is correct.

17. A   Difficulty: Medium

Category: Higher Math / Number and Quantity

Getting to the Answer: You can use your calculator to quickly find the fourth root of 90, or you can compare the fourth power of the integers in the answer choices. Stop when the result is greater than 90.

$$2^4 = 16, \, 3^4 = 81, \, 4^4 = 256$$

If $x^4 = 90$, then x must be between 3 and 4 because 90 is between 81 and 256, or 3^4 and 4^4. This makes (A) the correct answer.

18. G   Difficulty: High

Category: Higher Math / Number and Quantity

Getting to the Answer: Taking the square root of a complex number is not a concept you are likely to have learned, so you'll need to work backward to answer this question. Square the answer choices (using FOIL) until you find one that gives you $8 - 6i$. Start with F:

$$(3 + i)^2 = (3 + i)(3 + i)$$
$$= 9 + 6i + i^2$$
$$= 9 + 6i - 1$$
$$= 8 + 6i$$

That's not it, but it's close, so try G next.

$$(3 - i)^2 = (3 - i)(3 - i)$$
$$= 9 - 6i + i^2$$
$$= 9 - 6i - 1$$
$$= 8 - 6i$$

Choice (G) is correct.

19. B   Difficulty: High

Category: Higher Math / Number and Quantity

Getting to the Answer: Even if you're not sure how to perform operations on matrices, you can probably reason out the answer. The number of people who will leave Marketing is $0.13(300) = 39$. You can compute the number for each department, then add them all together. This will give you the same result as multiplying the matrices.

$$\begin{bmatrix} 300 \ 200 \ 600 \ 100 \end{bmatrix} \begin{bmatrix} 0.13 \\ 0.15 \\ 0.12 \\ 0.14 \end{bmatrix} = 300(0.13) + 200(0.15) \\ + 600(0.12) + 100(0.14)$$

$$= 39 + 30 + 72 + 14 = 155$$

Choice (B) is correct. Note that even though the information is expressed in matrices, you do not need to know how to multiply matrices to answer the question.

20. J   Difficulty: Medium

Category: Higher Math / Number and Quantity

Getting to the Answer: Adding vectors is very straightforward. Add the first coordinates together and add the second coordinates together:

$$\mathbf{u} + \mathbf{v} = \langle 2 + 0, 0 + (-2) \rangle = \langle 2, -2 \rangle$$

Choice (J) is correct.

CHAPTER 11

PRACTICE

13. E Difficulty: Medium

Category: Higher Math / Algebra

Getting to the Answer: You're told that the y-intercept of line t is -3, so you can eliminate C and D right away. (Each of these lines has a y-intercept of $+3$.) Now think about slope: Parallel lines have the same slope, so use the given line to find the slope of line t. To do this, rewrite the given equation in slope-intercept form:

$$3x - 5y = 4$$
$$-5y = -3x + 4$$
$$y = \frac{-3x}{-5} + \frac{4}{-5}$$
$$y = \frac{3}{5}x - \frac{4}{5}$$

The slope of the given line is $\frac{3}{5}$, which means the slope of line t is also $\frac{3}{5}$, so (E) is correct.

14. K Difficulty: Medium

Category: Higher Math / Algebra

Getting to the Answer: Creativity is key to getting the right answer to this question. Rather than multiplying just one equation by a factor, you'll need to multiply both by a factor to use combination. Which factors do you pick? It depends on which variable you want to eliminate. Suppose you want to eliminate x. The coefficients of the x terms are 2 and 5, so you need to multiply the equations by numbers that will give you -10 and 10 as your new x term coefficients. To do this, multiply the first equation by -5 and the second equation by 2:

$$-5(2x + 5y = 49)$$
$$2(5x + 3y = 94)$$

Add the resulting equations:

$$\begin{array}{r} -10x - 25y = -245 \\ + \quad 10x + 6y = 188 \\ \hline -19y = -57 \\ y = 3 \end{array}$$

Next, plug 3 back in for y in either equation and solve for x, which gives $x = 17$. Multiplying x and y together yields 51, which is (K).

15. C Difficulty: Low

Category: Higher Math / Algebra

Getting to the Answer: Determining how much greater A is than B means finding the difference between the two $(A - B)$. The basic setup is $(24xy + 13) - (8xy + 1)$; distribute the negative sign and combine like terms to get $16xy + 12$. Choice (C) is correct.

16. J Difficulty: High

Category: Higher Math / Algebra

Getting to the Answer: To find the amount of time it takes for the projectile to hit the ground, find the value of t for which $h = 0$. In other words, set the equation equal to 0 and solve for t. The fact that 16 divides evenly into 32 (and therefore into 320) is a big hint that you'll be able to factor.

$$0 = -16t^2 + 128t + 320$$
$$0 = -16\left(t^2 - 8t - 20\right)$$
$$0 = t^2 - 8t - 20$$
$$0 = (t - 10)(t + 2)$$

Setting each factor equal to 0 gives $t = 10$ or $t = 2$. However, because you need a positive solution, the answer is $t = 10$ seconds. Choice (J) is correct.

17. C Difficulty: High

Category: Higher Math / Algebra

Getting to the Answer: Pay attention to every word in a question like this. After you solve the equation, make sure you only count the solutions that are real and distinct. The equation is a polynomial, so the greatest number of roots (solutions) it can have is equal to the highest power on the variable, which is 3. This means you can eliminate E right away. That doesn't mean the answer is 3, though (because you're only counting distinct real solutions). To solve the equation, start by factoring out the GCF, which is $3x$. Then go from there. The resulting equation may be factorable, or you may need to use the quadratic formula.

$$3x^3 - 30x^2 + 75x = 0$$
$$3x(x^2 - 10x + 25) = 0$$
$$3x(x - 5)(x - 5) = 0$$

Setting each factor equal to 0 and solving for x yields $x = 0$, $x = 5$, and $x = 5$. This is only two distinct real solutions, 0 and 5, so (C) is correct.

18. J Difficulty: High

Category: Higher Math / Algebra

Getting to the Answer: If the absolute value of something is less than 8, then that something is between -8 and 8. Use this interpretation to rewrite the inequality without the absolute value symbols. Then solve the resulting compound inequality:

$$|4x + 3| < 8$$
$$-8 < 4x + 3 < 8$$
$$-11 < 4x < 5$$
$$\frac{-11}{4} < x < \frac{5}{4}$$
$$-2.75 < x < 1.25$$

There are four integers in that range: -2, -1, 0, and 1, so (J) is correct.

PERFORM

19. C Difficulty: Low

Category: Higher Math / Algebra

Getting to the Answer: The equation of a straight line is $y = mx + b$, where m is the slope and b is the y-intercept. The quickest way to get to the answer is by rewriting the given equation to get y in terms of x.

$$4x - 7y = 14$$
$$-7y = -4x + 14$$
$$y = \frac{4}{7}x - 2$$

The slope of the line given by this equation is the coefficient of x, which is $\frac{4}{7}$. Choice (C) is correct.

20. G Difficulty: Medium

Category: Higher Math / Algebra

Getting to the Answer: Both Backsolving and algebra work well here. If you choose to Backsolve this problem, be sure you plug in the answer choices for the number of hard questions, not the number of easy questions.

To solve algebraically, set up a system of equations—one equation that represents the *number of questions* of each type (e for easy and h for hard) and another that represents the *number of points* Nicole got. Because she correctly answered 21 questions, $e + h = 21$ and $e = 21 - h$. The number of points she got is $3e + 5h = 79$. Substitute $21 - h$ for e in the second equation and solve for h:

$$3(21 - h) + 5h = 79$$
$$63 - 3h + 5h = 79$$
$$2h = 16$$
$$h = 8$$

To Backsolve, start with H. If Nicole got 12 hard questions right, she got $21 - 12 = 9$ easy questions right for a total of $9(3) + 12(5) = 27 + 60 = 87$ points. This is too many, so she must have gotten fewer hard questions right. Try G. If she got 8 hard questions right, then she got $21 - 8 = 13$ easy questions right. This would give her a total of $13(3) + 8(5) = 39 + 40 = 79$ points—just right, so (G) is correct.

21. D Difficulty: Medium

Category: Higher Math / Algebra

Getting to the Answer: Because this question asks about the sum of the solutions of the equation, it cannot be Backsolved. You must factor the equation and solve for x. Start by moving all terms to the left of the equal sign so that the equation is equal to 0 on the right. Then factor out the GCF, which is 2. From there, you need to find the factors of the constant term that sum to the coefficient of the middle term.

$$2x^2 = 2x + 12$$
$$2x^2 - 2x - 12 = 0$$
$$2(x^2 - x - 6) = 0$$
$$x^2 - x - 6 = 0$$
$$(x - 3)(x + 2) = 0$$

Answers & Explanations

The product of the two factors will be 0 if either of the factors is 0, so $x = 3$ and $x = -2$ are the two solutions. The sum of the solutions is $3 + (-2) = 1$, which is (D).

Be sure not to pick A, which is one of the possible values of x. That's not what this question asks for.

22. G   Difficulty: High

Category: Higher Math / Algebra

Getting to the Answer: The absolute value of a number means its distance from 0 on a number line, which means the actual value can be positive *or* negative. Therefore, you'll need to set up two equations. Don't worry about the squared term until you have to. First, isolate the absolute value by adding 8 to both sides of the equation. Then, set the absolute value equal to both 8 and -8, remove the absolute value signs, and solve for x in each equation:

$$\left|x^2 - 28\right| - 8 = 0$$
$$\left|x^2 - 28\right| = 8$$

$$x^2 - 28 = \boxed{8}$$
$$x^2 = 36$$
$$x = \pm\sqrt{36} = \pm 6$$

$$x^2 - 28 = \boxed{-8}$$
$$x^2 = 20$$
$$x = \pm\sqrt{20} = \pm 2\sqrt{5}$$

The four possible values of x are 6, -6, $2\sqrt{5}$, and $-2\sqrt{5}$. Of those, 6 and -6 are not irrational, and $-2\sqrt{5}$ is not one of the options (this is not the same as $2\sqrt{-5}$), so (G) is correct.

ON YOUR OWN

1.   D   Difficulty: Low

Category: Higher Math / Algebra

Getting to the Answer: Use the graph to identify the y-intercept and the slope of the line, then write an equation in slope-intercept form, $y = mx + b$. Once you have

your equation, look for the answer choice that matches. The line crosses the y-axis at $(0, -4)$ so the y-intercept (b) is -4. The line rises 1 unit for every 3 units that it runs to the right, so the slope (m) is $\frac{1}{3}$. The equation of the line is $y = \frac{1}{3}x - 4$, which matches (D).

You could also graph each of the answer choices in your calculator to see which one matches the given graph, but this is not the most time-efficient strategy. You also have to be very careful when entering fractions—to graph (D), for example, you would enter $(1/3)x - 4$.

2.   K   Difficulty: High

Category: Higher Math / Algebra

Getting to the Answer: Perpendicular lines have negative reciprocal slopes. Using the slope formula, you can find that the slope of line m is $\frac{1 - 0}{-3 - 0} = -\frac{1}{3}$ and the slope of line n is $\frac{z - 1}{0 - (-3)} = \frac{z - 1}{3}$. Because the two lines are perpendicular, the slope of line n must be the negative reciprocal of the slope of m, $-\frac{1}{3}$; the slope of n is therefore 3. Set the expression equal to 3 and solve for z:

$$\frac{z - 1}{3} = 3$$
$$z - 1 = 9$$
$$z = 10$$

Choice (K) is correct.

3.   B   Difficulty: Medium

Category: Higher Math / Algebra

Getting to the Answer: The equation of a line is given by $y = mx + b$, where m is the slope of the line and b is the y-intercept. First, use the two points to find the slope of the line:

$$m = \frac{y_2 - y_1}{x_2 - x_1}$$
$$= \frac{6 - 4}{3 - (-3)}$$
$$= \frac{2}{6} = \frac{1}{3}$$

Answers & Explanations

Then use the slope to find the y-intercept. Substitute $\frac{1}{3}$ for m and either of the given points for x and y:

$$y = mx + b$$
$$4 = \frac{1}{3}(-3) + b$$
$$4 = -1 + b$$
$$5 = b$$

The slope-intercept form of the line is $y = \frac{1}{3}x + 5$. The answer choices are written in standard form, so rewrite the equation:

$$y = \frac{1}{3}x + 5$$
$$3(y) = 3\left(\frac{1}{3}x + 5\right)$$
$$3y = x + 15$$
$$-x + 3y = 15$$
$$x - 3y = -15$$

This matches (B). Note that you could also Backsolve to answer this question. To do this, substitute *both* of the points, one at a time, into each equation until you find the one that works. The equation must work for *both* points to be the correct equation.

4. J Difficulty: Medium

Category: Higher Math / Algebra

Getting to the Answer: This is a compound inequality, so whatever you do to one piece, you must do to all three pieces. Don't let the fraction intimidate you. Do easy operations first (subtract 3 from each piece), then worry about the fraction. Don't forget to flip the inequality symbols if you multiply or divide by a negative number.

$$2 \leq 3 - \frac{x}{4} \leq 4$$
$$-1 \leq -\frac{x}{4} \leq 1$$
$$-4(-1) \geq -4\left(-\frac{x}{4}\right) \geq -4(1)$$
$$4 \geq x \geq -4$$

Turn the inequality around so that smaller numbers come first to find that this matches (J).

5. D Difficulty: Medium

Category: Higher Math / Algebra

Getting to the Answer: Both Backsolving and algebra work well here. If you Backsolve, you can save time by noticing that C will be less than F (unless F is −40 or less). This lets you eliminate A, B, and C right away.

To solve algebraically, plug in 95 for C and solve for F:

$$95 = \frac{5}{9}(F - 32)$$
$$\frac{9}{5} \times 95 = \frac{9}{5} \times \frac{5}{9}(F - 32)$$
$$171 = F - 32$$
$$203 = F$$

Choice (D) is correct.

6. H Difficulty: Medium

Category: Higher Math / Algebra

Getting to the Answer: To get y in terms of x, you need to eliminate the t. So, solve the first equation for t (which will give you an expression that involves x) and plug this into the second equation for t. This should leave you with only x's and y's.

$$x = \frac{1}{3}t + 2$$
$$x - 2 = \frac{1}{3}t$$
$$3(x - 2) = t$$
$$3x - 6 = t$$

Now:

$$y = 4 - t$$
$$= 4 - (3x - 6)$$
$$= 4 - 3x + 6$$
$$= 10 - 3x$$

This matches (H). Note that you could also use Picking Numbers here, but it would be very time-consuming.

Answers & Explanations

7. C Difficulty: High

Category: Higher Math / Algebra

Getting to the Answer: This may look like a coordinate geometry question, but do you really have to graph the lines to find the point of intersection? Think algebraically instead: The point of intersection is the one point whose coordinates will satisfy *both* equations. In other words, treat the equations as a system and solve the system using either combination or substitution. If you happen to notice that the *y* terms have opposite coefficients (2 and −2), you'll most likely choose combination as the quickest route to the answer.

$$
\begin{aligned}
5x + 2y &= 4 \\
+ \quad x - 2y &= 8 \\
\hline
6x + 0y &= 12 \\
x &= 2
\end{aligned}
$$

Plug the value of *x* back into either of the original equations, and you'll find that $y = -3$. The point of intersection is $(2, -3)$, and the answer is (C).

8. H Difficulty: Medium

Category: Higher Math / Algebra

Getting to the Answer: Algebra and Backsolving both work well on word problems like this one. Use the method with which you are more comfortable.

To solve this problem algebraically, first translate it into a system of equations. At $8 per adult ticket and $5 per student ticket, the total amount of money collected can be written as $8a + 5s = 3{,}475$. Because there were 500 tickets total, $s + a = 500$, or $s = 500 - a$, is the other equation in the system. Plug $500 - a$ into the first equation for *s* and solve for *a*:

$$
\begin{aligned}
8a + 5(500 - a) &= 3{,}475 \\
8a + 2{,}500 - 5a &= 3{,}475 \\
3a &= 975 \\
a &= 325
\end{aligned}
$$

Choice (H) is correct.

To Backsolve, start with H. If there are 325 adult tickets, then there are $500 - 325 = 175$ student tickets. The total amount of money collected would be $\$325(8) + \$175(5)$,

or $\$2{,}600 + \$875 = \$3{,}475$. Because this is the total in the question stem, (H) is correct.

9. E Difficulty: Medium

Category: Higher Math / Algebra

Getting to the Answer: Distribute each term in the first factor to each term in the second factor (FOIL). Be careful with the signs.

$$
\begin{aligned}
(-x + 6)(2x - 3) &= -x(2x - 3) + 6(2x - 3) \\
&= -2x^2 + 3x + 12x - 18 \\
&= -2x^2 + 15x - 18
\end{aligned}
$$

Note that the question asks for the coefficient of *x*, not x^2, so the answer is 15, which is (E).

10. G Difficulty: Medium

Category: Higher Math / Algebra

Getting to the Answer: When finding solutions to a quadratic equation, always start by rewriting the equation to make it equal 0 (unless both sides of the equation are already perfect squares). Then take a peek at the answer choices—if they are all integers, then factoring is probably the quickest method for solving the equation. If the answers include messy fractions or square roots, then using the quadratic formula may be a better choice.

To make the equation equal 0, subtract 48 from both sides to get $x^2 + 8x - 48 = 0$. The answer choices are all integers, so factor the equation. Look for two numbers whose product is −48 and whose sum is 8. The two numbers are −4 and 12, so the factors are $(x - 4)$ and $(x + 12)$. Set each factor equal to 0 and solve to find that $x = 4$ and $x = -12$. The question states that $x > 0$, so *x* must equal 4. Before selecting an answer, don't forget to check that you answered the right question—the question asks for the value of $x - 5$, not just *x*, so the correct answer is $4 - 5 = -1$. This is a match for (G).

11. C Difficulty: Medium

Category: Higher Math / Algebra

Getting to the Answer: Taking the square root is the inverse operation of squaring, and both sides of this equation are already perfect squares, so take their square roots instead of FOILing the left side. Then solve the resulting equations. Remember, there will be two equations to solve.

$$(x + 1)^2 = \frac{1}{25}$$

$$\sqrt{(x + 1)^2} = \frac{\sqrt{1}}{\sqrt{25}}$$

$$x + 1 = \pm\frac{1}{5}$$

$$x = -1 \pm \frac{1}{5}$$

Now simplify each equation:

$$x = -1 + \frac{1}{5} = -\frac{5}{5} + \frac{1}{5} = -\frac{4}{5}$$

and

$$x = -1 - \frac{1}{5} = -\frac{5}{5} - \frac{1}{5} = -\frac{6}{5}$$

Choice (C) is correct.

12. F Difficulty: High

Category: Higher Math / Algebra

Getting to the Answer: If you don't know how to start a question that involves a quadratic equation, try factoring it.

You are given the value of $x + y$. To make use of it, reverse FOIL the equation $4x^2 + 6xy + 2y^2 = 32$ and try to factor out an $x + y$:

$$4x^2 + 6xy + 2y^2 = 32$$
$$(2x + 2y)(2x + y) = 32$$
$$2(x + y)(2x + y) = 32$$

Now substitute 4 for $x + y$ and solve for $2x + y$:

$$2(4)(2x + y) = 32$$
$$8(2x + y) = 32$$
$$2x + y = \frac{32}{8} = 4$$

Therefore, (F) is correct. Alternatively, you could simplify the original quadratic equation first by dividing both sides by 2 to get the lowest possible numbers to work with.

13. D Difficulty: Medium

Category: Higher Math / Algebra

Getting to the Answer: To solve an absolute value equation, consider the two possibilities: If $|2x - 3| = 13$, then what's inside the absolute value signs equals either 13 or −13:

$$2x - 3 = 13$$
$$2x = 16$$
$$x = 8$$
$$2x - 3 = -13$$
$$2x = -10$$
$$x = -5$$

Together, the two solutions form the solution set $\{-5, 8\}$, which is (D).

14. J Difficulty: High

Category: Higher Math / Algebra

Getting to the Answer: One approach to this question is to solve each of the answer choices to get a range of values for b and then see which one gives you the same range as that shown in the figure. A faster approach is to think of absolute value as a distance. You can see that the values in the figure are centered at 2 and include everything up to and including 3 units away from the center. Therefore, the distance between b and 2 must be less than or equal to 3, so $|b - 2| \leq 3$, which is (J).

You can confirm your choice by rewriting the absolute-value inequality as a compound inequality (because the symbol is $\leq$) and solving for b:

$$|b - 2| \leq 3$$
$$-3 \leq b - 2 \leq 3$$
$$-1 \leq b \leq 5$$

This inequality matches the number line perfectly.

15. A Difficulty: High

Category: Higher Math / Algebra

Getting to the Answer: You can't solve a quadratic inequality the same way you do a linear inequality because the squared term changes the sign of negative values of x. Instead, you need to factor the left side and then think about what "< 0" means. The left side factors to $(x - 3)(x - 2)$. This product will be positive (> 0) if both factors are negative or both factors are positive. The product will be negative (< 0, which is what you want) if one factor is negative and the other is positive. The smaller factor, $x - 3$, is negative and the larger factor, $x - 2$, is positive only for values of x between 2 and 3, or $2 < x < 3$. This matches (A).

Quadratic inequalities can be very confusing. Another approach is to graph $y = x^2 - 5x + 6$ in your graphing calculator and find the part of the graph that drops below the x-axis (because you want < 0), which is the part between 2 and 3.

16. G Difficulty: Low

Category: Higher Math / Algebra

Getting to the Answer: To find the slope of a line given by an equation in standard form, write the equation in slope-intercept form, $y = mx + b$. The coefficient of x gives you the slope.

$$-12x - 2y = 14$$
$$-2y = 12x + 14$$
$$y = \frac{12x}{-2y} + \frac{14}{-2y}$$
$$y = -6x - 7$$

The slope of the equation is -6, which is (G).

17. A Difficulty: Medium

Category: Higher Math / Algebra

Getting to the Answer: Here is another type of question in which you need to use the slope-intercept form of a line, $y = mx + b$. First, use the two given points and the slope formula to find the slope of the line (because you can't find b without first finding m):

$$m = \frac{y_2 - y_1}{x_2 - x_1} = \frac{31 - (-13)}{-10 - 1} = \frac{44}{-11} = -4$$

Now, plug this slope and the values of either point into $y = mx + b$ to find b (the y-intercept). Using $(1, -13)$, the result is $-13 = -4(1) + b$. Simplify the equation to get $b = -9$, which is (A).

Notice that B is a trap answer (it's the slope of the line, not the y-intercept). Double-check that you're answering the right question before you make your selection.

18. J Difficulty: Low

Category: Higher Math / Algebra

Getting to the Answer: Always take a second to look for relationships before diving into solve mode. Here, the quantity you're looking for, $3 - k$, is the opposite of the quantity you're given, $k - 3$. In other words, it's -1 times the given quantity: $-1(k - 3) = -k + 3$, or $3 - k$. This means you can multiply the right-hand side of the equation by -1 to find the answer: $-1\left(-\frac{5}{3}\right) = \frac{5}{3}$. Choice (J) is correct.

19. A Difficulty: Medium

Category: Higher Math / Algebra

Getting to the Answer: The first step to solving most questions about fractions set equal to each other is to cross-multiply. Your goal here is simply to get x by itself on one side of the equation.

$$\frac{3}{zy} = \frac{2y}{x}$$
$$3x = 2zy^2$$
$$x = \frac{2zy^2}{3}$$

This matches (A).

20. F Difficulty: Medium

Category: Higher Math / Algebra

Getting to the Answer: This can be a tricky question. If you arrive at an answer that isn't one of the choices, carefully consider which of the choices means the same thing in the context of the question. Don't just pick one that looks similar. And don't forget to flip the inequality symbol if you multiply or divide by a negative number.

$$-3x + 7 \leq 4$$
$$-3x \leq -3$$
$$x \geq 1$$

The solution to the inequality is not one of the answer choices, but think about what it means: If x is greater than or equal to 1 and it is an integer (per the question stem), then $x = 1, 2, 3, \ldots$, and the inequality $x > 0$ (when x is an integer) gives the same solution set. Choice (F) is correct.

21. D Difficulty: Medium

Category: Higher Math / Algebra

Getting to the Answer: Always read word problems carefully, particularly if you need to translate them into algebra problems.

Call the number of comic books in Brandy's collection c. Then translate the question stem into an equation. First, "she adds 15 to the number," means $c + 15$. Then she "multiplies the sum by 3" so you have $3(c + 15)$. "The result will be" indicates an equal sign, and "65 less than 4 times the number" is $4c - 65$. So this scenario can be modeled using the equation $3(c + 15) = 4c - 65$. Now solve for c by subtracting $3c$ from both sides and adding 65 to both sides. The result is $110 = c$, so (D) is correct.

You could also Backsolve, plugging each answer choice into the question stem until you find one that works with the information there.

22. G Difficulty: Medium

Category: Higher Math / Algebra

Getting to the Answer: Backsolving works well on many word problems.

Start with the middle choice, H. If Joy drove 96 miles, she would have paid $\$1.50 + \$0.25(96) = \$25.50$. This is too much, so go to G. If she drove 94 miles, she would have paid $\$1.50 + \$0.25(94) = \$25.00$. Choice (G) is correct.

You could also set up an equation. If m is the number of miles traveled, the toll is $\$1.50 + \$0.25m$. Joy paid $\$25.00$, so solve this equation:

$$\$1.50 + \$0.25m = \$25.00$$
$$\$0.25m = \$23.50$$
$$\frac{\$23.50}{\$0.25} = 94$$

This confirms that (G) is correct.

23. E Difficulty: High

Category: Higher Math / Algebra

Getting to the Answer: Take a look at the answer choices. The equations are given in slope-intercept form, so start by finding the slope. Substitute two pairs of values from the table (pick easy ones if possible) into the slope formula, $m = \dfrac{y_2 - y_1}{x_2 - x_1}$. Keep in mind that the projected number of pounds sold *depends* on the price, so the price is the independent variable (x) and the projected number of pounds is the dependent variable (y). Using the points (1.2, 15,000) and (2, 5,000), the slope is as follows:

$$m = \frac{5{,}000 - 15{,}000}{2 - 1.20}$$
$$= \frac{-10{,}000}{0.8}$$
$$= -12{,}500$$

This means you can eliminate A, B, and D because the slope is not correct. Don't let B fool you—the projected number of pounds sold goes *down* as the price goes *up*, so there is an inverse relationship, which means the slope must be negative. To choose between C and (E), you could find the y-intercept of the line, but this is a fairly time-intensive process. Instead, choose the easiest pair of values from the table, (2, 5,000), and substitute into C and (E) only. Choice (E) is correct because the equation $5{,}000 = -12{,}500(2) + 30{,}000$ is true.

24. G Difficulty: Low

Category: Higher Math / Algebra

Getting to the Answer: Either combination or substitution will work for a given system of equations, but one will usually be easier than the other. Because this question already has $+4y$ and $-4y$, combination is the best choice here.

$$3x + 4y = 31$$
$$+ \quad 3x - 4y = -1$$
$$\overline{\qquad 6x = 30 \qquad}$$
$$x = 5$$

The question asks for the value of x, so (G) is correct and there is no need to find the value of y.

25. A   Difficulty: Low

Category: Higher Math / Algebra

Getting to the Answer: The roots of a polynomial equation are the solutions to the equation. That is, for what value of x does $y = 0$? The equation here is already in factored form, so all that's left to do is to set each factor equal to 0. Technically, 2 is a factor, but 2 cannot equal 0, so you can ignore this factor (or divide both sides of the equation by 2 to get rid of it). The roots are as follows:

$$(x + 5) = 0 \rightarrow x = -5$$
$$(x - 1) = 0 \rightarrow x = 1$$
$$(x - 4) = 0 \rightarrow x = 4$$

Choice (A) is correct.

26. G   Difficulty: Medium

Category: Higher Math / Algebra

Getting to the Answer: Think "reverse FOIL": To factor $6x^2 - 13x + 6$, you need a pair of binomials whose "first" terms will give you a product of $6x^2$ and whose "last" terms will give you a product of $+6$. Because the middle term of the original expression is negative, the two last terms must both be negative. You know that one of the factors is among the answer choices, so you can use them in your trial-and-error effort to factor. You know you're looking for a factor with a minus sign in it, so the answer's either (G) or J.

Try (G) first: Its first term is $3x$, so the other factor's first term would have to be $2x$ (to get that $6x^2$ in the product). Choice G's last term is -2, so the other factor's last term would have to be -3. Check to see whether the factors $(3x - 2)$ and $(2x - 3)$ work:

$$(3x - 2)(2x - 3) = 3x(2x) + 3x(-3) + (-2)(2x) + (-2)(-3)$$
$$= 6x^2 - 9x - 4x + 6$$
$$= 6x^2 - 13x + 6$$

It works, so (G) is correct. There's no need to check J. Note that you could also use grouping to factor the expression.

27. D   Difficulty: Medium

Category: Higher Math / Algebra

Getting to the Answer: Use the acronym FOIL (First, Outside, Inside, Last) to multiply the binomials:

$$(4x - 1)(x + 5)$$
$$= 4x^2 + 20x - x - 5$$
$$= 4x^2 + 19x - 5$$

This matches (D). You can also find the answer by Picking Numbers. Use a small, positive number to substitute for x, like 2:

$$(4 \times 2 - 1)(2 + 5) = (7)(7) = 49$$

Now substitute 2 for x in the answer choices:

A: $4(2^2) + 8(2) = 16 + 16 = 32$ Eliminate.

B: $4(2^2) - 10(2) - 5 = 16 - 20 - 5 = -9$ Eliminate.

C: $4(2^2) + 15(2) + 5 = 16 + 30 + 5 = 51$ Eliminate.

D: $4(2^2) + 19(2) - 5 = 16 + 38 - 5 = 49$ Keep.

E: $4(2^2) + 19(2) + 5 = 16 + 38 + 5 = 59$ Eliminate.

This confirms that (D) is the correct answer.

28. H   Difficulty: Medium

Category: Higher Math / Algebra

Getting to the Answer: For questions with complex fractions, simplifying before multiplying will save you valuable time on Test Day.

Because $a = 4$, the fraction can be rewritten as $\dfrac{4(4)^4 + 64b}{16} = \dfrac{4^5 + 64b}{16}$. You could evaluate 4^5, but you'll save yourself some work if you notice that the denominator and the coefficient for b can both be written in base 4 as well. Rewriting the problem in base 4, you have the following:

$$\frac{4^5 + 4^3 b}{4^2} = 4^{(5-2)} + 4^{(3-2)}b = 4^3 + 4b = 64 + 4b$$

This matches (H).

29. A Difficulty: Medium

Category: Higher Math / Algebra

Getting to the Answer: To factor a quadratic expression, find factors of the last term that, when added together, equal the middle term. The factors of 24 that add to -11 are -8 and -3. Also keep in mind that $(a - b)$ is equivalent to $-(b - a)$.

$$\frac{x^2 - 11x + 24}{8 - x} = \frac{(x - 8)(x - 3)}{8 - x}$$
$$= \frac{-(8 - x)(x - 3)}{8 - x}$$
$$= -(x - 3)$$
$$= 3 - x$$

This matches (A).

30. G Difficulty: High

Category: Higher Math / Algebra

Getting to the Answer: You could use Picking Numbers here, but using algebra is probably quicker. To solve algebraically, you need to write the fractions in the denominator over a common denominator, x. Once you've accomplished that, you can simply flip the expression in the denominator to take out the "1 over" part of the original fraction.

$$\frac{1}{1 + \frac{1}{x}} = \frac{1}{\frac{x}{x} + \frac{1}{x}} = \frac{1}{\frac{x + 1}{x}} = \frac{x}{x + 1}$$

This matches (G).

31. E Difficulty: Medium

Category: Higher Math / Algebra

Getting to the Answer: There is no math to be done here. If you recall that absolute value represents distance on a number line and therefore cannot be negative, you'll immediately see that there are no values of x for which the equation is true (because the right-hand side is -4). Choice (E) is correct.

32. K Difficulty: High

Category: Higher Math / Algebra

Getting to the Answer: You could work out the algebra here, but it's not actually necessary. Because the symbol is $>$, the solution to the inequality will include all numbers that are less than a certain value and all numbers that are greater than a certain value. Regardless of what those values are, there will be infinitely many integers in the solution set. Choice (K) is correct.

33. E Difficulty: Medium

Category: Higher Math / Algebra

Getting to the Answer: Don't be fooled—the left side of this inequality cannot be factored (because of the $+$ between the terms), so you need to approach this question a bit differently. Think of what the graph would look like: The expression on the left is the standard quadratic (x^2) shifted up 9 units. Its graph, therefore, is a parabola (a U shape) that opens upward and has a minimum value of 9. (Note that parabolas will be covered in more detail in later chapters.) This means the graph never drops below the x-axis (which is where $y = 0$), so $x^2 + 9$ will never be less than 0. Choice (E) is correct.

You could also think about this algebraically: A number squared is either positive or 0 (if the number happens to be 0), and adding 9 to a number squared will certainly result in a positive number. Thus, $x^2 + 9$ is definitely a positive number and will never be less than 0.

34. J Difficulty: High

Category: Higher Math / Algebra

Getting to the Answer: Because the question has all variables in the answer choices, you could use the Picking Numbers strategy. However, there are lots of terms to evaluate, so solving algebraically is probably faster. Start by finding a common denominator, which happens to be the first denominator (you should recognize this as a difference of squares):

$$\frac{4x}{x^2-16}-\frac{3x}{x-4}=\frac{4x}{x^2-16}-\frac{3x}{x-4}\times\left(\frac{x+4}{x+4}\right)$$

$$=\frac{4x-3x(x+4)}{x^2-16}$$

$$=\frac{4x-3x^2-12x}{(x-4)(x+4)}$$

$$=\frac{-3x^2-8x}{x^2-16}$$

This matches (J).

35. D   Difficulty: High

Category: Higher Math / Algebra

Getting to the Answer: If an equation looks complicated enough that you'd get confused trying to solve it algebraically, use Backsolving instead. Answering this question algebraically would require finding a common denominator, FOILing, and several more steps, so Backsolving is definitely the quicker route.

As always, start with the middle answer choice, 0:

$$\frac{0+1}{0-3}-\frac{0+2}{0-4}=\frac{1}{-3}-\frac{2}{-4}=-\frac{1}{3}+\frac{1}{2}\neq0$$

Zero doesn't work, but it's hard to see whether a bigger or smaller number is necessary. If you're not sure which direction to go, just pick the one that looks easier to work with. In this case, that's 1:

$$\frac{1+1}{1-3}-\frac{1+2}{1-4}=\frac{2}{-2}-\frac{3}{-3}=-1-(-1)=0$$

Choice (D) is correct.

CHAPTER 12

PRACTICE

13. A Difficulty: Medium

Category: Higher Math / Functions

Getting to the Answer: Start by evaluating the function at $x = 25$ and at $x = 20$. Make sure you follow the correct order of operations as you simplify.

$$P(25) = 150(25) - (25)^2$$
$$= 3{,}750 - 625$$
$$= 3{,}125$$
$$P(20) = 150(20) - (20)^2$$
$$= 3{,}000 - 400$$
$$= 2{,}600$$

The question asks how much more profit *per unit* the company makes, so find the difference in the amounts of profit and divide by the number of units (150) to get

$$\frac{3{,}125 - 2{,}600}{150} = \frac{525}{150} = \$3.50, \text{ or (A)}.$$

14. H Difficulty: Medium

Category: Higher Math / Functions

Getting to the Answer: Piecewise functions look intimidating, but they are usually very simple functions—they're just written in pieces. The right-hand side of each piece of the function tells you what part of the domain (which *x*-values) goes with that particular expression. In this function, only values of *x* that are less than or equal to 0 go with the top expression, values of *x* greater than 0 and less than or equal to 3 go with the middle expression, and values of *x* that are greater than 3 go with the bottom expression. Because −3 is less than 0, plug it into the top expression and simplify:

$$f(-3) = (-3)^2 + 1$$
$$= 9 + 1$$
$$= 10$$

This matches (H).

15. C Difficulty: High

Category: Higher Math / Functions

Getting to the Answer: Consider the vertical translation first: If a function $f(x)$ is shifted up 4 units, the graph will be described by $f(x) + 4$. Here, the original function is $g(x) = (x - 1)^2$, so applying the vertical translation gives a new function of $(x - 1)^2 + 4$. Now for the horizontal translation: If a function $f(x)$ is shifted left 3 units, the graph will be described by $f(x + 3)$. Combining this with the first translation gives $h(x) = (x - 1 + 3)^2 + 4$, which simplifies to $h(x) = (x + 2)^2 + 4$, or choice (C).

16. F Difficulty: High

Category: Higher Math / Functions

Getting to the Answer: You'll need to rely on properties of logs to answer this question. All the bases in the question stem are the same (2), so you can totally ignore them. The given expression involves two different properties: It has an exponent and a product. As in algebra, deal with the exponent first: The relevant logarithm property is $\log_b x^y = y \log_b x$, which tells you to move the exponent down in front of the logarithm and multiply to get $\log_2 (MN)^3 = 3 \log_2 (MN)$. Next, use the property related to products: $\log_b (xy) = \log_b x + \log_b y$. The result is:

$$3\log_2(MN) = 3(\log_2 M + \log_2 N)$$

You now have enough information to answer the question because you're told that $\log_2 M = a$ and $\log_2 N = b$. Plug these values in to get $3(a + b)$, which is (F).

17. B Difficulty: Medium

Category: Higher Math / Functions

Getting to the Answer: When in doubt, draw it out! Set up the sequence using blanks in place of the numbers you don't know: 8, ___ , ___ , 36. If the common difference is −7, then the second term must be $8 + (-7) = 1$, and the third term must be $1 + (-7) = -6$. The sequence is 8, 1, −6, 36. To find the common ratio for the last part of the sequence, divide the fourth term by the third term; the result is −6, which is (B).

18. G   Difficulty: High

Category: Higher Math / Functions

Getting to the Answer: The values along the horizontal axis (the angle measures) are given in radians, but the angles in the question are given in degrees. Knowing common angle equivalents (radians/degrees) will save you time on Test Day, as will knowing the unit circle. However, you can also use the conversion $180° = \pi$ to convert the angle measures before reading the graph.

Convert each of the angles to radians and then read the corresponding y-values on the graph.

$$\cos 90° = \cos\left(90° \times \frac{\pi}{180°}\right) = \cos\left(\frac{\pi}{2}\right) = 0$$

$$\cos 180° = \cos\left(180° \times \frac{\pi}{180°}\right) = \cos(\pi) = -1$$

The sum is $0 + (-1) = -1$, which is (G).

PERFORM

19. D   Difficulty: Low

Category: Higher Math / Functions

Getting to the Answer: The notation $g(-2)$ means to find the value of the function when $x = -2$, so substitute -2 for each x in the function. Be sure to follow the correct order of operations as you simplify, and be careful of all the negative signs.

$$g(x) = 3x^2 - 5x - 7$$
$$g(-2) = 3(-2)^2 - 5(-2) - 7$$
$$= 3(4) + 10 - 7$$
$$= 12 + 10 - 7$$
$$= 15$$

Choice (D) is correct.

20. J   Difficulty: Medium

Category: Higher Math / Functions

Getting to the Answer: To determine the domain, look at the x-values. To determine the range, look at the y-values. For the domain, the graph is continuous and has arrows on both sides, so the domain is all real numbers. This means you can eliminate choices F and G. For the range,

the function's maximum is located at (0,5), which means the highest possible value of $f(x)$ is 5. The graph is continuous and opens downward, so the range of the function is $f(x) \leq 5$, making (J) correct.

21. A   Difficulty: Medium

Category: Higher Math / Functions

Getting to the Answer: If you remember your properties of logs, this question is very straightforward. Because $\log_b b^x = x$, the value of x is $\frac{3}{2} = 1.5$, which lies between 1 and 2. Choice (A) is correct.

If you don't remember this property, you'll have to rewrite the logarithmic equation as an exponential equation and solve: $\log_7 7^{\frac{3}{2}} = x$ is equivalent to the exponential form $7^x = 7^{\frac{3}{2}}$. The bases are the same (7), so the exponents must be equal. This means $x = \frac{3}{2}$, or 1.5, which lies between 1 and 2.

22. J   Difficulty: High

Category: Higher Math / Functions

Getting to the Answer: You could make a table of values, record the number of questions Winnie answered each day, and then add up all the numbers. This approach would be time-consuming (you would have to do 30 days), and you might make a mistake even with a calculator, but it is a straightforward process and would work.

You might also notice that this is an arithmetic sequence with $a_1 = 12$; a common difference, d, of 2; and $n = 30$ terms. You could then use the formula for finding the sum of an arithmetic sequence:

$$S_n = \frac{n}{2}\left[2a_1 + (n-1)d\right]$$
$$S_{30} = \frac{30}{2}\left[2(12) + (30-1)2\right]$$
$$= 15\left[24 + 29(2)\right]$$
$$= 15(82)$$
$$= 1{,}230$$

That is a lot of math questions to practice, and (J) is correct!

ON YOUR OWN

1. E Difficulty: Low

Category: Higher Math / Functions

Getting to the Answer: To find $f(4)$, substitute 4 for each x in the function and simplify using the correct order of operations:

$$f(x) = 3\sqrt{x^2 + 3x + 4}$$
$$f(4) = 3\sqrt{4^2 + 3(4) + 4}$$
$$= 3\sqrt{16 + 12 + 4}$$
$$= 3\sqrt{32}$$
$$= 3 \times 4\sqrt{2}$$
$$= 12\sqrt{2}$$

So the answer is (E).

2. F Difficulty: Medium

Category: Higher Math / Functions

Getting to the Answer: Evaluate the function at $t = 20$ and at $t = 10$, then subtract the results. Make sure you follow the correct order of operations as you simplify.

$$c(20) = -0.05(20)^2 + 2(20) + 2$$
$$= -0.05(400) + 40 + 2$$
$$= -20 + 40 + 2$$
$$= 22$$

$$c(10) = -0.05(10)^2 + 2(10) + 2$$
$$= -0.05(100) + 20 + 2$$
$$= -5 + 20 + 2$$
$$= 17$$

The question asks how many more parts per million are in a patient's bloodstream after 20 hours than after 10 hours, so subtract $22 - 17 = 5$. Choice (F) is correct.

3. A Difficulty: Medium

Category: Higher Math / Functions

Getting to the Answer: The notation $f(g(x))$ indicates a composition of two functions that is read "f of g of x." It means that the output when x is substituted into $g(x)$,

the inner function, becomes the input for $f(x)$. Substitute $\frac{1}{4}$ for x in $g(x)$, simplify, and then substitute the result into $f(x)$:

$$g\left(\frac{1}{4}\right) = \sqrt{\frac{1}{4}} + 2.5 = \frac{\sqrt{1}}{\sqrt{4}} + 2.5 = \frac{1}{2} + 2.5 = 3$$

$$f(3) = -4(3) + 1 = -12 + 1 = -11$$

Therefore, $f\left(g\left(\frac{1}{4}\right)\right) = -11$, which is (A).

4. K Difficulty: High

Category: Higher Math / Functions

Getting to the Answer: Just as you can substitute a number into a function or a composition of functions, you can substitute an expression into a function. Here, the notation $f(g(x))$ means to substitute the expression that defines $g(x)$, the inner function, for x in $f(x)$, the outer function. So, $f(g(x)) = (3x + 1)^2 + 1$. Use FOIL and then combine like terms to get the following:

$$f(g(x)) = (3x + 1)^2 + 1$$
$$= (3x + 1)(3x + 1) + 1$$
$$= 9x^2 + 3x + 3x + 1 + 1$$
$$= 9x^2 + 6x + 2$$

This matches (K).

5. E Difficulty: Low

Category: Higher Math / Functions

Getting to the Answer: The range of a function is the set of y-values generated by the function. In other words, the range describes how low the function goes to how high the function goes. Here, the lowest y-value that $h(x)$ takes on is -4. The highest y-value that $h(x)$ takes on is 2. There are no holes, gaps, or asymptotes in the graph, so the range is all real numbers between and including -4 and 2. This matches (E).

6. K Difficulty: Medium

Category: Higher Math / Functions

Getting to the Answer: Being able to translate function language into plain English is the key to answering this question: $h(x) = 0$ translates to "has a y-value of 0." In

Answers & Explanations

other words, the question is asking how many times the graph crosses the *x*-axis between −5 and 5. It crosses in 4 places, so (K) is correct.

7. D Difficulty: High

Category: Higher Math / Functions

Getting to the Answer: Vertical asymptotes correspond to the zeros of the denominator of a rational function that is written in simplest form. That is, given that there are no common factors shared by the numerator and denominator, you can set the denominator of a rational function equal to zero to find the vertical asymptotes. By doing this, you are finding the values of *x* for which the domain of the function is not defined.

$$x^2 - 16 = 0$$
$$x^2 = 16$$
$$x = \pm 4$$

Choice (D) is correct.

8. J Difficulty: High

Category: Higher Math / Functions

Getting to the Answer: Graphing piecewise functions can be tricky. Try describing the graph in words first and then find the matching function. Use words such as "to the left of" (which translates as *less than*) and "to the right of" (which translates as *greater than*).

First notice that there is a hole in the graph at *x* = 4. This means you can eliminate choice F right away because the inequality symbol in the top piece would include the endpoint at 4. To choose among the remaining answers, think about the shapes of some basic functions and transformations. To the left of *x* = 4, the graph is an absolute-value function (a V shape) that has been reflected vertically across the *x*-axis and then shifted up one unit. This means either H or J must be correct. Now look to the right of *x* = 4: The graph is a horizontal line, which means a line that has a slope of 0. The slope of the line in H is negative 3, so it can't be correct. This means (J) is correct. (The equation of a horizontal line always looks like *y* = *b*, or in this case, *g*(*x*) = −3.)

9. A Difficulty: Medium

Category: Higher Math / Functions

Getting to the Answer: You may encounter a strange-looking function and its definition on the ACT. Just follow the "rule" provided by the definition. Here, plug *a* = 64 and *b* = 3 into the definition:

$$a \downarrow b = \sqrt[b]{a}$$
$$64 \downarrow 3 = \sqrt[3]{64}$$
$$= \sqrt[3]{4 \times 4 \times 4}$$
$$= 4$$

Choice (A) is correct.

10. G Difficulty: Medium

Category: Higher Math / Functions

Getting to the Answer: Almost every logarithmic equation that you're likely to see on the ACT can be solved by rewriting the logarithm in its exponential form. Here, $\log_5 (25x) = 2$ is equivalent to the exponential form $5^2 = 25x$. This simplifies to 25 = 25*x*, or *x* = 1. Choice (G) is correct.

11. B Difficulty: Medium

Category: Higher Math / Functions

Getting to the Answer: The total difference between 12 and 32 is 32 − 12 = 20. This difference is spread over 4 parts: the difference between 12 and the first blank, the difference between the first and second blanks, the difference between the second and third blanks, and the difference between the third blank and 32. Therefore, each part has a difference of $\frac{20}{4} = 5$. So 12 + 5 = 17, 17 + 5 = 22, 22 + 5 = 27, and 27 + 5 = 32, and the missing numbers are 17, 22, and 27. Choice (B) is correct. Note that if you're not sure how to find the missing terms, Backsolving is a great alternative.

12. J Difficulty: High

Category: Higher Math / Functions

Getting to the Answer: In a geometric sequence, use the formula $a_n = a_1(r^{n-1})$, where *an* is the *n*th term in the sequence, a_1 is the first term in the sequence, and *r* is the amount by which each preceding term is multiplied to get the next term (called the common ratio).

The first two terms in this sequence are 3 and 12, so r is $\frac{12}{3} = 4$. You're given that a_1 is 3 and you're looking for the 24th term, so n is 24. Plug each of these values into the formula and simplify to get $a_{24} = 3(4^{24-1}) = 3 \times 4^{23}$. That's equivalent to (J).

13. C   Difficulty: High

Category: Higher Math / Functions

Getting to the Answer: The most direct way to answer this question is to recall the fact that the amplitude of the cosine (or sine) function when written in the form $g(x) = A \cos(Bx + C)$ is simply the absolute value of A. Here, that would be 2, making (C) the correct answer. Alternatively, you could recall that $y = \cos x$ normally has an amplitude of 1 (because it bounces back and forth between -1 and 1). Standard transformation rules tell you that the 2 in front of the cosine in the equation multiplies all the y-values of the graph by 2, which means the transformed graph bounces back and forth between -2 and 2, resulting in an amplitude of 2, which is (C).

14. J   Difficulty: High

Category: Higher Math / Functions

Getting to the Answer: While you may not know the values of most of the choices offhand, you don't need to. Every choice subtracts some value from 1, so the correct answer must subtract an expression that is equal to 0.5. Because secant is the reciprocal of cosine, $\cos G = \dfrac{1}{\sec G} = 0.5$, so (J) is correct.

15. E   Difficulty: High

Category: Higher Math / Functions

Getting to the Answer: Each answer choice involves a horizontal shift of the sine curve, so your job is to determine how much the graph has been shifted and in which direction. Don't forget—horizontal shifts are the opposite of what they look like. Think about a few key points on a standard sine curve: $(0,0)$, $\left(\frac{\pi}{2},1\right)$, $(\pi,0)$, and $\left(\frac{3\pi}{2},-1\right)$. Now, look for the corresponding points on the graph: $(0,1)$, $\left(\frac{\pi}{2},0\right)$, $(\pi, -1)$, and $\left(\frac{3\pi}{2},0\right)$. The sequence of points has

been shifted to the left by $\frac{\pi}{2}$, so the correct equation is $g(x) = \sin\left(x + \frac{\pi}{2}\right)$, which matches (E). Alternatively, you could graph each of the functions in your graphing calculator and look for the one that passes through $(0,1)$. Just make sure your calculator is set to radian mode.

16. H   Difficulty: Low

Category: Higher Math / Functions

Getting to the Answer: The notation $h(5)$ means the output value of the function when 5 is substituted for the input (x), and $h(2)$ means the output value of the function when 2 is substituted for the input (x). Substitute 5 and 2 into the equation, one at a time, and then subtract the results.

$$h(x) = 3x - 1$$
$$h(5) = 3(5) - 1 = 15 - 1 = 14$$
$$h(2) = 3(2) - 1 = 6 - 1 = 5$$

$$h(5) - h(2) = 14 - 5 = 9$$

Choice (H) is correct. Caution—this is not the same as subtracting 2 from 5 and then substituting 3 into the function.

17. E   Difficulty: Medium

Category: Higher Math / Functions

Getting to the Answer: The notation $f(2)$ means the value of f when $x = 2$. To evaluate the function at that value, you would simply substitute 2 for each x in the function. Here, you need to substitute $x + h$ for each x in the function and simplify. Be careful—you'll need to FOIL the squared expression and then combine like terms:

$$f(x) = x^2 + 3x - 5$$
$$f(x + h) = (x + h)^2 + 3(x + h) - 5$$
$$= (x + h)(x + h) + 3x + 3h - 5$$
$$= x^2 + xh + xh + h^2 + 3x + 3h - 5$$
$$= x^2 + 2xh + 3x + h^2 + 3h - 5$$

Choice (E) is correct.

18. J Difficulty: Medium

Category: Higher Math / Functions

Getting to the Answer: Many Function questions, like this one, rely on substituting given values for the variables. Here, plug in 3 for x in a(x), plug in 2 for x in b(x), and simplify. There is no need to simply the algebraic expressions before plugging in the numbers.

$$\frac{a(x)}{b(x)} = \frac{\sqrt{x^2 + 7}}{x^3 - 7}$$

$$\frac{a(3)}{b(2)} = \frac{\sqrt{3^2 + 7}}{2^3 - 7}$$

$$= \frac{\sqrt{9 + 7}}{8 - 7}$$

$$= \frac{\sqrt{16}}{1}$$

$$= 4$$

This matches (J).

19. A Difficulty: Medium

Category: Higher Math / Functions

Getting to the Answer: The notation g(h(x)) indicates a composition of two functions that can be read "g of h of x." It means that the output when x is substituted in h(x), the inner function and the table on the right, becomes the input for g(x), the outer function and the table on the left. First, use the table on the right to find that h(3) is 0. This is your new input. Now, use the table on the left to find g(0), which is −1, making (A) the correct answer.

20. J Difficulty: Medium

Category: Higher Math / Functions

Getting to the Answer: Read each answer choice carefully and compare it to the graph. Choice F indicates that the y-value on the graph of f is −4 when the x-value is 0, which is not true (at x = 0, the y-value of f is 2). Choice G indicates that the y-value on the graph of g is 0 when the x-value is 2, which is not true (at x = 2, the y-value of g is somewhere between 2 and 3). Choice H indicates that the graph of f is above (greater than) the graph of

g everywhere, which is not true (the bottom part of the V is below the graph of g). In (J), the notation f(x) = g(x) means the point at which the two graphs intersect. The graphs intersect in two places, one of which is (0,2), so (0,2) is a solution for f(x) = g(x), and (J) is correct.

There is no need to check K, but in case you're curious, the graph of f(x) touches the x-axis in only one place (between −1 and 0), so f(x) = 0 has exactly one solution, not two.

21. C Difficulty: Medium

Category: Higher Math / Functions

Getting to the Answer: The range of a function is the set of y-values that the function takes on. In other words, the range describes how low and how high the function goes. The graph of this function (which is quadratic) is a parabola that has been shifted down 9 units. The standard parabola, $y = x^2$, has a minimum value of 0 (because its vertex is at the origin and the graph opens upward), so the minimum value of this function is −9. Thus, the range of the function is all real numbers greater than or equal to −9, which is (C).

Note that you could also graph the function in your graphing calculator and find the minimum value to identify the range.

22. F Difficulty: High

Category: Higher Math / Functions

Getting to the Answer: Don't let piecewise functions intimidate you. The right-hand side of each piece of the function tells you what part of the domain (which x-values) goes with that particular expression. In this function, only values of x that are less than or equal to 0 go with the top expression, values of x greater than 0 and less than or equal to 6 go with the middle expression, and values of x that are greater than 6 go with the bottom expression. Because 6 is equal to 6, plug it into the middle expression and simplify:

$$f(6) = 2(6) - 9$$
$$= 12 - 9$$
$$= 3$$

This matches (F).

23. A   Difficulty: High

Category: Higher Math / Functions

Getting to the Answer: Graphing piecewise functions can be tricky. Try describing the graph in words first and then find the matching function. Use words like "to the left of" (which translates to *less than*) and "to the right of" (which translates to *greater than*).

First, notice that both pieces of the graph either start or stop at 0, but one has a closed dot and the other has an open dot. This means you can eliminate C right away because the inequality symbol in both equations would lead to open dots on the graph. To choose among the remaining answers, think about typical functions and transformations. To the left of $x = 0$, the graph is a line with a slope of $-\dfrac{3}{2}$ and a y-intercept of -4, so you can eliminate D and E because the slopes of the lines are incorrect. Now, look to the right of $x = 0$—the graph is a square root function (definitely not a line as in B) that has been moved down 1 unit, so its equation is $y = \sqrt{x} - 1$. This means (A) is correct.

24. G   Difficulty: Medium

Category: Higher Math / Functions

Getting to the Answer: You can think this one through conceptually. The expression $1 - x^2$ will be at its maximum when the x^2 that's subtracted from the 1 is as small as it can be. The square of a real number can't be any smaller than 0—and $x = 0$ is within the specified domain—so the maximum is $1 - 0 = 1$, which is (G).

25. D   Difficulty: High

Category: Higher Math / Functions

Getting to the Answer: Compare each answer choice to the graph, eliminating false statements as you go.

Choice A: Aaron went to the library first, so the library (not the post office) is about 5 miles from his home. Eliminate this choice.

Choice B: Aaron traveled 7 miles away from his home (between $t = 0$ minutes and $t = 30$ minutes) but then

also traveled 7 miles back (between $t = 45$ minutes and $t = 60$ minutes), so he traveled a total of 14 miles. Eliminate this choice.

Choice C: When Aaron reached the library, he was 5 miles from home; when he reached the post office, he was 7 miles from home. This means the post office must be about $7 - 5 = 2$ miles farther away. Eliminate this choice.

Choice (D): Aaron is the same distance from home (5 miles) between $t = 15$ minutes and $t = 25$ minutes, so he spent 10 minutes at the library. He is stopped once again (at the post office) between $t = 30$ minutes and $t = 45$ minutes, so he spent 15 minutes at the post office.

There is no need to check E, but in case you're curious or just not sure: Aaron spent $15 + 5 + 15 = 35$ minutes traveling to and from his destinations (represented by the portions of the graph that are not horizontal) and only $10 + 15 = 25$ minutes at his destinations, so E is not a true statement.

26. K   Difficulty: Medium

Category: Higher Math / Functions

Getting to the Answer: Although the notation may look intimidating, just follow the rule given in the question stem. Expand each factorial, cancel factors common to the numerator and denominator, and then simplify:

$$\frac{6!}{2!3!} = \frac{6 \times 5 \times 4 \times 3 \times 2 \times 1}{(2 \times 1) \times (3 \times 2 \times 1)}$$

$$= \frac{6 \times 5 \times 4 \times \cancel{3 \times 2 \times 1}}{2 \times \cancel{3 \times 2 \times 1}}$$

$$= \frac{6 \times 5 \times 4}{2} = \frac{120}{2} = 60$$

Choice (K) is correct.

27. C   Difficulty: Medium

Category: Higher Math / Functions

Getting to the Answer: Rewrite the logarithm in its exponential form: $2^{-3} = x$. To simplify the left side, recall that a negative exponent indicates taking the reciprocal of the base, so $2^{-3} = \dfrac{1}{2^3} = \dfrac{1}{8}$, which is (C).

Answers & Explanations

28. F Difficulty: High

Category: Higher Math / Functions

Getting to the Answer: Use the log property $\log_b x + \log_b y = \log_b(xy)$ to rewrite the left side of the equation. Then rewrite the entire equation in exponential form and solve for x:

$$\log_2 x + \log_2(8x) = 5$$
$$\log_2(8x^2) = 5$$
$$2^5 = 8x^2$$
$$32 = 8x^2$$
$$4 = x^2$$
$$x = \pm 2$$

Because $\log_b x$ is defined only for values of $x > 0$, -2 is not a valid solution. Thus, (F) is correct.

29. B Difficulty: Medium

Category: Higher Math / Functions

Getting to the Answer: For arithmetic sequences, use the formula $a_n = a_1 + (n - 1)d$, where n is the number of the term you're looking for, a_1 is the first term, and d is the common difference between consecutive terms (the number you're adding to each term to get the next term). Here, n is 20, a_1 is 25, and d is -4. Plug each of these values in the formula and simplify to get:

$$a_{20} = 25 + (20 - 1)(-4)$$
$$= 25 + (19)(-4)$$
$$= 25 - 76$$
$$= -51$$

Choice (B) is correct.

30. K Difficulty: Medium

Category: Higher Math / Functions

Getting to the Answer: You could use the general formula for a geometric sequence here, but you only need to go back four terms, so it's probably quicker to work backward. The common ratio (the number you're multiplying by each time to get to the next term) is $\frac{1}{3}$, which means working backward would require multiplying by 3

as you move to the previous term. This means the fourth term is 9, the third term is 27, the second term is 81, and the first term is 243, which is (K).

31. A Difficulty: High

Category: Higher Math / Functions

Getting to the Answer: This question is not as difficult as it may sound. You don't know the common difference between the terms, so call it d. Now, write out the five terms: 2, $2 + d$, $2 + 2d$, $2 + 3d$, and $2 + 4d$. The median is the middle term, which is $2 + 2d$. The mean is the sum of the terms, $10 + 10d$, divided by the number of terms, 5, which gives $2 + 2d$. Thus, the difference between the mean and the median is 0. Choice (A) is correct.

32. K Difficulty: Medium

Category: Higher Math / Functions

Getting to the Answer: The triangle in the figure is a 30°-60°-90° triangle. The hypotenuse is the radius of the circle, and point P is on the unit circle, so the hypotenuse is 1 unit long. That means that the shorter leg is $\frac{1}{2}$ and the longer leg is $\frac{\sqrt{3}}{2}$:

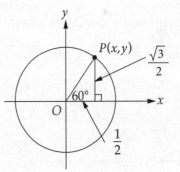

Therefore, $x + y = \frac{1}{2} + \frac{\sqrt{3}}{2} \approx 1.37$, making (K) the correct answer.

33. C Difficulty: High

Category: Higher Math / Functions

Getting to the Answer: Recall that $g(x) = 0$ means "crosses the x-axis," regardless of the type of function involved, which means you are looking for the x-intercepts. Study

Answers & Explanations

the graph carefully: The function crosses the x-axis six times, halfway between each of the labeled grid lines. Rather than finding the points using the radians given in the graph, convert the radians to degrees and then determine the halfway points:

$$-\pi\left(\frac{180°}{\pi}\right) = -180°,$$

$$\left(-\frac{2\pi}{3}\right)\left(\frac{180°}{\pi}\right) = -120°,$$

$$\left(-\frac{\pi}{3}\right)\left(\frac{180°}{\pi}\right) = -60°, \text{ and so on.}$$

Take a minute now to find the halfway points, because chances are that you don't have to do all the conversions. Halfway between $-180°$ and $-120°$ is $-150°$. Stop—that's all you need to know. The leftmost x-intercept is at $-150°$, which means (C) must be correct. If you want to check another value just to be sure, halfway between $-120°$ and $-60°$ is $-90°$, which is the second value in (C), confirming that it is correct.

34. G Difficulty: Medium

Category: Higher Math / Functions

Getting to the Answer: Substitute the given expressions into the square root for a and b, square each term carefully, and then use trig identities to simplify:

$$\sqrt{a^2 + b^2} = \sqrt{(x\cos\theta)^2 + (x\sin\theta)^2}$$
$$= \sqrt{x^2\left(\cos^2\theta + \sin^2\theta\right)}$$
$$= \sqrt{x^2 \cdot 1}$$
$$= |x|$$

It's given that $x > 0$, so $|x| = x$, which is (G).

35. D Difficulty: High

Category: Higher Math / Functions

Getting to the Answer: You should notice two things about the numerator of the expression: There's a tangent in each term (so it can be factored out), and there are squared trig functions. Start with that:

$$\frac{\tan\theta\cos^2\theta + \tan\theta\sin^2\theta}{\sin\theta} = \frac{\tan\theta\left(\cos^2\theta + \sin^2\theta\right)}{\sin\theta}$$
$$= \frac{\tan\theta\,(1)}{\sin\theta}$$
$$= \frac{\tan\theta}{\sin\theta}$$

Now, take a peek at the answer choices—each one is a single trig function, which means something in the result above must cancel. Use the trig ratios that you learned (SOHCAHTOA) to simplify your answer:

$$\frac{\tan\theta}{\sin\theta} = \frac{\dfrac{\text{opposite}}{\text{adjacent}}}{\dfrac{\text{opposite}}{\text{hypotenuse}}}$$
$$= \frac{\text{opposite}}{\text{adjacent}} \times \frac{\text{hypotenuse}}{\text{opposite}}$$
$$= \frac{\text{hypotenuse}}{\text{adjacent}}$$

Cosine is $\dfrac{\text{adj}}{\text{hyp}}$, and secant is the reciprocal of cosine, so the correct answer is (D).

CHAPTER 13

PRACTICE

17. B   Difficulty: Medium

Category: Higher Math / Geometry

Getting to the Answer: The cost per night in the hospital is the same as the unit rate, which is represented by the slope of the line. Use the grid lines and the axis labels to count the rise and the run from the y-intercept of the line, (0,26,000), to the next point that hits an intersection of two grid lines, (2,34,000). Pay careful attention to how the grid lines are marked (by 2s on the x-axis and by 2,000s on the y-axis). The line rises 8,000 units and runs 2 units, so the slope is $\frac{8,000}{2}$, which means it costs an average of $4,000 per night to stay in the hospital. Note that you could also use the slope formula and the two points to find the slope:

$$\frac{34,000 - 26,000}{2 - 0} = \frac{8,000}{2} = 4,000$$

Choice (B) is correct.

18. J   Difficulty: High

Category: Higher Math / Geometry

Getting to the Answer: Use what you know about parent functions and transformations to draw a quick sketch of the equation (or graph it in your graphing calculator).

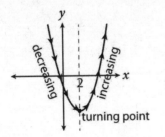

Based on the equation, the graph is a parabola that opens up with a vertex of (2,−5). A parabola changes direction at the x-coordinate of its vertex. This is all the information you need to answer the question. You can immediately

eliminate F, G, and K. To choose between H and J, take a closer look at the sketch. To the left of 2 (or $x < 2$), the parabola is decreasing, and to the right of 2 (or $x > 2$), it is increasing. This makes (J) correct.

19. A   Difficulty: Medium

Category: Higher Math / Geometry

Getting to the Answer: Start by drawing Marge's orchard and the fence she plans to build:

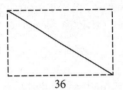

You know the length and the area of the field. Use these to find the width:

$$A = l \times w$$
$$540 = 36w$$
$$15 = w$$

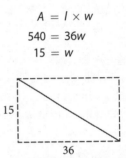

Now you know that the fence is the hypotenuse of a right triangle with legs of lengths 15 and 36. Before turning to the Pythagorean theorem, look for a Pythagorean triplet to lessen the required work. Indeed, this is a 5-12-13 triangle multiplied by 3. Therefore, the hypotenuse—and feet of fence needed—is $13 \times 3 = 39$, which is (A).

20. J   Difficulty: Low

Category: Higher Math / Geometry

Getting to the Answer: The volume of a cylinder is the area of its base times its height: $\pi r^2 h$. (You'll need to memorize this formula before Test Day.) This cylinder's height is 5 inches and its radius is 4 inches, so the volume is $\pi(4)^2(5) = 80\pi$. This matches (J).

Answers & Explanations

21. E Difficulty: Low

Category: Higher Math / Geometry

Getting to the Answer: The amount of paint needed to cover all the surface is the same as the total surface area of the solid. Add the areas of all six faces to find the surface area. The plank's dimensions are 3, 5, and 30 inches, so there are two surfaces of $3 \times 5 = 15$ square inches, two surfaces of $3 \times 30 = 90$ square inches, and two surfaces of $5 \times 30 = 150$ square inches. Therefore, the total surface area is $15 + 15 + 90 + 90 + 150 + 150 = 510$ square inches. Choice (E) is correct.

22. F Difficulty: Medium

Category: Higher Math / Geometry

Getting to the Answer: SOHCAHTOA helps you remember that:

$$\sin = \frac{\text{opposite}}{\text{hypotenuse}}, \cos = \frac{\text{adjacent}}{\text{hypotenuse}},$$

$$\tan = \frac{\text{opposite}}{\text{adjacent}}$$

$\overline{VX}$ is opposite the given angle and you are told the value of the hypotenuse, so the correct answer will involve the sine function:

$$\sin 55° = \frac{\text{opposite}}{\text{hypotenuse}}$$

$$\sin 55° = \frac{VX}{14}$$

Cross-multiply to find that $VX = 14 \sin 55°$. That's (F).

PERFORM

23. D Difficulty: Medium

Category: Higher Math / Geometry

Getting to the Answer: Don't let the triangle fool you—its presence is wholly irrelevant, as you only need $\overline{XZ}$ itself to answer the question. A bisector of a line segment cuts the segment in half, so it must intersect that segment at its midpoint. Therefore, you are actually looking for the

midpoint of $\overline{XZ}$. According to the figure, the coordinates of $\overline{XZ}$ are (4,8) for X and (10,4) for Z. Plug these points into the midpoint formula and solve:

$$
\begin{aligned}
\text{Midpoint} &= \left(\frac{x_1 + x_2}{2}, \frac{y_1 + y_2}{2} \right) \\
&= \left(\frac{4 + 10}{2}, \frac{8 + 4}{2} \right) \\
&= \left(\frac{14}{2}, \frac{12}{2} \right) \\
&= (7,6)
\end{aligned}
$$

Choice (D) is correct.

24. F Difficulty: High

Category: Higher Math / Geometry

Getting to the Answer: When a square is inscribed within another square, as the shapes are in this question, each of the inner square's vertices bisects one of the outer square's sides, so point Q bisects $\overline{AB}$ and point T bisects $\overline{AD}$. Therefore, $\overline{QA} = \overline{AT}$ and triangle QAT is an isosceles right triangle. Because $QRST$ is a square and $SR = 5$, QR, ST, and TQ also equal 5. Therefore, triangle QAT becomes an isosceles right triangle with a hypotenuse of 5. An isosceles right triangle has sides in the proportion $x:x:x\sqrt{2}$, so $\overline{QA}$ and $\overline{AT}$ each measure $\frac{5}{\sqrt{2}}$. Plug these into the area formula and solve:

$$
\begin{aligned}
\text{Area} &= \frac{1}{2}bh \\
&= \frac{1}{2} \times \left(\frac{5}{\sqrt{2}} \right)^2 \\
&= \frac{1}{2} \times \frac{25}{2} \\
&= \frac{25}{4} \\
&= 6.25
\end{aligned}
$$

That's (F).

25. D   Difficulty: Medium

Category: Higher Math / Geometry

Getting to the Answer: The question tells you that the circumference of the opening (which is a circle) is 8π, so substitute this value in the formula for circumference and solve for r:

$$C = 2\pi r$$
$$8\pi = 2\pi r$$
$$4 = r$$

You now have everything you need to find h, which in this case is the length of the tunnel. Use the formula $V = \pi r^2 h$:

$$2{,}048\pi = \pi(4)^2(h)$$
$$2{,}048 = 16h$$
$$128 = h$$

The tunnel is 128 feet long, which is (D).

26. J   Difficulty: Medium

Category: Higher Math / Geometry

Getting to the Answer: Glancing at the answer choices can help you figure out just what the question is asking for. Here, it's looking for the relationship between b and h that could be given by $\cos \theta$, so use the relationship $\cos \theta = \dfrac{\text{adjacent}}{\text{hypotenuse}}$. The side adjacent to θ is the base, b. You can find the hypotenuse, $\sqrt{b^2 + h^2}$, by using the Pythagorean theorem. Plug these into the equation for cosine to find $\cos \theta = \dfrac{b}{\sqrt{b^2 + h^2}}$, which is (J).

ON YOUR OWN

1.   C   Difficulty: Low

Category: Higher Math / Geometry

Getting to the Answer: You can use the two given points to find the slope:

$$\text{Slope} = \frac{y_2 - y_1}{x_2 - x_1}$$
$$= \frac{3 - 0}{0 - 6} = \frac{3}{-6} = -\frac{1}{2}$$

Choice (C) is correct.

2.   F   Difficulty: Medium

Category: Higher Math / Geometry

Getting to the Answer: Don't answer this question too quickly. The shading is below the line, but that does not necessarily mean that the symbol in the equation will be the less than symbol ($<$). Start by writing the equation of the dashed line shown in the graph in slope-intercept form. Then use the shading to determine the correct inequality symbol. The slope of the line shown in the graph is $\dfrac{1}{4}$ and the y-intercept is -3, so the equation of the dashed line is $y = \dfrac{1}{4}x - 3$. The graph is shaded below the boundary line, so use the $<$ symbol. When written in slope-intercept form, the inequality is $y < \dfrac{1}{4}x - 3$. The inequalities in the answer choices are given in standard form ($Ax + By = C$), so rewrite your answer in this form. Don't forget to reverse the inequality symbol if you multiply or divide by a negative number.

$$y < \frac{1}{4}x - 3$$
$$-\frac{1}{4}x + y < -3$$
$$\frac{1}{4}x - y > 3$$

Multiply everything by 4 to get whole numbers: $x - 4y > 12$. Choice (F) is correct.

3.   C   Difficulty: Medium

Category: Higher Math / Geometry

Getting to the Answer: In a real-world scenario, the slope of a line represents a unit rate, and the y-intercept represents a flat fee or a starting amount. The cost of one linear foot is the same as the unit rate (the cost per linear foot), which is represented by the slope of the line. Use the grid lines and the axis labels to count the rise and the run from the y-intercept of the line (0,150) to the next point that hits an intersection of two grid lines. Pay careful attention to how the grid lines are marked (by 5s on the x-axis and by 25s on the y-axis). The line rises 75 units and runs 5 units, so the slope is $\dfrac{75}{5} = 15$ dollars per linear foot of fence, which is (C). Note that you could also use the slope formula and two points from the graph to find the unit rate.

4.   K   Difficulty: Low

Category: Higher Math / Geometry

Getting to the Answer: To find the distance between two points, plug them into the distance formula and simplify:

$$\text{Distance} = \sqrt{(x_2 - x_1)^2 + (y_2 - y_1)^2}$$
$$= \sqrt{(-2 - 3)^2 + (6 - (-6))^2}$$
$$= \sqrt{(-5)^2 + 12^2}$$
$$= \sqrt{25 + 144}$$
$$= \sqrt{169}$$
$$= 13$$

Choice (K) is correct.

5.   A   Difficulty: Low

Category: Higher Math / Geometry

Getting to the Answer: The coordinates of the midpoint of a line segment with endpoints (x_1, y_1) and (x_2, y_2) are $\left(\frac{x_1 + x_2}{2}, \frac{y_1 + y_2}{2}\right)$. Setting $x_1 = -3$ and $y_1 = -8$, solve for x_2 and y_2. First, $1 = \frac{-3 + x_2}{2}$, or $2 = -3 + x_2$. Add 3 to both sides to get $x_2 = 5$. You can already select (A) based on this because none of the other x-coordinates are correct. To confirm your choice, find y_2 using the same process: $-5 = \frac{-8 + y_2}{2}$, or $-10 = -8 + y_2$. Add 8 to both sides to get $y_2 = -2$. Choice (A) is correct.

6.   G   Difficulty: High

Category: Higher Math / Geometry

Getting to the Answer: The area of a sector is equal to the area of the circle times the fraction of the circle represented by the sector. Start by finding the area of the whole circle: The diameter of the circle extends along the x-axis from -7 to 5, which is 12 units, meaning the radius is 6. Substitute this into the area formula:

$$A = \pi r^2$$
$$A = \pi(6)^2$$
$$A = 36\pi$$

There are 360 degrees in a whole circle, so the fraction of the circle represented by the sector is $\frac{60}{360} = \frac{1}{6}$. The area of the sector is $\frac{1}{6} \times 36\pi = 6\pi$ square units, (G).

7.   D   Difficulty: Medium

Category: Higher Math / Geometry

Getting to the Answer: The reflection of a point or figure is the mirror image of that point or figure. When point B is reflected over the line $y = 3$, the x-coordinate will not change. Point B is 4 units below the line $y = 3$, so it will become 4 units above the line. The new coordinates will be $(4, 3 + 4) = (4, 7)$, which is (D).

8.   J   Difficulty: Medium

Category: Higher Math / Geometry

Getting to the Answer: The set of points described in the question stem form a circle that has its center at $(-3, 4)$. The distance of 5 represents the length of the radius. This means you have everything you need to use the standard equation for a circle with center (h, k) and radius r. The equation is:

$$(x - h)^2 + (y - k)^2 = r^2$$
$$(x - (-3))^2 + (y - 4)^2 = 5^2$$
$$(x + 3)^2 + (y - 4)^2 = 25$$

The answer is (J).

9.   C   Difficulty: Low

Category: Higher Math / Geometry

Getting to the Answer: Because $LM = MN = NL$, triangle LMN is an equilateral triangle. In an equilateral triangle, each of the three interior angles has a measure of $60°$. Thus, $c = 60$. Because $NO = OL = LN$, triangle NOL is also an equilateral triangle, and $b = 60$. Therefore, $b - c = 60 - 60 = 0$, which is (C).

10. F   Difficulty: Medium

Category: Higher Math / Geometry

Getting to the Answer: Because one leg of the triangle is twice as long as the other, let x and $2x$ represent the lengths. Then, use the Pythagorean theorem to find the hypotenuse. Remember, a and b are the lengths of the two legs, and c is the length of the hypotenuse.

$$a^2 + b^2 = c^2$$
$$x^2 + (2x)^2 = c^2$$
$$x^2 + 4x^2 = c^2$$
$$\sqrt{5x^2} = \sqrt{c^2}$$
$$\sqrt{5x^2} = c$$

Although you can't find a numerical value for c, you do know that the number under the radical must be a multiple of 5, so (F) is correct.

11. E   Difficulty: Medium

Category: Higher Math / Geometry

Getting to the Answer: Two of the angles in the triangle have degree measures 30 and 90, which means the third angle must measure 60 degrees. This means you are dealing with a special right triangle and can use the 30°-60°-90° shortcut. In a 30°-60°-90° triangle, the sides are always in the ratio $x:x\sqrt{3}:2x$ (short leg to long leg to hypotenuse). The only length you know is the long leg—the side represented by the ground and the width of the bottom two steps. The ramp is to be placed 8 feet, or 96 inches, from the bottom step, and the steps themselves account for an additional 20 inches, which means this leg of the triangle is 116 inches long. Use the ratio to determine that you need to divide by $\sqrt{3}$ to find the length of the shorter leg. Then multiply the result by 2 to find the length of the hypotenuse, which represents the ramp.

$$116 \div \sqrt{3} = 66.97$$
$$66.97 \times 2 = 133.95$$

The result is about 134 inches, which matches (E).

12. K   Difficulty: High

Category: Higher Math / Geometry

Getting to the Answer: Start with what you know about the shaded square. Because its area is 12, each side must be $\sqrt{12} = 2\sqrt{3}$. Jot this down because you'll need it later.

Triangle ABC is an equilateral triangle, so each of its interior angles measures 60 degrees. This means that the two vertical sides of the square each represent the longer leg of a 30°-60°-90° triangle (the small white triangles on the sides). This leg has a length of $2\sqrt{3}$, making the short legs 2 each. You now have the length of the base of the large equilateral triangle: $2 + 2\sqrt{3} + 2 = 4 + 2\sqrt{3}$. Therefore, each side of the large equilateral triangle has length $4 + 2\sqrt{3}$. The perimeter is the sum of all three sides, so multiply by 3 to get $12 + 6\sqrt{3}$, making (K) correct.

13. C   Difficulty: Medium

Category: Higher Math / Geometry

Getting to the Answer: Because you aren't given values for the length and width of the flowerbed, you can Pick Numbers.

Say the width of the flowerbed is 2 and the length is 4. That means the area of the flowerbed will be 8. Double the width and the length to get the dimensions of the vegetable garden: 4 and 8. This gives the vegetable garden an area of 32, which is 4 times 8, the area of the flowerbed. So the answer is (C).

Algebraically: If the width of the flowerbed is w, its length is $2w$ and its area is $2w^2$. The vegetable garden's width is then $2w$ and its length is $4w$, so the area would be $8w^2$, which is 4 times the area of the flower bed.

14. J   Difficulty: Medium

Category: Higher Math / Geometry

Getting to the Answer: Begin by eliminating H, because $50 - 25\pi$ is a negative value, and that cannot be correct. Because the problem does not provide you with a figure, draw one to visualize what you are being asked.

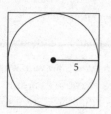

The circle is inscribed within the square, so its radius is half the side of the square. The circle has a radius of 5, so the square has a side of $2 \times 5 = 10$. Therefore, the area of the circle is $5^2\pi = 25\pi$, and the area of the square is $10^2 = 100$. The difference between the area of the square and that of the circle is $100 - 25\pi$, which is (J).

15. E   Difficulty: High

Category: Higher Math / Geometry

Getting to the Answer: You are given that the area of the triangle inside the circle is 24 and the length of the chord is 12. $\overline{OH}$ comes from the center and is perpendicular to $\overline{FG}$, so the former must be the perpendicular bisector of the latter and $\overline{FH} = \overline{HG} = 6$. Plug this into the area formula to find the length of $\overline{OH}$:

$$\text{Area} = \frac{1}{2}bh$$
$$24 = \frac{1}{2}(6)h$$
$$24 = 3h$$
$$8 = h$$

So $\overline{OH} = 8$, making triangle *HOG* a 3-4-5 right triangle with legs 6 and 8 and a hypotenuse of 10. The latter also happens to be the radius of the circle, so the circle's area is $\pi r^2 = \pi(10^2) = 100\pi$ square units. That's (E).

16. H   Difficulty: Medium

Category: Higher Math / Geometry

Getting to the Answer: To find the length of an arc, you will need the measure of the central angle as well as the circumference of the entire circle. In this question, the central angle is 45° and the circumference of the circle is $2\pi(5) = 10\pi$. Plug these values into the proportion and solve:

$$\frac{\text{central angle}}{360°} = \frac{\text{length of arc}}{\text{circumference}}$$
$$\frac{45°}{360°} = \frac{\text{length of arc}}{2\pi r}$$
$$\frac{1}{8} = \frac{\text{length of arc}}{10\pi}$$
$$8 \times (\text{length of arc}) = 10\pi$$
$$\text{length of arc} = \frac{5\pi}{4}$$

That matches (H).

17. C   Difficulty: High

Category: Higher Math / Geometry

Getting to the Answer: When calculating the area of an irregular shape, see if you can divide it into simpler shapes for which you know the area formulas.

The volume of the shovel will be the area of this cross section multiplied by the width of the shovel. Because you know the area formula for rectangles (base × height) and for triangles $\left(\frac{1}{2} \times \text{base} \times \text{height}\right)$, imagine that this figure is a rectangle with a right triangle cut out.

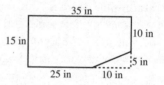

The area of the rectangle is $(15)(35) = 525$ square inches. The area of the triangle is $\frac{1}{2}(10)(5) = 25$ square inches. So the area of the cross section is $525 - 25 = 500$ square inches. Multiply this area by the third dimension, the width of the shovel, to get $(500)(40) = 20,000$ cubic inches. Choice (C) is correct.

18. G   Difficulty: Medium

Category: Higher Math / Geometry

Getting to the Answer: Remembering SOHCAHTOA alone can get you through a lot of trig questions. This question is essentially asking for the length of $\overline{BC}$. The only length you are given is that of the hypotenuse of the triangle, so eliminate J and K as tangent does not involve the hypotenuse. $\overline{BC}$ is opposite $\angle D$, the 37° angle, and adjacent to ∠*B*, the 90 − 37 = 53° angle, so you're looking for either sin 37° or cos 53° in the choices. The former is (G).

19. B   Difficulty: High

Category: Higher Math / Geometry

Getting to the Answer: The mnemonic SOHCAHTOA can help you remember the basic trig functions. Sketch a triangle that includes the information from the question. $\cos = \dfrac{\text{adjacent}}{\text{hypotenuse}}$, so the triangle described by $\cos \theta = \dfrac{5\sqrt{2}}{8}$ is:

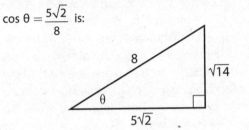

The opposite side can be found using the Pythagorean theorem:

$$\left(5\sqrt{2}\right)^2 + b^2 = 8^2$$
$$50 + b^2 = 64$$
$$b^2 = 14$$
$$b = \sqrt{14}$$

Now use SOHCAHTOA again:

$$\tan \theta = \frac{\text{opposite}}{\text{adjacent}}$$
$$= \frac{\sqrt{14}}{5\sqrt{2}}$$
$$= \frac{\sqrt{7} \cdot \sqrt{2}}{5 \cdot \sqrt{2}}$$
$$= \frac{\sqrt{7}}{5}$$

This matches (B).

20. H   Difficulty: High

Category: Higher Math / Geometry

Getting to the Answer: This question requires quite a bit of thought. The graph of a parabola is symmetric with respect to its axis of symmetry (the imaginary vertical line that passes through the *x*-coordinate of the vertex). This means that each *x*-intercept must be the same distance from the vertex. Take a careful look at the values in the table. The *y*-values start at 3.5, decrease to a minimum value of −4.5, and then turn around. The points on each side of the minimum have the same *y*-values (−4), which means you've found the vertex, (5,−4.5). The *x*-intercept given in the table is (2,0), which is 3 horizontal units to the left of 5. Therefore, the other *x*-intercept must be 3 horizontal units to the right of 5, which is (8,0). This means (H) is correct.

21. D   Difficulty: Medium

Category: Higher Math / Geometry

Getting to the Answer: You're given that $B\left(6,-\sqrt{3}\right)$ is the midpoint of $A\left(\sqrt{2},4\right)$ and $C(x, y)$, so 6 is the average of $\sqrt{2}$ and *x*, and $-\sqrt{3}$ is the average of 4 and *y*:

$$\frac{\sqrt{2} + x}{2} = 6$$
$$\sqrt{2} + x = 12$$
$$x = 12 - \sqrt{2} \approx 10.59$$

and:

$$\frac{4 + y}{2} = -\sqrt{3}$$
$$4 + y = -2\sqrt{3}$$
$$y = -2\sqrt{3} - 4 \approx -7.46$$

Choice (D) is correct.

22. F   Difficulty: High

Category: Higher Math / Geometry

Getting to the Answer: Don't get thrown off by the variables. If the question stem talks about distance, plug values into the distance formula. The distance between $(a,2)$ and $(16,a)$ is $\sqrt{(a - 2)^2 + (16 - a)^2} = 10$. The algebra required to solve this equation involves multiple

Answers & Explanations

steps, so Backsolving may be the quickest route to the correct answer. Trying (F) yields the correct answer:

$$\sqrt{(10-2)^2 + (16-10)^2} = \sqrt{8^2 + 6^2}$$
$$= \sqrt{64 + 36}$$
$$= \sqrt{100}$$
$$= 10$$

To solve algebraically, you would square both sides of the distance equation, FOIL out the parentheses and combine like terms, set the resulting equation equal to 0, and finally factor:

$$\sqrt{(a-2)^2 + (16-a)^2} = 10$$
$$(a-2)^2 + (16-a)^2 = 100$$
$$\left(a^2 - 4a + 4\right) + \left(256 - 32a + a^2\right) = 100$$
$$2a^2 - 36a + 260 = 100$$
$$2a^2 - 36a + 160 = 0$$
$$2\left(a^2 - 18a + 80\right) = 0$$
$$a^2 - 18a + 80 = 0$$
$$(a-8)(a-10) = 0$$

Setting each factor equal to 0 gives $a = 8$ or $a = 10$. This confirms that (F) is correct.

23. B Difficulty: High

Category: Higher Math / Geometry

Getting to the Answer: Did you notice that four of the five answer choices resemble the Pythagorean theorem? This should prompt you to try thinking about this word problem as a geometry question involving triangles. Remember, the answer choices can give you great clues about how to tackle a question.

First, figure out where each person has gone. Bob drove at 60 mph and went north for half an hour and then east for an hour, so he traveled 30 miles north and 60 miles east. Linda drove at 50 mph for 1 hour east and half an hour north, so she went 50 miles east and 25 miles north.

Drawing a diagram will be very helpful in making sense of this question:

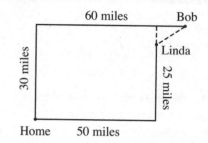

From the diagram, you can see that the distance between Bob and Linda when they both arrive at work is the hypotenuse of a right triangle. The shorter leg of the triangle is $(30 - 25)$, and the longer leg is $(60 - 50)$. Use the Pythagorean theorem, $a^2 + b^2 = c^2$, to get the equation $(30 - 25)^2 + (60 - 50)^2 = c^2$. Then determine which of the answer choices is equivalent to your expression. Because the answer choices haven't been simplified, there's no need to simplify your answer.

Take the square root of both sides of your equation to find that (B) is the correct answer. (Because any number squared is positive, $(30 - 25)^2$ is equivalent to $(25 - 30)^2$.)

24. J Difficulty: Low

Category: Higher Math / Geometry

Getting to the Answer: Visualize the situation and/or make a few sketches. Try to imagine as many points of intersection as possible. Here's a way to get four:

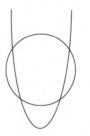

There's no way to get more, so (J) is correct.

25. B Difficulty: Medium

Category: Higher Math / Geometry

Getting to the Answer: According to the graph, one x-intercept is to the left of the y-axis, and the other is to the right. This tells you that one value of x is positive, while the other is negative, so you can immediately eliminate A, C, and E (both factors have the same sign). To choose between (B) and D, find the x-intercepts by setting each factor equal to 0 and solving for x. In (B), the x-intercepts are 7 and −3. In D, the x-intercepts are 1 and −10. Choice (B) is correct because the x-intercepts are exactly 10 units apart, while the x-intercepts in D are 11 units apart.

26. H Difficulty: High

Category: Higher Math / Geometry

Getting to the Answer: If you can tell at a glance that a question is going to take several minutes, save it until you've done all the easier problems.

In the equation of an ellipse, $\dfrac{(x-h)^2}{a^2} + \dfrac{(y-k)^2}{b^2}$, the center is at (h,k), the length of the horizontal axis is $2a$, and the length of the vertical axis is $2b$. Putting this together, the ellipse looks something like this:

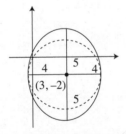

The largest circle possible is dotted on the diagram. Notice that it has the same center as the ellipse and has a radius of 4. In the standard equation for a circle, $(x-h)^2 + (y-k)^2 = r^2$, (h,k) is the center, and r is the radius. Plugging into the formula, this circle's equation is $(x-3)^2 + (y+2)^2 = 4^2 = 16$, which is (H).

27. B Difficulty: High

Category: Higher Math / Geometry

Getting to the Answer: Whenever two triangles have two equal angles, they are similar triangles. When you notice a triangle within a triangle, like the one in this figure, pay special attention to the angles that are shared by both triangles.

The triangle with hypotenuse b that is formed by the dotted line is similar to $\triangle PQR$. The sides of this triangle, therefore, will be in proportion to the sides of $\triangle PQR$. Your job, then, is to evaluate the answer choices to find which ratio describes the ratio of the smaller triangle to $\triangle PQR$. Side d is the shortest side of the smaller triangle, and a is the shortest side of $\triangle PQR$. Side c is the longer leg of the smaller triangle, and b is the longer leg of $\triangle PQR$. Therefore, the ratio between the two pairs of sides is the same, and $\dfrac{d}{a} = \dfrac{b}{c}$, which is (B).

28. F Difficulty: Medium

Category: Higher Math / Geometry

Getting to the Answer: Picking Numbers can make a theoretical question much more concrete. If you're not sure which answer choice makes the most sense, assume each side starts with length 1 and try each answer out. The area starts as $1 \times 1 = 1$, so triple the area is 3. As always, start with the middle choice:

H: area $= (1 \times 9)(1 \times 9) = 81$. This is too big, so try a smaller choice.

G: area $= (1 \times 3)(1 \times 3) = 9$. Still too big.

(F): area $= \left(1 \times \sqrt{3}\right)\left(1 \times \sqrt{3}\right) = \sqrt{3} \times \sqrt{3} = 3$. This is the correct answer.

29. D Difficulty: Medium

Category: Higher Math / Geometry

Getting to the Answer: If you have trouble keeping track of the variables, you can Pick Numbers, but many students will find it slightly faster to work with the variables in a question like this.

Use FOIL to find that the rectangle has an area of $(x+3)$ times $(x+7) = x^2 + 10x + 21$, and the square that is being removed has an area of x^2. The area after removing the square is $x^2 + 10x + 21 - x^2 = 10x + 21$, which is (D).

30. K Difficulty: Medium

Category: Higher Math / Geometry

Getting to the Answer: The formula for the area of a trapezoid is $A = \left(\dfrac{b_1 + b_2}{2}\right)h$, where b_1 and b_2 are the lengths of the parallel sides. Remember, you could think of it as the height times the average of the bases. You're given the height (3 inches), one base (8 inches), and enough information to figure out the other base. Notice that $\triangle ABE$ is a 3-4-5 triangle, so $AE = 4$ inches. And if you were to drop an altitude down from point C, you'd get another 3-4-5 triangle on the right:

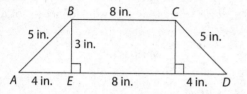

Now you can see that the bottom base is 16 inches. Plug these numbers into the formula:

$$A = \left(\frac{b_1 + b_2}{2}\right)h$$
$$= \left(\frac{8 + 16}{2}\right) \times 3$$
$$= 12 \times 3 = 36$$

The answer is (K). If you don't remember the whole equation on Test Day, note that you can also just find the areas of the two side triangles and the rectangle in the middle and add them all up.

31. D Difficulty: Medium

Category: Higher Math / Algebra

Getting to the Answer: At first glance, this looks like an esoteric geometry question. Who ever heard of such a formula? But when you think about the question a bit, you realize that you don't really have to understand the formula. You certainly don't have to remember it—it's right there in the question.

In fact, this is not really a geometry question at all. It's just an "evaluate the algebraic expression" question in disguise. All it really asks you to do is plug the given values, $h = 2$ and $c = 6$, into the formula:

$$A = \frac{2ch}{3} + \frac{h^3}{2c}$$
$$= \frac{2(6)(2)}{3} + \frac{(2)^3}{2(6)}$$
$$= 8 + \frac{2}{3} = 8\frac{2}{3}$$

Choice (D) is correct.

32. G Difficulty: Medium

Category: Higher Math / Geometry

Getting to the Answer: The central angle of minor arc AB is 40°, which is $\frac{1}{9}$ of the whole circle's 360°. The length of minor arc AB, therefore, is $\frac{1}{9}$ of the whole circle's circumference.

$$C = 2\pi r = 2\pi(9) = 18\pi$$
$$\frac{1}{9}C = \frac{1}{9}(18\pi) = 2\pi$$

The answer is (G).

33. B Difficulty: High

Category: Higher Math / Geometry

Getting to the Answer: To answer this question, sketch an "unfolded" drawing of the solid and add dimensions to your sketch as you reason through the information provided in the question:

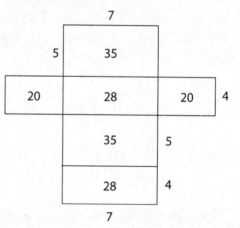

Opposite faces of a rectangular solid are congruent, so there are six faces, with the corresponding areas shown above. Look for factors that will produce the given areas. These factors are the dimensions of the solid: $7 \times 4 = 28$, $7 \times 5 = 35$, and $4 \times 5 = 20$. The dimensions are 7, 4, and 5. Use the volume formula to arrive at the correct answer: $V = lwh$, so $V = 7 \times 5 \times 4 = 140$ cubic centimeters, which is (B).

34. G Difficulty: Medium

Category: Higher Math / Geometry

Getting to the Answer: The cube is $6 \times 6 \times 6$, so its volume is 216. The sphere has radius 3, so:

$$\text{Volume of sphere} = \frac{4}{3}\pi r^3$$
$$= \frac{4}{3}\pi(3^3)$$
$$= 36\pi$$

The difference is $216 - 36\pi \approx 103$ cubic units, which is (G).

35. C Difficulty: High

Category: Higher Math / Geometry

Getting to the Answer: Use the given volume, 50, to get h in terms of x:

$$\text{Volume} = \text{length} \times \text{width} \times \text{height}$$
$$50 = x \cdot x \cdot h$$
$$h = \frac{50}{x^2}$$

The area you're looking for is equal to four lateral faces and one bottom face.

Each lateral face has area $x \cdot h = x \cdot \frac{50}{x^2} = \frac{50}{x}$, and the base has area x^2, so the total area you're looking for is:

$$4\left(\frac{50}{x}\right) + x^2 = \frac{200}{x} + x^2$$

This matches (C).

36. K Difficulty: High

Category: Higher Math / Geometry

Getting to the Answer: Use the given formula for finding the volume of a right circular cone. If the radius of cone B is x and the height is y, then the volume is $\frac{1}{3}\pi x^2 y$. The radius of cone A will be $\frac{1}{5}x$ and the height will be $\frac{1}{4}y$, so the volume is:

$$\frac{1}{3}\pi\left(\frac{1}{5}x\right)^2\left(\frac{1}{4}y\right) = \frac{1}{300}\pi x^2 y$$

The ratio of the volume of cone A to that of cone B is therefore:

$$\frac{\frac{1}{300}\pi x^2 y}{\frac{1}{3}\pi x^2 y} = \frac{1}{300} \div \frac{1}{3} = \frac{1}{100}$$

Choice (K) is correct.

37. D Difficulty: Medium

Category: Higher Math / Geometry

Getting to the Answer: You'll need to think logically to answer this question. It doesn't really matter that Quito lies on the equator. Because Earth makes a complete rotation about its axis in 24 hours, any point on its surface must rotate through 360 degrees in that time.

Quito rotates 360 degrees in the 24 hours from noon on January 1 to noon on January 2. There are 3 hours between noon on January 2 and 3:00 PM on January 2, so it rotates an additional $\frac{3}{24} \times 360 = 45°$, for a total of $360 + 45 = 405°$, which matches (D).

38. K Difficulty: Medium

Category: Higher Math / Geometry

Getting to the Answer: Don't try to do questions like this in your head. Set up an equation that relates the thing you're looking for to the things you know and then solve for the thing you're looking for.

You know the angle of elevation and the distance from the base of the flagpole, and you're looking for the height of the flagpole. That means you know one angle and the length of the side adjacent to it, and you're looking for the length of the side opposite it. Which trig function describes the relationship between an angle and the opposite and adjacent sides? Tangent does: $\tan 40° = \frac{f}{100}$, where f is the height of the flagpole.

Therefore, $100 \tan 40° = f$. The question tells you that $\tan 40°$ is approximately 0.839, so f is approximately $100(0.839) = 83.9$. The best approximation of this is (K).

39. A Difficulty: Medium

Category: Higher Math / Geometry

Getting to the Answer: Use the fact that $\sin = \dfrac{\text{opposite}}{\text{hypotenuse}}$ to sketch a right triangle and fill in the sides provided by $\sin \theta = \dfrac{\sqrt{11}}{2\sqrt{3}}$:

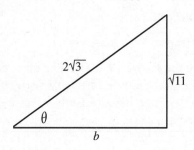

The length of side b can be found using the Pythagorean theorem:

$$\left(\sqrt{11}\right)^2 + b^2 = \left(2\sqrt{3}\right)^2$$
$$11 + b^2 = (4 \times 3)$$
$$b^2 = 12 - 11 = 1$$
$$b = 1$$

So if $b = 1$, $\cos \theta = \dfrac{1}{2\sqrt{3}}$. This matches (A).

40. K Difficulty: High

Category: Higher Math / Geometry

Getting to the Answer: On Test Day, be on the lookout for questions that simply ask you to plug values into a given formula. They may look tough, but they won't require you to do much math.

Here, the question is asking for the expression that represents the value of Z. With the values of two of the three angles known, you can determine that the unmarked angle has a measure of $180° - 35° - 45° = 100°$. You are given the length of $\overline{DS}$ along with its opposite angle, so plug that information into the law of sines to solve for Z:

$$\frac{\sin 45°}{7} = \frac{\sin 100°}{Z}$$
$$Z \sin 45° = 7 \sin 100°$$
$$Z = \frac{7 \sin 100°}{\sin 45°}$$

So (K) is correct.

Answers & Explanations

CHAPTER 14

PRACTICE

13. C   Difficulty: High

Category: Higher Math / Statistics and Probability

Getting to the Answer: Follow the steps for finding standard deviation:

Step 1: Find the mean of the data; it's 82.

Step 2: For each data point, subtract the mean and square the result; you get $(100 - 82)^2 = 324$, $(85 - 82)^2 = 9$, $(55 - 82)^2 = 729$, $(95 - 82)^2 = 169$, $(75 - 82)^2 = 49$.

Step 3: Find the average of all the squared results; it's 256.

Step 4: Take the square root of the result from Step 3; final answer = 16.

Choice (C) is correct.

14. J   Difficulty: Medium

Category: Higher Math / Statistics and Probability

Getting to the Answer: Break the question into steps. First, find how long it took Michael to fertilize one lawn. Then, use that amount to find how long it took him to fertilize all the lawns. According to the figure, he started the first house at 9:00 and the sixth house at 10:00, so it took him 1 hour, or 60 minutes, to fertilize the lawns of 5 houses (because he *started* the sixth house at 10:00, not *finished* it). This gives a unit rate of $60 \div 5 = 12$ minutes per house. Count the houses in the figure—there are 21. Multiply the unit rate by the number of houses to get $12 \times 21 = 252$ minutes to spray all the lawns. That's (J).

15. B   Difficulty: Low

Category: Higher Math / Statistics and Probability

Getting to the Answer: Read the question stem carefully, identifying parts of the graphic you need—the question asks about litters of 7 or more pups, so you'll only use the heights of the bars for 7, 8, and 9 pups. Of the 200 mice in the sample (which is given in the question stem, so you don't need to add the heights of all the bars), $25 + 14 + 5 = 44$ had a litter of 7 or more pups. This is

$\frac{44}{200} = \frac{22}{100} = 22\%$ of the mice in the sample. Choice (B) is correct.

16. H   Difficulty: Medium

Category: Higher Math / Statistics and Probability

Getting to the Answer: The expected number of returning bald eagles is the sum of the products of each number of returning eagles and its corresponding probability:

$$\begin{aligned} E = {} & 0(0.02) + 1(0.08) + 2(0.15) \\ & + 3(0.28) + 4(0.25) + 5(0.22) \\ = {} & 3.32 \end{aligned}$$

This is closest to 3, so (H) is correct.

17. A   Difficulty: High

Category: Higher Math / Statistics and Probability

Getting to the Answer: Start with the probability formula: $P = \frac{\text{\# desired outcomes}}{\text{\# possible outcomes}}$. Pay attention to numeric keywords such as "at least" to make sure you don't count the wrong items when setting up the probability formula. There are five coin flips, each with two possibilities, so the total number of outcomes is $2 \cdot 2 \cdot 2 \cdot 2 \cdot 2 = 32$. Because at least four of the five flips must be heads, simply writing out all desired outcomes won't take much time: HHHHH, HHHHT, HHHTH, HHTHH, HTHHH, THHHH.

There are six outcomes for which at least four of the flips are heads, so the answer is $\frac{6}{32} = \frac{3}{16}$. Choice (A) is correct.

18. J   Difficulty: Medium

Category: Higher Math / Statistics and Probability

Getting to the Answer: This is a permutation question because order matters. (Imagine the five desks in a row: Charlie, then Sam, then Katy is a different arrangement from Sam, then Charlie, then Katy, so order matters). The most direct approach is to use the Fundamental Counting Principle. Draw three blanks to represent the three students. How many desk options are there for the first student? How many for the second (now that one desk has already been taken)? And for the third? The correct answer is $5 \cdot 4 \cdot 3 = 60$, which is (J).

Answers & Explanations

PERFORM

19. B   Difficulty: Medium

Category: Higher Math / Statistics and Probability

Getting to the Answer: Start by writing the relevant formulas and then fill in the pieces of information you have from the question stem. Keep in mind that ACT questions will often ask you to work with the sum of the terms.

Write the Average formula: *Average = sum of terms* divided by *number of terms*. The average age of all employees will be the sum of the male ages plus the sum of the female ages divided by the total number of employees. To find this, you must find the sum of the male ages and the sum of the female ages independently. First the male employees:

$$42 = \frac{\text{sum of male ages}}{30}$$
$$1{,}260 = \text{sum of male ages}$$

Now the female employees:

$$37 = \frac{\text{sum of female ages}}{20}$$
$$740 = \text{sum of female ages}$$

Finally, put these together:

$$\text{Average age of all employees} = \frac{1{,}260 + 740}{30 + 20}$$
$$= \frac{2{,}000}{50} = 40$$

The correct answer is (B).

20. G   Difficulty: Low

Category: Higher Math / Statistics and Probability

Getting to the Answer: When working with two-way tables, always read the question carefully, identifying which pieces of information you need. Here, you need to focus on the "Against" column and the "1L" and "2L" rows. To stay organized, it may help to circle these pieces of information in the table. There are 58 1Ls and 64 2Ls in the survey sample, for a total of $58 + 64 = 122$ 1Ls and 2Ls. There are 16 1Ls and 12 2Ls against the policy, for a total of $16 + 12 = 28$. This means that 28 out of the 122 1Ls

and 2Ls are against the new policy. Written as a fraction, this is $\frac{28}{122}$, which reduces to $\frac{14}{61}$. Choice (G) is correct.

21. A   Difficulty: High

Category: Higher Math / Statistics and Probability

Getting to the Answer: The question asks for a number of positive four-digit integers. All integers must have 3 as the hundreds digit and either 5 or 9 as the ones digit. Think of the solution as four slots to be filled:

$$\underline{1–9} \ \ \underline{\ 3\ } \ \ \underline{0–9} \ \ \underline{5 \text{ or } 9}$$

If only a 3 can go in the hundreds slot, there is only one possibility. There are only two possibilities for the ones slot (5 and 9). There are 10 possibilities for the tens digit (0–9) but only 9 for the thousands slot (1–9). The total number of possibilities is $9 \times 1 \times 10 \times 2 = 180$, or choice (A).

22. H   Difficulty: High

Category: Higher Math / Statistics and Probability

Getting to the Answer: Little words such as "at least" make a big difference. Here, you need to find the probability of getting 2 or 3 heads. You can get exactly 2 heads three ways: THH, HTH or HHT. You can get exactly 3 heads one way: HHH. So you can get at least 2 heads in 4 ways. Each flip has 2 possible outcomes, so the probability of getting tails (or heads) on any one flip is $\frac{1}{2}$.

$$\text{Probability of THH} = \frac{1}{2} \cdot \frac{1}{2} \cdot \frac{1}{2} = \frac{1}{8}$$

$$\text{Probability of HTH} = \frac{1}{2} \cdot \frac{1}{2} \cdot \frac{1}{2} = \frac{1}{8}$$

$$\text{Probability of HHT} = \frac{1}{2} \cdot \frac{1}{2} \cdot \frac{1}{2} = \frac{1}{8}$$

$$\text{Probability of HHH} = \frac{1}{2} \cdot \frac{1}{2} \cdot \frac{1}{2} = \frac{1}{8}$$

The probability of any of these four combinations is $\frac{1}{8} + \frac{1}{8} + \frac{1}{8} + \frac{1}{8} = \frac{4}{8} = \frac{1}{2}$. This means (H) is correct.

ON YOUR OWN

1. C   Difficulty: Medium

Category: Higher Math / Statistics and Probability

Getting to the Answer: More difficult questions require that you work step-by-step. Make sure you know what the question is asking. Here, you need to use the average formula a couple of times.

Average cans per day for first four days:

$$10 = \frac{\text{sum of cans so far}}{4 \text{ days}}$$
$$40 = \text{sum of cans so far}$$

So, Mary has collected 40 cans so far, and she needs 160 more cans. She has 10 days left to collect them, so for the remaining days, she must average $\frac{160 \text{ cans}}{10 \text{ days}}$, or 16 cans per day, which is (C).

2. H   Difficulty: High

Category: Higher Math / Statistics and Probability

Getting to the Answer: Use the average formula: Average $= \frac{\text{sum of terms}}{\text{number of terms}}$. Set up an expression that can be solved to find the total number of class sessions. Let $x =$ the total number of sessions:

$$16 = \frac{19 + 17 + 15(x-2)}{x}$$
$$16x = 36 + 15x - 30$$
$$16x - 15x = 36 - 30$$
$$x = 6 \text{ sessions}$$

Choice (H) is correct.

3. B   Difficulty: Medium

Category: Higher Math / Statistics and Probability

Getting to the Answer: Always read the axis labels carefully when a question involves a chart or graph. *Frequency*, which is plotted along the vertical axis, tells you how many students missed the number of questions indicated under each bar. Evaluate each statement as efficiently as you can.

Choice A: Add the bar heights that represent students who missed 5 or more questions: $7 + 3 + 3 + 2 = 15$. Then, find the total number of students represented, which is the number who missed fewer than 5 questions plus the 15 you just found: $2 + 3 + 4 + 6 = 15$, plus the 15 you already found, for a total of 30 students. The statement is not true because 15 is exactly half (not more than half) of 30.

Choice B: This calculation will take a bit of time, so skip it for now.

Choice C: The tallest bar tells you which number of questions was missed most often, which was 5 questions, not 3 questions, so this statement is not true.

Choice D: The number of students from Mr. Foster's class who took the test that day is the sum of the heights of the bars, which you already know is 30, not 36.

Choice E: The question doesn't provide any information about passing scores, so there is no way to determine whether this statement is true.

This means (B) must be correct. Mark it and move on to the next question. In case you're curious, you find the mean by multiplying each number of questions missed by the corresponding frequency, adding all the products, and dividing by the total number of students, which you already know is 30:

$$\text{mean} = \frac{2 + 6 + 12 + 24 + 35 + 18 + 21 + 16}{30}$$
$$= \frac{134}{30} = 4.4\overline{6}$$

The mean is indeed between 4 and 5.

4. J   Difficulty: Low

Category: Higher Math / Statistics and Probability

Getting to the Answer: Start by finding the total amount of water. To make the calculations easier, add halves together and do the same for quarters. The total amount is:

$$\frac{1}{2} + \frac{1}{2} + 1\frac{1}{2} + 1\frac{1}{2} + 1\frac{1}{2} + 1\frac{1}{2} + 2\frac{1}{2} +$$
$$2\frac{1}{2} + \frac{3}{4} + \frac{1}{4} + 1 + 1 + 2 = 17 \text{ gallons}$$

Now divide by the number of campers, which you can find by counting the Xs in the plot: There are 12, so each camper should receive $\frac{17}{12} = 1\frac{5}{12}$ gallons of water each, which is (J).

5.   D   Difficulty: Medium

Category: Higher Math / Statistics and Probability

Getting to the Answer: There are more subcompact cars than any other type, so the largest section of the circle graph should represent 64 out of 320 cars. This means $\frac{64}{320} = \frac{1}{5}$ of the circle graph should represent subcompact cars. There are 360° in a full circle, so the angle measure of the subcompact car section should be one-fifth of that, or $\frac{1}{5} \cdot 360° = 72°$. Choice (D) is correct.

6.   H   Difficulty: Medium

Category: Higher Math / Statistics and Probability

Getting to the Answer: The median of a set of data is the middle term when the data are arranged in numerical order. The test grades are arranged in the table in grade intervals that are in order. Because there are 25 grades, the median will be the 13th term. There are $5 + 7 = 12$ grades in the first two intervals, which means the 13th grade must be in the next interval, C (71–80). Choice (H) is correct.

7.   D   Difficulty: Low

Category: Higher Math / Statistics and Probability

Getting to the Answer: This question tests your ability to read a probability distribution table. The probability that the randomly generated number will be odd is $P(X = 1)$ $+ P(X = 3)$, which is $\frac{1}{10} + \frac{3}{20} = \frac{2}{20} + \frac{3}{20} = \frac{5}{20}$. This simplifies to $\frac{1}{4}$, making (D) the correct answer.

8.   K   Difficulty: Medium

Category: Higher Math / Statistics and Probability

Getting to the Answer: The expected value of a random discrete variable is the weighted average of all possible

values that the variable can take on. The weights are determined by the probability distribution. To find the expected value, multiply each possible value by its given probability and then add the products:

$$E(X) = \frac{1}{5}(0) + \frac{1}{10}(1) + \frac{3}{10}(2) + \frac{3}{20}(3) + \frac{1}{4}(4)$$

$$= 0 + \frac{1}{10} + \frac{6}{10} + \frac{9}{20} + 1$$

$$= \frac{2}{20} + \frac{12}{20} + \frac{9}{20} + \frac{20}{20}$$

$$= \frac{43}{20} = 2\frac{3}{20}$$

Choice (K) is correct.

9.   D   Difficulty: Medium

Category: Higher Math / Statistics and Probability

Getting to the Answer: The probability that something will happen is the number of desired outcomes divided by the number of possible outcomes. Once Alicia has drawn the marble numbered 25, there are 49 marbles left in the box, or 49 possible outcomes. How many of these are desired outcomes? Alicia wins if she draws a marble with the same units digit (the number in the ones place) as the one she already drew, so there are 4 winning marbles (05, 15, 35, and 45). Therefore, the probability that she will win on her next draw is $\frac{4}{49}$, which is (D).

10.   H   Difficulty: Medium

Category: Higher Math / Statistics and Probability

Getting to the Answer: Think of each character as a slot to be filled and use the Fundamental Counting Principle. Each character can be 1 of 24 letters or 1 of 10 numbers, for a total of 34 possibilities for each character. Thus, the total number of possibilities is $34 \cdot 34 \cdot 34 \cdot 34 \cdot 34 \cdot 34$, which can be written as 34^6. Choice (H) is correct.

11.   C   Difficulty: Low

Category: Higher Math / Statistics and Probability

Getting to the Answer: The average is the sum of the terms divided by the number of terms, even when the terms are algebraic expressions.

Answers & Explanations

$$\frac{(2x + 5) + (5x - 6) + (-4x + 2)}{3} = \frac{3x + 1}{3}$$

$$= \frac{3x}{3} + \frac{1}{3}$$

$$= x + \frac{1}{3}$$

This matches (C).

12. G

Category: Medium

Difficulty: Higher Math / Statistics and Probability

Getting to the Answer: Use the formula for finding an average:

$$\text{Average} = \frac{\text{sum of the terms}}{\text{number of terms}}$$

If Brooks's average number of points per game is 30, then you can determine his number of points in Game 6, *x*, using the average formula.

$$30 = \frac{28 + 31 + 20 + 42 + 32 + x}{6}$$

$$30 = \frac{153 + x}{6}$$

$$180 = 153 + x$$

$$27 = x$$

Brooks's average was 30 points per game, so he scored 27 points, (G), in Game 6.

13. A Difficulty: Medium

Category: Higher Math / Statistics and Probability

Getting to the Answer: Read the question carefully: The largest *actual* increase is not necessarily the largest *percent* increase. Percent increase is the actual increase over the original amount, so you are looking for the largest increase, in dollar amounts, from the smallest original amount. Although the $8,000 increase from 1993 to 1994 is the largest dollar amount, it starts from a larger original amount than do increases in the other years and therefore may not be the largest *percent* increase. The increases from 1989 to 1990 and 1990 to 1991 are both $5,000, so you can already eliminate B, since its original amount is larger. Similarly, the increases from 1991 to 1992 and 1992 to 1993 are $3,000, and they both start from a larger original amount than (A). Evaluate the remaining answer choices:

Choice (A): $\frac{\$5,000}{\$20,000} \cdot 100\% = 25\%$

Choice E: $\frac{\$8,000}{\$36,000} \cdot 100\% = 22.2\%$

The percent increase from 1989 to 1990 is larger, so (A) is correct.

14. J Difficulty: Low

Category: Higher Math / Statistics and Probability

Getting to the Answer: A question like this tests your ability to read a graph and its key. Here, you want the percent of the participants who experienced severe side effects, regardless of whether they received the drug or the inert pills. That's sections C and F, so add 6.5% + 27.75% to arrive at the correct answer, 34.25%, which is (J).

15. B Difficulty: Medium

Category: Higher Math / Statistics and Probability

Getting to the Answer: There are several different ways to approach this question, but the quickest is to find the percents that fit the two categories (one of which you already calculated in the previous question), subtract, and then multiply by 400. You already know that 34.25% experienced severe side effects. Based on sections A and D of the circle graph, a total of 43.75% experienced mild or no side effects. That's a difference of 9.5%, so 0.095(400), or 38, more participants experienced mild or no side effects than severe side effects. Choice (B) is correct.

16. J Difficulty: High

Category: Higher Math / Statistics and Probability

Getting to the Answer: This question is a bit more involved. It's not asking what percent of *all* the participants were given the drug, so 50% is not the correct answer. Instead, you need to think only of the participants who experienced severe side effects. Of the 34.25% who experienced severe side effects, 27.75% were given the drug. That's 27.75% out of 34.25%, or $\frac{27.75}{34.25} \approx 0.8102$, which is about 81%. Choice (J) is correct.

Answers & Explanations

17. E   Difficulty: Medium

Category: Higher Math / Statistics and Probability

Getting to the Answer: Don't let the word *combination* confuse you. This is a very straightforward question. There are 90 females who could be chosen. For *each* of those 90 females, there are 125 males who could be chosen. That makes $90 \cdot 125 = 11{,}250$ different pairs of students who could be chosen. Choice (E) is correct.

18. K   Difficulty: High

Category: Higher Math / Statistics and Probability

Getting to the Answer: Distinct permutations are permutations without repetition. You need to find the number of unique orderings of the letters STATISTICS. If all 10 letters were different, the number of unique orderings would be 10!. Because the S and the T are each repeated three times and the I is repeated twice, you must divide by 3! to account for the repeated S, again by 3! to account for the repeated T, and by 2! to account for the repeated I. The result is $\dfrac{10!}{(3!)(3!)(2!)}$, which is (K).

Note that this process is the same as using the formula for "indistinguishable" outcomes: $\dfrac{n!}{a! \times b! \times \ldots}$. The number of letters is 10 (so $n = 10$), and there are 3 indistinguishable S's, 3 indistinguishable T's, and 2 indistinguishable I's (so $a = 3$, $b = 3$, and $c = 2$).

19. A   Difficulty: Medium

Category: Higher Math / Statistics and Probability

Getting to the Answer: The question asks for the probability of picking two green marbles. The probability of picking a green marble the first time is $\dfrac{7}{2 + 3 + 7} = \dfrac{7}{12}$.

Because one green marble is taken out of the bag, the probability of picking a green marble the second time is $\dfrac{7 - 1}{12 - 1} = \dfrac{6}{11}$. The probability of picking two green marbles is the product: $\left(\dfrac{7}{12}\right)\left(\dfrac{6}{11}\right) = \dfrac{42}{132} = \dfrac{7}{22}$. Choice (A) is correct.

Note that you could eliminate E right away because the probability that an event will occur cannot be greater than 1.

20. G   Difficulty: High

Category: Higher Math / Statistics and Probability

Getting to the Answer: There's a lot going on in this question, so find the most concrete point and begin there. You are told that the chance for a girl to win the scholarship is 0.55. Because this is more than half, there must be more girls than boys in the junior class, so eliminate H, J, and K. The value 0.55 isn't much greater than 0.5, so if you were low on time on Test Day, (G) would be a great guess.

To answer this question more formally, use the probability formula:

$$\text{Probability} = \frac{\text{number of desired outcomes}}{\text{number of possible outcomes}}$$

Because 0.55 is the probability that a girl would win, the 154 girls are the desired outcomes, and the total number of students (boys and girls) is the number of possible outcomes. Call this total x and use the formula to solve for x:

$$0.55 = \frac{154}{x}$$
$$x = \frac{154}{0.55}$$
$$x = 280$$

With 280 total students and 154 girls, there must be $280 - 154 = 126$ boys. That's (G).

21. E   Difficulty: Medium

Category: Higher Math / Statistics and Probability

Getting to the Answer: Completing at least 1 pass in the first 5 attempts and completing 0 passes are complementary events. Thus,

$$P(x \geq 1) = 1 - P(x = 0)$$
$$= 1 - 0.0219$$
$$= 0.9781$$

Choice (E) is correct.

22. G   Difficulty: High

Category: Higher Math / Statistics and Probability

Getting to the Answer: Determine the ratio that is not given and compare ratios to find the greatest. The ratio of buntings to total birds and the ratio of larks to total birds are given as 35:176 and 5:11, respectively. Assume that the total number of birds that have been counted in the meadow is 176. This automatically means that 35 buntings have been counted. The question also gives the information that 5 out of 11 of the birds are larks. Set up the proportion $\frac{5}{11} = \frac{x}{176}$, where x represents the number of larks in the field. Then:

$$x = 176 \times \frac{5}{11} = 80$$

Then find the number of sparrows, which is the number of birds remaining: $176 - 35 - 80 = 61$.

Because there are more larks in the meadow than any other type of bird (80 larks), the greatest probability is that a lark, (G), would be chosen at random.

23. C   Difficulty: High

Category: Higher Math / Statistics and Probability

Getting to the Answer: Probability is

$\frac{\#\text{ of desired outcomes}}{\#\text{ of possible outcomes}}$. Jamal wants the probability of selecting a white sock to be $\frac{1}{5}$. Because there are already 10 white socks, the ratio of desired outcomes (white socks) to possible outcomes (all socks) must be $\frac{1}{5} = \frac{10}{50}$. To get to 50 total socks, Jamal will need to add 40 black socks, or (C). Note that E is a trap. The question asks for the number of black socks Jamal needs to add, not the total number of socks that should be in the suitcase.

24. H   Difficulty: Medium

Category: Higher Math / Statistics and Probability

Getting to the Answer: The probability that an event will occur is the number of desired outcomes (number of available cars that have a rating of at least 25 mpg) divided by the number of total possible outcomes (total number of cars). "At least" means that much or greater, so find the number of cars represented by the two bars to the right of 25 in the histogram: $20 + 6 = 26$ cars. Now find the total number of available cars: $8 + 16 + 20 + 6 = 50$. Finally, divide to find the indicated probability: $\frac{26}{50} = \frac{13}{25}$. That's (H).

25. C   Difficulty: High

Category: Higher Math / Statistics and Probability

Getting to the Answer: This question actually has two parts: Find the expected attendance rate and then use that to find the expected number of occupied seats on any given day. The expected attendance rate is the sum of the products of each attendance rate and its corresponding probability:

$$E(\text{att. rate}) = 0.15(0.4) + 0.25(0.5)$$
$$+ 0.35(0.6) + 0.15(0.7) + 0.10(0.8)$$
$$= 0.58$$

To calculate the expected number of occupied seats, multiply the expected attendance rate by the total number of seats in the stadium. The result is $0.58(12,000) = 6,960$, which is (C).

CHAPTER 16

PRACTICE

Suggested Passage Map notes:

¶1: FLW: Notable architectural achievement, Fallingwater

¶2: Choosing site and techniques

¶3: Modern design + interaction w/nature

¶4: Critics' opinions; house connects people, nature

4. F   Difficulty: Low

Category: Key Ideas and Details / Inference

Getting to the Answer: Remember that the answer to an Inference question will always be directly supported by the text. Your Passage Map notes should point you to the second paragraph. The author writes that Kaufmann had originally planned to put the house on a flat site near the bottom of the waterfall, but Wright convinced him to accept a more daring location right over the waterfall. Predict that Kaufmann's original plans were not daring; they were basic. Choices G and H are the opposite of your prediction; Wright, not Kaufmann, had a daring or idealistic plan for the house. Choice J is a distortion; the passage never indicates the plans were architecturally unsound. The correct answer, which also matches your prediction, is (F).

5. D   Difficulty: Medium

Category: Key Ideas and Details / Inference

Getting to the Answer: When a narrow Inference question asks you to characterize an opinion, be sure to keep in mind whose opinion it is. The wrong way to approach this question would be to use your own impression of caves as your guide. It's the critics' notions of a cave that are important here. According to the cited sentence, critics compared Fallingwater to a cave because the house provided "a psychological and physical safe haven from a harsh, violent world" (lines 50–51). The critics' use of cave imagery alludes to a feeling of safety. Choices A, B, and C are distortions of what the critics alluded to in their characterization. Choice (D) is correct.

6. H   Difficulty: Medium

Category: Key Ideas and Details / Global

Getting to the Answer: Global questions often require you merely to combine central ideas and facts in the passage. At the end of the third paragraph, you learn that Wright's ideal dwelling for the waterfall site "was not simply a modern extravaganza or a direct extension of natural surroundings; rather, it was a little of both" (lines 42–44). Your answer must incorporate both elements. The passage offers no evidence that Kaufmann's money and position influenced Wright's thinking; F is incorrect. Choice G is out of scope; durability refers to a specific aspect of construction, but this Global question addresses more general issues. Choice J is a distortion; Wright wanted the house to be an "extension of natural surroundings," not a triumph over them. The correct answer is (H).

PERFORM

Suggested Passage Map notes:

¶1: 1st images of Mars: disappointing

¶2: Soil sample expert didn't find life forms

¶3: Reason for no life: radiation through thin atmos.

¶4: Limitation of landing sites

¶5: Comparing Mars, Antarctica

¶6: Influence on view of early life

7. D   Difficulty: Medium

Category: Key Ideas and Details / Inference

Getting to the Answer: The question stem does not point to any one paragraph definitively; the author discusses many differences between the two planets. When you receive limited help from the question stem, count on your Passage Map to help you confirm or rule out choices. Eliminate A, because according to Paragraph 2, no organic compounds were found in Martian soil. Choices B and C are distortions of the facts presented in the passage. The correct answer, then, is (D).

8. H **Difficulty:** Medium

Category: Key Ideas and Details / Global

Getting to the Answer: Use your Passage Map to answer questions on the main idea of a passage or paragraph. Your notes should indicate that Paragraph 2 discusses four experiments carried out by the Viking landers. These experiments were designed to detect signs of life but were inconclusive. Look for a match to this general prediction. Choices F and J are distortions of the facts within the passage. Choice G is out of scope; no such conclusions are suggested about Earth. The correct answer is (H).

9. A **Difficulty:** High

Category: Key Ideas and Details / Inference

Getting to the Answer: With generally worded question stems, skim your Passage Map and look for the choice that matches the general idea of the passage. *Martian rocks* are discussed in Paragraph 5: the author states that some scientists hypothesize that life on Mars may have "escaped worsening conditions by … seeking refuge in rocks" (lines 69–70), as happened on Earth. Predict that the way in which organisms may exist despite harsh conditions is similar on Earth and Mars. Choice (A) is correct; this matches the prediction and the main argument. Choices B and C are distortions of the facts in the passage. Choice D is incorrect because it suggests that the same organisms that survived in Antarctica could also survive on Mars. There's no suggestion that the organisms would be the same (blue-green algae), just that some type of organism could exist in rocks.

ON YOUR OWN

Suggested Passage Map notes:

¶1: N. Amer. suburb born out of need to "get away"

¶2: Suburbs near cities, which people use for work and play

¶3: What suburbs should be vs. what they are; lack community

¶4: Suburban structure; dependency on cars

¶5: Critics think no more suburbs; author disagrees → quality can improve

1. C **Difficulty:** Medium

Category: Key Ideas and Details / Global

Getting to the Answer: While reading every passage, you should be asking yourself the author's purpose. If you do, "main purpose" questions will be easy to answer: just pick the choice that matches your prediction. The author relates several negative aspects of suburbs but closes by speaking more hopefully. Predict something like "call for a better plan for suburbs." Choice A is too extreme; the author mentions several concerns but also possible solutions. Choice B is a distortion of the facts presented in the passage and D is out of scope. The correct answer, which matches the prediction, is (C).

2. H **Difficulty:** Medium

Category: Key Ideas and Details / Inference

Getting to the Answer: Inference questions require you to "read between the lines" or "connect the dots" between various points and the author's overall purpose. The author of this passage says that many people moved to the suburbs to get away from factories, because "factories before modern pollution and safety standards were horrific things to behold" (lines 8–9). Based on the clue *before*, predict that factories are not as bad as they once were. Eliminate F, which is too extreme for the author's position. Choice G is a distortion; the passage implies that people lived in the suburbs but continued to work in the cities. Choice J is a misused detail; suburban driving isn't mentioned until the fourth paragraph. The correct answer is (H).

3. A **Difficulty:** High

Category: Key Ideas and Details / Inference

Getting to the Answer: When a question is difficult to make a prediction for, or when your prediction isn't among the answer choices, eliminate choices that are definitely wrong and choose the answer that best matches the author's purpose. The sentence following the quoted statement describes what, ideally, a suburb should be: a nice place to live that's not too far away from the city. In the quoted statement, "All of this" refers to the previous paragraphs: the reasons suburbs exist and their limitations. You can infer from this that the author does not object to the original concept of a suburb but

Answers & Explanations

does have issues with how the concept has been carried out. Choice (A) fits the passage and is correct: the author thinks that suburbs are "logical and inevitable," so they must be providing some kind of service for those who live in them. Choices B and C are misused details that are discussed elsewhere in the passage, not in reference to line 19. Choice D is opposite; the author thinks that suburbs are necessary but are not currently well designed.

4. G   Difficulty: Medium

Category: Key Ideas and Details / Inference

Getting to the Answer: When the author makes a particularly complex or important point, you may see two questions that focus on different aspects of the same idea. Here, questions 3 and 4 are closely related. The writer says that the ideal suburb is removed from the unpleasant aspects of living in a city but is close enough to benefit from the positive aspects. Later, the writer complains that suburbs don't provide enough community necessities and public spaces. Predict that the ideal suburb would be "both convenient and interesting." Choice (G) fits well with the author's viewpoints and is correct. Choice F is a distortion; the author thinks that residents of the ideal suburb would still look beyond their own neighborhoods to the cities for culture, income, and entertainment. Choice H is the opposite of the prediction; suburban areas are not meant to mimic city life. Choice J is too extreme; the speaker wants suburbs to contain more than just housing.

5. C   Difficulty: Medium

Category: Key Ideas and Details / Inference

Getting to the Answer: Pay close attention to the lines surrounding a quoted line in a question stem. In the beginning of the paragraph, the author writes that "The structure of the modern suburb ... has created health and environmental risks of its own" (lines 32–34). These risks are caused by the necessity of driving between separate living and working spaces. Choice (C) is correct; "adverse environmental effects" fits with the *environmental risks* mentioned in the passage. Choices A and D are distortions of the facts presented in the passage. Choice B is out of scope; the author never discusses the effects on running a business.

6. G   Difficulty: Low

Category: Craft and Structure / Vocab-in-Context

Getting to the Answer: Look for context clues. The sentence says that walking to a local café is common for a city dweller, but that it is "rare or entirely alien" for a suburbanite. Predict that *alien* as used here must mean something like *rare*. Choice (G) matches this prediction. Choices F and H are out of scope; the passage never discusses extraterrestrial life or other countries. Choice J is too extreme; the passage never indicates residents would be confused by being able to walk to a café.

7. A   Difficulty: Medium

Category: Key Ideas and Details / Detail

Getting to the Answer: Your Passage Map notes for Paragraph 4 should help you make a prediction that incorporates the city planners' designs with modern Americans' strong connection to cars, as mentioned in lines 48–52. Since city planners cannot change the fact that Americans tend to love their cars, the correct answer is (A). Choice B is too extreme; although the passage refers to the separation of living and commercial spaces, city planners would not attempt to completely change this. Choice C is also too extreme; the passage mentions the distance from houses to suburban coffee shops, but does not indicate this should be a major concern for a city planner. Choice D is out of scope; the passage does not discuss problems with the parks' safety or locations.

8. J   Difficulty: Medium

Category: Key Ideas and Details / Inference

Getting to the Answer: Try summing up the cited lines in your own words when you make a prediction. Most of the passage concerns why people wanted to live in suburbs in the first place and the problems with the way suburbs actually are. In the last paragraph, the author speaks of the future, stating that suburbs could be great if we made some changes. (J) is correct and matches the author's tone. Choices F and H are out of scope; the author neither directly discusses city planning nor expresses an opinion about how much interest people take in their surroundings. Choice G is a distortion; the author thinks suburbs can be "fascinating and beautiful" but are not so in their current condition.

9. A   **Difficulty:** Medium

Category: Key Ideas and Details / Global

Getting to the Answer: Review all of your Passage Map notes and look for reasons to move out of cities. The first place in the passage that addresses the need to get away is Paragraph 1, which states that people wished to avoid the "city and all the noise, pollution, and general nastiness that went along with it" (lines 5–7). Predict that the suburbs would not have those specific problems. Choice (A) matches your prediction and is correct. Choice B is the opposite of your prediction and refers to a limitation of suburban life; line 48 mentions the "lack of daily exercise." Choice C is a distortion; lines 29–31 include information about the low number of community centers. Choice D is a distortion; while suburbs offer some jobs, the passage states that most residents commute to the city.

10. J   **Difficulty:** Medium

Category: Key Ideas and Details / Global

Getting to the Answer: To answer Global questions, use your entire Passage Map and look for themes in the passage. Lines 26–27 mention how "suburbs have grown to the size of sprawling towns." In lines 29–31, the author discusses the lack of retail and recreational spaces. Look for an answer that describes the broader ways in which suburbs have had major changes. Choice F is the opposite of your prediction; suburban families lack nearby spaces to spend their free time and shop. Choice G is a distortion; since World War II, suburbs have grown and changed. Choice H is a distortion; while the passage does mention the pollution caused by modern commutes, it does not state that the problem became worse. The correct answer is (J).

Suggested Passage Map notes:

¶1: Narrator's grandfather (G) proud of being Russian

¶2: G exiled, but still hoped for "new Moscow"

¶3: G moved to China then Am., didn't feel American right away

¶4: stability strange to G

¶5: G passionate about ownership (not allowed in R)

¶6: G openly against communism

¶7: G successful but giving ownership more imp. than $

¶8: G returned to R yearly, gained understanding

¶9: G's real estate career = offer sense of belonging to others

11. C   **Difficulty:** Medium

Category: Key Ideas and Details / Global

Getting to the Answer: The author frequently describes his grandfather's actions and their relationship to his heritage. Choice (C) fits this, as the other Russians in Paragraph 3 are also characterized as being naturally tied to Russia. Choice A distorts the grandfather's later visits to Russia; the passage does not imply that immigrants would prefer to be elsewhere. Choice B cites the opinions of American-born people, while the passage does not focus on those opinions. Choice D refers only to the grandfather, who was perpetually displaced; his story is addressed as being unique.

12. J   **Difficulty:** Low

Category: Key Ideas and Details / Detail

Getting to the Answer: The three specific locations mentioned are Moscow, Siberia, and China, in that order. Also, the author mentions that China was the longest stay. Choices F, G, and H all have errors: F puts the Russian Revolution in the wrong time period; G says he was exiled from Russia as an adult; and H says he settled in communist China, when he left during the revolution. Choice (J) is correct.

13. C   **Difficulty:** High

Category: Key Ideas and Details / Inference

Getting to the Answer: These line references both have to do with the grandfather's work in real estate. You can deduce that he sees real estate as providing stability for people, something he did not have earlier in his life. Choice (C) matches this very well. Choice A is part of his sales strategy, not his purpose. Choices B and D are never discussed as tasks he specifically attempts.

14. F   Difficulty: Medium

Category: Key Ideas and Details / Detail

Getting to the Answer: The grandfather is proud to be Russian and deeply influenced by his heritage, but he is also proud of doing his job and being a successful American. Choice (F) contradicts the grandfather's attitude because while he criticizes the government, he loves the country itself. Choice G suggests an unspoken pride among Russians, which is in line with the grandfather's characterization. Choices H and J both fit because he is critical of the communist government but still reverent regarding the country.

15. D   Difficulty: Medium

Category: Key Ideas and Details / Inference

Getting to the Answer: The passage deals heavily with displacement, and its implications, including its effects on people. Since Moscow was where the family was originally from, you can deduce that the answer will have something to do with belonging. Choice (D) fits this characterization well; Moscow is the family's native home, and all feel tied to Russia but are searching for places to live outside of Russia. Choices A and C are not implied at all in the passage. Choice B may be factually true but does not apply to the desires of the family.

16. F   Difficulty: Low

Category: Key Ideas and Details / Inference

Getting to the Answer: This selection refers to Russians saying, "I am American" in Russian. This contrasts with the fact that they are speaking Russian with other Russians, therefore suggesting that "playing the role" must mean becoming more accustomed to their new country. Choice (F) matches this perfectly. Choices G and H cannot be deduced from the information given, and J may be true, but it does not apply to "playing the role."

17. B   Difficulty: Medium

Category: Key Ideas and Details / Inference

Getting to the Answer: *Strategic compromise* applies to the grandfather's desire to sell homes, in spite of the current stigma against Russians. The tactics mentioned

by the author are informing the customer he was exiled and disagreed with the current Russian government and not responding to negative remarks regarding the entire country of Russia. Choice (B) fits this final part, as negative statements about Russia as a whole would offend the grandfather. Choices A and D are too extreme. Choice C is not mentioned.

18. H   Difficulty: Medium

Category: Key Ideas and Details / Inference

Getting to the Answer: According to the passage, this sort of trip "elucidates one's very existence" (line 92). This is the only result given; the rest of the details apply to the emotional strain involved. Choice (H) is the only choice that applies to this. Choices F and G are not even implied by the text, and J applies to the adoption analogy rather than to the grandfather.

19. B   Difficulty: Medium

Category: Key Ideas and Details / Detail

Getting to the Answer: The last sentence in the first paragraph (lines 11–13) states that the country came under new rule while the grandfather's mother was pregnant with him. He was therefore born after the revolution and under communist rule. Choice (B) is correct. The other choices contradict that factual sentence.

20. G   Difficulty: Medium

Category: Key Ideas and Details / Inference

Getting to the Answer: The need to rediscover a lost native land is what would be made unnecessary, so the correct answer would have to describe the opposite situation. Choice (G) fits this very well; having a sense of belonging would alleviate the need to search for it. Choice F is incorrect because the grandfather embodies the feelings he is potentially making unnecessary. Choice H is out of scope; the passage does not discuss young families. Choice J describes an unrelated achievement.

CHAPTER 17

PRACTICE

Suggested Passage Map notes:

¶1: Quasar very bright

¶2: Scientists studying Qs

¶3: Qs can be seen from very far away; brightness varies

¶4: Qs powered by energy; sci. cannot explain all

¶5: Observing 3C helps scientists understand Qs

¶6: Obs. 3C challenging

¶7: Radio waves emitted, became known as quasars

¶8: Schmidt mapped distance of 3C

4. G   Difficulty: Low

Category: Craft and Structure / Vocab-in-Context

Getting to the Answer: When answering a Vocab-in-Context question, reread the sentence without the word and make a prediction for the definition. Look for that prediction in the answer choices. In the passage context 3C 273 "possesses a very wide range of properties" (lines 40–41), so you can predict that *wealth* means *a great amount*. Choice (G) is correct. Choices F, H, and J are all valid definitions for *wealth*, but none has the correct meaning within this passage.

5. C   Difficulty: Medium

Category: Key Ideas and Details / Detail

Getting to the Answer: According to the Passage Map, the mystery behind quasars and scientists' lack of understanding is found in Paragraph 4. The last sentence in this paragraph states that "quasars exhibit many phenomena that cannot be explained." This matches answer choice (C). Answer choices A, B, and D are not cited in the passage as reasons that scientists do not understand quasars.

6. F   Difficulty: Medium

Category: Key Ideas and Details / Detail

Getting to the Answer: Use the Passage Map to identify places where observations and studying are discussed. Choice G is referred to as an extraordinary discovery, but the passage does not mention how that helped with understanding quasars. Choices H and J are cited in Paragraph 7 as helpful for identifying quasars, not understanding them. The passage does state in Paragraph 2 that monitoring the electromagnetic spectrum is a basis for understanding quasars. Choice (F) is correct.

PERFORM

Suggested Passage Map notes:

¶1: Intro Chomsky (C) and theory of Universal Grammar

¶2: Structure and head parameter rules help us understand other languages

¶3: ?s about U.G.

¶4: Opposing views to U.G. = biology/brain

7. B   Difficulty: Medium

Category: Key Ideas and Details / Detail

Getting to the Answer: When answering a Detail question, find the answer in the passage. The text following the cited phrase discusses the grammatical rules that help people understand the basic structure of any language. This aligns with the correct answer, (B). Choices A and C are too extreme; the passage never says humans can understand all languages or easily speak in multiple languages. Choices D is a misused detail.

8. H   Difficulty: Medium

Category: Key Ideas and Details / Detail

Getting to the Answer: Use the Passage Map to locate where in the passage *structure dependency* is located. Paragraph 2 explains that this rule means that all languages have a similar phrase structure regardless of the origin of the language. Choice (H) is correct.

9. D   Difficulty: Medium

Category: Craft and Structure / Vocab-in-Context

Getting to the Answer: For Vocab-in-Context questions, look at how the word is used in the context of the passage. Then predict a word that can be substituted for the cited word without changing the meaning of the sentence or passage. As used, *engage* means "to be a part of something." Choice (D) is correct. Choices A and C are trap answers based on common meanings of *engage*. Choice B is not supported by the passage.

10. G   Difficulty: Medium

Category: Craft and Structure / Vocab-in-Context

Getting to the Answer: With Vocab-in-Context questions, always predict a substitute word for the cited word. This will help avoid traps such as common meanings. Use that prediction to identify the correct answer. In this case, there is another word in the sentence, *oversimplified*, to aid with the context. Predict a word that works with *sterile* and *oversimplified* in context, such as *insignificant*. Choice (G) works perfectly in this context. Choices F and H are common meanings of *sterile* but are not correct here. Choice J does not fit within the context of the passage.

ON YOUR OWN

Suggested Passage Map notes:

¶1: Intro to ozone layer: purpose, issues

¶2: Ozone thickness

¶3: Scientific study of ozone

¶4: Seasonal variations

¶5: Causes of ozone hole, intro to CFCs

¶6: Economic interests in CFCs

¶7: Health issues

¶8: Montreal Protocol

¶9: Future effects

¶10: Subs for CFCs

1. D   Difficulty: Low

Category: Craft and Structure / Vocab-in-Context

Getting to the Answer: Use the text around the cited word to aid in predicting the answer for Vocab-in-Context questions. The rest of the paragraph discusses the harm being done to the ozone layer, suggesting that it is vulnerable. Choice (D) works correctly in this context. Choice A is the opposite of what the passage indicates, and C does not make sense in context. Choice B is a trap answer with a common meaning of *tenuous*.

2. J   Difficulty: Medium

Category: Key Ideas and Details / Global

Getting to the Answer: When answering a Global question, look at the Passage Map to determine the purpose: informative, persuasive, and so forth. This passage is informative regarding the ozone layer and the damage done to it. Use that prediction to locate the correct answer. Choice (J) is a match. The author is not persuading the reader to take action; H is incorrect. Choices F and G are details discussed in the passage, not the main purpose.

3. B   Difficulty: Medium

Category: Craft and Structure / Function

Getting to the Answer: This question is asking for the function of the cited phrase. Think about why the author uses that language in the passage. The author is conveying that the ozone protects life from harm, and in Paragraph 1 the passage says that harm comes from ultraviolet rays. Choice (B) is correct. Choice A is a misused detail; chlorofluorocarbons cause damage to the ozone layer. Choices C and D are both out of scope; the author does not make these points in this part of the passage.

4. F   Difficulty: Medium

Category: Craft and Structure / Function

Getting to the Answer: Refer to Paragraph 2 to find what the author says about the ozone layer's size. The author points out that while 25 kilometers may seem large, the ozone only comprises a few millimeters when compressed. Eliminate G, which is the opposite of what the author is stating. Choices H and J can also be eliminated; they are distortions of phrasing within the paragraph. The correct answer is (F).

5. D   Difficulty: Low

Category: Craft and Structure / Vocab-in-Context

Getting to the Answer: Read around the cited word to determine the context. The passage discusses people finally wanting to take action due to their emotional reaction. Predict that people need to become *upset* about something to take action. Choice (D) matches this prediction. Choice A is a common meaning of *roused* that is incorrect in context. Choices B and C do not convey the right tone.

6. G   Difficulty: High

Category: Craft and Structure / Writer's View

Getting to the Answer: Locate the paragraph that discusses the economic impact of CFCs—this is Paragraph 6. Predict that the author uses the market value and labor force costs to address the reasons not to halt the production of CFCs. Choice (G) matches this prediction. Choices F and H are the opposite of the author's stance. Choice J is too extreme and does not address the specific topic at hand.

7. B   Difficulty: Medium

Category: Craft and Structure / Writer's View

Getting to the Answer: For Writer's View questions, use the Passage Map to locate where the passage discusses the information in the question. In this case, the author discusses health issues in Paragraph 7. The author lists the health ailments and states they will only get worse with inaction concerning the ozone layer. This matches (B). Choices A and C are misused details; the author's emphasis is on future consequences if the condition of the ozone layer worsens. Choice D is too extreme; the author does not directly call on scientists to take action.

8. H   Difficulty: Medium

Category: Key Ideas and Details / Detail

Getting to the Answer: Use the Passage Map to locate the Montreal Protocol. Paragraph 8 discusses the protocol

itself and Paragraph 9 discusses its ramifications. In a post–CFC production era, there are still impacts on the ozone. As stated in the passage, it takes ten years for CFCs to reach the ozone layer, so they will continue to have a negative impact even after production ceases. Choice (H) sums up the challenge presented by the author. There is no evidence in the passage to support F, G, or J, which contain misused details.

9. C   Difficulty: Medium

Category: Key Ideas and Details / Detail

Getting to the Answer: This is a Detail question that requires a little research within the passage. The Montreal Protocol specified that the last year of CFC production for participating countries would be 2000. The next paragraph states it takes ten years for CFCs to reach the ozone. Therefore, if CFC production was halted in the year 2000, CFCs stopped reaching the ozone layer in the year 2010. This matches (C).

10. H   Difficulty: Medium

Category: Key Ideas and Detail / Detail

Getting to the Answer: The answer to a Detail question is directly in the passage. Use the Passage Map to locate the pros of CFCs, in Paragraph 5. The author lists them as nonflammable, nontoxic, and noncorrosive. Eliminate J because it is not mentioned as an advantage. Now look for the paragraph about CFC replacements (Paragraph 9) and compare their disadvantages to the pros of CFCs: some are toxic and some may be flammable. Eliminate F and G. Choice (H) is correct.

Suggested Passage Map:

¶1: Children of immigrants? Identity; travel and make art

¶2: Elders portray idealized homeland

¶3: Political stability enables visits; goal = idealized lands

¶4: Travels documented in art; theme = disappointment; can't relate

¶5: Author's view = not all are great art, but compelling, raise ?s

Answers & Explanations

11. D   Difficulty: Medium

Category: Key Ideas and Details / Global

Getting to the Answer: Reference your Passage Map to identify the main idea or purpose of a passage; Global questions that ask for a passage's main idea or purpose rarely require rereading the passage. Predict that the author is describing how children of immigrants, who often had idealized visions of their family homelands, created art that expressed their disappointment and identity questions. Though worded in more general terms, (D) matches this prediction. Eliminate B because of the verb *contrast*, as the author's primary purpose is never to contrast anything. While the author mentions both the quality of the artwork and the changing political situations that enabled travel, these are details and not the primary purpose of the passage; A and C are incorrect.

12. F   Difficulty: High

Category: Craft and Structure / Function

Getting to the Answer: When asked about the function of a portion of the passage, consider both the main idea of the relevant paragraph and the overall purpose of the passage; the function of the text in question must support both the paragraph's and passage's purposes. The overall passage describes how children of immigrants, who often have idealized visions of their family homelands, created art that expressed their disappointment and identity questions that arose from visiting their homelands. The paragraph in question serves this purpose by explaining that the children's idealized view came from their elders; this matches (F). Eliminate J because warning the reader is not the author's purpose. Eliminate G, which provides an opposite view from the passage; the children shared the same idealized view as the elders. Choice H is incorrect because the author never presents a detailed study of why shared mind-sets develop, instead only mentioning them to help explain the children's disillusionment.

13. A   Difficulty: Low

Category: Key Ideas and Details / Detail

Getting to the Answer: Use your Passage Map to locate the needed information for Detail questions. Since the question asks why the travelers went to their home countries, the relevant information will likely appear in Paragraphs 3 or 4, which discuss the journeys. Specifically, Paragraph 3 identifies the travelers' goals: "a journey toward a physical and spiritual homecoming" and an "imagined, idealized land" (lines 38–40). The first paragraph also states these children of immigrants "traveled in search of their identity" (lines 11–12). This matches (A). Choices B and D are out of scope for this passage, and C is incorrect because, although art was created, the art was a result of the emotional journeys, not the initial goal.

14. H   Difficulty: Medium

Category: Key Ideas and Details / Detail

Getting to the Answer: Use your Passage Map to locate this detail; the wording "The author states" in the question stem indicates that the answer is directly stated in the passage. Paragraph 4 discusses the creation of these works of art. The parenthetical statement in lines 46–48 claims "new digital technology . . . made these modern travelogues especially feasible." Therefore, (H) is correct. Choice F is the opposite of the correct answer; the author actually states that "not all of these travelogues are great art" (line 59). Choice G is incorrect because it is out of scope; *press restrictions* are neither mentioned in the passage nor would they impact the creation of art by individual artists. Choice J is a misused detail; the political environments of the countries directly facilitated travel to the lands, but not specifically the creation of art.

15. B   Difficulty: Low

Category: Key Ideas and Details / Detail

Getting to the Answer: Consult your Passage Map to locate this detail; the wording "According to the passage" indicates the correct answer is directly stated in the passage. Paragraph 4 discusses the creation of the artwork. In lines 42–44, the author states, "because of the deeply personal nature of these trips, many people documented their journeys." This matches (B). Choice A is out of scope, as the author never mentions any danger involved with the journeys. Choices C and D are distortions of information in the passage; the author mentions the political environment of the homelands but not the visitors' activism, and the elders are described as experiencing nostalgia but not as requesting stories about their homelands.

16. J   **Difficulty:** Medium

Category: Craft and Structure / Vocab-in-Context

Getting to the Answer: Check the lines before and after the cited word to determine the meaning in context of a Vocab-in-Context question. The Passage Map at this point indicates the artwork reflected disappointment about the homeland. The passage text indicates the travelers were surprised and dismayed that the lands did not match their "parents' gilded descriptions" (lines 52–53). Predict that *gilded* must mean unrealistically positive, as also indicated by the clue words *unspoiled* and *exotic* (line 52). This prediction matches (J). Choice F is a trap answer, giving a common meaning for the word that doesn't fit the context of the passage. Choice G is incorrect because the passage does not suggest the parents were trying to intentionally deceive, just that they had overly idealized visions of their homelands. Choice H is incorrect because the phrase *unnecessarily ornamented* is about overdecorating an object rather than too positively describing a location.

17. C   **Difficulty:** Low

Category: Craft and Structure / Vocab-in-Context

Getting to the Answer: Check the lines before and after the cited word to determine the meaning in context of a Vocab-in-Context question. The Passage Map indicates that when travelers arrived in their home countries, they found lands that "had decayed through years of strife" (lines 53–54). Choices B and D are trap answers; they contain common meanings for the word that don't fit the context of the passage. Choice A is incorrect, since it was the travelers who were disappointed, not the lands. The correct answer is (C).

18. F   **Difficulty:** High

Category: Craft and Structure / Writer's View

Getting to the Answer: Consider the author's overall view of the artwork. The Passage Map indicates that the final paragraph contains the author's view, as should be expected from most passages' concluding paragraphs. The author claims that although the works are not necessarily great art in a technical sense, they are "compelling, even heartbreaking" (line 62). The author ultimately claims we are "lucky . . . that they chronicled these journeys, so that we can share in this mystery" (lines 67–69). Choice (F) matches this prediction. Choice G is a distortion; the author acknowledges some of the work is boring but still thinks society is fortunate to have it. Choice H is out of scope because the author never describes any irony associated with the artwork or refers to it as beautiful. Choice J is also a distortion, as the author explains that the travelers were out of touch with people in their homelands but never implies this is disturbing.

19. D   **Difficulty:** Low

Category: Craft and Structure / Vocab-in-Context

Getting to the Answer: Check the lines before and after the cited word to determine the word's meaning in context for a Vocab-in-Context question. The Passage Map indicates that the art created by the travelers is varied in terms of skill level and the interest the art pieces evoke. Additionally the word *clumsy* is accompanied by the phrase *overly earnest* (line 60), which means "sincere and heartfelt to an exaggerated degree." Predict that in this context, *clumsy* means something along the lines of "made without professional skill." Choices A and C are trap answers; they contain common meanings for the word that don't fit the context of the passage. Choice B is too extreme for the author's tone and viewpoint. The correct answer, which matches the prediction, is (D).

20. H   **Difficulty:** Medium

Category: Craft and Structure / Writer's View

Getting to the Answer: Consider the author's viewpoint about the art throughout the passage. Typically, an author's overall viewpoint will be apparent in the beginning and/or conclusion of the passage; your Passage Map may also direct you to relevant parts of the text. In the first paragraph, the author describes the works of art as "a fascinating picture of the struggle to define one's self" (lines 16–17). Likewise, in the concluding paragraph, the author calls the art *compelling* in its portrayal of dismay and frustration (line 62). Choice (H) matches this prediction. Choices F and J depict the opposite of the author's view of the art: the author refers to the art as sometimes not very good and *overly earnest* (line 60) and the art movement as *small* (line 12). Choice G is out of scope, as the author never mentions any political impact the art may have had.

CHAPTER 18

PRACTICE

Suggested Passage Map notes:

¶1: Tourist towns not "typical" Mexico; terrain dictates difference

¶2: Beach areas require specialization but aren't representative

¶3: Beach regions not naturally suited to living; Mayans needed *cenotes*

¶4: Coast more limited and focused on tourists, *altiplano* more varied; example: gym vs. open market

¶5: Author's conclusion: better to visit "non-tourist" areas

5. B   Difficulty: Medium

Category: Craft and Structure / Function

Getting to the Answer: The author starts the introduction of the Mayans with "While the tourist," which suggests a comparison. The selection describes the Mayans' means of survival in contrast to what tourists find desirable. You can predict that the subject of the Mayans is used to illustrate the differences between what they looked for on the coast (water) with what tourists look for (beauty, tropical weather). Choice (B) is a good match for this idea. Choice A is a distortion; the Mayans lived on the coast, not the *altiplano*. Choice C is a distortion; the comparison is between the Mayans and the tourists, not the Mayans and current locals. Choice D is a distortion; the author is contrasting the experiences of the two groups, not criticizing tourists for not knowing cultural history.

6. H   Difficulty: Medium

Category: Craft and Structure / Function

Getting to the Answer: The paragraph indicates that a gymnasium provides a predictable and repeatable experience for its patrons, whereas the open market offers whatever happens to be available at a given time. You can predict that the reference is meant to show that the beach resort towns are set up more specifically for the needs of visitors than the *altiplano* is, as stated in (H).

Answer F is out of scope; there is no comparison between different classes of tourists. Answer G is opposite; the author is indicating that it is the beach towns that are set up for tourists, not the *altiplano*. Answer J is out of scope; the passage never compares the quantities of consumer goods in the different areas.

7. D   Difficulty: Medium

Category: Craft and Structure / Writer's View

Getting to the Answer: The author is rather critical of tourist-oriented beach towns, using such words as *artificial*, and the overall point is that these towns do not reflect the culture of the area. Look for an answer choice that makes a similar claim. Choice (D) is a match. Choice A is opposite; the author believes that these towns are not representative of their surroundings. Choice B is also opposite; the towns are compared to the gymnasium, which is said to be easy to navigate. Choice C is a distortion; Paragraph 3 contradicts the notion that the towns are not sufficiently supplied to accommodate visitors.

8. J   Difficulty: Low

Category: Craft and Structure / Writer's View

Getting to the Answer: The author describes the areas outside of the tourist-oriented beach towns as more typically representative of Mexico and its culture. Choice (J) matches this information. Choice F is too extreme; the author says that beach resorts are specifically set up to accommodate tourists but never refers to the *altiplano* as *inaccessible*. Choice G is opposite; the author makes the point that these more varied regions are more representative of Mexico's culture. Choice H is out of scope; the author never indicates this, instead advocating for visitors to explore the *altiplano*.

PERFORM

Suggested Passage Map notes:

¶1: W.M.'s identity based on her people; has desire to help them

¶2: Pride of Cherokee identity and Cherokee people overcoming hardships

Answers & Explanations

¶3: Tribe survived further difficulties; "second rebirth"

¶4: Parallel: tribal history and author's life, both survived "hardships"

¶5: Author's experience; tribal "self-help"

9. A   Difficulty: Low

Category: Craft and Structure / Function

Getting to the Answer: The author leads into this reference by describing her family's relocation experience. She explains how her family found a sense of belonging at this San Francisco community center. This fits with (A), the correct answer. Choices B, C, and D are all out of scope; the author does not mention the "size of the … community," "government" aid "after their relocation," or community centers "outside of . . . tribal lands."

10. H   Difficulty: Low

Category: Craft and Structure / Function

Getting to the Answer: The author describes this forced relocation to emphasize the Cherokees' history of overcoming hardships through their perseverance. Choice (H) closely matches this prediction. Choice F is too extreme. The author states that the obstacles were overcome; thus, they were not *insurmountable*. Choices G and J are misused details; the forced relocation occurred in the 1830s and was not part of the author's personal experience, and the Bell project happened after 1977 and was not related to this forced relocation.

11. D   Difficulty: High

Category: Craft and Structure / Writer's View

Getting to the Answer: Before looking at the answer choices, predict an answer that sums up the author's central argument. She begins the passage by speaking of the history of the Cherokee; that theme permeates the passage (lines 54–56): "my tribe's history has defined me, just as it has defined all Cherokee"). Look for an answer tying in Cherokee history, which is (D). Choice A is a distortion; the author briefly mentions gender and politics in Paragraph 1, but she never recommends a similar course of action for other women. Choice B is extreme; although the author implies that education has played a role in rebuilding Cherokee society, this implication is insufficient to support a claim that education is *vital* to the

rebuilding process. Choice C is out of scope; the author never explicitly invokes "traditional cultural values" in the context of rebuilding the Cherokee community.

12. G   Difficulty: Medium

Category: Craft and Structure / Writer's View

Getting to the Answer: Mankiller talks about the BIA relocation as a hardship, parallel to her ancestors' removal to the Indian Territory. Predict something like *distressed* or *disturbed*. These predictions match (G). Choice F is a distortion; the author is not *resigned* to the situation but believes her people are capable of helping themselves without government assistance. Choices H and J are opposites; both are too positive.

ON YOUR OWN

Suggested Passage Map notes:

¶1: Am. conflict w/ Brit. & France

¶2: Pres. Jefferson tried peaceful solution

¶3: 1811 Battle of Tippecanoe = outbreak

¶4: Am. unprepared

¶5: 1814 Am. losing

¶6: victories for Am. and Brit.

¶7: end of war = ↑ Am. confidence

1. D   Difficulty: Medium

Category: Key Ideas and Details / Inference

Getting to the Answer: The correct answer will be consistent with the author's purpose and tone. Choice (D) is correct; Paragraph 4 clearly states that American war preparations were inadequate, which is one example of how the Americans were "ill-prepared to assert their rights." Choice A is a distortion; while the passage certainly implies that the United States faced *mounting adversity*, the author does not emphasize the bravery of the Americans. The passage is more concerned with the reverses they suffered. Choice B is also a distortion; Jackson fought on the American side. Choice C is out of scope; the passage never mentions the prospect of such future conflicts.

2. H   **Difficulty:** Medium

Category: Craft and Structure / Writer's View

Getting to the Answer: Consider the author's overall reasoning regarding the conflict. Choice (H) reflects the author's view that both nations played a hand in beginning the conflict. Choice F is out of scope because the author never mentions such an arrangement. Choice G is a distortion; the author notes American territorial desires (Paragraph 3). Choice J is out of scope; the effect of the conflict on Native Americans is not directly addressed in the passage.

3. B   **Difficulty:** Medium

Category: Craft and Structure / Function

Getting to the Answer: Your Passage Map should help you see that Paragraph 3 deals primarily with two things: alleged British support of Native American populations and the desire of Western U.S. citizens for free land. Predict that the correct answer choice will address the cause of the war and/or place blame on both parties. Choice (B) fits with both aspects of your prediction. Choice A is out of scope because the author makes no mention of representation of frontiersmen. Choice C is a distortion; this leaves out the discussion of the U.S. role in the conflict. Choice D is a misused detail; this appears elsewhere but is not the function of the cited sentence.

4. H   **Difficulty:** Medium

Category: Key Ideas and Details / Detail

Getting to the Answer: Paragraph 2's opening sentence directly states that Jefferson thought a peaceful solution with the British could be achieved. You can predict that the correct answer will address the idea of peaceful resolution. Choice (H) matches. Choice F is extreme; nothing in this part of the passage can be described as *hostile* (this comes in Paragraph 3). Choice G is opposite; the passage refutes this idea, since the Americans eventually go to war. Choice J is out of scope; the passage doesn't support this contention.

5. B   **Difficulty:** Medium

Category: Craft and Structure / Function

Getting to the Answer: In Paragraph 4, the author describes a number of battlefield failures on the part of the United States, a concept not foreshadowed before this point. Look for a choice that captures this emphasis. Choice (B) matches. Choice A is a misused detail; nothing in the paragraph refers to the treaties, which the author discusses in the final paragraph. Choice C is out of scope; the paragraph does discuss this occurring once, but doesn't go so far as to extend this to other conflicts. Choice D is a misused detail; the reference to Hull is of limited importance in the paragraph.

6. F   **Difficulty:** High

Category: Craft and Structure / Function

Getting to the Answer: The author states that the victory after the end of the war "was important in restoring American confidence." Look for a choice that incorporates this idea. Choice (F) fits well with the text and represents a logical reasoning. Choice G is out of scope because the author never suggests what impact this battle may have had on Jackson's future fame. Choices H and J are distortions; they may seem logical, but the author does not directly suggest either idea.

7. C   **Difficulty:** High

Category: Craft and Structure / Writer's View

Getting to the Answer: The author states that difficulties with the British "were more apparent," so you can predict that the behavior of the French was not as intentionally damaging to American interests. Choice (C) matches. Choice A is out of scope; the author never discusses whether these actions were *justified*. Choice B is out of scope; the author never implies this in the paragraph. Choice D is a distortion; the British were the ones conscripting American sailors.

8. F   **Difficulty:** Low

Category: Key Ideas and Details / Detail

Getting to the Answer: The cited lines state that "the desire of the frontiersmen for free land" was a cause of the war, which matches (F). Choice G is opposite; the paragraph states that the British were aiding Native Americans. Choice H is out of scope; the author doesn't refer to "deteriorating relations with the Spanish," only the desire to obtain territory under Spanish control. Choice J is a misused detail; this comes from Paragraph 1.

9. B   **Difficulty:** Medium

Category: Key Ideas and Details / Detail

Getting to the Answer: The passage states directly that President Jefferson "hoped to achieve a peaceful settlement" (lines 16–17), which matches (B). Choice A is out of scope; the author doesn't suggest such fear on the part of the United States. Choice C is out of scope; this may seem like a viable option, but the passage never mentions the British perceiving such a threat. Choice D is extreme; the United States wanted to stand up for its rights, not simply *gain revenge*.

10. F   **Difficulty:** Medium

Category: Craft and Structure / Function

Getting to the Answer: As you read around the cited lines, you should see that little in the passage has indicated how disastrous the American performance would be in these battles. The author also references the fact that war supporters expected a quick victory, but were met with crushing defeat. Predict that the phrase emphasizes how shocking and devastating the losses were. Choice (F) matches well. Choice G is a distortion; the author makes no such connection to Jackson's victory. Choice H is opposite; the passage makes clear that these parties were wrong. Choice J is out of scope; the author never suggests this. The war success of British forces indicates that the British must have been doing most things right.

Suggested Passage Map notes:

¶1: Contemp. mov't = land art (nat. deteriorates)

¶2: Started in 1960s as backlash

¶3: Use natural materials

¶4: Massive scale

¶5: All land art is short-lived

11. B   **Difficulty:** Medium

Category: Craft and Structure / Writer's View

Getting to the Answer: The first paragraph states that building works of art that last was a particular challenge to ancient artists. Choice (B) matches. Choice A is a distortion; while land artists might agree with this choice, there is no indication that the author does. Choice C is extreme;

while the author does indicate that most artists seek to create lasting works, she never states that such creation is necessary. Choice D is out of scope; the author never expresses a clear opinion about works of art that last, only that such works were challenging to create.

12. G   **Difficulty:** Low

Category: Key Ideas and Details / Detail

Getting to the Answer: The first paragraph describes materials available to ancient artists as *perishable* (line 6). Choice (G) matches this prediction. Choice F is a misused detail; the passage describes land art as a contemporary movement. Choice H is out of scope; there is no mention of patrons in the passage. Choice J is out of scope; while the passage does describe ancient media as *perishable*, there is no mention of the elements of nature.

13. D   **Difficulty:** Medium

Category: Key Ideas and Details / Detail

Getting to the Answer: The second paragraph discusses the influences that led to the land art movement as a "backlash . . . against the seclusion of art from the real world" (lines 17–19), which matches (D). Choice A is a misused detail; the passage never states that *Spiral Jetty* was the first land artwork. Choice B is a distortion; the first paragraph discusses the impermanence of land art, but the author never suggests that land art was directly a reaction to permanent art. Choice C is extreme; the passage does mention the use of natural materials in land art, but never suggests that land art originated specifically from a desire to use such materials.

14. G   **Difficulty:** Low

Category: Key Ideas and Details / Detail

Getting to the Answer: The passage states that *Spiral Jetty* was allowed to "deteriorate *in situ*." It, therefore, does not state that the artist deliberately destroyed it. Choice (G) agrees with your prediction. Choice F is mentioned in lines 37–39. Eliminate H and J; the passage states that *Spiral Jetty* was submerged by water for decades and that Smithson did not try to preserve his work.

15. A   **Difficulty:** Medium

Category: Craft and Structure / Writer's View

Getting to the Answer: The purpose of the paragraph is to discuss the massive scale of land art works. Choice (A) matches well. Choice B is a misused detail; the two works are compared, but that is not the author's main purpose for including this detail. Choice C is opposite; the passage describes *Rhythms of Life* as massive, not diminutive. Choice D is a misused detail; the passage states that this work is the largest, but that is not the author's purpose.

16. F   **Difficulty:** Medium

Category: Craft and Structure / Function

Getting to the Answer: The last paragraph, more than anything, describes the consequences of creating short-lived artwork, so (F) is correct. Choice G is out of scope; the author does address criticism, but not for the entire paragraph. Choice H is out of scope; this comparison is made, but that is not the purpose of the whole paragraph. Choice J is out of scope; the author does not provide any examples in this paragraph.

17. C   **Difficulty:** High

Category: Craft and Structure / Function

Getting to the Answer: The author quotes Christo to support the explanation of artists' reasons for allowing their work to be destroyed. Christo's characterization of ephemeral art as *legendary* demonstrates his motivation for creating impermanent art. Choice (C) captures this suggestion. Choice A is extreme; the passage never states that *no* successful artworks still exist. Choice B is opposite; the paragraph cites similarities between land artists and Christo and Jeanne-Claude, not differences. Choice D is out of scope; artists' feelings about wasting resources are never discussed.

18. G   **Difficulty:** Medium

Category: Key Ideas and Details / Detail

Getting to the Answer: Lines 73–78 state that the materials from land art are taken from nature and returned to nature. Choice (G) matches. Choice F is out of scope; the passage does not discuss recycling. Choice H is a distortion; the passage describes *nature* as the rightful owner of the materials, not any specific person. Choice J is out of scope; the passage does not describe the reuse of land art materials.

19. D   **Difficulty:** High

Category: Key Ideas and Details / Inference

Getting to the Answer: Lines 67–73 in the last paragraph state that some critics and art lovers feel access to a work of art should not be limited to a brief period of time. Therefore, you can infer that the art world will take notice every time *Spiral Jetty* reemerges from the lake. Choice (D) matches this prediction. Choice A is a distortion; the passage states that *Rhythms of Life* is unsurpassed in size, not popularity. Choice B is opposite; the passage states that Christo and Jeanne-Claude do not *eschew*, or avoid, synthetic materials. Choice C is extreme; the passage states that most, not all, land artists need considerable funding.

20. J   **Difficulty:** Medium

Category: Craft and Structure / Writer's View

Getting to the Answer: The tone of this passage is mostly descriptive, but there are instances when the author's support for land art comes through. In the last paragraph, the author presents a defense of land art. Choice (J) is correct. Choice F is opposite; the passage does not dismiss land art but explores it thoroughly. Choice G is out of scope; nothing in the passage indicates a lack of trust, or skepticism. Choice H is extreme; while the tone is generally positive, *zealous* is too strongly positive.

Answers & Explanations

CHAPTER 19

PRACTICE

Suggested Passage Map notes:

Passage A ¶1: Recent urbanization rate ↑, will continue to ↑

Passage B ¶1: Urb. caused by: jobs in dev. countries, ↑ health in less-dev. countries

5. C   Difficulty: Medium

Category: Craft and Structure / Vocab-in-Context

Getting to the Answer: Use what you know of the definition of the cited word, as well as what you can gain from its context within the passage. In this case, *wedded* describes the relationship between a rural lifestyle and "the surrounding land and natural resources" (lines 2–3). Since the passage is describing a shift toward *greater urbanization* (line 9), then it is likely a rural life was characterized by a devotion to the land. Because the tone of the passage is neutral, A, B, and D are incorrect. The correct answer is (C).

6. J   Difficulty: Medium

Category: Key Ideas and Details / Inference

Getting to the Answer: When asked what a word or phrase implies, make sure your selection directly answers the question. The author is describing urbanization and massive migrations to disease-infested urban areas. The author's use of the word *nonetheless* suggests that the opportunity for employment was an attraction despite these dangerous conditions. Choice (J) matches this prediction. Choice F may have been tempting, but it is incorrect because the author suggests that concerns about employment were more powerful than concerns about disease, not that few people had such concerns.

7. A   Difficulty: Medium

Category: Key Ideas and Details / Inference

Getting to the Answer: When an Inference question asks you to determine one author's response to the information presented by the other, first determine what the first author feels about the issue. Author B states that cities in developed countries grew because of migration to jobs, while cities in less-developed nations

have grown because of falling death rates. In other words, urbanization can occur for different reasons. So, Author B would probably disagree with Author A's statement that "less-developed nations continue to experience the same causes of urbanization." Choice (A) correctly captures this disagreement.

8. H   Difficulty: High

Category: Key Ideas and Details / Global

Getting to the Answer: When a question asks about the passage as a whole, use your Passage Map to form a prediction. However, be aware that the answer choices to Global questions often discuss aspects of the passage you may not have included in your Passage Map. In that case, use the process of elimination. Passage A discusses urbanization as a relatively recent trend, whereas Passage B discusses the causes of urbanization. There is no obvious match among the answer choices for this prediction, so evaluate the answer choices and eliminate those not supported by the text. Choice F is a distortion; while this statement captures the second passage, the author of Passage A never mentions "a lack of rural land." Choices G and J are out of scope; neither author expresses an opinion regarding "the merits of urbanization," nor does either encourage it. One of the most noticeable differences between the first and second passages is that the first cites specific numbers, while the second approaches the issue with less quantifiable, more general conclusions. Thus, (H) is correct.

PERFORM

Suggested Passage Map notes:

Passage A

¶1: Pol. ads important, effective

Passage B

¶1: Pol. ads convenient, ↓ voters' power

9. C   Difficulty: Low

Category: Key Details and Ideas / Global

Getting to the Answer: By reading actively, you've already asked yourself about the author's purpose before you even get to this question. The author of Passage A claims that political advertisements are "the most direct and effective way" (lines 11–12) to present key issues to voters and that they play "a crucial part in the political process" (lines 7–8). Look for a choice that emphasizes this point. Choice (C) is correct because it emphasizes this central role.

10. H   Difficulty: High

Category: Craft and Structure / Function

Getting to the Answer: When asked about the function of a part of the passage, consider the overall tone and purpose of the passage. The author is implying that we shouldn't think of government as a product that we buy because of advertising, as we do meals and cars. Thus, meals and cars are used as examples of consumer products. Choice (H) expresses this function correctly. Watch out for incorrect answer choices that describe the passage but do not answer the question. Choice G is a misused detail; the electorate's unwillingness to examine government is mentioned later, but it is not illustrated by these examples.

11. A   Difficulty: Medium

Category: Integration of Knowledge and Ideas / Synthesis

Getting to the Answer: Look for areas in Passage B that deal with the same issues as the quote from Passage A. Author B feels that commercials take away from the process of the "disciplined—and often inconvenient—examination of government" (lines 23–24) that is so important. In other words, Author B thinks that people should work harder to understand the "rules and rhetoric" of government. Choice (A) correctly expresses this reasoning. Choice B might have been tempting, but it distorts the author's purpose; the author is concerned with criticizing, not improving, the typical political advertisement.

12. H   Difficulty: Medium

Category: Integration of Knowledge and Ideas / Synthesis

Getting to the Answer: This Global question tests your knowledge of the overall purpose of both authors. Even though they disagree on its merits, both authors talk about the great significance of the political commercial. Predict an answer that reflects this significance without

making a judgment. Choice (H) is correct; while the authors take different sides on the question of how good or bad these commercials are, they would certainly agree that such commercials play a key role.

ON YOUR OWN

Suggested Passage Map notes:

Passage A

¶1: Horrible flight; trouble speaking German

¶2: More language trouble

¶3: Intimidated but goes for walk

¶4: Beautiful Berlin has impressive architecture

¶5: Content with trip in silence

Passage B

¶1: Bare room, disoriented

¶2: Greg (G) takes lead, Paisan = Narrator (N)

¶3: Why churches?

¶4: Bone churches

¶5: N doesn't understand

¶6–8: N impressed by St. Peter's / acts unimpressed

¶9: G enthusiastic about Rome

¶10: Late night with locals

¶11: N has rough morning but interesting experience

1. B   Difficulty: Medium

Category: Craft and Structure / Function

Getting to the Answer: Every part of a passage contributes to the purpose of the larger section. According to the Passage Map, the interaction with the cab driver shows the author having more language troubles, which is a theme throughout the passage. Choice (B) reflects this purpose. Although A and D describe features of Paragraph 1, they do not reflect the reason the author included the interaction.

2. F **Difficulty:** Medium

Category: Key Ideas and Details / Detail

Getting to the Answer: To answer a Detail question, find the section of the passage that provides the answer. In the third paragraph, the author mentions being "Thoroughly intimidated by the locals and their language" when describing his decision to go for a walk. This phrase makes a good prediction, and it matches (F). Thus, (F) is correct.

3. C **Difficulty:** Medium

Category: Key Ideas and Details / Inference

Getting to the Answer: The answer to an Inference question is not directly stated in the passage, but it is supported by the passage. Use what you know about the tone and purpose to help you eliminate answer choices. Choice A is a misused detail; even though the narrator couldn't describe the scene well in German, he would choose not to even in English. The tone of the final paragraph is one of contentment, which suggests that the author is no longer frustrated with his inability to speak German. Thus, B is incorrect. Choice D merely repeats that the narrator sat quietly, without explaining why. Only (C) is supported by the contented tone, and it is therefore correct.

4. H **Difficulty:** Medium

Category: Key Ideas and Details / Detail

Getting to the Answer: Because you've already noted the main point of each paragraph in your Passage Map, use the note for the final paragraph as your prediction. The Passage Map states that the narrator had a rough morning, but that the previous day was an interesting experience. Choices F, G, and J are all off in tone. Choice F is too negative, whereas G and J are too positive. Only (H) accurately expresses that the previous night was an interesting experience without adding an extreme emotion.

5. B **Difficulty:** Medium

Category: Key Ideas and Details / Inference

Getting to the Answer: For an Inference question that asks about a relationship, use what you know about that relationship to form your prediction. The narrator expresses mixed feelings about going along with Greg. In the first paragraph, the narrator suggests some ambivalence when he wonders, "Why had I picked up with Greg, anyway?" (lines 52–53). However, the narrator follows Greg all day and half the night, and he admits to enjoying St. Peter's. When a character has mixed feelings, watch out for answer choices that are too extreme, such as A. Choice C is the opposite of how the narrator sees Greg; Greg seems to enjoy Rome immensely. Choice D is not supported by the passage; although Greg does want to tour historical churches, nothing about his stated reasons for doing so suggests religious fanaticism. Choice (B) is correct. The narrator is compelled by Greg's behavior and tour-guide tendencies, and he thereby remains curious enough to stay with Greg through the entire night's tour.

6. J **Difficulty:** Medium

Category: Craft and Structure / Function

Getting to the Answer: This Function question asks about the purpose of a particular part of Passage B in relation to the whole. In short, why does the author reveal that the narrator is unwilling to admit to Greg an admiration of St. Peter's? The function of a part of a Literary Narrative passage usually has to do with the characters' feelings, values, and relationships. The fact that the narrator isn't going to admit his enjoyment to Greg shows that the narrator is enjoying himself more than he is willing to reveal. Choice (J) matches this prediction, and it is correct. When answering Function questions, watch out for answer choices that describe the passage without revealing the cited text's function within the passage. Because the narrator is willing to follow Greg all day, F is incorrect. While the narrator's attitude may call attention to St. Peter's, the point of the passage is not to praise St. Peter's; it is to describe two characters and their interaction. Thus, H is incorrect. Choice G is incorrect because nothing in the text indicates that the narrator sees admiration of churches as a private matter.

7. D **Difficulty:** Medium

Category: Integration of Knowledge and Ideas / Synthesis

Getting to the Answer: When asked to compare two passages as a whole, use the main focus of each passage to form your prediction. Passage A focuses on the narrator's frustrations with the language barrier in Berlin, whereas

Passage B describes a whirlwind tour through Rome. The correct answer is (D). While the narrator of Passage B mentions "conversations that mixed French, Greek, Italian, and Martian" (lines 94–95), language is not a major theme in Passage B as it is in Passage A.

8. H **Difficulty:** High

Category: Integration of Knowledge and Ideas / Synthesis

Getting to the Answer: The tone of a passage includes the author's or narrator's attitudes toward the subject matter. Pay attention to shifts in attitude. Both narrators are anxious at the start of their respective passages, but both come to appreciate their individual experiences in a foreign country. Thus, (H) is correct. Choice F is a distortion; Passage A has a more polished quality, but that does not mean it is impersonal or historical. Nothing about Passage B makes it more nostalgic than Passage A. Choice G mixes up the passages; Passage A is more serious and introspective than Passage B, while Passage B is more animated and comical. Choice J is a distortion; while Passage B is humorous in the beginning, Passage A has a more serious tone.

9. A **Difficulty:** Medium

Category: Integration of Knowledge and Ideas / Synthesis

Getting to the Answer: The question stem mentions the style of Passage A, so your prediction should focus on the distinctive features of Passage B's style. Passage B uses dialogue featuring very casual, everyday language, in contrast to the more formal writing of Passage A. Choice (A) matches this prediction and is therefore correct. Choice B is an opposite answer choice; the passage is not particularly informative, merely recounting the narrator's personal experience with his friend in Rome. Choice C is out of scope; nothing about Passage B is intended to instruct the reader. Choice D is an opposite answer choice; Passage B is very personal.

10. J **Difficulty:** High

Category: Integration of Knowledge and Ideas / Synthesis

Getting to the Answer: When asked to compare details in two passages, use your Passage Maps to form a prediction. According to the map for Passage A, the narrator is impressed by Berlin's architecture and feels

content. According to the map for Passage B, its narrator questions why he and his companion are visiting so many churches and hides his appreciation for St. Peter's. Choice F is incorrect because Narrator B is secretly in awe of St. Peter's, which shows that he is not indifferent. Choice G is incorrect because Narrator A does notice the architecture and Narrator B is not entirely captivated by it. Choice H is incorrect because Narrator A does not grow tired of the architecture. Only (J) matches the prediction; it describes Narrator A's contentment and Narrator B's more complicated response. Thus, (J) is correct.

Suggested Passage Map notes:

Passage A

¶1: Author thought history was all factual

¶2: Author now knows history includes biases

Passage B

¶1: 1950s textbooks praised US

¶2: Current textbooks reflect pol. problems

¶3: Adults hope for objective truth

¶4: Adults want truth, want history to not change

11. C **Difficulty:** Medium

Category: Craft and Structure / Vocab-in-Context

Getting to the Answer: Use the surrounding text to predict the meaning of the word in context. The author is talking about a *nagging distinction*. Because the vanishing of this distinction is depicted as beneficial, you can predict that *nagging* means *annoying*, which matches (C). Choices A and B are out of scope; *carping* means "difficult to please" and *complaining* doesn't make sense in context. Choice D is opposite because *nagging* is considered undesirable rather than *manageable*.

12. J **Difficulty:** Medium

Category: Key Ideas and Details / Detail

Getting to the Answer: In the first sentence of the second paragraph, the author says that the picture of Greece is defective because it is based on the accounts of "a tiny group of people" (line 26), which matches (J). Choice F is out of scope because the author does not imply that the population of Greece was small. Choice G is opposite; the author specifically says that our incomplete understanding is not because information has been lost. Choice H is a misused detail; this is a statement from the end of the first paragraph that is not relevant here.

13. D   Difficulty: Medium

Category: Craft and Structure / Function

Getting to the Answer: Use the key words around the cited text to make a prediction. In the preceding sentences, the author asks why we believe a certain assumption about the Middle Ages—that people were religious—and wonders whether or not this is true. The author refers to "generations of chroniclers" to explain the author's reason for this assumption, which matches (D). Choice A is out of scope; the author never attempts to compare historical methods. Choice B is a misused detail because while this is discussed in the first paragraph, it isn't relevant here. Choice C is opposite; the author is questioning this theory, not supporting it.

14. G   Difficulty: Medium

Category: Craft and Structure / Vocab-in-Context

Getting to the Answer: Use the information surrounding the word to identify its use in context. In the part of the sentence before the colon, the author tells you that "the country never changed" (line 54), which matches (G). Choices F, H, and J are out of scope; *regular* does not convey a sense of unchanging, *constant* is not being used in the sense of something *faithful*, and *unremitting* means "never relaxing or slackening," which does not fit the context.

15. A   Difficulty: Medium

Category: Key Ideas and Details / Global

Getting to the Answer: The author opens the second paragraph with the claim that "now the texts have changed," and the rest of the paragraph expands on this idea. Choice (A) matches perfectly. Choice B is a misused detail; *social problems* are mentioned only briefly in the paragraph. Choices C and D are out of scope; the author never attempts to discuss the influence of presidents on history, and the author is describing a personal view of the subject rather than making recommendations.

16. J   Difficulty: Medium

Category: Key Ideas and Details / Inference

Getting to the Answer: Treat this like a Vocab-in-Context question; interpret the phrase as it is used in context. In the preceding part of the sentence, the author writes that people are hoping for "some reliable authority," which serves well as a prediction and matches (J). Choice F is a misused detail; the author mentions journalists, but not in relation to this sentence. Choice G is out of scope; the author never discusses anything regarding science. Choice H is opposite because *original interpretation* would run counter to something that is *reliable* or *fixed*.

17. B   Difficulty: Medium

Category: Integration of Knowledge and Ideas / Synthesis

Getting to the Answer: Both authors focus mainly on changes in how history is written, which matches (B). Choices A, C, and D are out of scope. Inaccuracies in history books are discussed solely in Passage A, and only Passage B discusses journalism. While Author B discusses the relevance of studying history, Author A does not.

18. G   Difficulty: Medium

Category: Integration of Knowledge and Ideas / Synthesis

Getting to the Answer: Because you need to infer Author A's attitude toward a statement in Passage 2, look for answers that match the first author's purpose and tone. Author A discusses "the illusion of having all the facts" in the first paragraph (lines 15–16), making the point that it is necessary to be skeptical of all histories because many writers filter facts. Because Author B is talking about texts that remained unchanged and unchallenged, Author A would most likely suggest that these texts be challenged. This matches (G). Choice F is a misused detail; this is discussed in Passage B and has no relevance to the attitude of the first author. Choice H is out of scope because neither author seems to think that reading more textbooks would be very helpful. Choice J is a misused detail; the *Middle Ages*, mentioned in Passage A, has no relevance here.

19. D   **Difficulty:** High

Category: Integration of Knowledge and Ideas / Synthesis

Getting to the Answer: The quote from Passage A is relaying the idea that the view of medieval man is now unalterable. In the final paragraph of Passage B, the author states that today some still yearn for unchanging history, which matches (D). Choice A is out of scope because it is not supported in Passage B. Choice B is opposite because its author implies that all age groups yearn for a history that is unchanging. Choice C is out of scope; the author of Passage B is not making any recommendations, only observations.

20. F   **Difficulty:** Medium

Category: Integration of Knowledge and Ideas / Synthesis

Getting to the Answer: Both authors state in their opening paragraphs that, in their younger days, they were rather naïve and unquestioning about history, which matches (F). Choice B is out of scope because neither author discusses any subject except history. Choice C is a misused detail; only Author B discusses the "pace of social change." Choice D is opposite because both authors talk about how they did not question the material.

CHAPTER 21

PRACTICE

12. H   Difficulty: Low

Category: Interpretation of Data

Getting to the Answer: Start with Figure 1. Trace the vertical line up from 800 g, which equals 0.8 kg, on the x-axis to the curve that represents Earth. Then from the point of intersection, draw a horizontal line to the y-axis to determine the expected displacement. The displacement is approximately 15 cm, so (H) is the correct answer. Choice F would be the displacement for a spring on Titan, and J would be the displacement for a spring on Jupiter.

13. D   Difficulty: Medium

Category: Interpretation of Data

Getting to the Answer: Use your pencil to extend the lines in graphs when required. This question directs you to Figure 2. What are the patterns in that data? For Earth, mass (m) increases as the period of oscillation (T) increases. When you extend the trend line of m, it's clear that the mass must be greater than 1,000 g. Only one answer, choice (D), has a mass that fits, so (D) is correct.

14. F   Difficulty: Medium

Category: Interpretation of Data

Getting to the Answer: To determine the relationship between g and x, you have to combine the information from Figure 1 with that of Table 1, which lists g for each planet or moon. For any given m greater than 0 in Figure 1, the spring's displacement is the highest for Jupiter, in the middle for Earth, and the lowest for Titan. According to Table 1, Jupiter has the highest gravitational acceleration at 24.9 m/sec^2, followed by Earth at 9.8 m/sec^2, followed by Titan at 1.4 m/sec^2. Thus, as gravitational acceleration increases, the spring's displacement increases. The correct answer is (F). If displacement stayed the same as gravitational acceleration increased, as H says, then the lines for Jupiter, Earth, and Titan would lie on top of each other, which is obviously not the case.

15. A   Difficulty: Medium

Category: Interpretation of Data

Getting to the Answer: Approach questions methodically and you'll eliminate careless mistakes. According to Figure 1, a spring will have a displacement of 10 cm on Jupiter's surface when a mass (m) of 200 g is attached. What m would give the same spring on Earth a displacement of 10 cm? Trace the horizontal line that corresponds to 10 cm until it intersects the curve for Earth. The intersection occurs around an m of 500 g. 500 g divided by 200 g is 2.5. Thus, to give the same displacement on Earth, m would have to be 2.5 times greater than the m for Jupiter. The correct answer is (A). Watch out for B, which suggests that m would be 2.5 times *less*.

16. J   Difficulty: High

Category: Interpretation of Data

Getting to the Answer: Make sure you understand how new data fits into the existing data before you attempt to answer the question. Figure 1 shows x is approximately 25 cm on Jupiter for a spring with k = 50 N/m, L = 2 cm, and m = 500 g. According to Figure 3, when L = 20 cm, k = 5 N/m. Thus, k has decreased by a factor of 10 from 50 N/m (the spring constant from Figure 1) to 5 N/m. The equation given in the passage is F = kx = mg, which can be rearranged to solve for displacement as follows: x = mg/k. Because m and g remain constant (at 500 g and 24.9 m/s^2, respectively) but k is decreasing by a factor of 10, x should *increase* by a factor of 10, going from 25 cm (the displacement from Figure 1 for a mass of 500 g on Jupiter) to 250 cm. Choice (J) is thus correct. You can also see that (J) is correct simply by noticing that it's the only answer choice showing an increase compared to the original displacement of 25 cm, which is required because k has decreased and k and x are inversely related.

PERFORM

17. D   Difficulty: Low

Category: Interpretation of Data

Getting to the Answer: Table 1 is organized alphabetically, which makes answering this question relatively simple. Locate *Arthrospira fusiformis* in the table and read across. In the presence of potassium silicate and at

30°C, its generation time is 103 minutes. Because this is greater than 90 minutes, (D) is correct. Choices A, B, and C are too low.

18. G   **Difficulty:** Medium

Category: Interpretation of Data

Getting to the Answer: You already examined the figures in Step 2 of the Kaplan Method for Data Representation passages, so you should know where to go to find the answer. Figure 1 plots algae density against generation time for *Dactylococcopsis salina*, so start there. Trace the line up from 400 on the *x*-axis to the curve, and then follow the horizontal line at the point of intersection to the *y*-axis. 400 algae/cm² corresponds to a generation time of about 50 minutes, which matches (G). Choice F can't be correct because the generation time never drops below roughly 30 minutes. Choice H would be the generation time for a density of about 600 algae/cm². Choice J would be the generation time for a density of about 725 algae/cm².

19. A   **Difficulty:** Medium

Category: Interpretation of Data

Getting to the Answer: Time is of the essence in ACT Science, so work quickly but carefully. As you locate each variety of algae in Table 1, jot its generation time down next to the answer choice. Then you won't have to remember which was the highest. *Merismopedia glauca* has the longest generation time at 751 minutes. The correct answer is (A).

20. G   **Difficulty:** Medium

Category: Interpretation of Data

Getting to the Answer: Be careful when converting units on ACT Science questions. Jot down the generation time next to each answer choice to eliminate any chance for error. *Kalagnymene spiralis* is closest to 2 hours, at 131 minutes. The correct answer is (G). You can eliminate F and H because they were grown in NH_4NO_3, not Na_3PO_4.

21. C   **Difficulty:** High

Category: Interpretation of Data

Getting to the Answer: There are plenty of chances to make mistakes on questions that involve multiple figures, so work carefully. Start with Table 1 and find the

generation time of *Dactylococcopsis salina* listed there: 259 minutes. Now, move to Figure 1 and draw a line from 259 on the *y*-axis across until you intersect the curve. Draw a line down from that point to the *x*-axis. It lands slightly below 800 algae/cm², which is closest to correct answer (C).

22. F   **Difficulty:** Low

Category: Interpretation of Data

Getting to the Answer: When you're looking for the relationship between two variables in a line graph, check to see if they go up or down together, if one remains constant as the other changes, or if one goes down as the other goes up. All six lines rise from left to right across the graph, indicating that solubility goes up as temperature goes up. Choice (F) is correct.

23. A   **Difficulty:** Low

Category: Interpretation of Data

Getting to the Answer: Unless the question stem specifically tells you to make guesses about what might happen beyond the range of a figure, consider only the given data when answering questions. The question stem limits you to the range between 0°C and 60°C. The phrase "exhibits the greatest variation in solubility" means "has the biggest change in solubility." KNO_3 starts very low (about 0.15 g/mL at 0°C) and comes close to 1.1 g/mL at 60°C, so it shows the greatest increase in solubility over the specified range. The solutes in B, C, and D have much smaller changes in solubility over the given temperature range. The correct answer is (A).

24. G   **Difficulty:** Medium

Category: Interpretation of Data

Getting to the Answer: When you're asked to look for trends between pairs on a line graph, mark up the graph so that you can easily distinguish one pair from the next— for example, you could circle the NaCl and KCl labels. Start by looking at the solubility curves of $NaClO_3$ and $KClO_3$. They have similar shapes, but the Na salt's solubility line is much higher than the K salt's solubility line. With $NaNO_3$ and KNO_3, the Na salt solubility line is again higher than the K salt solubility line—even though the steeper curve on the KNO_3 curve makes it seem that the two lines may intersect eventually, they do not do so within

Answers & Explanations

the range of values depicted in the graph. NaCl and KCl are the only pair of salts whose solubility lines cross, at a little below 30°C. Below that temperature, NaCl is more soluble; above it, KCl is more soluble. That makes NaCl and KCl different from the other two pairs of salts, whose Na salt solubilities are always above their corresponding K salt solubilities in the graph. Therefore, (G) is correct. Choice F contradicts the information in the graph—the Na salts are more soluble than the K salts, not the other way around. Choices H and J are incorrect because all of the salts are soluble in water.

25. C   Difficulty: Medium

Category: Interpretation of Data

Getting to the Answer: When a question gives you a specific range of values for the x- or y-axis, make sure you focus your attention within that range. To find the solubility of the different salts at 55°C, draw a vertical line up from the x-axis. To find solubilities greater than 0.65 g/mL, draw a horizontal line across the graph from the y-axis. Only three of the solubility curves ever rise above 0.65 g/mL: those for $NaClO_3$, $NaNO_3$, and KNO_3. None of the answer choices includes all three of those salts, but (C) lists two of the three, so (C) is the correct answer. The other three answer choices contain at least one salt with a solubility below 0.65 g/mL at 55°C.

26. J   Difficulty: High

Category: Interpretation of Data

Getting to the Answer: The question stem tells you where in the figure you'll find your answer. This question asks about a solution at 50°C, so start there. Trace the vertical line up from the x-axis at 50°C until it crosses the curve for KNO_3. Find the solubility of KNO_3 by drawing a horizontal line from the point of intersection to the y-axis. The solubility is about 0.84 g/mL. For $KClO_3$, repeat the process to find that the solubility is about 0.18 g/mL. The difference is $0.84 - 0.18 = 0.66$ g/mL. Note, however, that the volume given in the question stem is not 1 mL, but 1 L (or 1,000 mL), so you'll need to multiply the difference by 1,000: 0.66 g/mL × 1,000 mL = 660 g. Choice (J) is correct. Choice G is a trap that you might fall into if you forget to check your units. Choices F and H are incorrect because they represent the amount of $KClO_3$ dissolved in 1 mL and in 1 L, respectively.

ON YOUR OWN

1. C   Difficulty: Low

Category: Interpretation of Data

Getting to the Answer: Pay attention to which data points go with which axis—altitude is on the top x-axis. The question asks for gravitational acceleration at 500 m above sea level. On Figure 1, locate 500 m on the top x-axis and trace the vertical line down to the data point that represents altitude (represented by a solid triangle). Then from that point, draw a horizontal line to the y-axis to determine the gravitational acceleration. The gravitational acceleration is 9.76 m/s², as in (C).

2. G   Difficulty: Low

Category: Interpretation of Data

Getting to the Answer: To determine the relationship between two variables on a graph, check the trend of the data. Do the variables go up or down together, does one stay constant as the other changes, does one go down as the other goes up, or is there a more complex pattern? According to Figure 1, as altitude increases, gravitational acceleration always decreases, so the correct answer is (G).

3. C   Difficulty: Low

Category: Interpretation of Data

Getting to the Answer: On Figure 1, draw a horizontal line from 9.81 m/s² over to the data for latitude and draw a vertical line from the point of intersection down to the x-axis to determine the degrees of latitude. At 9.81m/s², the latitude falls somewhere between 40°N and 60°N. The only answer choice in that range is (C).

4. F   Difficulty: Medium

Category: Interpretation of Data

Getting to the Answer: Table 1 lists locations and their corresponding gravitational acceleration. Therefore, to determine which location is closest to the equator, you need to first determine the gravitational acceleration at the equator (0° latitude). (The question stem suggests that you can assume the locations are at sea level, so there's no need to worry about altitude.) According to Figure 1, at 0°, g is about 9.78 m/s². Look up g values in Table 1 for Singapore, Anchorage, London, and Oslo: Singapore is 9.776 m/s^2, Anchorage is 9.826 m/s^2, London is 9.816 m/s^2, and Oslo is 9.825 m/s^2. The location with a g value closest to 9.78 m/s^2 is 9.776 m/s^2, which corresponds to Singapore. The correct answer is (F).

5. D   **Difficulty:** Medium

Category: Interpretation of Data

Getting to the Answer: At the same latitude, variations in g will be due to altitude. On Table 1 look up g values for Chicago, Denver, and Washington D.C.: Chicago is 9.804 m/s^2, Denver is 9.798 m/s^2, and Washington D.C. is 9.801 m/s^2. According to Figure 1, altitude and g are inversely related: as altitude increases, g decreases. Thus, a lower g corresponds to a higher altitude. To rank the locations from highest to lowest elevation above sea level, simply order the g values for the 3 locations from lowest to highest: 9.798 m/s^2 (Denver), 9.801 m/s^2 (Washington D.C.), 9.804 m/s^2 (Chicago). The correct answer is (D).

6. H   **Difficulty:** High

Category: Interpretation of Data

Getting to the Answer: A parabola with a minimum at 0° will have an axis of symmetry at 0°. This means g for latitude in the Northern Hemisphere will equal g for latitude in the Southern Hemisphere, as long as the two locations share the same altitude. Figure 1 shows that at 35°N, g is 9.80 m/s^2 at sea level. Given the symmetry of the parabola, g at 35°S will also be 9.80 m/s^2 at sea level. The correct answer is (H).

7. A   **Difficulty:** High

Category: Interpretation of Data

Getting to the Answer: The students in the study measured gravitational acceleration as a function of altitude at 15°N latitude. If the students had measured gravitational acceleration at the North Pole instead, the degrees latitude would be greater (specifically, 90°N). According to Figure 1, as latitude increases, gravitational acceleration at sea level increases. Thus, the gravitational acceleration measured at the North Pole should be higher for any given altitude than it would be at 15°N latitude. The correct answer is (A).

8. G   **Difficulty:** Low

Category: Interpretation of Data

Getting to the Answer: Examine the figure carefully to answer this question. In Figure 2, carbon dioxide becomes a liquid around –57°C when the pressure is about 4,000 mm Hg and remains a liquid up to about 31°C at pressures over 50,000 mm Hg. The correct answer is (G).

9. D   **Difficulty:** Medium

Category: Interpretation of Data

Getting to the Answer: First determine the phase of water at 13°C and 28 mm Hg. According to Figure 1, at 13°C and 28 mm Hg, H_2O exists as a liquid. Eliminate A and C. Next determine the phase of carbon dioxide at 13°C and 28 mm Hg. According to Figure 2, CO_2 exists as a gas at that temperature and pressure. Thus, the correct answer is (D).

10. J   **Difficulty:** Medium

Category: Interpretation of Data

Getting to the Answer: The phase diagram for water is shown in Figure 1. To determine how water transitions from liquid to gas, hold one variable steady while changing the other. For instance, at a constant temperature of 20°C, liquid will only become gas when pressure decreases. That means F and G can be eliminated. Now hold pressure steady. At 15 mm Hg, liquid transitions to gas when temperature increases. Thus, the correct answer is (J).

11. B   **Difficulty:** Medium

Category: Interpretation of Data

Getting to the Answer: The freezing point is the point where liquid transitions to solid at a given pressure. In Figure 2, 70,000 mm Hg is beyond the range of the graph. Extend the y-axis to 70,000 mm Hg and continue the solid-liquid boundary line (its slope suggests that, for every increase of 10,000 mm Hg in pressure, there is a temperature increase of a degree or two in the freezing point). Because the freezing point at a pressure of 50,000 mm Hg is just under –50°C, you can expect that the freezing point at 70,000 mm Hg would be only a few degrees higher than that, or roughly –50°C, as in (B).

12. J   **Difficulty:** Medium

Category: Interpretation of Data

Getting to the Answer: On Figure 1, look at the area above 5 mm Hg and ignore the area below. Above 5 mm Hg, as temperature decreases, water transitions from gas directly to liquid and then from liquid directly to solid. Since the transition from gas to liquid is not an option, the correct answer is (J), liquid to solid.

13. A   **Difficulty:** Medium

Category: Interpretation of Data

Getting to the Answer: Use the information in the passage to help you interpret the graphs correctly. According to the passage, the triple point is the temperature and pressure at which the three phases of a substance exist in equilibrium. In Figure 2, the triple point is where the solid-liquid, liquid-gas, and solid-gas boundary lines meet. The temperature and pressure at this point is approximately –55°C and 4,000 mm Hg, respectively. The correct answer is (A).

14. H   **Difficulty:** Medium

Category: Interpretation of Data

Getting to the Answer: A substance melts when it transitions from solid to liquid. The solid-liquid boundary for H_2O falls along 0°C while the solid-liquid boundary for CO_2 falls between about –57°C and –51°C. Because –51°C is less than 0°C, H_2O always melts at a higher temperature than CO_2. The correct answer is (H).

CHAPTER 22

PRACTICE

8. G   **Difficulty:** Medium

Category: Scientific Investigation

Getting to the Answer: It's important to determine for yourself what factors would support the given hypothesis or cause it to be rejected. In this case, the hypothesis would be supported only if the results of Experiment 2 showed higher Hg concentrations in the swordfish and the shark than in the cod and the crab. The results in Table 2 do show this, so the hypothesis is confirmed, as in (G). In F, the "Yes" part is correct, but the reason given contradicts the data in Table 2 (the swordfish actually had the highest concentration), so it is incorrect. Choices H and J both represent the information in the table accurately, but they are both incorrect because they suggest the hypothesis would not be supported.

9. C   **Difficulty:** Medium

Category: Scientific Investigation

Getting to the Answer: The factors that researchers vary intentionally are the independent variables; independent variables are modified to determine the effect on the dependent variables, which are measured. Look back at Table 2. It shows that researchers tested four different kinds of animals and measured the Hg concentrations of 8 specimens of each. Because species is the independent variable, (C) is correct. The volume of tissue was held constant according to the passage, so A is incorrect. All four species in Experiment 2 were extracted from water of the same temperature by the same method, so B is incorrect. CVAFS is the only method of analysis mentioned, so D is incorrect too.

10. F   **Difficulty:** Medium

Category: Scientific Investigation

Getting to the Answer: Based on the results provided, the Hg concentrations for the shark are higher in Table 1 (cold water) than in Table 2 (warm water). Thus, the relationship between water temperature and Hg

concentration is inverse: as water temperature decreases, Hg concentration increases. Sharks at the coldest location will have the largest Hg concentration. The location with the coldest average water temperature is the Northern Atlantic Ocean at 33°F. The correct answer is (F).

11. D   **Difficulty:** High

Category: Scientific Investigation

Getting to the Answer: Refer to the description of CVAFS to understand the process in this question. The passage mentions that CVAFS "indicates the relative concentrations of various elements and compounds." A properly working CVAFS, then, should be able to measure accurately the relative concentrations of Hg and Pb. If lead were interfering with the detection of mercury, how would that affect the reading of Hg concentration? It would make the value measured by the CVAFS differ in some way from the actual value. Using a sample of known concentrations of Hg and Pb, as in (D), would support or reject the accuracy of the CVAFS in detecting the presence of Hg. Thus, (D) is correct. Flooding the sample with Pb would not give you more information about how Pb interferes with Hg readings, so A is incorrect. Choices B and C also would not help, because measuring additional samples with unknown Pb and Hg concentrations would reveal nothing about the accuracy of the CVAFS.

12. G   **Difficulty:** Medium

Category: Scientific Investigation

Getting to the Answer: To identify the animal most likely to have the highest Hg concentration in a new measurement, compare the average values found in Tables 1 and 2. The results suggest that the swordfish have higher Hg concentrations than any other species and that a species from cold water tends to have a higher Hg concentration than the same species from warm water. Therefore, a swordfish caught in cold water would likely have the greatest Hg concentration, making (G) correct.

13. D   **Difficulty:** High

Category: Scientific Investigation

Getting to the Answer: What is concentration? It's the amount of something per unit volume. So what effect would the situation described in the question stem have

Answers & Explanations

on the measured concentration? Consider a simpler example: say you had a cup of sugar water. If you add a cup of sugar-free water to the solution, you will dilute it, reducing the concentration of the sugar. By similar reasoning, adding volume to the samples (without adding more mercury) would result in a lower Hg concentration measurement, regardless of whether the sample is from warm water or cold water. Thus, the correct answer is (D).

PERFORM

14. G   Difficulty: Low

Category: Interpretation of Data

Getting to the Answer: To find the answer to this question, you have to look at Tables 1 and 2. Table 1 shows the conductivity when 10.0 g of each solute is dissolved in 100 mL of water, and Table 2 shows the conductivity when the amount of solute is tripled. Check each answer choice individually, and remember that you're looking for the solute that does NOT increase in conductivity as its concentration increases. NaCl increases from 73.6 mS/cm to 129.7 mS/cm, so eliminate F. $C_{12}H_{22}O_{11}$ measures 0.0 mS/cm in both tables. It shows no increase in conductivity as its concentration increases, so it's the exception, making (G) correct. The conductivity of KI and HCOOH also increase from 119.2 to 371.8 mS/cm and 3.6 to 4.8 mS/cm, respectively, so H and J are incorrect too.

15. D   Difficulty: Medium

Category: Interpretation of Data

Getting to the Answer: This question requires you to extrapolate from the results of the three experiments. You know from comparing the NaCl values in Tables 1 and 2 that the conductivity is higher for 30.0 g of NaCl than for 10.0 g. You also know from comparing values in Tables 2 and 3 that higher temperatures result in higher conductivity measurements. Thus, to find the NaCl solution that conducts the most electricity (in other words, the one with the highest conductivity), you should look for the choice with the most solute and the highest temperature. Choice (D) is thus correct.

16. H   Difficulty: Medium

Category: Interpretation of Data

Getting to the Answer: To determine which solute reached saturation, you need to determine which solution exhibited a decrease in conductivity when more solute was added. An increase in concentration was studied in Experiment 2, so compare the values in Table 1 to those in Table 2. The only solute whose conductivity decreased is $MgCl_2$, so the correct answer is (H).

17. A   Difficulty: Medium

Category: Scientific Investigation

Getting to the Answer: You're not given any data for conductivity at 50°C, but you are given the conductivity of each of the solutes at 20°C in Table 2 and at 70°C in Table 3. What's important to notice from these results is that there is a direct relationship between temperature and conductivity for all of the electrolytes (the solutions that don't have conductivity measurements of 0.0), even $MgCl_2$: as temperature increases, conductivity always increases. Thus, because 50°C is higher than the 20°C temperature used in Experiment 2, you should expect all the conductivity measurements at 50°C to be higher, too. Choice (A) is correct.

18. F   Difficulty: High

Category: Scientific Investigation

Getting to the Answer: What do you know about the role of water in these experiments? According to the passage, water was the solvent in each experiment. Measuring the conductivity of water by itself shows how much of each conductivity measurement can be attributed to water. In other words, the water serves as a control in the experiment. Choice (F) is thus correct. Choice G is incorrect because the passage states that water is the solvent in each experiment, so there's no need to test this. Choice H is incorrect because measuring the conductivity of water alone would reveal nothing about water's ability to dissolve the salts. Choice J is incorrect because pure water does not conduct electricity, as indicated by its consistent conductivity of 0.0.

19. C   **Difficulty:** High

Category: Scientific Investigation

Getting to the Answer: It's difficult to predict an answer to this question, so go straight to the answer choices. Experiment 3 already tested the effect of temperature change on conductivity, so eliminate A. There's nothing in the passage that suggests color has any impact on conductivity, so eliminate B. The effect of water on conductivity was already measured in all three experiments, so eliminate D. The only possibility that remains is (C). And, indeed, replacing water with different solvents would reveal information about conductivity that was not investigated in these experiments. Choice (C) is thus correct.

20. G   **Difficulty:** Low

Category: Scientific Investigation

Getting to the Answer: Bus 3 (built in 2006) is much newer than Bus 1 (1994) or Bus 2 (1992). Do the data in Table 1 support the hypothesis that newer buses emit a smaller percentage of hydrocarbons than older buses? Yes. For any sample time, Bus 3 emits a lower volume of hydrocarbons than either Bus 1 or Bus 2, and on average Bus 1 is lower than Bus 2. Answer (G) is a match. Be careful about choice H. It's true that the highest percentage of hydrocarbons was emitted by the 1992 bus, but H and J are both incorrect because they wrongly suggest that the results of Experiment 1 do not support the hypothesis from the question stem.

21. C   **Difficulty:** Low

Category: Scientific Investigation

Getting to the Answer: This question is asking for an independent variable from Experiment 1. In that experiment, students took exhaust samples at intervals of 30 seconds from buses of the same model that were built in different years. So time after starting and age of bus are the two independent variables. Only (C) mentions either of these variables, so it is correct. Choice A is tempting because it mentions time, but it does so incorrectly: the exhaust samples were collected at 30-second intervals, but the time of day at which they were collected wasn't mentioned. Choice B is incorrect because the same method of collection was used for each sample with each bus. Choice D is incorrect because you're told that 5 mL of each exhaust sample were injected into the gas chromatograph.

22. G   **Difficulty:** Low

Category: Scientific Investigation

Getting to the Answer: The goal is to test emissions when hydrocarbons are at their peak, so check Table 1 and Table 2 and determine the time at which each bus emits the highest percentage of hydrocarbons. Bus 1 emits peak hydrocarbons (12%) at 90 seconds, Bus 2 at 120 seconds (22.9%), and Bus 3 at 90 seconds (6%). This matches (G).

23. C   **Difficulty:** Medium

Category: Scientific Investigation

Getting to the Answer: Based on the description of Experiment 2, its purpose was to find the percentage of hydrocarbons in the exhaust of the same three buses used in Experiment 1 after they had idled for 15 minutes. This would enable the students to compare emissions during idling to emissions after starting. Choice (C) is thus correct. Choice A is incorrect because the experiment tests only hydrocarbons, not nitrogen oxides. Choice B is incorrect because no suggestion is made that the chromatograph isn't already calibrated—in fact, comparisons to samples with known hydrocarbon concentrations occurred during Experiment 1, suggesting the apparatus was calibrated then. Choice D is incorrect because no question is ever raised about the effectiveness of the bag used.

24. F   **Difficulty:** Medium

Category: Scientific Investigation

Getting to the Answer: The students were collecting exhaust samples to determine what percentage of the exhaust was composed of hydrocarbons, so they'd want to keep each exhaust sample as pure as possible. A bag attached to the tailpipe would collect the exhaust before it mixed with, and was diluted by, the outside air. So choice (F) is correct. Choice G violates the students' purpose. They wanted to compare the percentages of hydrocarbons in the exhaust, but adding air and other gases would make their results unreliable. Choice H is incorrect because you know that the collection bag captures all of the exhaust, not only hydrocarbons. Choice J is incorrect because you're given no reason to assume the bag filters anything from the exhaust.

25. D   **Difficulty:** High

Category: Scientific Investigation

Getting to the Answer: If the student wants to investigate whether carbon monoxide gas is affecting the hydrocarbon readings, the student would have to run some kind of test that determines whether the gas chromatograph correctly measures hydrocarbons when carbon monoxide is also present. Testing a control sample with known percentages of carbon monoxide and hydrocarbons, as in (D), would certainly tell the student whether the gas chromatograph was giving correct readings. Choice A won't work. Adding hydrocarbons to the collection bag would increase the percentage of hydrocarbons in the exhaust, but it wouldn't address the carbon monoxide issue. Choice B won't work either. The teacher's car won't tell the student anything new about measuring hydrocarbons when carbon monoxide is present. Choice C is also incorrect. Nothing in the passage suggests that testing oxygen will tell the student anything about carbon monoxide and hydrocarbons.

ON YOUR OWN

1. D   **Difficulty:** Low

Category: Scientific Investigation

Getting to the Answer: Understanding the scientific method will help you score points on questions like these. An independent variable is one that is altered directly by the researchers. The description of Experiment 1 states that the researchers "varied the temperatures," so (D) is correct. Choice A is incorrect because the surface area of each basin is constant. Choice B is incorrect because the rate of algal growth was not directly manipulated by the researchers, although it certainly had an impact on their results. Choice C is incorrect because the number of algal blooms was actually the dependent variable, the one measured by the researchers.

2. F   **Difficulty:** Low

Category: Scientific Investigation

Getting to the Answer: According to Tables 1 and 2, for any of the temperatures studied, the combination of sodium bicarbonate, carbon, and nitrogen yielded greater

algal blooms than any other combination of additives tested. Thus, this combination would be expected to yield the greatest production in a new study, making choice (F) correct. Choices G and H yielded lower production of blooms in the experiments, while J was not studied.

3. A   **Difficulty:** Low

Category: Scientific Investigation

Getting to the Answer: When a question asks you to find a broad trend, make sure you check every relevant experiment before you draw conclusions. For both experiments, within both basins, algal bloom density increases as temperature increases, so the correct answer is (A).

4. H   **Difficulty:** Medium

Category: Scientific Investigation

Getting to the Answer: This question requires you to predict the results of a new measurement, extrapolating beyond what was tested in the experiments from the passage. Sodium bicarbonate was used only in Basin A during Experiment 2, so that's where to look to find the answer. Since algal bloom density increased with temperature during the experiment, and since 40°C is a little higher than the highest temperature recorded, the average number of algal blooms in one square meter of surface area could reasonably be expected to be a little bit greater than the density of 0.78 blooms per square meter that was recorded at 35°C. Therefore, (H) is the most likely value, making it correct. Choices F and G are too low, while J is far too high.

5. A   **Difficulty:** Medium

Category: Scientific Investigation

Getting to the Answer: Carbon dioxide (CO_2) is not listed in either table, but it is mentioned in the paragraph for Experiment 2 as a product of sodium bicarbonate ($NaHCO_3$) and water. In that experiment, the addition of $NaHCO_3$ was the only difference between Basins A and B. The higher algal bloom density at each temperature in Basin A can therefore be attributed to the addition of the $NaHCO_3$ and the consequent production of CO_2. Hence, you can infer that carbon dioxide encourages the growth of algae. The correct answer is (A).

6. G   **Difficulty:** Medium

Category: Scientific Investigation

Getting to the Answer: The extra information in this question stem could be a bit distracting, but you're simply looking for a choice that would decrease algal bloom density. Decreasing the amount of detergent would decrease the amount of phosphorus in the water, which would in turn reduce algal blooms (based on the results of Experiment 1) and the associated pollution. Choice (G), then, is correct. Choices F and H would probably increase the growth of algal blooms. Choice J might also increase the growth, though the combination of phosphorus and sodium bicarbonate was not directly studied in the experiments from the passage.

7. A   **Difficulty:** High

Category: Scientific Investigation

Getting to the Answer: What role did Basin A play in Experiment 1? It acted as the control, or the baseline case, which allowed researchers to isolate the effects of phosphorus on algal bloom density. In Experiment 2, the experimenters wanted to be able to isolate the effect of adding sodium bicarbonate. Therefore, they used the same fertilizers in Basin B to allow for the same kind of comparison as in the first experiment. The correct answer is (A). The passage does not mention how much fertilizer is used, so B is incorrect. Choice C might be tempting because the results of Experiment 2 for Basin B are the same as those of Experiment 1 for Basin B, but this is not the main reason the experimenters repeated the conditions. Choice D is incorrect since it is never suggested in the passage.

8. F   **Difficulty:** Low

Category: Interpretation of Data

Getting to the Answer: This question is essentially asking you to combine parts of the graphs in Figures 1 and 2 into a single graph. Notice that Figure 1 shows the solubility of RNase increasing until it hits a peak at about 135°C, after which it rapidly drops off. Figure 2 shows RNase with no solubility at higher temperatures, but then a rapid increase just before a relatively smaller peak at about 115°C, followed by a more gradual decline as the temperature cools. Thus, the correct graph should look

like two hills separated by a valley, with the larger peak coming first. This corresponds to the graph in (F), the correct answer. Choice G is incorrect because it shows only the first peak, but not the second one as RNase renatures. Choice H is incorrect because it shows a single increase followed by a plateau, which corresponds to nothing in Figures 1 and 2. Choice J is incorrect because it places the first peak too high and at too low of a temperature, even though it captures the second peak accurately.

9. B   **Difficulty:** Low

Category: Interpretation of Data

Getting to the Answer: Normally, you would draw a line up from where 0°C would be in Figure 1, but 0°C is the y-axis. Extend the curve representing Case until it intersects the 0°C line (the y-axis). The value at that intersection should be a bit less than 0.05 g/mL. Thus, the correct answer is (B). Choice A can't be correct, because it is higher than the solubility at 20°C, and solubility clearly drops with decreasing temperature. Choices C and D would be too low.

10. J   **Difficulty:** Low

Category: Interpretation of Data

Getting to the Answer: According to Table 1, no renaturation temperature range is listed for Hase, so you can infer Hase did not renature upon cooling after heating. The correct answer is (J). Choice F corresponds to Hase's denaturation temperature range, and G and H correspond to the renaturation temperatures of Case and RNase, respectively.

11. C   **Difficulty:** Medium

Category: Interpretation of Data

Getting to the Answer: Solubility curves are found in Figure 1, where solubility is a function of temperature, so you can eliminate A and B (also, nothing in the passage suggests that molecular weight changes during denaturation or renaturation). Piecing together Table 1 with Figure 1, you can see that maximum solubility falls within the denaturation temperature range, so the correct answer is (C).

12. J   Difficulty: Medium

Category: Scientific Investigation

Getting to the Answer: Molecular weight and denaturation temperature can both be found in Table 1. The average denaturation temperature would fall in the middle of the denaturation temperature range. First rank the proteins from highest to lowest molecular weight: Hase is highest, Case is in the middle, and RNase is lowest. Then match the denaturation temperature ranges to the reordered proteins: Hase is 80–95°C, Case is 150–155°C, and RNase is 135–145°C. Case has the highest temperatures in its denaturation range but its molecular weight falls in the middle, so there is no correlation and the hypothesis is not supported. The correct answer is (J). Choice H is incorrect because it suggests an inverse relationship that is not supported by the data.

13. C   Difficulty: High

Category: Scientific Investigation

Getting to the Answer: What would best explain why the peak solubility is lower after Case denatures and then renatures? The passage states that "some proteins can fold back (renature) into their original conformation when the temperature is decreased," which suggests that not all of the molecules of a particular protein will necessarily renature after denaturing. The correct answer is (C). Choices A, B, and D are not supported by the passage.

14. J   Difficulty: High

Category: Scientific Investigation

Getting to the Answer: This question requires you to predict the results of repeating Experiment 2 with a new protein. You are given its denaturation and renaturation ranges and are asked to figure out where its solubility would peak. For the original experiments, the ranges appear in Table 1 and peak solubility can be found in Figure 1. Each protein's solubility peaks at the lower end of its denaturation range. So, you should expect that the solubility of ovalbumin will peak at the lower bound of its range at 115°C. Thus, the correct answer is (J).

CHAPTER 23

PRACTICE

10. J **Difficulty:** Medium

Category: Evaluation of Models, Inferences, and Experimental Results

Getting to the Answer: When you're reading Conflicting Viewpoints passages, it's important to note both what scientists agree and disagree about. Scientist 1 states that the surface of Triton is "covered with a thick layer of methane and nitrogen ice," while Scientist 2 mentions "the glacier-like movement of the methane-nitrogen polar ice caps," so both would agree that Triton's surface contains methane and nitrogen ice. Choice (J) is correct. Choices F and G are incorrect because only Scientist 1 proposes volcanic activity and internal heating by radioactive decay. Choice H is incorrect because only Scientist 2 proposes 'snowfall' as the cause of the dark streaks.

11. C **Difficulty:** High

Category: Evaluation of Models, Inferences, and Experimental Results

Getting to the Answer: To answer this question, first go back to the passage and reread the part where Scientist 2 discusses higher-resolution images. Scientist 2 proposes that small craters—which constitute some of Triton's surface features—arose from the impact of small meteorites over a long period of time, so (C) is correct. You could eliminate A immediately because Scientist 2 doesn't discuss planetoids. Choice B is incorrect because the impact of meteorites has nothing to do with volcanic activity (and that's Scientist 1's view anyway). Choice D is incorrect because nowhere in Scientist 1's argument does it say that lower-resolution images were used.

12. H **Difficulty:** Medium

Category: Evaluation of Models, Inferences, and Experimental Results

Getting to the Answer: First consider item I. There is no need for a chemical analysis of Triton's surface because both scientists agree that there is a layer of nitrogen and methane on the surface. Therefore, item I is false. Choice (H) is the only choice that does NOT include item I, so (H) must be correct. Items II and III are both true because subsurface temperature measurements and core radioactivity readings could both help to settle the question of whether Triton could sustain volcanic activity—as Scientist 1 notes, a source of internal heat such as radioactive decay is necessary for volcanic activity.

13. B **Difficulty:** Low

Category: Evaluation of Models, Inferences, and Experimental Results

Getting to the Answer: If you can't recall the points of disagreement, research the answer choices one by one. The scientists most clearly disagree about the physical processes responsible for the features found on Triton. Scientist 1 claims that a number of geological features are caused by volcanic activity, whereas Scientist 2 believes the same features are caused by glacier-like movement of ice caps and 'snowfall.' The correct answer is (B). The scientists do agree on what features are observed and the chemical composition of the surface of Triton, so A and C are incorrect. Choice D is incorrect because the origin of Triton is discussed only by Scientist 2.

14. H **Difficulty:** Medium

Category: Evaluation of Models, Inferences, and Experimental Results

Getting to the Answer: You should have answered this question first, before reading Scientist 2's viewpoint. To answer this question, you must know Scientist 1's central claim: a number of features on Triton arise from volcanic activity. Therefore, if evidence of an active volcano were found in the images, this hypothesis would be supported, so (H) is correct. Choice F would not support this hypothesis; the fact that the surfaces of the three moons are composed of the same elements doesn't prove that they all must exhibit volcanic activity. It is clear from Scientist 1's viewpoint that volcanic activity requires an internal heat source, so the external characteristics of the moon are not relevant. Choice G is incorrect because Scientist 1 doesn't discuss the images of small craters. Choice J is incorrect because it pertains to Scientist 2's viewpoint.

15. A   Difficulty: High

Category: Evaluation of Models, Inferences, and Experimental Results

Getting to the Answer: Consider how this new information affects both Scientist 1's and Scientist 2's viewpoints. Scientist 1 believes that radioactive decay may provide the heat for volcanic eruptions on Triton, but Scientist 2 says that Triton has been cooling in a stable orbit and is too small to support a source of internal heating. If new research suggested that slow radioactive decay could, in fact, continue in small bodies for up to 10 billion years, this information would support the view of Scientist 1 only. The correct answer is (A).

16. J   Difficulty: High

Category: Evaluation of Models, Inferences, and Experimental Results

Getting to the Answer: The correct answer must be consistent with what Scientist 2 stated in the passage. Go back and reread what Scientist 2 said about Triton's orbit. The third sentence of the paragraph states that Triton's "unusual orbit—it revolves in the direction opposite to the planet's rotation—indicates that it was captured by Neptune." If Triton's orbit is unusual in that it revolves in the direction opposite Neptune's rotation, then most moons must revolve in the same direction as their planet's rotation, as in (J). Choice F might be tempting because Scientist 2 does state that Triton's original orbit must have been highly elliptical before it settled into its current circular orbit. However, there is no indication in the passage that circular orbits are typical of other moons. Choices G and H are irrelevant to the information presented in the passage.

PERFORM

17. D   Difficulty: Low

Category: Evaluation of Models, Inferences, and Experimental Results

Getting to the Answer: Scientist 2 mentions that research has shown that the giant panda's DNA is far more similar to a bear's DNA than to that of any other family. Choice (D) paraphrases this idea. Scientist 1, not Scientist 2, mentions the lack of size disparity between

male and female pandas, so A is incorrect. Choice B is a distortion: Scientist 2 discusses the similar aggressive behaviors of bears and pandas; Scientist 1 discusses the similar greeting behaviors of raccoons and pandas. Scientist 2 never discusses the eating habits of pandas or bears, so C is incorrect as well.

18. J   Difficulty: Low

Category: Evaluation of Models, Inferences, and Experimental Results

Getting to the Answer: Both scientists make their arguments by comparing the physical, behavioral, and genetic traits of the giant panda to the characteristics of either the bear or the raccoon family. Therefore, both scientists would agree that animals should be classified into families based on these criteria. The correct answer is (J). Neither scientist suggests that pandas should be classified in a separate family, so F is incorrect. Scientist 1 argues that the giant panda is closely related to the raccoon, so G is not a point of agreement. Scientist 1 also describes ways in which the behavior of raccoons and giant pandas differ from the behavior of bears, which means H is incorrect too.

19. B   Difficulty: Low

Category: Evaluation of Models, Inferences, and Experimental Results

Getting to the Answer: Scientist 1 explains that both raccoons and pandas cover their eyes with their front paws when intimidated. Thus, the correct answer is (B). Scientist 1 mentions that pandas, like raccoons, have a greeting that consists of bleats and barks, but the scientist does not connect bleating and barking with a panda's behavior when frightened, so A is incorrect. Scientist 2, not Scientist 1, discusses the panda's aggressive behavior of swatting with its forepaws and tendency to walk pigeon-toed, so C and D are both incorrect.

20. H   Difficulty: Medium

Category: Evaluation of Models, Inferences, and Experimental Results

Getting to the Answer: Scientist 1 states that *Ursidae* (bears) have 36 pairs of chromosomes, while Scientist 2 cites the similarity between giant panda and bear DNA as a reason to classify pandas as bears, so statement I would support the classification of a mammal as a bear. This rules out G and J. Scientist 1 also explains that male bears can be up to twice the size of female bears, whereas male and female raccoons are the same size. Statement III, therefore, also supports the classification of a mammal as a bear. Choice (H) must be correct, and you don't even have to look at statement II (which would support classification as a raccoon, not as a bear).

21. A   Difficulty: Medium

Category: Evaluation of Models, Inferences, and Experimental Results

Getting to the Answer: This question asks you to determine which of the four choices would provide support for the viewpoint expressed by Scientist 2. Similarities between the blood proteins of giant pandas and several bear species would certainly provide evidence for Scientist 2's theory that pandas should be classified as bears, so (A) is correct. Watch out for choices that support the other position in questions like this: choices B and D, for instance, are incorrect because they support Scientist 1's argument that pandas should be classified as raccoons, not as bears. Choice C, meanwhile, is inconclusive because it only gives a reason against Scientist 1's hypothesis, not a reason in favor of Scientist 2's.

22. F   Difficulty: Low

Category: Evaluation of Models, Inferences, and Experimental Results

Getting to the Answer: If giant pandas and raccoons both had scent-releasing glands, this evidence would support the viewpoint of Scientist 1, who thinks that giant pandas are closely related to raccoons. Thus, the correct answer is (F). Choice G contains a contradiction: Scientist 2 argues that giant pandas should be classified as bears, but the evidence given in G that bears do not have scent-releasing glands would indicate a major difference between pandas and bears. It is unclear how either a raccoon's poor sense of smell or a bear's scent marking would be directly related to the existence of scent-releasing glands, so H and J are incorrect.

23. B   Difficulty: High

Category: Evaluation of Models, Inferences, and Experimental Results

Getting to the Answer: Scientist 2 contends that giant pandas display the same aggressive behavior as bears do: they both swat and try to grab adversaries with their forepaws. Only (B) presents an effective counterclaim that concerns the aggressive behavior of pandas. According to (B), an aggressive panda's behavior is like a raccoon's behavior, not a bear's, in that the panda bobs its head up and down. Choices A and C are examples that Scientist 2 uses to argue that giant pandas should be classified as bears, so Scientist 1 could not use these same examples to counter Scientist 2's claims. The number of chromosomes for a giant panda, discussed in D, is not connected to Scientist 2's claim that giant pandas and bears display similar aggressive behaviors.

24. F   Difficulty: Low

Category: Evaluation of Models, Inferences, and Experimental Results

Getting to the Answer: You know that Scientist 1 claims that hyperacidity in the stomach from a highly acidic diet and prolonged stress cause gastric ulcers, so you can predict Scientist 1 would suggest acid-suppressing drugs to treat the ulcers. Scientist 2 claims that *H. pylori* infection causes gastric ulcers, so you can predict Scientist 2 would suggest antibiotics to treat the ulcers. Choice (F) correctly matches this prediction. Choice G reverses the treatments, and H and J mention NSAIDs, which Scientist 3 suggests are the cause of ulcers, not a treatment.

25. C   Difficulty: Low

Category: Evaluation of Models, Inferences, and Experimental Results

Getting to the Answer: The gastric mucosa is defined in the introductory paragraph. Choices A, B, and D are all stated explicitly: the gastric mucosa "protects the stomach from digestive juices . . . [and] also removes hydrogen ions and secretes bicarbonate ions to maintain a neutral environment." Necrosis of cells is mentioned by Scientist 1 and is caused by stress; the gastric mucosa does NOT promote necrosis of cells. Thus, the correct answer is (C).

26. H   **Difficulty:** Medium

Category: Evaluation of Models, Inferences, and Experimental Results

Getting to the Answer: According to Scientist 3, the cause of ulcers is chronic use of NSAIDs, which "disrupts the production of prostaglandins in the stomach and leads to an increase in gastric acid." You can infer from this that a disruption in the production of prostaglandins leads to lower levels of prostaglandins. Therefore, an increase in gastric ulcers would correspond with a decrease in prostaglandins in the stomach. Thus, the correct answer is (H). Choices F and G refer to the viewpoints of Scientist 1 and 2, respectively, and J states the opposite of what Scientist 3 would suggest. According to Scientist 3, decreased use of NSAIDs would cause a decrease in gastric ulcers.

27. C   **Difficulty:** Medium

Category: Evaluation of Models, Inferences, and Experimental Results

Getting to the Answer: According to Scientist 1, gastric ulcers are caused by lifestyle habits such as diet and stress, while Scientist 2 blames the bacterium *H. pylori*. To strengthen Scientist 1's theory while weakening Scientist 2's, you would need evidence showing the cause-and-effect relationship between diet or stress and ulcers in the absence of *H. pylori*. Only (C) provides such evidence.

28. J   **Difficulty:** Medium

Category: Evaluation of Models, Inferences, and Experimental Results

Getting to the Answer: Information found in the introductory paragraph or mentioned by all of the viewpoints can generally be considered points of agreement in a Conflicting Viewpoints passage. Only Scientist 3 states that consuming NSAIDs causes gastric ulcers, so eliminate F. Choice G combines key terms from the accounts of Scientist 2 and Scientist 3, but neither scientist makes this claim. Choice H is directly challenged by the study cited by Scientist 2. All 3 scientists do, however, suggest that consuming caffeinated drinks and spicy foods aggravates existing gastric ulcers, so (J) is correct.

29. D   **Difficulty:** Medium

Category: Evaluation of Models, Inferences, and Experimental Results

Getting to the Answer: Remember to keep straight who said what. If a person 65 years old with arthritis developed a gastric ulcer, Scientist 1 would likely conclude the person experiences chronic stress, Scientist 2 would likely conclude the person is infected with *H. pylori*, and Scientist 3 would likely conclude the person chronically uses NSAIDs. The only answer choice that correctly matches the predicted information is (D).

30. G   **Difficulty:** High

Category: Evaluation of Models, Inferences, and Experimental Results

Getting to the Answer: Scientist 2 argues against the effectiveness of acid-suppressing drugs in treating ulcers by citing the results of a study: "When people with gastric ulcers were administered only acid-suppressing drugs, 80% experienced recurrence of ulcers." To challenge this evidence, Scientist 1 would have to explain how the actual cause of the recurrence had to do with a change in lifestyle, rather than the effects of *H. pylori*. Choice F supports Scientist 2's claim, so it can be eliminated. Choice (G) suggests that taking the drugs caused the patients additional stress, which Scientist 1 suggests leads to "increased gastric acidity, necrosis of mucosal cells, and changes in the mucous barrier," all of which could lead to the recurrence of ulcers without requiring the presence of *H. pylori*. Choice (G) is thus correct. Choice H would be an argument to support Scientist 3's explanation. Choice J is a true statement but does not counter Scientist 2's argument.

ON YOUR OWN

1. D   **Difficulty:** Low

Category: Evaluation of Models, Inferences, and Experimental Results

Getting to the Answer: Scientists 1 and 2 disagree about whether the universe is open or closed, whether mass measurements that have been taken are accurate, and whether luminosity can be used to calculate mass and density. They do not disagree about the fact that a density greater than the critical density results in a closed universe, so eliminate A. *Luminosity* is just a technical term for *brightness* introduced in Scientist 1's account, which Scientist 2 doesn't dispute, so B is also incorrect. The scientists agree that some matter has been detected and some has not (Scientist 1 mentions *detectable matter*, implying that there is also some matter that has not yet been detected), so eliminate C too. Scientist 1 concludes that the universe is still open based on calculations from luminosity measurements, whereas Scientist 2 concludes that there is some mass that is not revealed by these measurements. Thus, (D) is the correct answer.

2. H   Difficulty: Low

Category: Evaluation of Models, Inferences, and Experimental Results

Getting to the Answer: Scientist 1 argues that the universe "will continue to expand." Scientist 2 argues that the universe "will eventually stop expanding." Both suggest the universe is currently expanding, so choice (H) is correct. Choice F is incorrect because nothing in the passage suggests a static universe. Choice G is incorrect because the scientists disagree about whether the universe will *eventually* collapse, but neither suggests that it is *currently* collapsing. Neither scientist disputes the value of the critical density provided in the opening paragraph, so J is also incorrect.

3. C   Difficulty: Low

Category: Evaluation of Models, Inferences, and Experimental Results

Getting to the Answer: Scientist 2 states that observations of stars in other galaxies suggest more mass than the value endorsed by Scientist 1 and that this "missing mass must be non-luminous matter that cannot be detected by luminosity measurements." This directly matches (C). Choice A is the opposite of what Scientist 2 suggests, while B is too extreme—just because it has not been detected by luminosity measurements does not mean it will never be detected. Choice D is a distortion: being non-luminous does not necessarily make the matter *alien*.

4. F   Difficulty: Medium

Category: Evaluation of Models, Inferences, and Experimental Results

Getting to the Answer: Scientist 1 determines the average density of the universe by calculating the collected mass of all matter in a large part of the universe detected by luminosity measurements. Statement I is thus true, which allows you to eliminate G and J. Statement II does not appear in the remaining answer choices, so you do not need to evaluate it, but it is false since Scientist 1 never discusses planetary motions. Statement III is false because Scientist 1 never mentions non-luminous matter, so eliminate H. Because only statement I is true, (F) is correct.

5. A   Difficulty: Medium

Category: Evaluation of Models, Inferences, and Experimental Results

Getting to the Answer: What is Scientist 2's hypothesis? The combined density of luminous and non-luminous matter exceeds the critical value. How could Scientist 2 support this hypothesis? If she could determine the mass of non-luminous matter in a large volume of the universe, she could add it to the mass of luminous matter detected, and use the total sum to show that the average density of the universe exceeds the critical value. Choice (A) matches this prediction. Choice B would challenge her hypothesis, while C and D are irrelevant.

6. G   Difficulty: High

Category: Evaluation of Models, Inferences, and Experimental Results

Getting to the Answer: Scientist 1's estimate of the size of the universe comes from evaluating "a large volume of the universe." If this volume is not representative of the whole universe and there are other parts of the universe with greater amounts of luminous matter, then all the new mass need NOT be from non-luminous matter, so eliminate F. Scientist 1's mass calculation accounted for 5% of the critical density. If new measurements show that the universe has passed the critical density, the new mass must account for at least 95% of the critical density. Therefore, the correct answer is (G). Scientist 2 suggests that the motion of the stars in other galaxies was consistent with the idea that the universe had reached critical density, so H is incorrect. Choice J is incorrect because the new information suggests that the universe is closed, not open.

7. B   Difficulty: High

Category: Evaluation of Models, Inferences, and Experimental Results

Getting to the Answer: According to the evidence cited by Scientist 1, the density of the universe is much lower than the critical value, so the universe is open. Choice A is incorrect because Scientist 1 never suggests that there is a discrepancy between the universe's density and current calculations. Scientist 1 concludes that the average density of the universe is currently 5% of the critical value, meaning the critical value is 20 times greater than its actual density, so (B) is correct. Choice C contradicts Scientist 1's viewpoint, which is based on calculating mass (and density) using measurements of brightness. Scientist 1 does not discuss non-luminous matter, so D is also incorrect.

8. H   Difficulty: Low

Category: Evaluation of Models, Inferences, and Experimental Results

Getting to the Answer: Information found in the introductory paragraph of a Conflicting Viewpoints passage can generally be considered as a point of agreement between the different viewpoints. The opening paragraph here states that "mitochondria are surrounded by two membranes, contain their own DNA, and divide independently from the host cell." Therefore, both scientists would agree that mitochondria possess their own DNA, making (H) correct. Choice F is Scientist 2's view, while G is Scientist 1's. Choice J contradicts the opening paragraph, so neither scientist would agree with it.

9. D   Difficulty: Low

Category: Evaluation of Models, Inferences, and Experimental Results

Getting to the Answer: According to Scientist 1, "as the oxygen levels in the atmosphere rose, some prokaryotes evolved into aerobes to utilize the free oxygen. Since anaerobic prokaryotes could not metabolize oxygen, they engulfed the aerobic prokaryotes." This resulted in an endosymbiotic relationship. Therefore, the correct answer is (D). Choice A is a distortion (anaerobic bacteria were the ones that could not utilize free oxygen), and B and C are true but irrelevant.

10. F   Difficulty: Low

Category: Evaluation of Models, Inferences, and Experimental Results

Getting to the Answer: The answer can be found directly stated in the passage. Scientist 1 states that "aerobic prokaryotes evolved into mitochondria. For that reason, mitochondrial DNA differs both genetically and structurally from the DNA in the eukaryotic cell's nucleus." Therefore, the correct answer is (F). Choices G and H correspond to Scientist 2's viewpoint. Choice J contradicts the opening paragraph, which states that mitochondria have 2 membranes.

11. A   Difficulty: Medium

Category: Evaluation of Models, Inferences, and Experimental Results

Getting to the Answer: Scientist 1 states that "aerobic prokaryotes evolved into mitochondria" but Scientist 2 claims that "the DNA...of mitochondria differ from those of bacteria." Thus, the statement that mitochondrial DNA has the same structure as prokaryotic DNA would strengthen Scientist 1's viewpoint but weaken Scientist 2's. The correct answer is (A).

12. J   Difficulty: Medium

Category: Evaluation of Models, Inferences, and Experimental Results

Getting to the Answer: Scientist 2 states that mitochondrial DNA and ribosomal proteins differ from those of bacteria, concluding from these facts that "mitochondria could not have evolved from the endosymbiosis of two prokaryotes." This matches (J). Choice F is incorrect because it's the exact opposite of Scientist 2's conclusion. Choice G is incorrect because Scientist 2 never discusses the "aerobic capacity of mitochondria." Choice H is incorrect because genetic complexity is never an issue in the passage.

13. B   **Difficulty:** High

Category: Evaluation of Models, Inferences, and Experimental Results

Getting to the Answer: What is each Scientist's hypothesis? Scientist 1 states that "mitochondria-containing eukaryotes developed from an endosymbiotic relationship between two types of prokaryotes" and that "aerobic prokaryotes evolved into mitochondria." Scientist 2 claims that "mitochondria developed from the membrane of the [eukaryotic] cell," which evolved from a single prokaryote. Choice A states that mitochondria originated from aerobic *eukaryotes*, which is a view suggested by neither scientist, making it incorrect. Choice (B) correctly states Scientist 1's view that mitochondria originated from aerobic prokaryotes. Moreover, a study that shows mitochondria divide by binary fission, much like bacteria, would definitely support Scientist 1. Thus, the correct answer is (B). Choice C assigns a view from Scientist 1 to Scientist 2, so it is incorrect. Choice D correctly describes Scientist 2's viewpoint, but it would not be supported by the study.

14. G   **Difficulty:** High

Category: Evaluation of Models, Inferences, and Experimental Results

Getting to the Answer: Scientist 2's claim is that *most* mitochondrial proteins are synthesized from genes in the nucleus, not *all*, so F is incorrect. Scientist 1 could explain the role of the nucleus in synthesizing mitochondrial proteins by arguing that many mitochondrial genes were transferred to the nucleus after the two independent prokaryotes became one organism. Therefore, the correct answer is (G). Choice H is irrelevant, and J is false because the passage states that mitochondria possess their own DNA and synthesize some of their own enzymes.

CHAPTER 25: ACT WRITING IN-DEPTH

PRACTICE

¶3: 2nd body paragraph

Continue supporting your **thesis** <u>Important to study leaders and their decisions</u>

Provide 2nd example/reasoning: include specific, relevant information <u>Lincoln not like every Ameri-</u><u>can but made lasting impact</u>

¶4: 3rd body paragraph

Explain how your thesis compares and contrasts with **Perspectives One, Two, and/or Three** <u>com-</u><u>bines 1 and 2 for most effective way of teaching history, disagrees with 3</u>

Strengths/Weaknesses of the perspective(s)

- Insights offered / Insights not considered <u>general knowledge of dates helps understand event</u><u>impacts, learn from past /</u> knowing dates alone does not explain effects; can learn from past, but need more than dates to understand context/impact

- Persuasive / Not persuasive <u>3 is not persuasive</u>

Example or Reasoning: provide specific, relevant information <u>knowing date of EP or 0 inauguration</u><u>not enough to explain impact of events</u>

¶5: Conclusion paragraph

Recap your **thesis** <u>best approach = examine how imp. leaders affect dev. of entire population</u>

Recap how your thesis compares and contrasts with **Perspectives One, Two, and/or Three** <u>study</u><u>of history = better decisions; the best way = study how leaders' decisions affect society as a whole</u>

PERFORM

The following includes an example of a high-scoring student response for ¶3, ¶4, and ¶5.

Especially in American history, where most of the important leaders were democratically elected by a majority of the population, major historical characters could be considered as representative of the nation as a whole, because voters are unlikely to choose candidates with values and backgrounds much different from their own. However, this view overlooks the very exceptionality built into the electoral process. In order to persuade the majority of people to vote for him, a candidate must possess attributes or talents that distinguish him, and make him preferable to his opponent. The example of Abraham Lincoln is illustrative. While Lincoln came from a humble background, similar to that of many rural Americans of his time, his penetrating thinking and persuasive

Answers & Explanations

oratory set him apart and were not characteristic of the population as a whole. Lincoln's personal history is an important backdrop to the decisions he made that shaped US history; however, what is most necessary for Americans to understand and appreciate are the changes he brought to the entire nation through his leadership of the North during the Civil War, and through his Emancipation Proclamation. This is why it is necessary to supplement the study of the lives of national leaders with the understanding of how their decisions affected the population as a whole.

The study of history enables us to understand how societies progress, and to use the knowledge of the past to make better decisions in the present. The least valuable understanding of history comes through memorization of dates and events. Although some argue that knowledge of dates and events is necessary for us to learn from the past, if a person could recite the precise date of the signing of the Emancipation Proclamation, or the dates of Barack Obama's inaugurations, that knowledge would be insufficient to describe or explain the effects of those events. A general knowledge of the approximate time of major events is enough to analyze their impact, and again, their impact is best measured by evaluating the development or progress of the population of the nation as a whole.

The most effective way to learn from history is to study how leaders' decisions of the past have impacted society as a whole. In order to make the best decisions, we must have some metric to evaluate the success of the choices made in the past, both the decisions of society's influential leaders and society's acceptance of those decisions. The welfare of the society as a whole is an excellent measure, and should be the focus of teaching history.

ON YOUR OWN

Sample Student Essays

Prompt 1

Score of 6

With the explosion in information technology, many companies are developing applications to enhance students' learning. Some of these companies are profit-based and some are non-profit, entering this endeavor to benefit students and society, not themselves. Because the personal data of technology users is marketable, three perspectives have arisen about the usage of the students' personal information. Some believe this data should never be shared, because it is collected from persons below the legal age of consent. Others believe that the data can be shared, but only among not-for-profit developers who will use the data for further non-profit projects. Finally, some believe that use of this technology, with realtime feedback, implies that the user understands and agrees that the information they provide will be freely available to anyone, for any purpose. Because disclosure of personal information can have serious consequences, and because the students using this software cannot legally consent to a contract, personal information obtained from educational technology should never be shared without consent from the students' parents or guardians.

Even though the information collected by ed tech software has the potential to be utilized to further aid student learning through new applications, this potential benefit is not great enough to permit the sharing of students' personal data in light of its great risks. One doesn't have to look very far to find examples of harm caused by personal information obtained improperly from the internet. My uncle's identity was stolen from his

PayPal account, and, while the money that was stolen was replaced, he had to close all his bank accounts and change all his credit cards. Recently, the major company Sony was hacked and their company e-mails were posted on the internet. Educational technology companies should keep the welfare of their student users foremost and not share information obtained through the use of their software. Perhaps I might want to try to take a difficult course online, and then fail it because either the course was too hard, or because I wasn't able to learn it well from the technology. If that information were shared and published on the internet, it might negatively affect my college applications, even though I was just taking an extra class to try to improve myself. Because of the potential harm caused by abuse of personal information, educational technology companies should not share their students' information freely.

In addition to the risks posed by the sharing of student data, such sharing should only be done when one has obtained express consent—and such consent is not usually obtained by ed tech companies. Some believe that students using educational technology understand and agree that, because they're using a real-time application with continuous data sharing, their information can be shared indiscriminately with any organization, for any purpose. This perspective is severely flawed in two ways: it assumes that students would think about and agree to this sharing, and it permits the obtaining of permission for this sharing (however indirectly) from students who are below the legal age of consent. Because most websites offer some privacy protection—for example, any shopping, credit card, or banking site is protected—technology users tend to assume their data is protected. Even Facebook and Google, which rely on users sharing information, encourage their subscribers to limit those who can observe or contribute to their accounts. Students are far more likely to assume their data on educational websites is similarly protected, rather than to think that they are agreeing to limitless distribution of their information. Even if students actually agreed to this sharing, if they are under the age of 18, they're not able to legally consent to this activity. Therefore, educational technology companies should not distribute student information.

Some would argue that the information generated by students' activity on the educational software provides valuable information to improve the technology and should be shared with non-profit entities working to improve educational outcomes. While this may seem to be an acceptable compromise, this view assumes that the sensitive personal data obtained from students will never be stolen or misused. Again, from current events, we know that employees can steal data, as did Edward Snowden, and that even sophisticated systems such as PayPal and Sony can be hacked. If non-profit educational technology companies want to share data, they could strip off all personal identifiers and share information such as number of users, average scores, average time spent, etc. as long as there were no way to trace any information back to the individual student. This could further the goal of developing educational technology while preserving the privacy of students. Without protecting the identities of individual students, this data should not be shared, even with not-for-profit entities.

If educational technology companies want to use the personal information of their subscribers to further improve their products without putting students at risk, they have two options. First, they could disclose their proposed usages and obtain permission from the parents or legal guardians of their users. Second, they could strip off any information that could personally identify the students and use that information in any way they choose. The tremendous success of Khan Academy, a free non-profit educational website that only collects an email address from its users, indicates that these technologies can be developed and improved rapidly without risking the harm to students that could be generated from data sharing. Through the examples of my uncle's identity theft, the hacking of Sony, and Edward Snowden, it is clear that there are many potential problems facing students if their personal information is shared. These risks exist whether they are used to generate profits or for altruistic purposes. Student information obtained from educational websites should not be distributed to other entities without the permission of the student's parents or guardians.

Score of 5

Educational technology companies are generating extensive data through the use of their programs. Non-profit companies want to use this information to improve their offerings more quickly, and for-profit companies want to defray some of the costs of developing these products through the sale of their users' information. Some people believe that any data collected from students under the age of 18 should be completely protected, others believe that that data may be shared among non-profit companies, and others believe that the data may be shared with anyone, because the students are using a real-time system and thus have no expectation of privacy. Because of all the problems that may arise if information is used inappropriately, and because products can be improved without sharing data, student data obtained from educational technology should not be shared.

Those who say student data should be completely protected are correct, because of the many problems that can arise if data is misused. E-mail bullying has caused many students to suffer. If students' scores were ever stolen from an educational website, and published, it could lead to similar trauma. We know from experience that personal information obtained by a company is not safe from hackers. Student data should be completely protected because of these risks.

Many non-profit educational technology companies want to share student data among themselves to share ideas and more quickly improve their products, but this sharing is not necessary to improve their products. After all, Khan Academy is a very successful educational technology program that has risen up very quickly on its own. From one man producing YouTube videos for his niece, Khan Academy is rapidly growing to fulfill its goal of providing a free education to anyone in the world. Their success indicates that data sharing is not necessary to produce excellent educational technology.

Some people think that sharing student data should be an expected outcome of using educational technology. However, students use educational technology to learn; they don't expect to be targeted by advertisers as a result of their search for knowledge or self-improvement. To assume that students know that their information will be shared, just because they're using a real-time application, doesn't make any sense. When we buy something from the internet, our important identity and financial data are protected. Yes, we may later see an advertisement or a recommendation for another product, but even though the sale was made in real-time, our personal information is protected. Users of educational technology sites would expect no less.

Because so many serious problems can arise from the misuse of personal information, data from students under the age of 18 on educational websites should be completely protected. To allow non-profit companies to use it still exposes innocent students to harmful consequences. To allow any company to use it is not only wrong, but unnecessary. Since the protection of minors should be our highest priority and effective education technology can be created without it, student data from ed tech companies should never be shared.

Score of 4

Educational technology companies are considering sharing the data they collect. Some think any data sharing is wrong, because most of the students who generate that data are under the age of 18. Some think that it's acceptable to share data among non-profit companies to improve their products, while some believe that the data can be shared with anyone for any reason. Data shouldn't be shared because of the dangers that may arise when students' data is shared.

The safest route is for educational technology companies to never share their student data. Any time data is shared, there's a risk that it will be stolen and misused. My mom had to get a new Target credit card last year after one of their employees stole a lot of credit card numbers. Perhaps an employee of an educational technology company might do the same thing, and my test scores or home address could be posted on the internet. It's not worth taking that chance. When I'm using an educational website, I expect my information will remain private.

Sharing students' data might not even be legal. People under 18 are considered minors and are not able to consent to their information being used. These products do not ask for consent from parents, so using the data they collect would be wrong. Students are using these sites to improve themselves and to learn. To take that opportunity to use their personal information just to make more money is taking advantage of them. Educational websites should never sell or make money from their students.

Non-profit educational technology companies are trying to help people learn and improve, so some argue that they should be allowed to share student data to modify and improve their products more quickly—but again, any data sharing brings risks. The more people have access to data, the more likely it is that there may be someone who would steal or misuse it. The risks of the harm that may come about from sharing the information are greater than the benefits that may arise.

Student data is personal and private, and it's important for companies to recognize that. Even nonprofit companies should protect students' information and privacy. The risk of damage that may occur if personal information is misused is greater than any advantage that might come from sharing that data, and sharing it might not be legal anyway.

Score of 3

Three perspectives have been offered in regards to ed tech companies sharing the data they collect from elementary and high school students. Some people believe students data should be wholly protected, some people believe it can be shared as long as it's just being used to make the programs better, and some think that everyone should be able to use the data however they like. I agree that students data should be wholly protected because a lot of times, when your information is on the internet, it can cause problems.

My mom is always checking my computer to make sure I don't use the internet wrong. She doesn't let me put our address in my Facebook, even if I just want my friends to be able to come over. She says that somehow crooks could find out where we live. If my school was giving my address out, she'd be upset.

I bet the companies would want to share students information to be able to make their programs better, but it's not worth the risk. Why should I have to worry about bad stuff happeneing to me just because I use some companies website?

And of course companies want to make more money, but I don't want them to make money by making my life more dangerous. That's not fair. Why should they make money off my information? I'm just doing what I have to for my classes.

So the only right thing is for companies to protect student information. This way, students can learn more, and still be safe.

Score of 2

There's three perspectives on sharing student information. First, it should be wholly protected. Second, it should be exclusively available to not-for-profit tech developers. Third, it can be used by anyone. I think it should be protected.

I use the Khan Academy website a lot, and really like it. It enables me to review tough subjects that were covered in my classes and to get in some extra math practice. All I needed to do to use Khan Academy was provide an email account. I used my "trash" email account because I didn't want a lot of extra spam coming to my regular email. But to my surprise, I didn't get any spam from them. I'm more likely to use their site now that I know my information is safe, and that they are not using my email to send me a lot of unwanted advertisements. If I thought they might give my information to other companies, I wouldn't sign up.

Score of 1

I don't want anyone, from any company to have my personal information. I don't want people to know where I live or what I'm doing. I certainly don't want anyone to know my grades if I don't tell them. Privacy is important, and just because I'm trying to learn on the internet, and not in a classroom, I shouldn't have to give up my privacy.

Prompt 2

Score of 6

The costs of a college education are rising rapidly, and have made a college degree prohibitively expensive for many students. To alleviate this problem, three approaches have been suggested. The first would provide low-interest loans to students, and remove any responsibility from the states to provide reduced tuition; the second would provide funding for employment programs to enable graduates to find work so they could repay their tuition loans; and the last would offer reduced tuition to in-state students as part of the state's responsibility to improve the welfare of society as a whole. Because state colleges and universities receive substantial funding from state taxes, and because these state taxes are paid by residents of the state, state colleges and universities should offer substantial tuition discounts to in-state students.

One important reason why the state has a responsibility to provide discounted tuition to residents is that the discount is paid by residents themselves in the form of taxes. Some might consider such discounts to be undeserved handouts, but that viewpoint couldn't be further from the truth. The very source of funding for state colleges and universities is the citizens of the state itself. Because state residents (or their parents) have paid state taxes for years to support their local colleges, they should be eligible for reduced tuition. Given the high burden posed by paying for a college education, it is only just that students receive the benefit of their tax dollars in relieving this burden.

States should provide reduced tuition to their residents as an extension of the social contract. The founding fathers of our country insisted on the provision of education to every citizen and demanded that states offer free public education. In today's world, a high-school diploma is no longer sufficient for many jobs. The increasing complexity of technology, and our dependence on it, demands more highly trained workers in engineering, computer science, management sciences, economics, and social systems. As demands on our nation's workers increase, the level of education supported by the state must also increase. Providing a lower-cost tuition to in-state students is not only fair because of the support residents have provided these schools through their taxes, but also because a well-educated population will improve the welfare of the citizens of the state as a whole. Businesses will be more willing to open factories and operations in states where well-educated employees are available. Technology companies are known to "cluster" in areas like Northern California, Austin, Texas, and the North Carolina Triangle where major state-sponsored colleges generate qualified graduates. More businesses mean more taxes to generate funds for the state, as well as more support services such as restaurants, retail operations and personal services that provide even more employment opportunities for the state's residents. Because residents of the state have provided the funds that have supported local colleges and universities, and because a better-educated population will lead to improvements in the general welfare of the entire state, local residents should be offered reduced tuition to state schools.

Some might argue that the funds dedicated to state colleges should be used for employment programs so graduates are able to find work and pay off their loans, thus learning about responsible financial planning. This view would create an entire new tier of administrators between graduates and their potential employers. The money that could be used for lower tuition would instead be dedicated to paying the salaries of the advisors and administrators who would be assisting the graduates. It would be a much more efficient use of the state's resources to simply provide lower tuition to in-state students. In addition, the value of this plan in generating financial responsibility and fiscal planning skills is overstated. Tuition, while substantial, is only one part of the costs of a college education. Students will still learn financial responsibility and fiscal planning as they pay for books, equipment, housing, transportation, food, and other living expenses. Providing an employment-assistance service to college graduates is not a wise use of taxpayers' funds dedicated to education.

As states and students struggle with the rising costs of education, states must recognize the value of a well educated population, invest in their residents, and use the money raised by state taxes to provide reduced tuition to in-state students. Ultimately, other schemes such as low-cost loans or employment-assistance services divert the money residents have paid to fund education to banks, administrators, and program managers. These funds are more efficiently and appropriately used to directly support residents through low-cost tuition to state colleges and universities. Offering tuition reduction more directly benefits the taxpayers, and it benefits the community as well by encouraging economic growth.

Score of 5

College costs are rising quickly, even much faster than the overall cost of living. Because the high costs are making it impossible for many qualified students to attend college, some have proposed that states offer support to students to enable accepted students to attend state colleges and universities. Three forms of this support have been proposed: low-cost student loans, employment assistance for graduates, and lower cost tuition to state residents. Because an educated population benefits the state as a whole, and because funds to support state colleges and universities are generated by taxes paid by state residents, states should assist qualified students with tuition assistance.

An educated population benefits everyone, but these benefits cannot be fully realized unless tuition discounts are implemented. For most non-technical degrees, the tuition costs alone for college can come to more than $50,000. For scientific and technical degrees, like engineering and medicine, the costs are much higher because these degree programs take longer to complete. My sister graduated 5 years ago with a degree in elementary education, and college loans of $70,000. Her starting salary was under $30,000. Even with a lower interest rate than she's paying, it would take her many years to pay off her loans. During this time, she won't be able to buy a house, a new car, or have much discretionary spending. My sister teaches fourth grade in a public school. She's an example of a hard-working person whose education is contributing to the welfare of society as a whole. If she could buy a home or hire a housekeeper once a month, these types of modest expenditures would contribute to strengthening the local economy. Low-cost student loans as a solution to the problem of higher tuition are short-sighted. They may seem to relieve the burden on the students, but they actually prevent dedicated graduates from contributing to local economies for extended periods of time.

Furthermore, the funds that support public education are the result of taxpayers' contributions to the government. State residents should receive the most direct benefit from the use of these taxes, and one impactful way to use this money would be to relieve the burden of college tuition by reducing tuition for in-state residents. These residents (or their parents) have already contributed to the funds that would be used in this way, and the benefit is clear. This use of state funds would enable students to graduate with much more manageable tuition loans, thus allowing them to make fuller economic contributions back into the system from which they received the benefit of a reduced tuition.

While some argue that schools should divert their funds to employment services rather than tuition discounts, there are many problems with this apparent solution. Offering employment services to students assumes that graduates are not able to find work to pay off their loans. But for the students who are contributing the most to the welfare of society, like my sister, this is not the case. Almost every municipality is looking for more excellent teachers, nurses, doctors, police officers, computer programmers, and other well-educated professionals. Locating suitable employment is not the problem; the problem is the large amount of debt graduates accumulate through their college careers. Even if jobs were hard to find, this plan doesn't guarantee graduates a position. What if the state located a position far away from a graduate's family? Or found a position that paid substantially below the average market rate for that job? Would the student have to accept whatever position the state identified? The faulty assumptions behind this plan make it a poor choice.

The best solution to rising tuition is for states to offer qualified resident students tuition discounts. While it may seem to be the most expensive option, that is a short-term view. In the long run, it may even generate enough money to pay for itself through the improved business climate. If major companies relocated to the state because of the excellent, qualified workforce created by the reduced tuition program, the tax revenues generated by that company could not only defray many tuition subsidies, but also contribute to the state's general revenue. To improve their business environment, and thus, improve the overall welfare of the community, states should enable their qualified students to attend local colleges and universities. The best way to defray the ever-rising costs of tuition is for the states to offer tuition discounts to these students that are funded by taxes. Low-cost loans and job-placement programs are insufficient to provide qualified students the assistance they need and deserve, and the funds have already been paid by residents in the form of taxes.

Score of 4

The cost of going to college is so high, it's keeping many good students from attending, so it's been suggested that states should come up with some ways to assist student in funding their high education. To address the question of whether states should assist students or not, three views have been presented. Some say the states have no obligation to help because students will be able to repay their student loans once they start working. Others say that the states should start and support job placement services that enable graduates to find work quickly; others believe the states should assist students with tuition discounts. I think the best approach is for states to offer their students reduced tuition to state colleges and universities because the money used to support state schools is raised from taxes paid by the residents, and this will enable state residents to become better educated, improving the society as a whole.

I think the best solution is for the states to use taxes to provide lower-cost tuition for graduates. My parents have paid property taxes here my whole life, and we pay sales tax on everything we buy. Part of those taxes should be used to support the state colleges and universities. My sister graduated from college 5 years ago and has been teaching fourth grade ever since. But she says that after paying for her rent, car, food, and insurance she only has enough left over to make the minimum payment on her student loans. She says it's going to take her another 12 years to finish paying her student loans. States should use the money raised by our taxes to help its residents.

Educated people help improve our communities, which is another reason the state should help reduce tuition. My sister is helping the state by working in a public school educating children. It is the responsibility of the state to assist its residents. Because my sister's job helps her students and so makes our state a better place to live, the state should've helped her graduate without the burden of a large debt from student loans. The state has a responsibility to help our best and brightest improve our communities, and reducing student tuition is a major way the state can help achieve that goal.

Some believe that states should use some of the money they raise for schools for setting up job placement services that will enable their college graduates to find work quickly, but in my opinion, this will not be very helpful. My sister was able to find a job quickly, but still struggles to pay off her loans, so this idea wouldn't help her at all. For many people, the problem isn't finding a job, but in the large amount of money they've had to borrow to finish college. These loans become a great burden over time, and reducing tuition would help more than employment services.

College tuition goes up every year. It's important for states to assist their residents because more educated people make the state a better place to live. Those who say the state has no responsibility to help ignore the benefits that come to the society as a whole from a more educated population. Those who say the state should assist college students by providing an employment service after graduation are assuming that the graduates can't find work, and this is not always the case. States should assist their residents with lower tuitions funded by state taxes.

Score of 3

Going to college is very, very expensive. Because the cost of tuition can prevent some students from going college, three views have been presented to assist them. These are: first, for states to offer low-cost loans, second, for states to provide services that will assist graduates to secure employment so they can repay their loans, and finally, for states to offer tuition discounts to residents. I think that states should give us lower tuition.

Because our parents have paid taxes, and the out-of-state students haven't, I think that it's only fair that we get lower tuitions. That way, any student who is accepted will be able to attend college. I live in Florida and the television ads are always saying that the state lottery contributes a lot of money to education, so some of that money can be used for lower tuition.

If you get a student loan, you have to pay it back and it's easy to end up with huge student loans, so I don't think low-cost student loans are a good idea. The state should do more to help us because we are going to live and work here and make the state a better place. If we're improving the community by getting a good education, the state should help us to do this. Just as the state builds roads to help us get around, and hospitals to take of us when we're sick, and pays police and firemen to keep us safe, the state should help us get a good education. These are all things that make our communities better places to live.

Having a job service for college graduates shouldn't be needed. If you can't get a job, why would you go to college? For the state to find you a job after college seems unnecessary. And that doesn't do anything about the high cost of college. States should be doing something to help make college less expensive so more of us can go.

Because educating it's citizens makes the state a better place to live, just like having good roads, good hospitals and good public services, the states should provide free or reduced tuition for all students who receive acceptance letters. Low-cost student loans and job-placement services are not enough help.

Score of 2

I'm hoping to go to college, but I don't know . . . it's very expensive and my family is already paying for my brother's college. My parents say that I'll have to come up with some way to help them. Just like my brother, he works in the dorm and over the summer he works with a landscape company. There are 3 ideas to help students like me go to college, their can be low-cost loans from the state or the state can help people find jobs or the state can give students free tuition. My parents say some states give the students that live there a discount on tuitions, and I think that's a very good idea. After all, we live here and will work here, and so it's good for the state if we have college degrees. People with college degrees can become engineers or computer programmers, and if you don't have a degree, you can't. We need more engineers and programmers because so many things run on computers.

If there are a lot of people with college degrees in our state, then that's good for the state. More people will want to come here to live, and that means more people will be buying houses, cars and food etc here. That will create more jobs for other people like saleman and store clerks, and that will help the state. I don't think low-cost loans or job programs will be that helpful.

Score of 1

I think paying for college will be hard, because it's so expensive. I think it would be a good thing for the state to provide lower tuition because if I go to college, I'll be able to get a good job, get married and raise a family. I won't be able to take care of my family as well without a college degree. If I do go to college, I want to make sure my kids have a good life. I don't want to owe a lot of money. It's too hard to pay back. So, it would be good if tuition cost less.